Working on your car can be dangerous. This page shows just some of the potential risks and hazards, with the aim of creating a safety-conscious attitude.

General hazards

Scalding

• Don't remove the radiator or expansion tank cap while the engine is hot.
• Engine oil, automatic transmission fluid or power steering fluid may also be dangerously hot if the engine has recently been running.

Burning

• Beware of burns from the exhaust system and from any part of the engine. Brake discs and drums can also be extremely hot immediately after use.

Crushing

• When working under or near a raised vehicle, always supplement the jack with axle stands, or use drive-on ramps. ***Never venture under a car which is only supported by a jack.***
• Take care if loosening or tightening high-torque nuts when the vehicle is on stands. Initial loosening and final tightening should be done with the wheels on the ground.

Fire

• Fuel is highly flammable; fuel vapour is explosive.
• Don't let fuel spill onto a hot engine.
• Do not smoke or allow naked lights (including pilot lights) anywhere near a vehicle being worked on. Also beware of creating sparks (electrically or by use of tools).
• Fuel vapour is heavier than air, so don't work on the fuel system with the vehicle over an inspection pit.
• Another cause of fire is an electrical overload or short-circuit. Take care when repairing or modifying the vehicle wiring.
• Keep a fire extinguisher handy, of a type suitable for use on fuel and electrical fires.

Electric shock

• Ignition HT voltage can be dangerous, especially to people with heart problems or a pacemaker. Don't work on or near the ignition system with the engine running or the ignition switched on.

• Mains voltage is also dangerous. Make sure that any mains-operated equipment is correctly earthed. Mains power points should be protected by a residual current device (RCD) circuit breaker.

Fume or gas intoxication

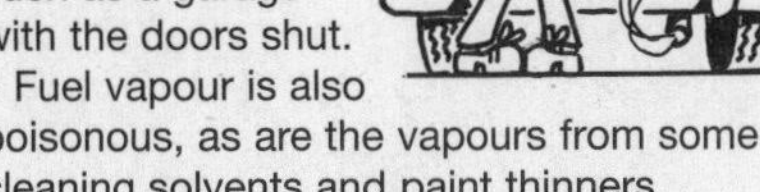

• Exhaust fumes are poisonous; they often contain carbon monoxide, which is rapidly fatal if inhaled. Never run the engine in a confined space such as a garage with the doors shut.
• Fuel vapour is also poisonous, as are the vapours from some cleaning solvents and paint thinners.

Poisonous or irritant substances

• Avoid skin contact with battery acid and with any fuel, fluid or lubricant, especially antifreeze, brake hydraulic fluid and Diesel fuel. Don't syphon them by mouth. If such a substance is swallowed or gets into the eyes, seek medical advice.
• Prolonged contact with used engine oil can cause skin cancer. Wear gloves or use a barrier cream if necessary. Change out of oil-soaked clothes and do not keep oily rags in your pocket.
• Air conditioning refrigerant forms a poisonous gas if exposed to a naked flame (including a cigarette). It can also cause skin burns on contact.

Asbestos

• Asbestos dust can cause cancer if inhaled or swallowed. Asbestos may be found in gaskets and in brake and clutch linings. When dealing with such components it is safest to assume that they contain asbestos.

Special hazards

Hydrofluoric acid

• This extremely corrosive acid is formed when certain types of synthetic rubber, found in some O-rings, oil seals, fuel hoses etc, are exposed to temperatures above 400ºC. The rubber changes into a charred or sticky substance containing the acid. *Once formed, the acid remains dangerous for years. If it gets onto the skin, it may be necessary to amputate the limb concerned.*
• When dealing with a vehicle which has suffered a fire, or with components salvaged from such a vehicle, wear protective gloves and discard them after use.

The battery

• Batteries contain sulphuric acid, which attacks clothing, eyes and skin. Take care when topping-up or carrying the battery.
• The hydrogen gas given off by the battery is highly explosive. Never cause a spark or allow a naked light nearby. Be careful when connecting and disconnecting battery chargers or jump leads.

Air bags

• Air bags can cause injury if they go off accidentally. Take care when removing the steering wheel and/or facia. Special storage instructions may apply.

Diesel injection equipment

• Diesel injection pumps supply fuel at very high pressure. Take care when working on the fuel injectors and fuel pipes.

Warning: Never expose the hands, face or any other part of the body to injector spray; the fuel can penetrate the skin with potentially fatal results.

Remember...

DO

• Do use eye protection when using power tools, and when working under the vehicle.

• Do wear gloves or use barrier cream to protect your hands when necessary.

• Do get someone to check periodically that all is well when working alone on the vehicle.

• Do keep loose clothing and long hair well out of the way of moving mechanical parts.

• Do remove rings, wristwatch etc, before working on the vehicle – especially the electrical system.

• Do ensure that any lifting or jacking equipment has a safe working load rating adequate for the job.

DON'T

• Don't attempt to lift a heavy component which may be beyond your capability – get assistance.

• Don't rush to finish a job, or take unverified short cuts.

• Don't use ill-fitting tools which may slip and cause injury.

• Don't leave tools or parts lying around where someone can trip over them. Mop up oil and fuel spills at once.

• Don't allow children or pets to play in or near a vehicle being worked on.

Dimensions

Overall length	4051 mm (159.5 in)
Overall width (excluding mirrors)	1628 mm (64.1 in)
Overall height	1376 to 1395 mm (54.2 to 54.9 in)
Wheelbase	2469 mm (97.2 in)

Weights

Kerb weight:	
1.1, 1.3 and 1.4 litre 3-door models	835 to 870 kg (1841 to 1918 lb)
1.1, 1.3 and 1.4 litre 5-door models	850 to 910 kg (1874 to 2006 lb)
1.6 litre automatic transmission models, 1.6 XSI	910 to 930 kg (2006 to 2050 lb)
SRI, GRI and GTI models	930 to 950 kg (2050 to 2094 lb)
All other 1.6 litre models	870 to 890 kg (1918 to 1962 lb)
Towing weights	Differ according to model and year - refer either to vehicle's Owner's Handbook or to Peugeot dealer
Maximum tow hitch load	50 kg (110 lb)
Maximum roof rack load	75 kg (165 lb)

Capacities

Engine oil (including filter):	
1.1 and 1.3 litre models (E1A and G1A engines)	3.3 litres (5.8 pints)
1.1 and 1.4 litre models (TU engines)	3.5 litres (6.2 pints)
1.6 and 1.9 litre models (XU engines)	5.0 litres (8.8 pints)
Cooling system:	
1.1 and 1.3 litre models (E1A and G1A engines)	6.6 litres (11.6 pints)
1.1 litre models (TU1 engines)	5.7 litres (10.0 pints)
1.4 litre models (TU3 engines)	7.5 litres (13.2 pints)
1992-on 1.6 GL Automatic (XU5M3/Z and XU5M3/L engines)	6.1 litres (10.7 pints)
All other 1.6 and 1.9 litre models (XU engines)	7.5 to 8.0 litres (13.2 to 14.1 pints)
Fuel tank (approximate)	55 litres (12.1 gallons)
Transmission:	
Manual - all types	2.0 litres (3.5 pints)
Automatic - at fluid change	2.4 litres (4.2 pints)
Automatic - at overhaul	6.2 litres (10.9 pints)
Power-assisted steering system (approximate)	0.65 litre (1.1 pints)
Washer reservoir (approximate):	
Front - with headlamp washers	6.6 litres (11.6 pints)
Front - without headlamp washers	1.8 litres (3.2 pints)

Jump starting

HAYNES HiNT ***Jump starting will get you out of trouble, but you must correct whatever made the battery go flat in the first place. There are three possibilities:***

1 The battery has been drained by repeated attempts to start, or by leaving the lights on.

2 The charging system is not working properly (alternator drivebelt slack or broken, alternator wiring fault or alternator itself faulty).

3 The battery itself is at fault (electrolyte low, or battery worn out).

When jump-starting a car using a booster battery, observe the following precautions:

- ✔ Before connecting the booster battery, make sure that the ignition is switched off.
- ✔ Ensure that all electrical equipment (lights, heater, wipers, etc) is switched off.
- ✔ Make sure that the booster battery is the same voltage as the discharged one in the vehicle.
- ✔ If the battery is being jump-started from the battery in another vehicle, the two vehcles MUST NOT TOUCH each other.
- ✔ Make sure that the transmission is in neutral (or PARK, in the case of automatic transmission).

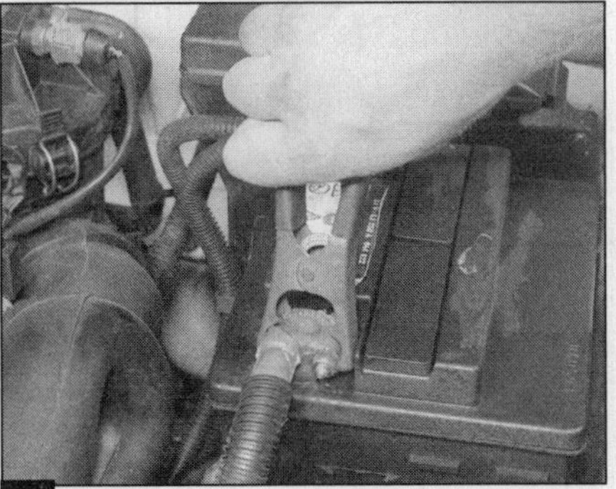

1 Connect one end of the red jump lead to the positive (+) terminal of the flat battery

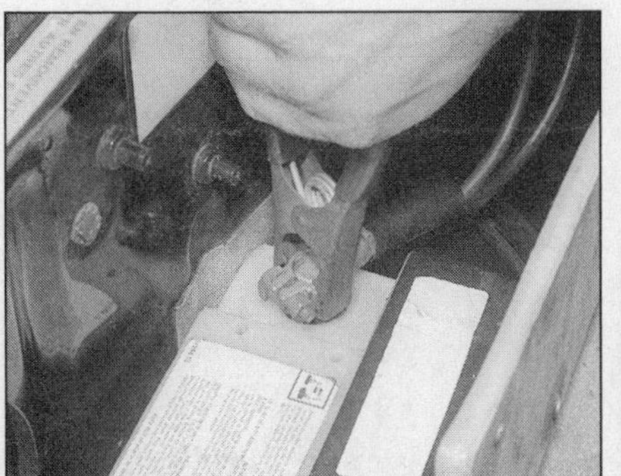

2 Connect the other end of the red lead to the positive (+) terminal of the booster battery.

3 Connect one end of the black jump lead to the negative (-) terminal of the booster battery

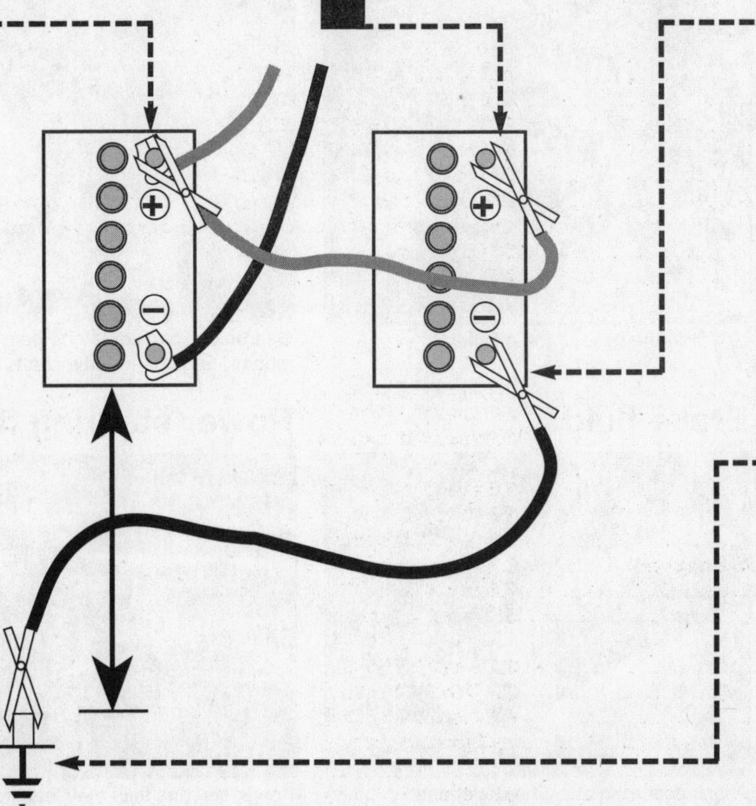

4 Connect the other end of the black jump lead to a bolt or bracket on the engine block, well away from the battery, on the vehicle to be started.

5 Make sure that the jump leads will not come into contact with the fan, drive-belts or other moving parts of the engine.

6 Start the engine using the booster battery, then with the engine running at idle speed, disconnect the jump leads in the reverse order of connection.

Identifying leaks

Puddles on the garage floor or drive, or obvious wetness under the bonnet or underneath the car, suggest a leak that needs investigating. It can sometimes be difficult to decide where the leak is coming from, especially if the engine bay is very dirty already. Leaking oil or fluid can also be blown rearwards by the passage of air under the car, giving a false impression of where the problem lies.

Warning: Most automotive oils and fluids are poisonous. Wash them off skin, and change out of contaminated clothing, without delay.

The smell of a fluid leaking from the car may provide a clue to what's leaking. Some fluids are distinctively coloured. It may help to clean the car carefully and to park it over some clean paper overnight as an aid to locating the source of the leak.

Remember that some leaks may only occur while the engine is running.

Sump oil

Engine oil may leak from the drain plug...

Oil from filter

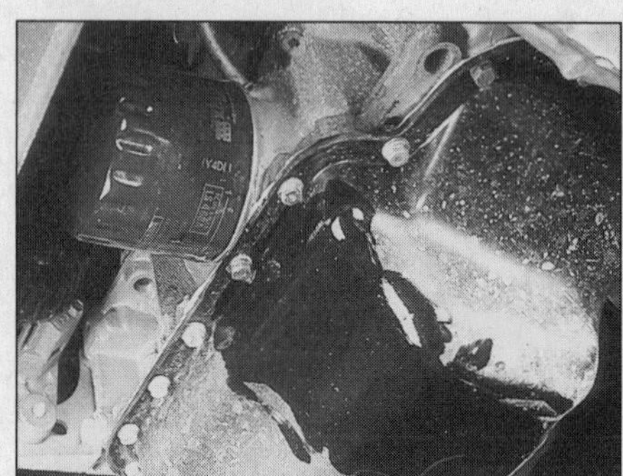

...or from the base of the oil filter.

Gearbox oil

Gearbox oil can leak from the seals at the inboard ends of the driveshafts.

Antifreeze

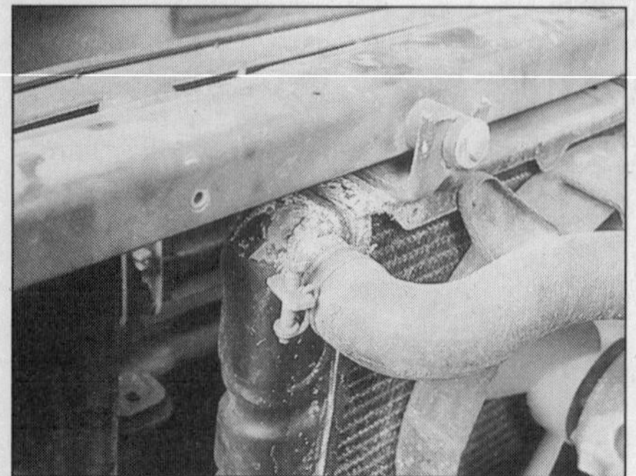

Leaking antifreeze often leaves a crystalline deposit like this.

Brake fluid

A leak occurring at a wheel is almost certainly brake fluid.

Power steering fluid

Power steering fluid may leak from the pipe connectors on the steering rack.

Jacking and towing

The jack supplied with the car by the manufacturers is designed for use only when changing a roadwheel. The jack locates under the body sill on the side concerned at the jack point to the rear of the front wheel arch or to the front of the rear wheel arch as applicable.

Before jacking up the car to change the roadwheel, loosen the roadwheel retaining bolts first. Ensure that the jack is securely located and standing on firm level ground. The car should be in gear and the handbrake fully applied.

View showing jack storage location and fitting position on the body sill. Note alternative jack types supplied – according to model

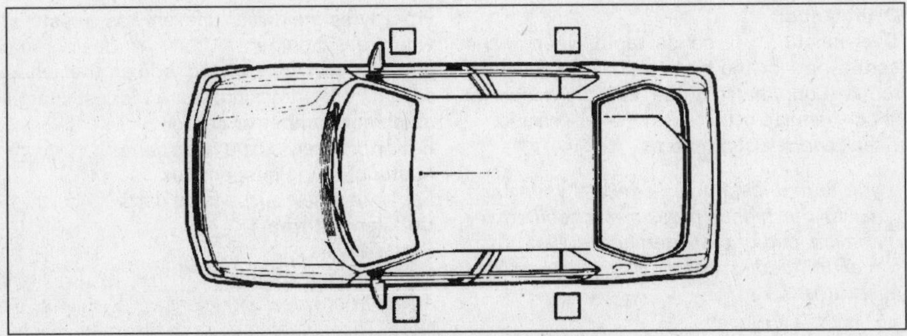

Jack location points

If you are going to carry out work under the car it is preferable to position the car over an inspection pit. If this is not available use a workshop trolley jack or substantial screw or bottle type hydraulic jack. *Always supplement a jack with axle stands.* The sill jacking points or their adjacent reinforced areas should be used as jacking points for raising the car. A beam may be placed under the front subframe and the front end jacked up under that. The side-members of the front subframe should be used as axle stand support points. The rear side-members may be used in a similar way.

Towing and being towed

Front and rear anchorage points are provided for securing the car during transportation on a car transporter, boat, train and so on (photo). These points can also be used for towing the car or for towing another in an emergency. For permanent towing requirements a tow-bar is necessary, properly attached to the vehicle.

Ensure that the ignition key is in the steering unlocked position (A or M as required).

On some models the blanking plate in the front bumper will need removal for access to the towing eye.

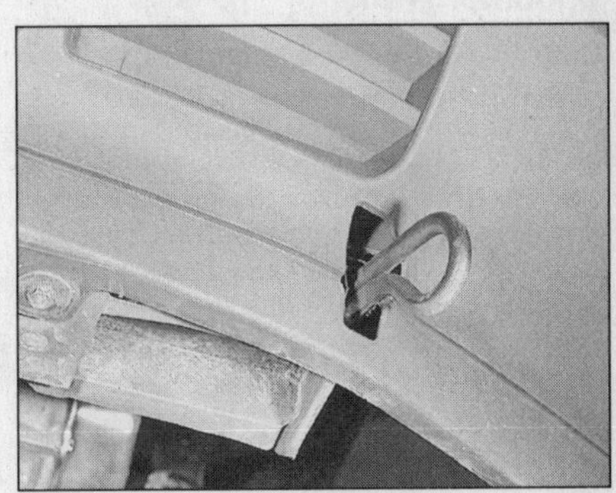

Front towing eye

Tyre condition and pressure

It is very important that tyres are in good condition, and at the correct pressure - having a tyre failure at any speed is highly dangerous. Tyre wear is influenced by driving style - harsh braking and acceleration, or fast cornering, will all produce more rapid tyre wear. As a general rule, the front tyres wear out faster than the rears. Interchanging the tyres from front to rear ("rotating" the tyres) may result in more even wear. However, if this is completely effective, you may have the expense of replacing all four tyres at once!

Remove any nails or stones embedded in the tread before they penetrate the tyre to cause deflation. If removal of a nail does reveal that the tyre has been punctured, refit the nail so that its point of penetration is marked. Then immediately change the wheel, and have the tyre repaired by a tyre dealer.

Regularly check the tyres for damage in the form of cuts or bulges, especially in the sidewalls. Periodically remove the wheels, and clean any dirt or mud from the inside and outside surfaces. Examine the wheel rims for signs of rusting, corrosion or other damage. Light alloy wheels are easily damaged by "kerbing" whilst parking; steel wheels may also become dented or buckled. A new wheel is very often the only way to overcome severe damage.

New tyres should be balanced when they are fitted, but it may become necessary to re-balance them as they wear, or if the balance weights fitted to the wheel rim should fall off. Unbalanced tyres will wear more quickly, as will the steering and suspension components. Wheel imbalance is normally signified by vibration, particularly at a certain speed (typically around 50 mph). If this vibration is felt only through the steering, then it is likely that just the front wheels need balancing. If, however, the vibration is felt through the whole car, the rear wheels could be out of balance. Wheel balancing should be carried out by a tyre dealer or garage.

1 Tread Depth - visual check

The original tyres have tread wear safety bands (B), which will appear when the tread depth reaches approximately 1.6 mm. The band positions are indicated by a triangular mark on the tyre sidewall (A).

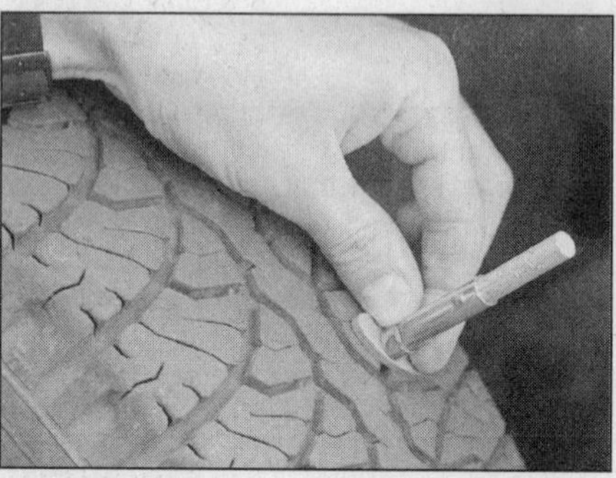

2 Tread Depth - manual check

Alternatively, tread wear can be monitored with a simple, inexpensive device known as a tread depth indicator gauge.

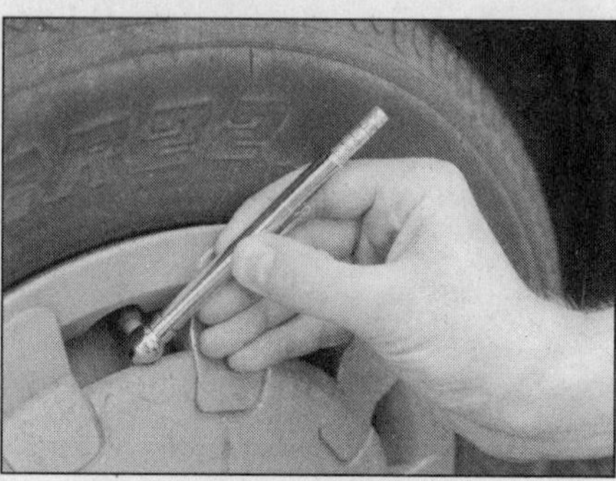

3 Tyre Pressure Check

Check the tyre pressures regularly with the tyres cold. Do not adjust the tyre pressures immediately after the vehicle has been used, or an inaccurate setting will result.

Tyre tread wear patterns

Shoulder Wear

Underinflation (wear on both sides)
Under-inflation will cause overheating of the tyre, because the tyre will flex too much, and the tread will not sit correctly on the road surface. This will cause a loss of grip and excessive wear, not to mention the danger of sudden tyre failure due to heat build-up.
Check and adjust pressures
Incorrect wheel camber (wear on one side)
Repair or renew suspension parts
Hard cornering
Reduce speed!

Centre Wear

Overinflation
Over-inflation will cause rapid wear of the centre part of the tyre tread, coupled with reduced grip, harsher ride, and the danger of shock damage occurring in the tyre casing.
Check and adjust pressures

If you sometimes have to inflate your car's tyres to the higher pressures specified for maximum load or sustained high speed, don't forget to reduce the pressures to normal afterwards.

Uneven Wear

Front tyres may wear unevenly as a result of wheel misalignment. Most tyre dealers and garages can check and adjust the wheel alignment (or "tracking") for a modest charge.
Incorrect camber or castor
Repair or renew suspension parts
Malfunctioning suspension
Repair or renew suspension parts
Unbalanced wheel
Balance tyres
Incorrect toe setting
Adjust front wheel alignment
Note: *The feathered edge of the tread which typifies toe wear is best checked by feel.*

For information applicable to later models, see Supplement at end of manual

Every 250 miles (400 km) or weekly - whichever comes first

- ☐ Check the engine oil level using the dipstick. The oil level must be maintained between the high and low markings at all times. Top up when necessary but do not overfill
- ☐ Check the coolant level. Top up if necessary
- ☐ Check for signs of leaks, and hose/pipe security
- ☐ Check the level of brake fluid in the fluid reservoir. The level must be kept between the high and low markings on the reservoir wall. Top up if necessary
- ☐ Check the tyre pressures, and examine them for wear and damage
- ☐ Check and if necessary top up the fluid level in the windscreen and tailgate washer reservoirs, adding a screen wash

Every 6000 miles (9500 km) or six months - whichever comes first

- ☐ Renew the engine oil and filter
- ☐ Check the brake pads for wear. Renew if necessary
- ☐ Check the battery electrolyte level. Top up if necessary (not usually required on low maintenance type)

Every 12 000 miles (19 000 km) or 12 months - whichever comes first

In addition to the 6000 miles service

- ☐ Clean the engine oil filler cap filter mesh (if applicable)
- ☐ Adjust and lubricate the throttle and choke cables (if applicable)
- ☐ Renew the spark plugs
- ☐ Lubricate the distributor
- ☐ Check for ignition system cable security
- ☐ Adjust the clutch pedal/cable
- ☐ Check brake shoes for wear. Renew if necessary
- ☐ Adjust the handbrake
- ☐ Check the power steering fluid level (if applicable)
- ☐ Adjust the power steering pump drivebelt (if applicable)
- ☐ Check the bodywork condition. Repair as necessary
- ☐ Adjust alternator/coolant pump drivebelt tension

Maintenance is essential for ensuring safety and is desirable for the purpose of getting the best in terms of performance and economy from the car. Over the years the need for periodic lubrication - oiling and greasing has been drastically reduced, if not totally eliminated. This has unfortunately tended to lead some owners to think that because no such action is required the components either no longer exist or will last for ever. This is a serious delusion. If anything, there are now more places, particularly in the steering and suspension, where joints and pivots are fitted. Although you do not grease them any more you still have to look at them - and look at them just as often as you may previously have had to grease them. The largest initial element of maintenance is visual examination. This may lead to repairs or renewal.

Every 24 000 miles (38 000 km) or 2 years - whichever comes first

In addition to the 12 000 miles service

- ☐ Renew the coolant
- ☐ Renew the air cleaner element
- ☐ Clean the fuel pump filter (if applicable)
- ☐ Renew the in-line filter-carburettor models (if applicable)
- ☐ Adjust the ignition timing
- ☐ Renew the gearbox oil
- ☐ Check for driveshaft damage and wear
- ☐ Renew the brake fluid
- ☐ Check the wheel bearings for wear and damage
- ☐ Check the steering and suspension balljoints for wear and damage
- ☐ Check the shock absorbers for operation and leaks
- ☐ Renew the automatic transmission fluid

Every 36 000 miles (57 000 km)

- ☐ Renew the camshaft (timing) drivebelt (if applicable)

Every 60 000 miles (95 000 km) or 5 years - whichever comes first

- ☐ Renew the fuel filter - fuel injection models

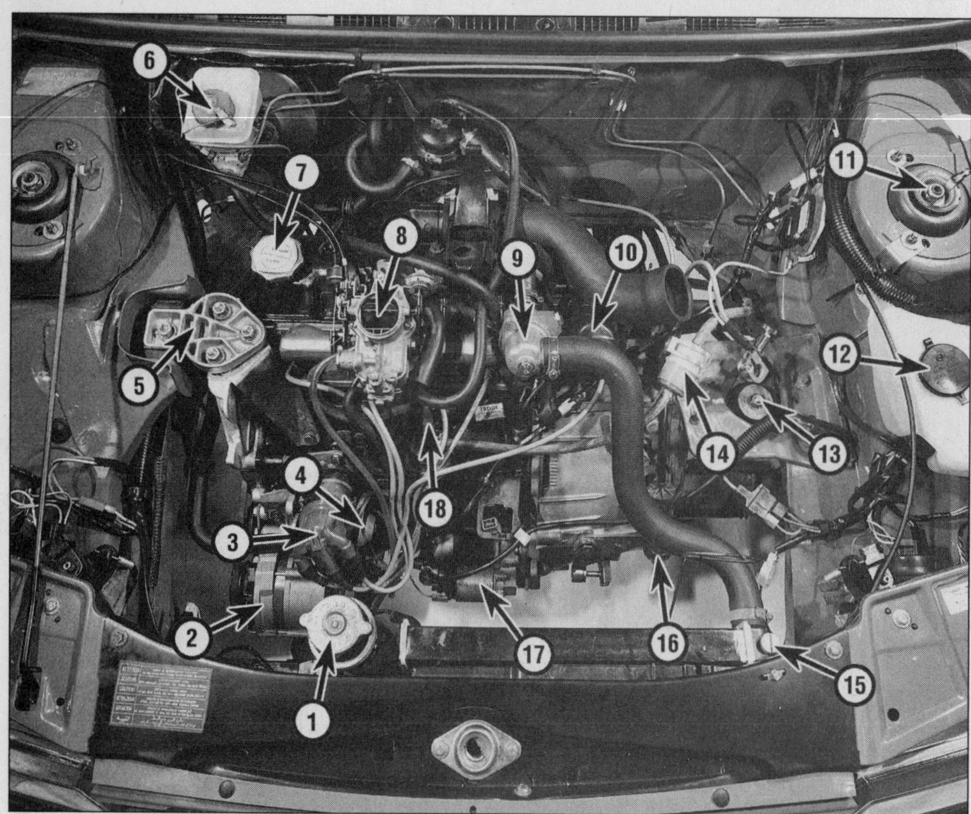

Under bonnet view – 1.3 litre engine

1 *Radiator filler cap*
2 *Alternator*
3 *Distributor*
4 *Engine oil dipstick*
5 *Right-hand engine mounting*
6 *Brake hydraulic system master cylinder*
7 *Engine oil filler cap*
8 *Carburettor (air filter removed)*
9 *Cooling system thermostat housing*
10 *Ignition coil*
11 *Front suspension strut top mounting (left-hand side)*
12 *Washer system reservoir*
13 *Engine/transmission mounting (shown with battery removed)*
14 *Fuel filter (in-line)*
15 *Cooling system bleed screw*
16 *Clutch adjuster*
17 *Starter motor*
18 *Fuel pump*

Under bonnet view – 1.6 litre SR Injection engine

1 *Alternator*
2 *Injectors*
3 *Engine mounting (right-hand)*
4 *Fuel filter*
5 *Brake hydraulic system master cylinder*
6 *Air filter*
7 *Engine oil dipstick*
8 *Cooling system expansion tank and filler cap*
9 *Ignition coil*
10 *Ignition distributor*
11 *Front suspension strut top mounting (left-hand side)*
12 *Washer system reservoir*
13 *Battery*
14 *Radiator cap*
15 *Throttle housing*
16 *Engine oil filler*
17 *Inlet manifold*

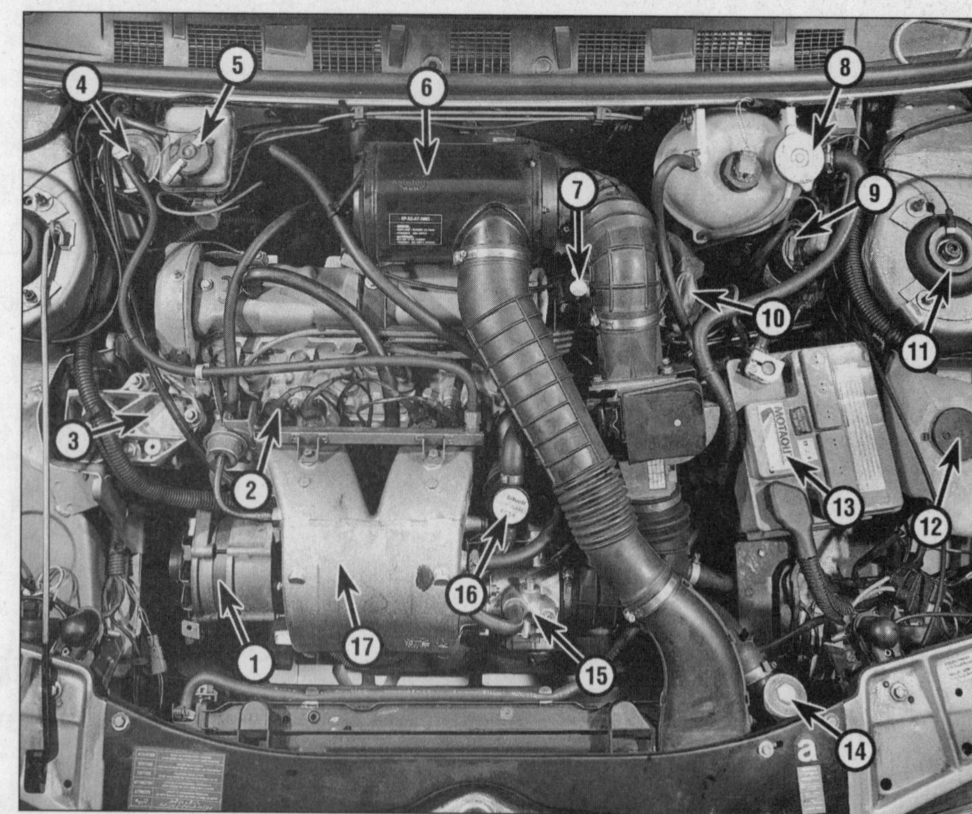

View of front underside of car with engine undershield removed – 1.3 litre engine

1 Alternator/coolant pump drivebelt
2 Starter motor
3 Gearbox
4 Differential housing
5 Suspension arm
6 Anti-roll bar
7 Track rod
8 Exhaust pipe
9 Exhaust manifold
10 Driveshaft
11 Torque reaction link
12 Brake caliper
13 Sump drain plug
14 Engine coolant drain plug (OHV engines only)

View of rear underside of car – 1.3 litre model

1 Spare wheel
2 Towing eye
3 Shock absorber
4 Suspension arm
5 Suspension cross tube
6 Handbrake cable
7 Heat shield
8 Fuel tank
9 Torsion bar (right-hand)
10 Torsion bar (left-hand)
11 Brake backplate
12 Exhaust rear silencer

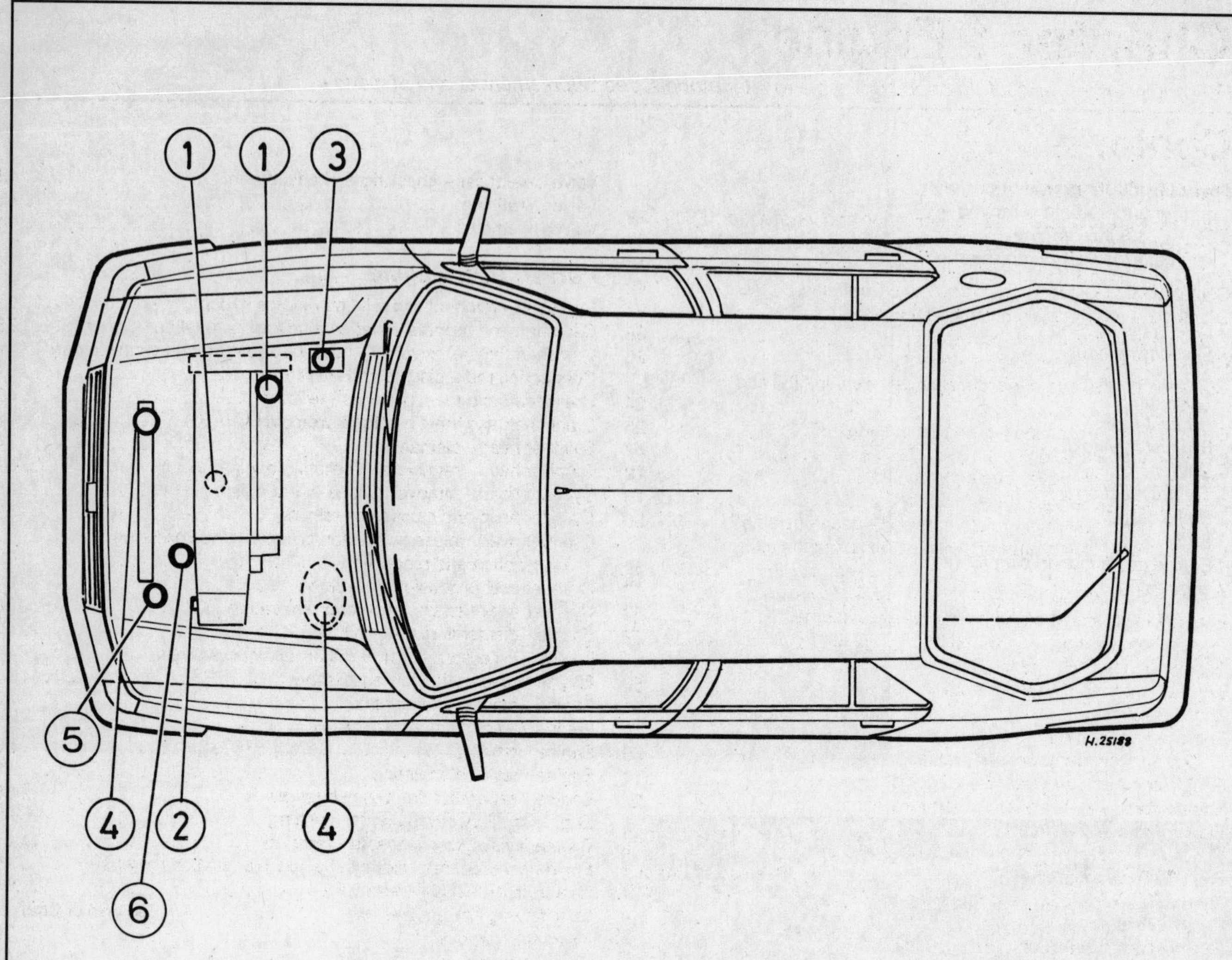

Component or system	Lubricant type/specification
1 Engine	Multigrade engine oil, viscosity SAE 10W/40 or 15W/40
2 Manual gearbox*	
Up to October 1987	Multigrade engine oil, viscosity SAE 10W/40 or 15W/40
October 1987 on	Gear oil, viscosity SAE 75W/80
3 Braking system	Hydraulic fluid to SAE J1703C
4 Cooling system	Ethylene glycol based antifreeze coolant mixture
5 Power steering	Dexron II type ATF
6 Automatic transmission	Dexron II type ATF

**On cars manufactured after October 1987, the manual gearbox is 'sealed for life', and renewing the oil is no longer required. It is essential to use only the specified type of oil when topping-up.*

Chapter 1 Engine

For modifications, and information applicable to later models, see Supplement at end of manual

Contents

Part A: OHV engines

Part B: OHC engine

Degrees of difficulty

Easy, suitable for novice with little experience 	**Fairly easy,** suitable for beginner with some experience 	**Fairly difficult,** suitable for competent DIY mechanic 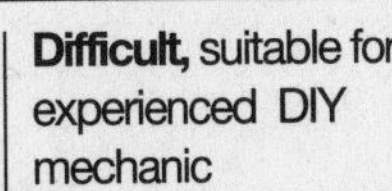	**Difficult,** suitable for experienced DIY mechanic 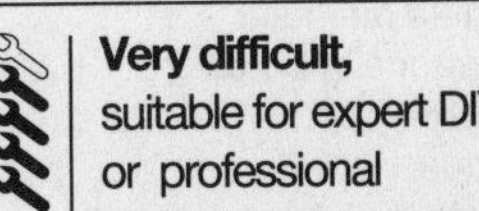	**Very difficult,** suitable for expert DIY or professional

Specifications

Part A: OHV engines

General

Type	Four-cylinder, in-line, overhead valve (OHV), water-cooled, transverse mounting	
Engine type references:		
1.1 litre engine	E1A (1E1A)	
1.3 litre engine	G1A (1G1A)	
Bore X stroke:		
EIA engine	74 x 65 mm	
GIA engine	76.7 x 70 mm	
Capacity:		
EIA engine	1118 cc	
GIA engine	1294 cc	
Compression ratio:		
EIA engine	9.6 : 1	
GIA engine	9.5 : 1	
Firing order	1 - 3 - 4 - 2 (No 1 at flywheel end)	

Cylinder block

Cylinder bore diameter:	**1118 cc**	**1294** cc
Class A	73.9920 to 73.9995 mm	76.6870 to 76.6945 mm
Class B	73.9995 to 74.0070 mm	76.6945 to 76.7020 mm
Class C	74.0070 to 74.0145 mm	76.7020 to 76.7095 mm
Class D	74.0145 to 74.0220 mm	76.7095 to 76.7170 mm
Bore oversizes	+ 0.1 mm, + 0.4 mm	+ 0.1 mm, + 0.4 mm
Width of centre bearing bore	26.58 to 26.62 mm	26.58 to 26.62 mm
Camshaft bore diameter (bearings fitted):		
No 1 (flywheel end)	35.484 to 35.520 mm	35.484 to 35.520 mm
No 2	40.984 to 41.020 mm	40.984 to 41.020 mm
No 3	41.484 to 41.520 mm	41.484 to 41.520 mm

Crankshaft and connecting rods

Number of main bearings	5
Main bearing journal diameter	51.966 to 51.976 mm
Undersizes for regrinding	0.1, 0.2 and 0.5 mm
Main bearing running clearance	0.04 to 0.078 mm
Big-end journal diameter	40.949 to 40.957 mm
Undersizes for regrinding	0.1, 0.2 and 0.5 mm
Big-end running clearance	0.03 to 0.064 mm
Crankshaft stroke:	
1118 cc	65 mm
1294 cc	70 mm
Crankshaft endfloat	0.09 to 0.27 mm
Thrustwasher thickness	2.31 to 2.36 mm
Connecting rod endfloat	0.010 to 0.027 mm

Camshaft and valve gear

Camshaft journal diameter:	
No 1 (flywheel end)	35.439 to 35.459 mm
No 2	40.939 to 40.959 mm
No 3	41.439 to 41.459 mm
Camshaft endfloat	0.10 to 0.20 mm
Valve timing:	
Inlet opens	16° 30' BTDC
Inlet closes	37° 06' ABDC
Exhaust opens	52° BBDC
Exhaust closes	16° 20' ATDC
Inlet cam lift	5.41 mm
Exhaust cam lift	5.71 mm
Cam followers (tappets):	
Outside diameter	22.974 to 23.000 mm
Clearance in bores	Zero to 0.047 mm
Length	39.5 to 40.5 mm
Pushrods:	
Length (to bottom of rocker arm ball seat)	201 mm

Pistons

	1118 cc	1294 cc
Material	Aluminium alloy	
Number of rings	2 compression, 1 oil control	
Maximum weight difference between any two pistons	3g	
Piston diameter:		
Class A	73.9625 to 73.9700 mm	75.6575 to 76.6650 mm
Class B	73.9700 to 73.9775 mm	76.6650 to 76.6725 mm
Class C	73.9775 to 73.9850 mm	76.6725 to 76.6800 mm
Class D	73.9850 to 73.9925 mm	76.6800 to 76.6875 mm
Piston oversizes	+ 0.1 mm, + 0.4 mm	+ 0.1 mm, + 0.4 mm
Piston-to-bore clearance (nominal)	0.22 to 0.037 mm	0.22 to 0.037 mm
Piston ring end gap:		
Compression rings	0.025 to 0.45 mm	0.025 to 0.45 mm
Oil control ring	0.020 to 0.40 mm	0.020 to 0.40 mm

Gudgeon pin

Material	Steel
Outside diameter	21.991 to 21.995 mm
Inside diameter	13 mm
Length:	
1118cc	64mm
1294cc	66.7 mm
Fit	Clearance in piston, interference in connecting rod

Cylinder head

	1118 cc	1294 cc
Maximum amount to be skimmed from gasket face	1.0 mm	0.6 mm
Gasket thickness for use with machined head	2.2 mm	1.8 mm
Standard gasket thickness	1.2 mm	1.2 mm
Valve guides:		
Material	Cast iron	Cast iron
Inside diameter	8.022 to 8.040 mm	8.022 to 8.040 mm
Valve seats/face angle	44° to 44° 30'/45°	44° to 44° 30'/45°
Valve lift:		
Inlet	8.12 mm	8.12 mm
Exhaust	8.58 mm	8.58 mm

Valves

Valve clearances - cold:	
Inlet	0.25 mm (0.010 in)
Exhaust	0.30 mm (0.012 in)
Valve sequence (from flywheel end)	I,E,I,E,E,I,E,I
Inlet valves:	
Stem diameter	7.970 to 7.985 mm
Stem-to-guide clearance	0.037 to 0.070 mm
Exhaust valves:	
Stem diameter	7.950 to 7.965 mm
Stem-to-guide clearance	0.057 to 0.090 mm
Valve springs free length	48.4 mm

Lubrication system

Oil pressure (minimum) at pressure switch take-off:	
At idle speed:	
Oil temperature of 40° to 80°C (104° to 176°F)	2.6 bar (37.7 lbf/in^2)
Oil temperature of 120°C (248°F)	1.2 bar (17.4 lbf in^2)
At 3000 rpm:	
At temperature of 40° to 120°C (104° to 248°F)	3.6 to 5.6 bar (52.2 to 81.2 lbf/in^2)
Oil pump	Externally mounted gear type
Endfloat - oil pump driveshaft	0.05 to 0.50 mm
Pump driveshaft bush diameter	12.030 to 12.055 mm
Oil type/specification	Multigrade engine oil, viscosity SAE 10W/40 or 15W/40
Oil filter	Champion H101

Torque wrench settings

	Nm	lbf ft
Rocker cover	5	4
Spark plugs	30	22
Main bearing cap bolts	65	48
Big-end cap bolts	38	28
Flywheel to crankshaft	55	41

Torque wrench settings (continued)

	Nm	lbf ft
Crankshaft pulley	150	111
Inlet manifold	15	11
Exhaust manifold	20	15
Timing cover to block:		
7 mm bolts	13	10
8 mm bolts	30	22
Timing cover	20	15
Sump to block	13	10
Sump baseplate	10	7
Oil pump to block	13	10
Oil pressure relief valve plug	40	30
Oil pump strainer to block	13	10
Camshaft sprocket	15	11
Camshaft thrust plate bolt	15	11
Crankshaft oil seal housing	13	10
Oil strainer gauze to housing	15	11
Sump drain plug	35	26
Cylinder block coolant drain plug	4	3
Engine to right mounting support nuts	50	37
Flexible mounting nuts	20	15
Gearbox (left-hand) mounting support nuts	35	26
Suspension lower balljoint bolts	35	26
Bearing to housing	17	13
Engine lower mounting bolt (on engine side)	45	33
Engine lower mounting bolt (crossmember side)	55	41
Front hub nuts	265	196
Cylinder head bolts:		
Stage 1	50	37
Stage 2	70	52
Stage 3 (after running engine - see Section 47) - loosen bolts in turn and retighten to	70	52

Part B: OHC engine

General

Type	Four-cylinder, in-line, overhead camshaft (OHC), water cooled, transverse mounting
Engine type references:	
1.6 litre engine, carburettor	XU51C (B1A/A)
1.6 litre engine, fuel injection	XU5JA (B6D)
Bore	83 mm
Stroke	73 mm
Capacity	1580 cc
Compression ratio	9.39 : 1
Firing order	1-3-4-2 (No 1 at flywheel end)

Camshaft

Drive	Toothed belt
Action	Directly onto bucket tappets
Endfloat (not adjustable)	0.07 to 0.16 mm
Lift:	
Early models	10.4 mm
Later models	9.7 mm

Connecting rods

Type	Forged steel
Big-end bore	48.655 to 48.671 mm
Small-end bore	21.959 to 21.971 mm

Cylinder liners

Type	Wet, removable, matched to piston
Protrusion from block (without seal)	0.08 to 0.15 mm
Protrusion difference between liners	0.05 mm max
Coding mark	One, two or three slashes

Crankshaft and main bearings

Number of main bearings	5
Main bearing bore in crankcase	63.708 to 63.727 mm
Main journal diameter:	
New	59.981 to 60.000 mm
After regrinding	59.681 to 59.700 mm
Crankpin diameter:	
New	44.971 to 44.990 mm
After regrinding	44.671 to 44.690 mm
Journal or crankpin out-of-round	0.007 mm max
Endfloat	0.07 to 0.27 mm
Thrust washer thicknesses available	2.30, 2.35, 2.40, 2.45 and 2.50 mm

Pistons

Type	Aluminium alloy with three compression rings and one scraper; matched to liner
Fitting orientation	DT mark and arrow point towards timing case end of engine
Coding marks:	
For gudgeon pin	Figure 1 (blue), 2 (white) or 3 (red)
For liner	One, two or three slashes

Gudgeon pin

Nominal diameter	22 mm
Coding mark	Coloured paint (see piston specs)
Fit	Clearance in piston, interference in connecting rod

Cylinder head

Material	Aluminium alloy
Warp limit	0.05 mm
Number of camshaft bearings	5
Cylinder head gasket thickness (service exchange)	1.4 mm
Cylinder head gasket thickness (new engine)	1.2 mm
Maximum amount to be skimmed from gasket face	0.20 mm

Valves

Head diameter:	
Inlet	40 mm
Exhaust	32.95 mm
Stem diameter:	
Inlet	7.965 to 7.980 mm
Exhaust	7.945 to 7.960 mm
Length:	
Inlet	109.29 mm
Exhaust	108.72 mm
Valve clearances (cold):	
Inlet	0.15 to 0.25 mm (0.006 to 0.010 in)
Exhaust	0.35 to 0.45 mm (0.014 to 0.018 in)
Adjustment method	Shims between tappet and valve stem

Valve timing

Inlet opens	10° 16’ BTDC
Inlet closes	28° 26’ ABDC
Exhaust opens	41° 20’ BBDC
Exhaust closes	4° 37’ ATDC

Lubrication system

Type	Wet sump, pressure feed and splash
Oil pressure (at oil temperature of 80°C/176°F):	
Minimum at 900 rpm	1.4 bar (20.3 lbf/in^2)
Minimum at 4000 rpm	3.5 bar (50.8 lbf/in^2)
Oil pressure warning light operation:	
Bulb extinguished above pressure of	0.8 bar (11.6 lbf/in^2)
Bulb lights if pressure falls below	0.6 bar (8.7 lbf/in^2)
Oil type/specification	Multigrade engine oil,viscosity SAE10W/40 or 15W/40
Filter type	Full flow, disposable cartridge (Champion F104)

Torque wrench settings

	Nm	lbf ft
Cam cover	10	7
Cylinder head bolts:		
Stage 1 (All bolts, in sequence)	60	44
Stage 2: Slacken bolt 1, then	20 +120°	15 +120°
Repeat Stage 2 on remaining bolts in sequence		
Camshaft bearing caps	15	11
Camshaft sprocket bolt (M10)	40	30
Camshaft sprocket bolt (M12)	80	59
Crankshaft pulley bolt	110	81
Camshaft thrust plate	10	7
Main bearing cap nuts and bolts	50	37
Main bearing side bolts	25	18
Big-end cap bolts	50	37
Oil pump-to-block bolts	20	15
Oil seal carrier	15	11
Sump bolts	20	15
Suction drain pipe (oil)	5	4
Flywheel to crankshaft*	50	37
Engine mounting bracket bolts (timing case end)	20	15
Engine mounting nut (centre) - left-hand mounting	35	26
Coolant pump bolts	20	15
Timing cover bolts	15	11
Timing belt tensioner	15	11
Oil pressure switch	25	18
Clutch housing bolts	45	33
Starter motor bolts	35	26

**Apply locking solution to bolt threads*

Part A: OHV engines

1 General description

The Peugeot 309 models fitted with the overhead valve type engine are the XE and GE models (1.1 litre engine), and the XE, XL, GE, GL, Style and GR Profile models (1.3 litre engine). Whichever engine type is fitted, the basic design is the same, being a water-cooled, four-cylinder, four-stroke petrol engine. The different engine capacities are obtained by using different cylinder bore diameters and lengths of piston stroke.

The engine is located in a transverse position and is inclined rearwards at an angle of 38°. This lowers the centre of gravity and also improves accessibility to the ancillary components mounted on the front of the engine.

The combined crankcase and cylinder block is of cast iron construction and houses the pistons, connecting rods, crankshaft and camshaft. The cast aluminium alloy pistons are retained on the connecting rods by gudgeon pins which are an interference fit in the connecting rod small-end bore. The connecting rods are attached to the crankshaft by renewable shell type big-end bearings.

The forged steel crankshaft is carried in five main bearings, also of the renewable shell type. Crankshaft endfloat is controlled by semi-circular thrust washers on the upper half of the centre main bearing.

The camshaft runs in three bearings recessed into bores in the cylinder block. Camshaft drive is by a double row timing chain from a sprocket on the crankshaft.

The cylinder head is an aluminium alloy die-casting of crossflow configuration. Inclined inlet and exhaust valves operate in renewable valve guides pressed into the cylinder head. Valve actuation is by rocker arms, pushrods and cam followers activated by the camshaft lobes.

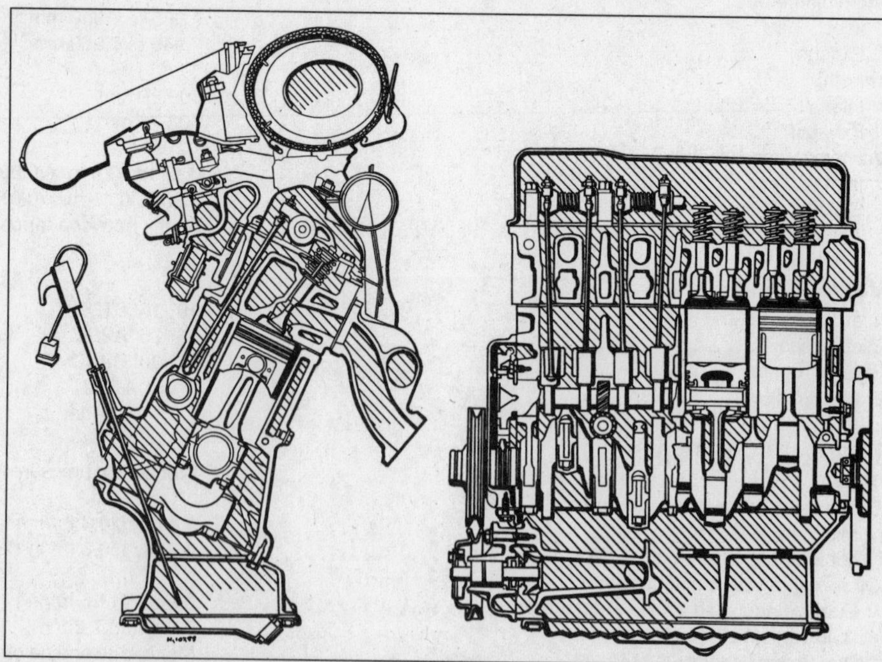

Fig. 1.1 Side and end section views of the OHV engine (Sec 1)

2.3 Topping-up the engine oil (OHV engine)

2.4 Engine oil drain plug (OHV engine)

2.10 Oil filler cap showing filter mesh (OHC engine shown)

2 Routine maintenance

The following maintenance procedures must be carried out at the intervals given in Routine Maintenance at the beginning of the manual.

1 The oil level in the engine should be checked with the car standing on level ground, with the engine switched off and preferably when the engine is cold.

2 The manufacturers specify a normal oil consumption figure of 0.5 litre per 1000 km (700 miles per pint), but this will depend on the condition of the engine and the conditions under which it is driven, therefore check the engine oil level at the intervals specified.

3 Withdraw the dipstick, wipe it clean, re-insert it and then withdraw it for the second time. The oil level should be between the high and low marks. If it is too low, top up through the filler cap (photo), but take care not to overfill. Refit the filler cap.

4 To drain the engine oil it is preferable for the engine to be hot. First raise the front of the car on ramps or with a jack. Unscrew the socket-headed plug in the sump, remove the filler cap and allow the oil to drain into a suitable container (photo).

5 When the oil has drained, wipe clean the drain plug then refit and tighten it.

6 If the oil filter is due for renewal, now is the time to change it. The removal and refitting details are described in Section 4.

7 Lower the car to the ground then fill the engine with the specified quantity and grade of oil.

8 Start the engine. There will be a short delay before the oil warning lamp goes out. This is normal and is caused by the new filter having to fill with oil.

9 Switch off the engine, wait ten minutes and check the oil level and top up if necessary.

10 Periodically, particularly on an engine which has covered a high mileage, remove the engine oil filler cap and, if fitted, check the filter mesh incorporated in the cap (photo). The filter is a breather for the crankcase ventilation system and should be cleaned or renewed if it is blocked with sludge.

3 Lubrication system - description

An external spur type oil pump is bolted to the rear face of the cylinder block and is driven by a skew gear off the camshaft. Oil is pumped through a full-flow filter to the crankshaft main oil gallery and then through drillings in the cylinder block to the camshaft, timing gears and valve train. The cylinder bores, gudgeon pins and valve stems are splash lubricated by oil thrown off the moving parts.

4 Oil filter - removal and refitting

1 The oil filter is of disposable cartridge type. Unscrew it with an oil filter wrench, but first wrap it in cloth as some oil will run out. If a proper wrench is not available a large worm drive hose clip can be fitted to the filter and the screw used as a gripping point. If all else fails, a screwdriver can be driven right through the cartridge and this used as a lever to unscrew it.

2 It is very important to purchase and fit the correct type of filter as some engines have a bypass valve incorporated in the filter mounting base of the crankcase whilst others have the valve incorporated in the filter cartridge.

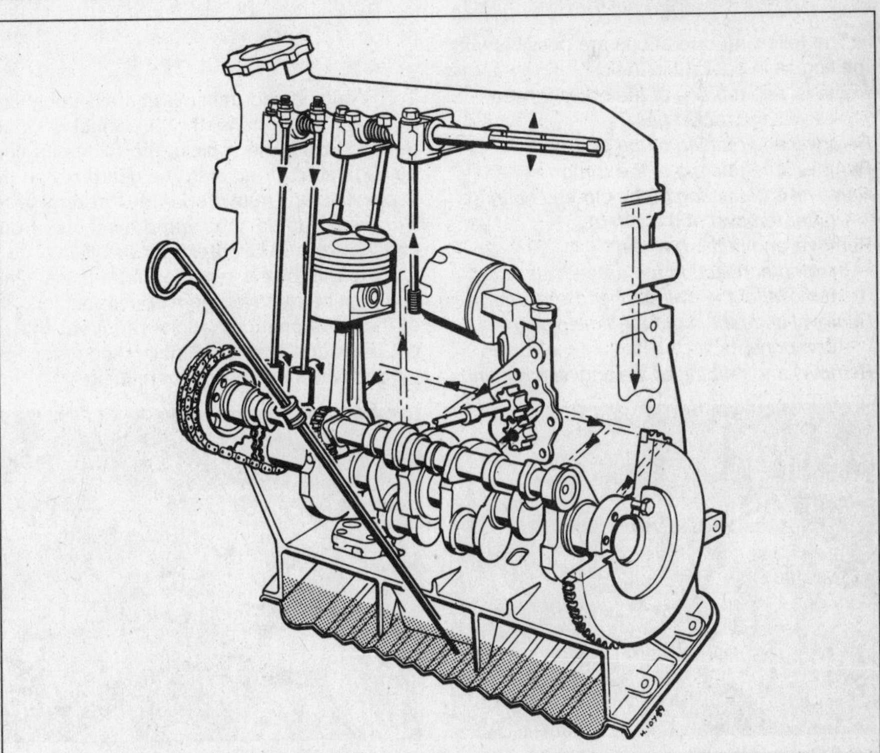
Fig. 1.2 Engine lubrication system circuit – OHV engine (Sec 3)

1

4.4 Lubricate filter seal with oil before fitting

3 No problem will arise if genuine Peugeot filters are used as they all incorporate a bypass valve. This will have no bearing upon the fact that a valve may already be built into the crankcase.
4 Clean the filter mounting ring on the crankcase and apply engine oil to the rubber seal on the cartridge. Do not use grease as it may make the filter difficult to unscrew (photo).
5 Check that the threaded sleeve is tight on the crankcase, offer up the new filter and screw it on using hand pressure only.
6 Top up the engine oil, run the engine and check for any signs of oil leakage from the filter seal.

5 Major operations possible with engine in car

The following operations are possible with the engine in position in the car.
Removal and refitting of the cylinder head, valves and rocker gear
Removal and refitting of the oil pump
Removal and refitting of the sump
Removal and refitting of the big-end bearings (after removal of the sump)
Removal and refitting of the piston/connecting rod assemblies (after removal of the cylinder head and sump)
Removal and refitting of the timing gear components
Removal and refitting of the engine mountings

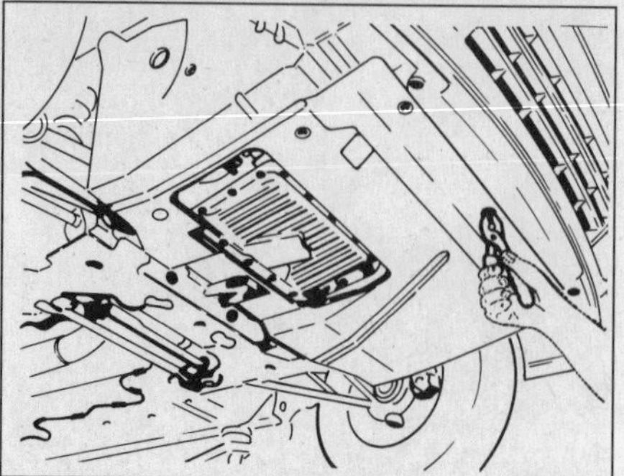

Fig. 1.3 Engine undershield and side shield removal – pull on clips to withdraw them (Sec 8)

Removal and refitting of the flywheel (after removal of the gearbox)
Removal and refitting of the major ancillary components - inlet and exhaust manifolds, starter motor, water pump, distributor, alternator and oil filter

6 Major operations requiring engine removal

The following operations can only be carried out with the engine removed from the car.
Removal and refitting of the main bearings
Removal and refitting of the crankshaft
Removal and refitting of the camshaft

7 Engine removal methods

1 The engine and transmission assembly are removed from beneath the vehicle. Once removed from the vehicle, the two units can be separated. If required the gearbox can be separated and removed with the engine *in situ*, but again its withdrawal is from underneath (see Chapter 6 for details).
2 If the gearbox is removed first, the engine can then be removed from above, but in view of the additional operations required, this is not a method that is normally recommended for removal and subsequent refitting.

8.1 Unbolt and remove the bonnet

8 Engine/transmission - removal

1 Open and support the bonnet in the full open position (photo).

HAYNES HiNT ***It is advisable though not necessary, to unbolt and remove the bonnet (see Chapter 11) to prevent damaging it and to improve access***

2 Disconnect and remove the battery as described in Chapter 12.
3 Remove the air cleaner unit and ductings (Chapter 3).
4 Remove the engine undershield and side shields, then drain the cooling system as described in Chapter 2.
5 Undo the sump drain plug and drain the engine oil into a suitable container for disposal.
6 Undo the two drain plugs and drain the oil from the gearbox and differential unit into a suitable container for disposal (see Chapter 6).
7 Disconnect and remove the radiator top hose.
8 Disconnect the heater hose at the thermostat and at the three-way connector on the front side of the engine (photo).
9 Disconnect the vacuum servo hose at the

8.8 Detach the hoses indicated from the three-way connector

8.11A Disconnect the LT lead connector, and distributor cap and HT leads . . .

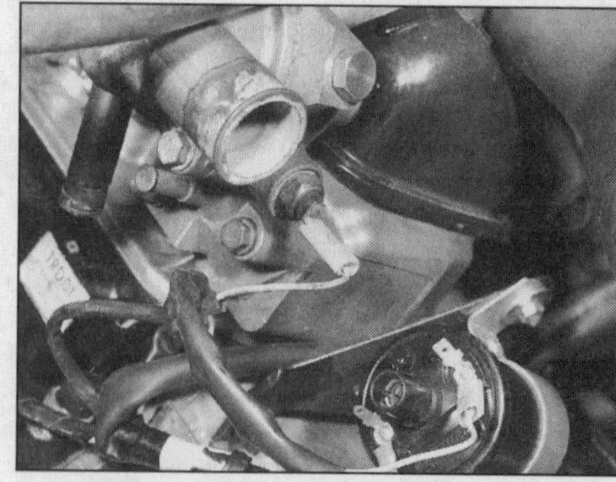

8.11B . . . from the distributor and coil

8.27 Torque reaction link and right-hand driveshaft

8.31 Lowering the engine and transmission from the car

9.5 Engine and transmission separation

inlet manifold and release it from the guide clip on the rocker cover.

10 Disconnect the fuel supply and return hose from the location bracket on the left-hand mounting and move the hose out of the way.

11 Disconnect the ignition HT leads from the coil and the spark plugs. Detach the LT lead connector from the distributor body. Remove the distributor cap and leads (photos).

12 Disconnect the accelerator and choke cables at the carburettor (see Chapter 3).

13 Disconnect the following items from the transmission:

(a) Reverse stop cable (unscrew)
(b) Clutch cable (see Chapter 5)
(c) Speedometer cable (see Chapter 12)
(d) Earth cable (note connection point)
(e) Reversing light switch wire

14 Disconnect the oil pressure and level switch leads, also the temperature switch leads, noting their connections. Detach the wiring harness from the clip on the gearbox, the diagnostic socket bracket and the clip on the coolant hose between the inlet manifold and the three-way connector.

15 Whilst the vehicle is still free-standing, loosen (but do not remove at this stage) the front wheel hub nuts.

16 If they are available, fit Peugeot special cables No 0903 to the front suspension struts as described in Chapter 9 (Section 4).

17 Raise and support the vehicle at the front end and rear end using safety (axle) stands for support. There should be a minimum front skirt-to-ground clearance of about 27 inches (686 mm) to allow engine and transmission removal clearance. The following operations are carried out underneath the vehicle, so ensure that it is securely supported.

18 Refit the drain plugs to the engine and transmission.

19 Unbolt and detach the exhaust downpipe from the manifold flange.

20 Unclip the heat shield from the gear control relay lever then detach the gear control rods from the gearbox at their balljoints by prising them free using needle-nosed pliers or an open-ended spanner.

21 Pivot the gearbox relay lever through 90° (either direction) to ensure that it is out of the way when removing the engine.

22 Detach the radiator bottom hose at the engine end, and the heater return hose at the radiator end.

23 Detach the wiring connectors from the starter motor and the alternator, also the coolant level indicator sensor on the radiator.

24 Undo the clamp bolt from the steering stub axle lower balljoint on each side and withdraw the bolts. Note that the bolts are fitted from the front. With the bolts removed, prise free the joints by levering down on the suspension arm. Take care not to damage the gaiters.

25 Remove the balljoint protector shields. If strut retainer cables were not fitted (as suggested in paragraph 16), it will be necessary to unbolt and remove the suspension arm inner pivot bolt in order to allow the full separation of the balljoint. Turn the hub onto full lock when separating the balljoint in this manner.

26 Undo the left-hand front hub nut, then detach and remove the left-hand drive shaft (see Chapter 7).

27 Unbolt and remove the torque reaction link from its location between the engine and the subframe on the right-hand side (photo).

28 Remove the right-hand driveshaft as described in Chapter 7.

29 Fit the lift sling to the engine and transmission. Lift sling attachment eyes are located at the right-hand side mounting and on the rear of the transmission on the left-hand side above the selector shaft. Attach the lift hoist to the sling and take up any slack but do not raise the engine/transmission.

30 Undo the left and right-hand mounting nuts.

31 Check that all attachments are clear of the engine and transmission, then carefully lower the engine and transmission unit (photo). As the two assemblies are separated from their mountings, collect the special flat washer from the left-hand mounting and the standard flat washer from the right-hand mounting.

32 When fully lowered, withdraw the engine and transmission from the front end of the vehicle. Lowering onto a suitable trolley will ease removal.

9 Engine - separation from the transmission

1 If the engine has been removed complete with the transmission assembly, it is necessary to separate the two units before dismantling work on the engine can begin.

2 To do this, first undo and remove the bolts securing the starter motor flange to the bellhousing and the bolt securing the lower support bracket to the cylinder block. Lift away the starter motor.

3 Undo and remove the bolts securing the ignition coil mounting plate to the bellhousing and lift off this assembly.

4 Unbolt and remove the clutch housing cover plate with the TDC wire and sensor (where fitted). Loosen the small bolt and pivot the plate free.

5 Support the gearbox, remove any retaining bolts remaining. The gearbox can now be withdrawn from the engine but as they are separated, do not allow the weight of the transmission to hang on the input shaft. Recover any loose dowels (photo).

10 Engine - dismantling (general)

1 Ideally, the engine is mounted on a proper stand for overhaul but it is anticipated that most owners will have a strong bench on which to place it. If a sufficiently large strong bench is not available then the work can be done at ground level. It is essential, however, that some form of substantial wooden surface is available. Timber should be at least 3/4 inch thick, otherwise the weight of the engine will cause projections to punch holes straight through it.

2 It will save a great deal of time later if the engine is thoroughly cleaned down on the exterior before any dismantling begins. This can be done by using paraffin and a stiff brush or more easily, probably, by the use of a water soluble solvent which can be brushed on and then the dirt swilled off with a water jet. This

11.1 General view of the 1.3 litre engine prior to dismantling

will dispose of all the heavy grease and grit once and for all so that later cleaning of individual components will be a relatively clean process and the paraffin bath will not become contaminated with abrasive metal.

3 As the engine is stripped down, clean each part as it comes off. Try to avoid immersing parts with oilways in paraffin as pockets of liquid could remain and cause oil dilution in the critical first few revolutions after reassembly. Clean oilways with wire or, preferably, an air jet.

4 Where possible, avoid damaging gaskets on removal, especially if new ones have not been obtained. They can be used as patterns if new ones have to be specially cut.

5 It is helpful to obtain a few blocks of wood to support the engine while it is in the process of dismantling. Start dismantling at the top of the engine and then turn the block over and deal with the sump and crankshaft etc, afterwards.

6 Nuts and bolts should be refitted in their locations where possible to avoid confusion later. As an alternative keep each group of nuts and bolts together in a jar or tin.

7 Many items which are removed must be refitted in the same position, if they are not being renewed. These include valves, rocker arms, cam followers, pistons, pushrods, bearings and connecting rods. Some of these are marked on assembly to avoid any possibility of mixing them up during overhaul. Others are not, and it is a great help if adequate preparation is made in advance to classify these parts. Suitably labelled tins or jars and, for small items, egg trays, tobacco tins and so on, can be used. The time spent in this operation will be amply repaid later.

8 Other items which will be useful are a notebook and pencil, masking tape (for labelling components) and a good supply of plastic bags.

Make notes of the positions of washers, shims, etc - you may think you will remember as you are dismantling but it can be a different story when the time comes for reassembly!

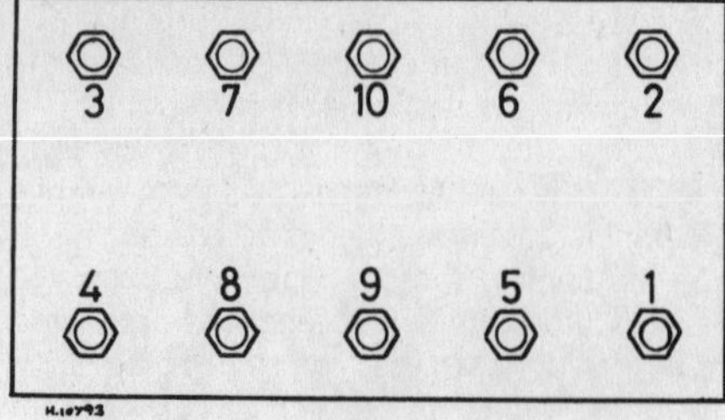

Fig. 1.4 Numerical sequence for loosening the cylinder head bolts – OHV engine (Sec 12)

11 Engine ancillary components - removal

1 Before engine dismantling begins it is necessary to remove the externally mounted ancillary components. The extent and sequence of their removal is dependent on the amount to which the engine is being dismantled. If the engine is being fully dismantled, the following items must be removed (photo).

(a) Thermostat housing complete - refer to Chapter 2 for details
(b) Inlet manifold with carburettor - refer to Chapter 3 for details
(c) Exhaust manifold - refer to Chapter 3 for details
(d) Fuel pump - refer to Chapter 3 for details
(e) Distributor - refer to Chapter 4 for details
(f) Alternator and mounting bracket - refer to Chapter 12 for details
(g) Clutch unit - refer to Chapter 5 for details
(h) Engine oil filter - refer to Section 4 for details

2 With the major ancillary components removed, the engine sub-assemblies can now be dismantled as required, as described in the following Sections.

12 Cylinder head - removal (engine in car)

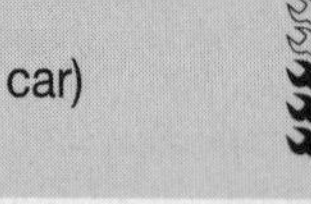

1 Disconnect the battery earth terminal and then drain the cooling system as described in Chapter 2.

2 Remove the air cleaner assembly as described in Chapter 3.

3 Undo and remove the nuts securing the exhaust front pipe to the manifold flange and recover the heat shield and gasket. If it is necessary to jack up the car for this operation, make sure that it is well supported on axle stands.

4 Slacken the retaining clip and remove the brake servo vacuum hose from the inlet manifold.

5 Undo and remove the two nuts and one bolt securing the air cleaner hot air box to the rocker cover. Lift off the air box.

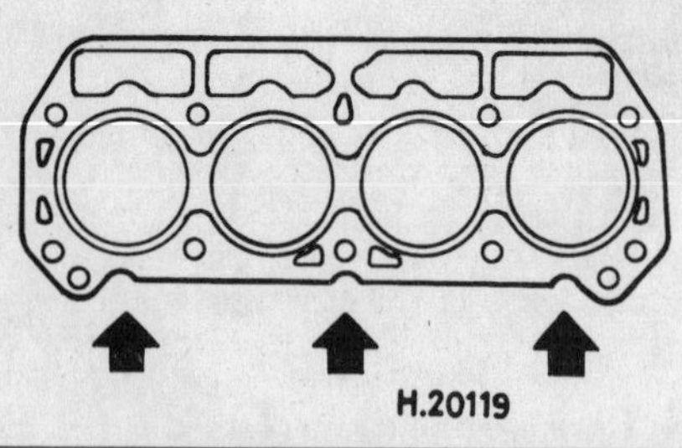

Fig. 1.5 Cylinder head gasket identification - OHV engines (Sec 12)

E series (1.1 litre) engine – 2 notches
G Series (1.3 litre) engine – 3 notches

6 Slacken the retaining clips and withdraw the radiator top hose and heater hose from their outlets on the thermostat housing.

7 Slacken the hose clips and detach the coolant hoses from the inlet manifold and carburettor as necessary.

8 Mark the positions of the HT leads and then pull them off the spark plugs. Note that No 1 cylinder is nearest to the flywheel.

9 Detach the fuel inlet pipe and distributor vacuum advance pipe from the carburettor.

10 Refer to Chapter 3, and disconnect the accelerator cable and choke cable from the carburettor.

11 Detach the electrical lead from the temperature gauge transmitter at the rear of the cylinder head.

12 Undo and remove the remaining securing nuts and lift off the rocker cover complete with breather hose. Recover the rocker cover gasket. The engine must be cold before proceeding any further to avoid distortion of the cylinder head.

13 Slacken all the cylinder head bolts one turn at a time in the order shown in Fig. 1.4 and then undo and remove them completely.

14 Lift off the rocker shaft assembly, holding it at both ends to prevent it springing apart. After removal, secure the assembly with wire to keep it together.

15 Lift out each pushrod in turn, using a twisting motion to release them from the cam followers.

Punch eight holes in a stiff piece of cardboard, number them one to eight and place the pushrods in order of removal through the cardboard.

16 The cylinder head, complete with manifolds and carburettor, can now be removed by lifting it upwards. If the head is stuck, try to rock it to break the seal or strike it sharply with a hide or plastic mallet. Under no circumstances should the head be struck directly with a metal hammer, nor should any attempt be made to prise it apart from the cylinder block using a screwdriver or cold chisel.

Cranking the engine on the starter motor may be effective in breaking the seal of a stubborn gasket.

17 Having removed the cylinder head, lift out the cam followers. Withdraw them one at a time, keeping each follower in its correct order of removal so that it can be fitted in its original bore.
18 If further work is to be carried out on the cylinder head, remove the thermostat housing and manifolds before proceeding.
19 It should be noted that the cylinder head gasket must be renewed when refitting and it is essential that the correct type is fitted according to model (see Figure 1.5).

13 Cylinder head - removal (engine out of car)

Remove the engine ancillary components as described in Section 11, and then proceed as directed in paragraphs 12 to 17 inclusive of the previous Section.

14 Valves - removal

With the cylinder head removed from the engine, the valves can be removed as follows.
1 First remove the spark plugs.
2 Using a conventional valve spring compressor, compress each valve spring in turn until the two halves of the collets can be removed. Release the compressor and remove the spring and spring cup, valve oil seal, spring seat and the valve itself.
3 As before, identify all the parts so that they may be refitted into the same positions from which they were taken.

If when the valve spring compressor is screwed down, the valve spring cup refuses to free and expose the split collets, do not screw the compressor further down in an effort to force the cup free. Gently tap the top of the tool directly over the spring cup with a light hammer. This will usually free the cup. Whilst tapping the tool, hold the compressor firmly with your other hand to prevent the tool jumping off the cup when it is released.

15 Sump - removal

1 The sump consists of two parts: a lower pressed steel baseplate, containing the drain plug, and a light alloy main body incorporating anti-surge baffles. A separate compartment on the front face of the main body houses the water pump and water inlet elbow.
2 If the sump is to be removed with the engine in the car it is first necessary to remove the engine undertray, then drain the engine oil and the cooling system. Also to be removed are the alternator dirt shield, alternator and water pump hoses. Full information covering these operations will be found in the relevant Sections and Chapters of this manual.
3 If the engine is out of the car and on the bench, turn it over on its side so that the sump bolts are accessible.
4 Undo and remove the fourteen baseplate retaining bolts and lift off the plate.
5 Undo and remove the three retaining bolts and withdraw the oil pick-up and strainer assembly (photo).
6 Undo and remove the bolts inside and along the outer edge of the main body and lift off this assembly. If it is stuck, tap it free using a hide or plastic mallet. Recover the cork and paper gaskets from the baseplate, main body and strainer mating faces.

16 Flywheel - removal

1 If this component is to be removed with the engine in the car, it will first be necessary to remove the bellhousing and gearbox assembly, and then the clutch, as described in Chapter 6 and Chapter 5 respectively.
2 If the engine is on the bench, turn it the right way up and stand it on wooden blocks positioned beneath the crankcase.
3 Lock the flywheel to prevent it turning by engaging a strip of angle iron with the ring gear teeth and resting it against a bar inserted through the rear engine-to-bellhousing retaining bolt hole.
4 Undo and remove the flywheel retaining bolts in a progressive, diagonal sequence, recover the seating plate, and lift off the flywheel. Be careful not to drop it, it is heavy.

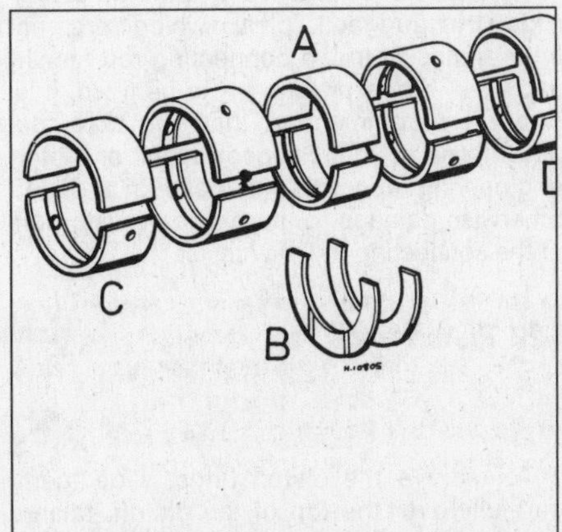

Fig. 1.6 Using a spring compressor to release the valve collets (Sec 14)

17 Timing cover, gears and chain - removal

1 Remove the sump as described in Section 15.
2 Place a block of wood between the crankshaft and the side of the crankcase to prevent rotation of the crankshaft.
3 Using a socket and extension bar, undo and remove the crankshaft pulley retaining bolt and then lever off the pulley using two screwdrivers. The retaining bolt is very tight.
4 Undo and remove the timing cover retaining bolts, ease the cover off its locating dowels and remove it from the front face of the engine.
5 Undo and remove the three bolts securing the camshaft sprocket to the camshaft.
6 Lift off the camshaft sprocket complete with chain and then using two screwdrivers, lever off the crankshaft sprocket. Recover the Woodruff key from the end of the crankshaft.

18 Camshaft and oil pump driveshaft - removal

It is theoretically possible to remove the camshaft with the engine in the car. However, the preliminary work is so extensive - removal of cylinder head, sump, starter motor, oil pump and fuel pump, followed by the lowering of the front of the engine - that the procedure is not recommended. With the engine on the bench and the camshaft sprocket removed as described in Section 17, proceed as follows.
1 Undo and remove the two bolts that secure the distributor mounting plate to the side of the cylinder block and lift off the plate.
2 Withdraw the distributor driving dog from the splined end of the oil pump driveshaft.
3 Prior to removing the shaft, if a dial gauge is available, the driveshaft endfloat should be checked and noted (also the camshaft).
4 Using a pair of pliers, extract the small circlip from the end of the shaft, lift out the driven gear and washer, and then slide out the driveshaft from the oil pump side of the cylinder block.

15.5 Oil pick-up and strainer shown with sump baseplate removed

5 Rotate the camshaft until the cut-outs on the front flange are aligned with the thrust plate retaining bolts. Relieve the locktabs (if applicable), then undo and remove the thrust plate retaining bolts.

6 Lift off the thrust plate and then carefully withdraw the camshaft from the front of the engine. Take care to avoid scratching the soft bearing surfaces with the camshaft lobes.

19 Piston and connecting rod assemblies - removal

1 This operation may be carried out with the engine in the car after removal of the cylinder head, described in Section 12, and the sump, described in Section 15.

2 Before removing the piston and connecting rod assemblies, clean off all traces of carbon from the top of the cylinder bores. If a wear ridge can be felt, reduce this as much as possible, using a suitable scraper, to avoid damaging the pistons and rings during removal.

3 Rotate the crankshaft in the normal direction of rotation until No 1 piston is at the bottom of its stroke.

4 Undo and remove the big-end bearing nuts on No 1 connecting rod and take off the cap and lower bearing shell. If the cap is tight, tap it gently from side to side using a hammer.

5 Push the piston and connecting rod assembly up through the bore and withdraw it from the top of the cylinder block. Take care not to score the crankshaft journal with the big-end bolts.

6 Refit the bearing cap and lower shell to the connecting rod and secure with the nuts finger tight. Make sure that the upper and lower bearing shells are not interchanged if they are to be re-used. Identification numbers may be stamped on the connecting rod and big-end cap to indicate the cylinder to which they are fitted.

HAYNES HiNT

If numbers are not visible, suitably mark the cap and rod using a centre punch.

7 Repeat the above procedure for the remaining three piston and connecting rod assemblies, turning the crankshaft as necessary to gain access to the big-end nuts.

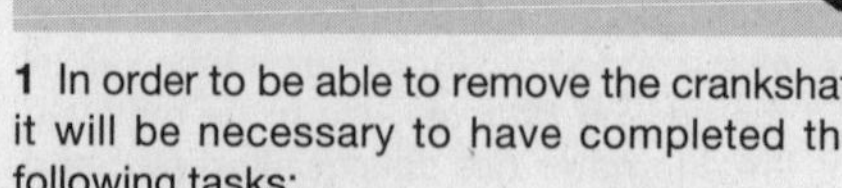

20 Crankshaft and main bearings - removal

1 In order to be able to remove the crankshaft it will be necessary to have completed the following tasks:

(a) Removal of engine
(b) Separation of engine from transmission
(c) Removal of cylinder head
(d) Removal of sump and flywheel
(e) Removal of timing cover, gears and chain
(f) Removal of big-end bearings

2 It is not essential to have extracted the pistons and connecting rods, but it makes for a less cluttered engine block during crankshaft removal.

3 Before removing the crankshaft, it is advisable to check the crankshaft endfloat as described in Section 38. If the crankshaft endfloat is in excess of the maximum amount specified, it is indicative of excessive wear of the crankshaft and bearings. Remove the crankshaft as follows.

4 Begin by removing the five retaining bolts and lifting off the oil seal housing at the rear of the crankshaft and cylinder block.

5 Check that the main bearing caps have identification numbers marked on them; No 1 should be at the flywheel end and No 5 at the timing gear end. If identification is not visible, use a centre punch to mark the caps. Also note the direction of fitting of the caps.

6 Slacken the main bearing cap retaining bolts by one turn only to begin with. Once all have been loosened, proceed to unscrew and remove them.

7 The bearing caps can now be lifted away, together with the shells inside them. Finally the crankshaft can be removed, followed by the upper shells seated in the crankcase.

21 Gudgeon pins - removal

The pistons are retained on the connecting rods by gudgeon pins, which are an interference fit in the connecting rod small-end bore. If new pistons are to be fitted, it is strongly recommended that you take the assemblies to your Peugeot dealer or motor engineering specialist to have this done, otherwise damage to the piston or distortion of the connecting rod may result.

22 Piston rings - removal

1 To remove the piston rings, slide them carefully over the top of the piston, taking care not to scratch the aluminium alloy; never slide them off the bottom of the piston skirt. It is very easy to break the cast iron piston rings if they are pulled off roughly, so this operation should be done with extreme care. It is helpful to make use of an old 0.5 mm (0.020 in) feeler gauge.

2 Lift one end of the piston ring to be removed out of its groove and insert under it the end of the feeler gauge.

3 Slide the feeler gauge slowly round the piston and, as the ring comes out of its groove, apply slight upward pressure so it rests on the land above. It can then be eased off the piston with the feeler gauge stopping it from slipping into an empty groove if it is any but the top piston ring that is being removed.

4 Repeat the procedure on the remaining piston rings. Keep the rings with their pistons if they are to be re-used (photo).

23 Engine components - examination for wear

When the engine has been stripped down and all parts properly cleaned, decisions have to be made as to what needs renewal. The following Sections tell the examiner what to look for. In any border-line case it is always best to decide in favour of a new part. Even if a part may still be serviceable, its life will have to be reduced by wear and the degree of trouble needed to renew it in the future must be taken into consideration. However, these things are relative and it depends on whether a quick 'survival' job is being done or whether the car as a whole is being regarded as having many thousands of miles of useful and economical life remaining.

24 Crankshaft, main and big-end bearings - examination and renovation

1 With careful servicing and regular oil and filter changes, bearings will last for a very long time. But they can still fail for unforeseen reasons. With big-end bearings, an indication is a regular rhythmic loud knocking from the crankcase. The frequency depends on engine speed and is particularly noticeable when the engine is under load. This symptom is

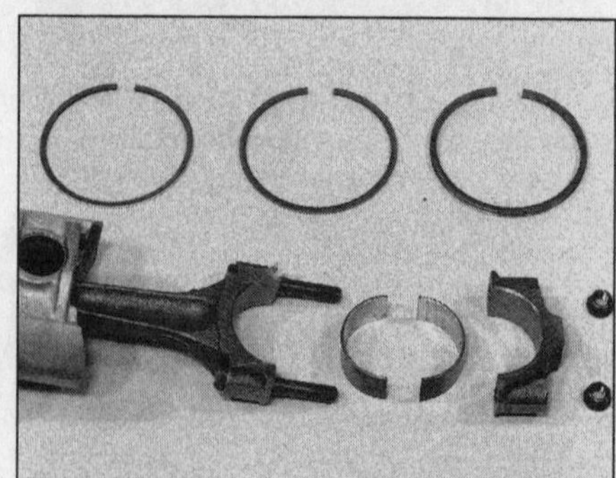

22.4 Piston, connecting rod and piston rings dismantled for inspection

accompanied by a fall in oil pressure, although this is not normally noticeable unless an oil pressure gauge is fitted. Main bearing failure is usually indicated by serious vibration, particularly at higher engine revolutions, accompanied by a more significant drop in oil pressure and a 'rumbling' noise.

2 Big-end bearings can be removed with the engine still in the car. If the failure is sudden and the engine has a low mileage since new or overhaul, this is probably worth doing. Bearing shells in good condition have bearing surfaces with a smooth, even matt silver/grey colour all over. Worn bearings will show patches of a different colour when the bearing metal has worn away and exposed the underlay. Damaged bearings will be pitted or scored. It is always well worthwhile fitting new shells as their cost is relatively low. If the crankshaft is in good condition, it is merely a question of obtaining another set of standard size shells (but see below). A reground crankshaft will need new bearing shells as a matter of course (photo).

3 Look at the main bearing journals and the crankpins. If there are any deep scratches or score marks, the shaft will need regrinding. Such conditions will nearly always be accompanied by similar deterioration in the matching bearing shells.

4 Each bearing journal must also be perfectly round and can be checked with a micrometer (photo) or caliper gauge around the periphery at several points. If there is more the 0.02 mm (0.001 in) of ovality, regrinding is necessary.

5 A main Peugeot agent or motor engineering specialist will be able to decide to what extent regrinding is necessary and also supply the special oversize shell bearings to match whatever may need grinding off.

6 Before taking the crankshaft for regrinding, check also the cylinder bore and pistons as it may be advantageous to have the whole engine done at the same time.

7 If the crankshaft is not being reground, but the bearings are to be renewed, take the old shells along to your supplier and check that you are getting the correct size bearings.

8 Check the spigot bush in the end of the crankshaft for wear, and if necessary renew it.

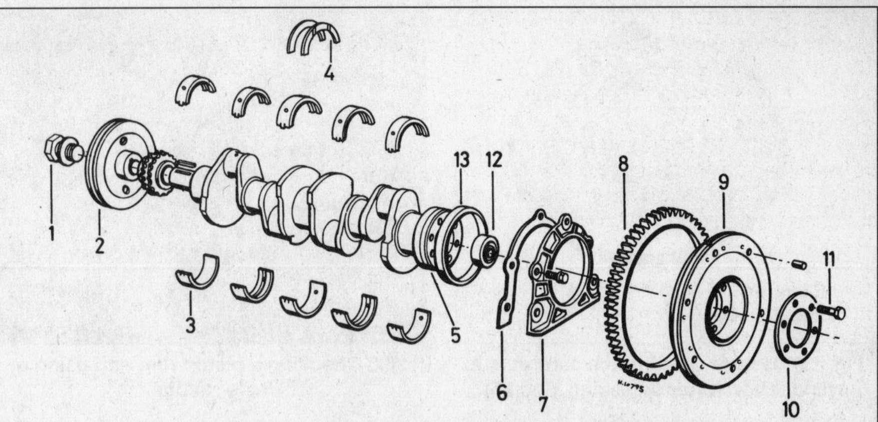

Fig. 1.7 Crankshaft and flywheel assembly (Sec 24)

1 Pulley retaining bolt
2 Pulley
3 Shell bearing
4 Thrust washers
5 Crankshaft
6 Gasket
7 Oil seal cover
8 Starter ring gear
9 Flywheel
10 Locking plate
11 Flywheel bolt
12 Spigot bush
13 Crankshaft rear flange seal

To remove the bush, fill it with grease and then drive in a close-fitting rod. The bush will come out by the hydraulic pressure generated.

25 Cylinder bores - examination and renovation

1 A new cylinder is perfectly round and the walls parallel throughout its length. The action of the piston tends to wear the walls at right-angles to the gudgeon pin due to side thrust. This wear takes place principally on that section of the cylinder swept by the piston rings.

2 It is possible to get an indication of bore wear by removing the cylinder head with the engine still in the car. With the piston down in the bore, first signs of wear can be seen and felt just below the top of the bore where the top piston ring reaches and there will be a noticeable lip. If there is no lip it is fairly reasonable to expect that bore wear is not severe and any lack of compression or excessive oil consumption is due to worn or broken piston rings or pistons.

3 If it is possible to obtain a bore measuring micrometer, measure the bore in the thrust plane below the lip and again at the bottom of the cylinder in the same plane. If the difference is more than 0.15 mm (0.006 in), a rebore is necessary. Similarly, a difference of 0.08 mm (0.003 in) or more between two measurements of the bore diameter taken at right angles to each other is a sign of ovality, calling for a rebore.

4 Any bore which is significantly scratched or scored will need reboring. This symptom usually indicates that the piston or rings are damaged also. In the event of only one cylinder being in need of reboring it will still be necessary for all four to be bored and fitted with new oversize pistons and rings. Your

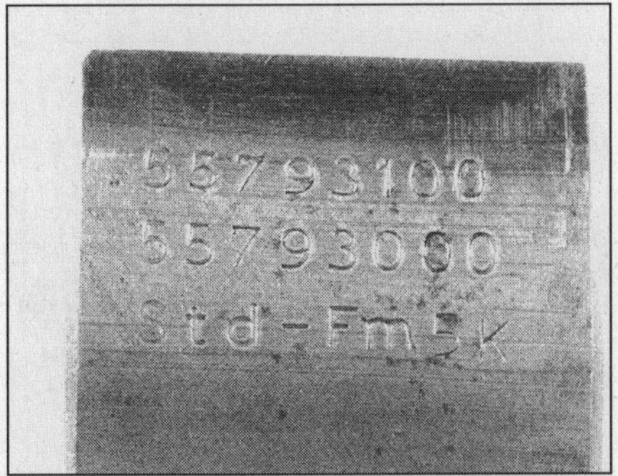

24.2 Bearing shell identification mark (on rear face of shell)

24.4 Measure crankshaft journals for wear using a micrometer

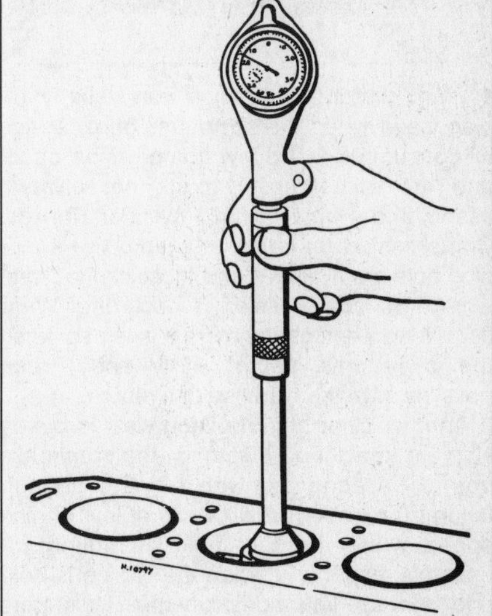

Fig. 1.8 Measuring cylinder bore wear with bore gauge (Sec 25)

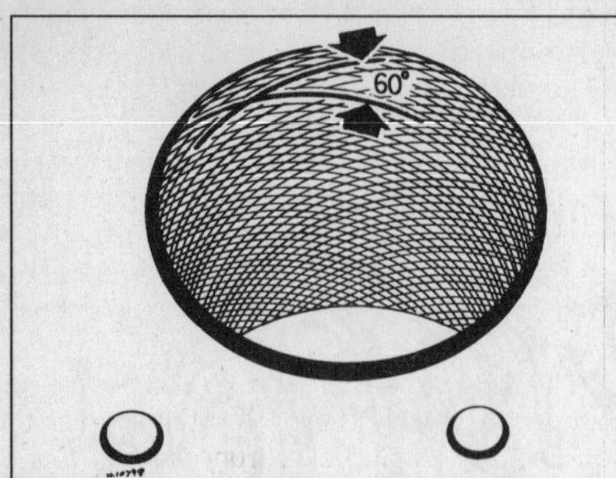

Fig. 1.9 Desired cross-hatch pattern in a cylinder bore after deglazing (Sec 25)

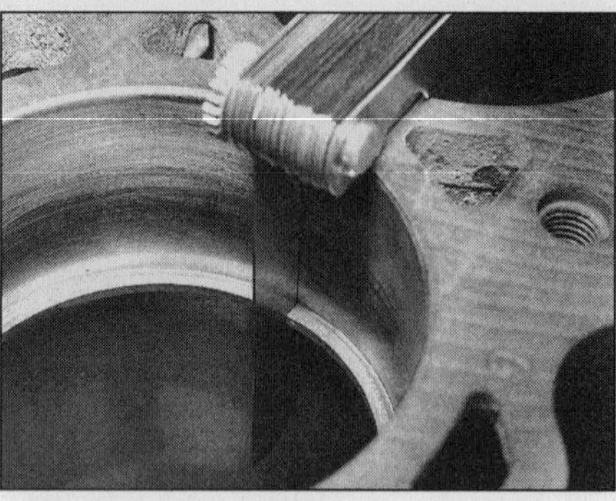

26.3 Checking a piston ring gap using a feeler gauge

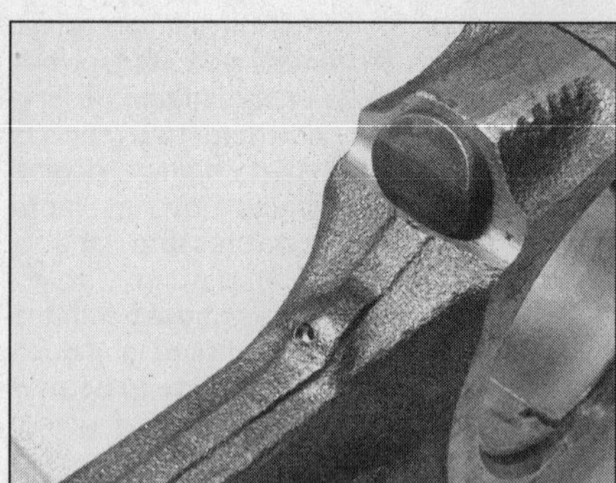

27.3 Connecting rod oil squirt hole

Peugeot agent or local motor engineering specialist will be able to rebore and obtain the necessary matched pistons. If the crankshaft is undergoing regrinding also, it is a good idea to let the same firm renovate and reassemble the crankshaft and pistons to the block. A reputable firm normally gives a guarantee for such work.

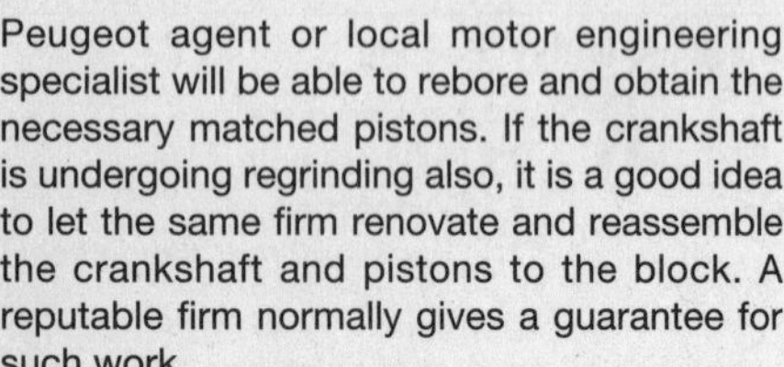

5 If the cylinders are in a satisfactory condition and a rebore is not necessary but new pistons and/or rings are to be fitted, the cylinder bores must be deglazed. This entails removing the high surface polish or glaze on the cylinder walls which will otherwise prevent the new rings from properly bedding in, with resultant high oil consumption.

6 Deglazing can be carried out using a fine grade emery cloth wrapped around a suitable former. Use liberal amounts of paraffin to keep the emery unclogged and use a criss-cross action so that the resulting finish is of a cross-hatch pattern. On completion thoroughly wash the block and remove all traces of emery grit.

26 Piston and piston rings - examination and renovation

1 Worn pistons and rings can usually be diagnosed when the symptoms of excessive oil consumption and low compression occur and are sometimes, though not always, associated with worn cylinder bores. Compression testers that fit into the spark plug hole are available and these can indicate where low compression is occurring. Wear usually accelerates the more it is left so when the symptoms occur, early action can possibly save the expense of a rebore.

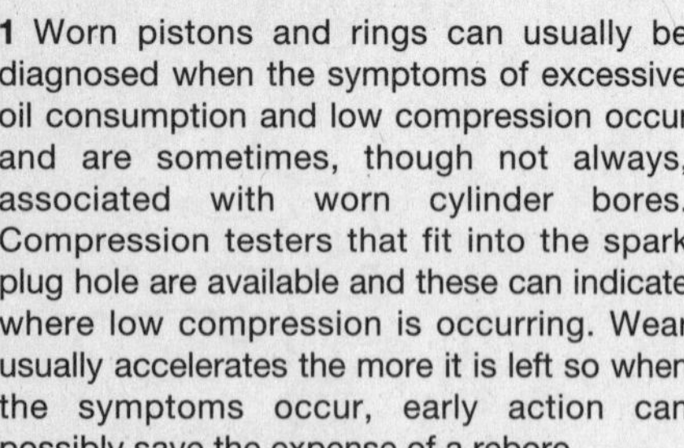

2 Another symptom of piston wear is piston slap - a knocking noise from the crankcase not to be confused with big-end bearing failure. It can be heard clearly at low engine speed when there is no load (idling for example) especially when the engine is cold and is much less audible when the engine speed increases. Piston wear usually occurs in the skirt or lower end of the piston and is indicated by vertical streaks in the worn area which is always on the thrust side. It can also be seen where the skirt thickness is different.

3 Piston ring wear can be checked by first removing the rings from the pistons as described in Section 22. Then place the rings in the cylinder bores from the top, pushing them down about 38 mm (1.5 in) with the head of a piston (from which the rings have been removed) so that they rest square in the cylinder. Now measure the gap at the ends of the rings with a feeler gauge and compare the dimension obtained with the figures given in Specifications. It the gaps are excessive the rings must be renewed (photo).

4 The grooves in which the rings locate in the pistons can also become enlarged in use. These clearances can be measured with the rings in position on the piston after cleaning away any carbon deposits. Excessive clearances may be overcome by fitting thicker piston rings, but the grooves will need to be machined out to suit. This is a specialist's job and must therefore be entrusted to a Peugeot dealer or automotive machine shop.

5 If any of the pistons are excessively worn or damaged they must be renewed as a set. Removal of the pistons from the connecting rods whether for repair or renewal is a task which must be entrusted to your Peugeot dealer or motor engineering specialist (see Section 21).

6 If the engine has been using an excessive amount of oil, but no significant wear or defects can be found in the cylinder bores and/or the pistons and rings, consult your Peugeot dealer or motor engineering specialist concerning the possibility of fitting a ring expander to the oil control rings, or fitting an alternative type of oil control ring.

27 Connecting rods - examination and renovation

1 The connecting rods are not subject to wear but can, in the case of engine seizure, become bent or twisted. If any distortion is visible or suspected, have the rods checked for alignment by your Peugeot dealer or motor engineering specialist. A small amount of twist or distortion of the rods can usually be straightened, but again this must be entrusted to a specialist. If the rods are excessively twisted, distorted or are damaged in any way they must be renewed as a set.

2 Removal of the pistons and gudgeon pins from the connecting rods is a specialist task (see Section 21).

3 Check that the oil squirt hole is clear (photo).

28 Camshaft and camshaft bearings - examination and renovation

1 The camshaft lobes and bearing journals should be carefully examined for any indications of flat spots, deep scoring, pitting or breakdown of the surface hardening. If any of these conditions exist the camshaft must be renewed, together with a complete set of cam followers.

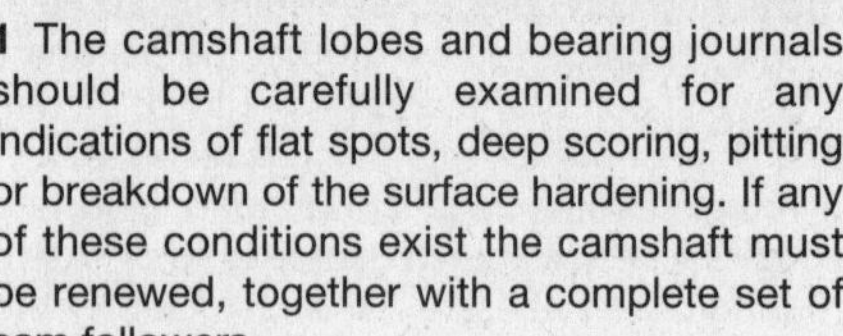

2 If only very slight scoring marks on the lobes are noticed, these can be removed by a very gentle rubbing down with fine emery cloth or an oil stone. The greatest care should be taken to keep the cam profiles smooth.

3 Removal of the camshaft bearings in the cylinder block can be carried out using the following method.

4 First drive out the camshaft bearing sealing plug from the flywheel end bearing, using a long tubular drift (Fig. 1.10).

5 Removal of the front, rear and centre camshaft bushes is best accomplished by the

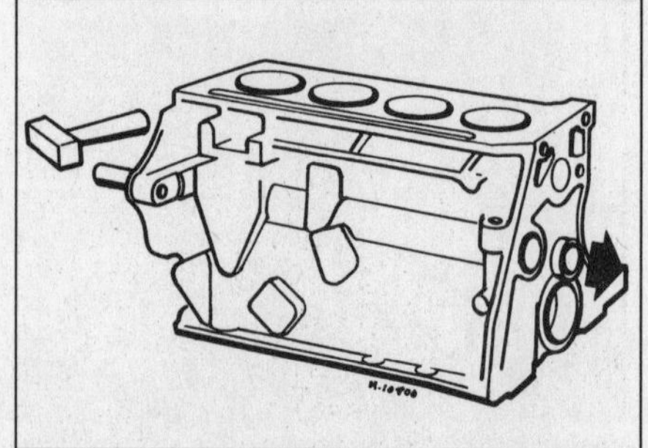

Fig. 1.10 Removing the camshaft sealing plug (Sec 28)

use of a length of threaded rod and nuts with suitable tubular distance pieces (Fig. 1.11).

6 Note the precise positioning of each bearing bush before removal and ensure that the bearing seats are not damaged during the removal operation.

7 Fit the new bearing bushes using the same method as for removal, starting with the centre one. It is essential that the bearing oil hole is in exact alignment with the one drilled in the bearing seat and marks should be made on the edge of the bearing bush and seat before pulling into position.

8 Fit a new camshaft front bearing sealing cap.

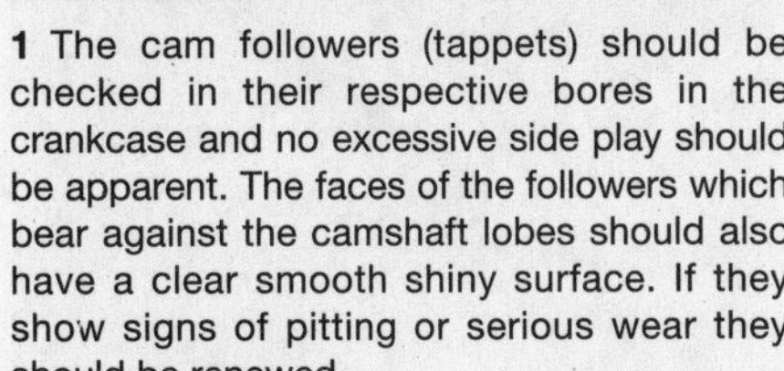

29 Cam followers and pushrods - examination and renovation

1 The cam followers (tappets) should be checked in their respective bores in the crankcase and no excessive side play should be apparent. The faces of the followers which bear against the camshaft lobes should also have a clear smooth shiny surface. If they show signs of pitting or serious wear they should be renewed.

2 The pushrods should be checked for straightness by rolling them along a flat surface. Also check for wear of the ball end which locates in the cam follower, and the cup end that accepts the rocker adjusting ball. Renew as necessary.

30 Cylinder head, valves and piston crowns - decarbonising

1 When the cylinder head is removed, either in the course of an overhaul or for inspection of bores or valve condition when the engine is in the car, it is normal to remove all carbon deposits from the piston crowns, cylinder head and valves.

2 This is best done using a scraper, but when working on the cylinder head and piston crowns, take care not to damage the relatively soft alloy in any way.

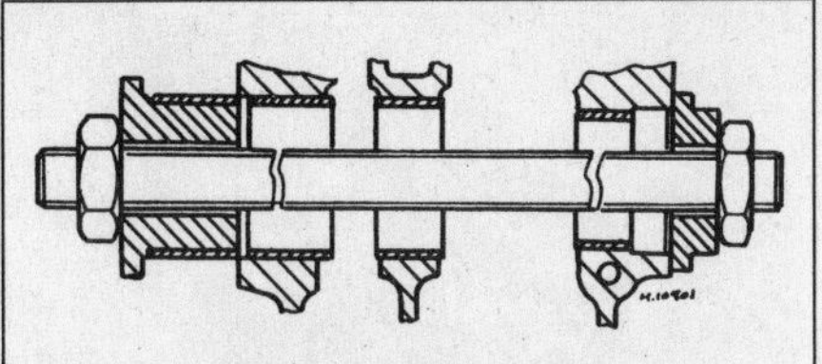

Fig. 1.11 Camshaft bush removal using a threaded rod, nuts and distance pieces (Sec 28)

3 When the engine is in the car, certain precautions must be taken when decarbonising the piston crowns in order to prevent dislodged pieces of carbon falling into the interior of the engine which could cause damage to the cylinder bores, piston and rings, or if allowed into the water passages, damage to the water pump. Turn the engine so that the piston being worked on is at the top of its stroke and then mask off the adjacent cylinder bores and all surrounding orifices with paper and adhesive tape. Press grease into the gap all round the piston to keep the carbon particles out and then scrape all carbon away. When completed, carefully clear out the grease around the rim of the piston with a matchstick or something similar bringing any carbon particles with it. Repeat the process on the other piston crown. It is not recommended that a ring of carbon is left round the edge of the piston on the theory that it will aid oil consumption. This was valid in the earlier days of long stroke, low revving engines but modern engines, fuels and lubricants cause less carbon deposits anyway, and any left behind tends merely to cause hot spots.

4 The valves are best cleaned using a rotary wire brush.

31 Cylinder head, valves and rocker gear - examination and renovation

1 Examine the cylinder head for signs of cracks around the valve seats or spark plug holes and for water erosion around the passages and outlets in the cylinder head face. Also check for distortion of the cylinder head face using a straight-edge. If any cracks are apparent the head must be renewed. Minor erosion or distortion of the cylinder head face can be rectified by having the face skimmed by a motor engineering specialist or machine shop. If this work is carried out, refer to the Specifications for the maximum amount of metal that can be removed from the head face and note also that a thicker gasket must be used on reassembly.

2 The valve seats should be examined for signs of pitting or ridging. Slight pitting can be ground away using carborundum paste and an *old* valve (photo). New valves are specially plated and **must not** be used to grind in the seats. If the valve faces are burnt or cracked, new valves must be obtained. If the valve seats require re-cutting ensure that the seat width and seat angle are maintained (Fig. 1.12).

3 The rocker gear should be dismantled and thoroughly cleaned of the sludge deposits which normally tend to accumulate on it. The gear is dismantled by simply sliding the pedestals, springs and rockers off the shafts (photo). The shafts may be removed from the centre pedestal after drifting out the retaining roll pin.

4 The rocker arms should be a slide fit over the shaft with very little play. If play is excessive, or if ridges are apparent in the shaft, renew these components. Also check the domed ends of the rocker adjusting screws for wear and renew any that are deformed. The pad of the rocker that bears against the valve stem should also be examined. It is normal to detect a slight wear ridge using the edge of your fingernail. If the ridge is visibly apparent then it has penetrated the surface hardening of the pad and the rocker arm should be renewed. A very slight ridge can be dressed with an oilstone.

5 Refit the valve into its guide in the head and note if there is any sideways movement which denotes wear between the stem and guide. Here again the degree of wear can vary. If excessive, the performance of the engine can be noticeably affected and oil consumption increased. Wear is normally in the guide rather than on the valve stem but check a new valve in the guide if possible first. Valve guide

31.2 Valve seat refacing using an old valve and carborundum paste

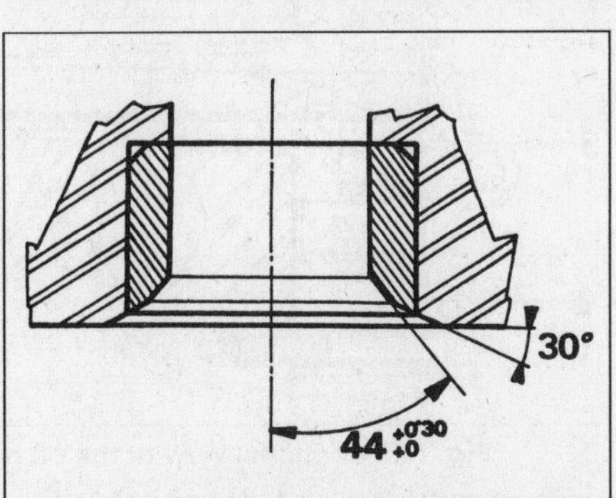

Fig. 1.12 Valve seat angles (Sec 31)

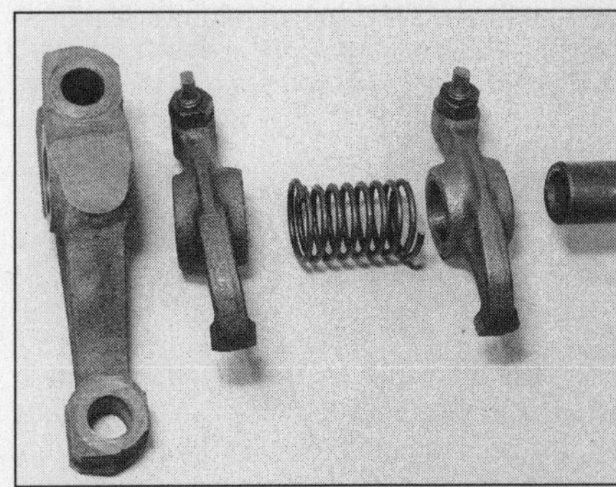

31.3 Check the rocker gear for excessive wear

32.1A Separate the two halves of the oil pump . . .

32.1B . . . and remove the gears to check for excessive wear

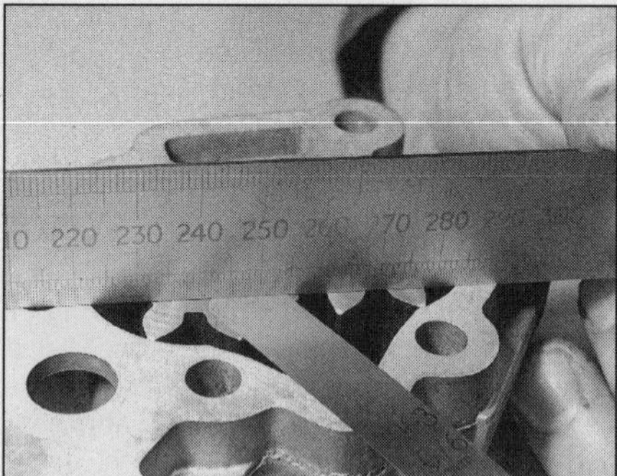

32.1C Checking the gears for excessive endfloat

renewal is a tricky operation and should be left to a Peugeot dealer.

6 Check that the end face of the valve stem is not 'hammered' or ridged by the action of the rocker arm. If it is, dress it square and smooth with an oilstone.

32 Oil pump - examination and renovation

1 Separate the two halves of the oil pump body and examine the gears and internal walls of the housing for scoring, pitting or wear ridges. Check for excessive endfloat of the gears using a straight-edge and feeler gauges as shown (photos). Peugeot do not stipulate any allowable wear tolerances for the endfloat of the gears and it will therefore be necessary to compare the amount of wear present against a new pump to assess if excessive wear is present. If in doubt, renew the pump unit.

2 Remove the domed nut and sealing washer and then, using an Allen key, unscrew the pressure relief valve plunger. Take out the plunger, spring and ball. Thoroughly clean away any sludge deposits from the relief valve and then check the ball and housing for pitting or ridging (photos).

3 If the oil pump or pressure relief valve are worn or in any way suspect, renew the pump or worn parts as necessary. It is always a good idea to renew the pump if the engine is being overhauled or reconditioned, particularly if it has covered a high mileage.

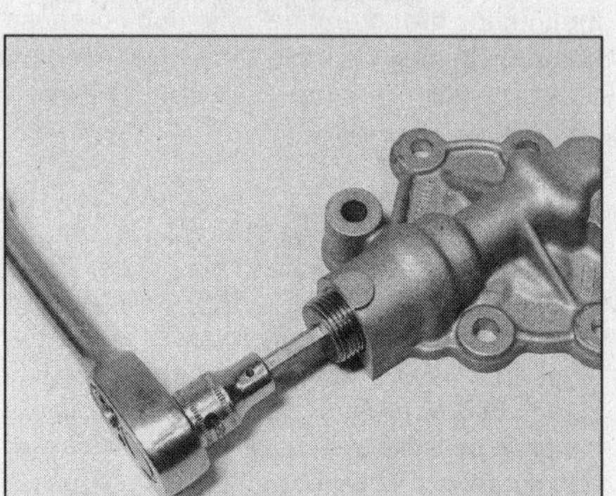

32.2A Unscrew the pressure relief valve plunger . . .

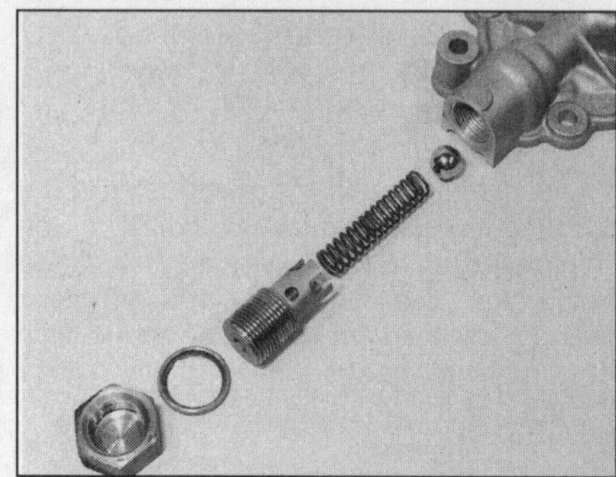

32.2B . . . to withdraw the ball and spring

33 Oil pump driveshaft bushes - examination and renovation

1 The two bushes in the cylinder block in which the oil pump/dipstick driveshaft runs should be examined for wear by refitting the shaft and checking for excessive side play (unless checked when dismantling).

2 If wear has taken place the bushes should be renewed. To remove them, draw each one out using a threaded rod, nuts, and distance piece as shown in Fig. 1.14.

3 New bushes can be fitted using the following procedure.

4 Fit the shorter bush to the distributor side, pulling it in tight to the machined surface of the cylinder block. It is vital that the oil hole in the bush aligns with the crankshaft bearing oil passage.

5 Fit the bush to the oil pump side, again using the threaded rod and nut method and avoid damage to the bush just fitted. There is no need to align the oil hole on this bush as it opens into a circular oil chamber in the cylinder block.

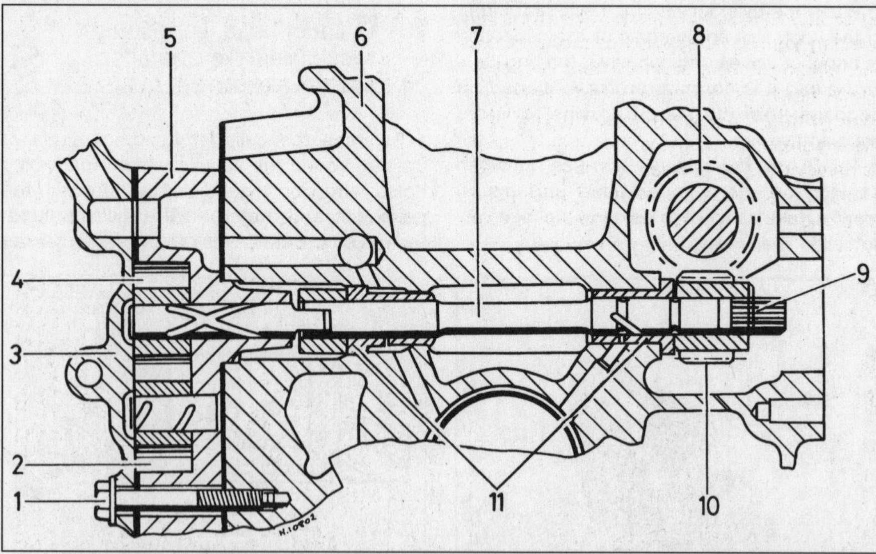

Fig. 1.13 Sectional view of the oil pump and driveshaft assembly (Sec 33)

1 Fixing bolt
2 Idler gear
3 Cover
4 Driven gear
5 Body
6 Crankcase
7 Driveshaft
8 Camshaft
9 Circlip
10 Drivegear
11 Driveshaft bushes

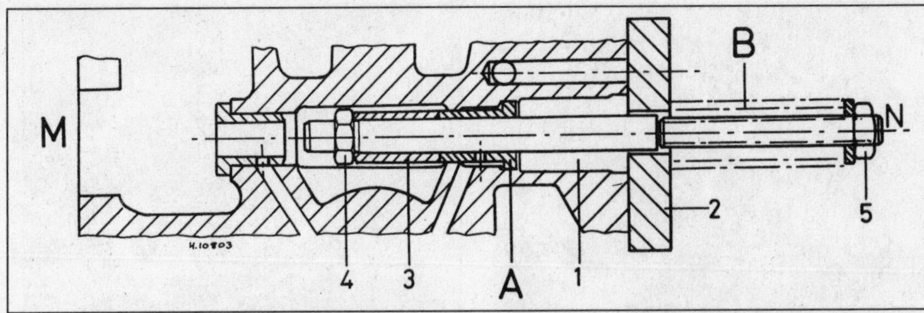

Fig. 1.14 Extracting the oil pump driveshaft bushes (Sec 33)

1 Rod
2 Plate
3 Sleeve
4 Nut
5 Nut
A Shaft bush
B Old gudgeon pin
M Side towards distributor
N Side towards oil pump

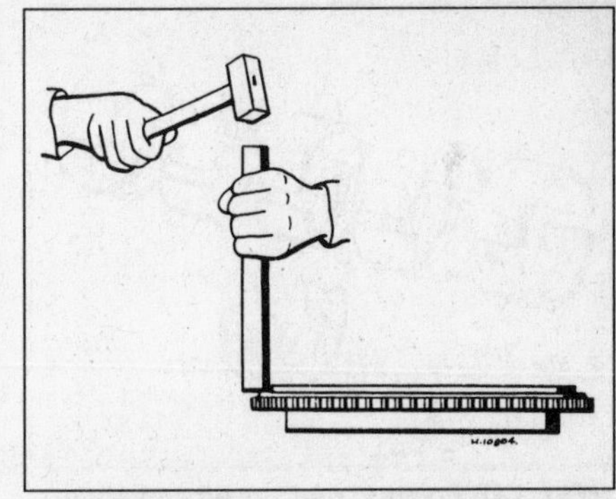

Fig. 1.15 Drifting off the flywheel ring gear (Sec 34)

6 Test the driveshaft in the bushes for ease of rotation. A hard spot will indicate misalignment or distortion.

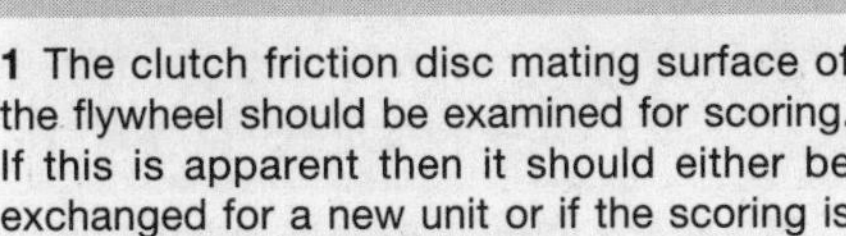

34 Flywheel - examination and renovation

1 The clutch friction disc mating surface of the flywheel should be examined for scoring. If this is apparent then it should either be exchanged for a new unit or if the scoring is very light it may be skimmed.

2 The starter ring gear should be examined and if the teeth are worn or chipped, it must be renewed.

3 To remove the ring, support the flywheel and drive off the ring gear using a bronze or steel bar (Fig. 1.15).

4 Take care not to damage the flywheel locating dowels during this operation or they will have to be renewed.

5 To fit a new ring gear requires heating the ring to 220°C (428°F). This can be done by polishing four equal spaced sections of the gear, placing it on a suitable heat resistant surface (such as fire bricks) and heating it evenly with a blow lamp or torch until the polished areas turn a light yellow tinge. Do not overheat, or the hard wearing properties will be lost. The gear has a chamfered inner edge which should go against the shoulder when put on the flywheel. When hot enough, place the gear in position quickly, tapping it home if necessary, and let it cool naturally without quenching in any way.

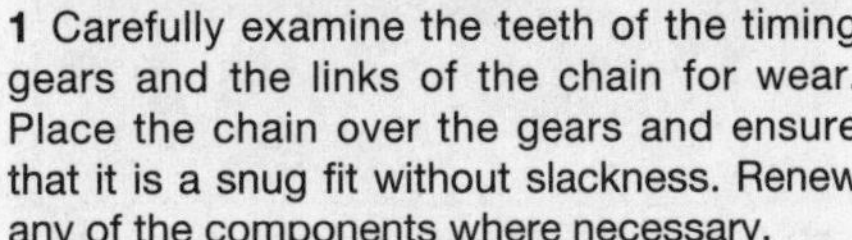

35 Timing gears, chain and cover - examination and renovation

1 Carefully examine the teeth of the timing gears and the links of the chain for wear. Place the chain over the gears and ensure that it is a snug fit without slackness. Renew any of the components where necessary.

2 The camshaft timing chain sprocket has an anti-rattle band located in its central groove. Check this for deterioration and renew it if necessary (photo).

3 The crankshaft front oil seal in the timing cover should be renewed as a matter of course. The old seal may be drifted out using a hammer and a suitable tube, or levered out with a screwdriver or stout bar. Tap a new seal into position using a hammer and a block of wood. The lips of the seal must face toward the engine when installed (photo).

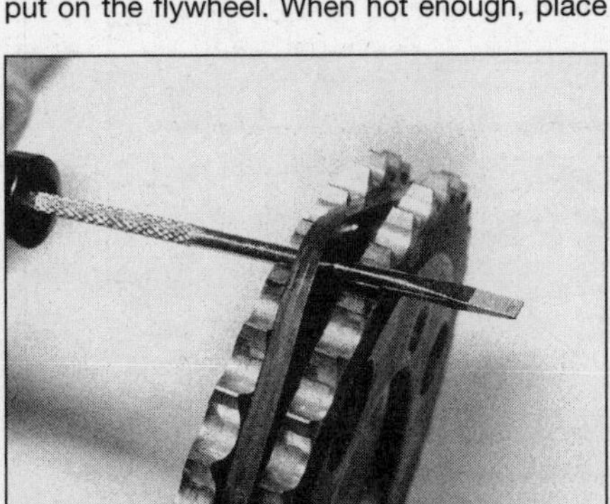

35.2 Camshaft sprocket showing the anti-rattle band

35.3 Renew the timing cover oil seal

36 Engine - reassembly (general)

1 It is during the process of engine reassembly that the job is either made a success or a failure. From the word go there are certain basic rules which it is folly to ignore, namely:

(a) *Absolute cleanliness. The working area, the components of the engine and the hands of those working on the engine must be completely free of grime and grit. One small piece of carborundum dust or swarf can ruin a big-end in no time. and nullify all the time and effort you have spent*

(b) *Always, no matter what the circumstances may be, use new gaskets, locking tabs, seals, nyloc (self-locking) nuts and any other parts mentioned in the Sections in this Chapter. It is pointless to dismantle an engine, spend considerable money and time on it and then waste all this for the sake of something as small as a failed oil seal. Delay the rebuilding if necessary.*

(c) *Don't rush it. The most skilled and experienced mechanic can easily make a mistake if he is rushed.*

(d) *Check that all nuts and bolts are clean and in good condition and ideally renew all spring washers, lockwashers and tab washers as a matter of course. A supply of clean engine oil and clean cloths (to wipe excess oil off your hands) and a torque spanner are the only things which should be required in addition to all the tools used in dismantling the engine.*

(e) *The torque wrench is an essential requirement when reassembling the engine (and transmission) components. This is because the various housings are manufactured from aluminium alloy and whilst this gives the advantage of less weight, it also means that the various fastenings must be accurately tightened as specified to avoid distortion and/or damage to the components.*

37 Engine - preparation for reassembly

1 Assuming that the engine has been completely stripped for reconditioning and that the block is now bare, before any

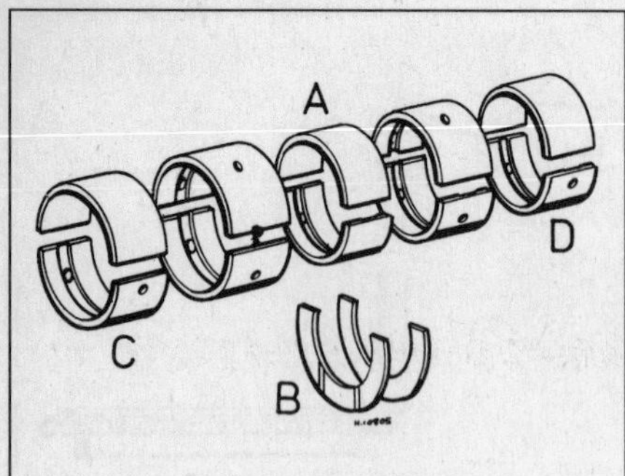

Fig. 1.16 Position of grooved and plain main bearing shells (Sec 38)

A Lower (cap) shells
B Upper (cylinder block) shells
C Timing cover end
D Flywheel end

reassembly takes place it must be thoroughly cleaned both inside and out.

2 Clean out the oilways using a bottle brush, wire or other suitable implement, and blow through with compressed air. Squirt some clean engine oil through to check that the oilways are clear.

3 If the core plugs are defective and show signs of weeping, they must be renewed at this stage. To remove, carefully drive a punch through the centre of the plug and use the punch to lever the plug out. Clean the aperture thoroughly and prior to fitting the new plug, smear the orifice with sealant. Use a small-headed hammer and carefully drive the new core plug into position with the convex side outwards. Check that it is correctly seated on completion.

4 As the components are assembled, lubricate them with clean engine oil and use a suitable sealant where applicable.

5 Make sure that all blind tapped holes are clean, with any oil mopped out of them. This is because it is possible for a casting to fracture when a bolt is screwed in owing to hydraulic pressure.

6 Before fitting the retaining bolts, their threads must be cleaned and lightly oiled, unless otherwise stated or where a locking compound or sealant is specified.

38.1 Check that the crankcase and oilways are clean prior to reassembly

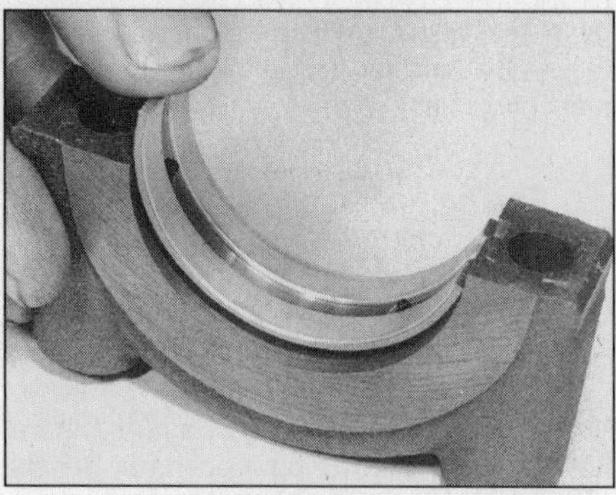

38.4 . . . and the lower shells in the caps

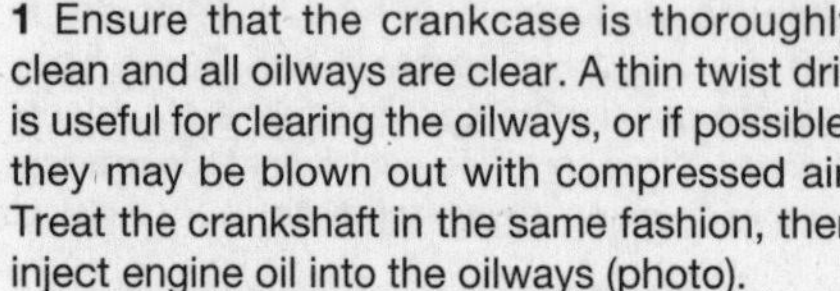

38 Crankshaft and main bearings - refitting

1 Ensure that the crankcase is thoroughly clean and all oilways are clear. A thin twist drill is useful for clearing the oilways, or if possible, they may be blown out with compressed air. Treat the crankshaft in the same fashion, then inject engine oil into the oilways (photo).

2 Wipe the bearing shell seats in the crankcase clean, then fit the upper halves of the new main bearing shells into their seats (photo). All upper half shells have oil grooves in them but the cap shells differ in that numbers 2 and 4 have oil grooves, whilst numbers 1, 3 and 5 are plain shells.

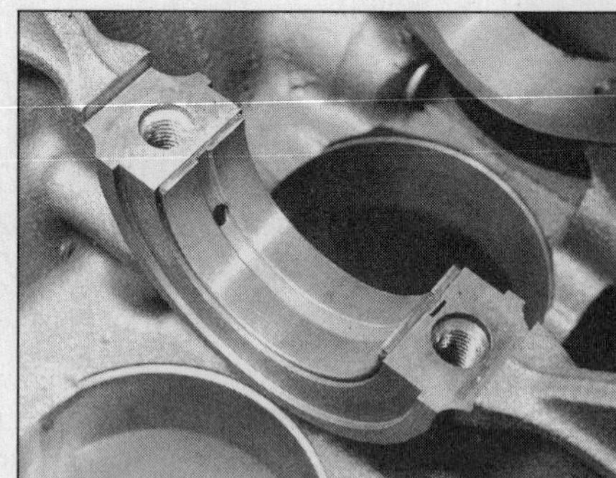

38.2 Locate the main bearing upper shells in the crankcase . . .

38.5 Fit the thrust washers with the oil grooves facing out

3 Note that there is a tab on the back of each bearing shell which engages with a groove in the seating.

4 Wipe the seats in the main bearing caps clean and fit the remaining shells to their seats (photo).

5 Fit the semi-circular thrust washers to each side of the centre main bearing in the crankcase. Retain the thrust washers with a smear of grease and position them with the oil grooves facing outwards (photo) .

6 Liberally lubricate the main bearing shells in the crankcase and then carefully lower the crankshaft into position (photos).

7 Lubricate the bearing shells in the caps and then refit the caps and retaining bolts to their correct locations in the crankcase (photos).

8 With all the caps in place, tighten the

38.6A Lubricate the bearings . . .

38.6B . . . then lower the crankshaft into position . . .

38.7 . . . and fit the main bearing caps

38.8 Tighten the cap retaining bolts to the specified torque

retaining bolts progressively to the specified torque wrench setting (photo). Check the crankshaft for ease of rotation. If new bearing shells have been fitted, it may be fairly stiff to turn, but there should be no high spots.

9 Should the crankshaft be very stiff to turn or possess high spots, a most careful inspection should be made - preferably by a skilled mechanic - to trace the cause of the trouble. It is very seldom that trouble of this nature will be experienced when fitting the crankshaft.

10 Using a screwdriver, ease the crankshaft fully forward and measure the endfloat, with feeler gauges, between the side of the crankshaft centre journal and the thrust washers. Ensure that the clearance is within the limits given in the Specifications. Oversize thrust washers are available (photo).

11 Position a new oil seal housing gasket, lightly smeared with jointing compound, on the rear face of the crankcase.

12 Lubricate the lips of the oil seal and then carefully ease it over the crankshaft flange using a twisting action (photo).

13 Refit the oil seal housing retaining bolts finger tight, rotate the crankshaft one full turn to centralise the seal and then progressively tighten the bolts to the specified torque wrench setting.

39 Gudgeon pins - refitting

As interference fit gudgeon pins are used (see Section 21), this operation must be carried out by your Peugeot dealer or motor engineering specialists.

40 Piston rings - refitting

1 Check that the piston ring grooves and oilways are thoroughly clean and unblocked. Piston rings must always be fitted over the head of the piston and never from the bottom.

2 The easiest method to use when fitting rings is to wrap a 0.38 mm (0.015 in) feeler gauge round the top of the piston and place

38.10 Check the crankshaft endfloat using a feeler gauge

the rings one at a time, starting with the bottom oil control ring, over the feeler gauge (photo).

3 The feeler gauge, complete with ring, can then be slid down the piston over the other piston ring grooves until the correct groove is reached. The piston ring is then slid gently off the feeler gauge into the groove.

4 An alternative method is to fit the rings by holding them slightly open with the thumbs and both of the index fingers. This method requires a steady hand and great care, as it is easy to open the ring too much and break it.

5 The top compression ring and oil control ring may be fitted either way up; however the second ring must be fitted with the word TOP uppermost (photo). (Fig. 1.17).

40.2 Method used to refit the piston rings

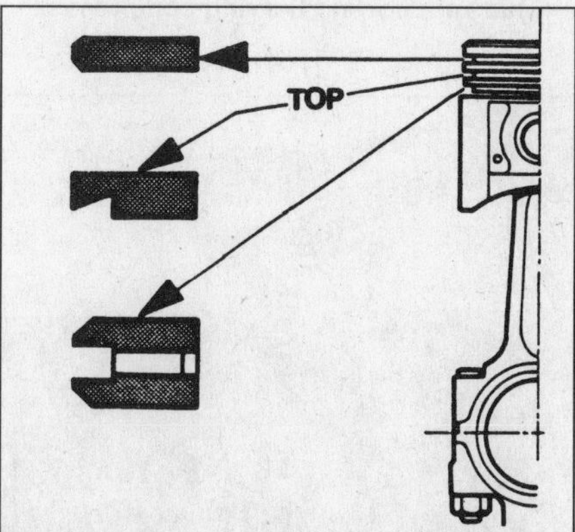

Fig. 1.17 Piston ring identification (Sec 40)

38.12 Fit the crankshaft rear oil seal

6 When all the rings are in position on the pistons, move them around to bring each ring gap approximately 120° away from the adjacent ring (Fig. 1.18).

7 If special oil control rings are being fitted, follow the maker's instructions closely.

41 Piston and connecting rod assemblies - refitting

1 Clean the cylinder bores with a non-fluffy rag and then liberally lubricate them with engine oil.

2 Apply clean engine oil to the piston rings of

40.5 Orientation and size mark on the top piston ring

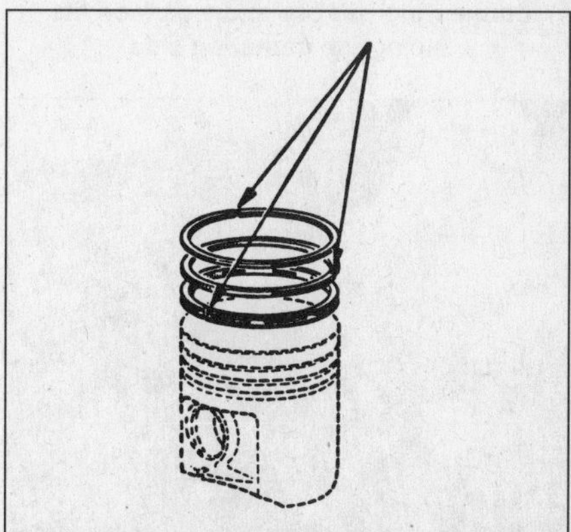
Fig. 1.18 Space the ring gaps when fitted as indicated (Sec 40)

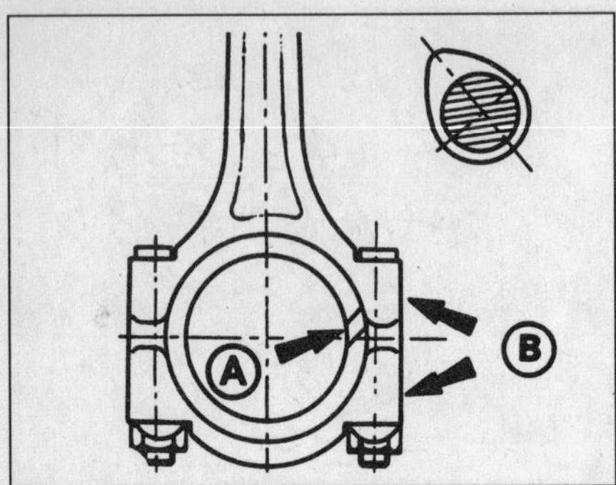

Fig. 1.19 Connecting rod orientation when fitting (Sec 41)

A Oil groove towards camshaft side
B Identification marks

No 1 piston and insert this piston connecting rod assembly into No 1 cylinder bore (photo).

3 It is essential that the piston and rod assemblies are correctly orientated when fitted, with lubrication groove on the big-end face and the connecting rod and cap identity marks facing towards the camshaft side of the engine (Figs. 1.19 and 1.20) (photo).

4 Make sure that the piston ring gaps are still correctly staggered and then compress the rings using a piston ring compressing tool.

A large diameter worm drive hose clip will serve as a ring compressor if a proper tool is not available.

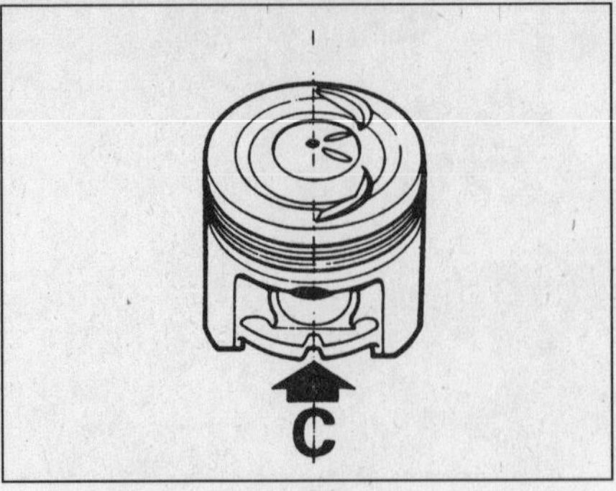

Fig. 1.20 Piston orientation when fitting. Slot C must face the timing cover end (Sec 41)

5 Now tap the top of the piston down through the ring compressor and into the cylinder using a block of wood or hammer handle (photo). Guide the big-end of the connecting rod near to its position on the crankshaft, taking care not to scratch the crankpin with the big-end bolts.

6 Wipe the shell seat in the big-end of the connecting rod clean, and the underside of the new shell bearing. Fit the shell into position in the connecting rod with its locating tongue engaged with the appropriate groove in the big-end.

7 Generously lubricate the crankpin journals with engine oil and turn the crankshaft so that it is in its most advantageous position for the rod to be drawn onto it.

8 Wipe the bearing shell seat in the bearing cap clean, and then the underside of the new shell. Fit the shell into the cap, engaging the shell tongue with the groove in the cap.

41.2 Inserting a piston and connecting rod into its bore

9 Draw the big-end of the connecting rod onto the crankpin, then fit the cap into position (photo). Make sure it is the correct way around, then fit new nuts.

10 Tighten the nuts progressively to the specified torque wrench setting (photo) and then check that the crankshaft is still free to rotate without tight spots. (A certain additional amount of resistance is to be expected from the friction between piston rings and cylinder bore).

11 Repeat this procedure for the remaining piston/connecting rod assemblies.

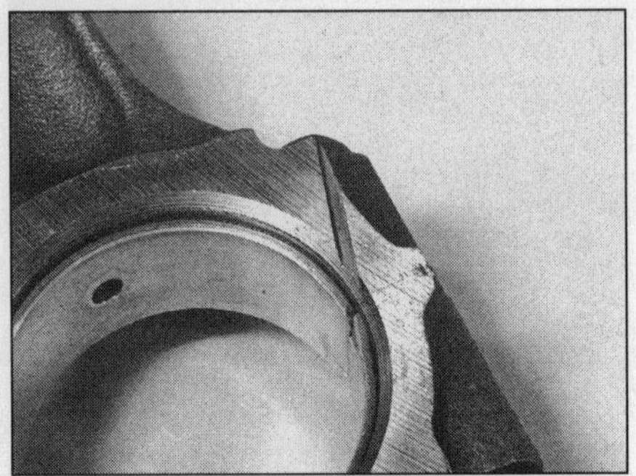

41.3 The lubrication groove on the connecting rod big-end side face fits facing the camshaft side

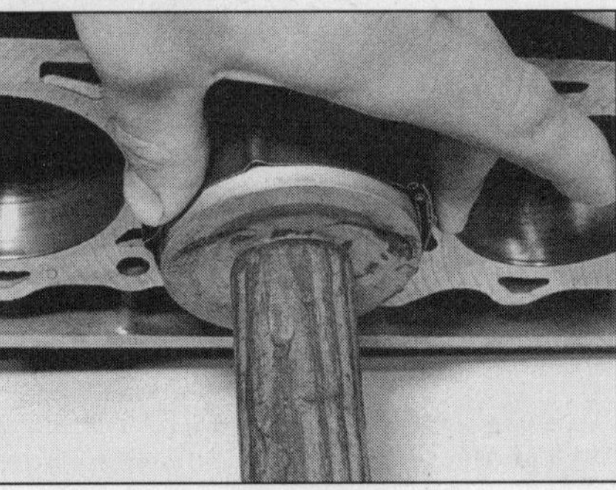

41.5 Tap the piston and rod down the bore whilst supporting the ring compressor

42 Camshaft, timing gears, chain and cover - refitting

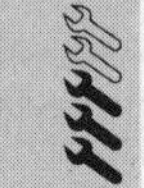

1 Liberally lubricate the camshaft bearings and insert the camshaft, taking care not to damage the bearings as the cam lobes pass through them (photos).

2 Engage the camshaft thrust plate with the groove behind the camshaft flange (photo), and refit the retaining bolts, tightened to the specified torque wrench setting (photo). Knock up the lockwasher tabs (if fitted).

3 Pull the camshaft fully forward and check the endfloat using feeler gauges inserted

41.9 Fit the connecting rod big-end bearing cap . . .

41.10 . . . and tighten the cap retaining bolts to the specified torque

42.1A Lubricate the camshaft bearings . . .

42.1B . . . and fit the camshaft

42.2A Locate the camshaft thrust plate . . .

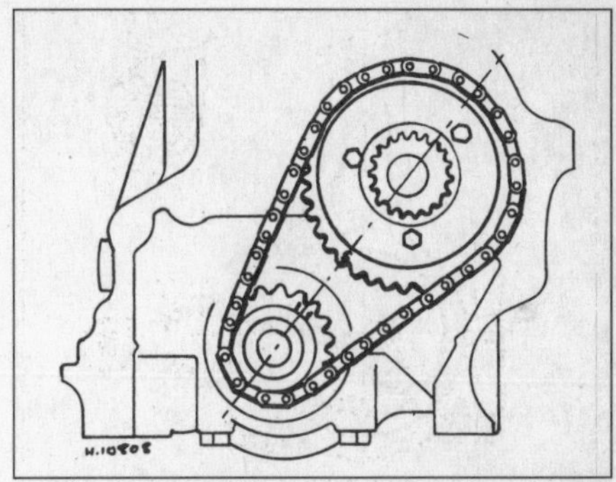
Fig. 1.21 Alignment of timing marks and sprockets (Sec 42)

between the thrust plate and flange (photo). If the endfloat is outside the specified tolerance, various sizes of thrust plate are available.

4 Rotate the crankshaft until Nos 1 and 4 pistons are at TDC.

5 Refit the Woodruff key to the slot in the crankshaft and slide on the crankshaft sprocket (photo).

6 Temporarily position the camshaft sprocket on the camshaft and align the bolt holes.

7 Rotate the camshaft and sprocket until the dot on the edge of the sprocket is aligned between the two lines on the crankshaft sprocket.

8 Remove the camshaft sprocket without rotating the camshaft and lift the timing chain over both sprockets. Refit the camshaft sprocket and check that the timing marks are still in alignment, using a straight-edge if necessary (photo). (Fig. 1.21).

9 Refit the three camshaft sprocket retaining bolts and tighten to the specified torque wrench setting (photo). Knock up the tabs of the lockwashers (if used).

10 Lightly smear a new timing cover gasket with jointing compound and position it on the cylinder block. Refit the timing cover and retaining bolts and then tighten the bolts to the specified torque (photos). Note that the engine mounting support is returned by the upper bolts, and this can be fitted at this stage.

42.2B . . . fit and tighten the retaining bolt to the specified torque

42.3 Check the camshaft endfloat

42.5 Fit the crankshaft sprocket

42.8 Fit the camshaft sprocket and chain, aligning the timing marks on the sprockets

42.9 Tighten the camshaft sprocket retaining bolts

42.10A Position a new gasket on the endface of the crankcase . . .

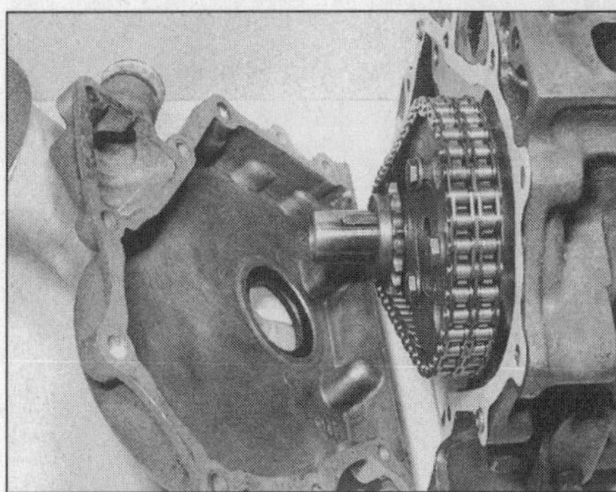
42.10B . . . then fit the timing cover

43.2 Insert the oil pump driveshaft

43.3 Fit the driven gear onto the driveshaft. . .

43.4 . . . and secure it with the circlip

43 Oil pump driveshaft - refitting

1 Temporarily refit the crankshaft pulley and then rotate the crankshaft until the notch on the pulley is aligned with the specified BTDC mark on the timing scale of the timing cover. No 1 cylinder must be on its compression stroke, ie the cam lobes for No 1 cylinder will point downwards.

2 Smear the oil pump driveshaft with engine oil and insert it into its bushes from the oil pump side of the cylinder block (photo).

3 With the shaft in position, slide on the washer and driven gear from the distributor side of the cylinder block, ensuring that the flanged side of the gear faces outward (photo).

4 Secure the gear and shaft with the circlip and then check that the endfloat of the shaft is as specified (photo).

5 With the crankshaft positioned as described above (paragraph 1), slide the distributor driving dog onto the end of the shaft, so that when installed the dog slot positioned as shown (photo); three teeth anti-clockwise from vertical.

6 Refit the distributor mounting plate so that its boss is towards the timing cover and secure with the retaining bolts (photo).

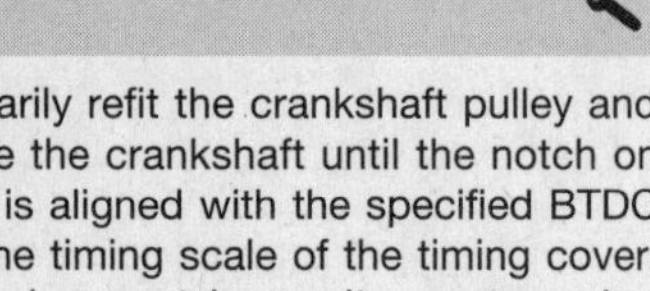
43.5 Fit the distributor driving dog with the slot positioned as shown

43.6 Refit the distributor mounting plate

44 Flywheel and crankshaft pulley - refitting

1 Place the flywheel in position on the crankshaft flange and turn it as necessary until all the offset bolt holes are aligned.

2 Apply a drop of thread locking compound to the retaining bolts and then refit the bolts and seating plate (photo).

3 Lock the flywheel using a piece of angle iron and bar engaged in the ring gear, or a block of wood between the crankshaft and crankcase.

4 Tighten the flywheel retaining bolts in a diagonal sequence to the specified torque wrench setting (photo).

5 Lubricate the lips of the timing cover oil seal and slide on the crankshaft pulley.

6 Refit the retaining bolt and tighten to the specified torque wrench setting (photos).

45 Sump - refitting

1 Ensure that the mating surfaces of the sump and crankcase are clean, smear both sides of the new gasket with jointing compound and position it on the crankcase.

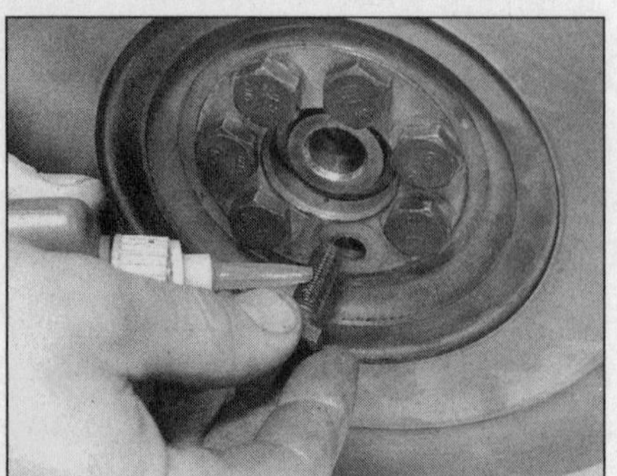
44.2 Fit the flywheel and retaining bolts. Apply locking compound to the bolt threads

44.4 Tighten the retaining bolts to the specified torque

44.6 Fit the crankshaft pulley and retaining bolt

45.2 Refit the sump main body

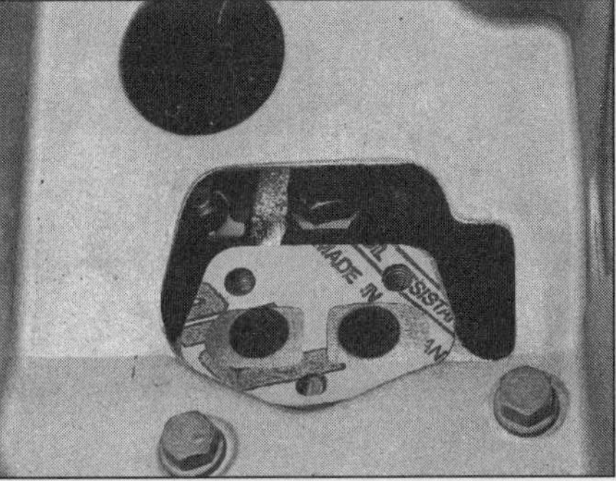
45.3A Locate the oil pick-up gasket

45.3B Assemble the pick-up and strainer unit . . .

2 Place the sump main body over the gasket and secure with the internal and external retaining bolts (photo), using thread locking compound.
3 Smear the oil pick-up/strainer assembly gasket with jointing compound, position it on the sump and refit the pick-up/strainer assembly (photos).
4 Finally refit the baseplate, again using a new gasket with jointing compound, and secure with the retaining bolts, correctly tightened (photo),

46 Valves - refitting

1 Place new oil seals over the valve guides (photo).
2 Liberally lubricate the valve stems and then insert them into the valve guides from which they were removed (photo).
3 Refit the lower spring seat, valve spring and spring cup over the valve stem and then position the spring compressor over the assembly (photos) .
4 Compress the spring sufficiently to allow the cotters to be slipped into place in the groove machined in the top of the valve stem (photo). Now release the spring compressor.
5 Repeat this operation until all eight valves have been assembled into the cylinder head.

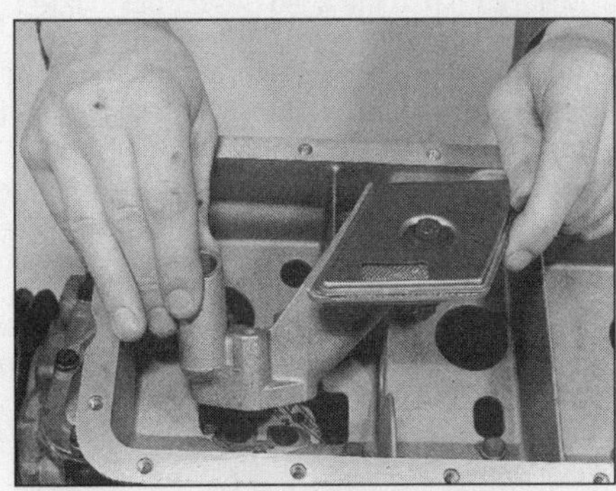
453C . . . then fit it into position . . .

45.3D . . . and tighten the securing bolts

45.4 Refit the sump baseplate

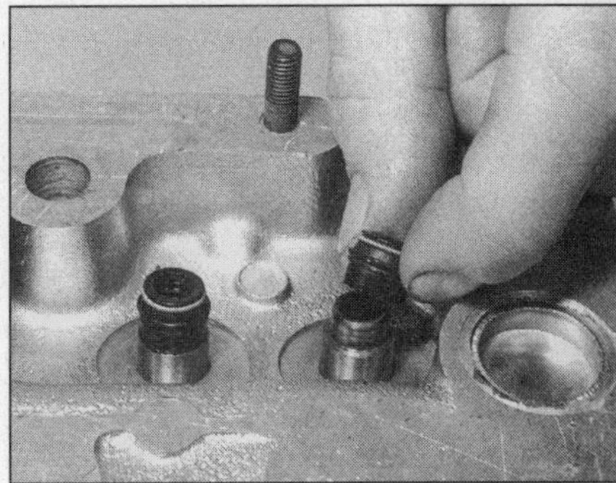
46.1 Fit the new oil seals onto the valve guides

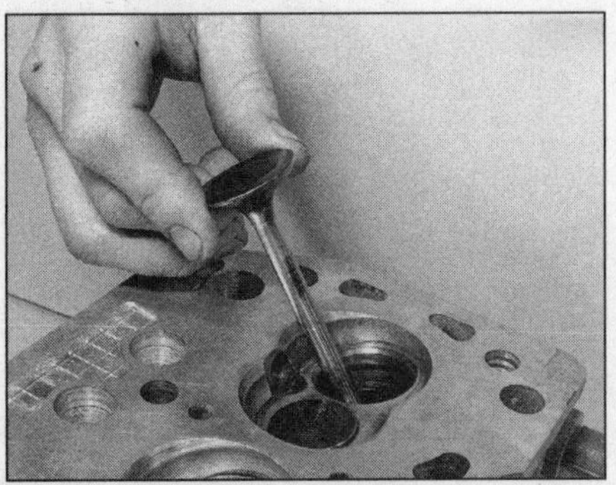
46.2 Insert the valves . . .

46.3A . . . fit the lower spring seat . . .

46.3B . . . spring and upper cup . . .

46.4 . . . then locate the compressor and fit the collets

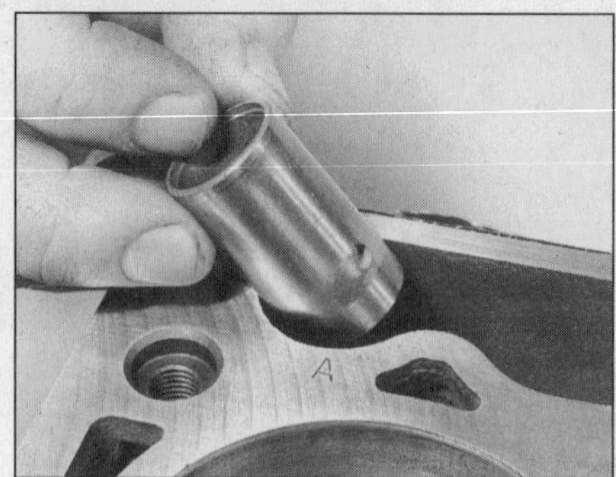
47.1 Fit the cam followers into their original positions

47.2 Alignment dowels must be securely fitted

6 With all the valves installed, gently tap the top of the valve stems once or twice, using a soft-faced mallet, to seat the cotters and centralise the components.

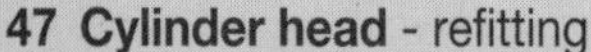

47 Cylinder head - refitting

1 Before refitting the cylinder head, insert the cam followers, liberally lubricated, into their original bores in the cylinder block (photo).

2 Make sure that the two alignment dowels are in position on the cylinder block face and then wipe the block and cylinder head faces with a petrol-moistened rag. Allow time to air dry (photo).

3 Make sure that the head gasket being fitted is of the correct type. If any machining operations have been carried out on the cylinder head face, a gasket of the correct thickness must be used (see Specifications).

4 Locate the new cylinder head gasket in position on the block, ensuring that the word ALTO is visible on the upper surface (photos). The gasket should normally be fitted dry, but if there has been evidence of water leaks from the previous head gasket, or if there is slight eroding of the aluminium face around the water passages, then a thin film of a suitable sealant (eg Hylomar) should be applied to both sides of the gasket. This is a non-setting jointing compound, particularly resistant to oil, water and heat, and will also provide protection against further erosion of the head. Refer to Fig. 1.5 and check that the gasket type is correct.

5 Lower the cylinder head gently into position on the cylinder block and engage the locating dowels (photo).

6 Fit the pushrods in their correct locations, carefully engaging their lower ends in the cam followers (photo).

7 If the rocker shaft has been dismantled for removal of worn components, it should be reassembled with the parts fitted in the sequence shown in Fig. 1.22. Note that the shafts are assembled with their plugged ends facing outward.

8 Make sure that the rocker pillar alignment dowels are in position and lower the rocker gear into place over the dowels (photo). Make sure that the adjusting screw ball on each

47.4A Position cylinder head gasket with ALTO marking uppermost

47.4B New cylinder head gasket fitted into position

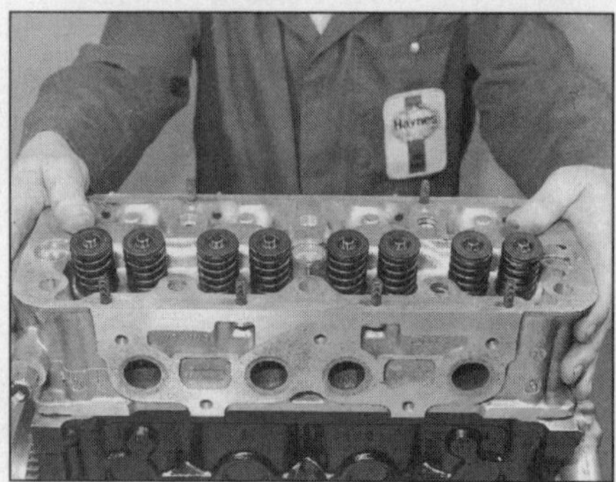
47.5 Refitting the cylinder head

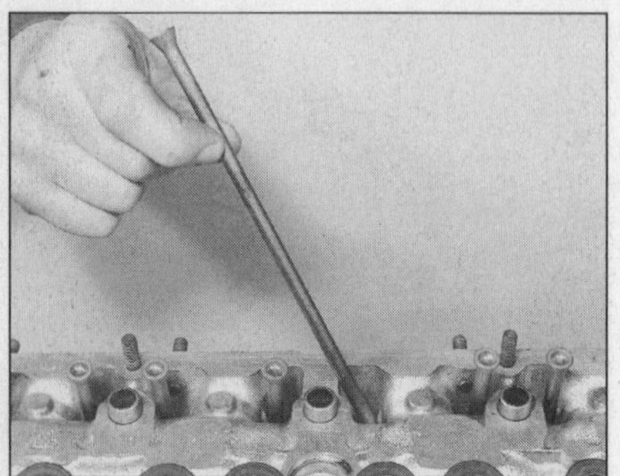
47.6 Locate the pushrods into their original positions

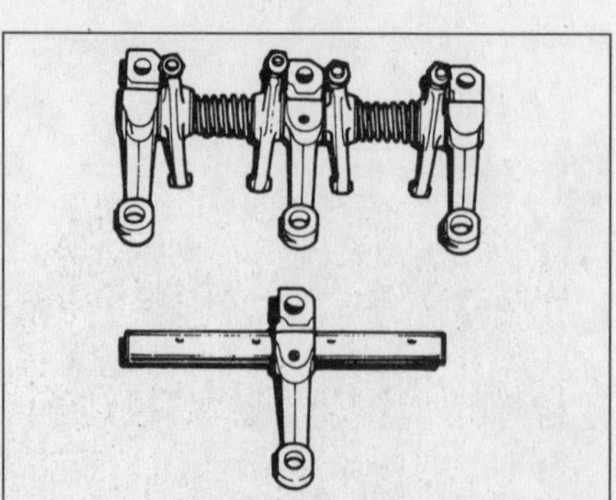
Fig. 1.22 Correct reassembly of the rocker gear (Sec 47)

47.8 Refit the rocker gear assembly

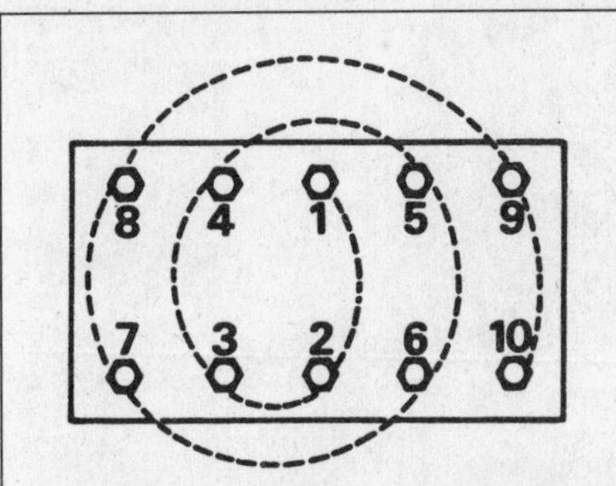

Fig. 1.23 Tightening sequence for cylinder head retaining bolts (Sec 47)

rocker arm engages with its respective pushrod.

9 Refit the cylinder head retaining bolts, having first cleaned their threads with a wire brush. Oil the threads also.

10 Using a torque wrench, tighten the cylinder head bolts progressively and evenly, in the sequence shown in Fig. 1.23, to the torque wrench setting given in the Specifications (photo), but note that the tightening procedure for all OHV engine models must be as follows whenever the cylinder head is being refitted:

(a) Tighten to the Stage 1 torque
(b) Tighten to the Stage 2 torque
(c) After the engine has been restarted, run it up to its operating temperature (but do not exceed 3000 rpm), then switch it off and allow it to cool for a minimum period of 6 hours
(d) Final tightening: Loosen each head bolt in turn and retighten it to the Stage 3 torque in the specified order of sequence. Readjust the valve clearances

48 Valve clearances - checking and adjusting

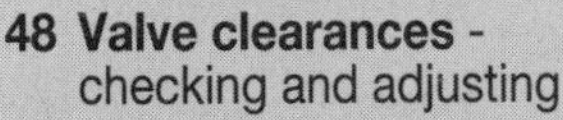

1 The importance of correct rocker arm/valve stem clearance cannot be over-stressed as it vitally affects the performance of the engine. If the clearances are set too wide, the efficiency of the engine is reduced as the valves open later and close earlier than intended. If, however, the clearances are too tight, there is a danger that as the valve stems expand with heat there will be insufficient clearance to allow the valves to close properly. This will cause loss of compression and possible burning of the valve head and seat.

47.10 Tighten the cylinder head bolts to the specified torque

2 Valve clearances must only be adjusted with the engine cold. With the engine in the car, access to the rockers is gained after removing the air cleaner, as described in Chapter 3, and the rocker cover as described in Section 12 of this Chapter. The crankshaft can be rotated for adjustment of the clearances by engaging a socket on the crankshaft pulley bolt.

3 It is important that the clearances are adjusted only when the appropriate piston is at TDC on the compression stroke. The following table shows the order in which the valves should be adjusted (which also avoids turning the crankshaft more than necessary):

Valves rocking on cylinder No	Adjust valves on cylinder No
4	*1*
2	*3*
1	*4*
3	*2*

4 Turn the crankshaft in the normal direction of rotation and observe the movement of the exhaust valves. (Counting from the flywheel end, exhaust valves are Nos 2, 4, 5 and 7). When one is moving upward to its closed position, continue turning slowly until the inlet valve on the same cylinder just starts to open. This is the 'valves rocking' position. The piston in the appropriate cylinder shown in the table is now at TDC on the compression stroke and its valve clearances can be checked and if necessary adjusted.

5 Insert a feeler blade of the specified thickness into the gap between the valve stem and the rocker arm. The blade should be a firm sliding fit.

6 If adjustment is necessary, slacken the hexagon locknut on the rocker arm, then screw the adjusting screw in or out as necessary until the feeler blade is a firm sliding fit (photo). Hold the adjusting screw to prevent it turning further and tighten the locknut, then recheck the clearance. Repeat the operation if necessary.

7 Check the adjacent valve of that cylinder in the same way and then repeat the procedure until all eight valves have been adjusted.

8 If the engine is in the car, refit the rocker cover on completion, using a new gasket if the old one was damaged during removal, and then the air cleaner assembly (photo).

1

49 Engine ancillary components - refitting

1 Begin by refitting the clutch assembly to the flywheel. Full details of the fitting procedure and centralisation of the clutch friction disc are given in Chapter 5.

2 Place a new gasket, lightly coated with jointing compound, in position on the water pump housing and then refit the pump and retaining bolts. With the pump in position refit the pulley, and the pump-to-timing cover water hose. (Refer to Chapter 2 for full details).

3 Fit the alternator mounting bracket and plate (photo).

4 The alternator and drivebelt can be fitted and adjusted at this stage or later after the engine is fitted. Refer to Chapter 12 for details.

5 Position new gaskets on both sides of the

48.6 Adjusting the valve-to-rocker arm clearance

48.8 Refitting the rocker cover (note new gasket)

49.3 Refit the alternator mounting bracket and plate

49.6A Reassemble the oil pump . . .

49.6B . . . locate the new gasket and fit the pump unit . . .

49.6C . . . and secure the retaining bolts

fuel pump insulator block. Hold the block in place on the engine and refit the fuel pump, ensuring that the operating arm goes over the camshaft eccentric, not under it. Secure the pump with the two bolts.

6 Liberally lubricate the oil pump gears and the inside of the housing. Place a new gasket between the two halves of the pump body and join them together. Using another new gasket refit the pump to the cylinder block and secure with the retaining bolts (photos).

7 Smear clean engine oil onto the rubber seal of a new oil filter and screw the filter onto its housing on the oil pump (photo). Tighten the filter by hand only. Do not use any tools.

8 Refit the distributor to the engine, using the procedure described in Chapter 4 to ensure that the ignition timing is correct.

9 Refit the oil pressure switch using a new washer (photo).

10 Fit the three-way coolant connector to the side of the sump using a new gasket smeared with sealant (photo).

11 Refit the inlet manifold (together with carburettor if applicable) and reconnect the coolant hoses. Use a new manifold gasket.

12 Stick a new gasket onto the thermostat housing, engage the housing with the hose from the inlet manifold and refit the bolts. Secure the hose clip in position. Fit the down hose between the inlet manifold and the three-way connector.

13 If not already fitted, locate the right-hand engine mounting bracket and its support plate as shown (photos).

14 Refit the driveshaft bearing/torque reaction link bush housing (photo).

15 Refit the exhaust manifold using a new gasket. Ensure that both mating faces are clean before fitting.

16 Refit the fault diagnosis socket retaining bracket.

17 The engine is now reassembled and ready for reconnection to the gearbox and refitting to the car.

49.7 Fit the new oil filter to the pump

49.9 Oil pressure switch location

49.10 Coolant three-way connector

49.13A Right-hand engine support bracket . . .

49.13B . . . and support plate

49.14 Driveshaft bearing/torque reaction link bush housing

50 Engine - reconnecting to gearbox

1 If the engine and transmission were removed from the car as a unit, the two assemblies must now be reconnected before being refitted to the car.

2 The reconnecting procedure is a straightforward reverse of the removal sequence. On no account allow the weight of the gearbox to hang unsupported on the input shaft.

If difficulty is experienced engaging the manual gearbox input shaft splines, engage a gear by moving the shift rod and then rotate the crankshaft slightly. This should align the clutch friction disc and input shaft splines and allow the shaft to enter the disc.

51 Engine - refitting

1 Refitting the engine is a reversal of the removal procedure. A little trouble taken in getting the engine properly slung (so it takes up a suspended angle similar to its final position) will pay off when it comes to locating the engine mountings. Note the following special points when refitting the engine and transmission unit to the car.

(a) Ensure that all loose leads, cables, hoses, etc. are tucked out of the way. If not, it is easy to trap one and cause additional work after the engine is refitted in the car

(b) An assistant will be required to help guide the power unit into position

(c) Fit the special washer to the centre stud in the left-hand engine mounting. This washer prevents the engine from placing the mounting under excessive tension. Tighten the mounting nuts to the specified torque settings

(d) Use a final drive oil seal protector when inserting the right-hand driveshaft. Remove the protector when the driveshaft is fitted. See Chapter 7 for full details

(e) Adjust the clutch cable with reference to Chapter 5

(f) Adjust the throttle cable with reference to Chapter 3

(g) Tighten the exhaust flange bolts as described in Chapter 3

(h) Ensure that the heater hose is located in the strap attached to the bracket on alternator upper retaining bolt. This is necessary to keep the hose clear of the alternator drive pulley (Fig. 1.24).

(i) Refill and bleed the cooling system as described in Chapter 2

(j) Top up the engine and gearbox oil levels (see Chapters 1 and 6)

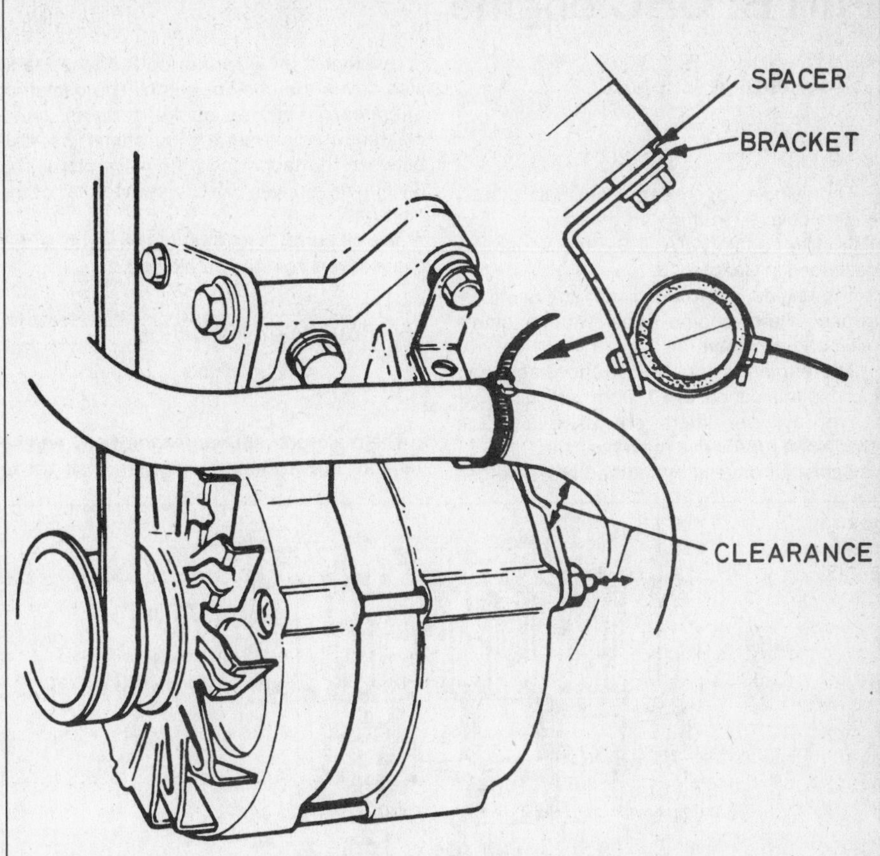

Fig. 1.24 Heater hose arrangement to clear alternator and drivebelt (Sec 51)

52 Engine - initial start-up after major repair or overhaul

1 Make sure that the battery is fully charged and that all lubricants, coolant and fuel are replenished.

2 If the fuel system has been dismantled, it will require several revolutions of the engine on the starter motor to pump petrol to the carburettor. It will help to remove the spark plugs, which will enable the engine to turn over much easier, and enable oil to be pumped around the engine before starting it.

3 Refit the spark plugs and as soon as the engine fires and runs, keep it going at a fast tickover only (no faster) and bring it up to normal working temperature.

4 As the engine warms up, there will be odd smells and some smoke from parts getting hot and burning off oil deposits. Look for water or oil leaks which will be obvious if serious. Check also the clamp connection of the exhaust pipe to the manifold as these do not always find their exact gastight position until the warmth and vibration have acted on them, and it is almost certain that they will need tightening further. This should be done, of course, with the engine stationary.

5 When the engine running temperature has been reached, adjust the idling speed as described in Chapter 3.

6 Stop the engine and wait a few minutes to see if any lubricant or coolant leaks.

7 Road test the car to check that the timing is correct and that the engine is giving the necessary smoothness and power. Do not race the engine. If new bearings and or pistons and rings have been fitted, it should be treated as a new engine and run in at reduced revolutions for 500 miles (800 km).

8 Re-tighten the cylinder head bolts, with the engine cold, after the first 1000 miles have been covered. It is best to slacken each bolt 1/4 turn to break the 'stiction' before tightening. Follow the tightening sequence shown in Fig. 1.23 and check the valve clearances on completion.

9 Also after the first 1000 miles, it is a good idea to change the engine oil and filter if many new engine parts have been fitted. This is because the small metal particles produced by new components bedding in to each other will be circulating in the oil, or trapped in the filter.

Part B: OHC engine

53 General description

The single overhead camshaft (OHC) engine covered in this Part of Chapter 1 is of 1.6 litre capacity. A 1.9 litre variant is described in Chapter 13.

The engine is a four-cylinder (in-line), four-stroke, water-cooled type with a single overhead camshaft.

The engine is mounted transversely and inclined at an angle of 30° from vertical.

Wet cylinder liners are used and the crankshaft runs in five main bearings.

Camshaft drive is by toothed belt. The belt is tensioned by a spring-loaded wheel and also drives the coolant pump. The camshaft operates directly on bucket tappets; valve clearance adjustment is by shims inserted between the tappet and the valve stem. The distributor is driven directly from the tail of the camshaft.

The oil pump is located in the sump and is chain driven from the crankshaft.

54 Routine maintenance

The main procedures for the OHC engine variants are in general the same as those described for the smaller engine OHV variants in Section 2 of this Chapter. The dipstick and drain plug locations applicable to the OHC engine are shown in the accompanying photos.

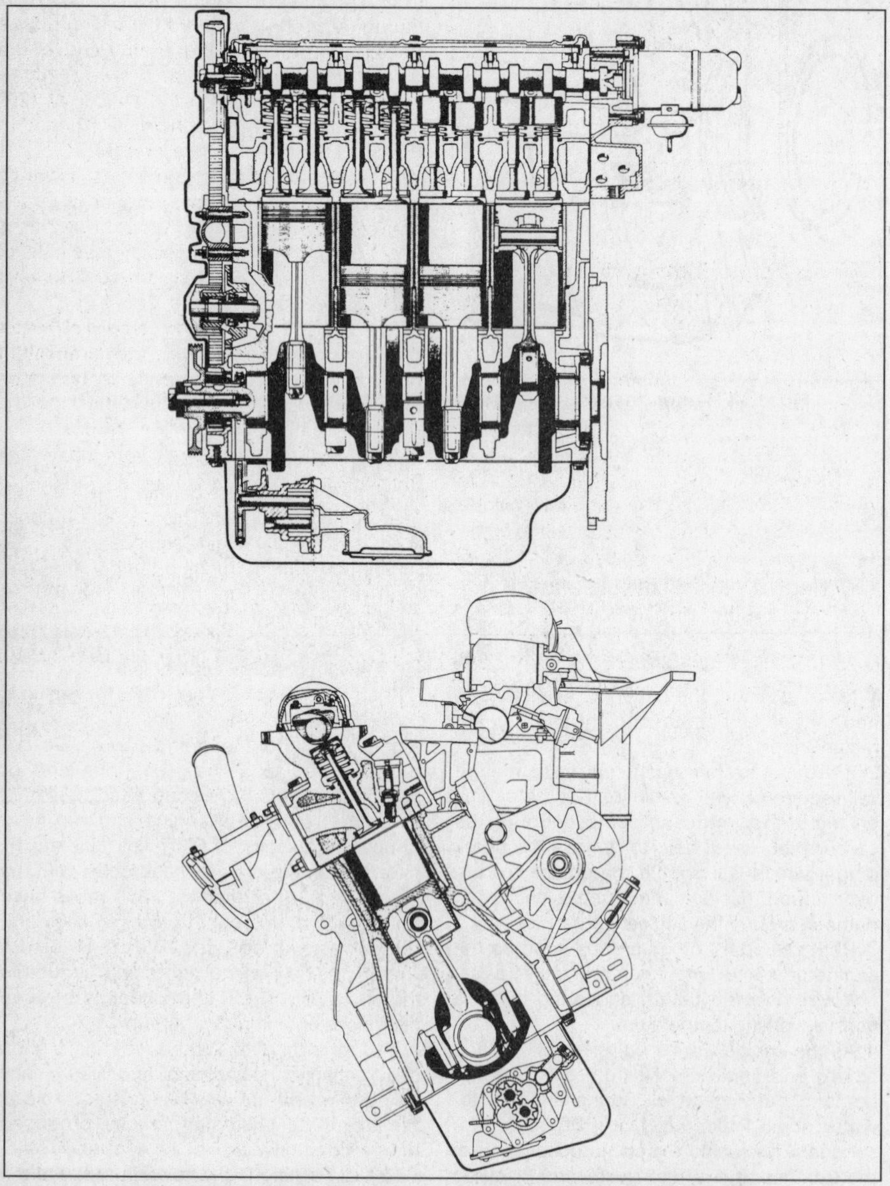

Fig. 1.25 Side and end section views of the OHC engine (Sec 53)

55 Lubrication system - description

The oil pump is located in the sump and is chain driven from the crankshaft. A forced feed lubrication system is employed. Oil from the pump passes to the oil filter then to the oil gallery, crankshaft and camshaft. The valve stems are lubricated by oil returning from the camshaft to the sump. The oil pump chain and sprockets are lubricated by oil in the sump. Fig. 1.26 shows the lubrication system circuit round the engine.

56 Oil filter - removal and refitting

1 The oil filter is located on the inlet manifold side of the engine in the lower side face of the crankcase. The filter must be renewed at the specified intervals (see Routine Maintenance at the front of the manual).

2 Removal and renewal of the oil filter is the

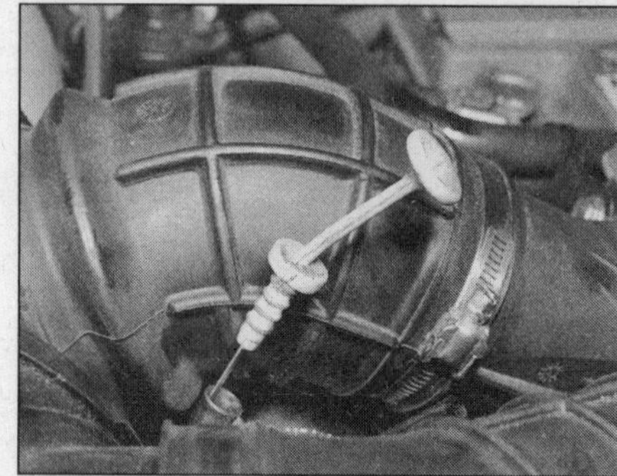

54.1A Engine oil dipstick location – OHC engine (SRi)

54.1B Engine oil drain plug removal – OHC engine

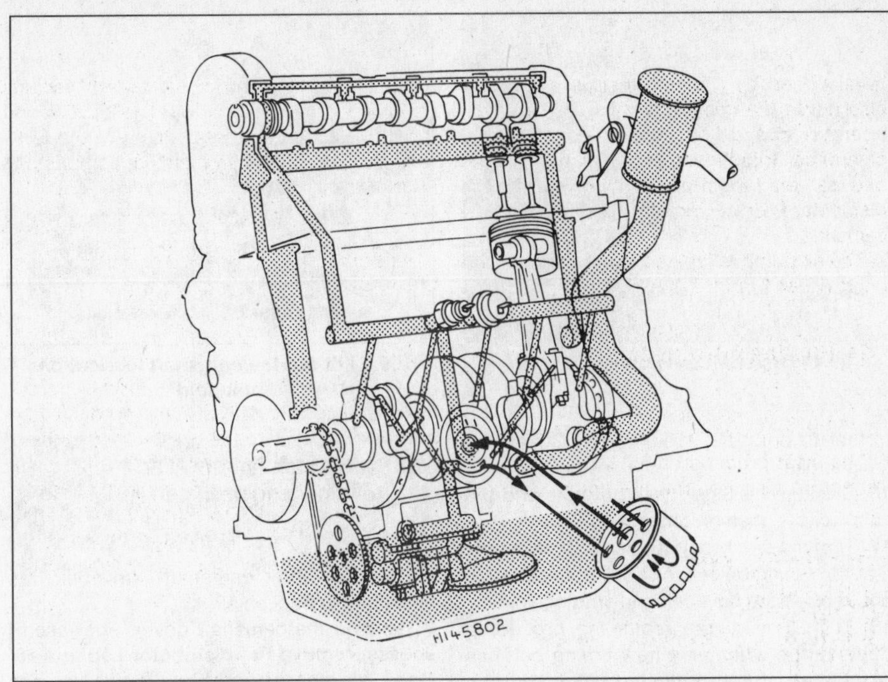

Fig. 1.26 Engine lubrication circuit – OHC engine (Sec 55)

same as that described for the smaller engine variants, therefore refer to Section 4. For access, remove the engine undertray and renew the filter from underneath (photo).

57 Major operations possible with the engine in the car

The following operations are possible with the engine in the car.

Valve clearances checking and adjustment
Camshaft drivebelt renewal
Camshaft removal and refitting
Cylinder head removal and refitting
Sump and oil pump removal and refitting
Big-end renewal (after removal of sump)
Piston and connecting rod assembles removal and refitting (after removal of sump and cylinder head)
Removal and refitting of engine mountings
Removal and refitting of major ancillary items such as inlet/exhaust manifolds, starter motor, water pump. etc
Clutch and flywheel removal and refitting (after removal of transmission)

58 Major operations requiring engine removal

The following operations can only be carried out with the engine removed from the car.

Main bearings renewal
Crankshaft removal and refitting

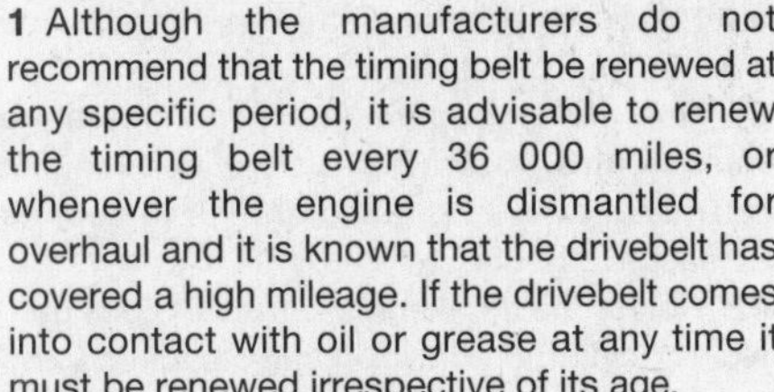

59 Camshaft (timing) drivebelt - removal and refitting (engine in car)

1 Although the manufacturers do not recommend that the timing belt be renewed at any specific period, it is advisable to renew the timing belt every 36 000 miles, or whenever the engine is dismantled for overhaul and it is known that the drivebelt has covered a high mileage. If the drivebelt comes into contact with oil or grease at any time it must be renewed irrespective of its age.
2 Disconnect the battery earth lead.
3 Remove the alternator drivebelt.
4 Remove the inner shield from the right-hand wheel arch and wedge the radiator bottom hose under the sump.
5 Remove the shield from the camshaft sprocket.

59.6 Timing dowels in position – shown with engine removed for clarity

56.2 Engine oil filter location – OHC engine

6 Turn the crankshaft until the dowel hole in the pulley is at about 12 o'clock and the hole in the camshaft sprocket is at about 7 o'clock. In this position a 10 mm dowel should pass through each hole and into the timing recess behind. Verify this and then remove the dowels (photo). Note that there are three holes in the crankshaft pulley spaced at 120° intervals but only one hole is 10 mm in diameter, the other two are larger.
7 Remove the clutch bottom shield. Have an assistant jam the starter ring gear while the crankshaft pulley bolt is undone. This bolt is very tight. **Do not** jam the pulley by means of the timing dowel: damage will result. Remove the bolt and washer.
8 Check that the 10 mm dowels will still enter the timing holes: adjust the crankshaft position if necessary by means of the starter ring gear. Remove the crankshaft pulley, retrieving the Woodruff key if it is loose.
9 Remove the plastic covers from the front of the camshaft drivebelt. Note the location of the various bolts.
10 Slacken the two nuts on the front of the drivebelt tensioner and the single nut at the rear. Use a spanner on the 6 mm square end of the tensioner cam spindle to turn the cam to the horizontal position and so compress the tensioner spring. Tighten the cam locknut (photo).
11 Remove the camshaft drivebelt, taking care not to kink it or contaminate it with oil if it is to be re-used.

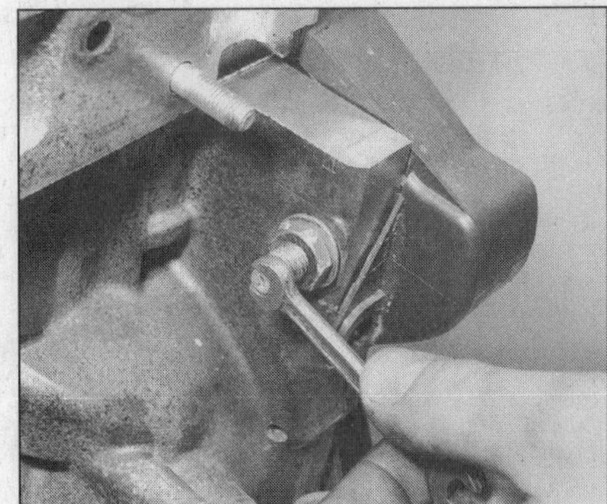

59.10 Turning the tension cam spindle

59.12 Line on belt aligns with mark on sprocket

59.14 Drivebelt tensioner front nuts

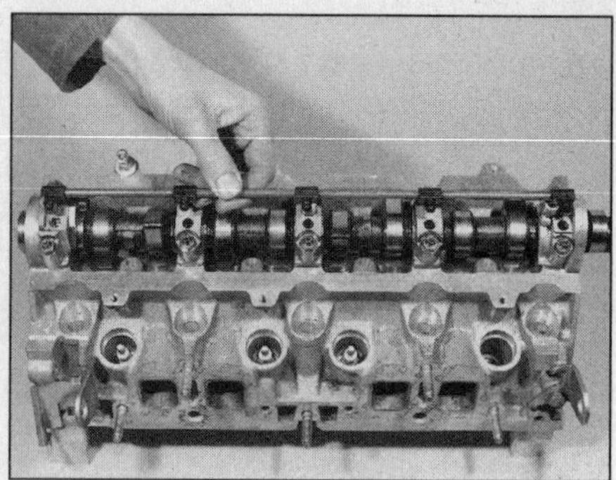

60.4 Lift out the camshaft lubrication manifold

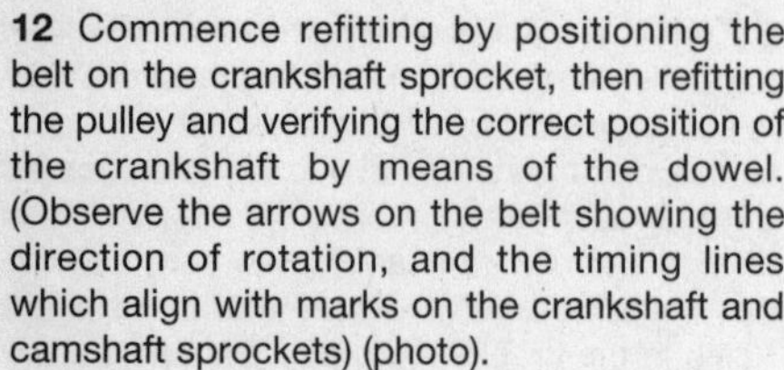

12 Commence refitting by positioning the belt on the crankshaft sprocket, then refitting the pulley and verifying the correct position of the crankshaft by means of the dowel. (Observe the arrows on the belt showing the direction of rotation, and the timing lines which align with marks on the crankshaft and camshaft sprockets) (photo).

13 Fit the belt to the camshaft sprocket, round the tensioner and to the coolant pump socket.

14 Release the tensioner cam locknut and turn the cam downwards to release the spring. Tighten the locknut and the tensioner front nuts (photo).

15 Remove the timing dowels and turn the crankshaft through two full turns in the normal direction of rotation. Turn the crankshaft further to bring No 1 piston to TDC on the firing stroke.

60.5A Camshaft sprocket locked with a 10 mm rod (or drill as in this case)

16 Slacken the tensioner front nuts and the cam locknut, then retighten them.

17 Turn the crankshaft further and make sure that the timing dowels can still be inserted. If not, remove the drivebelt and start again.

18 At this point, the remaining procedure depends on whether a new timing belt has been fitted. If the old timing belt is refitted, remove the crankshaft pulley and proceed from paragraph 23, but ignore the alternator drivebelt removal reference.

19 If a new belt has been fitted, it must be run in and retensioned as follows.

20 Tighten the crankshaft pulley bolt to the specified torque, then refit and tension the alternator drivebelt. Temporarily refit the camshaft sprocket cover.

21 Run the engine up to operating temperature, indicated by the cooling fan operating, then stop it and allow it to cool for at least two hours.

22 Rotate the crankshaft to the TDC position, No 1 cylinder firing, then slacken and retighten the tensioner nuts once more.

23 Remove the alternator drivebelt and the crankshaft pulley. Refit and secure the plastic covers, then refit the pulley and tighten its bolt to the specified torque. Refit and tension the alternator drivebelt.

24 Check the ignition timing and adjust if necessary.

60 Camshaft - removal and refitting (engine in car)

1 Remove the camshaft drivebelt as described in Section 59.

2 Remove the camshaft cover. For ease of access, remove the distributor cap and HT leads, air cleaner and brake servo vacuum hose.

3 Remove the distributor, as described in Chapter 4.

4 Remove the camshaft lubrication manifold (photo).

5 Lock the camshaft sprocket (eg with a timing dowel - see previous Section), and remove the sprocket retaining bolt. Remove the sprocket and the cover plate behind it. Remove the thrust plate (photos).

6 Progressively slacken the camshaft bearing cap securing nuts. Make identifying marks if necessary, then remove the caps. Be prepared for the camshaft to spring upwards. Remove the camshaft (photo).

7 Commence refitting by making sure that the crankshaft is in the correct (dowelled) position - if not, move it to this position to avoid possible piston/valve contact.

8 Lubricate the camshaft bearing journals with clean engine oil then fit the camshaft into position. On carburettor models fitted with a mechanical fuel pump, push the pump operating rod in as the camshaft is fitted.

60.5B Undo the retaining screw . . .

60.5C . . . and remove the camshaft thrust plate

60.6 Removing the camshaft (cylinder head removed in this instance)

60.8 Tighten the camshaft bearing cap nuts to the specified torque

60.10 Locate the cover plate with a 10 mm rod

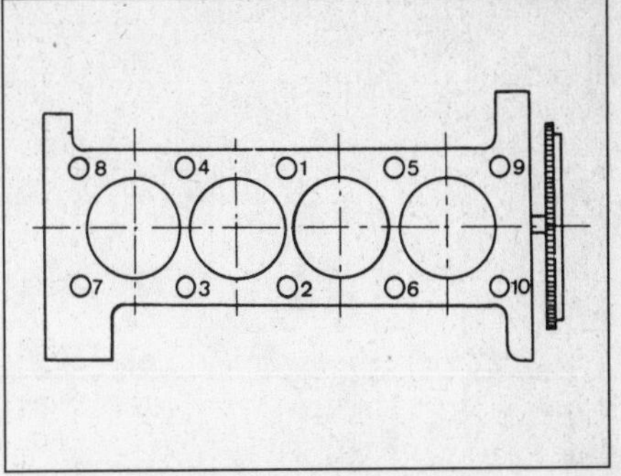

Fig. 1.27 Cylinder head bolt tightening sequence (Sec 61)

Lubricate and fit the camshaft bearing caps to their original positions as noted during removal. When fitting the No 1 bearing cap, smear the joint and lower mating faces with sealant. Tighten the cap nuts progressively to the specified torque. Refit and secure the thrust plate (photo).

9 Fit a new oil seal to the sprocket end of the camshaft.

10 Refit the sprocket rear cover plate, locate it correctly with a 10 mm dowel and tighten its fastenings (photo). Fit the camshaft sprocket, dowel it and tighten its securing bolt to the specified torque.

11 Check and if necessary adjust the valve clearances as described in Section 62.

12 Refit the lubrication manifold and distributor.

13 Refit the camshaft cover, HT leads and distributor cap, air cleaner and brake servo vacuum hose.

14 Refit the camshaft drivebelt (Section 59).

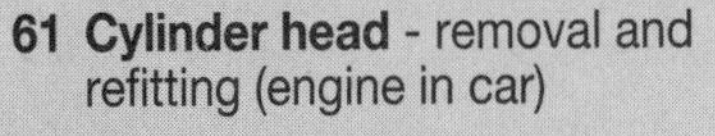

61 Cylinder head - removal and refitting (engine in car)

1 Disconnect the battery earth lead.

2 Drain the engine coolant as described in Chapter 2.

3 Remove the timing belt as described in Section 59.

4 Remove the air cleaner unit as described in Chapter 3.

5 Remove the distributor cap and leads then the distributor referring to Chapter 4 for details.

6 Working underneath the vehicle, remove the engine undertray then unbolt and detach the engine torque reaction link from the lower engine mounting (photo).

7 Unscrew and remove the right-hand engine mounting rubber retaining nut (photo).

8 Position a jack under the sump with a protector or suitable piece of wood located on the jack saddle to avoid damaging the sump. Raise the engine about 3 inches (70 to 80 mm) so that the two bolts securing the right-hand mounting bracket to the cylinder head can be removed, then lower the engine to its original position.

9 Disconnect the coolant and vacuum hoses from the cylinder head noting their fitting locations. Mark them to avoid confusion.

10 Referring to the appropriate Sections in Chapter 3 disconnect and remove the following (as applicable).

(a) *Carburettor and inlet manifold*

(b) *Fuel injectors, fuel feed tube rail and inlet manifold*

11 Unbolt and detach the exhaust downpipe from the exhaust manifold. If required the exhaust manifold can be removed together with, or separate from the cylinder head.

12 Disconnect all electrical leads from the cylinder head and note their connections.

13 Disconnect the oil filter spout and the engine oil dipstick guide tube location bolt from the cylinder head (bulkhead side).

14 Unbolt and remove the diagnostic socket/retainer.

15 Remove the camshaft cover from access to the cylinder head bolts. Loosen the head bolts in a progressive sequence in the reverse order of that shown for tightening (Fig. 1.27). Remove the bolts.

16 Before removing the cylinder head the following must be noted. The cylinder head is positioned during assembly by means of two dowels. When removing the cylinder head it is most important not to lift it directly from the cylinder block; it must be twisted slightly. This action prevents the cylinder liners from sticking to the cylinder head face and being lifted with it, thus breaking their bottom seals. Before the cylinder head can be twisted, the dowel at the flywheel end must be tapped down flush with the top of the cylinder block, using a drift. Tap the cylinder head at the flywheel end to twist it free.

17 Fit cylinder liner clamps, or large washers secured with nuts and bolts, to keep the liners in position (photo). *If the liners are disturbed, the engine will have to be removed for new seals to be fitted.*

18 Before refitting the cylinder head, ensure that the joint faces are clean, also the bolt hole threads. If possible, clean the threads with a suitable 11 x 50 mm thread tap. Commence refitting by fitting the dowels to

61.6 Torque reaction link and lower engine mounting

61.7 Right-hand engine mounting – undo nut arrowed

61.17 Cylinder liners clamped with washers and bolts

61.18A Dowel is retained with a nail or rod on its underside

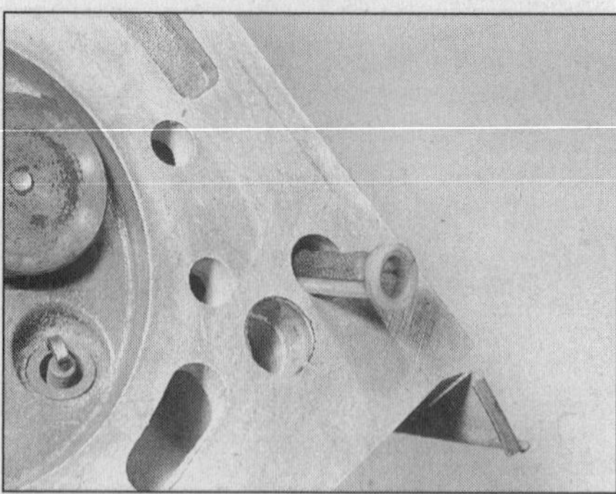

61.18B Oil filter gauze location in cylinder head oilway

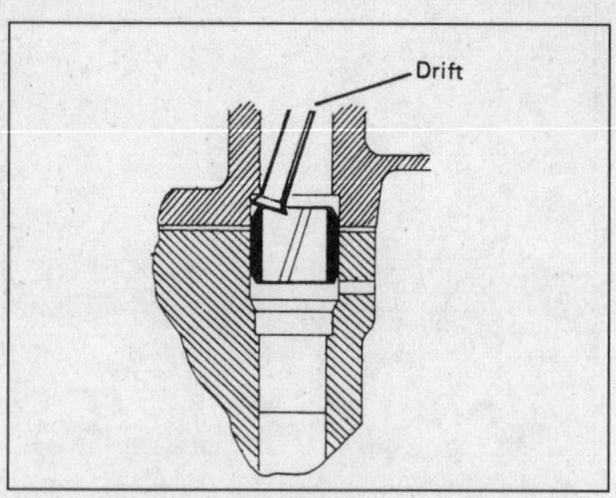

Fig. 1.28 Driving cylinder head dowel down flush with block (Sec 61)

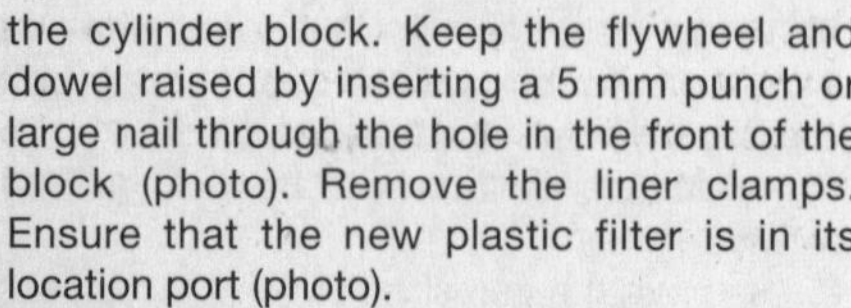

the cylinder block. Keep the flywheel and dowel raised by inserting a 5 mm punch or large nail through the hole in the front of the block (photo). Remove the liner clamps. Ensure that the new plastic filter is in its location port (photo).

19 Fit the new gasket, dry, with the tab at the flywheel end. Lower the cylinder head into position, making sure that it mates with the dowels. Remove the punch or nail.

20 Fit the cylinder head bolts, their threads clean and lightly oiled. Remember to fit the spacer to the bolt above the coolant pump (bolt number 8) (photo).

21 Progressively tighten the bolts in the order shown in Fig. 1.27 to the Stage 1 specified torque.

22 Raise the engine slightly and refit the two bolts which secure the righthand mounting bracket to the cylinder head. Tighten these bolts and slacken the one which holds the same bracket to the engine block. Lower the engine and tighten the right-hand mounting nut and the lower mounting rubber nut and bolt.

23 Slacken cylinder head bolt No 1, then immediately retighten it to the Stage 2 specified torque. Tighten further by the angle specified. Repeat for all the bolts, following the tightening sequence (photo).

24 Check the valve clearances and adjust if necessary (Section 62). After the engine is restarted follow the check procedures in Section 94.

25 Refit the remaining components in the reverse order of removal.

26 Refill and bleed the cooling system (Chapter 2).

27 Start the engine and warm it up until the cooling fan cuts in, then switch off and allow it to cool for at least two hours.

28 Retighten the cylinder head bolts as described in paragraphs 22 and 23 then recheck the valve clearances. If Torx type cylinder head bolts are fitted, note the different final tightening angle, and also that no subsequent re-tightening is required (see Chapter 13).

29 If a new camshaft drivebelt has been fitted, retension it as described in Section 59, Paragraph 19 on.

30 Tighten the engine mounting bracket bolt.

62 Valve clearances - checking and adjustment

Valve clearances - checking

1 The valve clearances must be checked with the engine cold; therefore do not run the engine for a minimum period of two hours prior to making the checks.

2 Detach the distributor cap and the spark plug leads.

3 Remove the camshaft cover; trying not to damage the gasket.

4 Prepare to rotate the crankshaft, either by jacking up one front wheel and turning the wheel with 4th or 5th gear engaged, or with a spanner on the crankshaft pulley bolt. The crankshaft will be easier to rotate if the spark plugs are first removed.

5 Have ready a pencil and paper to record the measured clearances.

6 Turn the crankshaft until the cam lobe nearest the pulley end of the engine is pointing vertically upwards. Use feeler gauges to measure the clearance between the base of the cam and the tappet (photo). Record the clearance.

7 Repeat the measurement for the other seven valves, turning the crankshaft as necessary so that the cam lobe in question is always vertically upwards.

8 Calculate the difference between each measured clearance and the desired value (see Specifications). Note that the value for inlet valves is different from that for exhaust. Counting from either end of the engine, the valve sequence is:

Exhaust - Inlet - Inlet - Exhaust - Exhaust - Inlet - Inlet - Exhaust

9 If any clearance measured is outside the specified tolerance adjustment must be carried out as described below.

10 If all clearances are within tolerance, refit

61.20 Fit and progressively tighten the cylinder head bolts to the Stage 1 torque setting. Note spacer location (arrowed)

61.23 Home-made disc used for measuring the Stage 3 cylinder head bolt tightening angle. Disc is fixed and pointer rotates

62.6 Measuring a valve clearance

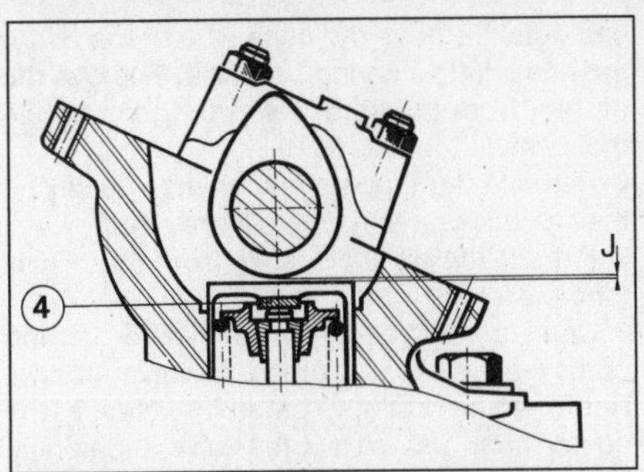

Fig. 1.29 Valve clearance is measured at point J and altered by selective thickness shim (4) (Sec 62)

the camshaft cover, using a new gasket if necessary. Note the copper washer under the bolt at the timing belt end.

Valve clearances - adjustment

11 Remove the camshaft as described in Section 60.

12 Lift off a tappet and its shim. Be careful that the shim does not fall out of the tappet. Clean the shim and measure its thickness with a micrometer (photos).

13 Refer to the clearance recorded for the valve concerned. If the clearance was larger than specified, a thicker shim must be fitted; if the clearance was too small, a thinner shim must be fitted.

Sample calculation - clearance too large:
- Desired clearance (A) 0.20 mm
- Measured clearance (B) 0.28 mm
- Difference (B-A) = + 0.08 mm
- Original shim thickness 2.62 mm
- Required shim thickness
  2.62 + 0.08 = 2.70 mm

Sample calculation - clearance too small:
- Desired clearance (A') 0.40 mm
- Measure clearance (B') 0.23 mm
- Difference (B'-A') = 0.17 mm
- Original shim thickness 2.86 mm
- Required shim thickness
  2.86 - 0.17 = 2.69 mm

14 Shims are available in thicknesses from 1.650 to 4.000 mm, in steps of 0.025 mm in the middle of the range and at the ends in steps of 0.075 mm. Clean new shims before measuring or fitting them.

15 Repeat the operations on the other tappets and shims, keeping each tappet identified so that it can be refitted in the same position.

16 When reassembling, oil the shim and fit it on the valve stem, then oil the tappet and lower it smoothly into position. If the tappet is raised at any stage the shim may be dislodged.

17 When all the tappets are in position with their shims, refit the camshaft. Check the valve clearances before refitting the camshaft drivebelt in case a mistake has been made and the camshaft has to be removed again.

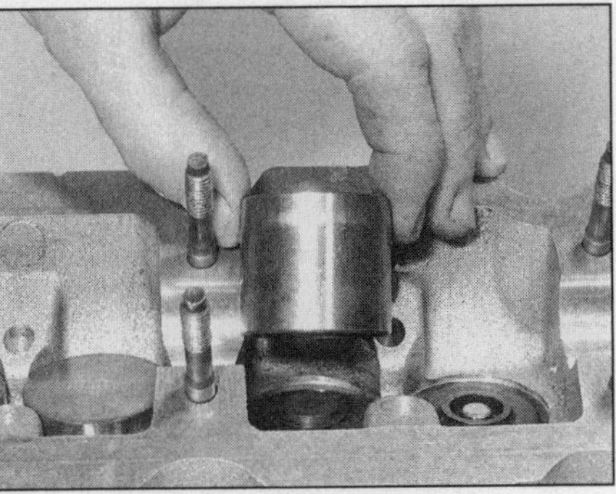

62.12A Lift off the tappet

63 Engine - removal methods

Refer to Section 7. The engine and transmission removal and refitting methods are the same as for the OHV variants.

64 Engine/transmission - removal

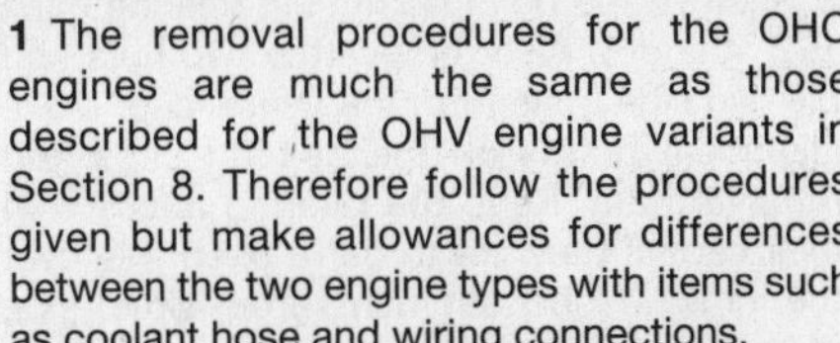

1 The removal procedures for the OHC engines are much the same as those described for the OHV engine variants in Section 8. Therefore follow the procedures given but make allowances for differences between the two engine types with items such as coolant hose and wiring connections.

2 On fuel injection models ignore references made to the carburettor and its associated components and remove or disconnect (as applicable) the following; with reference to Chapter 3 where necessary.

Throttle cable from the throttle body
Air cleaner unit
Air flow sensor unit
Throttle switch leads connection
Supplementary air device and temperature sensor leads
Pressure regulator and fuel supply hoses

65 Engine - separation from transmission

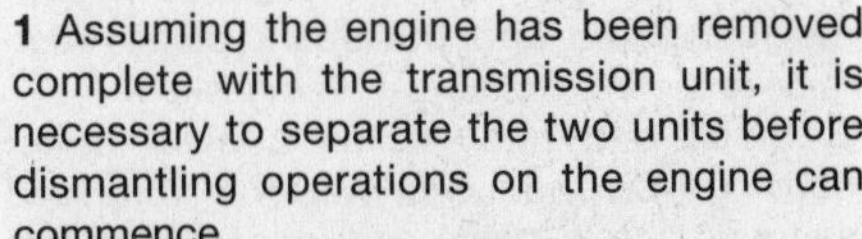

1 Assuming the engine has been removed complete with the transmission unit, it is necessary to separate the two units before dismantling operations on the engine can commence.

2 Unbolt and remove the starter motor as described in Chapter 12.

3 Remove the remaining engine-to-transmission bolts and note the position of any ancillary items which may be secured by the bolts, such as hose retaining clips.

4 Support the engine and pull the transmission away from it. Do not allow the weight of the transmission to hang on the input shaft during withdrawal of the transmission. Recover any loose location dowels.

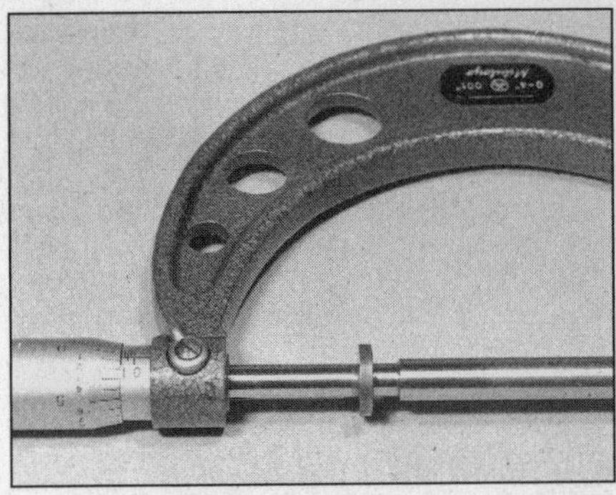

62.12B Measuring the thickness of a shim using a micrometer

66 Engine - dismantling (general)

Refer to Section 10 of this Chapter.

1

67 Engine ancillary components - removal

Refer to Section 11 of this Chapter.

68 Cylinder head - removal (engine out of car)

1 Slacken the ten cylinder head bolts, working in the reverse sequence of that used when tightening (Fig. 1.27). Remove the bolts and washers.

2 Remove the cylinder head. Refer to Section 61, paragraph 16.

3 Fit liner clamps if it is not proposed to remove the pistons and liners. See Section 61, paragraph 17.

69 Timing covers, timing belt and associated components - removal

1 Unbolt and remove the crankshaft pulley. Jam the flywheel teeth when undoing the pulley bolt to stop the crankshaft rotating.

2 Remove the camshaft drivebelt covers, noting the location of the various sizes of bolt.

3 Unbolt and remove the camshaft cover.

4 Rotate the crankshaft by means of the flywheel until a 10 mm diameter rod can be passed through the hole in the camshaft sprocket and into the timing recess. Nos 1 and 4 pistons are now at TDC.

5 Release the camshaft drivebelt tensioner by slackening its nuts (two at the front and one behind the front plate) and using the square end of the cam spindle to bring the cam into a horizontal position.

6 Remove the camshaft drivebelt, taking care not to kink it and noting its direction of travel if it is to be re-used.

7 Unbolt and remove the camshaft drivebelt tensioner.

8 Remove the belt side covers and crankshaft sprocket. Recover the Woodruff key.

9 Unbolt and remove the camshaft sprocket. Restrain the sprocket from turning if necessary using the 10 mm diameter rod inserted through the timing hole in the sprocket (see photo 60.5).

10 Unbolt and remove the engine mounting bracket, the camshaft sprocket backplate and the coolant pump.

70 Flywheel - removal

Refer to Section 16 of this Chapter. Note that the flywheel is located by dowels. If the dowels are loose they must be renewed.

71 Sump and oil pump - removal

1 If the engine is in the car, remove the engine undertray and drain the engine oil.

2 Remove the suction drain pipe from the side of the sump.

3 Unbolt and remove the sump. Note the location of the three Allen-headed bolts (photo).

4 Remove the bolts which secure the oil pump, noting the special centring bolt at the rear.

5 Unbolt and remove the oil seal carrier plate.

6 Lower the oil pump into the engine so that its chain can be removed. Withdraw the pump and recover the spacer, the dowel and the chain.

7 Pull the oil pump sprocket off the crankshaft and recover the Woodruff key.

71.3 Allen-head bolt locations on sump

72 Connecting rods, pistons and liners - removal

1 If the engine is in the car remove the sump (Section 71) and the cylinder head (Section 61).

2 Unscrew the connecting rod cap bolts. Before removing the caps check that they are marked in numerical order, also the connecting rods, liners and pistons. Mark them if they are not (1 to 4 from the flywheel end).

3 If the cylinder liners are being removed, then the pistons, rods and liners can be lifted out of the block as individual units, but mark their relative positions.

73 Crankshaft and main bearings - removal

1 Before removing the crankshaft, its endfloat should be checked and noted to assess for wear during examination and renovation procedures later. To check the endfloat proceed as described in Section 85.

2 Remove the bolts from main bearing caps 1, 2, 4 and 5. Also remove the two nuts and the two side bolts from the centre cap. Make alignment marks on the bearing caps and remove them. Keep the bearing shells with their caps if they are to be re-used. Recover the thrust washer segments from either side of No 2 bearing cap.

3 Remove the oil seal from the flywheel end of the crankshaft.

4 Lift the crankshaft out of the crankcase. Recover the upper half main bearing shells and the other two thrust washer segments.

5 If the cylinder liners have been left clamped in position in the cylinder block, their protrusions above the cylinder block face must be checked, as described in Section 81 before reassembling the engine.

74 Cylinder head - dismantling

1 If not already done, remove the distributor, the fuel pump and the spark plugs. Also remove the manifolds and their gaskets.

2 Unbolt and remove the coolant outlet housing. Do not overlook the recessed securing screw in the end (photo). Remove the thermostat elbow from the housing and withdraw the thermostat.

3 Lift out the camshaft lubrication manifold (photo 60.4).

4 Unbolt and remove the camshaft thrust fork plate (photos 60.5B and 60.5C).

5 Progressively slacken the camshaft bearing cap nuts. Remove the caps - be prepared for the camshaft to spring upwards. Remove the oil seal from the sprocket end, then remove the camshaft (photo 60.6).

6 Remove the tappets and shims, identifying their locations if they are to be re-used.

7 Extract the oil filter gauze from the oilway (photo 61.18B).

8 Use a universal type valve spring compressor to compress a valve spring. Remove the collets, carefully release the compressor and extract the valve and spring. Repeat for the other seven valves.

9 Using long-nosed pliers, carefully remove the valve stem oil seals from their locations in the head. Dismantling of the cylinder head is now complete.

75 Engine components - examination and renovation (general)

The inspection requirement procedures concerning the following engine components are as described for the equivalent items in Part A of this Chapter, but refer to the Part B Specifications for the tolerance requirements applicable to the OHC engine.

(a) General guidance on examination for wear - Section 23

(b) Crankshaft main and big-end bearings - Section 24

(c) Pistons and rings - Section 26

(d) Connecting rods - Section 27

(e) Gudgeon pins - Sections 21 and 39

(f) Flywheel - Section 34

76 Camshaft and tappets - examination and renovation

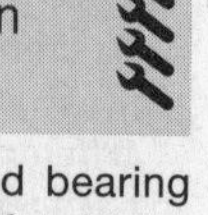

1 Inspect the camshaft lobes and bearing journals for wear and damage; if evident, renewal is probably necessary. Also inspect the bearing surfaces in the cylinder head and bearing caps.

2 Clean the camshaft lubrication manifold with solvent and then blow through it with

74.2 Undoing the recessed securing screw in the coolant outlet housing

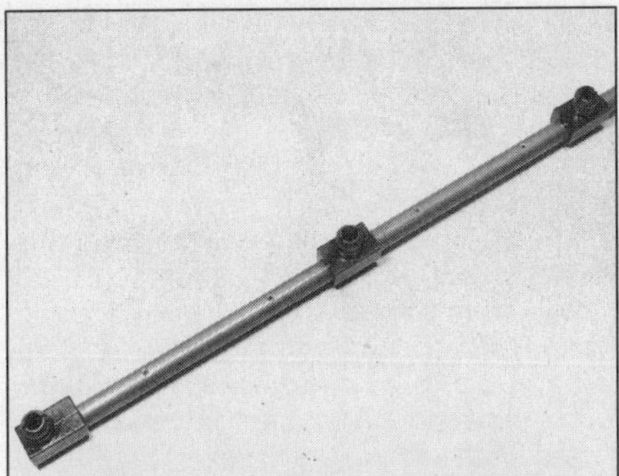

76.2 The pinholes in the camshaft lubrication manifold must be clear

compressed air. All the holes must be clear (photo).

3 Inspect the tappets for wear and scuffing; renew them as necessary. New tappets **must** be fitted if the camshaft is renewed; it is also advisable to renew the valve springs.

4 Renew the camshaft drivebelt as a matter of course unless it is in perfect condition and is known to have covered only a nominal mileage. Renew the sprockets if they are damaged.

77 Cylinder head, valves and piston crowns - decarbonising, examination and renovation

1 With the cylinder head and associated components dismantled they can be cleaned and examined as described in Sections 30 and 31 of this Chapter, but ignore the references to the rocker arms.

2 Note that, with the OHC engine, the manufacturers state that only 0.2 mm machining of the cylinder head surface is permitted. A badly warped head must therefore be renewed.

3 Factory exchange cylinder heads may have had 0.2 mm machined off the mating face. These heads are identified by the letter 'R' stamped on a boss at the distributor end of the head. A gasket 0.2 mm thicker than normal must be used with such a head; the thicker gasket is identified by a cut-out in the tab at the clutch end.

78 Timing belt, tensioner and sprockets - examination and renovation

1 Renew the drivebelt as a matter of course unless it is in perfect condition and is known to have covered only a nominal mileage.

2 Inspect the sprockets for any signs of damage. Renew them if necessary.

3 The drivebelt tensioner must be examined for roughness of the wheel bearing and wear or distortion of the spring. Renew as necessary. The wheel, bearing and backplate must be renewed as an assembly (photo).

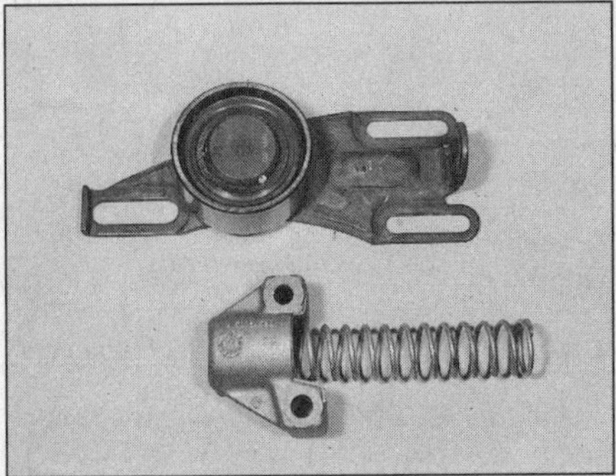

78.3 Camshaft drivebelt tensioner components

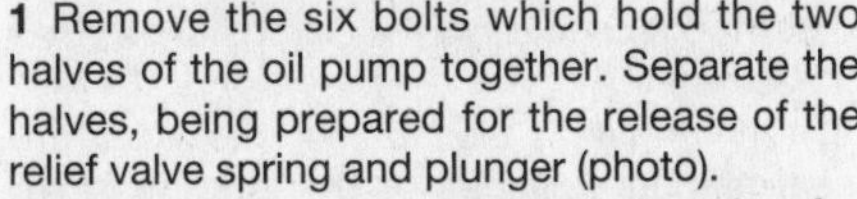

79 Oil pump, drive chain and sprockets - examination and renovation

1 Remove the six bolts which hold the two halves of the oil pump together. Separate the halves, being prepared for the release of the relief valve spring and plunger (photo).

2 Inspect the rotors and their housing for wear and damage. No wear limits are published for this pump; any visible wear on the moving parts suggests that renewal is necessary. With the exception of the relief valve spring and plunger, individual components are not available (photos).

3 Lubricate the pump components well before reassembly. Bolt the two halves together, being careful not to trap the spring.

4 If the pump is to be renewed it is wise to renew the chain and the crankshaft sprocket also.

5 Examine the teeth of both sprockets for wear. Each tooth on a sprocket is an inverted V-shape and wear is apparent when one side of the tooth becomes more concave in shape than the other. When badly worn, the teeth become hoop-shaped and the sprockets must be renewed.

6 If the sprockets need to be renewed then the chain will have worn also and should be renewed as well. If the sprockets are satisfactory, examine the chain and look for play between the links. When the chain is held out horizontally, it should not bend appreciably. Remember, a chain is only as strong as its weakest link, and being a relatively cheap item, it is worthwhile fitting a replacement anyway.

79.2A Inspect the oil pump gears for excessive wear

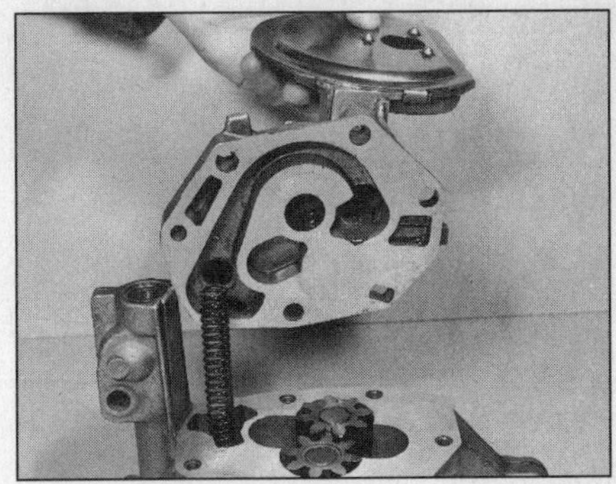

79.1 Separating the two halves of the oil pump

80 Cylinder liners - examination and renovation

1 The liner bores may be examined for wear either in or out of the engine block; the cylinder head must, of course, be removed in each case.

2 First of all examine the top of the cylinder about a quarter of an inch below the top of the liner and with a finger, feel if there is any ridge running round the circumference of the bore. In a worn cylinder bore a ridge will develop at the point where the top ring on the piston comes to the uppermost limit of its stroke. An excessive ridge indicates that the bore below the ridge is worn. If there is no ridge, it is reasonable to assume that the cylinder is not badly worn. Measurement of the diameter of the cylinder bore both in line with the piston gudgeon pin and at right angles to it, at the top and bottom of the cylinder, is another check to be made. A cylinder is expected to wear at the sides where the thrust of the piston presses against it. In time this causes the cylinder to assume an oval shape. Furthermore, the top of the cylinder is likely to wear more than the bottom of the cylinder. It will be necessary to use a proper bore

79.2b Oil pump relief valve spring and plunger

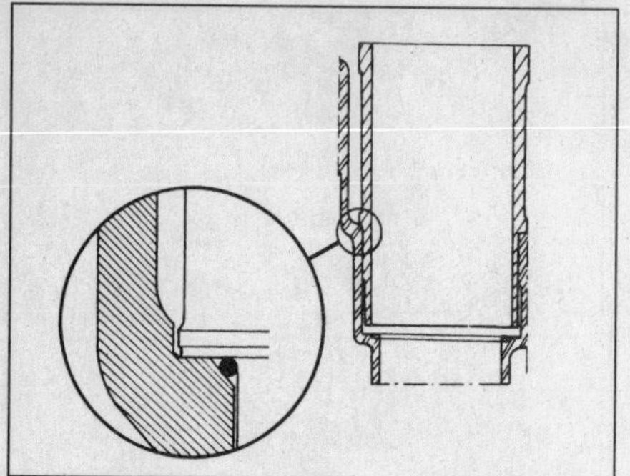

Fig. 1.30 Cylinder line O-ring seal location (Sec 81)

measuring instrument in order to measure the differences in bore diameter across the cylinder, and variations between the top and bottom ends of the cylinder. As a general guide it may be assumed that any variation more than 0.25 mm (0.010 in) indicates that the liners should be renewed. Provided all variations are less than 0.25 mm (0.010 in) it is probable that the fitting of new piston rings will cure the problem of piston-to-cylinder bore clearances. Once again it is difficult to give a firm ruling on this as so much depends on the amount of time, effort and money which the individual owner is prepared, or wishes to spend, on the task. Certainly if the cylinder bores are obviously deeply grooved or scored, the liners must be renewed, regardless of any measurement differences in the cylinder diameter.

3 If new liners are to be fitted, new pistons will be required also, as they are supplied as matched sets.

4 If the existing liners are to be refitted, it is advisable to check their protrusions when fitted at this stage rather than during engine reassembly. This is because the protrusion heights are not adjustable and if the old liners cannot meet the specified protrusion they may well have to be scrapped and new ones fitted. Consult your Peugeot dealer if in doubt. Refer to Section 81 for details on checking the protrusions of each liner.

81 Cylinder liner protrusion - checking

1 The protrusion of the cylinder liners when assembled to the block must be within prescribed limits so that a gastight seal can be achieved when the head is bolted on. One liner protruding too much or not enough will, despite the cylinder head gasket, make it impossible to secure a gas or watertight joint.

2 An O-ring seal is fitted between each liner mating flange and the cylinder block. These seals compress when the cylinder head is tightened down to effect a watertight seal (Fig. 1.30).

3 Although the actual liner protrusion check

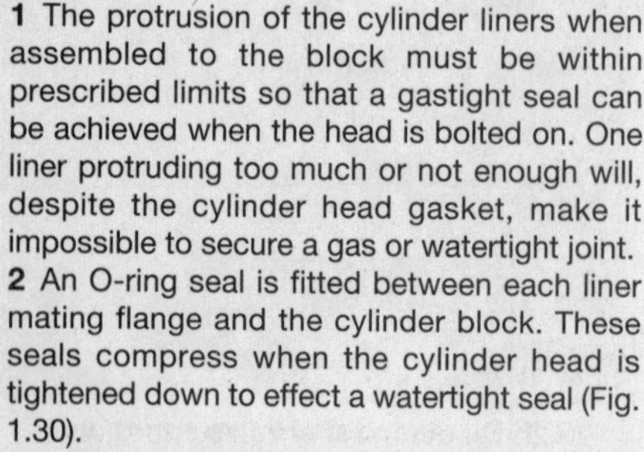

81.6 Measuring a cylinder liner projection

method is the same, the procedure differs if the engine is assembled or dismantled.

4 If the cylinder head has been removed with the engine *in situ* the liners must be held under compression with the use of liner clamps. Remove the dowels from the cylinder block top face to allow the clamps to be fitted, if necessary.

5 If the engine is dismantled, check that the seal mating surfaces of the liners and the cylinder block are clean, then insert each liner into its respective position in the cylinder block without its seal.

6 Check each liner protrusion in turn measuring the distance between the top face of the liner and the top face of the cylinder block. Use a dial test indicator if available but, failing this, use a metal rule and feeler gauges to assess the protrusion (photo).

7 As the protrusion of each liner in turn is checked, ensure that it is squarely located in the cylinder block. The protrusion of each liner should be within the limits specified (see Specifications at the start of this Chapter). New liners can be rotated half a turn (180°) and/or fitted in a different position in the block, to bring protrusion within tolerance. Old liners which will not produce the desired results are best scrapped. Consult a Peugeot dealer for advice.

8 Finally check the difference in height between adjacent liners. Use the dial test indicators or rule and feeler gauges to measure the difference in height, if any, between adjacent liners at a point on each lying along the centre axis parallel with the crankshaft on the top face. Each difference in level must not exceed the maximum specified.

9 If the checks reveal a discrepancy on an installed engine it will be necessary to renew the liner O-rings or even one or more liners.

10 Once the checks have shown the liners to be within limits of protrusion and squareness reassembling can continue or, if appropriate, temporary retainer clamps/straps should be fitted to hold them in position. *Don't turn the crankshaft if the liners are not restrained from movement.* Cover the exposed engine internal parts if there is likely to be a delay before completing reassembly.

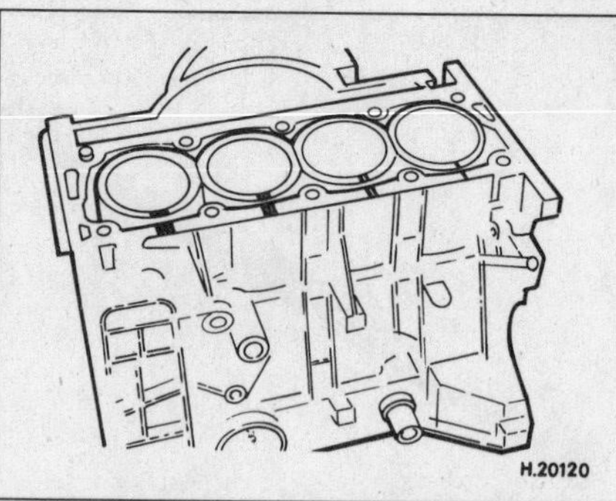

Fig. 1.31 Mark top of cylinders and block numerically from the flywheel end to ensure correct relocation (Sec 81)

11 With new liners, once correctly located, mark their sequence in the block (see Fig. 1.31) and withdraw them so that their piston/rods can be fitted.

82 Engine - reassembly (general)

Refer to Section 36 of this Chapter.

83 Engine - preparation for reassembly

Refer to Section 37 of this Chapter.

84 Pistons and liners - reassembly and refitting

1 Fit the piston rings to the pistons. Always fit the rings from the piston crown end. Use

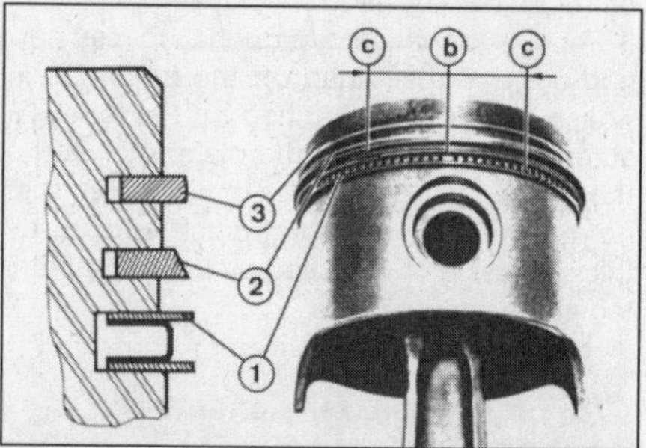

Fig 1.32 Positioning the piston ring gaps on assembly (Sec 84)

1 *Scraper ring*
   (b) *Expander gap on axis of gudgeon pin hole*
   (c) *Scraper rings gaps on alternate sides of gudgeon pin axis within 20 to 50 mm (0.79 to 1.96 in)*

2 *Tapered face ring gap 120° from gudgeon pin axis*

3 *Curved face ring gap 120° from gudgeon pin axis in opposite direction*

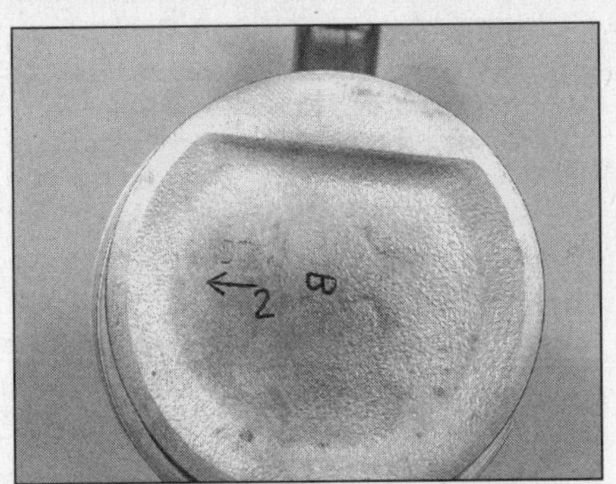

84.6 Arrow mark on piston crown must point towards the timing cover end of engine. Letter and number indicate the liner and gudgeon pin grade

three old feeler blades equally spaced behind the ring so that it will slide down to the lower grooves without dropping into the higher ones (see photo 40.2).

2 Make sure that the rings are correctly located and the right way up. If genuine Peugeot piston rings are being used, refer to Fig. 1.32. If special proprietary rings are being fitted, follow the manufacturer's instructions.

3 Twist the piston rings so that the gap in the oil control ring expander aligns with the gudgeon pin and the gaps in the rails are offset from the gudgeon pin by between 20.0 and 50.0 mm (0.79 and 1.97 in). The gaps in the top two compression rings should be equally spaced (120°) from the gap in the oil control expander around the piston.

4 If new piston/liner assemblies have been supplied, the identification marks on the piston and liner should be:

Piston	Liner
A	*One file mark on rim*
B	*Two file marks on rim*
C	*Three file marks on rim*

5 All four pistons should be of the same grading.

6 Fit the liners to the piston/connecting rod assemblies so that when installed in the cylinder block, the rim mark on the liner will be towards the oil gallery side and the arrow on the piston crown facing towards the timing cover end of the engine (photo). Piston-to-rod relationship is not important.

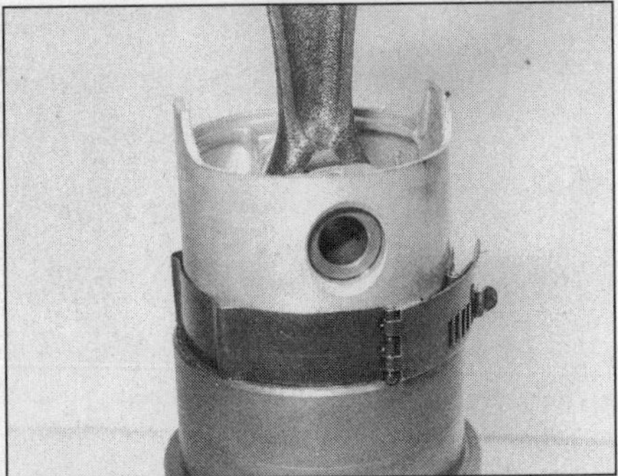

84.8 Insert the piston into its liner

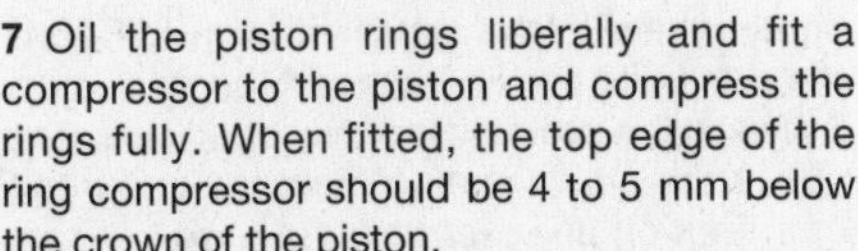

7 Oil the piston rings liberally and fit a compressor to the piston and compress the rings fully. When fitted, the top edge of the ring compressor should be 4 to 5 mm below the crown of the piston.

8 Lubricate the bore of the liner and insert the piston. As this is done, the compressor will be pushed off (photo).

9 Push the piston down so that the piston crown is level with or just below the top edge of the liner.

10 With the pistons and liners reassembled, fit a new O-ring seal over the bottom end of each liner in turn, ensuring that the seals are not twisted as they are fitted (photo).

11 Remove the big-end caps, wipe the recesses in rod and cap absolutely clean and fit the bearing shells. If the original shells are being used again, make sure that they are being returned to their original locations.

12 Push the liner/rod assemblies into the block, without disturbing the seals and aligning the location marks (photo).

13 Fit clamps to hold the liners in the block.

85 Crankshaft and main bearings - refitting

1 Position the cylinder block for access to the bottom end then fit the upper half main bearing shells, with grooved shells to the No 2 and No 4 main bearing.

2 Locate the 2.30 mm thick thrust washers to

84.10 Fit the liner O-ring seal

84.12 Installing piston/liner assembly

the No 2 bearing (from flywheel end), with its grooved face out (toward the crankshaft). Retain the washers each side of the bearing by smearing them with grease.

3 Oil the bearing shells and lower the crankshaft into position, taking care not to dislodge the thrust washer segments (photo). Inject some oil into the crankshaft oilways.

4 Check the crankshaft endfloat by pushing it in one direction then the other along its length. A dial gauge or feeler gauges should be used to measure the endfloat. If the endfloat measured is not within the specified limits change the thrust washer segments and fit alternatives of suitable thickness, but the four thrust washers used must all be of the same thickness. Thrust washers are available in a choice of four thicknesses.

5 Fit new side seals to No 1 main bearing cap. Carefully fit the cap with its bearing shell,

85.3 Fitting the crankshaft

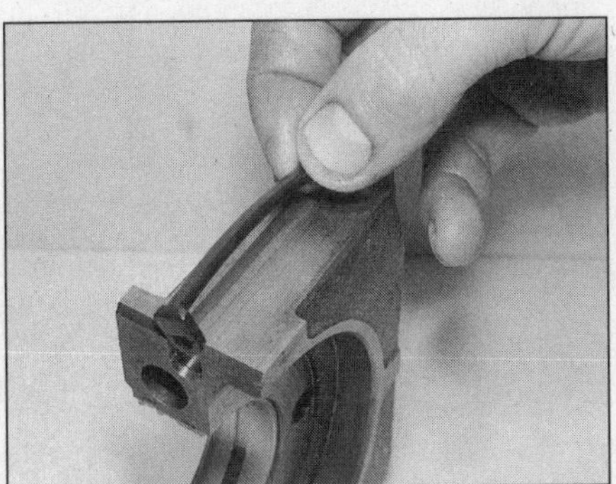

85.5A Fitting a side seal to No 1 main bearing cap

85.5B Protect the side seals with feeler blades

85.7 Tightening the No 3 main bearing side bolt

85.10 Crankshaft oil seal – flywheel end

lubricate the shell, the sides of the cap and the locating surfaces in the block. There is a risk of displacing or distorting the side seals as the cap is fitted, so protect them with a couple of feeler blades or thin strips of tin which can be withdrawn rearwards after fitting the cap (photos).

6 Fit the shells to the other main bearing caps, lubricate them and fit the caps. Fit the thrust washer segments (grooved side outwards) to the No 2 cap. Observe the mating marks made when dismantling; the lug on each bearing cap points towards the timing sprockets. Ensure that the thrust washer segment on each side of the number two main bearing cap is of equal thickness to the corresponding upper segment washer selected when setting the crankshaft endfloat.

7 Fit the main bearing cap nuts and bolts and tighten them to the specified torque. Tighten the side bolts on No 3 cap last (photo).

8 Check the protrusion of No 1 cap side seals above the sump mating face; it should be 2 mm. Trim off any excess.

9 Recheck the crankshaft endfloat (paragraph 4), and ensure that it rotates freely.

10 Fit a new oil seal, lips inwards and lubricated, to the flywheel end of the crankshaft. Drive it into place with a piece of tube (photo).

11 If not already fitted, fit new O-ring seals to the cylinder liners, then fit the pistons and liners with reference to paragraphs 10 to 13 inclusive in Section 84.

12 Push each piston down its liner and simultaneously engage the connecting rod with the crankshaft journal. Fit the mating big-end cap with the bearing and shells well lubricated. Ensure that the cap/rod match marks are in alignment to make sure that the shell tongues are correctly located on the same side.

13 Fit and tighten the big-end nuts to the specified torque, then check that the crankshaft can still be rotated. Extra effort will be required to turn the crankshaft.

86 Oil pump and sump - refitting

1 Fit the Woodruff key and oil pump drive sprocket to the crankshaft nose. Fit the chain over the sprocket (photos).

2 Make sure that the locating dowel is in position, then engage the oil pump sprocket in the chain and offer the pump to the block. Engage the pump on the dowel, then lift it up far enough to slide the L-shaped spacer in underneath it (photos).

3 Fit the oil pump securing bolts, remembering that the special centring bolt is nearest the flywheel, and tighten them to the specified torque. Generously lubricate the pump and the chain (photo).

4 Refit the pulley oil seal carrier plate, using silicone jointing compound on the block mating faces. Fit a new oil seal, lubricated lips inwards, and drive it home with a piece of tube.

5 Fit the sump, using a new gasket, and tighten its securing bolts progressively to the specified torque. Remember the correct location of the three Allen-headed bolts.

6 Refit the suction drain pipe, using a new O-ring. Do not overtighten the securing nuts, refer to the Specifications for the correct torque setting.

87 Flywheel and clutch - refitting

1 Fit the flywheel to the crankshaft flange and secure with new bolts, using thread locking compound. Tighten the bolts progressively to the specified torque.

2 Fit the clutch friction plate and pressure plate, as described in Chapter 5.

86.1A Fitting the oil pump drive sprocket

86.1B Locate the oil pump drive chain

86.2A Fitting the oil pump. Engage the chain first

86.2B Locate the oil pump spacer

86.3 Oil pump special bolt location

88 Valves - refitting

1 Commence reassembly by fitting new valve stem oil seals, then fit the valves, springs and collets. Oil the valve stems liberally; a smear of grease will hold the collets in position while the spring is compressed. The valve springs can be fitted either way up.
2 Lubricate the tappet bores. Secure each shim to its valve stem with a dab of grease and carefully fit the tappets. If new components have been fitted so that the valve clearances are unknown, fit the thinnest possible shims to all valves.

89 Cylinder head and camshaft - refitting

1 Refer to Section 61 and proceed as described in paragraphs 1 8 to 21 inclusive, then paragraph 23.
2 Refer to Section 60 and proceed as described in paragraphs 8 to 11 inclusive to fit the camshaft.
3 Note that the cylinder head bolts will need to be retightened again after the engine is restarted and warmed up (see Section 94 for details). This does not apply to Torx head bolts.

90 Timing covers, timing belt and associated components - refitting

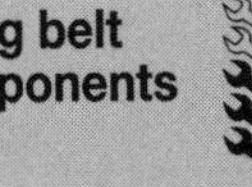

1 Fit the camshaft sprocket backplate, using a 10 mm rod through the timing hole to locate it precisely before tightening its securing bolts.
2 Fit the camshaft sprocket, washer and bolt. Use the 10 mm rod to lock the sprocket in the correct position and tighten the bolt to the specified torque. Remove the rod.

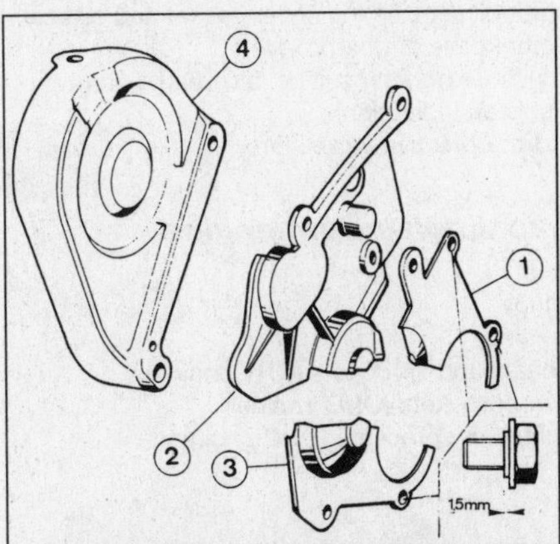

Fig. 1.34 Fit the timing covers in the numerical sequence shown (Sec 90)

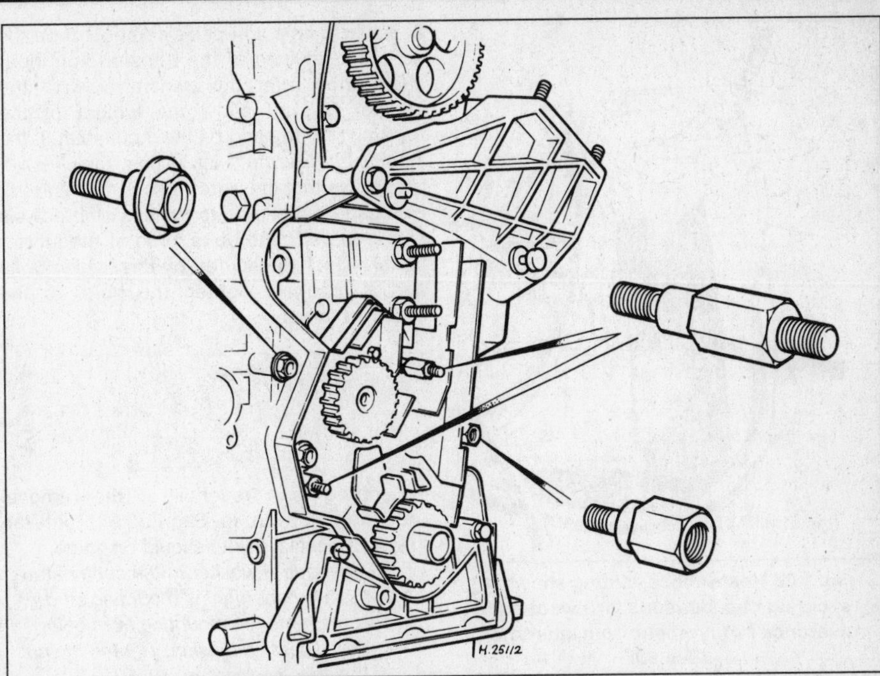

Fig. 1.33 Drivebelt cover special bolts (Sec 90)

3 Fit and secure the coolant pump, using a new gasket. Tighten the bolts to the specified torque (Chapter 2).
4 Fit the covers around the coolant pump, noting the locations of the various special bolts (Fig. 1.33). Smear the large bolt threads with sealant.
5 Fit the Woodruff key and the crankshaft sprocket.
6 Fit the camshaft drivebelt tensioner, but leave the nuts slack. Compress the spring by locking the cam in the horizontal position.
7 Temporarily fit the crankshaft pulley, its washer and bolt; lightly tighten the bolt. Carefully turn the crankshaft until a 10 mm rod will pass through the timing hole in the pulley and into the timing recess. If piston/valve contact occurs, back off and try again with the camshaft in a slightly different position. Do not try to force the crankshaft if a piston contacts a valve.
8 Use the 10 mm rod to position the camshaft sprocket, then remove the crankshaft pulley and fit the camshaft drivebelt. Be careful not to kink the belt as it is fitted, and observe the arrows showing the correct direction of rotation. The two white strips on the belt should align with the timing marks on the sprockets.
9 Withdraw the timing rod. Tension the belt by turning the tensioner cam so that it points downwards; secure it with its locknut. Tighten the two nuts at the front of the tensioner.
10 Turn the crankshaft through two full turns in the normal direction of rotation; rotate it further to bring Nos 1 and 4 pistons to TDC with the valves on No 1 cylinder open.
11 Slacken the two nuts and the cam locknut on the drivebelt tensioner, then retighten them.
12 Temporarily refit the crankshaft pulley, rotate the crankshaft and check that the timing rods can be inserted simultaneously in the crankshaft pulley and camshaft sprocket holes. If not, remove the belt and try again. Remove the pulley.
13 Fit the engine mounting bracket and tighten its bolts.
14 Refit the drivebelt covers, but note that they will have to be removed later to retension the drivebelt if a new one has been fitted (Fig. 1.34).
15 Fit the crankshaft pulley, washer and bolt, making sure that the Woodruff key is still in position. Jam the starter ring gear teeth and tighten the bolt to the specified torque.
16 If not already fitted, locate the camshaft oil lubrication manifold, then refit the camshaft cover, noting the copper washer at the sprocket end bolt. Use a new gasket.

91 Engine ancillary components - refitting

1 Refit the ancillary components listed below; it may be preferable to leave delicate items such as the alternator and distributor until after the engine is refitted:

(a) Oil filler/breather pipe
(b) Oil pressure switch
(c) Coolant housing and pipe
(d) Spark plugs, distributor and HT leads (refer to Chapter 4)
(e) Inlet and exhaust manifolds (Chapter 3)
(f) Alternator and drivebelt (Chapter 12)
(g) Oil filter (Section 56)

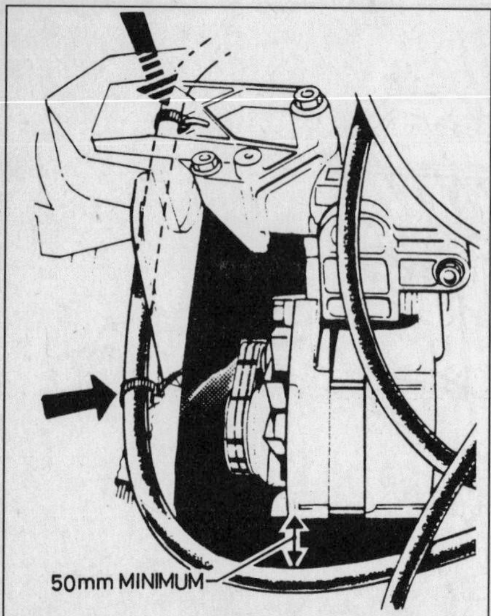

Fig. 1.35 Heater hose routing showing securing clip locations (arrowed) and clearance requirement from alternator (Sec 93)

92 Engine - reconnection to gearbox

1 Check that the clutch release components are correctly fitted in the gearbox and that the pressure plate and friction disc are fitted to the flywheel.

2 Smear a little anti-seize compound on the nose and splines of the transmission input shaft, then offer the transmission to the engine. Do not allow the weight of the transmission to hang on the input shaft. If the input shaft does not wish to pass the clutch, it is possible that the clutch disc is not centred.

3 Engage the engine-to-transmission dowels and loosely fit the bolts. Also fit the starter motor, which is secured by three Allen bolts and a bracket. Tighten the bolts to the specified torque.

93 Engine - refitting

1 Refitting is a reversal of the removal procedures given in Section 64, but the following special points should be noted.

(a) *Fit the special washer to the centre stud in the left-hand engine mounting stud. This prevents the mounting from being under excessive tension. Tighten the nut to the specified torque.*

(b) *Use a final drive oil seal protector when inserting the right-hand driveshaft. Remove the protector when the driveshaft is fitted (see Chapter 7 for full details).*

(c) *Adjust the clutch cable. with reference to Chapter 5, and the throttle cable, with reference to Chapter 3.*

(d) *Tighten the exhaust flange bolts, as described in Chapter 3.*

(e) *Refill and bleed the cooling system as described in Chapter 2.*

(f) *When refitting the heater hose, arrange it as shown in Fig. 1.35 and secure it with the retaining straps. When located the hose must be 50 mm clear of the alternator (at the front).*

(g) *Refer to Chapter 3 when reconnecting the fuel injection components on the SRi model.*

(h) *Top up the engine and gearbox oil levels with the correct grade and quantity of oils.*

94 Engine - initial start-up after major repair or overhaul

1 Refer to Section 52 of this Chapter, but when retightening the cylinder head bolts (not Torx type bolts) the procedure is as follows.

2 Allow the engine to cool for at least two hours. Loosen the bolt which secures the engine right-hand mounting bracket to the block then retighten the cylinder head bolts, as described in Section 61, paragraph 23.

3 Tighten the mounting bracket bolt on completion. No subsequent retightening is necessary.

4 Recheck the valve clearances, then refit the cam cover.

5 If a new camshaft drivebelt was fitted, retension it as described in Section 59, paragraphs 22 and 23.

Fault finding - all engines

Engine will not turn over when starter switch is operated

- ☐ Flat battery
- ☐ Bad battery connections
- ☐ Bad connections at solenoid switch and/or starter motor
- ☐ Starter motor jammed
- ☐ Defective solenoid
- ☐ Starter motor defective

Engine turns over normally but fails to fire and run

- ☐ No sparks at plugs
- ☐ No fuel reaching engine
- ☐ Too much fuel reaching engine (flooding)

Engine starts but runs unevenly and misfires

- ☐ Ignition and/or fuel system faults
- ☐ Incorrect valve clearance
- ☐ Burnt out valves
- ☐ Blown cylinder head gasket, dropped liners (if applicable)
- ☐ Worn out piston rings
- ☐ Worn cylinder bores

Lack of power

- ☐ Ignition and/or fuel system faults
- ☐ Incorrect valve clearances
- ☐ Burnt out valves
- ☐ Blown cylinder head gasket
- ☐ Worn out piston rings
- ☐ Worn cylinder bores

Excessive oil consumption

- ☐ Oil leaks from crankshaft oil seal, timing cover gasket and oil seal, rocker cover gasket, crankcase or gearbox joint
- ☐ Worn piston rings or cylinder bores resulting in oil being burnt by engine (smoky exhaust is an indication)
- ☐ Worn valve guides and/or defective valve stem
- ☐ Worn valve seals

Excessive mechanical noise from engine

- ☐ Wrong valve clearances
- ☐ Worn crankshaft bearings
- ☐ Worn cylinders (piston slap)
- ☐ Slack or worn timing chain and sprockets (OHV engine)
- ☐ Worn timing belt and/or sprockets (OHC engine)
- ☐ Worn oil pump drive chain or sprockets (OHC engine)

Chapter 2 Cooling system

For modifications, and information applicable to later models, see Supplement at end of manual

Contents

Degrees of difficulty

Easy, suitable for novice with little experience 	**Fairly easy,** suitable for beginner with some experience 	**Fairly difficult,** suitable for competent DIY mechanic 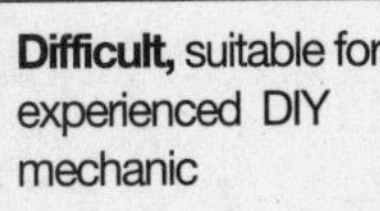	**Difficult,** suitable for experienced DIY mechanic	**Very difficult,** suitable for expert DIY or professional

2

Specifications

General

Type	Pressurised system with front-mounted radiator, electric cooling fan, water pump and thermostat	
System coolant capacity:		
1.1 and 1.3 litre (OHV) engines	6.6 litres (11.6 pints)	
1.6 litre (OHC) engines	7.5 to 8.0 litres (13.2 to 14.1 pints)	
Pressure cap setting	1.0 bar (14.5 lbf/in²)	
Thermostat opening temperature:		
1.1 and 1.3 litre (OHV engines)	89°C (192°F)	
1.6 litre (OHC) engine	82°C (180°F)	
Radiator cooling fan operating temperatures (°C/°F):	**On**	**Off**
1.1 litre (OHV) engine	95/203	86/187
1.3 litre (OHV) engine and 1.6 litre (OHC) carburettor engine:		
1st stage	93/199	88/190
2nd stage	97/207	92/198
1.6 litre (OHC) fuel injection engine:		
1st stage	97/207	92/198
2nd stage	101/214	96/205
Antifreeze type/specification	Ethylene glycol based antifreeze coolant mixture	
Antifreeze mixture:		
Protection to - 15°C (5°F)	27% antifreeze	
Protection to - 35°C (-31°F)	50% antifreeze	

Torque wrench settings

	Nm	lbf ft
OHV engines		
Coolant pump	12	9
Pump pulley bolts	15	11
Coolant pump drain plug	18	13
Coolant drain plug on crankcase	18	13
OHC engines		
Coolant pump	15	11
Coolant outlet housing (to cylinder head)	15	11

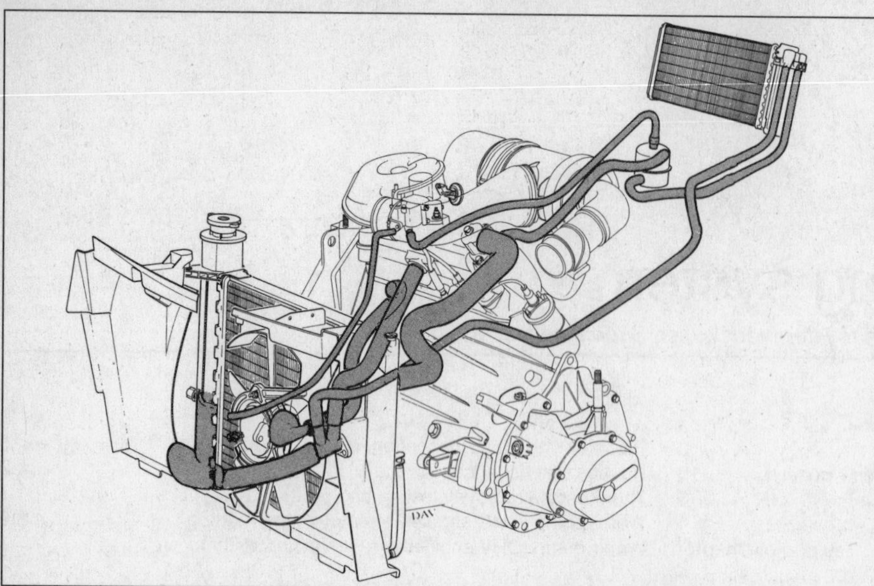

Fig. 2.1 Engine cooling system and heater system coolant circuits - OHV engine (Sec 1)

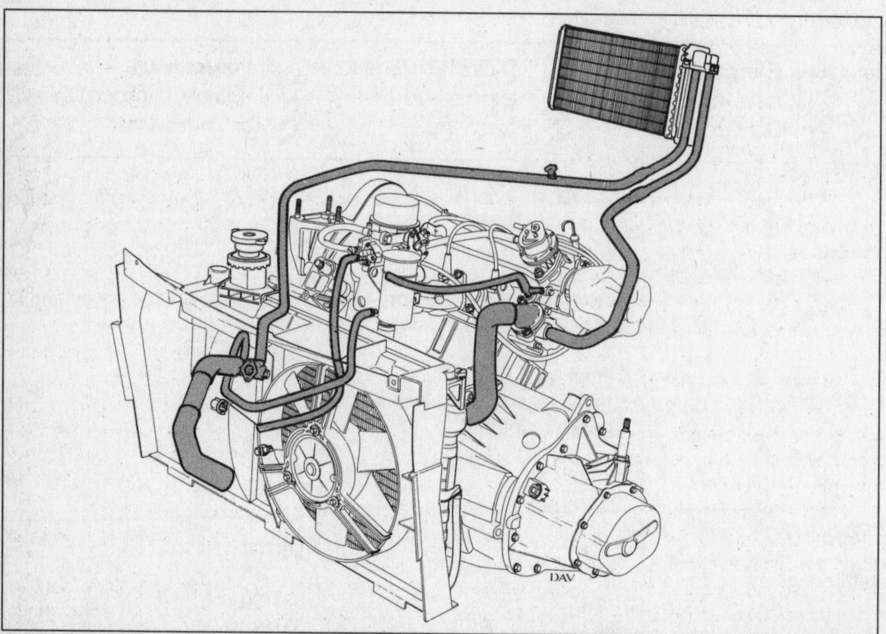

Fig. 2.2 Engine cooling system and heater system coolant circuits - OHC engine (Sec 1)

2.1 Coolant expansion tank (where fitted)

2.2 Top up the cooling system with specified antifreeze

1 General description

The cooling system is of the pressurised type. The system includes a front-mounted cross-flow radiator, thermoswitch controlled electric cooling fan, water pump and thermostat. The car interior heater matrix is supplied with a continuous supply of coolant since there is no water valve and the hot air supply is controlled by an air flap.

On OHV engine models, the water pump is driven in tandem with the alternator drivebelt. On OHC models the water pump is driven by the engine camshaft (timing) drivebelt.

The cooling system functions in the following way. After a cold start the thermostat valve is shut and coolant circulation is restricted to the engine and heater matrix. When the coolant reaches the normal engine operating temperature the thermostat starts to open and coolant circulation also flows through the radiator. The engine temperature is then controlled by the thermostat and the electric cooling fan located on the front of the radiator.

2 Routine maintenance

Carry out the following procedures at the intervals given in Routine Maintenance at the beginning of the manual.

1 With the engine cold, check the level of coolant in the radiator or the expansion tank (where applicable). Where an expansion tank is *not* fitted, the coolant level should be six inches below the top of the radiator filler neck. Where an expansion tank *is* fitted, a level guide is fitted inside the filler neck. Do not remove the filler cap when the engine is hot as the system will be pressurized and steam or coolant will be suddenly released under pressure and scalding could result. If it is essential to remove the cap with the engine hot, cover the cap with a cloth and slowly release the cap to its first position. Leave at this position until the pressure in the system is fully released before removing the cap, again covered with a cloth to guard against scalding (photo).

2 If necessary top up the cooling system level as required then refit the cap. Note that cold coolant must not be added to a hot engine (photo).

3 Check the cooling system hoses, thermostat housing and water pump for leakage and rectify as necessary.

4 Drain the coolant, flush the cooling system and fill with fresh coolant, as described in Section 4.

5 On OHV engine models, check the tension and condition of the alternator/coolant pump drivebelt (see Chapter 12).

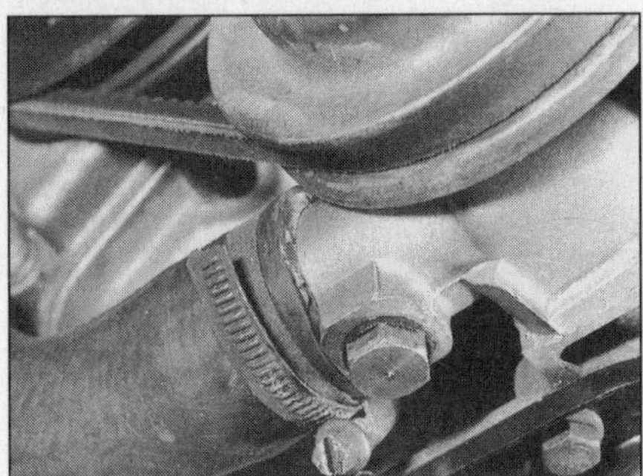
4.3A Coolant drain plug in the water pump – OHV engine

4.3B Coolant drain plug in the radiator – OHC engine

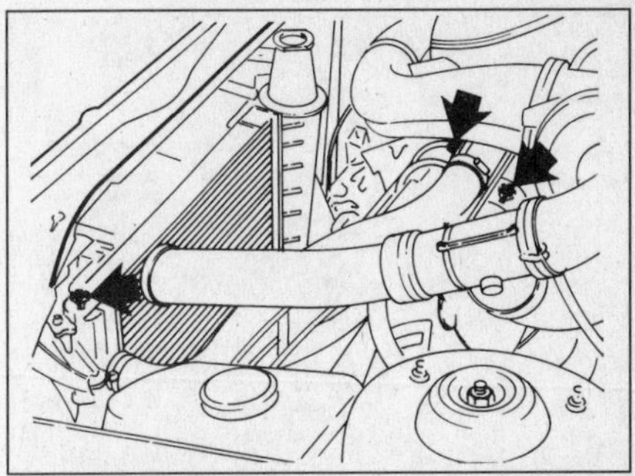
Fig. 2.3 Cooling system bleed screw locations (arrowed) – OHV engine (Sec 4)

3 Coolant mixture - general

1 Plain water should never be used in the cooling system. Apart from giving protection against freezing, an antifreeze mixture protects the engine internal surfaces and components against corrosion. This is very important in an engine with alloy components.

2 Always use a top quality glycol-based antifreeze which is recommended for alloy engines.

3 Ideally a 50% mixture of antifreeze and soft or demineralised water should be used to maintain maximum protection against freezing and corrosion. On no account use less than 25% antifreeze.

4 Renew the coolant at the specified intervals as the inhibitors contained in the antifreeze gradually lose their effectiveness.

5 Even when operating in climates where antifreeze is not required never use plain water, but add a corrosion inhibitor to it.

4 Cooling system - draining, flushing and refilling

1 If the engine is cold, remove the filler cap from the radiator/expansion tank by turning the cap anti-clockwise. If the engine is hot, then turn the filler cap very slightly until pressure in the system has had time to be released. Use a rag over the cap to protect your hand from escaping steam. If, with the engine very hot, the cap is released suddenly, the drop in pressure can result in the water boiling. With the pressure released the cap can be removed. Remove the engine undershield.

2 If antifreeze is used in the cooling system, drain into a bowl having the necessary capacity (see Specifications). If the system coolant is under two years old, it can be re-used, otherwise it must be discarded.

3 The drain plug location is dependent on model as follows:

(a) OHV engines: Radiator and coolant (water) pump base (photo)

(b) OHC engines: Radiator cylinder block and inlet manifold (photo)

When draining the radiator on both engine types, undo the small diameter expansion hose from the lower connection on the rear face of the radiator on the left-hand side.

4 When the coolant has finished draining, probe the drain points with a piece of wire to dislodge any sediment or rust particles which may cause blockage.

5 Remember that, without dismantling, it is impossible to drain the system dry as some coolant will be retained in the heater matrix. If there is no antifreeze in the system, frost damage is still possible in winter even though the system is 'drained'.

6 If you intend to re-use the coolant, cover it to prevent dust or other contaminants from affecting it.

7 To flush the cooling system, cover the engine and all electrical circuits with a sheet of plastic to stop water getting on them, as you are bound to cause some splashing. Insert a hose in the radiator filler neck and flush the system with fresh water for ten to fifteen minutes.

8 If the water still does not run clear, the radiator can be flushed with a good proprietary cleaning agent, and/or reverse flushed. In the latter case disconnect the bottom hose from the radiator and remove the thermostat (Section 7). Direct the hose into the thermostat housing so that water is forced through the engine coolant passages and out of the bottom hose. To reverse flush the radiator it is advisable to remove it as described in Section 5 and invert it whilst flushing.

2

9 Flushing should be continued until the water runs clear and you are satisfied that the system is clean; then close the drain tap and refit any components which were removed.

10 Whenever the engine coolant level is to be topped up or the coolant renewed, it is essential that the engine is cold.

11 Reconnect the radiator hoses and refit the drain plugs.

12 Loosen the cooling system bleed screws (Fig. 2.3), then refill the cooling system through the radiator filler neck (photos).

4.12A Radiator filler cap on SRI model fitted with an expansion tank. The cap should not be removed unless refilling or flushing the system

4.12B Cooling system bleeder on the inlet manifold (arrowed) – OHV engine

4.12C Cooling system bleed screw on the thermostat housing (arrowed) – OHC engine

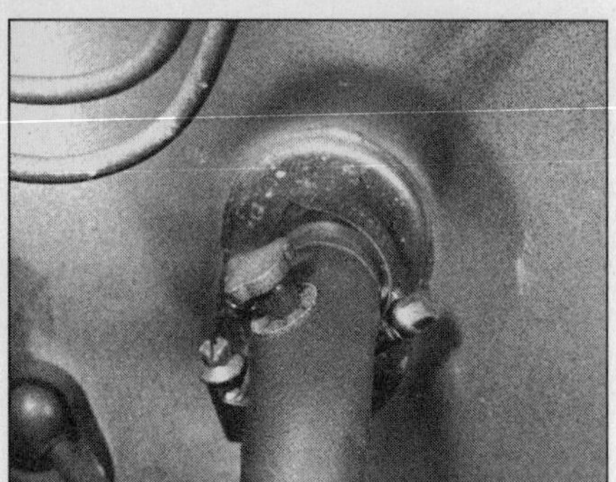

4.12D Cooling system bleed screw in heater hose at bulkhead – OHC engine

5.3A Coolant temperature switch location in radiator – OHV engine

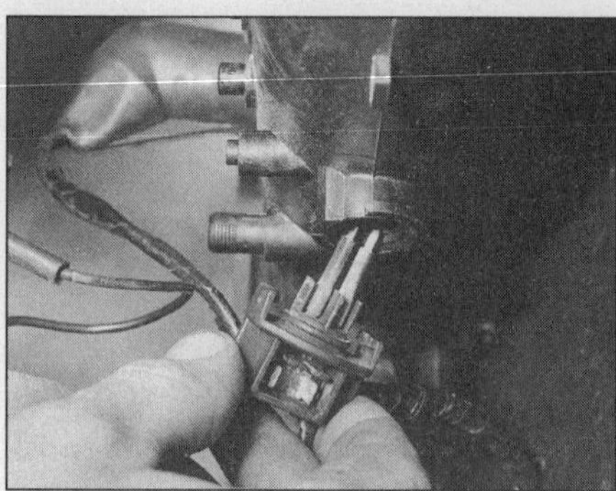

5.3B Coolant level warning switch removal from radiator – OHV engine

Ensure that the correct ratio of antifreeze is used (Section 3).

13 As the system is filled, coolant will flow from the bleed screws. When the flow of coolant from each screw is continuous, retighten the bleed screw.

14 Fill the system so that the coolant level reaches the top of the radiator filler neck, then refit the radiator cap. Wipe any spilt coolant from the paintwork.

15 On models with an expansion tank, refit the radiator filler cap then continue refilling the expansion tank to top up the level, then refit its cap.

16 Start the engine and run it up to its normal operating temperature and the cooling fan cuts in. Run the engine for a further five minutes and turn it off. Check for any signs of leaks and allow the engine to cool for about two hours, then recheck the coolant level in the radiator or expansion tank (as applicable). Top up if necessary.

17 The cooling system should be drained and flushed, then new antifreeze solution added at regular intervals (see Routine Maintenance).

5 Radiator - removal, inspection, cleaning and refitting

1 Drain the cooling system as described in Section 4.

2 Loosen the clips securing the top and bottom hoses to the radiator and carefully ease the hoses off the connecting tubes.

3 Disconnect the electrical leads to the fan thermal switch and the coolant level warning switch (photos).

4 Lift the radiator upwards to disengage its bottom location pegs from their holes in the body frame, on the left and right-hand sides. Then, when clear, pivot the radiator at the bottom towards the engine, pull it downwards and disengage the radiator from its upper fixings and lift it clear (photo).

5 Radiator repairs are best left to a specialist, although in an emergency, minor leaks from the radiator can be cured using a radiator sealant with the radiator *in situ*. The radiator matrix, header and bottom tanks should be thoroughly examined for signs of damage, deterioration and leakage; very often a rusty sediment will have been deposited where a leak has occurred.

6 After inspection, the radiator should be flushed as described in Section 4 and the matrix and exterior cleaned of dirt and dead flies with a strong jet of water.

7 Refitting the radiator is a reversal of the removal procedure but the following additional points should be noted:

(a) Examine and renew any clips, hoses and rubber mounting washers which have deteriorated

(b) Refill the cooling system as described in Section 4

6 Cooling fan - removal and refitting

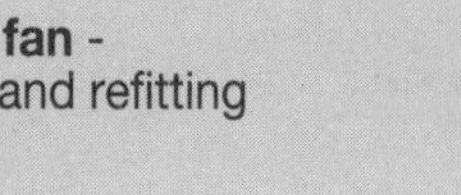

1 Disconnect the battery earth lead.

2 Remove the radiator as described in the previous Section.

3 Unbolt and remove the top front cross panel.

4 Detach the air intake duct from the locating wire at the front.

5 Disconnect the wiring from the cooling fan at the in-line connectors.

6 Lift out the cooling fan and the location frame (photo).

7 Undo the three retaining nuts to remove the fan unit from the frame (photo).

8 Refitting is a reversal of the removal procedure. If renewing the fan unit, note that the motor output is dependent on the engine type.

9 Check for satisfactory operation on completion by running the engine at a fast idle speed until the engine is warmed up when the fan should cut in, then out when the engine has cooled sufficiently.

7 Thermostat - removal, testing and refitting

1 Drain the cooling system as described in Section 4.

5.4 Radiator removal from the car – OHV engine

6.6 Cooling fan and location frame removal

6.7 Cooling fan retaining nuts removal

7.2 Thermostat housing and radiator top hose (arrowed) – OHV engine

7.3 Thermostat housing cover removal – OHC engine

7.8 Thermostat, showing temperature rating (arrowed) – OHC engine

2 Disconnect the radiator top hose from the thermostat housing (photo). On SRi models first remove the air inlet duct from the air cleaner.

3 Unscrew and remove the two thermostat housing cover bolts and remove the cover. This may need a little persuasion with a wooden or plastic-faced hammer (photo).

4 Remove the thermostat. If it is stuck, do not lever it out under its bridge piece, but cut around its edge with a sharp knife.

5 Remove the rubber ring(s) (if applicable) and clean the mating faces of the housing and cover.

6 If the thermostat is suspected of being faulty, suspend it in a container of water which is being heated. Using a thermometer, check that the thermostat starts to open at the specified temperature.

7 Remove the thermostat from the water and allow it to cool. The valve plate should close smoothly.

8 If the unit fails to operate as described or it is stuck open or shut, renew it with one of similar temperature rating (photo).

9 Refitting is a reversal of the removal procedure. On OHV engine models ensure that the locating tab on the thermostat is correctly aligned and use a new cover gasket. On OHC engine models use new rubber sealing ring(s).

10 Do not overtighten the cover bolts when tightening them.

11 Reconnect the coolant hose and refill the system and bleed it as described in Section 4.

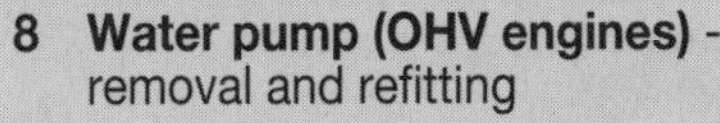

8 Water pump (OHV engines) - removal and refitting

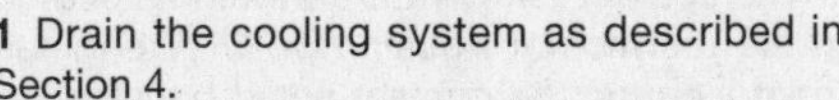

1 Drain the cooling system as described in Section 4.

2 Jack up the front of the car and support it securely on safety stands.

3 Unbolt and remove the engine under shield and side shield.

4 Loosen the alternator mounting and adjusting arm bolts, move the alternator towards the engine and disengage the drivebelt.

5 Undo and remove the three retaining bolts and withdraw the water pump pulley from the pump flange (photo).

8.5 Water pump pulley and retaining bolts – OHV engine

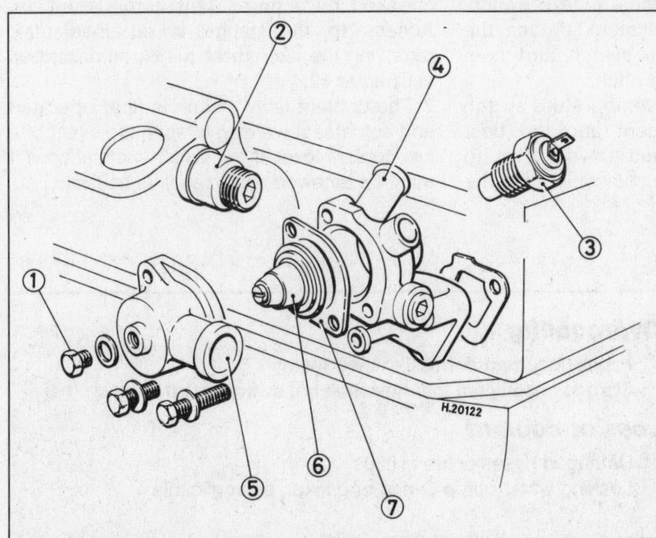

Fig. 2.4 Thermostat, housing and associated fittings – OHV engine (Sec 7)

1 Bleed screw and washer
2 End piece
3 Temperature sender unit
4 Coolant outlet housing and gasket
5 Housing cover
6 Thermostat
7 Gasket

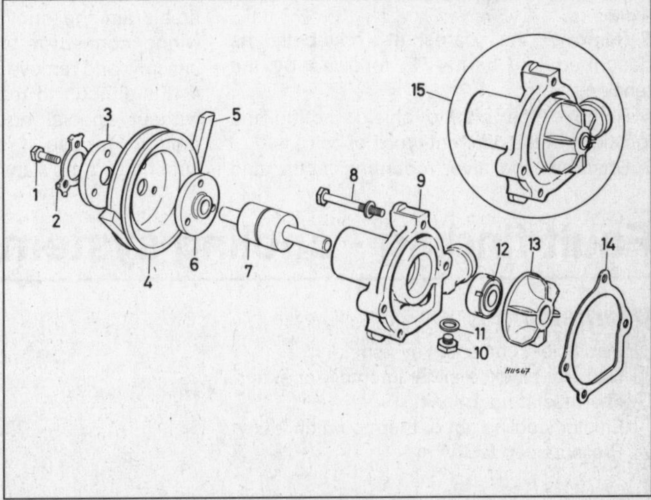

Fig. 2.5 Exploded view of the water pump – OHV engine (Sec 8)

1 Pulley retaining bolt
2 Lockplate
3 Plate
4 Pulley
5 Drivebelt
6 Hub
7 Shaft/bearing assembly
8 Bolt
9 Pump body
10 Drain plug
11 Drain plug seal
12 Seal
13 Impeller
14 Gasket
15 Assembled water pump

2

6 Disconnect the water hose from the outlet on the side of the pump.
7 Undo and remove the four retaining bolts and withdraw the water pump assembly from its location in the sump casting.
8 If the water pump is worn, noisy or leaks, it should be renewed by a new replacement unit. Although this type of water pump can be dismantled for inspection, any replacement parts may not be readily available and their cost may nearly equal that of a complete unit. Any repairs which may be possible should be entrusted to a Peugeot dealer who has the necessary experience and tools.
9 Refitting the water pump is the reverse sequence to removal, bearing in mind the following points:

(a) Ensure that the sump face and water pump mating surfaces are thoroughly clean and free from any traces of old gasket
(b) Use a new gasket lightly smeared on both sides with sealing compound (photo)
(c) Tighten the pulley and water pump retaining bolts to the torque settings shown in the Specifications
(d) Adjust the drivebelt tension as described in Chapter 12

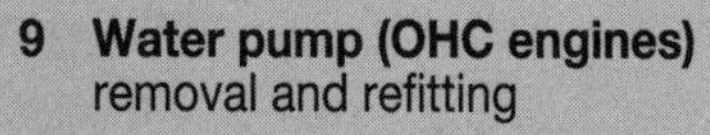

9 Water pump (OHC engines) - removal and refitting

1 Drain the cooling system as described in Section 4.
2 Jack up the car at the front and support it securely on safety stands.
3 Unbolt and remove the engine undershield.
4 Detach and remove the radiator bottom hose.
5 Remove the camshaft drivebelt, as described in Chapter 1, followed by the tensioner.
6 Remove the plastic shield, noting the locations of the different types of bolt.
7 Unscrew the five mounting bolts and remove the water pump from the cylinder block. Remove the gasket.
8 If the water pump is worn, noisy or leaks coolant it must be renewed, as repair is not possible.
9 Refitting is a reversal of removal, but clean the mating faces and always fit a new O-ring or gasket, as applicable. Fill the cooling system, as described in Section 4.

8.9 Refitting the water pump with new gasket located on body - OHV engine

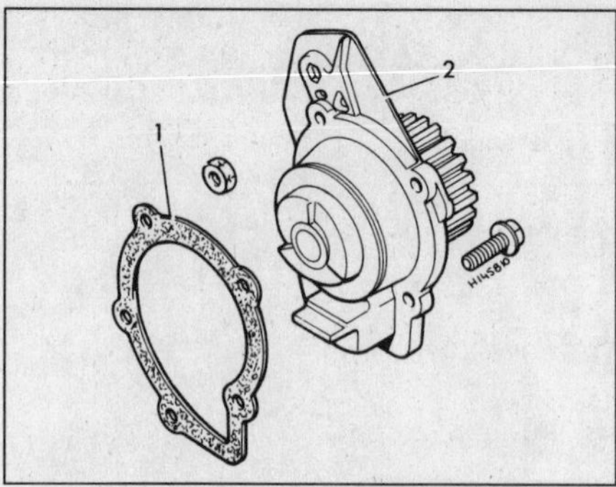

Fig. 2.6 Water pump - OHC engine (Sec 9)
1 Gasket 2 Pump unit

10.1 Coolant temperature switch location (arrowed) - OHV engine

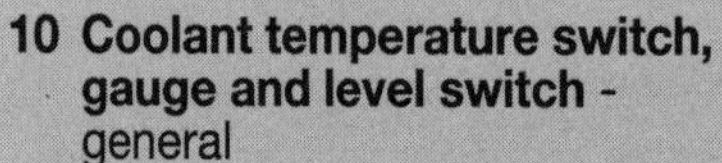

10 Coolant temperature switch, gauge and level switch - general

1 The coolant temperature switch is located in the thermostat housing on OHV engines (photo) and in the coolant outlet housing (on the end of the cylinder head) on OHC engine models.
2 The coolant level switch is located in the side of the radiator.
3 To remove the temperature or level switch, first drain the cooling system, detach the wiring connector to the switch and then unscrew and remove the switch.
4 It is difficult to test a temperature switch without special equipment and the best method to use if a fault develops is to substitute a new switch, but only after the wiring to the gauge had been thoroughly checked.
5 When refitting the switch, make sure that the seal is in good condition and do not overtighten it.
6 If the switch is changed and the gauge still does not register, then the gauge should be checked by a competent auto-electrician. Access to the gauge is obtained after removing the instrument panel, as described in Chapter 12.
7 The coolant level switch is float operated and actuates a warning lamp in the event of a low coolant level. If the switch malfunctions it must be renewed as no repair is possible.

Fault finding - cooling system

Overheating

- ☐ Insufficient coolant in system
- ☐ Radiator blocked either internally or externally
- ☐ Thermostat not opening
- ☐ Electric cooling fan or thermoswitch faulty
- ☐ Pressure cap faulty

Overcooling

- ☐ Faulty, incorrect or missing thermostat
- ☐ Electric cooling fan thermoswitch not switching off

Loss of coolant

- ☐ Damaged hoses or loose clips
- ☐ Leaking water pump O-ring or gasket, as applicable

Chapter 3 Fuel and exhaust systems

For modifications. and information applicable to later models, see Supplement at end of manual

Contents

Degrees of difficulty

Easy, suitable for novice with little experience 

Fairly easy, suitable for beginner with some experience 

Fairly difficult, suitable for competent DIY mechanic 

Difficult, suitable for experienced DIY mechanic 

Very difficult, suitable for expert DIY or professional

Specifications

Part A: Carburettor models

General

Air cleaner:	
Type	Dry type with replaceable element. Air temperature controlled inlet system
Element	Champion V401
Fuel pump	Mechanical diaphragm
Fuel octane rating	4-Star (97 RON)
Fuel tank capacity	55 litres (12.1 gal)

Carburettor*

Type:	
1118 cc engine	Weber 32 IBSH 13 or Solex 32 BISA 9 (393)
1294 cc engine	Weber 32 IBSH 14 or Solex 32 BISA (392)
1580 cc engine	Weber 36 TLP 1/100
Carburettor specifications:	**Weber 36 TLP 1/100**
Choke tube	28
Main jet	137 to 142
Float valve	1.5
Idle fuel jet	47 to 51
Air correction jet	145 ± 10
Emulsion tube	F80
Accelerator pump injector	50
Econostat fuel jet	65 to 80
Positive throttle opening	19° 30’
Idle speed	650 to 750 rpm
Idle mixture (CO)	1 to 2%

Carburettor specifications:	**Weber 32 IBSH 13**	**Weber 32 IBSH 14**
Choke tube	25	26
Main jet	130	142
Air correction jet	155	175
Emulsion tube	F102	F102
Fuel enrichment jet	50	50
Econostat	75	110
Idle jet	46	46
Idle air jet	185	175
Accelerator pump injector	40	40
Float valve	1.5	1.5
Float weight	11 g	11 g
Float level	7 mm	7 mm
Positive throttle opening	18° 30'	19°
Pneumatic opening	3.5 to 4.0 mm	4.0 to 4.5 mm
Idle speed	600 to 700 rpm	600 to 700 rpm
Idle mixture (CO)	1 to 2%	1 to 2%
Carburettor specifications:	**Solex 32 BISA 9 (393)**	**Solex 32 BISA 9 (392)**
Choke tube	25	26
Main jet	130 ± 5	132 ± 5
Air correction jet	170 ± 5	165 ± 5
Emulsion tube	EM	EM
Fuel enrichment	50 ± 10	55 ± 10
Econostat fuel	50 ± 10	50 ± 10
Econostat air	300	300
Idle fuel jet	48 ± 5	48 ± 5
Idle air jet	180 ± 5	180 ± 5
Progression slots	0.6x4.5	0.6x4.5
Accelerator pump injector	40 ± 5	40 ± 5
Accelerator pump bleed screw	35	35
Float valve	1.6	1.6
Float weight	5.7 g	5.7 g
Positive throttle opening	20° 10'	19° 40'
Pneumatic opening (high side)	4.3 mm	4.0 mm
Choke flap hole	8	5
Idle speed	600 to 700 rpm	600 to 700 rpm
Idle mixture (CO)	1 to 2%	1 to 2%

**A Bressel carburettor may be fitted. The Bressel unit is manufactured under licence from both Weber and Solex. and shares the same type numbers. They are in all respects otherwise identical to the equivalent Weber or Solex counterpart*

Torque wrench settings

	Nm	**lbf ft**
Fuel pump bolts	20	15
Carburettor bolts	15	11

Part B: Fuel injection models

General

System type	Rear-mounted fuel tank, Bosch LE2-Jetronic fuel injection system, electric fuel pump
Air cleaner element	Champion W175
Fuel filter	Champion L205
Fuel tank capacity	55 litres (12.1 gallons)
Fuel octane rating	4-star (97 RON)
Idling speed	850 to 900 rpm
CO at idling	0.5%
CO_2 at idling	10% minimum
Fuel pressure	2.9 to 3.1 bar (42.1 to 45.0 lbf/in^2)
Fuel pump delivery	540 cc/15 sec
Tachometric relay cut-out speed	6600 rpm
Fuel cut-off speed (decelerating)	Above 1600 rpm

Torque wrench setting

	Nm	**lbf ft**
Fuel filter base banjo type union hollow bolt	35	26

Part A: General description and routine maintenance

1 General description

The fuel system comprises a rear-mounted fuel tank. and a single downdraught carburettor or a Bosch LE2-Jetronic fuel injection system on the XU5-JA engine variant. On carburettor versions the fuel pump is a mechanical diaphragm type driven by an eccentric on the camshaft. On the fuel injection system the electric fuel pump is located in the fuel tank.

The air cleaner incorporates a dry element and the inlet air temperature is manually controlled.

2 Routine maintenance

Carry out the following procedures at the intervals given in Routine Maintenance at the beginning of the manual.

1 Check all fuel lines and hoses for damage and security, including those located on the underbody.

2 Check the accelerator pedal operation and the throttle cable for the correct adjustment.

3 Renew the air filter element (Section 3 or 18).

4 On carburettor engines, clean the fuel pump filter (if applicable), as described in Section 4. Some models have an in-line fuel filter instead. This must be renewed at the specified intervals, by unclipping and detaching the unit. An arrow on the body of the filter indicates the direction of flow when fitting the new filter (photo).

2.4 In-line fuel filter – carburettor engines

2.5 Fuel filter – fuel injection engines

5 On fuel injection engines, to renew the fuel filter first unscrew the union bolt from the top of the unit then place the bolt union and washers to one side and cover to prevent ingress of dirt. Unscrew the clamp bolt, then lift the filter and unscrew the bottom union. Fit the new filter using a reversal of the removal procedure; making sure that dust and dirt is prevented from entering the fuel lines (photo).

6 Lubricate the carburettor and choke cables.

Part B: Carburettor engines

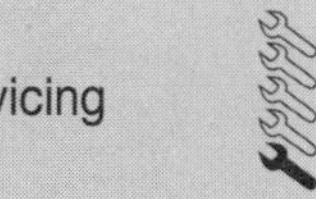

3 Air cleaner - description and servicing

1 All models are fitted with a renewable paper element air filter housed in a plastic casing on top of the engine which is retained by a quick-release strap. The filter element must be renewed at the specified intervals if engine efficiency and fuel economy are to be maintained.

2 The temperature of the air entering the air cleaner can be controlled by means of a selector lever on the intake duct. In the 'summer' position cold air is drawn into the air cleaner assembly via a hose leading in from the front wing, while the 'winter' position allows air to be drawn in through a hot air duct fitted over the exhaust manifold. An intermediate position provides mixed hot and cold air (photo).

3 To renew the filter element, release the spring clips to release the end cover/filter element (photos). Loosen the intake hose retaining clips to the end cover and detach the hose. Withdraw the end cover/element from the filter body.

4 The end cover is integral with the filter element and the complete assembly must be discarded.

5 When fitting the new filter and end cover, ensure that the arrows on top of the cover and the filter housing are in alignment before fastening the clips and refitting the intake hose. Also ensure that the new filter is of the same make as the old; several different types have been fitted and not all are interchangeable (photo).

3.2 Air cleaner inlet temperature control lever

3.3A Release the end cover retaining clips . . .

3.3B . . . to remove the cover/element

3.5 Align the arrows of the body and end cover

3.6 Air cleaner-to-carburettor adaptor cover showing the two retaining nuts (arrowed)

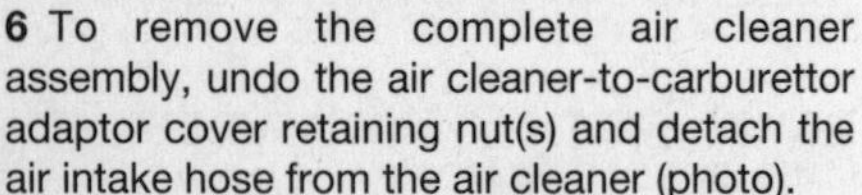

6 To remove the complete air cleaner assembly, undo the air cleaner-to-carburettor adaptor cover retaining nut(s) and detach the air intake hose from the air cleaner (photo).

7 Release the strap securing the air cleaner body, disengage the locating peg from its grommet and lift off the air cleaner assembly. Disconnect the vacuum hose(s) noting their connections (photos).

8 Refitting the air cleaner is the reverse of the removal procedure. When fitting the carburettor adaptor cover into position on the carburettor, ensure that the O-ring seal(s) are correctly located (Fig. 3.1 or 3.2). Smear the ring seals with Vaseline to ease fitting.

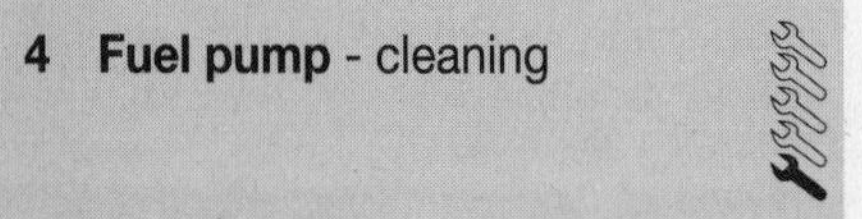

4 Fuel pump - cleaning

This only applies to models with a fuel pump with an integral filter. Fully sealed units will have an in-line filter (see Section 2)

1 Detach the fuel supply hose from the pump and plug the hose to prevent loss of fluid.

2 Unscrew the top cover retaining screw(s) and carefully lift the cover off the pump.

3 Withdraw the filter gauze and wash it thoroughly in petrol. If it is badly contaminated it is best to renew it.

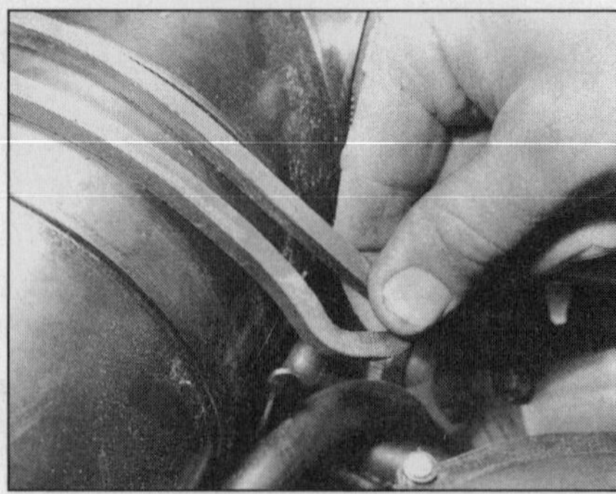

3.7A Disengage the air cleaner body retaining strap . . .

4 Remove all traces of dirt and sediment from the interior of the pump chamber.

5 Refit the filter to the pump body, place the cover gasket in position and refit the cover. Tighten but do not use excessive force on the retaining screw(s).

6 Reconnect the fuel hose, start the engine and check for leaks.

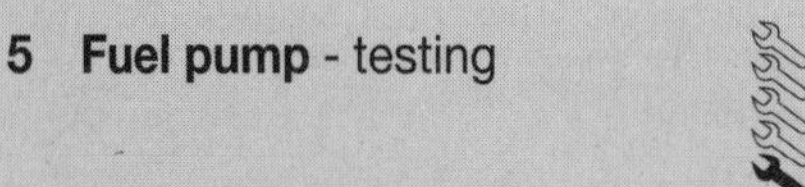

5 Fuel pump - testing

1 If the performance of the fuel pump is in doubt, first examine for fuel leaks and check that the fuel line connections are all sound.

2 Disconnect the fuel hose at the carburettor inlet connection and disconnect the high tension lead from the coil. Ensure that the tank contains fuel.

3 Direct the fuel feed hose into a suitable container and have an assistant operate the starter to crank the engine. A good spurt of fuel should be delivered on every second revolution of the engine. If not, check that the hose is not blocked. If that is clear the pump will need removal for examination or renewal.

3.7B . . . and the cleaner body from the location peg

6 Fuel pump - removal, overhaul and refitting

1 Disconnect the fuel hoses from the pump (photo). Plug the inlet hose.

2 Unscrew the pump mounting bolts/nuts and lift the pump away (photo).

3 An insulator block with a gasket each side is fitted between the pump flange and the

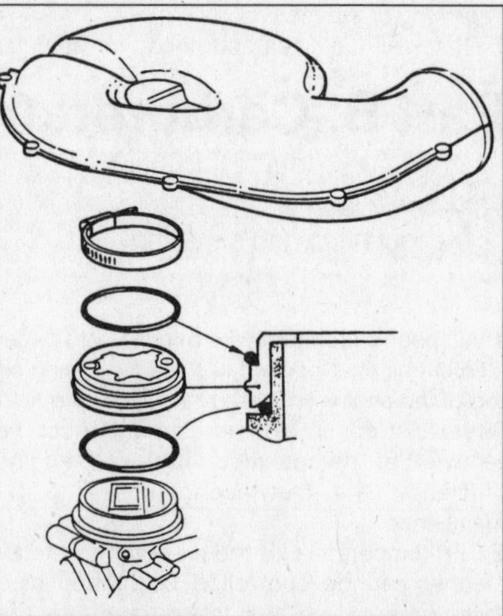

Fig. 3.2 O-ring seal locations in the carburettor adaptor cover – OHC engine (Sec 3)

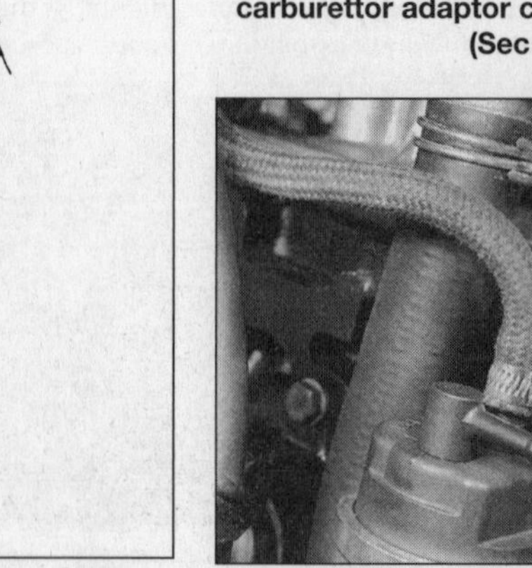

6.1 Disconnect the fuel hoses ..

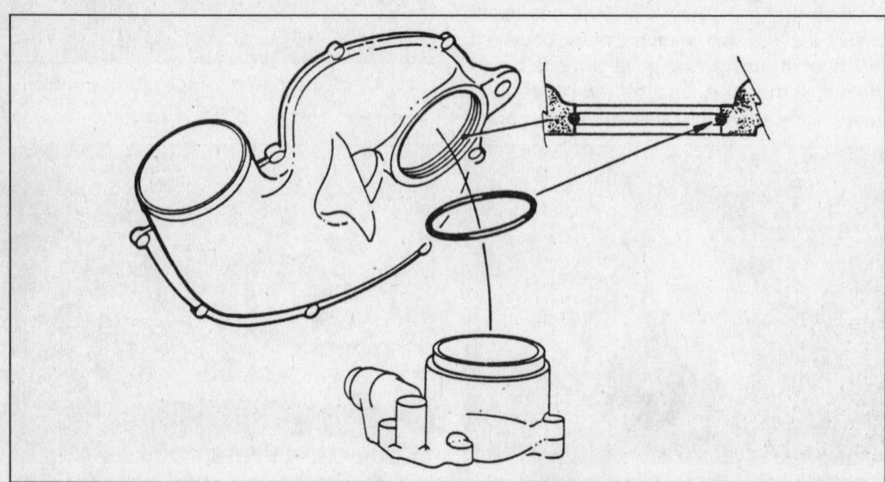

Fig.3.1 O-ring seal location in the carburettor adaptor cover – OHV engine (Sec 3)

6.2 . . . unbolt and remove the fuel pump (OHV engine)

mounting flange on the engine. The gaskets must be renewed when refitting the fuel pump.

4 Where applicable, withdraw the pump operating pushrod.

5 Further dismantling may not be possible on some types of pump. Even if it is, it should only be attempted if you have a repair kit. First mark the top and bottom halves of the pump for reassembly and then progressively loosen and remove the screws holding the two halves together. The diaphragm is connected to the operating mechanism beneath, and details will vary with different pumps. Note the sequence of assembly so that reassembly can be achieved in the same order.

6 Renew all defective parts; the kit will contain a variety of seals or gaskets which should automatically be fitted in place of the originals regardless of the fact that they may appear fit for further use.

7 Reassembly is the reverse of the dismantling sequence. Make sure that the upper and lower halves of the pump body are aligned and tighten the joint screws progressively and diagonally. Don't overtighten the top cover screws.

8 Before refitting the pump, check that the operating pushrod is in position (where applicable). Locate a new gasket each side of the insulator and refit the pump.

9 Tighten the securing bolts and make sure that the fuel hoses are reconnected to their correct pump connections.

7 Fuel level transmitter - removal and refitting

1 Disconnect the battery earth lead.

2 Fold the rear seat forwards and remove the insulator mat.

3 Prise free the circular plastic cover to expose the fuel level transmitter and disconnect the wiring from it (photo).

4 Before removing the transmitter from the fuel tank the safety precautions detailed in paragraph 2 in Section 8 should be observed.

5 Using a suitable tool, unscrew the transmitter mounting plate to release it from

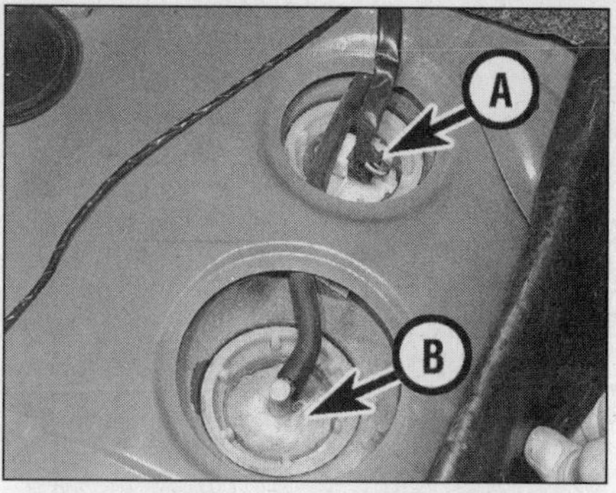

7.3 Fuel level transmitter unit (A) and fuel supply hose connector unit (B)

the securing tabs. Withdraw the transmitter unit.

6 Refitting is a reversal of removal, but use a new sealing ring if there is any doubt about the condition of the original one.

8 Fuel tank - removal and refitting

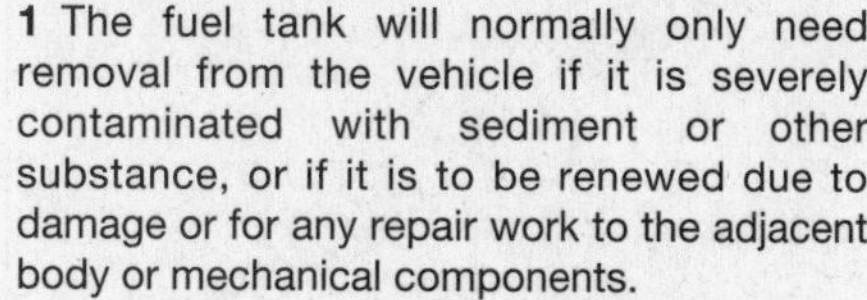

1 The fuel tank will normally only need removal from the vehicle if it is severely contaminated with sediment or other substance, or if it is to be renewed due to damage or for any repair work to the adjacent body or mechanical components.

2 As there is no drain plug incorporated in the tank, the best time to remove it is when it is nearly empty. If this is not possible, syphon as much fuel as possible from the tank into a container which can be sealed, but before doing so, observe the following precautions:

(a) *Disconnect the battery*

(b) *Do not smoke or allow any naked lights near the working area*

(c) *Avoid placing the vehicle over an inspection pit as the fuel vapour is heavier than air; raise the vehicle at the rear and support it on safety stands, supporting under the jacking point on the left-hand side and the rear crossmember on the right-hand side. Release the handbrake*

3 From within the vehicle at the rear. disconnect the wiring from the fuel level transmitter (see previous Section).

4 Disconnect the fuel supply and return pipes from the fuel tank top face, but mark them for identification to ensure correct reconnection during refitting. Plug the pipes to prevent leakage and the ingress of dirt.

5 Remove the exhaust system (Section 16).

6 Unbolt and remove the heat shield(s).

7 Detach the fuel supply and vent hoses to the tank under the wheel arch .

8 Undo the two mounting strap bolts and carefully tilt the tank downwards at the rear. Detach the breather and bleed pipes on the right-hand side and further lower the fuel tank so that it rests on the handbrake cables.

9 The fuel tank can now be removed by passing it under the right-hand side of the vehicle. Get an assistant to help manoeuvre it free and support it as it is withdrawn.

10 If the tank is leaking or damaged it should be renewed or, if any repairs are possible, entrust them to your Peugeot dealer or a specialist.

11 If the tank contains sediment, remove the fuel level transmitter and wash out the tank using paraffin, then rinse it out with clean fuel. Refit in the reverse order of removal. Ensure that all hose connections are securely made. Renew the rubber mounting washers.

9 Carburettor - description

1 In production a Weber carburettor is fitted as standard, the type being in accordance with the engine fitted (see Specifications at the start of the Chapter).

2 The Solex carburettors listed are supplied as an alternative replacement unit for the original Weber. A third type of carburettor which may be fitted is the Bressel, which is a direct equivalent of the Weber or Solex counterpart.

3 In each case, the carburettor is of downdraught, single choke design, the main differences between the types being the jet sizes and the drillings in the carburettor body.

4 These carburettors comprise three main assemblies, namely the throttle block, the main body and the top cover. The throttle block embodies the throttle plate and control linkages and incorporates a water-heated jacket connected to the engine cooling system to provide pre-heating of the carburettor.

5 The main body incorporates the choke tube (sometimes known as the venturi or throttle barrel), the float chamber, accelerator pump and the jets, also the distributor vacuum and crankcase breather connections.

6 The top cover carries the choke plate, fuel inlet connection and needle valve.

7 The cold start enrichment device comprises a strangler type choke, which is operated manually by the driver. The choke plate is held open by a linkage when the control is pushed in; however, when the control is pulled out, the linkage is released and the choke plate is closed by a spring. When the engine starts, the depression in the carburettor overcomes the spring tension and automatically opens the choke plate slightly. Thus once the engine is running the mixture will be weakened by the additional air past the choke plate.

8 The accelerator pedal is connected via a cable to the linkage of the carburettor and operates the throttle plate. The depression created in the carburettor choke tube causes fuel to be drawn from the jets and out through the various drillings in the carburettor body. The fuel mixes with the incoming air to form a combustible mixture, the strength of which is controlled by the jet diameter.

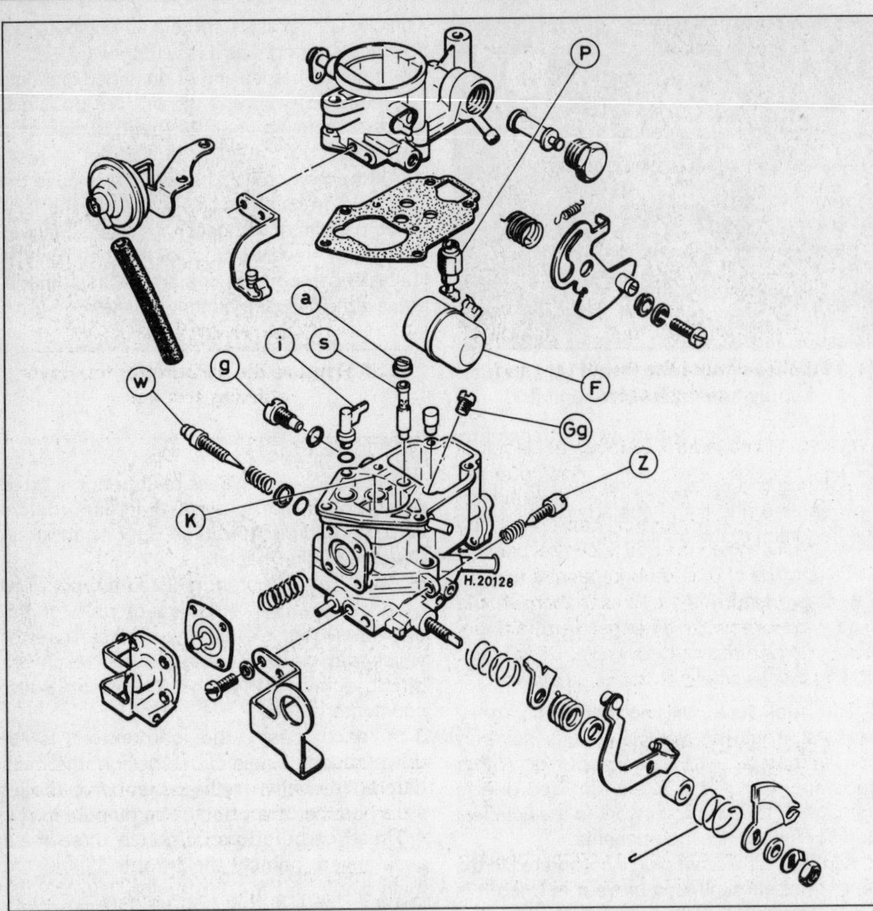

Fig. 3.3 Exploded view of the Weber 32 IBSH carburettor fitted to OHV engines (Sec 9)

a Air correction jet
F Float
g Idle jet
Gg Main jet
I Accelerator pump injector
K Choke tube
P Float valve
S Emulsion tube
W Idle mixture adjuster
Z Throttle stop screw

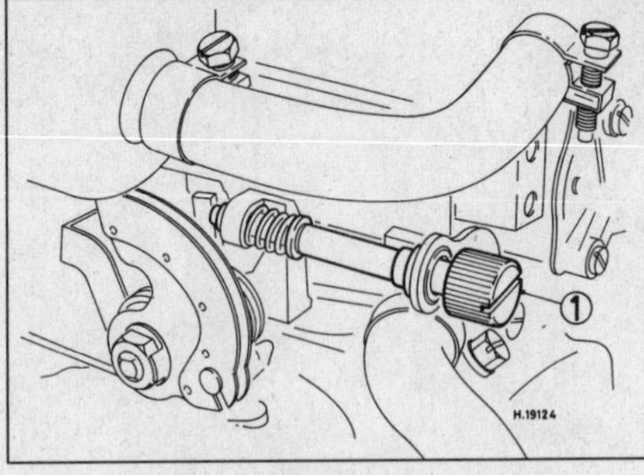

Fig. 3.4 Throttle stop screw position (1) on the Weber 36 TLP carburettor – OHC engine (Sec 10)

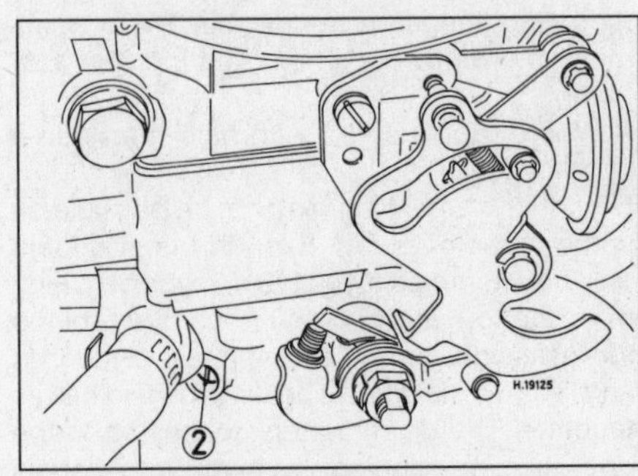

Fig. 3.5 Mixture setting screw location (2) on the Weber 36 TLP carburettor – OHC engine (Sec 10)

9 When the accelerator is depressed quickly, a spring-loaded rod attached to the throttle spindle operates an accelerator pump which provides a jet of neat fuel into the choke tube. This creates the slightly richer mixture demanded by the engine during initial acceleration and eliminates flat spots.

10 Engine speed at tickover is adjustable by an idle speed control screw acting directly on the throttle control linkage.

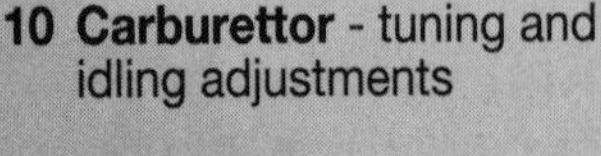

10 Carburettor - tuning and idling adjustments

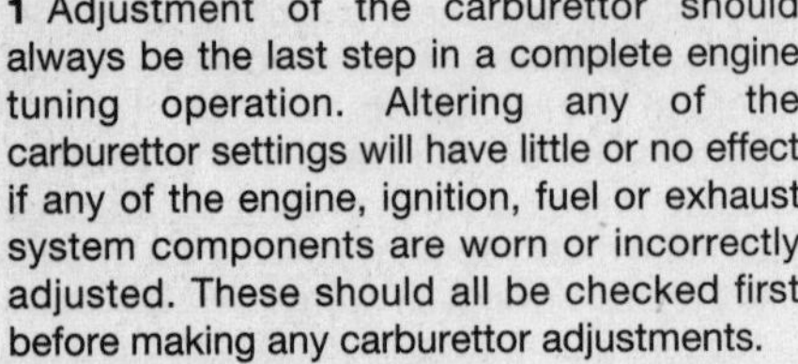

1 Adjustment of the carburettor should always be the last step in a complete engine tuning operation. Altering any of the carburettor settings will have little or no effect if any of the engine, ignition, fuel or exhaust system components are worn or incorrectly adjusted. These should all be checked first before making any carburettor adjustments.

2 Make sure that the engine is at normal working temperature, that the manual choke control is pushed fully in, and that the air cleaner assembly is in position on the carburettor. Adjustment of the various carburettors is as follows.

3 Connect a tachometer to the engine, following its manufacturer's instructions, then start the engine and allow it to idle.

4 Adjust the throttle stop screw until the correct engine rpm, as shown in the Specifications, is obtained. Refer to the photo or Fig. 3.4 for the location of the throttle stop screw.

5 Normally this is the only adjustment required. The mixture screw is set on production and should not need altering. If the idling is unsatisfactory, and all other engine variables described at the beginning of this Section are in order, the mixture may be adjusted as follows.

6 First break off the tamperproof cap on the end of the mixture screw, taking care not to bend the screw.

7 Start the engine and check that the idling speed is still at the specified rpm. Adjust the throttle stop screw if necessary.

8 Turn the mixture screw in or out until the highest possible idling speed is obtained (photo or Fig. 3.5).

9 Bring the idling speed back to the specified setting by adjusting the throttle stop screw.

10.4 Throttle stop screw adjustment – arrowed (Weber carburettor)

10.8 Mixture screw adjustment (Weber carburettor)

11.4 Weber carburettor showing hose connections (1.3 litre engine)

11.5 Disconnect the throttle (A) and choke (B) cables

12.5A Remove the carburettor top cover retaining screws

10 Reduce the idling speed very slightly by screwing in the mixture screw, but without going so far as to cause uneven running.

11 Finally reset the idling speed again by altering the throttle stop screw. Switch off the engine and disconnect the tachometer.

11 Carburettor - removal and refitting

1 Disconnect the battery earth lead.

2 Unclip and detach the air ducting between the carburettor and the air cleaner unit.

3 Disconnect the wire from the idle cut-off solenoid.

4 Disconnect the fuel supply and return hoses from the carburettor. Plug the hoses (photo).

5 Detach the accelerator inner cable from the quadrant and the outer cable from its support at the carburettor and fold it back out of the way (photo) .

6 Detach the choke cable by loosening the inner cable clamp screw. Unscrew the outer cable location clamp bolt and move the cable out of the way.

7 Where applicable, disconnect the vacuum hose from the carburettor.

8 Unscrew the carburettor retaining nuts and then lift it clear of the manifold. Retrieve the old joint gasket and place a piece of clean cloth over the aperture in the manifold to prevent dirt or anything from accidentally falling into it while the carburettor is removed.

9 Refitting the carburettor is the reverse of the removal procedure. Remove all traces of the old gasket and use a new one on installation. After fitting the carburettor, reconnect the accelerator cable and the choke cable. When the choke control cable is fitted and the choke knob is pushed fully in, the flap should be fully open and there should be a small amount of possible additional movement on the control knob. Check that the flap closes when the control is pulled.

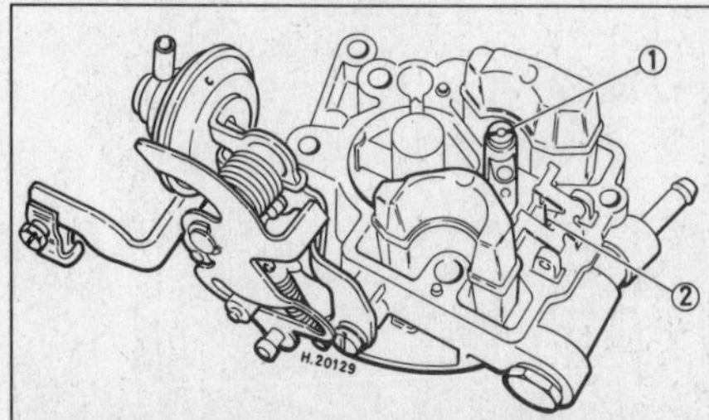

Fig. 3.6 Weber 36 TLP 1/100 carburettor showing the main jet (1) and float valve (2) locations (Sec 12)

12 Carburettor (Weber) - dismantling, reassembly and adjustment

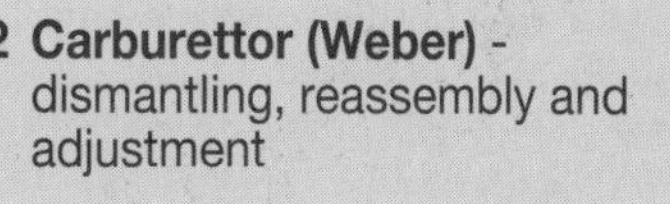

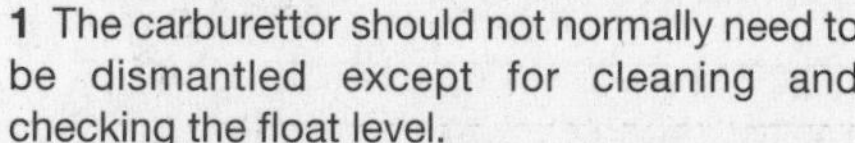

1 The carburettor should not normally need to be dismantled except for cleaning and checking the float level.

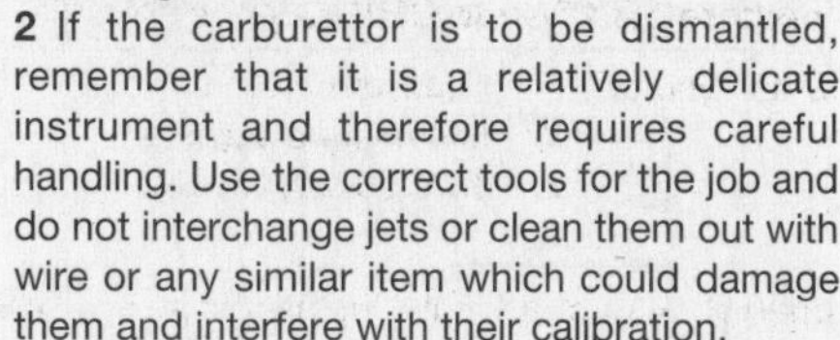

2 If the carburettor is to be dismantled, remember that it is a relatively delicate instrument and therefore requires careful handling. Use the correct tools for the job and do not interchange jets or clean them out with wire or any similar item which could damage them and interfere with their calibration.

3 Before dismantling the carburettor. or any part of it, first clean the outside and prepare a clean work area. When taking anything mechanical apart. and this applies particularly to such components as carburettors, it is always sound policy to make sure that the individual parts are put back exactly where they came from, and even the same way round if it is possible to do otherwise. even though they may appear to be interchangeable.

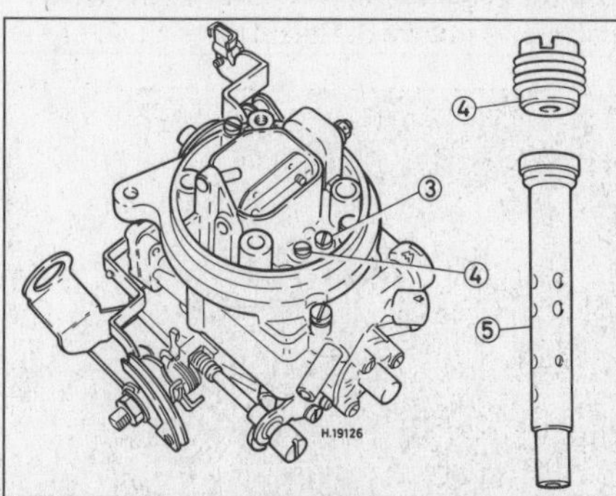

Fig. 3.7 Weber 36 TLP 1/100 carburettor showing positions of the idle fuel jet (3) air correction jet (4) and emulsion tube (5) (Sec 12)

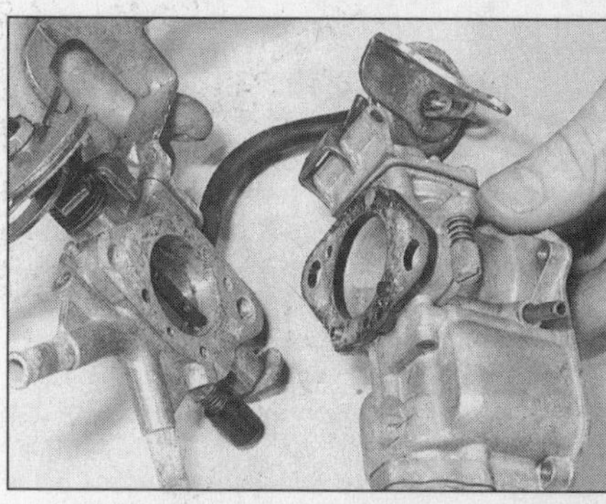

12.5B Throttle body separation from the carburettor main body. Note insulation spacer

3

4 To help in this procedure, mark or label items, put small parts in boxes or tins so that they don't get mixed up, and lay parts out in order of assembly on clean paper.

5 Undo the retaining screws and lift the carburettor top cover away from the main body (photo), and the main body from the throttle body - if required (photo).

6 The float can be removed by pushing out the hinge pin and then the needle valve assembly can be unscrewed from the cover. Unscrew the end bolt near the fuel inlet connection and remove the gauze filter. Examine the filter for contamination and blockage. Soak the filter in petrol to clean it (photos).

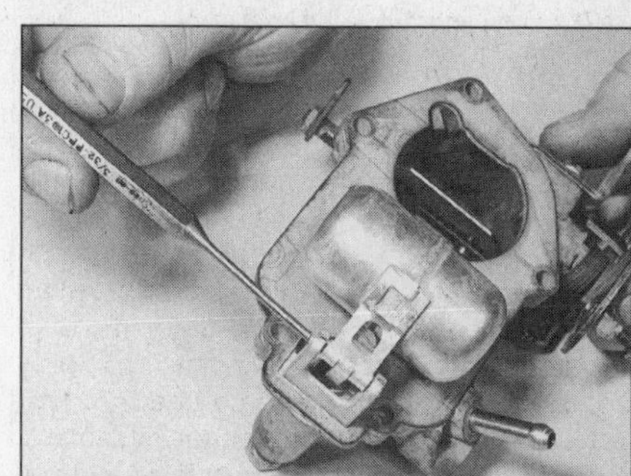

12.6A Press out the hinge pin . . .

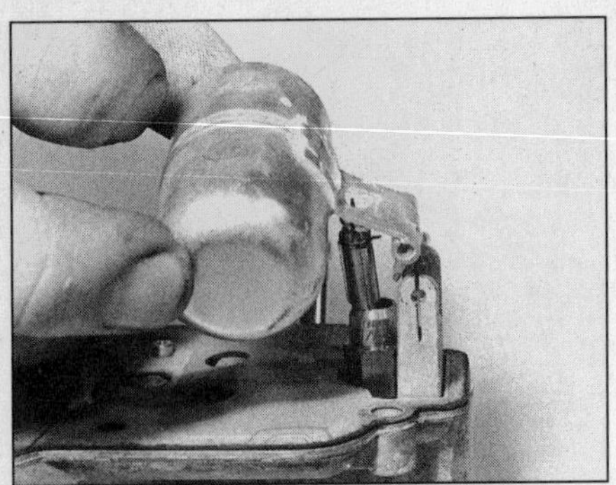

12.6B . . . and remove the float

7 Carefully remove the accelerator pump valve, the main jet, the idle jet and the mixture adjustment screw; noting their respective fitting positions. When removing the idle jet and mixture setting adjusters, count the number of turns required to remove them so that they can be refitted in approximately the same position and give a provisional adjustment position (photo).

8 Do not disturb the choke flap and throttle butterfly valve or spindles. Their actuating mechanisms are external and normally require no attention unless excessively worn. If the spindles are worn in the carburettor body then serious consideration should be given to renewing the complete carburettor. Such wear is an indication that the carburettor is due for renewal and it would be false economy to refit the original instrument. Air leaks around worn spindles make it impossible to tune the carburettor correctly and poor performance and impaired economy will inevitably result.

9 The respective chambers, passages and jet seats can be brush cleaned using clean fuel and they should then be blown dry, if an air supply is available, or allowed to dry naturally. Don't use rag or cloth. Clean and blow through the jets in a similar manner.

10 Reassembly is the reverse of the dismantling procedure. Whenever possible use new washers, gaskets, or seals wherever fitted. During reassembly check and adjust the float level.

11 Check the float level with the top cover removed and held vertically on its side with the float hanging down (photo). The cover gasket must be fitted on the flange face of the cover. With the tongue of the float arm in light contact with the ball of the needle valve, the dimension from the gasket bottom face to the lower part of the float is the float level. The correct dimension for the various carburettor types is given in the Specifications at the start of this Chapter (Fig. 3.8).

12 To adjust the float level setting, carefully bend the float arm as required .

13 On the Weber 36 TLP carburettor, the procedure for checking the float level differs slightly in that you will need to fabricate a check gauge to the shape and dimensions shown in Fig. 3.9. With the top cover removed and the gasket in position, support the carburettor with the top of the float chamber vertical and position the check gauge as shown in Fig. 3.10. The floats should just contact the gauge. If adjustment is necessary bend the tongue and/or the bars to suit (Fig. 3.11).

14 Another check which can be made on the Weber 36 TLP carburettor is the positive throttle valve opening, but this is best entrusted to your Peugeot dealer.

15 Before refitting the carburettor, check that the filter is clean, insert it into its aperture and fit the retaining bolt (photos).

12.7 View inside the carburettor main body showing location of jets, the accelerator pump injector and the emulsion tube

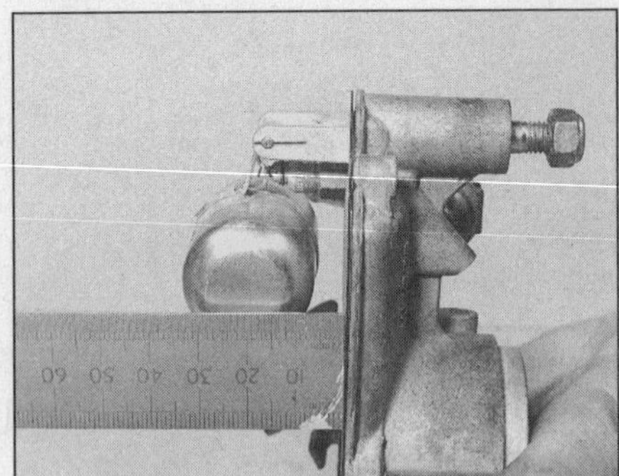

12.11 Float level check method

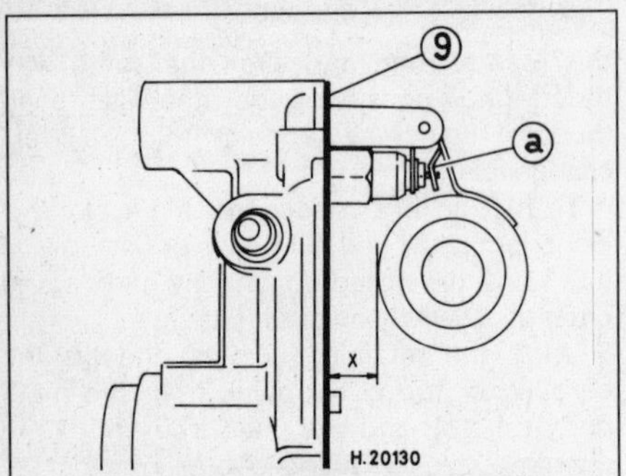

Fig. 3.8 Float level adjustment check – Weber 32 IBSH carburettor (Sec 12)

a Float arm tongue (in contact with ball)
9 Gasket (must be fitted when checking)
X = 7mm

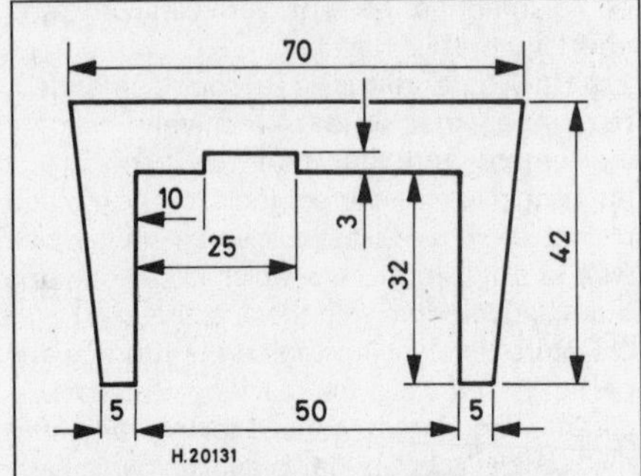

Fig. 3.9 Float level check gauge required for the Weber 36 TLP carburettor showing shape and dimensions (in mm) (Sec 12)

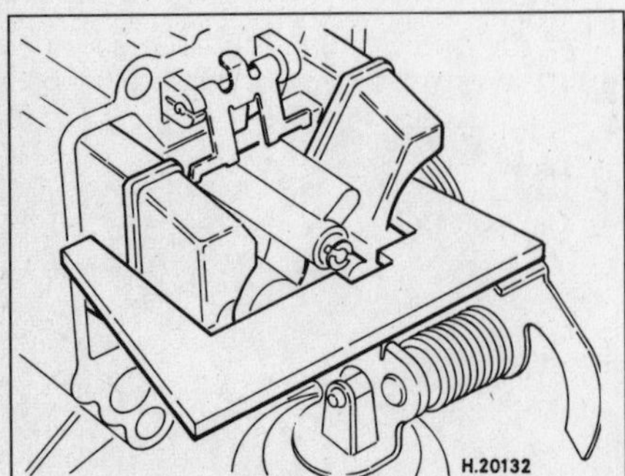

Fig. 3.10 Float level check using gauge – Weber 36 TLP carburettor (Sec 12)

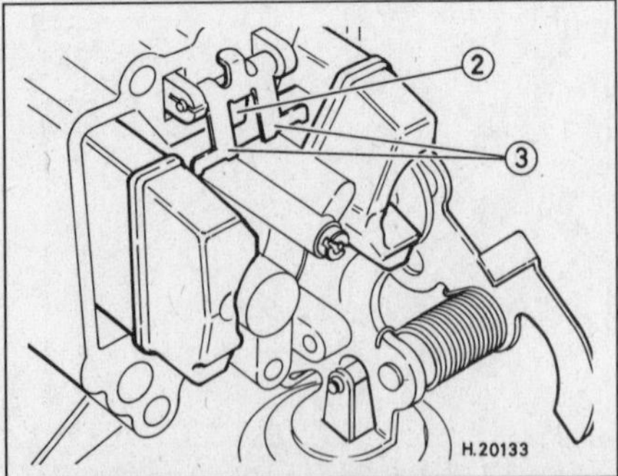

Fig. 3.11 Float level adjustment is made at tongue (2) or bars (3) – Weber 36 TLP carburettor (Sec 12)

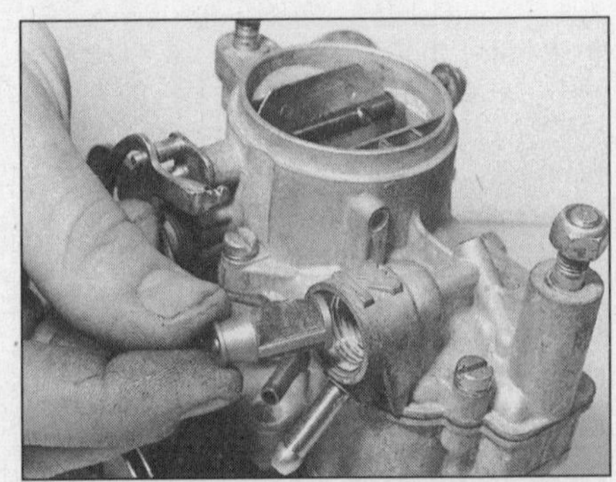

12.15A Insert the filter . . .

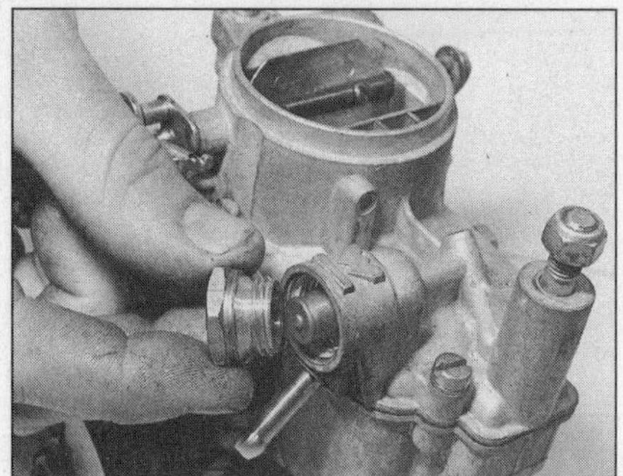
12.15B .. . and fit the securing bolt

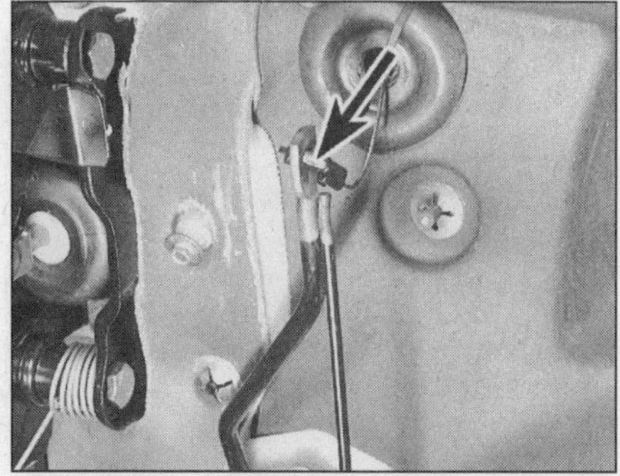
14.3 Throttle pedal and cable end fitting (arrowed)

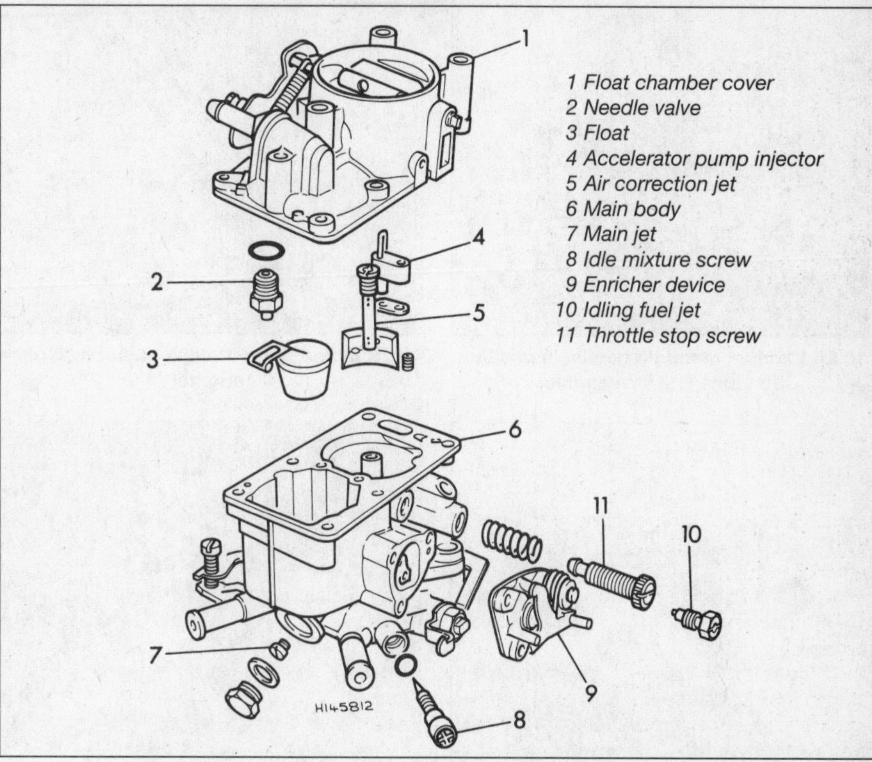

Fig. 3.12 Exploded view of the Solex BISA carburettor (Sec 13)

3

13 Carburettor (Solex) - dismantling, reassembly and adjustment

1 Refer to Section 12, paragraphs 1 to 3 inclusive for some general observations prior to dismantling the carburettor.

2 An exploded view of the Solex 32 BISA carburettor is shown in Fig. 3.12.

3 Remove the screws and lift off the float chamber cover.

4 Unscrew the air correction jet followed by the main jet and the idling fuel jet.

5 Unscrew the accelerator pump valve and remove the pump injector.

6 Remove the enrichment valve.

7 Unscrew the needle valve.

8 Clean the float chamber and removed components with fuel and blow through the internal channels using an air line if possible.

9 Obtain a repair kit of gaskets then reassemble the carburettor in reverse order. The float level is not adjustable.

10 The only adjustment possible is the fast idle setting of the throttle valve, but this is best checked and if necessary adjusted by a Peugeot dealer.

11 When the carburettor is refitted to the car, check it for correct adjustment as described in Section 10.

14 Throttle cable - removal and refitting

1 Extract the spring retaining clip from the adjustment ferrule at the throttle cable support bracket at the carburettor.

2 Detach the throttle cable (inner) from the throttle quadrant of the carburettor (see photo 11.5).

3 Working inside the car, disconnect the cable end fitting from the top of the accelerator pedal arm (photo).

4 Release the cable from the bracket on the carburettor.

5 Withdraw the throttle cable through the bulkhead grommet.

6 Refitting is a reversal of removal, but adjust the cable at the ferrule to remove all but the slightest amount of play. Check that full throttle can be obtained with the accelerator pedal fully depressed.

15 Choke cable - removal and refitting

1 At the carburettor end, undo the inner cable-to-choke lever pinch-bolt and the outer cable support pinch-bolt (photo 11.5). Disconnect the cable from the lever and support.

2 Working inside the car, reach up behind the choke control cable lever and compress the clips to allow the control lever to be withdrawn from the facia. It is advisable to remove the lower facia trim panel on the drivers' side for access.

3 Detach the inner cable nipple from the control lever (photo) and withdraw the cable from the control lever unit (photo). Remove the cable.

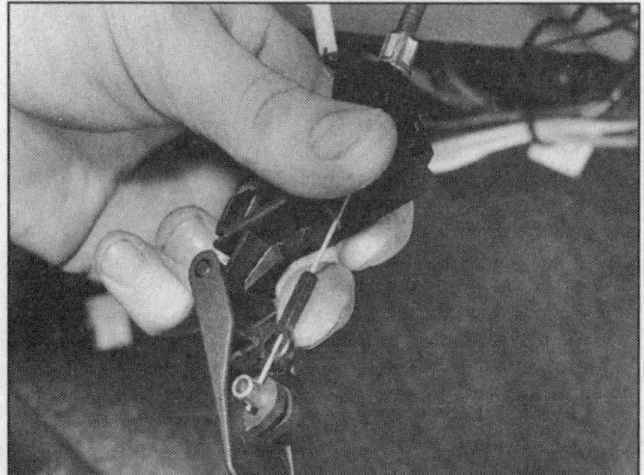
15.3A Detach the inner cable nipple . . .

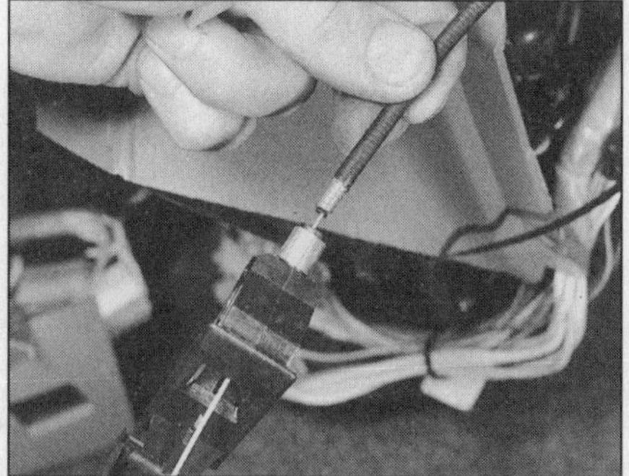
15.3B . . . and remove the cable from the choke control

16.2A Exhaust manifold gasket in position on studs (1.3 litre engine)

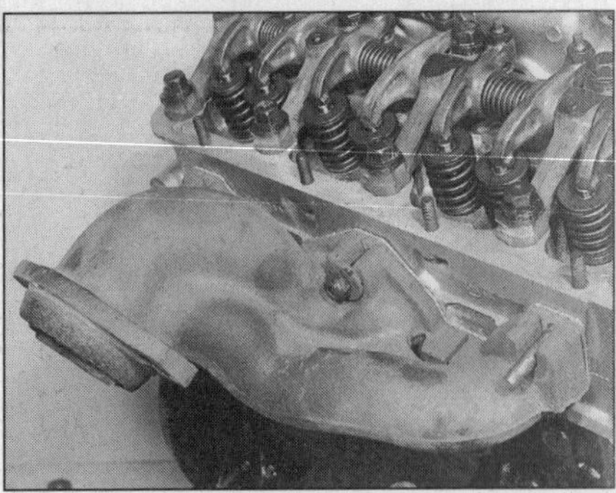

16.2B Exhaust manifold in position (1.3 litre engine)

16.3A Inlet manifold gasket in position (1.3 litre engine)

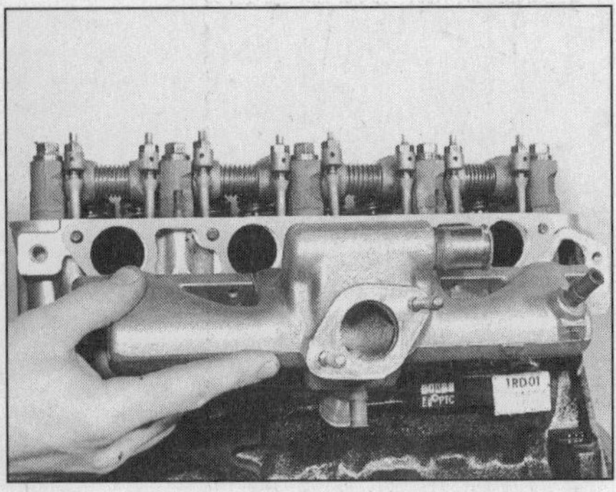

16.3B Inlet manifold fitting (1.3 litre engine)

16.4 Typical exhaust system mounting

16.6 Exhaust manifold-to-downpipe connection view from underneath (1.3 litre engine)

4 Refitting is a reversal of removal, but adjust the cable at the carburettor end so that, when the control knob is pushed fully in, the choke valve plate is fully open.

16 Manifolds and exhaust system - general

1 The inlet and exhaust manifolds are located on opposite sides of the cylinder head.
2 The exhaust manifold is simply bolted into position with a common flange gasket for each port (photos).
3 The inlet manifold has coolant connections and before it can be removed, the cooling system should be at least partially drained to avoid any coolant running into the cylinder bores as the manifold is removed. Always renew the gasket when refitting the manifold (photos) .
4 The exhaust system is in sections and the mountings are of the flexible rubber type (photo).
5 Even if only one section of the system is to be renewed, it is recommended that the complete system is removed from under the car with the car supported on axle stands.
6 When fitting the exhaust system tighten the flange mounting nuts evenly so that the special springs are compressed equally; the joint should be lubricated with grease (photo). Ensure that an insulating washer is positioned between each spring and the flange face (Fig. 3.13).

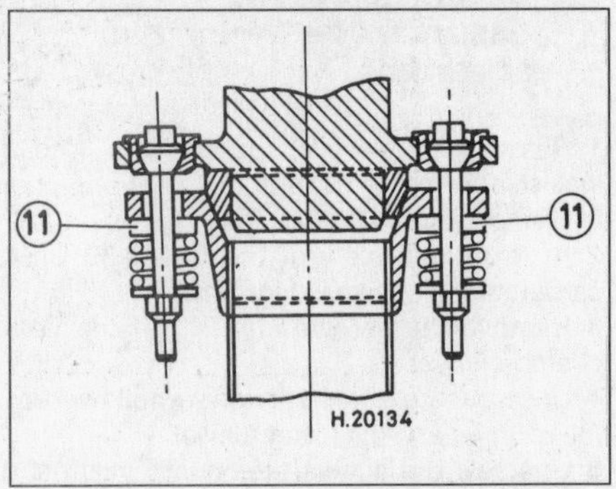

Fig. 3.13 Sectional view of the exhaust manifold-to-downpipe flange joint showing location for the insulating washers (11) (Sec 16)

Part C: Fuel injection engine

17 Fuel injection system - general description and precautions

Fuel injection system components are shown in Fig. 3.14 and 3.15. A roller type electric pump located in the fuel tank pumps fuel through the filter to the injectors via a distribution pipe. The electronic control unit which is triggered by the ignition circuit sends impulses to the injectors which operate simultaneously and inject fuel in the vicinity of the inlet valves. The electronic control unit is provided with sensors to determine engine temperature, speed and load, and the quantity of air entering the engine. This information is computed to determine the period of injection.

For cold starting, additional fuel is provided and, to compensate for this, additional air is provided by a supplementary air device.

The following Sections describe the procedures which can be carried out by the home mechanic. Work involving the use of pressure gauges is not included.

In order to prevent damage to the electrical components of the system the battery must **never** be disconnected with the engine running, the electronic control unit must not be disconnected with the ignition on, and a test lamp must not be used for checking the circuits.

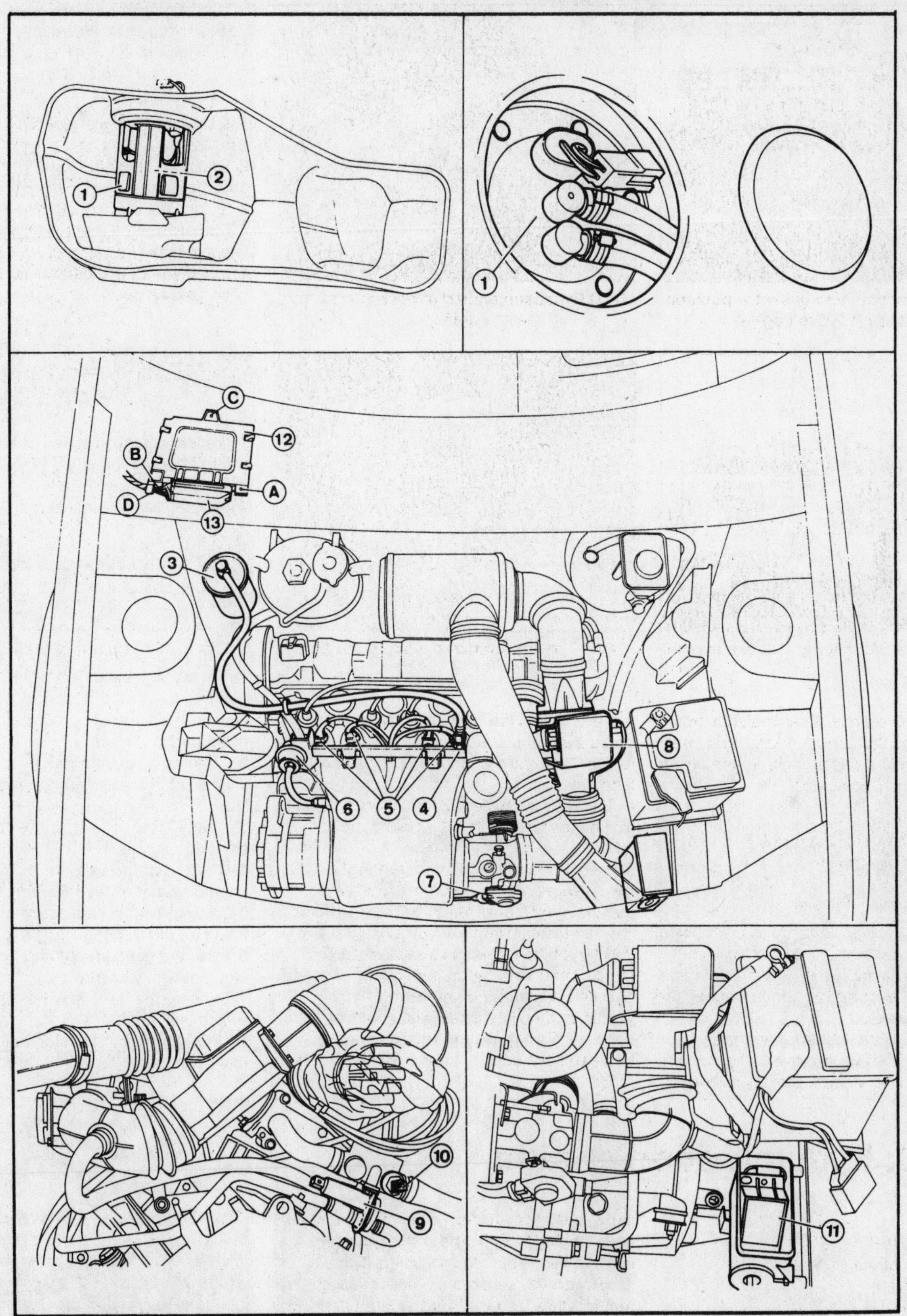

Fig. 3.14 Fuel injection system component locations in the engine compartment (LH drive shown) (Sec 17)

A Securing screw
B Securing screw
C Securing screw
D ECU connector
1 Fuel pump housing
2 Fuel pump
3 Fuel filter
4 Distribution pipe
5 Injectors
6 Fuel pressure regulator
7 Throttle switch unit
8 Airflow sensor
9 Supplementary air device
10 Temperature cover
11 Tachometric relay and engine speed limiter
12 Electric control unit
13 Connector

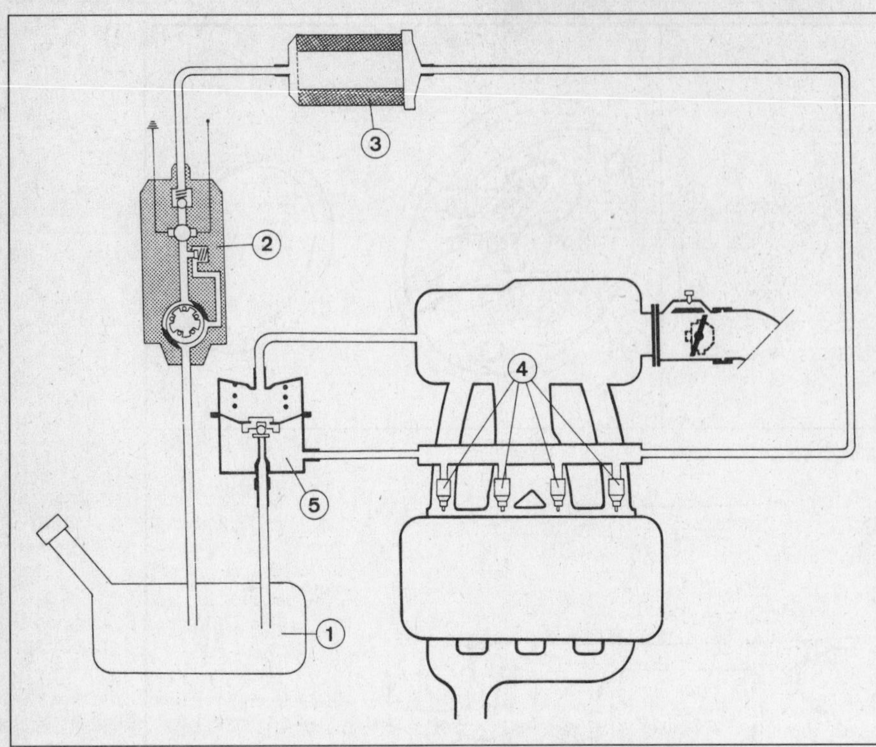

Fig. 3.15 Fuel injection system main components (Sec 17)

1 Fuel tank
2 Fuel pump (electric)
3 Fuel filter
4 Distribution pipe and injectors
5 Fuel pressure regulator

18.2 Filter end cover and retaining nuts (arrowed)

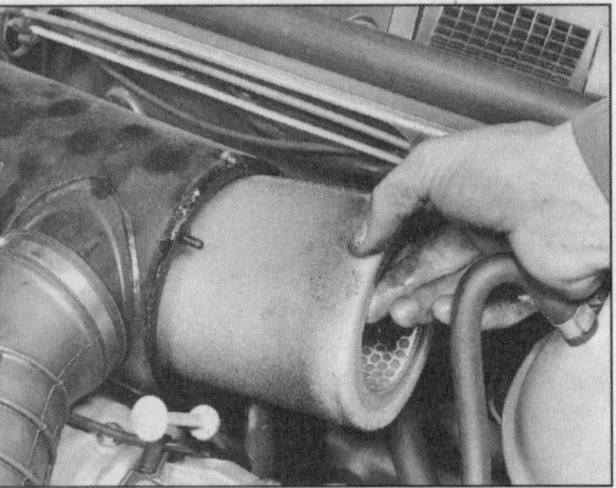

18.3 Removing the filter element

18 Air cleaner element - renewal

1 Disconnect the air duct from the end of the air cleaner.

2 Unscrew the nuts and remove the end cover (photo).

3 Extract the element (photo).

4 Discard the element and wipe the casing interior clean.

5 Insert the new element then refit the end cover and air duct.

19 Air cleaner - removal and refitting

1 Disconnect the inlet and outlet ducts.

2 Unscrew the mounting bolts and lift the air cleaner from the engine.

3 Refitting is a reversal of removal.

20 Throttle initial position - checking and adjustment

1 Run the engine to normal operating temperature - indicated when the electronic cooling fan has cut in and out twice. The ignition timing must be correctly adjusted, as described in Chapter 4.

2 Connect a vacuum gauge to the test point (Fig. 3.16) in the distributor vacuum advance line.

3 Check that the throttle movement is smooth.

4 Check that the vacuum reading at the test point does not exceed 50 mm Hg (65 mbar).

5 If adjustment is necessary, stop the engine then turn the air screw fully in (photo).

6 Prise the tamperproof cap from the throttle stop adjustment screw.

7 Loosen the two screws on the throttle switch unit (photo).

8 Unscrew the throttle stop adjustment screw then retighten it until it just touches the

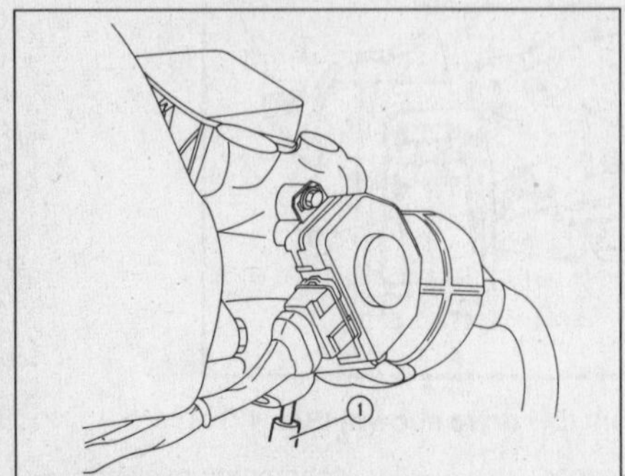

Fig. 3.16 Vacuum gauge test point (1) (Sec 20)

20.5 Throttle housing showing position of the (1) air screw (idle adjustment screw) and the throttle stop screw (2)

20.7 Throttle switch unit and retaining screw (arrowed)

21.7 Mixture adjustment using an Allen key

throttle lever. Tighten the screw a further four complete turns.

9 Adjust the idling speed and mixture, as described in the following Section.

21 Idle speed and mixture - adjustment

1 Connect a tachometer and an exhaust gas analyser to the engine.

2 With the throttle initial position set, as described in Section 20, run the engine at idle speed.

3 Turn the air (idle speed) adjustment screw to obtain an idle speed of 650 rpm. Check that the vacuum reading does not exceed 50 mmHg (65 mbar) and if necessary adjust the idle speed adjustment screw.

4 Stop the engine and adjust the throttle switch, as described in Section 22.

5 With the engine at normal operating temperature, unscrew the air screw to set the idling speed between 850 and 900 rpm.

6 Check that the CO reading is between 1 and 2% and the CO_2 reading is more than 10%.

7 If adjustment is necessary, prise out the tamperproof cap on the airflow sensor (photo) and use a 5 mm Allen key to adjust the mixture. Turn the screw in to richen the mixture and out to weaken it.

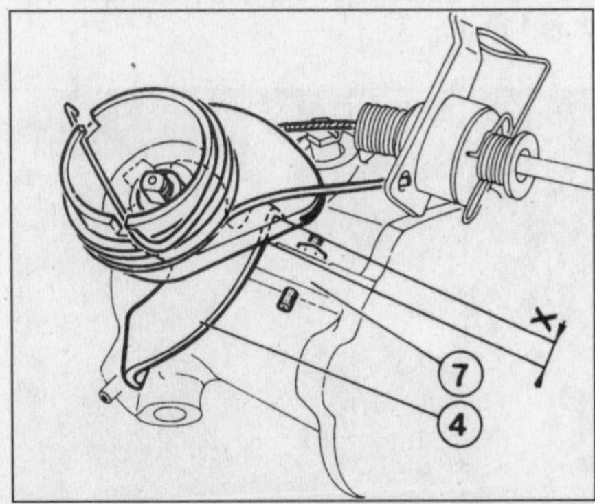

Fig. 3.18 Full throttle dimension X (Sec 22)

4 Throttle lever *X = 4.0 mm (0.158 in)*
7 Throttle housing

22.1 Disconnect the throttle switch wiring connector

8 Blip the throttle two or three times and then recheck that the idle speed and mixture is correct.

9 If the CO_2 reading is less than 10% check that the air filter is clean and that there are no leaks in the inlet or exhaust systems.

22 Throttle switch - checking and adjustment

1 Pull the connector from the throttle switch (photo).

2 Connect a voltmeter between the middle terminal on the connector and earth.

3 Pull the connector from the ignition distributor then operate the starter motor and check that there is a reading of at least 9 volts.

4 Disconnect the air hose from the throttle housing.

5 Position a 0.30 mm (0.012 in) feeler blade between the throttle stop adjustment screw and the throttle lever (Fig. 3.17).

6 Loosen the two throttle switch screws.

7 Connect an ohmmeter between terminals 18 and 2 on the throttle switch, then rotate the switch until the internal contacts

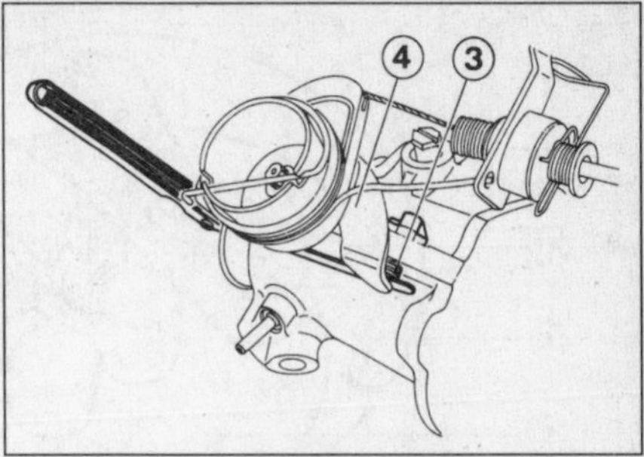

Fig. 3.17 Adjusting the throttle switch (Sec 22)

3 Throttle stop screw *4 Throttle lever*

close and the reading is zero ohms. Tighten the screws with the switch in this position .

8 Remove the feeler blade and insert in its place a 0.70 mm (0.028 in) feeler blade. The internal contacts should now be separated and the reading on the ohmmeter infinity. If not, repeat the procedure in paragraph 7.

9 Remove the feeler blade.

10 Check the full throttle operation by connecting an ohmmeter between terminals 18 and 2, then fully opening the throttle so that dimension X (Fig. 3.18) is 4.0 mm (0.158 in). The internal contacts should close and the ohmmeter reading be zero.

11 If the switch does not operate correctly it should be renewed.

23 Air intake system - checking for leaks

1 For the correct operation of the airflow sensor there must be no air entering the system upstream of the sensor.

2 Check that there is no leakage at the points arrowed in Fig. 3.19 or at the inlet manifold gasket.

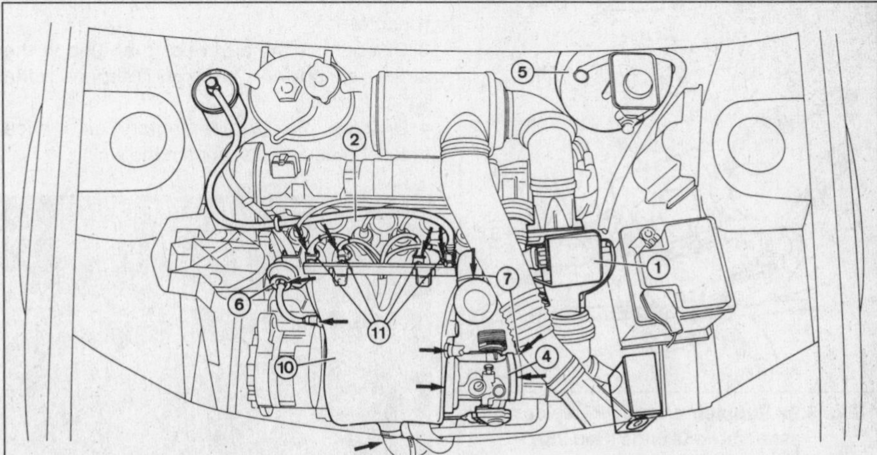

Fig. 3.19 Areas (arrowed) for checking air intake leakage (LH drive shown) (Sec 23)

1 Airflow sensor
2 Cylinder head
4 Throttle housing
5 Brake vacuum servo
6 Fuel pressure regulator
7 Crankcase breather hose
10 Air distribution manifold
11 Injectors

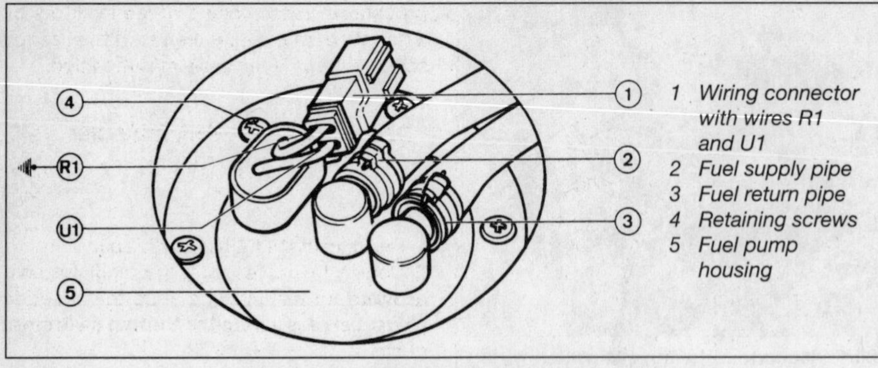

Fig. 3.20 Fuel pump connections (Sec 24)

3 If an air line is available, disconnect the airflow sensor inlet hose and use an adaptor to blow air through the intake system while fully opening the throttle, blocking the exhaust pipe and pinching the crankcase breather hose. If the points indicated in paragraph 2 are then brushed with soapy water any bad seals will be immediately evident.

24 Fuel pump - removal and refitting

1 Remove the rear seat or tilt it forward, prise up the right-hand plastic cover then disconnect the wiring, and the fuel supply and return pipes, noting their location (Fig. 3.20).

2 Note the safety precautions given in Section 8 of this Chapter.

3 Unscrew the retaining screws and lift the fuel pump housing from the fuel tank.

4 Release the filter from the bottom of the housing, followed by the collar (Fig. 3.21).

5 Disconnect the wiring and release the fuel pump from the upper collar.

6 Refitting is a reversal of removal, but fit new collars and make sure that the wiring terminals are positioned away from the pump terminals. Always fit a new gasket between the pump housing and fuel tank.

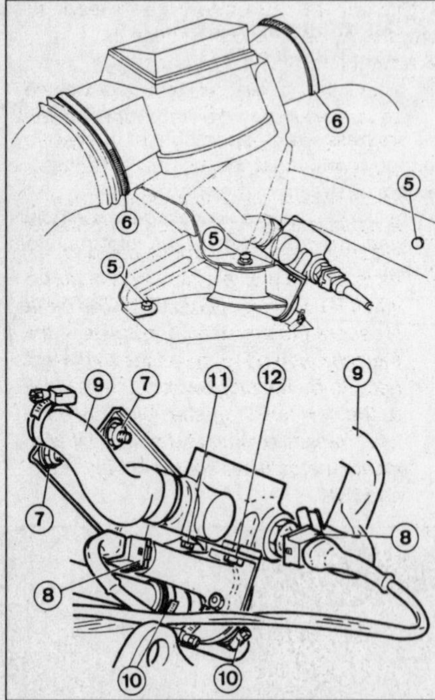

Fig. 3.22 Supplementary air device and associated fittings (Sec 25)

5 *Mounting bracket screws*
6 *Hose clips*
7 *Nuts*
8 *Connectors*
9 *Coolant hoses*
10 *Air hose unions*
11 *Retaining bolt*
12 *Retaining bolt*

25 Supplementary air device (cold start) - removal and refitting

1 The supplementary air device unit is located beneath the distributor and is attached to the flywheel end of the engine. Access is poor both from above and from underneath, but removal of the following will enable it to be inspected or removed.

2 Disconnect and remove the battery (Chapter 12).

3 Disconnect the air hoses then unbolt the airflow sensor and bracket. Disconnect the wiring (photos).

4 Unscrew the supplementary air device bracket nuts and disconnect the wiring.

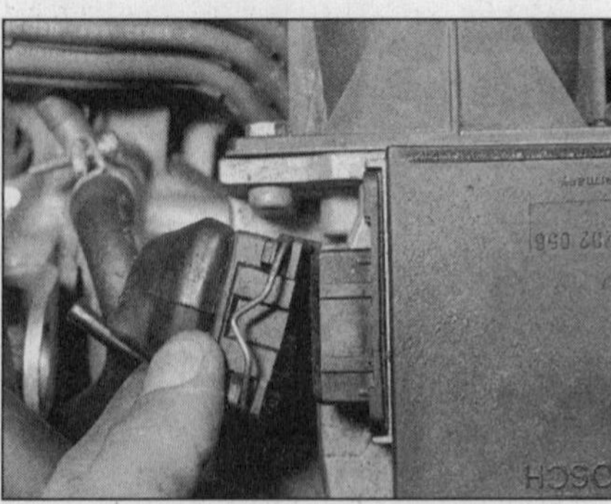

25.3A Disconnect the wiring connector from the airflow sensor

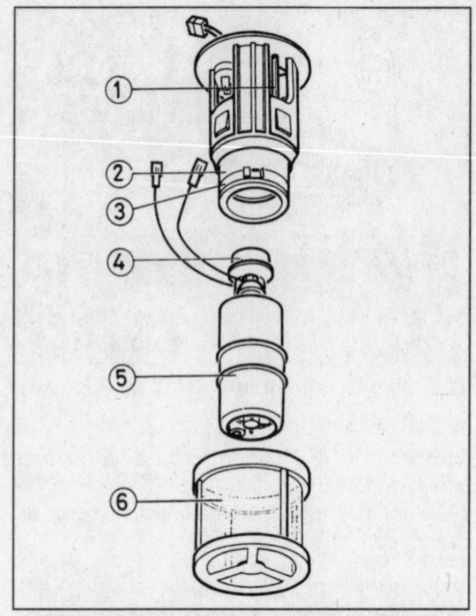

Fig. 3.21 Fuel pump components (Sec 24)

1 *Bleed tube*
2 *Bracket*
3 *Collar*
4 *Collar*
5 *Fuel pump*
6 *Filter*

5 Tilt the assembly and coolant outlet housing (without disconnecting the coolant hoses) and remove the concealed mounting bolt (Fig. 3.22).

6 Disconnect the air hoses, then remove the remaining mounting bolt and withdraw the unit.

7 Refitting is a reversal of removal.

26 Fuel injection system - complete test

1 Pull the connector from the airflow sensor and connect a voltmeter between wire 18A and earth.

2 Disconnect the ignition control unit then operate the starter motor and check that a minimum of 9 volts is obtained.

3 Disconnect the battery negative lead.

4 Connect an ohmmeter between wire M18 and earth and check that the reading is less than 1 ohm.

25.3B Airflow sensor mounting bracket and retaining bolts

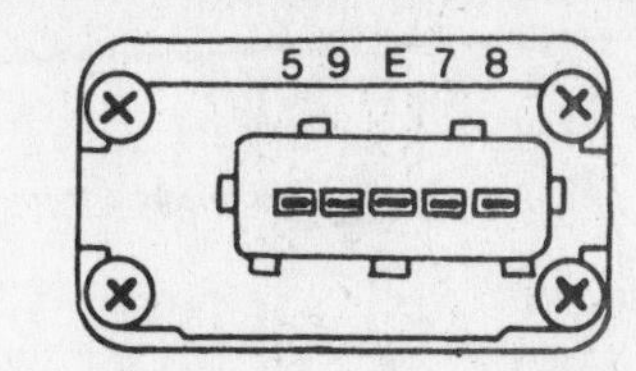

Fig. 3.23 Airflow sensor terminals (Sec 26)

5 Disconnect the airflow sensor inlet hose and use a screwdriver to open and close the sensor flap. The movement should be free. Clean the interior of the sensor if necessary.
6 Connect an ohmmeter between terminals 5 and 8 on the airflow sensor (Fig. 3.23) and check that a reading of 340 to 450 ohms is obtained.
7 Connect the ohmmeter between terminals 9 and 8 and check that the reading is now between 160 and 300 ohms.
8 Connect the ohmmeter between terminals 5 and 7, then move the flap with a screwdriver. The resistance should vary between 60 and 1000 ohms.
9 Connect the ohmmeter between the terminal on the engine temperature sensor (above the supplementary air device) and earth. The reading should be less than 1 ohm.
10 Pull off the temperature sensor connector and connect the ohmmeter across the two terminals on the sensor. If the reading is infinity, renew the sensor.
11 Connect a voltmeter between wire 48 on the supplementary air device connector and earth (Fig. 3.24).
12 Disconnect the ignition control unit then operate the starter motor and check that the reading is at least 9 volts.
13 With the battery disconnected, connect an ohmmeter between wire M24 on the connector and earth. The reading should be less than 1 ohm.
14 Remove the supplementary air device (Section 25), and check that, at an ambient temperature of 20°C (68°F), the opening in the diaphragm is visible through the end of the unit.
15 Connect an ohmmeter across the terminals of the unit and check that a reading of 45 to 55 ohms is obtained at an ambient temperature of 20°C (68°F).

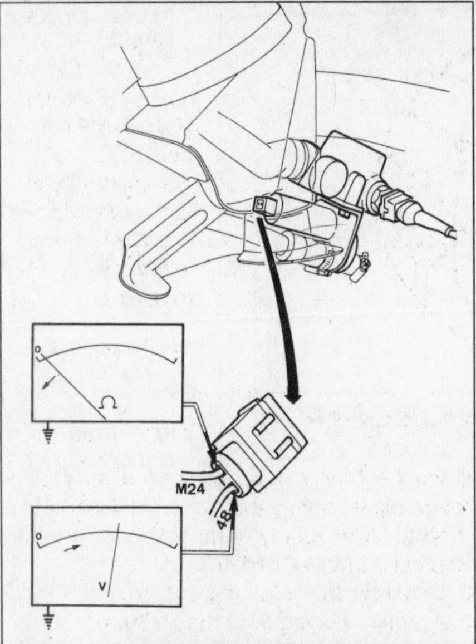

Fig. 3.24 Checking the supplementary air device wiring (Sec 26)

16 Connect a 12 volt supply to the terminals of the unit. After five minutes the diaphragm must completely block the airflow aperture.

27 Fuel injectors and distribution pipe - removal and refitting

1 Disconnect the battery earth lead.
2 Unbolt and disconnect the fuel pressure unit from the end of the distribution pipe.
3 Unclip and detach the wiring connectors from each injector. If they are not marked for identity, label them numerically as they are detached (photo) .
4 Prise free the retaining clip from each injector connection (under the distribution pipe).
5 Unbolt and remove the feed pipe.
6 Pull free the injectors as required from the cylinder head.
7 When refitting the injectors and reconnecting the fuel feed lines and distribution pipe, ensure that no dirt is allowed to enter the system.
8 Refitting is a reversal of the removal procedure. Ease refitting of the injectors by lubricating the O-ring seals with a soapy solution. New O-ring seals must be fitted.

28 Fuel pressure regulator unit - removal and refitting

1 Disconnect the battery earth lead.
2 Detach the hoses from the regulator unit, allowing for fuel spillage. Plug the hoses to prevent excess leakage of fuel and the ingress of dirt.
3 Unbolt and remove the pressure regulator unit, noting how the hose bracket is attached to the upper bolt.
4 Refit in the reverse order of removal. Check for signs of fuel leakage on completion and when the engine is restarted.

29 Fuel level transmitter - removal and refitting

Refer to Section 7.

30 Fuel tank - removal and refitting

3

1 Disconnect the battery earth lead, then proceed as described in Section 8.
2 Note the following differences:
(a) *There is an additional vent valve located separately and to the rear of the fuel tank near the rear towing eye (photo). This valve is secured by a clip.*
(b) *The fuel tank has a drain plug (photo).*
(c) *A baffle is fitted to the moulded stiffener within the tank, its purpose being to maintain the fuel level around the pump when the vehicle is cornering. The baffle is secured to the stiffener by clips. If the fuel tank is to be renewed the baffle will need to be transferred from the old tank to the new tank, together with the fuel level transmitter unit and pump. Fit and locate the baffle as shown in Figs. 3.25 and 3.26.*

27.3 Detach the injector wiring connection

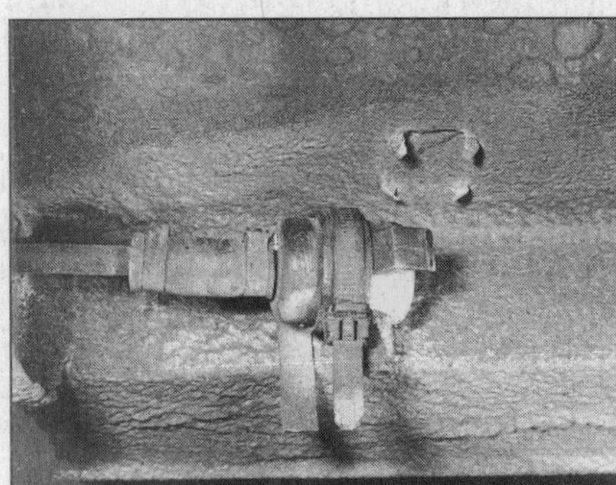

30.2A The fuel tank vent valve

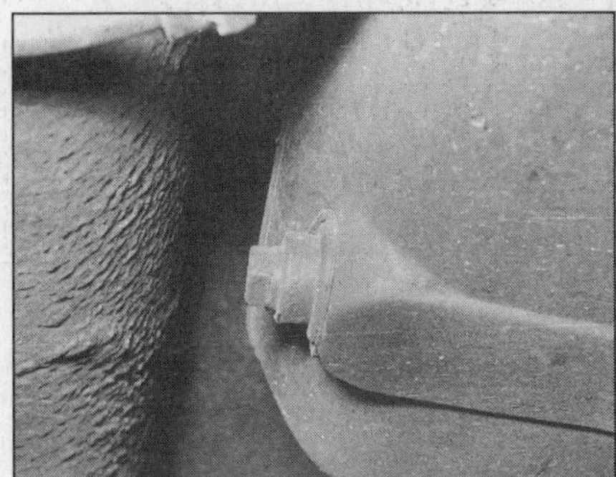

30.2B Fuel tank drain plug

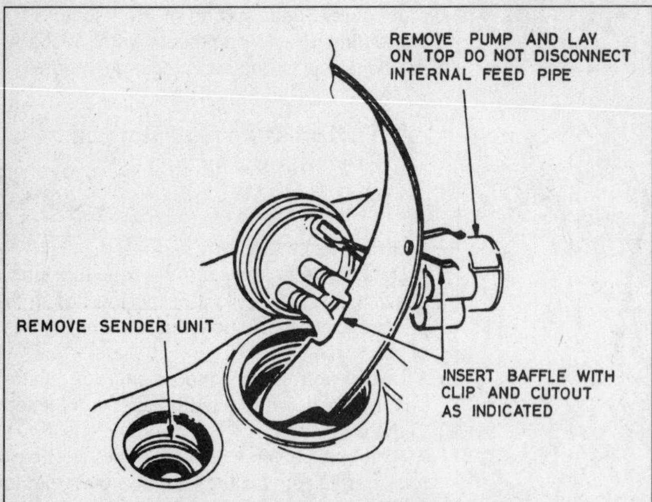

Fig. 3.25 Fuel tank baffle replacement (Sec 30)

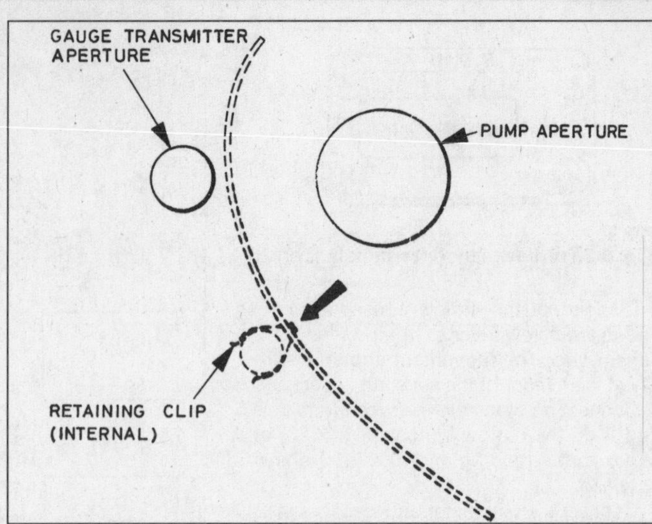

Fig. 3.26 Locate the baffle as shown (when fitted) (Sec 30)

31.1 Throttle cable and adjustment ferrule

31 Throttle cable - removal and refitting

The procedure is similar to that described in Section 14, but the adjustment ferrule is located beneath the inlet manifold (photo).

32 Manifolds and exhaust system - general

Inlet manifold

1 Removal of the inlet manifold necessitates access from underneath as well as from above and the engine undershield should therefore be removed.

2 From the underside, disconnect the crankcase breather hose and unbolt and remove the support bracket and arm.

3 From above, remove the injection distribution pipe (Section 27) together with the pressure valve. Detach the throttle switch wire connector and the throttle cable, also the vacuum and air hoses.

4 The manifold retaining bolts can now be removed and the manifold withdrawn from the cylinder head. Remove the old gasket.

5 Renew the gasket when refitting the manifold. Refitting is otherwise a reversal of the removal procedure.

Exhaust system

6 The exhaust system is similar to that fitted to carburettor models. combining a manifold and sectional pipe system (see Section 16).

7 When removing the manifold, remove the air filter unit to gain access to the upper retaining nuts and remove the engine undershield to provide access to the lower manifold retaining nuts from underneath.

8 Removal is relatively easy and it is therefore recommended that the complete system is removed, at least from the manifold flange, whenever any work or repairs to the exhaust system are necessary. Ensure that the vehicle is securely supported when raised for working underneath the vehicle.

9 Always renew the manifold-to-cylinder head flange gasket, and refer to Section 16 when reconnecting the downpipe to the manifold.

Fault finding - fuel and exhaust systems

Difficult starting from cold

- ☐ Choke control inoperative (carburettor)
- ☐ Fuel pump fault
- ☐ Blocked fuel line or filter
- ☐ Needle valve sticking (carburettor)
- ☐ Supplementary air device fault (fuel injection)
- ☐ Temperature sensor faulty or disconnected (fuel injection)

Difficult starting when hot

- ☐ Choked air filter
- ☐ Choke control sticking (carburettor)
- ☐ Fuel pump faulty

Excessive fuel consumption

- ☐ Mixture setting incorrect
- ☐ Excessive fuel pressure (fuel injection)
- ☐ Temperature sensor faulty (fuel injection)
- ☐ Airflow sensor faulty (fuel injection)

Uneven idling

- ☐ Mixture setting incorrect
- ☐ Air leak in intake system
- ☐ Throttle switch out of adjustment (fuel injection)
- ☐ Loose electronic control unit connector (fuel injection)

Hesitation after cornering

- ☐ Displaced baffle in fuel tank (fuel injection)

Chapter 4 Ignition system

For modifications, and information applicable to later models, see Supplement at end of manual

Contents

Degrees of difficulty

Easy, suitable for novice with little experience 	**Fairly easy,** suitable for beginner with some experience 	**Fairly difficult,** suitable for competent DIY mechanic	**Difficult,** suitable for experienced DIY mechanic	**Very difficult,** suitable for expert DIY or professional

Specifications

System type	12 volt, electronic (breakerless) system	
Distributor		
Make	Ducellier or Bosch	
Firing order	1-3-4-2 (No 1 cylinder at flywheel end)	
Rotation:		
OHV engines	Clockwise	
OHC engines	Anti-clockwise	
Ignition coil		
Make and type	Bosch or Ducellier, BTR01	
Ignition amplifier module		
Make and type	Bosch or Ducellier, MTR01	
Ignition timing		
Vacuum hose disconnected (and plugged):		
OHV engines	8° BTDC at 650 rpm	
OHC engines	10° BTDC at 700 rpm	
Spark plugs		
Type:		
OHV models	Champion C9YCC or C281YC	
OHC models up to 1987 model year	Champion S9YCC or S281YC	
Electrode gap:		
C9YCC and S9YCC	0.8 mm (0.032 in)	
C281YC and S281YC	0.6 mm (0.024 in)	
HT leads		
Type:		
OHV models up to 1987	Champion LS-03	
OHC models up to 1988	Champion LS-12	
Torque wrench settings	**Nm**	**lbf ft**
Spark plugs:		
OHV engines	20 to 30	15 to 22
OHC engines	17	18

4

1.2 Ignition amplifier module

3.1 Distributor showing cap retaining clips (arrowed) - OHV engine

3.4 Scribe alignment marks on distributor body and mounting bracket - OHV engine

1 General description

On all models the ignition system is of electronic breakerless type, which provides a high degree of reliability combined with the minimum of service requirements.

The system components comprise the ignition amplifier module, ignition coil, distributor (incorporating a pulse generator) and the spark plugs (photo).

It should be noted that the spark plugs used on the OHC engine variants have a tapered seat with no sealing washers fitted.

In order that the engine may run correctly it is necessary for an electrical spark to ignite the fuel/air mixture in the combustion chamber at exactly the right moment in relation to the engine speed and load.

Basically the ignition system functions as follows. Low tension voltage from the battery is fed to the ignition coil. where it is converted into high tension voltage. The high tension voltage is powerful enough to jump the spark plug gap in the cylinder many times a second under high compression, providing that the ignition system is in good working order.

The ignition system consists of two individual circuits known as the low tension (LT) circuit and high tension (HT) circuit.

The low tension circuit (sometimes known as the primary circuit) comprises the ignition switch, primary ignition coil windings, and amplifier module. The high tension circuit (sometimes known as the secondary circuit) comprises the secondary ignition coil windings, distributor cap, rotor arm, spark plugs and HT leads.

The primary circuit is initially switched on by the amplifier module and a magnetic field is formed within the ignition coil. At the precise point of ignition the pulse generator causes the amplifier module to switch off the primary circuit, and high tension voltage is then induced in the secondary circuit and fed to the spark plug via the distributor cap and rotor arm.

The ignition is advanced and retarded automatically by centrifugal weights and a vacuum capsule to ensure that the spark occurs at the correct instant in relation to engine speed and load.

Note: *When working on the ignition system remember that the high tension voltage can be considerably higher than on a conventional system and in certain circumstances could prove fatal.*

2 Routine maintenance

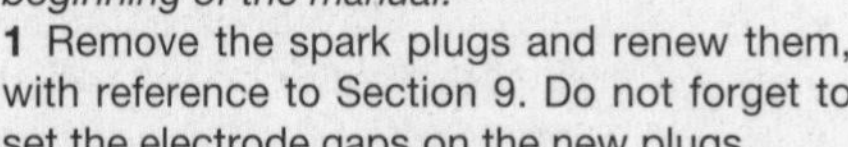

Carry out the following procedures at the intervals given in Routine Maintenance at the beginning of the manual.

1 Remove the spark plugs and renew them, with reference to Section 9. Do not forget to set the electrode gaps on the new plugs.

2 Check and, if necessary, adjust the ignition timing, as described in Section 6.

3 Periodically inspect the ignition system HT and LT wiring for security at their connection points and their general condition.

4 Periodically the condition of the distributor cap and rotor should be checked .

5 Remove the protective boot from around the distributor cap, release the two spring clips or unscrew the two retaining screws and lift off the cap.

6 Clean the inside and outside of the cap with a clean cloth and check the centre contact and four segments on the inside of the cap for excessive wear or burning. If evident the cap should be renewed.

7 Carefully lift the rotor off the distributor shaft and check the end of the brass segment for burning. Renew if necessary.

8 The air gap between the vane tips and the magnetic pick-up point is preset. It cannot be adjusted and requires no maintenance.

9 Apply a few drops of clean engine oil to the felt pad in the top of the distributor shaft.

10 Refit the rotor and distributor cap followed by the protective boot.

3 Distributor (OHV engine) - removal and refitting

1 Release the retaining clips and detach the distributor cap and leads from the distributor (photo).

2 Disconnect the vacuum hose from the distributor vacuum advance unit.

3 Disconnect the low tension wires at the in-line connector.

4 Using a small sharp screwdriver or similar instrument, carefully scribe an alignment mark between the distributor body and the crankcase mounting bracket (photo).

5 Undo the distributor clamp bolt, remove the clamp and lift out the distributor from the engine (photo).

6 To refit the distributor, enter it into the crankcase mounting bracket and then turn the distributor rotor until the tongue on the distributor shaft engages with the slot in the driveshaft (photo).

3.5 Remove distributor clamp bolt (arrowed) - OHV engine

3.6 Refitting the distributor - OHV engine

7 Rotate the distributor body to line up the previously made scribe marks, refit the clamp and tighten the securing bolt.
8 Refit the remaining distributor components using the reverse sequence to removal. After completing the installation it is advisable to check the ignition timing as described in Section 6.
9 If a new distributor is being fitted or if for any reason the alignment marks scribed between the distributor body and mounting bracket have been lost, it will be necessary to time the distributor to the engine, before fitting, as described below.
10 Pull off the HT lead and remove No 1 spark plug (nearest the flywheel end of the engine).
11 Place a finger over the spark plug hole and rotate the engine until pressure is felt, indicating that the piston is on the compression stroke. (Rotate the engine by means of a large socket on the crankshaft pulley bolt, or put the car in gear and move it forwards). The direction of engine rotation is clockwise viewed from the timing cover end.
12 With the No 1 cylinder at TDC on its firing stroke, the slot in the distributor drive collar on the distributor driveshaft will be set at the angle shown in Fig. 4.1 (three teeth anti-clockwise from the vertical). The TDC position can be further checked by observing the position of the timing notch in the crankshaft pulley. The notch should be aligned with the 0 (TDC) mark on the timing case (photos). This check will require the removal of the engine side cover from the right-hand wheel arch for access.
13 Temporarily place the distributor cap in position on the distributor and make a mark on the distributor body, with pencil or crayon adjacent to the No 1 HT segment of the cap.
14 Remove the cap and turn the distributor rotor so that it is pointing toward the mark.
15 Refit the distributor to the crankcase mounting bracket and engage the offset drive dog of the distributor with the slot in the drive collar. When in position the vacuum advance unit should be positioned on the underside of the distributor (towards the sump).
16 Relocate the distributor retaining clamp and bolt, but only hand tighten the bolt at this stage. Full tighten the bolt when the timing has been checked.
17 Check and adjust the timing as described in Section 6.

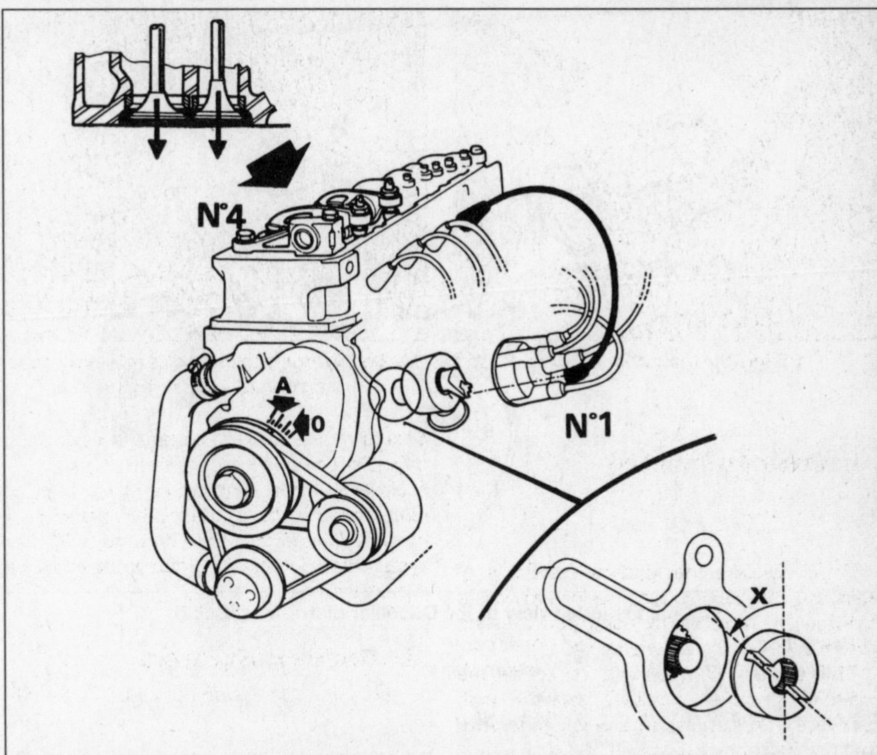

Fig. 4.1 Distributor refitting requirements – OHV engine (Sec 3)
Slot angle X = 3 teeth from vertical

3.12A Flywheel timing mark and timing scale marks on the clutch housing – OHV engine

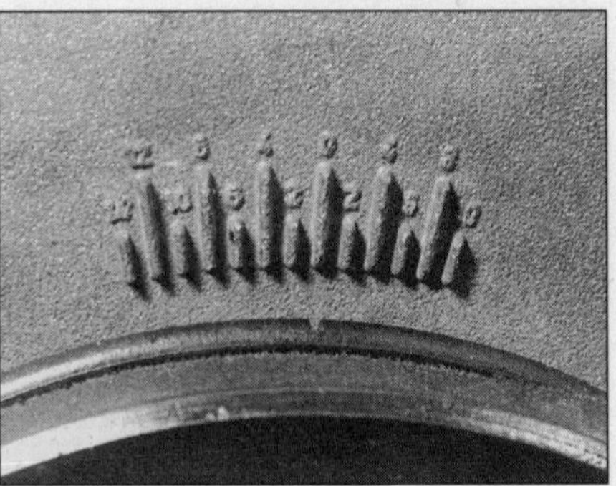

3.12B Align the pulley notch with appropriate timing mark (shown at TDC) – OHV engine

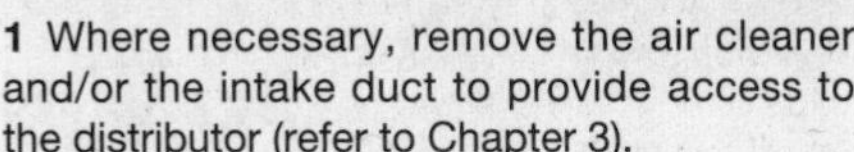

4 Distributor (OHC engine) - removal and refitting

1 Where necessary, remove the air cleaner and/or the intake duct to provide access to the distributor (refer to Chapter 3).
2 Identify the HT leads for position then disconnect them from the spark plugs.
3 Slide off the ignition coil cover and disconnect the HT lead from the coil.
4 Pull back the plastic cover then unclip and remove the distributor cap (photo).
5 Disconnect the wiring at the connector, where necessary pulling out the spring clip first.
6 Pull the hose from the vacuum advance unit.
7 Mark the relative positions of the distributor and mounting flanges for positional reference when refitting.

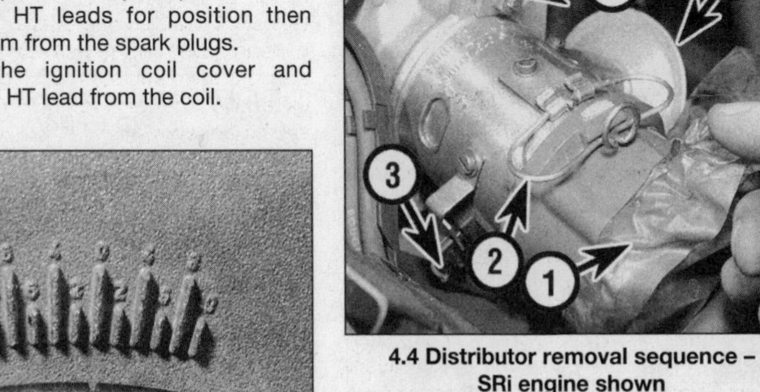

4.4 Distributor removal sequence – SRi engine shown

1 Withdraw the cover
2 Release cap clips
3 Detach wiring connector
4 Detach vacuum advance hose
5 Mark relative positions of flanges
6 Remove retaining nuts and flat plate washers

4

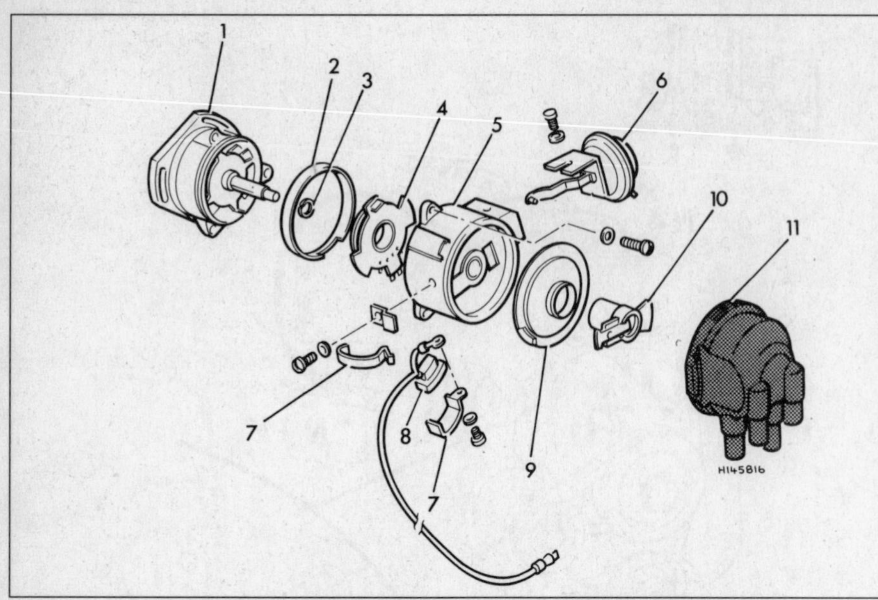

Fig. 4.2 Exploded view of the Ducellier distributor (Sec 5)

1 Lower body
2 Plastic ring
3 Circlip
4 Magnetic coil
5 Upper body
6 Vacuum unit
7 Clips
8 Wiring plug
9 Cover
10 Rotor arm
11 Distributor cap

8 Unscrew the mounting nuts, remove the small plates, and withdraw the distributor.
9 Check the condition of the O-ring on the mounting flange and renew it if necessary.
10 Refitting is a reversal of removal, but turn the rotor arm as required to align the lugs with the offset slot in the camshaft. If the old distributor is being refitted, align the previously made marks before tightening the mounting nuts. If fitting a new distributor, 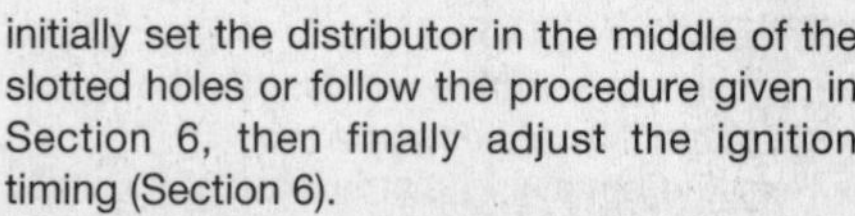initially set the distributor in the middle of the slotted holes or follow the procedure given in Section 6, then finally adjust the ignition timing (Section 6).

5 Distributor - overhaul

1 Clean the exterior of the distributor.
2 Pull off the rotor arm and remove the plastic cover, where fitted.

Ducellier

3 Extract the screw and remove the clamp and wiring plug (photo).
4 Extract the three body screws. The lugs are offset so the body sections cannot be misaligned when reassembled. Separate the body sections (photo).
5 Invert the body upper section, pull out the plastic ring and lift out the magnetic coil (photos).
6 From the body upper section, extract the circlip and the thrust washer (photo).
7 Extract the vacuum unit screw and then lift out the baseplate at the same time unhooking the vacuum link (photos).
8 Extract the circlip and shim from the body lower section (photo).
9 Lift out the counterweight assembly.
10 The drive dog is secured to the shaft by a pin.

5.3 Clamp and wiring plug (Ducellier)

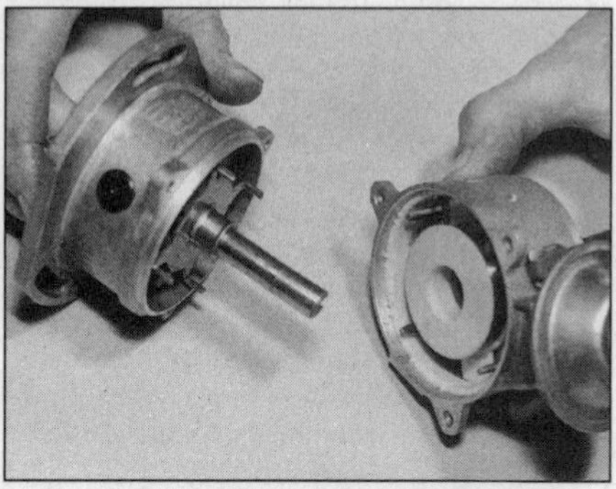

5.4 Separating the body sections (Ducellier)

5.5A Remove the plastic ring . . .

5.5B . . . and the magnetic coil (Ducellier)

5.6 Remove the circlip and thrust washer (Ducellier)

5.7A Vacuum unit and screw (Ducellier)

5.7B Baseplate removal (Ducellier)

5.8 View showing reluctor, centrifugal weights and securing circlip – arrowed (Ducellier)

5.11 Hole marked for engagement of vacuum unit link (Ducellier)

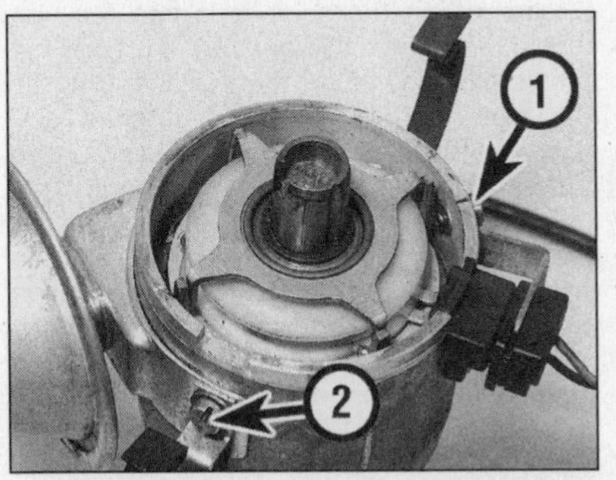

5.12A General view of the Bosch distributor fitted to 1.1 and 1.3 litre models

1 Wiring connector plug and retaining screw
2 Vacuum advance/cap clip retaining screw

5.12B Vacuum advance unit removal from Bosch distributor (1.1 and 1.3 litre models)

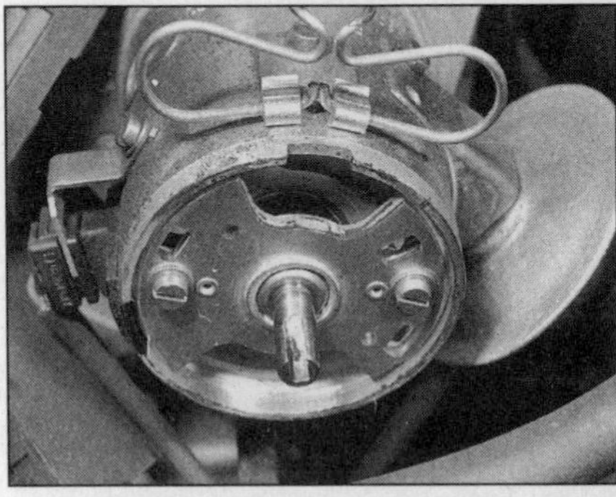

5.12C Bosch distributor showing bearing plate (SRi model)

11 Reassembly is a reversal of dismantling, but note that one baseplate hole is marked by engagement of the vacuum unit link rod (photo).

Bosch

12 The procedure is similar to that for the Ducellier distributor but the body is in one piece. Refer to Fig. 4.3 (photos).

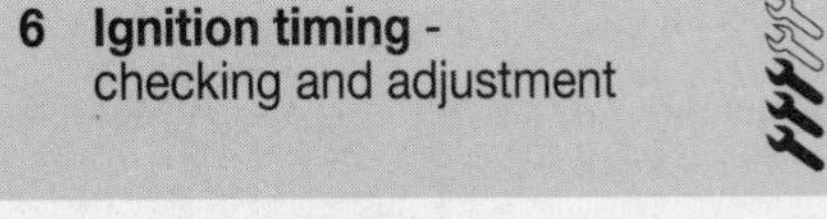

6 Ignition timing - checking and adjustment

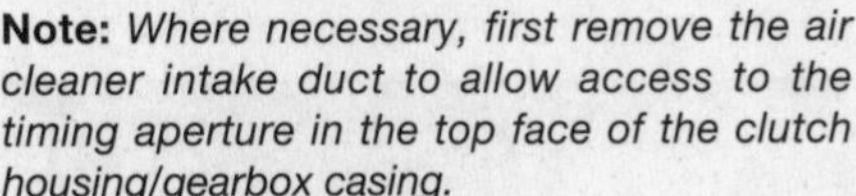

Note: *Where necessary, first remove the air cleaner intake duct to allow access to the timing aperture in the top face of the clutch housing/gearbox casing.*

Static ignition timing

1 To set the ignition timing statically so that the engine can be started, first remove No 1 spark plug (nearest clutch) and turn the engine in the normal rotational direction until pressure is felt indicating that the piston is commencing the compression stroke. The pressure can be felt using a suitable wooden rod or piece of cork placed over the spark plug hole.

2 While looking into the timing aperture in the clutch housing/gearbox casing, continue

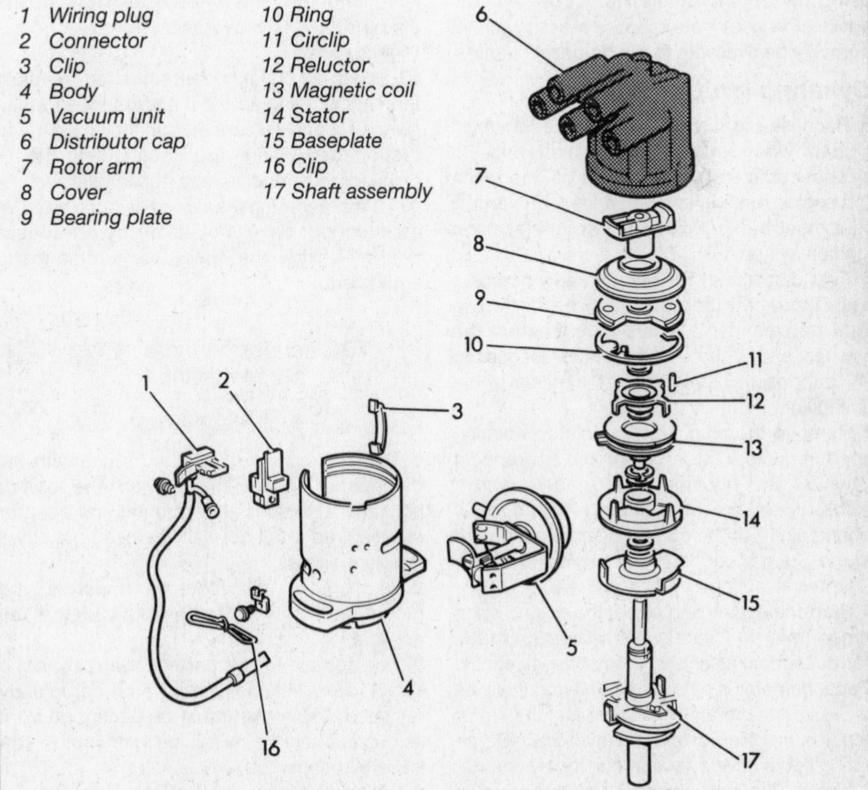

Fig. 4.3 Exploded view of the Bosch distributor (Sec 5)

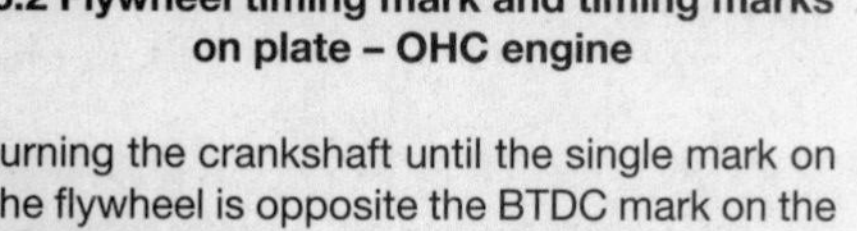

6.2 Flywheel timing mark and timing marks on plate – OHC engine

7.1 TDC sensor location in the clutch housing closing (belly) plate

7.4 TDC sensor showing the three extensions on the inner face

turning the crankshaft until the single mark on the flywheel is opposite the BTDC mark on the timing plate (see photo 3.12A or 6.2).

3 Check that the distributor rotor arm is facing the No 1 HT lead segment position in the distributor cap. To do this, remove the cap and mark the outside in line with the segment, then put it back on the distributor noting which way the rotor arm is facing.

4 If necessary, loosen the mounting nuts and turn the distributor body to bring the segment and rotor arm in line, then tighten the nuts. Refit No 1 spark plug. The ignition timing should now be checked dynamically as described below. For this you will need a stroboscopic timing light. Alternatively the ignition timing may be checked and adjusted using the engine diagnosis socket, but the special Peugeot instrument necessary will not normally be available to the home mechanic.

Dynamic ignition timing

5 Because the distributor only gives a timing signal when the shaft is rotating, a stroboscopic timing light must be used with the engine running at idling speed. The timing light must be suitable for use with electronic ignition systems.

6 First disconnect the vacuum advance pipe from the distributor and connect the timing light between No 1 spark plug (nearest the flywheel end of the engine) and its associated HT lead, or as instructed by the maker of the timing light.

7 Remove the plug from the clutch housing aperture (where fitted). Clean the appropriate flywheel and housing timing marks with a piece of rag and mark them with a spot of white paint. For the correct degree mark, refer to the Specifications at the beginning of this Chapter.

8 Start the engine and adjust the engine idling speed (refer to Chapter 3 if necessary) to the correct setting as shown in the Specifications. If a tachometer is not fitted to the car, it will be necessary to obtain a unit that is suitable for use on electronic ignition systems. Some timing lights have a tachometer incorporated.

9 Aim the timing light at the clutch housing aperture and observe the timing marks. They will appear stationary, and if the timing is correct, the mark on the flywheel will be adjacent to the appropriate degree mark on the scale. If this is not the case, slacken the clamp bolt at the base of the distributor and then turn the distributor slowly in the desired direction (clockwise to retard the timing, anti-clockwise to advance it) until the mark on the flywheel is in line with the appropriate mark on the scale. Tighten the clamp bolt and recheck that the marks are still in alignment.

10 To check the centrifugal advance, increase the engine speed and note whether the white mark on the flywheel moves away from the mark on the scale. If it does, the centrifugal advance is functioning.

11 To check the vacuum advance, reconnect the vacuum pipe to the distributor. If the unit is functioning, this should also cause the timing marks to move away from each other slightly.

12 When all checks are completed, readjust the engine idling speed if necessary and then switch off and disconnect the timing light and tachometer (where applicable). Refit the air cleaner intake duct (where applicable).

13 If the centrifugal advance is suspected of malfunction, have it checked by a Peugeot dealer using the necessary diagnostic equipment.

7 TDC sensor - removal and refitting

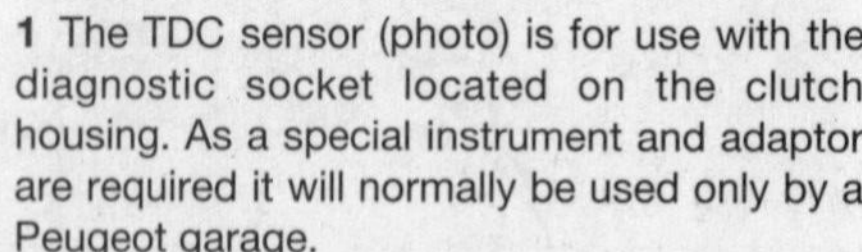

1 The TDC sensor (photo) is for use with the diagnostic socket located on the clutch housing. As a special instrument and adaptor are required it will normally be used only by a Peugeot garage.

2 To remove the sensor, unscrew the mounting screw or release the clamp (as applicable).

3 The sensor forms part of the diagnostic socket assembly so, if it is to be completely removed, the socket must be unclipped from its bracket and the remaining wiring and earth leads disconnected.

4 Refitting is a reversal of removal, but the adjustment procedure for new and used sensors differs. New sensors have three extensions on the inner face and the unit should be inserted through the clamp until the extensions just touch the flywheel (photo). The clamp screw is then tightened and clearance is provided as the flywheel rotates and wears the ends of the extensions. This method should not be used when refitting a used sensor. In this case, cut off the extensions completely then temporarily insert the sensor until it touches the flywheel; remove it and reposition it in the clamp 1.0 mm (0.04 in) further out.

8 Ignition coil - general

1 The maintenance of the coil is minimal and is limited to periodically wiping its surfaces clean and dry and ensuring that the lead connectors are secure. High voltages generated by the coil can easily leak to earth over its surface and prevent the spark plugs from receiving the electrical pulses. Water repellent sprays are now available to prevent dampness causing this type of malfunction (photo).

2 Wipe clean and spray the HT leads and distributor cap also.

3 Special equipment is required to test a coil and is best left to an auto-electrician. Substitution of another coil is an alternative method of fault tracing.

8.1 Ignition coil and connections – SRi model

9.2 Spark lead removal – grip and pull on the insulator/end fitting – not the lead

9 Spark plugs, HT leads and distributor cap - general

1 The correct functioning of the spark plugs is vital for the correct running and efficiency of the engine. It is essential that the plugs fitted are appropriate for the engine, and the suitable type is specified at the beginning of this chapter. If this type is used and the engine is in good condition, the spark plugs should not need attention between scheduled replacement intervals. Spark plug cleaning is rarely necessary and should not be attempted unless specialised equipment is available as damage can easily be caused to the firing ends.

2 To remove the plugs, first open the bonnet and pull the HT leads from them. Grip the rubber end fitting not the lead, otherwise the lead connection may be fractured. Also remove the extensions (photo).

3 The spark plugs are recessed in the cylinder head and it is recommended that dirt is removed from the recesses using a vacuum cleaner or compressed air, before removing the plugs, to prevent dirt dropping into the cylinders.

4 Unscrew the plugs using a suitable box spanner, such as the Peugeot type shown (photo). On some models, it will be necessary to remove the air filter intake duct to allow the No 1 spark plug to be removed.

5 Examination of the spark plugs will give a good indication of the condition of the engine. If the insulator nose of the spark plug is clean and white, with no deposits, this is indicative of a weak mixture, or too hot a plug (a hot plug transfers heat away from the electrode slowly, a cold plug transfers heat away quickly).

9.4 Spark plug removal using Peugeot box spanner

6 If the tip and insulator nose are covered with hard black-looking deposits, then this is indicative that the mixture is too rich. Should the plug be black and oily, then it is likely that the engine is fairly worn, as well as the mixture being too rich.

7 If the insulator nose is covered with light tan to greyish brown deposits, then the mixture is correct and it is likely that the engine is in good condition.

8 The spark plug gap is of considerable importance as, if it is too large or too small, the size of the spark and its efficiency will be seriously impaired. For the best results the spark plug gap should be set in accordance with the Specifications at the beginning of this Chapter.

9 To set it, measure the gap with a feeler gauge, and then bend open, or close, the outer plug electrode until the correct gap is achieved. The centre electrode should never be bent, as this may crack the insulation and cause plug failure, if nothing worse.

10 Special spark plug electrode gap adjusting tools are available from most motor accessory shops.

11 Screw in the spark plugs by hand where possible, then tighten them to the specified torque. Take extra care to enter the plug threads correctly as the cylinder head is of aluminium.

12 The OHC engine variants use a taper seat type spark plug which do not use washers. When tightening this type of plug, take care not to overtighten them. If a torque wrench is not available, tighten them as much as possible by hand, then a further 1/15 th of a turn using the box wrench. Overtightening of this plug type will make them difficult to remove and damage would easily result.

13 Fit the extensions followed by the HT leads making sure that the latter are in their correct order of 1-3-4-2 (No 1 nearest the clutch end of the engine) in relation to the normal rotation of the rotor arm.

14 The HT leads and their connections should always be kept clean and dry and arranged neatly in the special holder. If any lead shows signs of cracking or chafing of the insulation it should be renewed.

15 If the engine fails to start due to either damp HT leads or distributor cap, a moisture dispersant can be very effective.

16 Check the distributor cap whenever it is removed. If there are any very thin black lines running between the electrodes this indicates tracking and a new cap should be fitted. Check the rotor arm in a similar way. Where applicable check that the spring-tensioned carbon brush in the centre of the cap is free to move and is not worn excessively.

HAYNES HiNT

It's often difficult to insert spark plugs into their holes without cross-threading them. To avoid this possibility, fit a short piece of rubber hose over the end of the spark plug. The flexible hose acts as a universal joint, to help align the plug with the plug hole. Should the plug begin to cross-thread, the hose will slip on the spark plug, preventing thread damage.

Fault finding - ignition system

Starter turns but engine will not start

- ☐ Faulty or disconnected leads
- ☐ Faulty spark plug
- ☐ Fault in ignition coil
- ☐ Fault in pick-up/starter unit

Engine starts but runs erratically

- ☐ Incorrect timing
- ☐ Fouled spark plug
- ☐ Incorrectly connected HT leads
- ☐ Crack in distributor cap or rotor
- ☐ Poor battery, engine and earth connections

Notes

Chapter 5 Clutch

For modifications, and information applicable to later models, see Supplement at end of manual

Contents

Degrees of difficulty

Easy, suitable for novice with little experience 

Fairly easy, suitable for beginner with some experience 

Fairly difficult, suitable for competent DIY mechanic 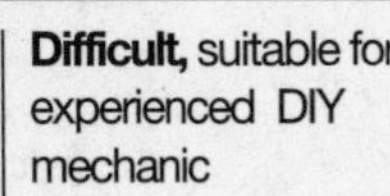

Difficult, suitable for experienced DIY mechanic

Very difficult, suitable for expert DIY or professional

Specifications

General

Type	Single plate with diaphragm spring. Cable operation
Driven plate clutch disc outer diameter:	
OHV engines	181 mm (7.13 in)
OHC engines	200 mm (7.87 in)
Adjustment:	
Clutch pedal travel	140 mm (5.5 in)

Torque wrench settings

	Nm	lbf ft
Clutch cover bolts:		
OHV engines	15	11
OHC engines	25	18

1 General description

The clutch is of diaphragm spring, single dry plate type with cable actuation.

The clutch pedal pivots in a bracket mounted under the facia and operates a cable to the clutch release arm (or fork). The release lever operates a thrust bearing (clutch release bearing) which bears on the diaphragm spring of the pressure plate, and releases the clutch driven plate from the flywheel. The driven plate (or disc) is splined to a shaft which transmits the drive to the gearbox.

The clutch release mechanism consists of a fork and bearing which are in permanent contact with release fingers on the pressure plate assembly. The fork pushes the release bearing forwards to bear against the release fingers, so moving the centre of the diaphragm spring inwards. The spring is sandwiched between two rings which act as fulcrum points. As the centre of the spring is pushed in, the outside of the spring is pushed out, so moving the pressure plate backwards and disengaging it from the clutch driven plate.

When the clutch pedal is released, the diaphragm spring forces the pressure plate into contact with the friction linings on the driven plate and at the same time pushes the driven plate a fraction of an inch forwards on its splines so engaging it with the flywheel. The driven plate is now firmly sandwiched between the pressure plate and the flywheel, so the drive is taken up.

As wear takes place on the driven plate friction linings the diaphragm fingers move outwards and the pedal stroke decreases; the cable mechanism incorporates an adjustment to compensate for this wear.

2 Routine maintenance

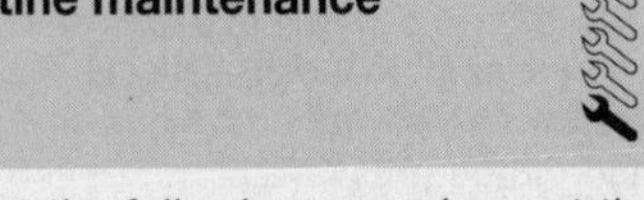

Carry out the following procedures at the intervals given in Routine Maintenance at the beginning of the manual.

1 Depress the clutch pedal fully three times then, using a rule, measure the total stroke of the pedal pad.

2 If the stroke is not as given in the specifications it will be necessary to adjust the clutch cable.

3 To make the adjustment, loosen the locknut at the gearbox end of the cable, turn the adjusting nut as required, then retighten the locknut.

4 Before checking the adjustment, fully operate the clutch pedal three times.

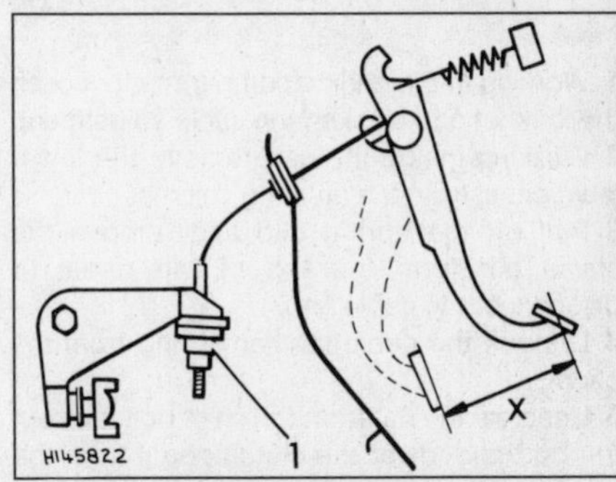

Fig. 5.1 Clutch pedal stroke (X) adjustment diagram (Sec 2)

1 Adjustment nut and locknut

5

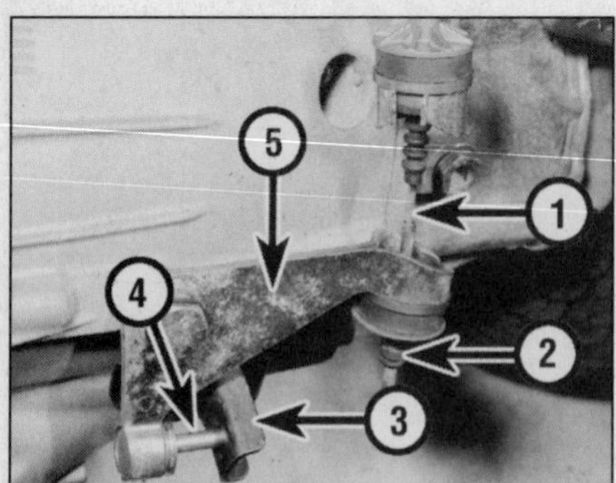

3.1 Clutch cable and associated fittings at the transmission end

1 *Clutch cable*
2 *Adjustment and locknuts*
3 *Release lever*
4 *Pushrod (where applicable)*
5 *Relay lever*

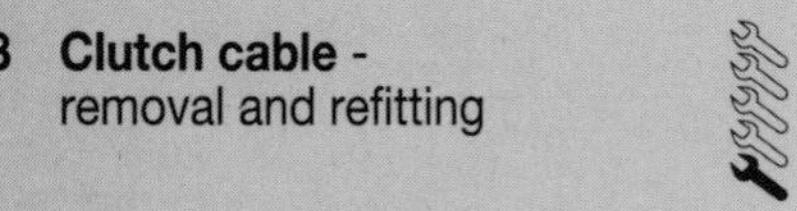

3 Clutch cable - removal and refitting

1 Working in the engine compartment, loosen the locknut and slacken the cable adjustment (photo).
2 Release the cable end fitting from the intermediate lever. Recover the pushrod (where applicable).
3 Remove the metal clip which secures the clutch cable to the underside of the car.
4 Working inside the car, remove the lower facia panel from the steering column.
5 Pull off the spring clip and remove the clevis pin from the top of the pedal to disconnect the cable end.
6 Release the cable from the bulkhead by twisting the plastic grommet through a quarter of a turn and withdraw it into the engine compartment.
7 Refitting is a reversal of removal, but finally adjust the pedal stroke, as described in Section 2.

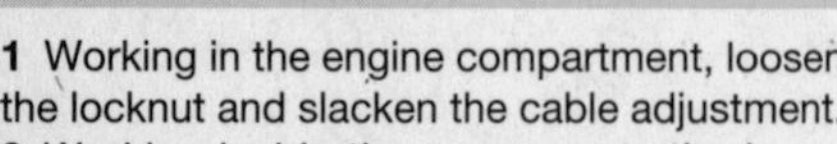

4 Clutch pedal - removal and refitting

1 Working in the engine compartment, loosen the locknut and slacken the cable adjustment.
2 Working inside the car, remove the lower facia panel from the steering column.
3 Pull off the spring clip and remove the clevis pin from the top of the pedal to disconnect the cable end.
4 Unhook the cable tension spring from the pedal.
5 Unscrew the nut from the pivot bolt, pull out the bolt and lower the clutch pedal from the bracket.
6 Examine the pedal bushes for wear and renew them if necessary.
7 Refitting is a reversal of removal, but lightly

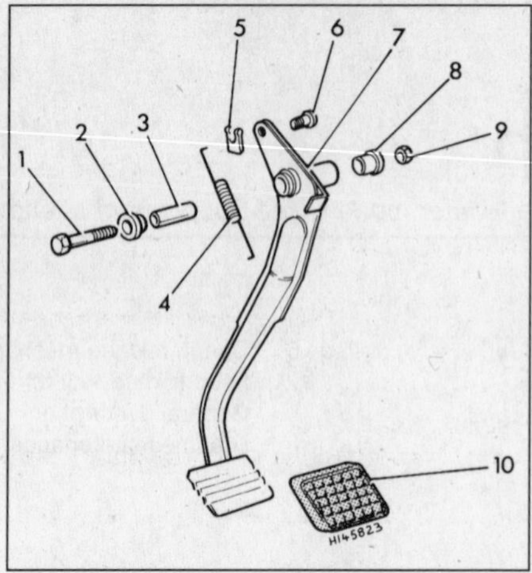

Fig. 5.2 Clutch pedal components (Sec 4)

1 *Pivot bolt*
2 *Bush*
3 *Spacer*
4 *Tension spring (circular type on some models)*
5 *Clip*
6 *Clevis pin*
7 *Pedal*
8 *Bush*
9 *Nut*
10 *Pad*

grease the bushes and clevis pin, finally adjust the pedal stroke, as described in Section 2.

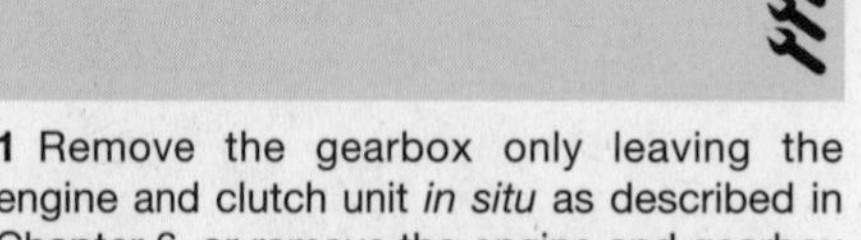

5 Clutch - removal

1 Remove the gearbox only leaving the engine and clutch unit *in situ* as described in Chapter 6, or remove the engine and gearbox units combined, then separate as described in Chapter 1.
2 Mark the clutch pressure plate in relation to the flywheel then progressively loosen the bolts. If necessary hold the flywheel stationary using a screwdriver engaged with the starter ring gear.
3 With all the bolts removed lift the pressure plate assembly from the location dowels followed by the driven plate. Note the orientation of the driven plate to ensure correct refitting.

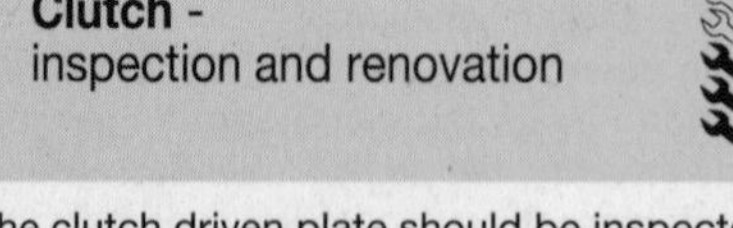

6 Clutch - inspection and renovation

1 The clutch driven plate should be inspected for wear and for contamination by oil. Wear is gauged by the depth of the rivet heads below the surface of the friction material. If this is less than 0.6 mm (0.024 in) the linings are worn enough to justify renewal.
2 Examine the friction faces of the flywheel and clutch pressure plate. These should be bright and smooth. If the linings have worn too much it is possible that the metal surfaces may have been scored by the rivet heads. Dust and grit can have the same effect. If the

7.1 Locating the driven plate – note direction of fitting

scoring is very severe it could mean that even with a new clutch driven plate, slip and juddering and other malfunctions will recur. Deep scoring on the flywheel face is serious because the flywheel will have to be removed and machined by a specialist, or renewed. If the pressure plate is worn excessively it must be renewed. If the driven plate friction linings are contaminated with oil, the plate must be renewed and the source of the oil traced and rectified.
3 Replacement of the crankshaft rear oil seal is possible after removing the flywheel and is described in Chapter 1. If the oil leak is from the gearbox, renew the input shaft oil seal as described in Chapter 6. If in doubt, renew both the crankshaft rear oil seal and the gearbox input shaft seal.
4 If the reason for removal of the clutch has been because of slip and the slip has been allowed to go on for any length of time, it is possible that the heat generated will have adversely affected the diaphragm spring in the cover with the result that the pressure is now uneven and/or insufficient to prevent slip, even with a new driven plate. Where this occurs, the friction surfaces on the flywheel and pressure plate will often show a blue discoloration necessitating the renewal of the pressure plate.
5 With the clutch removed, the release bearing should be checked for excessive wear and noise, and renewed if necessary. Also check the spigot bush in the crankshaft rear flange for wear and, if necessary, renew it.

7 Clutch - refitting

1 Ensure that the friction surfaces are clean of dirt and free from grease then commence refitting by offering the driven plate to the flywheel (photo), making sure it is the right way round. It will only fit one way. Retain the disc in position by inserting a centring mandrel. Various proprietary centring tools are available, or alternatively one can be made from a piece of dowel or bar built up with tape.

7.4 Centralising the driven plate and tightening the clutch cover bolts

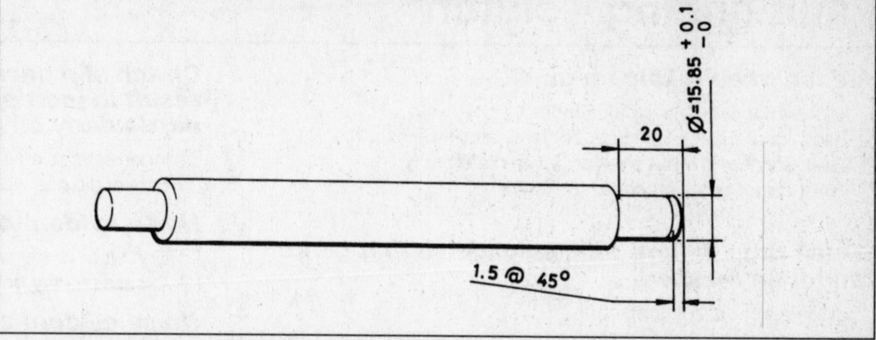

Fig. 5.3 Clutch disc centralizing tool showing dimension requirements (in mm) (Sec 7)

2 Fit the pressure plate, observing the alignment marks made when dismantling if the old plate is being refitted. Insert the six bolts and just nip them up so that the driven plate is lightly nipped.

3 Make sure that the driven plate is accurately centred, either by visual inspection or by inserting an old gearbox input shaft. If the plate is not centred it will not be possible to refit the gearbox.

4 With the centring mandrel in position, tighten the pressure plate securing bolts progressively to the special torque. Remove the centring mandrel (photo).

5 Prior to refitting the gearbox, lubricate the clutch mechanism components (release bearing tube, fork balljoint and fingers, and shaft splines) with Molykote 321R, but take great care not to get any lubricant onto the clutch friction surfaces.

6 Refit the gearbox referring to Chapter 1 or 6 as applicable.

8 Clutch release mechanism - overhaul

1 Remove the gearbox, as described in Chapter 6.

2 Release the spring clips and slide the bearing from the guide sleeve.

3 Withdraw the release fork from the ball-stud.

4 Where applicable, the pivot bush may be removed as follows. First drill out the rivets which secure the old bush. Remove the bush and discard it. Position the new bush on the fork and pass its rivets through the holes. Heat the rivets with a cigarette lighter or a low powered blowlamp, then peen over their heads while they are still hot.

5 Lightly coat the bush with grease, then refit the release fork. Press it onto the ball-stud until it snaps home.

6 If the ball-stud requires renewal, remove it with a slide hammer having a suitable claw. Support the casing and drive in the new stud using a soft metal drift.

7 Refit the remaining components using a reversal of the removal procedure.

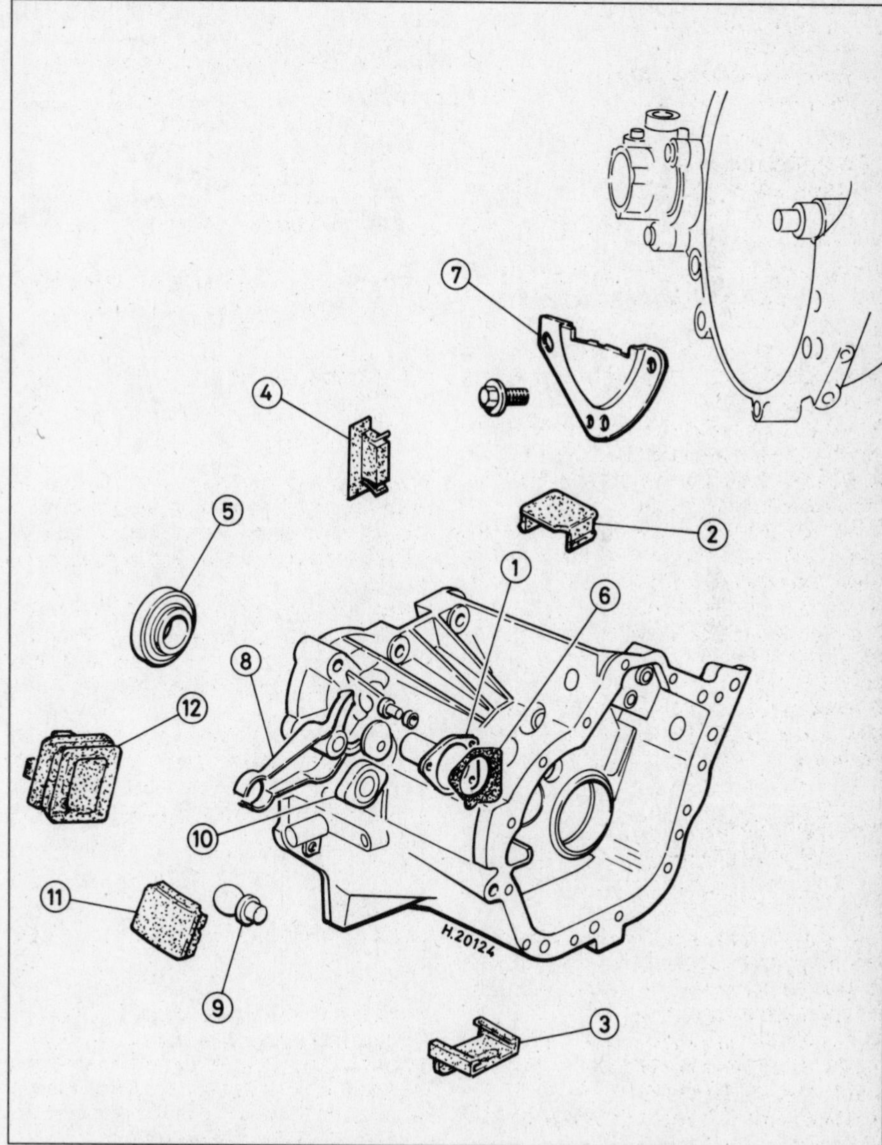

Fig. 5.4 Clutch release mechanism and associated components (Sec 8)

1 Guide sleeve
2 Plug – OHC engine
3 Lower plug – OHC engine
4 Protective boot
5 Gasket
6 Gasket
7 Locking plate
8 Fork lever
9 Ball-stud
10 Seal cap
11 Plug
12 Release fork gaiter

Fault finding - clutch

Judder when taking up drive

- ☐ Loose engine/gearbox mountings
- ☐ Badly worn friction linings or contaminated with oil
- ☐ Worn splines on input shaft or driven plate hub
- ☐ Worn spigot bush in crankshaft flange

Clutch drag (failure to disengage so that gears cannot be meshed)

- ☐ Incorrect cable adjustment
- ☐ Rust on splines (may occur after vehicle standing idle for long periods)
- ☐ Damaged or misaligned pressure plate assembly
- ☐ Cable stretched or broken

Clutch slip (increase in engine speed does not result in increase in vehicle road speed - particularly on gradients)

- ☐ Incorrect cable adjustment
- ☐ Friction linings worn out or oil contaminated

Noise evident on depressing clutch pedal

- ☐ Dry, worn or damaged release bearing
- ☐ Excessive play between drive plate hub splines and shaft splines

Noise evident as clutch pedal released

- ☐ Distorted driven plate
- ☐ Broken or weak driven plate cushion coil springs
- ☐ Release bearing loose on retainer hub

Chapter 6 Transmission

For modifications, and information applicable to later models, see Supplement at end of manual

Contents

Degrees of difficulty

Easy, suitable for novice with little experience 	**Fairly easy,** suitable for beginner with some experience 	**Fairly difficult,** suitable for competent DIY mechanic	**Difficult,** suitable for experienced DIY mechanic 	**Very difficult,** suitable for expert DIY or professional

Specifications

General

Type	Manual gearbox with 4 or 5 forward speeds plus reverse. All forward speeds have synchromesh	
Identification codes:		
4-speed	BE1/4	
5-speed	BE1/5	
Ratios:	**BE1/4**	**BE1/5**
1st	3.31:1	3.31:1
2nd	1.88:1	1.88:1
3rd	1.15:1	1.28:1
4th	0.80:1	0.97:1
5th	0.76:1	
Reverse	3.33:1	3.33:1
Final drive ratios:		
1.1 litre	4.43:1	
1.3 litre	4.06:1	
1.6 litre	3.81:1	

Lubrication

Oil type/specification	Multigrade engine oil, viscosity SAE 10W/40 or 15W/40
Capacity	2.0 litre (3.5 pints)

Torque wrench settings	**Nm**	**lbf ft**
Rear cover bolts (use thread locking compound)	12	9
Input and output shaft nuts	50	37
Rear bearing retainer bolts	15	11
Selector rod backplate bolt	15	11
End casing to main casing bolts	12	9
Reverse idler spindle bolt	20	15
Selector shaft spring bracket	15	11
Reverse selector spindle nut	20	15
Breather	15	11
Reversing lamp switch	25	18
Drain plug (gearbox)	9	7
Drain plug (final drive)	30	22
Speedometer pinion adaptor	12	9
Final drive extension housing bolts	15	11
Crownwheel securing bolts	65	48
Final drive half housing bolts, 10 mm	41	30
Final drive half housing bolts, 7 mm	12	9
Clutch release bearing guide tube bolts	12	9
Mounting stud nut	100	74

1 General description

A four or five-speed gearbox will be fitted depending on the vehicle model. The 5th speed gears of the BE1/5 gearbox are located on the primary and secondary shafts, but otherwise both gearbox types are similar in construction.

The transmission is of conventional two shaft constant-mesh layout. There are four pairs of gears, one for each forward speed. The gears on the primary shaft are fixed to the shaft, while those on the secondary or pinion shaft float, each being locked to the shaft when engaged by the synchromesh unit. The reverse idler gear is on a third shaft.

On five-speed units, the 5th speed gears are of fixed type with an extra synchromesh assembly.

The gear selector forks engage in the synchromesh unit; these slide axially along the shaft to engage the appropriate gear. The forks are mounted on selector shafts which are located in the base of the gearbox.

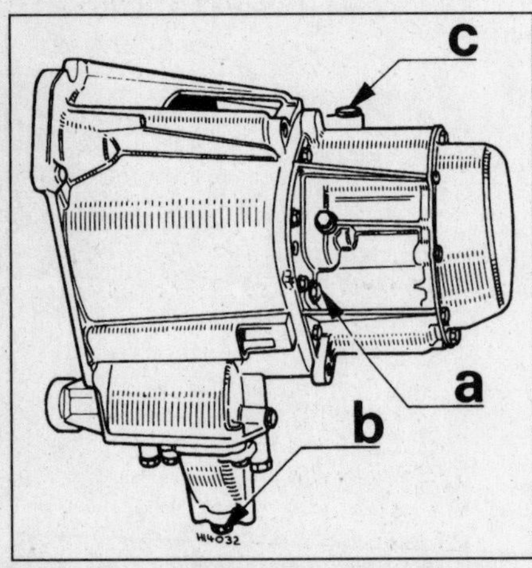

Fig. 6.1 Oil drain and filler plug positions – early 1986 models (Sec 2)

a *Gearbox drain plug*
b *Final drive drain plug*
c *Oil filler plug*

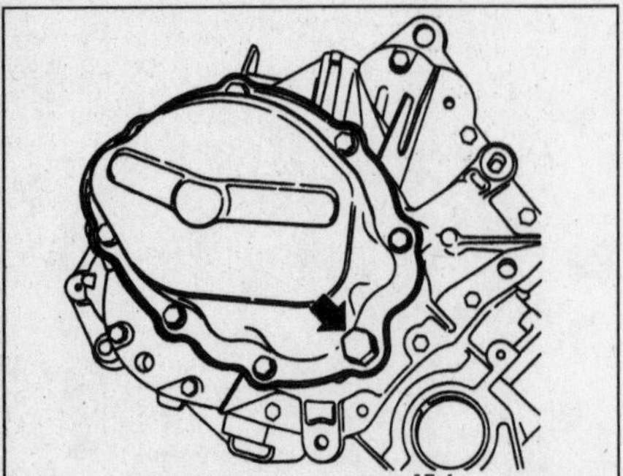

Fig. 6.2 Gearbox/final drive level plug location (arrowed) – 1986 on (Sec 2)

The helical gear on the end of the pinion shaft drives directly onto the crownwheel mounted on the differential unit. The latter differs from normal practice in that it runs in shell bearings and the end play is taken up by thrust washers in a similar manner to the engine crankshaft.

2 Routine maintenance

1 The only regular maintenance required is to change the transmission oil at the specified intervals. The oil level, drain and filler plug locations differ in accordance with the model year and are shown in Figs. 6.1 and 6.2.
2 On earlier models there is no transmission level plug, and to check the level the oil must be drained completely by removing the gearbox and final drive drain plugs, then measuring the total amount drained to see if it complies with the amount specified.
3 When draining later models, the removal of the differential unit drain plug drains both the differential and gearbox housing oils. As a combined level/filler plug is fitted to later models, draining is only necessary when removing the transmission unit or when renewing the transmission oil.
4 When checking the oil level in the transmission on later models with a combined level/filler plug, the oil level must be up to the base of the plug hole.
5 On earlier models, a differential level plug was fitted, but this was deleted with the introduction of the reverse lock mechanism (in early 1986), when the breather location was also changed (Fig. 6.3).
6 Access to the oil drain and filler/level plugs may necessitate the removal of the engine undertray and the side shields.
7 Do not overfill the transmission and use only the specified grade of oil. On completion ensure that the drain and filler plugs are secured to the specified torque wrench settings.
8 On earlier models, where the oil filler plug does not act as a level gauge as well, measure out the required amount of oil before filling.
9 Apart from the regular oil change at the specified intervals the oil should be changed in a new or reconditioned unit after the first 1000 to 1500 miles, and in any unit after detection and rectification of an oil leak.

3 Gearchange linkage - general

1 The gearchange linkage assemblies are shown in Figs. 6.4 and 6.5.
2 The gear selector and engagement rods have balljoint connections. The balljoints can be detached by prising them free from the lever balls, using an open-ended spanner.
3 The balljoints are 'long-life' types and as such require no maintenance, but if gear selection becomes difficult, the joints should be checked for excessive wear, and if necessary renewed.
4 The balljoint at one end of the selector and engagement rod is screwed onto the rod and secured by a locknut. If the balljoint is to be removed at any time, first measure the length of the rod between the balljoint centres and make a note of it. When refitting the balljoint to the rod set it at the distance noted to retain the adjustment and secure with the locknut. When reconnecting the balljoints, the use of self-locking pliers will facilitate the job.
5 Access to the gearlever can be obtained after removing the floor console and gaiter.
6 The gearchange rods should be set to the following lengths (centre-to-centre of ball end fittings)

Engagement rod 283.0 to 285.0 mm
Selection rod 110.0 to 113.0 mm

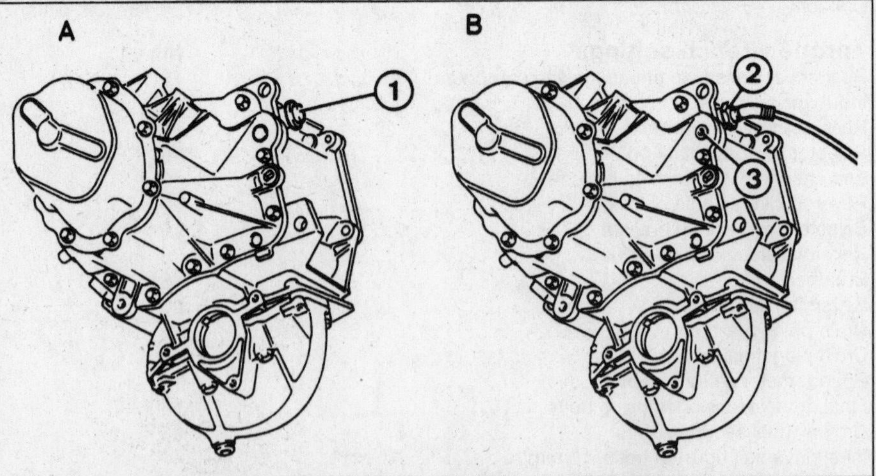

Fig. 6.3 Early (A) and late (B) type gearboxes (Sec 2)

1 Breather *2 Reverse lock mechanism* *3 Breather*

Fig. 6.4 Gearchange selector rods and associated components (Sec 3)

1 Layshaft (pivot bolt)
2 Bush
3 Spring
4 Ball-head screw
5 Bush
6 Snap ring
7 Lever (gear selection)
8 Lever (gearshift passage)
9 Countershaft
10 Protector cap
11 Heat shield
12 Engagement rod
13 Gear selection rod

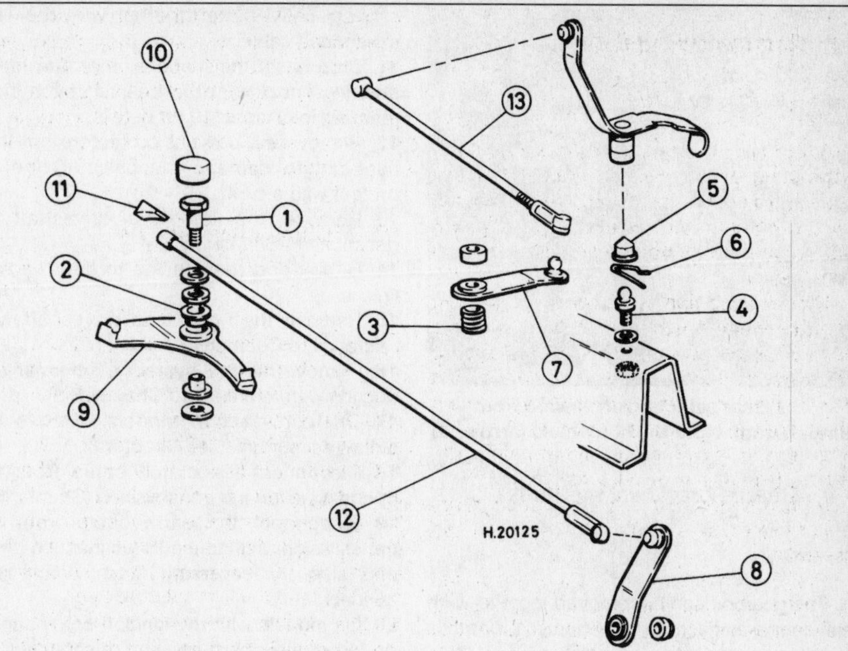

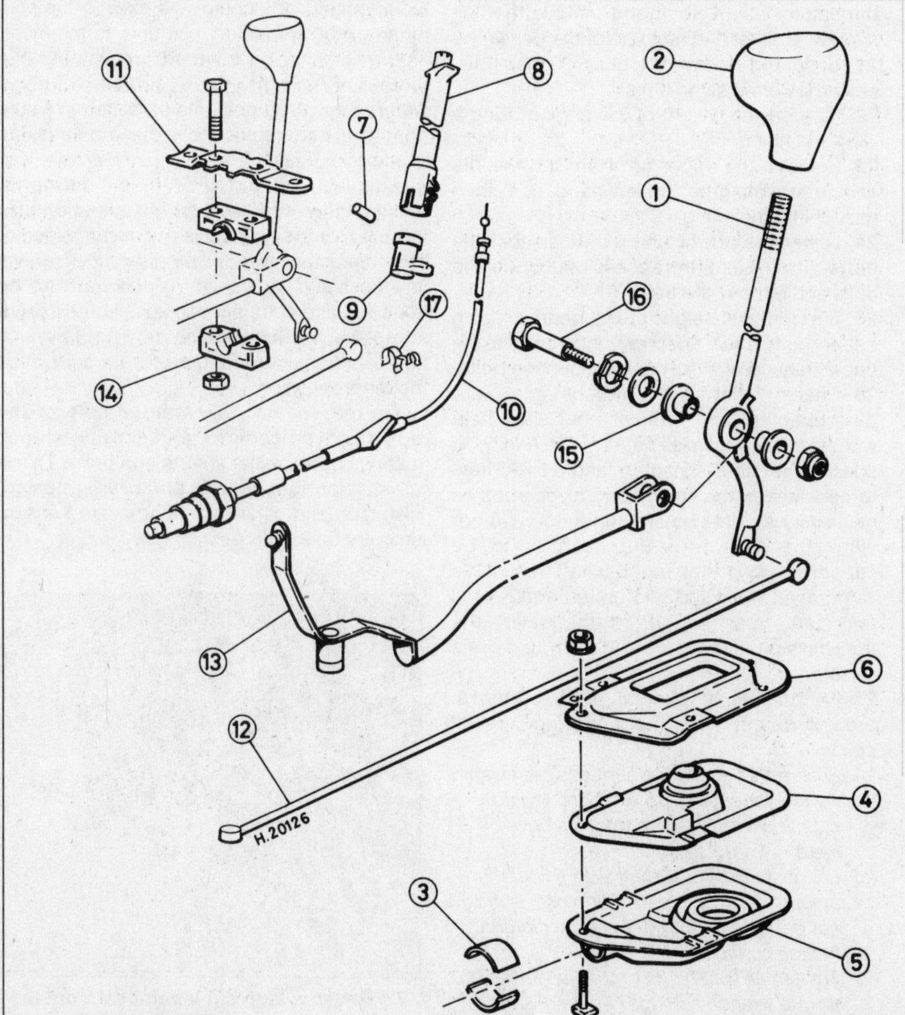

Fig. 6.5 Gear lever and associated components (Sec 3)

1 Gear selector lever
2 Gear lever knob
3 Half-bearing
4 Boot
5 Gasket
6 Plate
7 Rubber dowel
8 Upper sleeve
9 Lower sleeve
10 Reverse stop cable
11 Bearing support
12 Gearshift passage bar
13 Gear selector bar
14 Half-bearing
15 Lever bush
16 Lever shaft
17 Cable support clip

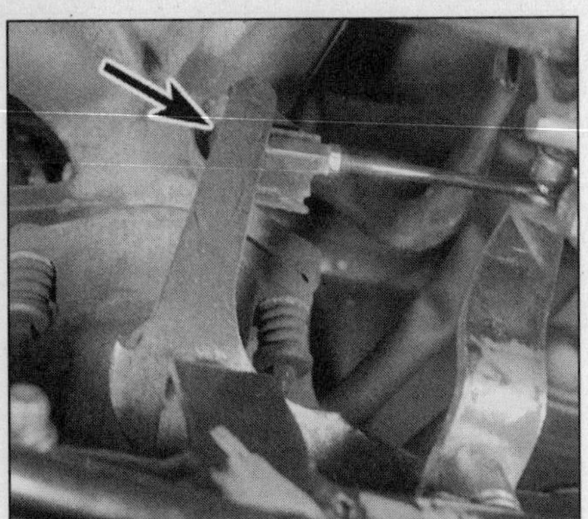

5.7 Gear selector rod viewed from underneath. Note the heatshield (arrowed)

4 Gearbox removal methods

1 The gearbox can be removed together with the engine as described in Chapter 1, or on its own leaving the engine in position.

2 Whichever method is employed. the gearbox will have to be withdrawn from underneath the vehicle and requires the vehicle to be raised at the front end to allow sufficient working clearance.

3 Safety stands will be required to support the vehicle at the front end and the manufacturers recommend that the front suspension be retained with special cables as described in Chapter 9, Section 4.

5 Gearbox - removal and refitting

1 Disconnect the battery earth lead, then the positive lead and remove the battery.

2 Remove the engine undertray and the side shield under the left-hand wheel arch.

3 Drain the transmission oil, with reference to Section 2, then refit the drain plug(s). The oil should be drained into a suitable container for disposal.

4 Retain the suspension strut each side at the front using the Peugeot special tool (see Chapter 9, Section 4).

5 Undo the front hub nut each side, then raise and support the front end of the vehicle on safety stands.

6 Working underneath the vehicle, undo the retaining nuts and detach the exhaust downpipe from the manifold flange.

7 Disconnect the gearchange rod and selector rod from the gearbox by prising free the balljoints (photo).

8 Disconnect the speedometer cable and the reverse stop cable at the gearbox.

9 Remove the starter motor as described in Chapter 12.

10 Unbolt and remove the clutch housing closing (belly) plate together with the TDC sensor and cable.

11 Disconnect the suspension arm from the steering knuckle at the balljoint each side, referring to Chapter 10 for details.

12 Remove the balljoint protectors but take care not to damage the balljoint boots - protect with a cloth.

13 Remove the left-hand driveshaft as described in Chapter 7.

14 Unbolt and remove the torque reaction link.

15 Remove the right-hand driveshaft with reference to Chapter 7.

16 Remove the fuel system air cleaner and ducting with reference to Chapter 3.

17 On fuel injection models, remove the airflow sensor unit (see Chapter 3).

18 Disconnect the clutch cable from the operating lever and transmission (Chapter 5).

19 Disconnect the earth cable from the transmission unit (noting its connection point) and also the reversing light switch wire connector.

20 On models with the ignition coil mounted on top of the clutch housing, disconnect the coil leads and unclip the wiring harness from the battery tray. Unbolt and remove the coil support bracket and refit one of the bolts.

21 Undo and remove the clutch housing-to-engine lower retaining bolts.

22 Support the weight of the engine using a sling and hoist.

23 Remove the upper nut from the flexible engine mounting on the left-hand side, then remove the mounting.

24 Lower the power unit a little so that the battery tray bolts are accessible. Undo the bolts and remove the tray.

25 Support the weight of the gearbox from underneath, then unscrew and remove the upper transmission-to-engine mounting bolts.

26 Check that all attachments are disconnected and out of the way then withdraw the transmission from the engine. If possible get an assistant to lend a hand here to help steady the engine and/or gearbox as necessary as the two are separated. Do not allow the weight of the gearbox to be supported by the input shaft as it is withdrawn. Keep the two units parallel until they are disengaged, then lower the transmission and withdraw it from under the vehicle.

27 Refitting is a reversal of the removal procedure but note the following special points.

(a) Ensure that all mating surfaces are clean

(b) Renew the drain plug washers, Nylstop nuts, lockwashers and the final drive oil seals

(c) Lubricate the input shaft with a liberal amount of Molykote 321R grease, but do not get grease onto or near the clutch friction surfaces

(d) Tighten all fastenings to their specified torque wrench settings (where given)

(e) Do not remove the engine support hoist until the engine and transmission units are securely located

(f) Refer to Chapter 7 when refitting the driveshafts

(g) Refer to Chapter 10 when refitting the lower suspension arm to the left-hand steering knuckle

28 On completion top up the gearbox/final drive oil level with the specified grade and quantity of oil (see Section 2).

6 Gearbox - preliminary overhaul notes

Although the transmission system employed is relatively simple, a few words of warning must be stressed before any inexperienced dismantlers start work to make sure that they know what they are letting themselves in for.

First of all decide whether the fault you wish to repair is worth the time and effort involved. Secondly bear in mind that, if the transmission is well worn, then the cost of the necessary component parts could well exceed the cost of an exchange factory unit and, furthermore, you will get a guaranteed job without the bother of having to do it yourself. Thirdly, if you are intent on doing it yourself, make sure that you understand how the transmission works.

Special care must be taken during all dismantling and assembly operations to ensure that the housing is not overstressed or distorted in any way. When dismantled, check the cost and availability of the parts to be renewed and compare this against the cost of a replacement unit, which may not be much more expensive and therefore would be a better proposition.

On reassembly, take careful note of the tightening procedures and torque wrench settings of the relevant nuts and bolts. This is most important to prevent overtightening, distortion and oil leakage, and also to ensure smooth, trouble-free running of the unit.

7.1 Reverse stop cable removal from the gearbox

7 Reverse stop cable - removal and refitting

1 At the gearbox end of the cable, undo the black plastic retainer and detach the cable from the gearbox (photo).

2 Working within the car, undo the two screws and remove the floor console away from the gear lever, (tilt it to one side).

3 Disconnect the reverse stop cable from the gear lever by detaching the nipple (photo).

4 Loosen the nuts securing the lower support plate to the floor, lift the plate and remove the cable by pulling it through into the engine compartment.

5 Refit in reverse, passing the cable under the floor carpet and support plate and attach it to the gearbox reverse stop release sleeve. Screw the front end of the cable into the gearbox and then check for satisfactory operation before refitting the console.

7.3 Reverse stop cable nipple and outer cable clip on gear lever (arrowed)

Fault finding - transmission

Weak or ineffective synchromesh

- ☐ Synchromesh units worn, or damaged

Excessive noise

- ☐ Incorrect grade of oil or oil level too low
- ☐ Gearteeth excessively worn or damaged
- ☐ Intermediate gear thrust washers worn allowing excessive end play
- ☐ Worn bearings

Jumps out of gear

- ☐ Gearchange mechanism worn
- ☐ Synchromesh units badly worn
- ☐ Selector fork badly worn

Difficulty in engaging gears

- ☐ Clutch pedal adjustment incorrect
- ☐ Worn selector components
- ☐ Worn synchromesh units

Notes

Chapter 7 Driveshafts

For modifications, and information applicable to later models, see Supplement at end of manual

Contents

Degrees of difficulty

Easy, suitable for novice with little experience 	**Fairly easy,** suitable for beginner with some experience 	**Fairly difficult,** suitable for competent DIY mechanic 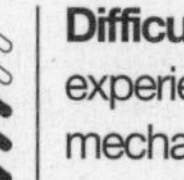	**Difficult,** suitable for experienced DIY mechanic 	**Very difficult,** suitable for expert DIY or professional

Specifications

Type .... Open, with constant velocity joint at each end. Right-hand driveshaft has intermediate bearing

Torque wrench settings	**Nm**	**lbf ft**
Front hub nut	265	196
Lower suspension balljoint	35	26
Right-hand intermediate bearing bolt	18	13

1 General description

Drive to the front wheels is transmitted from the final drive unit to the front hubs by two driveshafts. The driveshafts incorporate inner and outer joints to accommodate suspension and steering angular movement.

The inner ends of the driveshafts are splined to the final drive/differential side gears, and the outer ends are splined to the front hubs.

The right-hand driveshaft is longer than the left-hand driveshaft and it has additional support by means of an intermediate bearing carried in a support bracket bolted to the engine.

2 Routine maintenance

Carry out the following procedures at the intervals given in Routine Maintenance at the beginning of the manual.

1 Jack up the front of the car and support on axle stands. Apply the handbrake.

2 Thoroughly examine the rubber bellows at each end of the driveshafts for splitting, damage and grease leakage (photo). If evident the bellows will need renewal, refer to Chapter 13.

3 Check the right-hand driveshaft intermediate housing for excessive wear by attempting to move the driveshaft up and down. Also turn the right-hand wheel and listen for excessive noise which would indicate pitted tracks or balls. Renew the bearing if necessary.

4 If the driveshaft joints are excessively noisy, perhaps more noticeable when turning corners, renew the driveshaft or obtain an exchange unit.

3 Driveshafts - removal and refitting

1 Unclip and remove the engine/gearbox undershield.

2 Place a container beneath the gearbox and final drive casing then remove the drain plug(s) and drain the oil. Clean the drain plugs then refit and tighten them (refer to Section 2 in Chapter 6).

3 Fully apply the handbrake then remove the roadwheel trim on the side concerned and loosen the hub nut. Do not apply the footbrake when loosening the hub nut as damage can occur to the brake disc retaining screws.

4 If available fit Peugeot special retaining cables to the front suspension strut(s), as described in Chapter 9. Although not absolutely necessary they do ease the driveshaft removal and refitting procedures by restraining the suspension movement when the vehicle is raised.

5 Raise the car so that the roadwheels are clear of the ground and to provide a suitable working clearance underneath. Support the vehicle on safety stands.

6 Unscrew the clamp bolt securing the front suspension lower balljoint to the bottom of the hub carrier then pull the lower suspension arm down from the carrier. **Do not** lever the clamp slot open to separate the suspension arm from the carrier. As they are separated, take care not to damage the driveshaft bellows (gaiters). If the Peugeot retaining cables mentioned in paragraph 4 were not fitted, it may be necessary to unbolt the suspension arm at its inner pivot to allow the lower arm balljoint clamp to be separated from the carrier.

2.2 Examine the driveshaft rubber bellows

Fig. 7.1 Special oil seal protector for use when renewing the final drive housing right-hand oil seal (Sec 3)

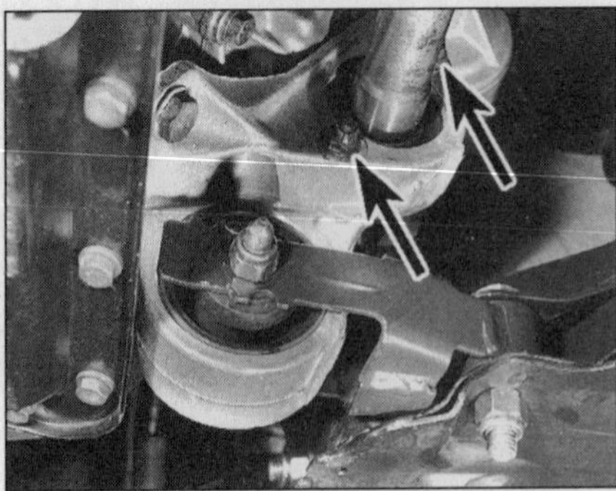

3.12 Right-hand driveshaft intermediate bearing and retaining nuts (arrowed)

3.14 Right-hand driveshaft removal from the wheel hub

7 Unbolt the balljoint guard plate from the hub carrier.

Left-hand driveshaft

8 Turn the front wheels to full right-hand lock, and remove the hub nut.

9 Pull the hub carrier outwards and at the same time withdraw the outer end of the driveshaft from the hub.

10 Withdraw the inner end of the driveshaft from the final drive unit.

11 Note that the weight of the car **must not** be taken by the front wheels with the driveshaft(s) removed otherwise damage may occur to the hub bearings.

Right-hand driveshaft

12 Loosen the two nuts retaining the intermediate bearing in the bracket bolted to the rear of the cylinder block, then turn the bolts so that their heads move through 90° (photo).

13 Turn the front wheels to full left-hand lock, and remove the hub nut.

14 Pull the hub carrier outwards and at the same time withdraw the outer end of the driveshaft from the hub (photo).

15 Withdraw the inner end of the driveshaft from the final drive unit and guide it through the intermediate bearing bracket.

16 Note the caution given in paragraph 11.

3.18 Stake punch the hub nut to lock it

Both driveshafts

17 With the driveshafts removed, the opportunity should be taken to renew the oil seal in the final drive housing. To do this, prise out the old seal and wipe clean the recess. Fill the space between the new oil seal lips with grease then use a suitable block of wood to tap it into the housing. The right-hand oil seal should be flush with the housing, but the left-hand oil seal recessed. Fit the special protector to the right-hand oil seal (Fig. 7.1).

18 Refitting is a reversal of removal, but tighten all nuts and bolts to the specified torque. When refitting the right-hand driveshaft, make sure that the lugs on the intermediate bearing bolt heads are located over the bearing outer track, and after tightening the nuts remove the special protector from the oil seal. After tightening the hub nut lock it by staking the shoulder into the groove on the end of the driveshaft (photo).

19 Remove the strut retainer(s) (if fitted).

20 Check that the gearbox/final drive drain plug(s) are securely fitted, then top up the gearbox and final drive oil with reference to Section 2 in Chapter 6.

4 Driveshaft intermediate bearing - renewal

1 Refer to the previous Section and remove the right-hand driveshaft.

2 Undo the retaining bolts and remove the torque reaction link.

3 Unbolt and remove the engine mounting/intermediate bearing carrier. If the bearing did not come away with the driveshaft, press it and its sealing ring out of the carrier.

4 Fit the new bearing and sealing ring, refit the carrier and the driveshaft. Tighten all fastenings to the specified torque, using new nuts on the steering and suspension balljoints.

5 Refit the torque reaction link.

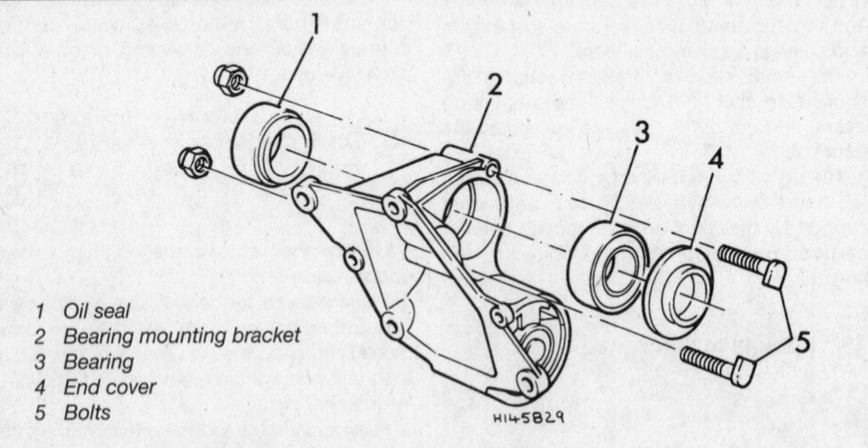

Fig. 7.2 Driveshaft intermediate bearing components (Sec 4)

Fault finding - driveshafts

Knocking noise, particularly on full lock

☐ Worn driveshaft joints

Metallic grating, varying with roadspeed

☐ Worn intermediate bearing on the right-hand driveshaft

Chapter 8 Braking system

For modifications, and information applicable to later models, see Supplement at end of manual

Contents

Degrees of difficulty

Easy, suitable for novice with little experience 	**Fairly easy,** suitable for beginner with some experience 	**Fairly difficult,** suitable for competent DIY mechanic	**Difficult,** suitable for experienced DIY mechanic	**Very difficult,** suitable for expert DIY or professional

Specifications

Type	Front disc brakes, rear drum brakes, (self-adjusting). Servo assistance on all models. Rear brake compensator. Cable-operate handbrake on rear wheels
Brake fluid type/specification	Hydraulic fluid to SAE J1703C

Disc brakes

Disc diameter	247 mm (9.72 in)
Disc thickness	10 mm (0.39 in)
Minimum disc thickness (after regrind)	8.5 mm (0.335 in)
Maximum disc run-out	0.07 mm (0.0028 in)
Caliper type	DBA (IV) or Girling
Front brake cylinder diameter	48 mm (1.89 in)
Disc pad wear limit	2 mm (0.08 in)

Rear drum brakes

Drum diameter	180 mm (7.09 in)
Maximum drum Internal diameter (after regrind)	181.0 mm (7.13 m)
Lining width	40 mm (1.57 in)
Lining thickness:	
New	5 mm (0.20 in)
Wear limit	1 mm (0.04 in)
Rear wheel cylinder diameter:	
OHV engine models	17.5 mm (0.69 in)
OHC engine models	22.0 mm (0.87 in)
Brake compensator type	DBA or Automotive Products (fixed)

Master cylinder

Type	DBA Bendix or ATE Teves
Bore diameter	19 mm (0.75 in)
Stroke	30 mm (1.18 in)

Servo unit

Pushrod-to-master cylinder mounting face	22.3 mm (0.88 in)
Pushrod length - servo-to-clevis eye (at brake pedal)	88.0 mm (3.46 in)
Servo unit diameter	177.8 mm (7.00 in)

Torque wrench settings

	Nm	lbf ft
Rear wheel hub nut	215	159
Caliper mounting bolts:		
Girling	97	72
DBA	120	88

8

1 General description

The braking system is of hydraulic type with discs on the front and drums on the rear. The handbrake is cable-operated on the rear wheels.

The hydraulic circuit is of two independent sections so that, in the event of the failure of one section, the remaining section is still functional. The master cylinder has a primary and secondary barrel; the primary operating the rear brakes, the secondary the front brakes, thus splitting the hydraulic circuit operation front and rear.

A compensating valve fitted to some models reduces the hydraulic pressure to the rear brakes under heavy applications of the brake pedal in order to prevent rear wheel lock-up.

A vacuum servo unit is fitted to all models, and is mounted between the master cylinder and engine compartment bulkhead.

Precautions

All work undertaken on the braking system, including routine maintenance, must be to the highest standard. It is vitally important to maintain the integrity of the system and to use the right fasteners with correct locking devices where appropriate. Adjustments must be within specified limits where these apply and spare parts must be new or in faultless condition. Absolute cleanliness when assembling hydraulic components is essential. New seals and fresh hydraulic fluid must be used and any fluid drained or removed from the system must be discarded. Remember that your life and possibly the lives of others could depend on these points; if you are in any doubt at all concerning what to do or how to do it, get professional advice or have the job done by an expert.

If the brake system tell-tale warning light comes on and the handbrake is not applied, immediately check the level of the brake fluid. If the level is satisfactory check the setting of the handbrake warning switch.

2 Routine maintenance

Carry out the following procedures at the intervals given in Routine Maintenance.

1 Thoroughly clean the external surfaces of the reservoir and its filler cap. The reservoir is made of semi-transparent plastic and the fluid can be seen without removing the cap. However, you should only rely on this check once you have satisfied yourself that an accurate indication of the fluid level is possible. If necessary top up with fresh fluid, but make allowances for the change in level that will occur when the cap, with its switch and float, is refitted. The level in the reservoir will rise to some extent due to displacement by the switch assembly. Check that the vent hole in the filler cap is clear. Any need for regular topping-up must be viewed with suspicion and the whole hydraulic system inspected for signs of leaks. A *small,* slow fall in the level as the disc pads wear is normal.

2 Inspect the front disc pads for wear (see Section 3). The wear indication grooves in the pads should be visible, indicating that adequate pad material remains.

3 Remove the rubber inspection plugs in the rear brake backplates and inspect the shoe linings for wear. All four shoes will need renewing if the thickness of any one lining is below 1.0 mm (0.04 in) (photo).

4 Check the operation of the handbrake. The brakes should lock the wheels when the lever has been moved six to eight notches.

5 Check the clearance between the brake foot pedal and the floor when the brakes are applied, to make sure that the pedal is not bottoming.

6 Examine the hydraulic circuit lines and hoses for damage and deterioration, and for any signs of leakage. There is no need to retighten union nuts as this may distort the sealing faces.

7 Renew the brake fluid at the specified intervals.

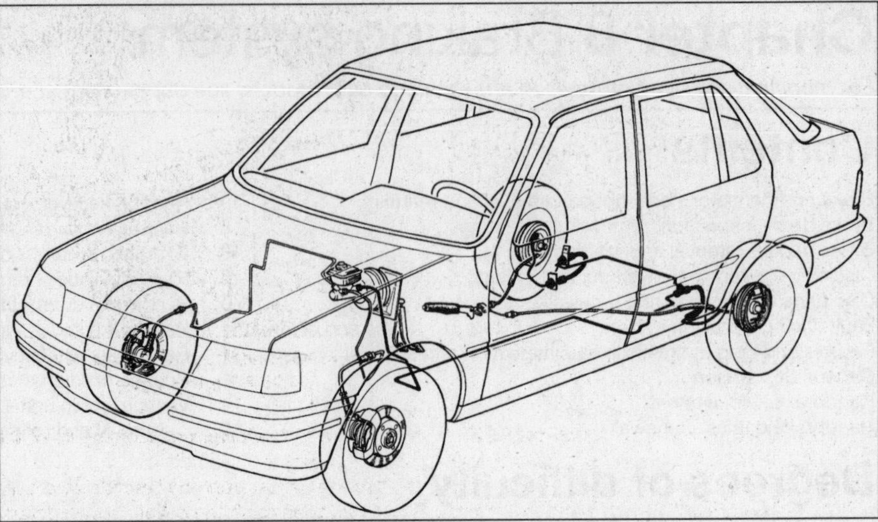

Fig. 8.1 Braking system layout (LH drive model) (Sec 1)

3 Disc pads - inspection and renewal

1 Jack up the front of the car and support on axle stands. Apply the handbrake and remove the roadwheels.

2 If the friction material has worn down to 2.0 mm (0.08 in) (this is indicated if the groove in the pad has disappeared) then the pads must be renewed as an axle set. The removal and refitting operations will vary according to the type of caliper, but first reduce the fluid level in the reservoir to allow for displacement of fluid when the pistons are pushed back into their calipers. Syphon a small amount of fluid from the reservoir but do not spill the hydraulic fluid on paintwork or fittings. Wipe any spillage of fluid clean. Do not allow the fluid reservoir to be emptied.

DBA Bendix disc caliper

3 Remove the clip from the end of the upper sliding key (photo). Disconnect the pad wear wiring as necessary (photo).

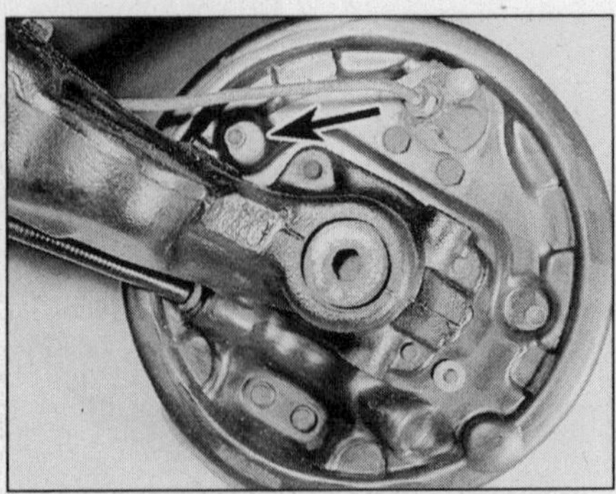

2.3 Inspection plug location in rear brake backplate (arrowed)

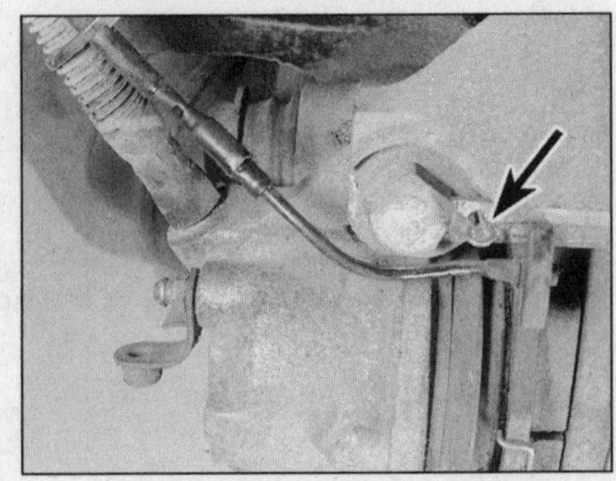

3.3A Pad sliding key clip-arrowed (DBA Bendix type)

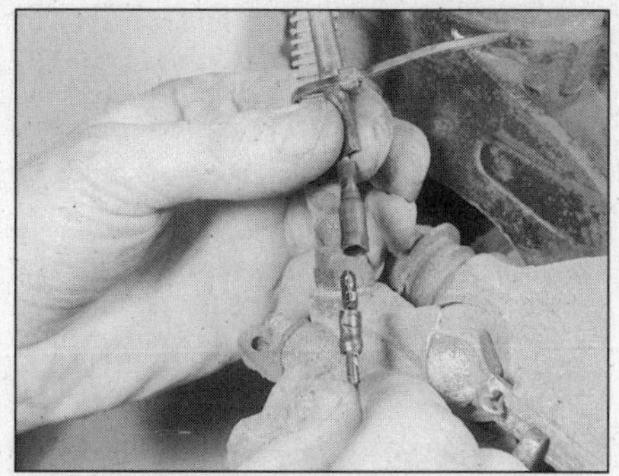
3.3B Disconnecting the pad wear wiring (DBA Bendix type)

3.4 Remove the pad sliding key (DBA Bendix type)

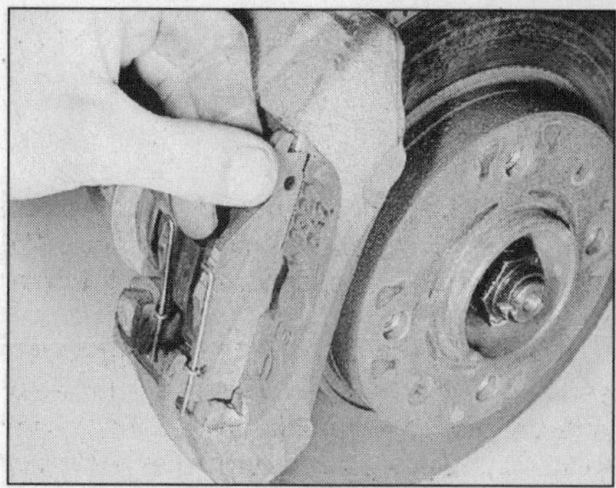
3.5 Remove the outer pad

4 Pull out the upper sliding key (photo).

5 Using a lever against the front suspension strut, push the cylinder towards the brake disc so that the outer pad can be withdrawn from the caliper (photo).

6 Push back the caliper and withdraw the inner pad (photo).

7 Clean away all dust and dirt from the caliper. **Do not** inhale the dust, as it may be injurious to health. Check for brake fluid leakage around the piston dust seal and, if evident, overhaul the caliper, as described later in the Chapter. Check the brake disc for wear and also check that the rubber bellows on the cylinder sliding rods are in good condition.

8 Clean the backs of the disc pads and apply a little anti-squeal brake grease. Also apply the grease to the lower pad locating lip of the caliper (photo).

9 With the caliper pushrod inwards, insert the inner pad then push the caliper outwards and insert the outer pad.

10 Check that the pads are correctly located on the caliper lip (photo) then tap in the upper sliding key to lock them. Fit a new sliding key clip.

Girling disc caliper

11 Extract the spring clips and tap out the pad retaining pins. Disconnect the pad wear wiring as necessary. Release the pad anti-knock spring (photos).

12 Lever the cylinder outwards and withdraw the outer pad then push in the caliper and withdraw the inner pad (photos).

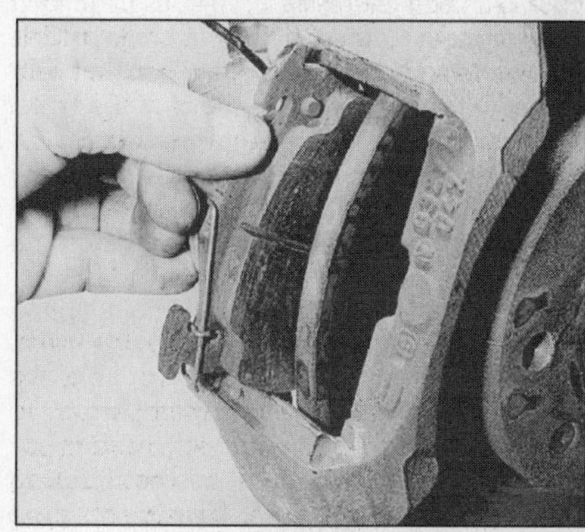
3.6 Remove the inner pad

3.8 Applying anti-squeal brake grease to the pad locating lip on the caliper

3.10 Correct location of the anti-rattle clips on the disc pads (DBA Bendix type)

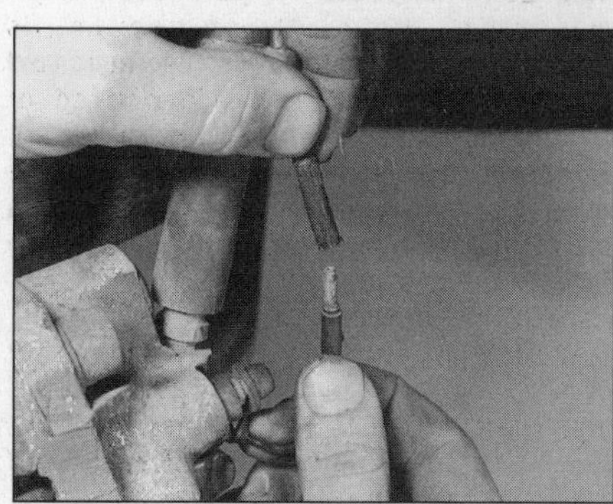
3.11A Disconnecting the pad wear wiring (Girling type)

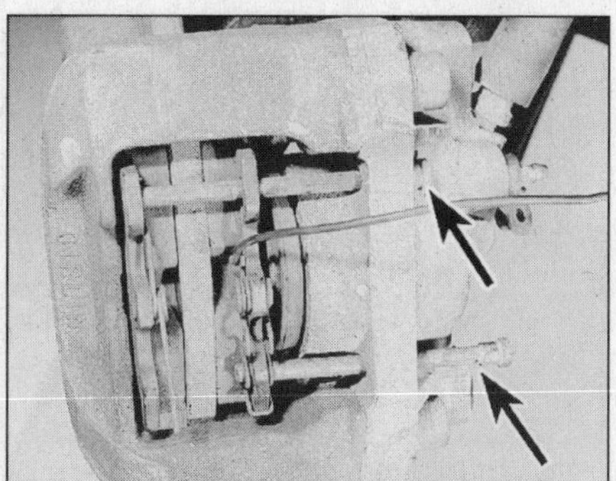

3.11B Withdraw the pad retaining pins (Girling type)

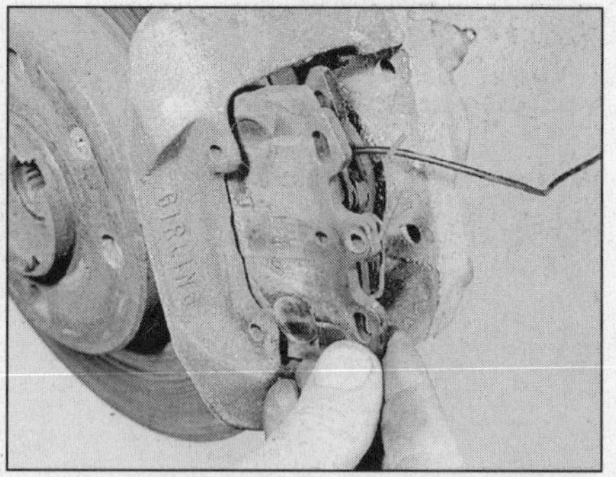

3.12A Remove the outer pad (Girling type)

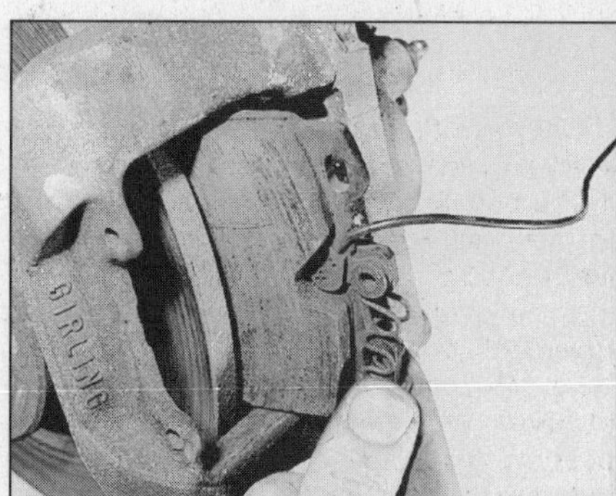

3.12B Remove the inner pad (Girling type)

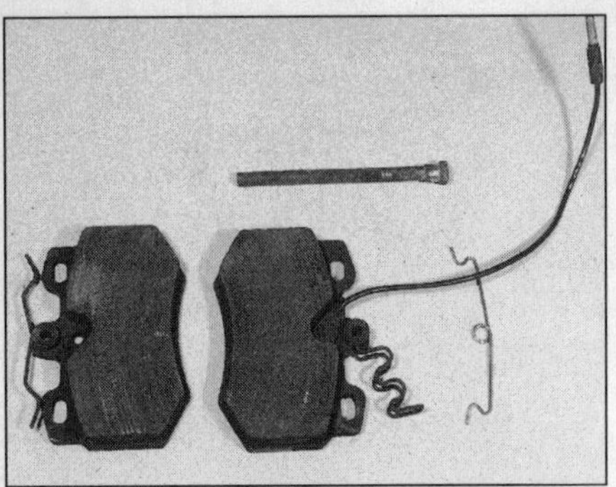

3.12C Pads, springs and retaining pins removed for inspection (Girling type)

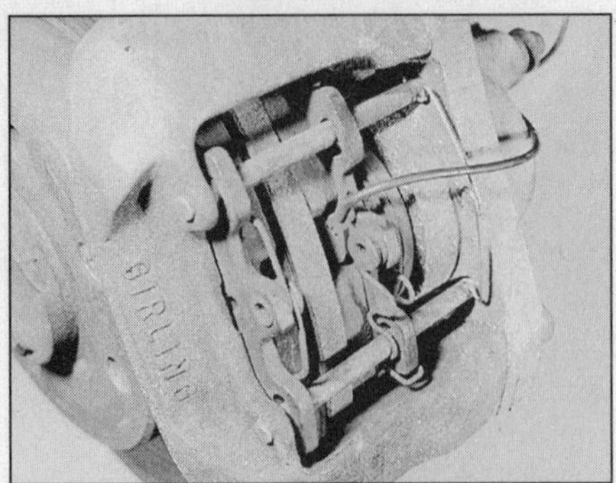

3.15 Reassembled brake pads (Girling type)

13 Clean and check the caliper, as described in paragraph 7, then clean the backs of the disc pads and apply a little anti-squeal brake grease.

14 With the caliper pushed inwards, insert the inner pad then push the caliper outwards and insert the outer pad.

15 Tap in the pad retaining pins and fit the spring clips (photo).

16 Where fitted, hook the anti-knock spring on the lower pad retaining pin (Fig. 8.2).

DBA Bendix and Girling disc calipers

17 Repeat the operations on the opposite disc caliper.

18 Apply the footbrake several times to position the pads against the discs.

19 Top up the master cylinder reservoir to its correct level.

20 Refit the roadwheels and lower the car to the ground.

21 The new pads supplied by Peugeot are special in that they have an abrasive top surface skin. The object of the thin abrasive coating is to clean the surface of the discs and remove any minor imperfections in their friction surfaces during the initial braking applications. These brake pads require careful running in, ideally as follows:-

(a) *For the first three miles (5 km), drive at low speeds and apply the brakes intermittently under a light pressure*

(b) *During the first 120 miles (200 km) of use, avoid (where possible) any heavy or prolonged braking*

4 Rear brake shoes - inspection and renewal

DBA or Girling type rear brakes may be fitted. The two types are shown in Figs. 8.3 and 8.4. The photos which accompany this Section show the DBA type. The inspection and renewal procedures for both types are similar, but where differences occur they are described.

1 Jack up the rear of the car and support it on axle stands. Chock the front wheels and release the handbrake.

2 The lining thickness may be checked without removing the drums/hubs. Pull out the rubber plugs from the backplates by the handbrake cables and use a torch, if necessary, to check the lining thickness (photo 2.3). If it is at or near the specified minimum remove the drums and make a more thorough inspection.

3 Remove the rear roadwheels.

4 Tap off the grease cap, taking care not to damage its outer lip, then unscrew the staked nut from the end of the stub axle and remove the washer (photos). Should the stub axle rotate within the trailing arm, hold it stationary with a 12 mm splined key on the inner end (photo).

5 Withdraw the hub/drum from the stub axle. If difficulty is experienced, due to the shoes wearing grooves in the drum, proceed as follows according to type.

DBA: Insert a screwdriver through one of the wheel bolt holes and depress the handbrake

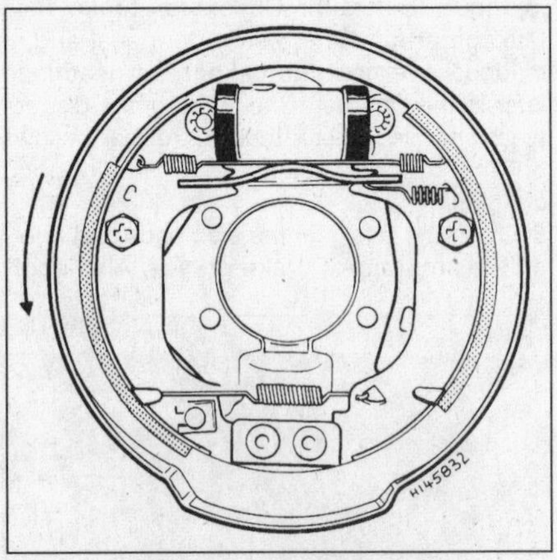

Fig. 8.3 Diagram of the DBA Bendix type rear brake (Sec 4)

Arrow indicates wheel rotation

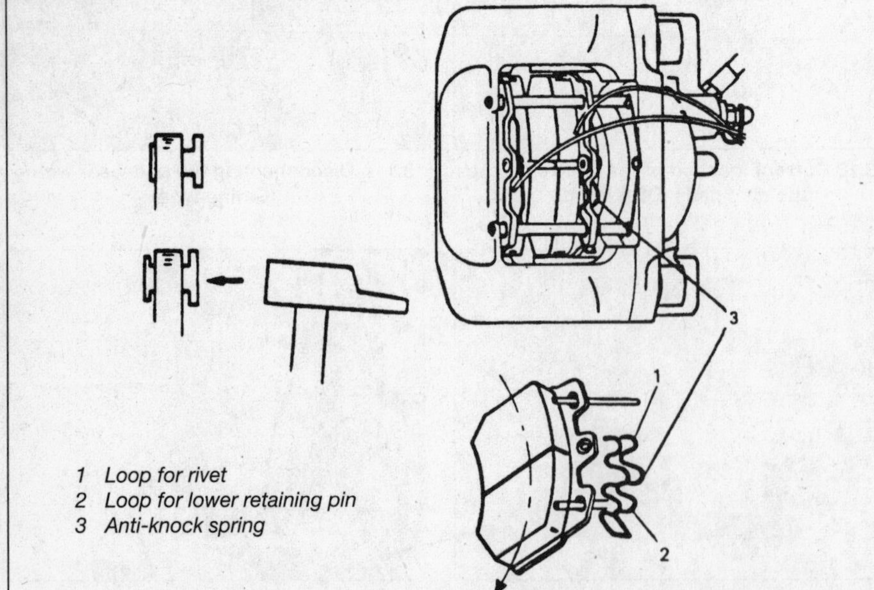

Fig. 8.2 Method of fitting anti-knock spring to Girling inner disc pad (Sec 3)

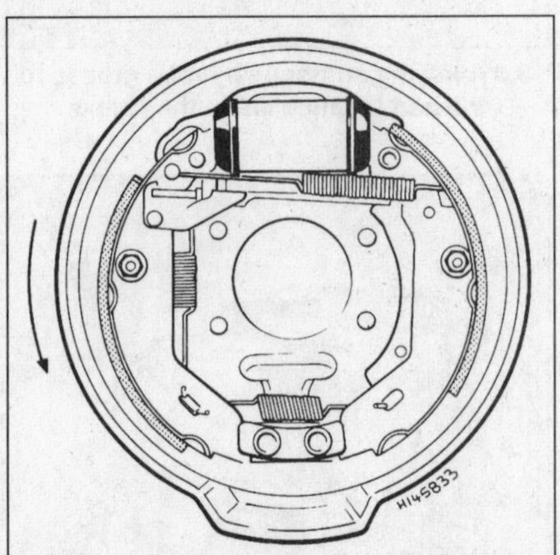

Fig. 8.4 Diagram of the Girling type rear brake (Sec 4)

Arrow indicates wheel rotation

4.4A Prise free the grease cap . . .

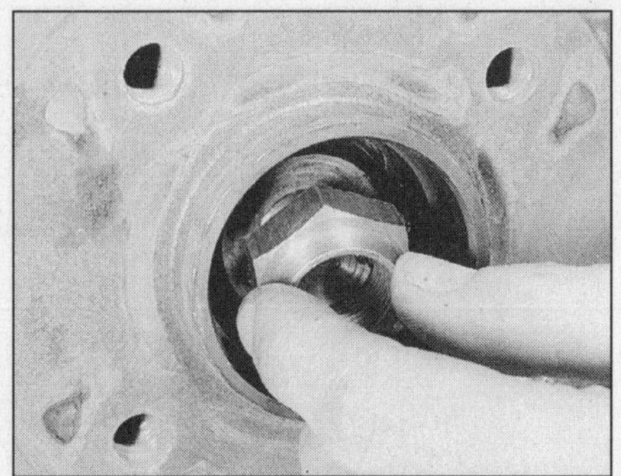
4.4B . . . then unscrew the staked nut . . .

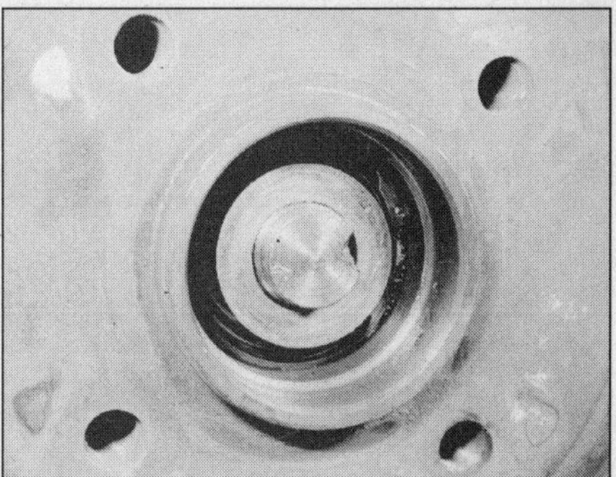
4.4C . . . and remove the washer

lever on the rear brake shoe so that it slides back behind the shoe (photos).

Girling: Insert a punch through one of the wheel bolt holes and drive out the roll pin from the handbrake lever (Fig. 8.5). With the brake shoes retracted the hub/drum can be withdrawn. Lay the drum down so that the hub oil seal faces upwards (if faced downwards it could be damaged) .

6 Brush the dust and dirt from the shoes, backplate and drum. **Do not** inhale it, as it may be injurious to health.

7 It is now possible to inspect both shoe linings for wear. If either is worn down the specified minimum amount, renew them both.

8 Note the position of each shoe and the location of the return and steady springs (photos).

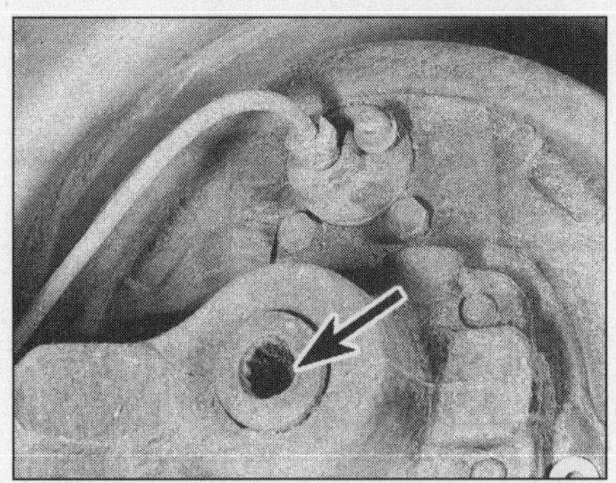
4.4D Inner end of rear stub axle (arrowed) which can be held with a splined key

9 Unhook and remove the upper return spring (photo).

10 Remove the steady springs using pliers to depress the outer cups and turn them through 90° (photo). Remove the pins from the backplate.

4.5A Insert a screwdriver through the wheel bolt hole . . .

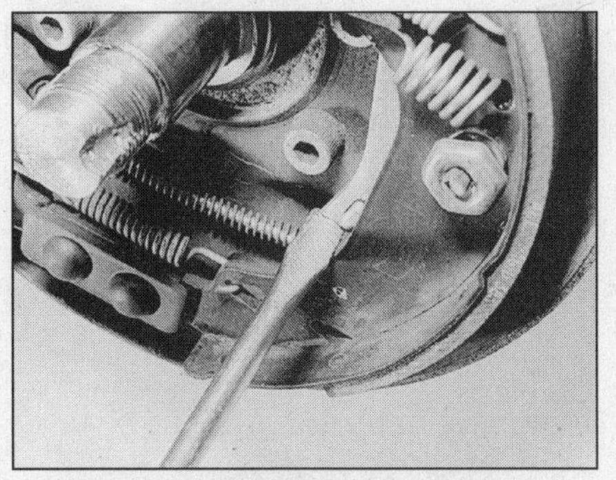
4.5B . . . and push the handbrake lever behind the shoe (DBA Bendix type)

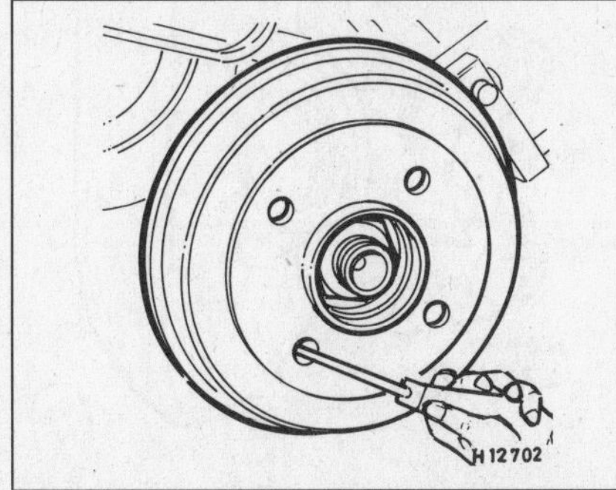

Fig. 8.5 Roll pin removal from the handbrake lever on the Girling drum brake (Sec 4)

4.8A Rear brake assembly – DBA type

4.8B Rear brake assembly – Girling type

4.9 Upper return spring location

4.10 Shoe steady spring (arrowed)

4.11 Automatic adjuster lever (arrowed) and bottom return spring location

4.24A Tighten the rear hub nut . . .

4.24B . . . then stake it to the stub axle

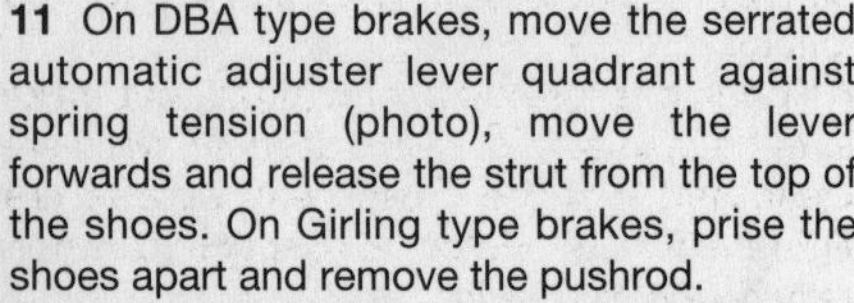

11 On DBA type brakes, move the serrated automatic adjuster lever quadrant against spring tension (photo), move the lever forwards and release the strut from the top of the shoes. On Girling type brakes, prise the shoes apart and remove the pushrod.

12 Expand the shoes over the wheel cylinder then release them from the bottom anchor.

13 Unhook the lever return spring and the handbrake cable.

14 If necessary, position a rubber band over the wheel cylinder to prevent the pistons coming out. Should there be evidence of brake fluid leakage from the wheel cylinder, renew it or overhaul it, as described in Section 7.

15 Transfer the handbrake and automatic adjuster levers to the new shoes as required. Note that the levers and strut on each rear wheel are different, and that the leading and trailing shoes are fitted with different grade linings. On Girling types, ensure that the roll pin is refitted to the handbrake operating lever (the pin acts as a stop).

16 Place the shoes on the bench in their correct location and fit the lower return spring.

17 Apply brake grease sparingly to the metal contact points of the shoes, then position them on the backplate and reconnect the handbrake cable. Locate the shoe ends on the bottom anchor.

18 Engage the strut with the slots at the top of the shoes, making sure it is located correctly on the automatic adjuster lever. Engage the upper shoe ends on the wheel cylinder pistons.

19 Insert the steady spring pins in the backplate and through the shoe webs, then fit the springs and outer cups.

20 Fit the upper return spring.

21 Move the serrated automatic adjuster lever quadrant against the spring tension to set the shoes at their minimum diameter.

22 Check that the handbrake lever on the rear brake shoe is positioned with the lug on the edge of the shoe web and not behind the shoe.

23 Fit the hub/drum on the stub axle and retain with the washer and nut. Always renew the nut.

24 Tighten the nut to the specified torque then lock it by staking the nut flange into the groove on the stub axle (photos).

25 Tap the grease cap into the hub/drum.

26 Repeat all the operations on the opposite rear brake then refit the roadwheels and lower the car to the ground.

27 Apply the footbrake several times to set the shoes in their adjusted position.

28 Adjust the handbrake, as described in Section 14.

5 Disc caliper - removal, overhaul and refitting

1 Remove the disc pads, as described in Section 3.

2 Fit a brake hose clamp to the flexible hose connected to the caliper. Alternatively remove the brake fluid reservoir filler cap and tighten it

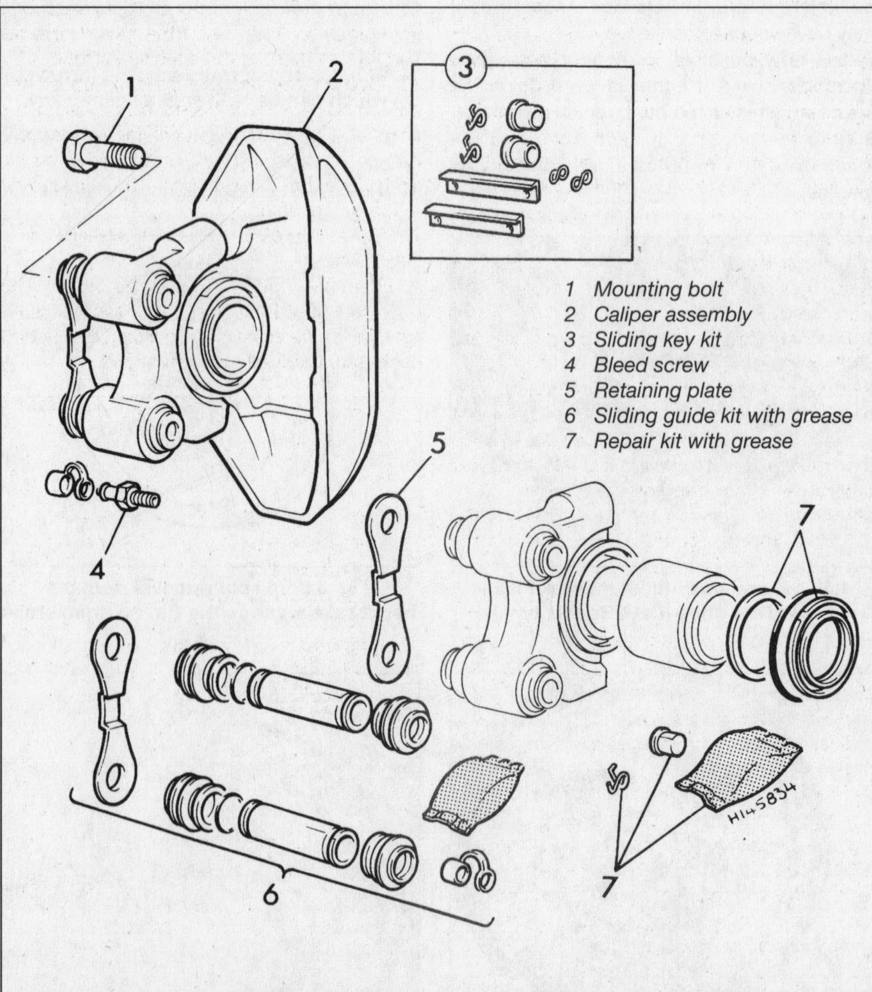

Fig. 8.6 Bendix type disc caliper components (Sec 5)

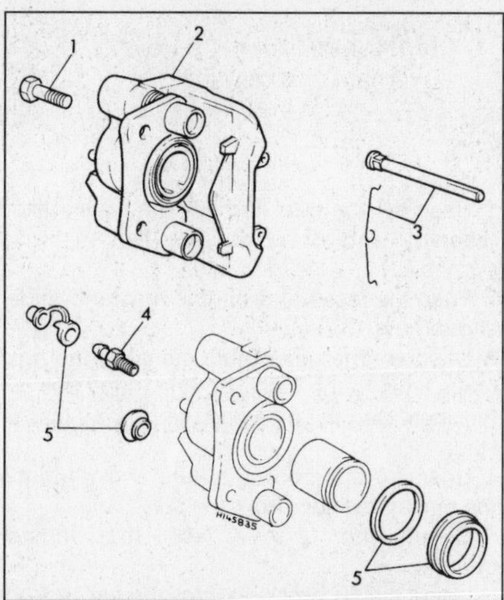

Fig. 8.7 Girling type disc caliper components (Sec 5)

1 Mounting bolt
2 Caliper assembly
3 Pad retaining pin and spring
4 Bleed screw
5 Repair kit

down onto a piece of polythene sheeting to reduce the loss of fluid when disconnecting the caliper.

3 Loosen the flexible hose union connection at the caliper.

4 Unscrew the two mounting bolts, withdraw the caliper from the disc then unscrew the caliper from the flexible hose. Plug the hose to prevent loss of fluid.

5 Clean the exterior of the caliper.

6 On the DBA type, unbolt the caliper frame from the cylinder.

7 Prise the dust cover and ring from the end of the piston.

8 Withdraw the piston from the cylinder. If necessary use air pressure from a foot pump in the fluid inlet to force the piston out.

9 Prise the seal from inside the cylinder, taking care not to damage the cylinder wall.

10 If required, dismantle the sliding guides. On the DBA type, unbolt the endplate from the guides and remove the rubber dust covers. Keep the guides identified for location.

11 Clean all the components using methylated spirit or clean brake fluid then examine them for wear and damage. Check the piston and cylinder surfaces for scoring, excessive wear and corrosion, and if evident renew the complete caliper assembly. Similarly check the sliding guides. If the components are in good condition obtain a repair kit which will contain all the necessary rubber seals and other renewable items.

12 Dip the new seal in fresh brake fluid then locate it in the cylinder groove using the fingers only to manipulate it.

13 Dip the piston in brake fluid and insert it in the cylinder, twisting it as necessary to locate it in the seal.

6.3 Disc retaining screws (arrowed)

14 Fit the dust cover and ring over the end of the piston and cylinder.

15 Lubricate the sliding guides with the grease supplied and refit them, together with the new seals. On the DBA type, refit the endplate and tighten the bolts.

16 On the DBA type, refit the caliper frame and tighten the bolts.

17 To refit the caliper, first screw it onto the flexible hose and locate it over the brake disc so that the hose is not twisted.

18 Clean the mounting bolt threads and apply locking fluid. Insert the mounting bolts and tighten them to the specified torque.

19 Tighten the flexible hose union on the caliper. Check that the hose is clear of the strut and surrounding components and, if necessary, loosen the rigid pipe union on the body bracket, reposition the hose and retighten the union.

20 Refit the disc pads, as described in Section 3.

21 Remove the brake hose clamp or polythene sheeting and bleed the hydraulic system, as described in Section 12. It is only necessary to bleed the front circuit.

6 Brake disc - inspection, removal and refitting

1 Remove the disc pads, as described in Section 3.

2 Using a dial gauge or feelers and a fixed block, check that the disc run-out is within the specified limit. Do not confuse wheel bearing endfloat with disc wear. Also check the condition of the disc, for scoring. Light scoring is normal, but if excessive either renew the disc or have it ground.

3 To remove the disc, unscrew the two cross-head screws (where fitted) and withdraw the disc at an angle from the caliper and hub (photo) .

4 Refitting is a reversal of removal, but make sure that the disc-to-hub mating surfaces are clean and that the cross-head screws are tightened fully. Refer to Section 3 when refitting the disc pads.

7 Rear brake wheel cylinder - removal, overhaul and refitting

1 Jack up the rear of the car and support on axle stands. Chock the front wheels and remove the relevant rear wheel.

2 Remove the hub/drum, as described in Section 4.

3 Note the location of the brake shoe upper return spring then unhook and remove it.

4 Pivot the brake shoes away from the wheel cylinder and wedge them in this position. If a suitable wedge, or sufficient clearance between each shoe and the brake wheel cylinder pistons cannot be obtained, the brake shoes will need to be removed as

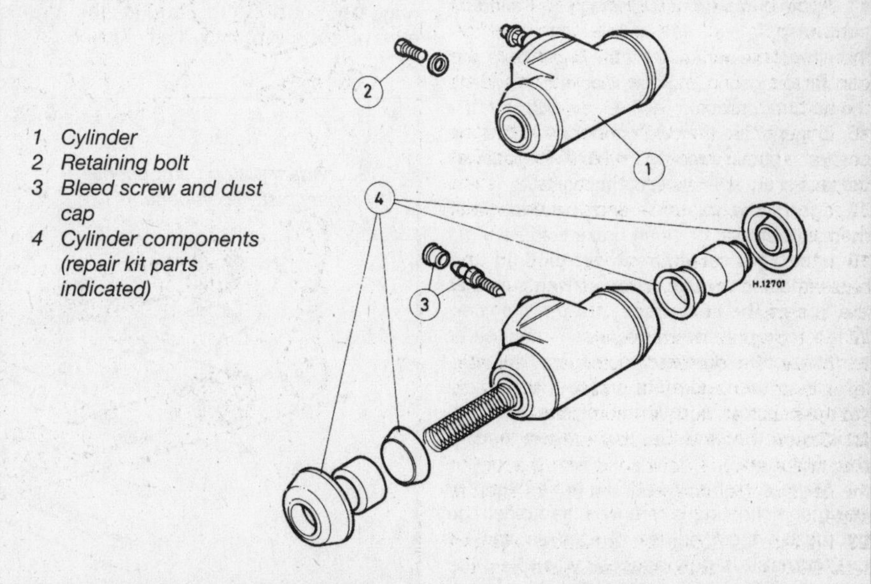

1 Cylinder
2 Retaining bolt
3 Bleed screw and dust cap
4 Cylinder components (repair kit parts indicated)

Fig. 8.8 Exploded view of the DBA Bendix type rear wheel cylinder (Sec 7)

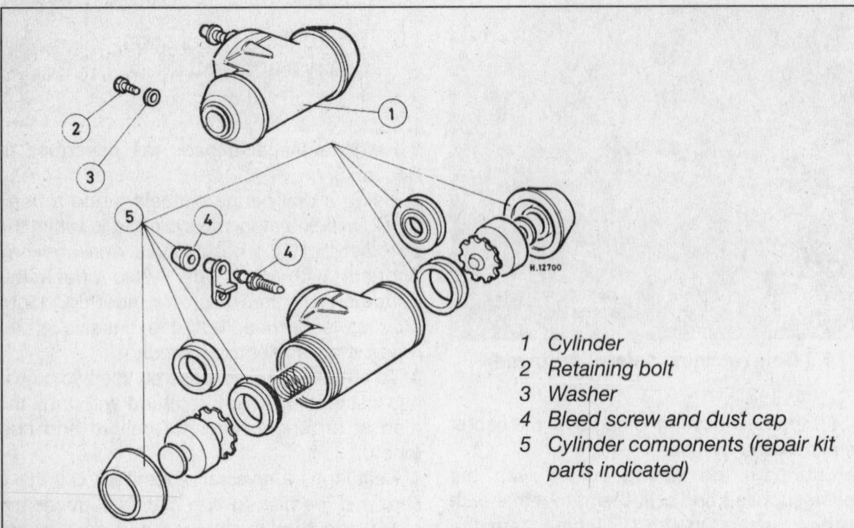

Fig. 8.9 Exploded view of the Girling type rear wheel cylinder (Sec 7)

described in Section 4. Avoid damage or distortion to the brake components.

5 Fit a brake hose clamp to the flexible hose supplying the rear brakes. Alternatively remove the brake fluid reservoir filler cap and tighten it down onto a piece of polythene sheeting to reduce the loss of fluid when disconnecting the wheel cylinder.

6 Unscrew the hydraulic pipe union nut from the rear of the wheel cylinder.

7 Unscrew the two mounting bolts and withdraw the wheel cylinder from the backplate. Take care not to spill any brake fluid on the brake shoe linings.

8 Clean the exterior surfaces of the wheel cylinder before dismantling it. The cylinder will be of Girling or DBA Bendix manufacture (see Figs. 8.8 or 8.9).

9 Pull off the dust excluders.

10 Extract the pistons, seals and return spring; keeping each component identified for location.

11 Check the surface of the cylinder bore and pistons for scoring and corrosion and, if evident, renew the complete wheel cylinder. If the components are in good condition discard the seals and obtain a repair kit which will contain all the necessary renewable components.

12 Clean the pistons and cylinder with methylated spirit or clean brake fluid then dip each component in fresh brake fluid and reassemble in reverse order, making sure that the lips of the seals face into the cylinder. When completed, wipe clean the outer surfaces of the dust excluders.

13 Clean the backplate and refit the wheel cylinder using a reversal of the removal procedure. Refer to Section 4 when refitting the hub/drum.

14 Make sure that the brake hose clamp or polythene sheeting is removed then bleed the hydraulic system, as described in Section 12; noting that it is only necessary to bleed the rear circuit (if only the rear brakes have been disturbed).

8 Rear brake drum - inspection and renovation

1 Whenever the hub/brake drum is removed to check the linings, take the opportunity to inspect the interior of the drum.

2 If the drum is grooved, owing to failure to renew worn linings or after a very high mileage has been covered, then it may be possible to regrind it, provided the maximum internal diameter is not exceeded.

3 Even if only one drum is in need of grinding, both drums must be reground to the same size in order to maintain even braking characteristics.

4 Judder or a springy pedal felt when the brakes are applied can be caused by a distorted (out-of-round) drum. Here again it may be possible to regrind the drums, otherwise a new drum will be required.

9 Master cylinder - removal, overhaul and refitting

1 Unscrew the filler cap from the brake fluid reservoir and draw out the fluid using a syringe.

2 Prise the reservoir from the master cylinder and remove the seals.

3 Unscrew the union nuts securing the rigid brake lines to the master cylinder and pull out the lines. Cap the pipe ends to prevent loss of fluid.

4 Unscrew the mounting nuts and withdraw the master cylinder from the servo unit.

5 Clean the exterior of the master cylinder.

6 Using circlip pliers, extract the circlip from the mouth of the cylinder.

7 Remove the primary and secondary piston components noting their locations. If necessary tap the cylinder on a block of wood.

8 Clean all the components in methylated spirit. Check the surfaces of the cylinder bore and pistons for scoring and corrosion, and if evident renew the complete master cylinder. If the components are in good condition remove and discard the seals and obtain a repair kit which will contain all the necessary renewable components.

9 Dip the new seals in fresh brake fluid and fit them to the pistons using the fingers only to manipulate them.

10 Reassemble the master cylinder in reverse order to dismantling and make sure that the circlip is fully engaged with the groove in the mouth of the cylinder.

11 Refitting is a reversal of removal. Take care to align the brake line unions correctly or cross threading may occur. On completion, bleed the complete hydraulic system as described in Section 12.

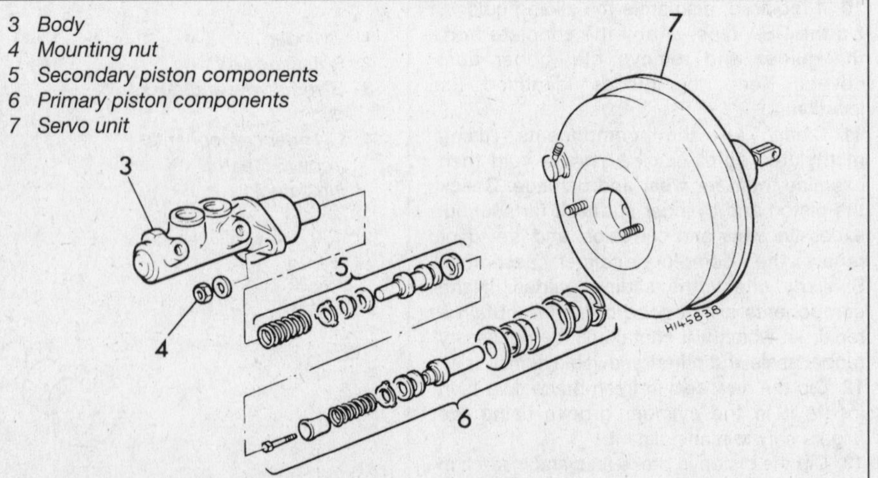

Fig. 8.10 Master cylinder components (Sec 9)

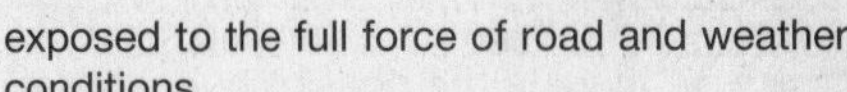

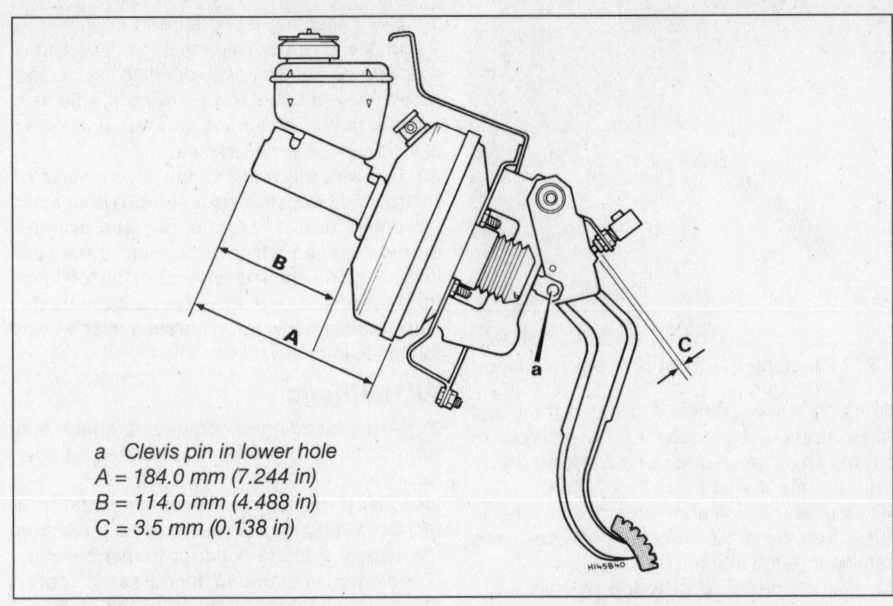

Fig. 8.11 Master cylinder, servo unit and brake pedal assembly (Sec 9)

10 Brake compensator - description, removal and refitting

1 The OHC engine models have a brake compensator fitted in the rear brake hydraulic system and it is located under the car floor just forward of the rear suspension. Its purpose is to maintain equal braking effect on the front and rear wheels and prevent the rear brakes from locking up (photo).

2 If you find that, on applying the brakes, the effect is mainly on the front wheels and that it is impossible to lock the rear brakes without using the handbrake or, alternatively, if you find that the rear brakes invariably lock under heavy braking, it is likely that the compensator is defective.

3 A Peugeot agent will have to test the component if its performance is in doubt as pressure test equipment is necessary. No attempt must be made to dismantle the unit.

4 Renewal of a brake compensator is a straightforward removal and refitting procedure followed by bleeding of the hydraulic system. Ensure that the unit is correctly orientated when fitted.

11 Flexible and rigid hydraulic lines - inspection and renewal

1 Examine all the unions for signs of leaks. The look at the flexible hoses for signs of fraying and chafing (as well as for leaks). This is only a preliminary inspection of the flexible hoses as exterior condition does not necessarily indicate interior condition which will be considered later.

2 The steel pipes must be examined equally carefully. They must be thoroughly cleaned and examined for signs of dents or other percussive damage, rust and corrosion. Rust and corrosion should be scraped off and, if the depth of pitting in the pipes is significant, they will need renewal. This is most likely in those areas underneath the chassis and along the rear suspension arms where the pipes are exposed to the full force of road and weather conditions.

3 Rigid pipe removal is usually quite straightforward. The unions at each end are undone and the pipe drawn out of the connection. The clips which may hold it to the car body are bent back and it is then removed. Underneath the car exposed unions can be particularly stubborn, defying the efforts of an open-ended spanner. As few people will have the special split ring spanner required, a self-grip wrench is the only answer. If the pipe is being renewed, new unions will be provided. If not then one will have to put up with the possibility of burring over the flats on the union and use a self-grip wrench for replacement also.

4 Flexible hoses are always fitted to a rigid support bracket where they join a rigid pipe, the bracket being fixed to the chassis or rear suspension arm (photo). The rigid pipe unions must first be removed from the flexible union, then the retaining plate must be pulled out and the flexible hose and fitting released from the bracket.

5 Whenever a part of the hydraulic system is disconnected, clamp the hose (photo) or plug the pipe end connections to prevent leakage of fluid and the possible ingress of dirt.

6 Depending upon the make of the particular caliper, the flexible hose may be connected simply by screwing it into its tapped hole or by using a hollow bolt with banjo end fitting. Use a new copper sealing washer on each side of the banjo union.

7 Once the flexible hose is removed, examine the internal bore. If clear of fluid it should be possible to see through it. Any specks of rubber which come out, or signs of restriction in the bore, mean that the inner lining is breaking up and the hose must be renewed.

8 Rigid pipes which need replacement can usually be purchased at any local garage where they have the pipe, unions and special tools to make them up. They will need to know the pipe length required and the type of flare used at the ends of the pipe. These may be different at each end of the same pipe.

9 Installation of the pipes is a reversal of the removal procedure. The pipe profile must be preset before fitting. Any acute bends must be

10.1 Rear brake compensator (AP type)

11.4 Rear brake pipe-to-hose junction and rigid support bracket on rear suspension arm

11.5 Method of clamping brake hose using two sockets and clamp to prevent damaging the hose

put in by the garage on a bending machine, otherwise there is the possibility of kinking them and restricting the fluid flow.

10 All hose and pipe threads and unions are to metric standards. Screw in new components by hand initially to ensure that the threads are compatible.

11 Remember that a metric hose end fitting seals at the tip of its threaded section and will leave a gap between the hexagon of the end fitting and the surface of the component. Do not attempt to overtighten the hose end fitting in order to eliminate the gap.

12 The hydraulic system must be bled on completion of hose or rigid pipe renewal.

12 Hydraulic system - draining and bleeding

1 To renew the hydraulic fluid, remove the filler cap from the reservoir and use a syringe to remove the fluid. Fill the reservoir with new hydraulic fluid and bleed the complete system as described later. If the master cylinder or connecting pipes have been removed, the complete hydraulic system must be bled, but if only a caliper or wheel cylinder has been removed then only that particular circuit need be bled.

2 If the complete system is being bled, the sequence of bleeding should be as follows:

LH rear wheel and brake compensator (if fitted)
RH rear wheel
LH front wheel
RH front wheel

3 Unless the pressure bleeding method is being used, do not forget to keep the fluid level in the master cylinder reservoir topped up to prevent air from being drawn into the system which would make any work done worthless. Before commencing operations, check that all system hoses and pipes are in good condition with unions tight and free from leaks.

4 Take great care not to allow hydraulic fluid to come into contact with the vehicle paintwork as it is an effective paint stripper. Wash off any spilled fluid immediately with cold water.

5 To dissipate any vacuum assistance from the brake system, apply the brake pedal several times in quick succession (with the engine switched off).

Bleeding - two man method

6 Gather together a clean jar and a length of rubber or plastic tubing which will be a tight fit on the brake bleed screws.

7 Engage the help of an assistant.

8 Push one end of the bleed tube onto the first bleed screw and immerse the other end in the jar which should contain enough hydraulic fluid to cover the end of the tube.

9 Open the bleed screw one half a turn and have your assistant depress the brake pedal fully then slowly release it. Tighten the bleed screw at the end of each pedal downstroke to obviate any chance of air or fluid being drawn back into the system.

12.12 Bleeding the front brake disc caliper

10 Repeat this operation until clean hydraulic fluid, free from air bubbles, can be seen coming through into the jar.

11 It is important to dislodge air trapped in the inertia compensator (if fitted). To do this, open the bleed screw again and have your assistant fully depress and release the brake pedal rapidly 4 or 5 times, finally keeping the pedal depressed before tightening the bleed screw.

12 With the bleed screw tightened, remove the bleed tube and proceed to the next wheel (photo).

Bleeding - using one-way valve kits

13 There are a number of one-man, one-way brake bleeding kits available from motor accessory shops. It is recommended that one of these kits is used wherever possible as it will greatly simplify the bleeding operation and also reduce the risk of air or fluid being drawn back into the system, quite apart from being able to do the work without the help of an assistant. To use the kit, connect the tube to the bleed screw and open the screw one half a turn.

14 Depress the brake pedal fully then slowly release it. The one-way valve in the kit will prevent expelled air from returning at the end of each pedal downstroke. Repeat the operation several times to be sure of ejecting all the air from the system. Some kits include a translucent container which can be positioned so that the air bubbles can actually be seen being ejected from the system.

15 Tighten the bleed screw, remove the tube and repeat the operations on the remaining brakes, but first carry out the procedure described in paragraph 11.

16 On completion, depress the brake pedal. If it still feels spongy, repeat the bleeding operations as air must still be trapped in the system.

Bleeding - using a pressure bleeding kit

17 These kits are available from motor accessory shops and are usually operated by air pressure from the spare tyre.

18 By connecting a pressurised container to the master cylinder fluid reservoir, bleeding is then carried out simply by opening each bleed screw in sequence and allowing the fluid to run out, rather like turning on a tap, until no air is visible in the expelled fluid.

19 By using this method, the large reserve of hydraulic fluid provides a safeguard against air being drawn into the master cylinder during bleeding which may occur if the fluid level in the reservoir is allowed to fall too low.

20 Pressure bleeding is particularly useful when bleeding the complete system at time of routine fluid renewal.

All methods

21 When bleeding is completed, check and top up the fluid level in the master cylinder reservoir.

22 Check the feel of the brake pedal. If it feels at all spongy, air must still be present in the system and the need for further bleeding is indicated. Failure to bleed satisfactorily after a reasonable repetition of the bleeding operations may be due to worn master cylinder seals.

23 Always discard brake fluid which had been bled from the system. It is almost certain to be contaminated with moisture, air and dirt, making it unsuitable for further use.

24 Clean fluid should always be stored in an airtight container as it absorbs moisture readily which lowers its boiling point and could affect braking performance under severe conditions.

13 Vacuum servo unit - description, testing, maintenance, removal and refitting

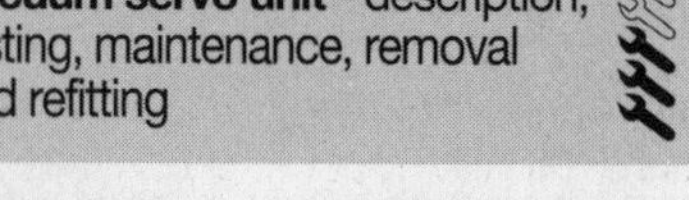

Description

1 The vacuum servo unit is fitted into the brake hydraulic circuit in series with the master cylinder to provide power assistance to the driver when the brake pedal is depressed.

2 The unit operates by vacuum obtained from the engine induction manifold and consists of, basically, a booster diaphragm and non-return valve.

3 The servo unit and the master cylinder are connected so that the servo piston rod acts as the master cylinder pushrod.

4 The driver's braking effort is transmitted from the brake pedal to the servo unit piston and its integral control system.

5 The forward chamber of the servo unit is held under vacuum at all times whilst the rear chamber is held under vacuum conditions only when the brake pedal is in the released position. When the pedal is depressed, the rear chamber opens to atmospheric pressure which causes the servo piston to move forward and so operate the master cylinder pushrod.

6 It is emphasised that a servo unit provides

13.21 Brake stop-lamp switch (arrowed)

assistance only and, should a fault occur, the normal hydraulic braking system is unaffected except that the need for higher pedal pressure will be noticed.

Testing

7 With the engine switched off, depress the brake pedal several times. The distance by which the pedal moves should now alter over all applications.

8 Depress the brake pedal fully and hold it down then start the engine. The pedal should be felt to move downward slightly.

9 Hold the pedal depressed with the engine running, switch off the ignition and continue to hold the pedal depressed for 30 seconds during which period the pedal should neither rise nor drop.

10 Start the engine whilst the brake pedal is released, run it for a minute and switch off. Give several applications of the brake pedal. The pedal travel should decrease with each application.

11 Failure of the brake pedal to act in the way described will indicate a fault in the servo unit.

12 The servo unit should not be serviced or overhauled beyond the operations described in this Section and in the event of a fault developing, renew the servo complete.

13 Periodically check the condition of the vacuum hose and security of the clips.

14 Renew the hose if necessary.

15 If the servo hose right-angled non-return valve is loose in its sealing grommet, or if the grommet shows evidence of cracking or perishing, renew it. Apply some hydraulic fluid to the rubber to facilitate fitting.

Air filter renewal

16 Although not a specified operation, the air filter through which the pushrod passes at the rear of the servo can become clogged after a high mileage. Disconnect the rod from the pedal, cut the filter diagonally having slipped the dust excluder off the rod. Fit the new filter.

Removal and refitting

17 Remove the master cylinder, as described in Section 9. Disconnect the servo vacuum hose. On fuel injection models it is also necessary to remove the fuel filter unit (see Chapter 3).

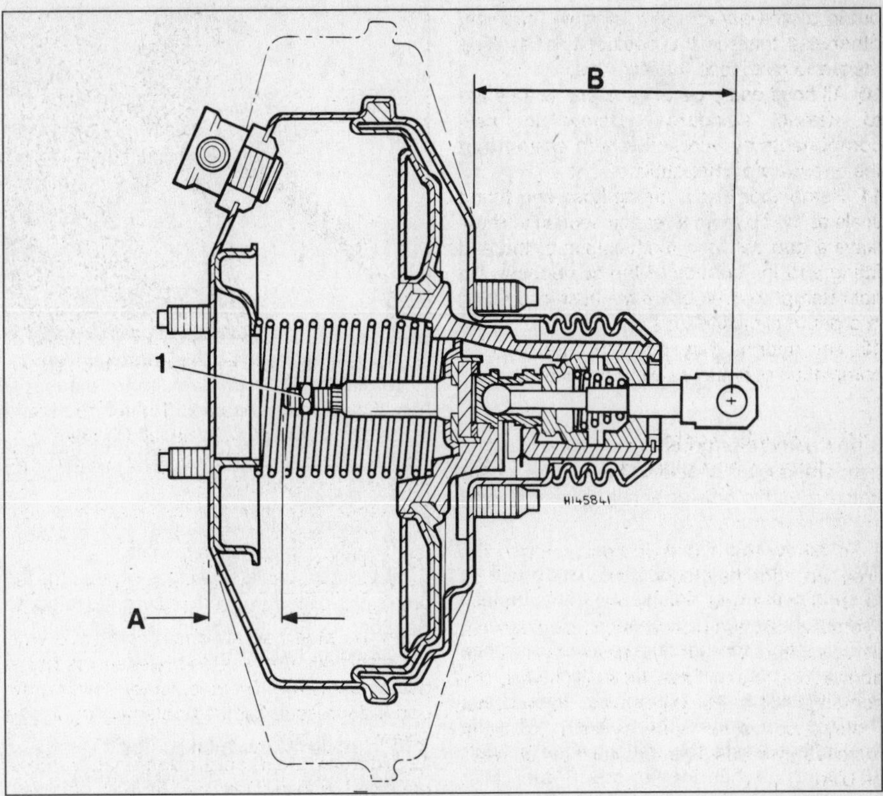

Fig. 8.12 Cross-section of the vacuum servo unit showing pushrod adjustment dimensions (Sec 13)

1 Adjustment screw

A = 22.2 to 22.4 mm (0.874 to 0.882 in) *B = 86.5 to 89.5 mm (3.406 to 3.524 in)*

18 Working inside the car, disconnect the pushrod from the brake pedal; noting that it is on the lower hole.

19 Unscrew the mounting nuts behind the pedal bracket then withdraw the servo unit into the engine compartment. Remove the gasket.

20 Before fitting a servo unit, check the pushrod dimensions shown in Fig. 8.12 and adjust where possible.

21 Refitting is a reversal of removal, but fit a new gasket and fully tighten the mounting nuts. Refer to Section 9 when refitting the master cylinder. Finally, with the brake pedal released, check that the clearance between the stop-lamp switch threaded shank and pedal is 3.5 mm (0.138 in). If necessary loosen the locknuts, adjust the switch and tighten the locknuts (photo).

14 Handbrake - adjustment

1 The handbrake is normally kept adjusted by the action of the automatic adjusters on the rear brake shoes. However, in due course the cables will stretch and will have to be adjusted in order to fully apply the handbrake.

2 Access to the adjuster is obtained after removing the handbrake cover. To do this unbolt and remove the driver's seat, pull free the fuel filler cap release handle from its shaft, then undo the retaining screws and remove the cover from the handbrake.

3 Jack up the rear of the car and support it on axle stands. Chock the front wheels.

4 Release the handbrake then move the lever to the third notch position. Loosen the adjuster locknut.

5 Turn the adjustment nut on the rear of the cable equaliser so that both rear wheels are just binding on the brake shoes (photo).

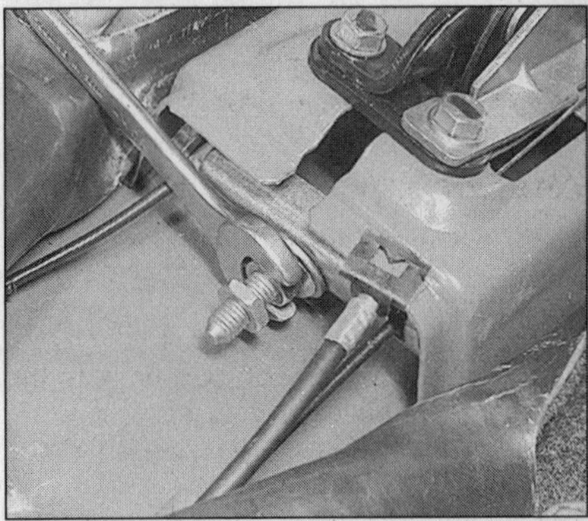

14.5 Adjusting the handbrake

15.3 Unhook the handbrake cable(s) from the equaliser

6 The number of notches through which the handbrake lever should be able to be pulled from fully-off to fully-on should be as follows:

With rear drums 5 to 7
With rear discs 6 to 8

7 On no account adjust the handbrake to operate over fewer notches, or the automatic brake adjusters will not operate.

8 Fully apply the handbrake lever, and then check that both rear wheels are locked.

9 Fully release the handbrake, then check that the rear wheels rotate freely. With the adjustment satisfactory, retighten the locknut.

10 Refit the handbrake cover, fuel filler release handle and driver's seat, then lower the car.

15 Handbrake cables - renewal

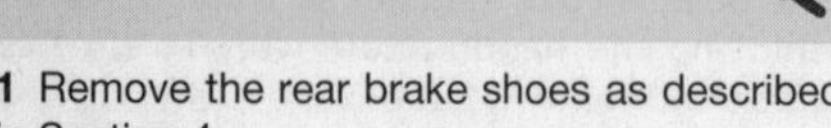

1 Remove the rear brake shoes as described in Section 4.

2 Remove the handbrake cover as described in paragraph 2 of Section 14.

3 Undo the handbrake lever retaining nuts and bolts and lift the lever to gain access to the handbrake cable and equaliser. Unhook the cables from the equalizer (photo).

4 Release the cable(s) from the retaining clips, the floor, the fuel tank, and the rear brake backplate(s) and withdraw from under the car (photos) .

5 If renewing both cables, note that the right-hand cable is longer than the left.

6 Fit the new cable(s) using a reversal of the removal procedure with reference also to Section 4. Finally adjust the cable(s) as described in Section 14.

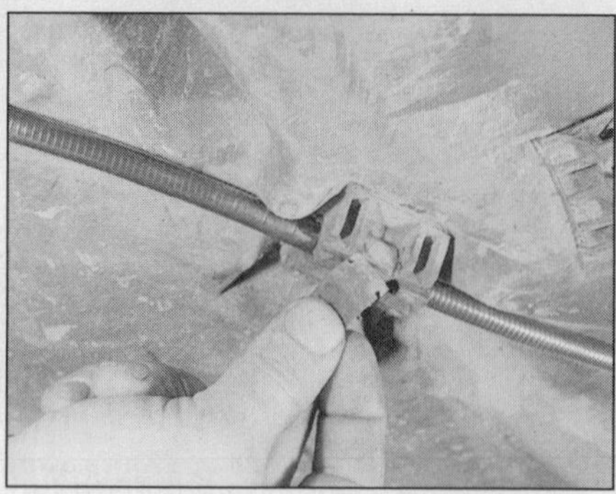
15.4A Handbrake cable removal from retaining clip – remove clip to release cable

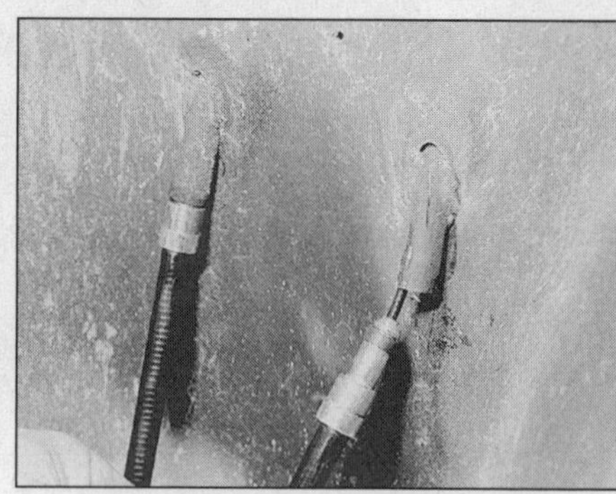
15.4B Pull cable(s) through the floor from the underside

16 Handbrake warning light switch - removal and refitting

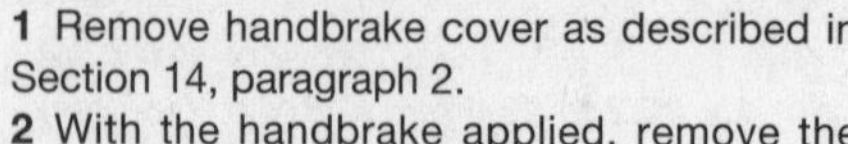

1 Remove handbrake cover as described in Section 14, paragraph 2.

2 With the handbrake applied, remove the mounting screw, withdraw the switch and disconnect the wiring (photo).

3 Refitting is a reversal of removal.

17 Handbrake lever - removal and refitting

1 Remove the handbrake cover as described in paragraph 2 of Section 14.

2 Undo the handbrake lever retaining nuts and bolts. Move the fuel filler release lever to one side (photo).

3 Disconnect the handbrake cables from the equalizer and then remove the handbrake lever.

4 Refit in the reverse order of removal. Adjust the handbrake as described in Section 14, paragraphs 5 to 7.

18 Brake pedal - removal and refitting

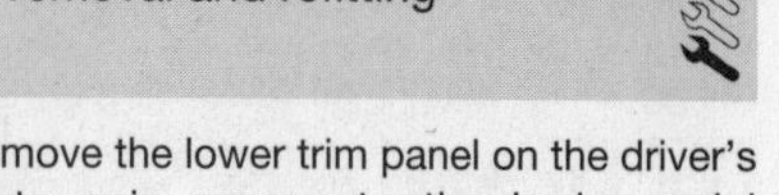

1 Remove the lower trim panel on the driver's side to gain access to the brake pedal assembly.

2 Remove the clevis pin and disconnect the pushrod from the brake pedal. Note that the pushrod is on the lower hole (photo).

3 Unscrew the self-locking nut from the pivot bolt, pull out the bolt and lower the brake pedal.

4 Examine the pedal bushes for wear and renew them if necessary.

5 Refitting is a reversal of removal, but lightly grease the bushes and clevis pin and renew the self-locking nut.

16.2 Handbrake warning light switch

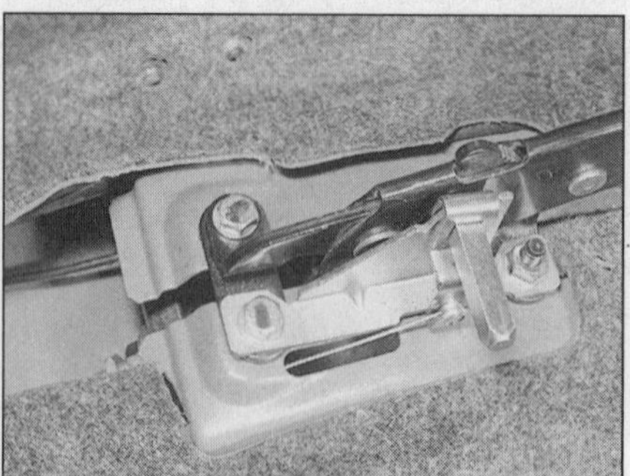
17.2 Handbrake lever/fuel filler release lever retaining bolts and nut

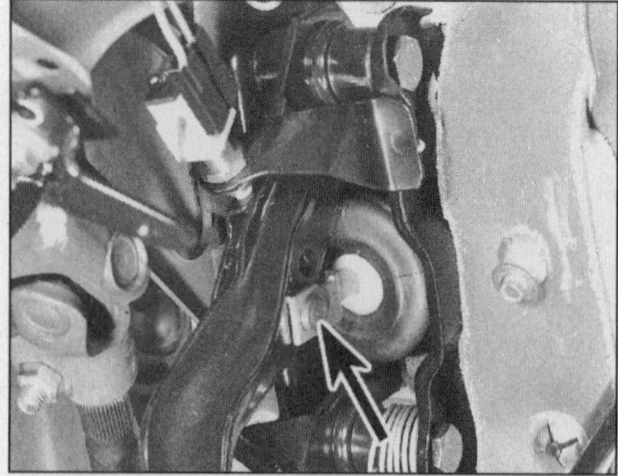
18.2 Pushrod to brake pedal clevis pin arrowed (note location of clevis pin hole used)

Fault finding - braking system

Before diagnosing faults from the following chart check that any braking irregularities are not caused by:
(a) Uneven and incorrect tyre pressures
(b) Incorrect mix of radial and crossply tyres
(c) Wear in the steering mechanism
(d) Misalignment of the chassis geometry

Pedal travels a long way before the brakes operate

- ☐ Brake shoes set too far from the drums due to faulty self-adjusting mechanism

Stopping ability poor, even though pedal pressure is firm

- ☐ Linings/pads and/or drums/disc badly worn or scored
- ☐ One or more wheel hydraulic cylinders or caliper pistons seized resulting in some brake shoes/pads not pressing against the drums/discs
- ☐ Brake linings/pads contaminated with oil
- ☐ Wrong type of linings/pads fitted (too hard)
- ☐ Brake shoes/pads wrongly assembled
- ☐ Faulty servo unit

Car veers to one side when the brakes are applied

- ☐ Brake linings/pads on one side are contaminated with oil
- ☐ Hydraulic wheel cylinder/caliper on one side partially or fully seized
- ☐ A mixture of lining materials fitted between sides
- ☐ Unequal wear between sides caused by partially seized wheel cylinders/pistons

Pedal feels spongy

- ☐ Air in the hydraulic system

Pedal feels springy when the brakes are applied

- ☐ Braking linings/pads not bedded into the drums/discs (after fitting new ones)
- ☐ Master cylinder or brake backplate mounting bolts loose
- ☐ Out-of-round drums or discs with excessive run-out

Pedal travels right down with little or no resistance and brakes are virtually non-operative

- ☐ Leak in hydraulic system resulting in lack of pressure for operating wheel cylinders/caliper pistons
- ☐ If no signs of leakage are apparent the master cylinder internal seals are failing to sustain pressure

Binding, juddering, overheating

- ☐ One or a combination of causes given in the foregoing sections
- ☐ Handbrake over-adjusted
- ☐ Handbrake cable(s) seized

Lack of servo assistance

- ☐ Vacuum hose leaking
- ☐ Non-return valve defective or leaking grommet
- ☐ Servo internal fault

Notes

Chapter 9
Suspension, hubs, wheels and tyres

For modifications and information applicable to later models, see Supplement at end of manual

Contents

Degrees of difficulty

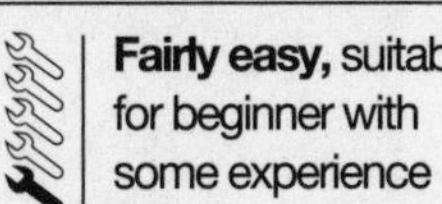

Easy, suitable for novice with little experience

Fairly easy, suitable for beginner with some experience

Fairly difficult, suitable for competent DIY mechanic

Difficult, suitable for experienced DIY mechanic

Very difficult, suitable for expert DIY or professional

Specifications

Front suspension

Type	Independent, MacPherson struts, coil springs and anti-roll bar
Front suspension geometry	*Refer to Chapter 10*
Anti-roll bar diameter	20 mm, 22 mm or 23 mm (dependent on model)

Rear suspension

Type	Independent, trailing arms, torsion bars, inclined shock absorbers. Anti-roll bar on OHC engine models
Rear suspension geometry:	
Toe-in	0.5 ± 1 mm (0.02 ± 0.04 in)
Camber	-1° ± 30'
Rear suspension ride height	436 to 450 mm (17.2 to 17.7 in)
Maximum allowable difference in ride height, side to side	10 mm (0.4 in)

Roadwheels and tyres

Wheels:		
GE	4 1/2 B steel	
GL, GR, GR Profile and SR	5B steel	
SRI	5 1/2 J alloy	
Tyres:		
GE and GR Profile	145 SR 13	
GL GR and SR	165/70 SR 13	
SRi	175/65 HR 14	
Tyre pressures (cold):	**Front**	**Rear**
All models except SRI	28 lbf/in^2 (1.9 bar)	31 lbf/in^2 (2.1 bar)
SRI	28 lbf/in^2 (1.9 bar)	26 lbf/in^2 (1.8 bar)

9

Torque wrench settings

	Nm	lbf ft
Front suspension		
Top mounting	12	9
Shock absorber piston rod	45	33
Crimped nuts	70	52
Strut clamp bolt	58	43
Anti-roll bar clamp	35	26
Anti-roll bar end	75	55
Bottom balljoint	35	26
Lower suspension arm pivot bolt	35	26
Subframe mounting self-locking nuts (use new nuts)	52	39
Subframe rear mounting-to-floor bolts	75	55
Front hub nut	265	195
Rear suspension		
Suspension to body mountings	45	33
Suspension front mounting pivot	80	59
Hub nut	215	159
Cable support bracket bolt	35	26
Roadwheels		
Roadwheel bolts (steel or alloy wheels)	85	63

1 General description

The front suspension is of independent type; incorporating McPherson struts with coil springs and integral shock absorbers. An anti-roll bar is fitted to all models.

The rear suspension is also of independent type; incorporating a cross-tube with trailing arms set in each end and supported on needle or plain bearings. Torsion bars are fitted to the trailing arms and, on certain models, an anti-roll bar located inside the cross-tube stabilizes the car when cornering. The telescopic shock absorbers are inclined with their top mountings attached to the suspension side-members. A rubber cone bump stop is provided on each side for times of excessive movement of the trailing arms (photo).

1.3 Rear suspension bump stop

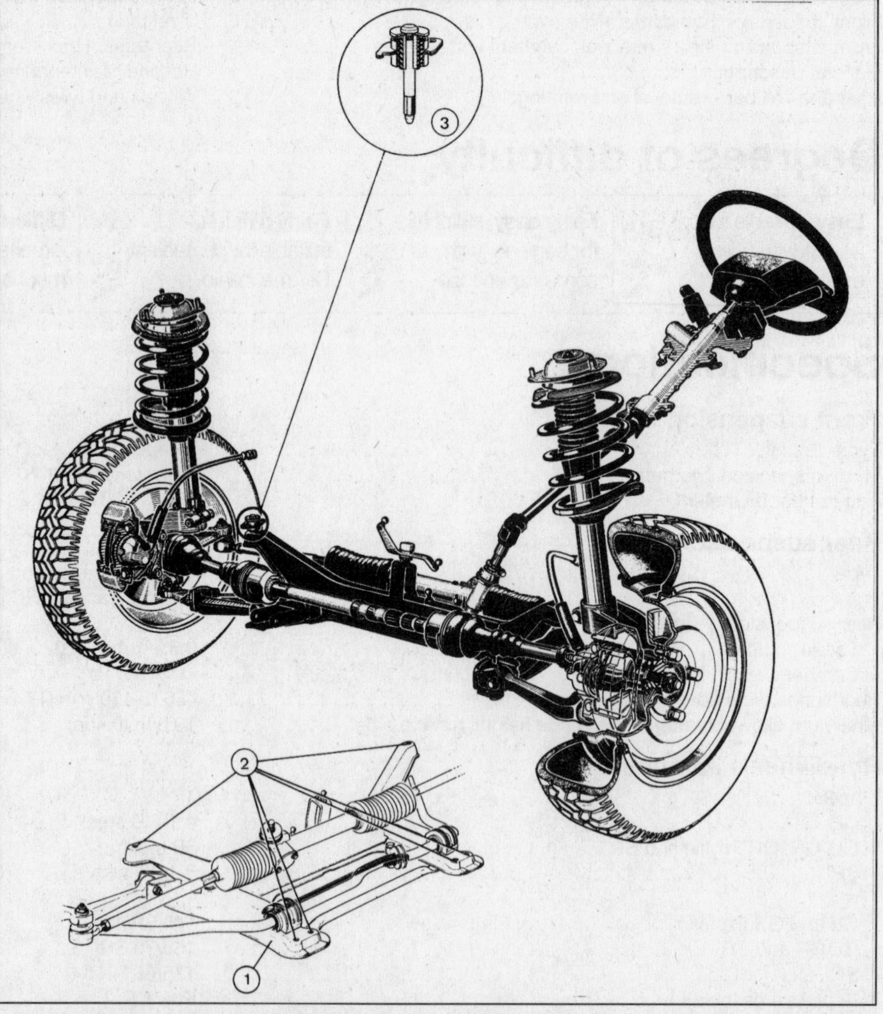

Fig. 9.1 Front suspension assembly showing the subframe (1) and mounting points (2) with silentbloc mounting at 3 (Sec 1)

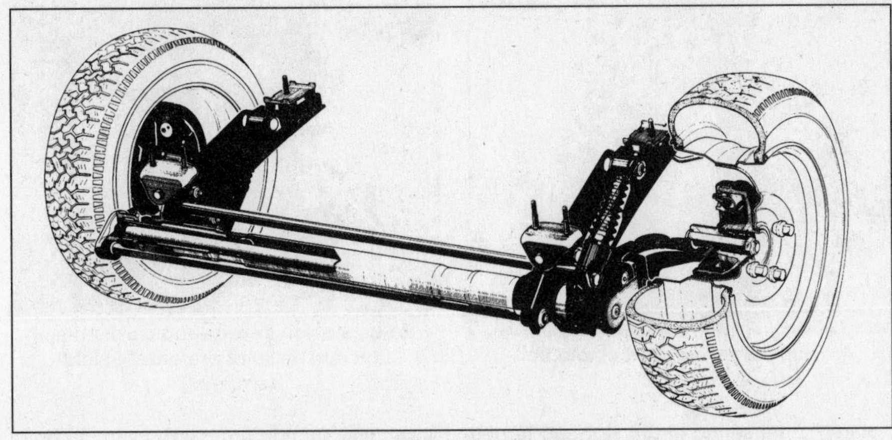

Fig. 9.2 Rear suspension assembly (Sec 1)

2 Routine maintenance

Carry out the following procedures at the intervals given in Routine Maintenance at the beginning of the manual.

1 Check and adjust the tyre pressures and make sure that the caps are securely fitted to the valves.

2 Thoroughly examine the tyres for wear, damage and deterioration. When making this check, raise the vehicle so that each wheel in turn is clear of the ground so that a complete check can be made.

3 Check the hub bearings for excessive wear. With the wheels clear of the ground, grip the top and bottom and attempt to rock the wheel. Any excessive play indicates wear in the hub bearings although, on the front wheels, check that the movement is not due to a worn lower suspension balljoint.

4 Place the car on ramps or jack it up and support on axle stands, then check the front and rear shock absorbers for leakage of fluid. If evident, renew the shock absorber or strut as necessary. The efficiency of the shock absorbers can be checked as described later in this Chapter.

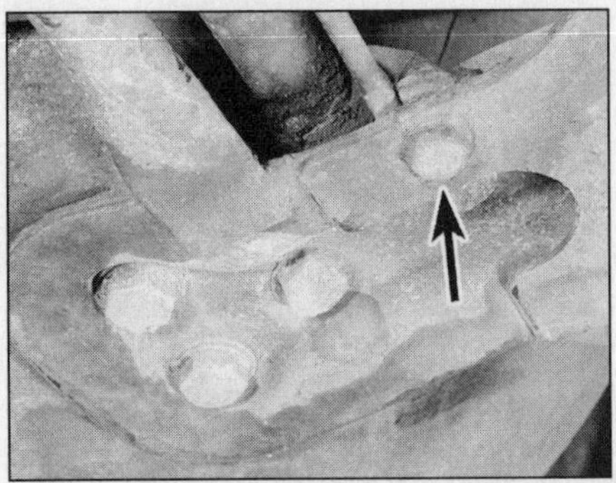

3.4 Anti-roll bar guide bar bolt (arrowed)

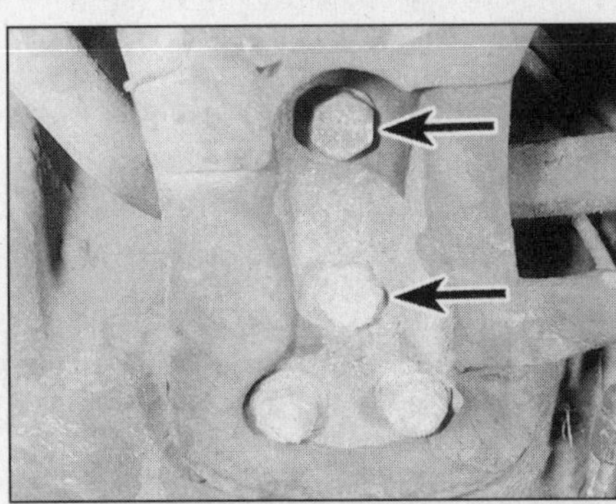

3.5 Anti-roll bar mounting clamp bolts (arrowed)

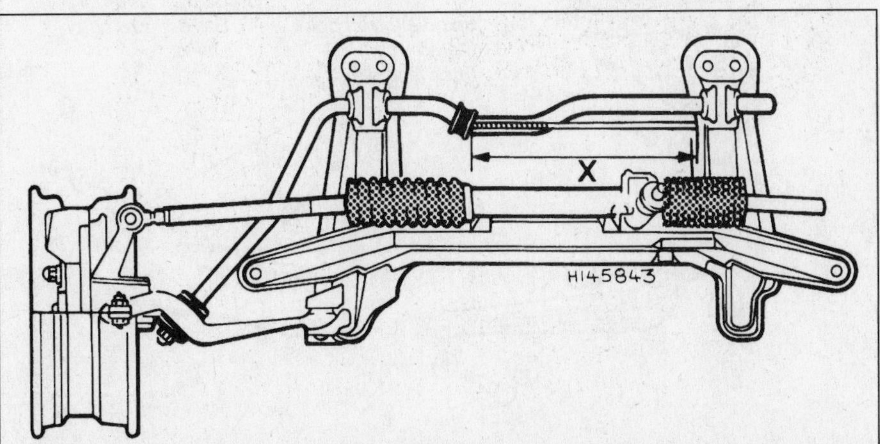

Fig. 9.3 Top view of front suspension showing measuring points for anti-roll bar guide dimension (X) (Sec 3)

3 Front anti-roll bar - removal and refitting

1 Detach and remove the engine undershield.

2 Measure and note the distance 'X' between the subframe and guide bar bush shown in Fig. 9.3, then remove the lower suspension arm from one side, as described in Section 5.

3 Unscrew the nut securing the remaining end of the anti-roll bar to the other suspension arm and recover the washer.

4 Unbolt the guide bar from the subframe (photo).

5 Unscrew the mounting clamp bolts (photo) and withdraw the anti-roll bar over the subframe.

6 Examine the nylon mounting bushes and the rubber bushes in the suspension arms for damage or excessive wear and renew them as necessary. The bushes in the suspension arms can be prised or driven out.

7 Refitting is a reversal of removal, but delay fully tightening the clamp bolts until the full weight of the car is on the suspension. The guide bar bolts should also remain loosened until after the bearing clamp bolts have been tightened and its length should be suitably set (see Fig. 9.3, as noted during removal).

4 Front suspension strut - removal, overhaul and refitting

1 Before raising the car it is recommended that a retaining tool is fitted to the coil spring to enable easier removal of the strut. Peugeot garages use two special cables inserted through the holes at the top of the front suspension tower and engaged with further holes in the bottom coil spring seat (Fig. 9.4).

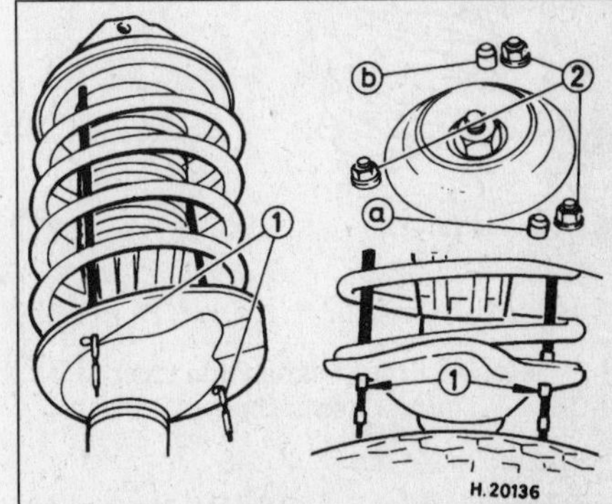

Fig. 9.4 Front suspension strut showing Peugeot special retaining cables (1), upper cable locations (a and b) and the strut securing nuts (2) (Sec 4)

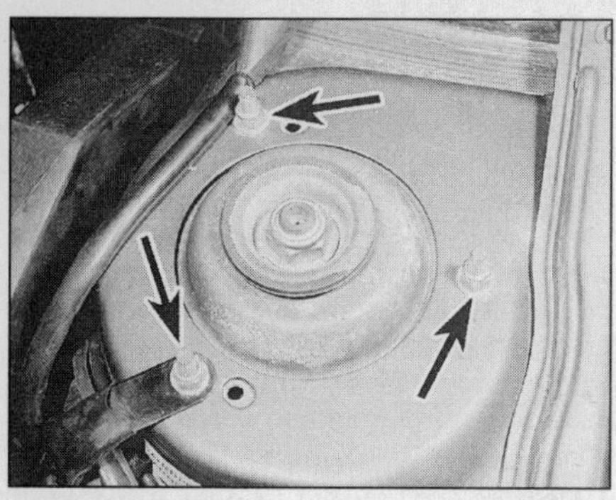

4.2 Front suspension top mounting nuts (arrowed)

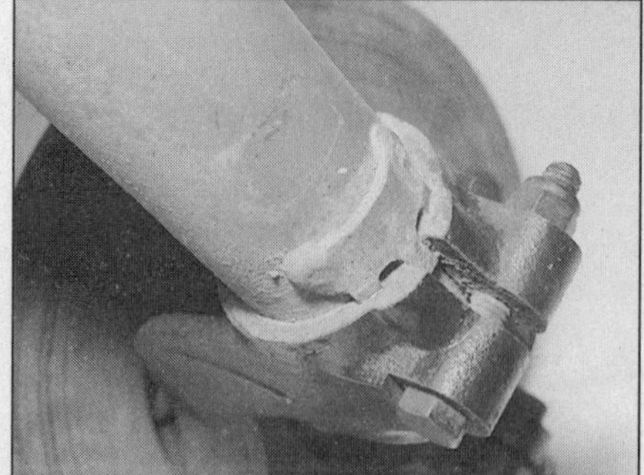

4.4 Hub carrier-to-strut clamp bolt

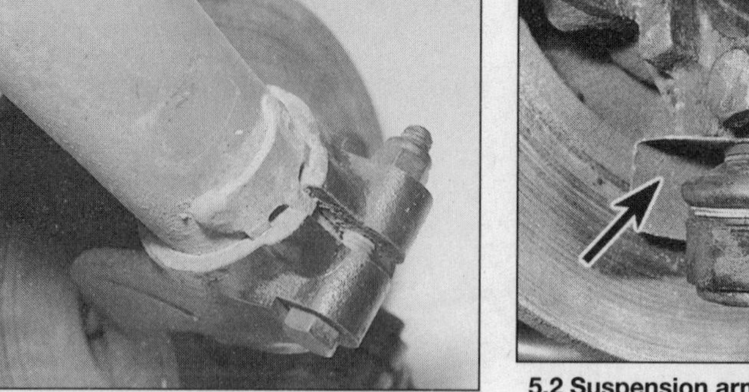

5.2 Suspension arm-to-hub carrier clamp bolt and balljoint protector shield (arrowed)

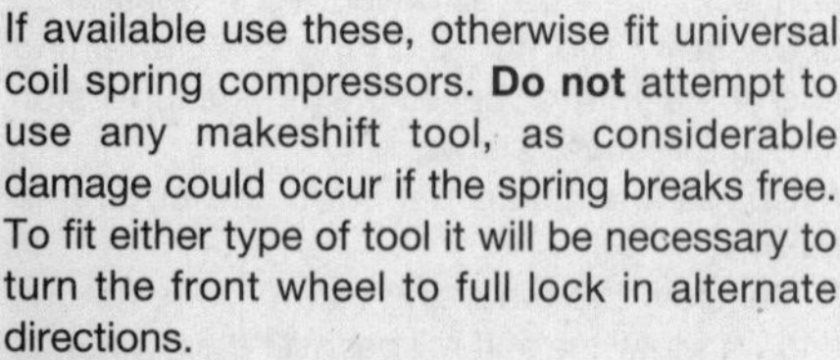

If available use these, otherwise fit universal coil spring compressors. **Do not** attempt to use any makeshift tool, as considerable damage could occur if the spring breaks free. To fit either type of tool it will be necessary to turn the front wheel to full lock in alternate directions.

2 Loosen, but do not remove, the three top strut mounting nuts (photo) .

3 Jack up the front of the car and support on axle stands. Apply the handbrake and remove the roadwheel on the relevant side.

4 Unscrew the clamp bolt securing the hub carrier to the bottom of the strut (photo).

5 In order to prevent any damage to the driveshaft joints, fit a length of wire from the top of the hub carrier to the subframe.

6 Drive a suitable wedge into the slot on the hub carrier and slide the carrier from the bottom of the strut. If available, use the special Peugeot tool which consists of a cranked rod inserted in the slot and turned through 90°.

7 Support the strut then unscrew the top mounting nuts and withdraw it from under the wing. Recover the washers.

8 Clean away all external dirt from the strut and coil spring.

9 Fit spring compressors to the coil spring (if applicable) and tighten them evenly until the spring is released from the upper mounting. If applicable, remove the Peugeot cables.

10 Unscrew the piston rod nut, if necessary using a 7 mm Allen key to hold the rod stationary.

11 Remove the washer and upper mounting, followed by the coil spring. The spring may remain in the compressed state ready for refitting to the strut. If the spring is to be renewed, release the compressors very gently and evenly until they can be removed and fitted to the new spring.

12 If necessary, remove the gaiter and bump stop from the piston rod. Note the location of each component to ensure correct refitting.

13 Check the strut for signs of fluid seepage at the piston rod seal. Temporarily refit the upper mounting to the piston rod and, with the bottom of the strut gripped in a vice, fully extend and retract the piston rod. If the resistance is not firm and even in both directions, or if there are signs of leakage or damage, the strut must be renewed.

14 Refitting is a reversal of removal, but note that the bump stop must be fitted with the largest diameter uppermost. Renew the piston rod nut and tighten it to the specified torque. Make sure that the strut fully enters the hub carrier; if there is any doubt about this loosen the clamp bolts with the full weight of the car on the suspension and the strut will be forced fully home. Retighten the bolt to the specified torque.

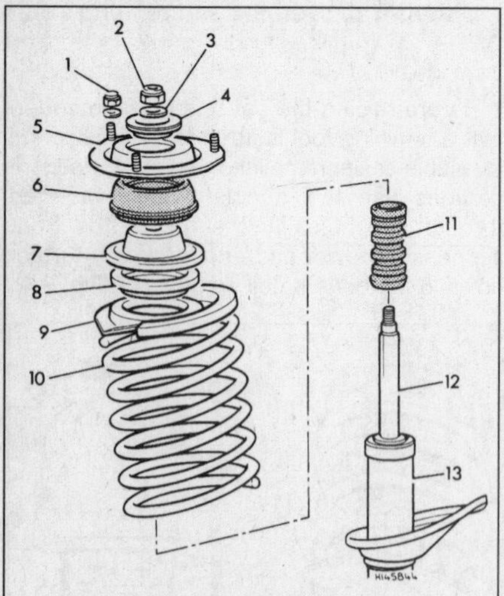

Fig. 9.5 Front suspension strut components (Sec 4)

1 *Top mounting nut*
2 *Piston rod nut*
3 *Washer*
4 *Spacer*
5 *Top mounting*
6 *Pad*
7 *Cap*
8 *Stop*
9 *Coil spring*
10 *Bump stop*
11 *Piston rod*
12 *Strut*

5 Front lower suspension arm - removal, overhaul and refitting

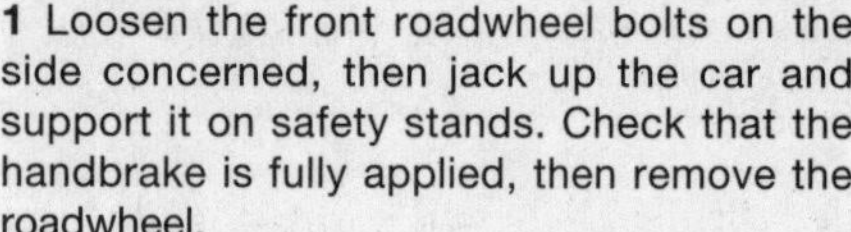

1 Loosen the front roadwheel bolts on the side concerned, then jack up the car and support it on safety stands. Check that the handbrake is fully applied, then remove the roadwheel.

2 Unscrew the hub carrier-to-arm clamp bolt and withdraw it from the front. Remove the balljoint protector shield (photo).

3 Unscrew the retaining nut from the

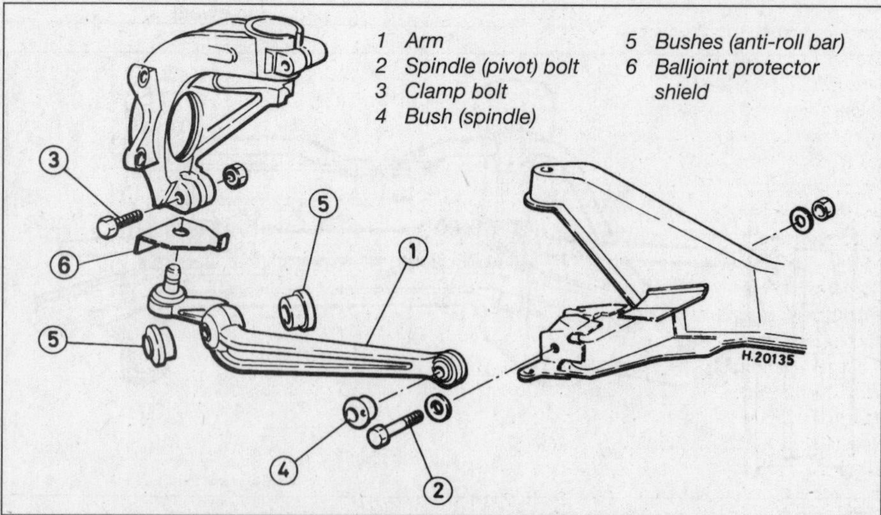

Fig. 9.6 Front lower suspension arm components (Sec 5)

5.3 Suspension arm inner pivot bolt and nut

6.6 Unbolt the brake caliper from the hub carrier

7.3 Front hub bearing and circlip

suspension arm inner pivot bolt, remove the washer, then withdraw the pivot bolt (photo).

4 Turn the hub onto full left-hand lock, then lever down on the suspension arm to separate it from the hub carrier. if necessary drive a suitable wedge into the slot in the carrier to ease separation.

5 Undo the anti-roll bar nut and withdraw the suspension arm from the anti-roll bar.

6 Check the inner pivot and anti-roll bar bushes for wear and deterioration. Check the lower balljoint on the outer end of the arm for excessive wear indicated by up and down movement of the ball in the socket. Check the arm for damage or deterioration. The bushes may be renewed using a simple puller consisting of a metal tube and washers, together with a long bolt and nut, it is not possible to renew the balljoint separately.

7 Refitting is a reversal of removal, but delay tightening the inner pivot bolt until the full weight of the car is on the suspension.

6 Front suspension hub carrier - removal and refitting

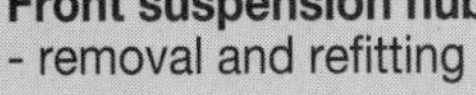

Before removing the hub, it should be noted that a new bearing must always be fitted whenever the hub is removed and refitted. If available, use the special Peugeot tools referred to in the text.

1 Detach the wheel trim from the wheel concerned, then undo the driveshaft nut.

2 Fit the Peugeot restraining cables or a suitable retaining tool to the strut coil spring, as described in paragraph 1 of Section 4.

3 Loosen the roadwheel bolts, raise the front of the car and support it on safety stands. Remove the front roadwheel.

4 Unscrew and remove the bolt securing the hub carrier to the bottom of the strut.

5 Drive a suitable wedge into the slot on the hub carrier and slide the carrier from the bottom of the strut. If available use the Peugeot special tool which consists of a cranked rod inserted in the slot and turned through 90°. As the stub axle is lowered, disconnect the driveshaft from it. Tie up or rest the driveshaft on something for support.

6 Unbolt and remove the brake caliper as described in Chapter 8. The hydraulic hose can be left attached providing the caliper is supported (photo).

7 Unscrew the two retaining screws and remove the brake disc.

8 The hub bearings can be checked or renewed at this stage, or the hub carrier fully detached and the bearings removed later, as required (see Section 1).

9 Unscrew the nut and use a balljoint removal tool to separate the track rod arm from the steering arm.

10 Unscrew and remove the lower suspension arm-to-hub carrier clamp bolt and detach the lower suspension arm from the hub carrier (see Section 5).

11 Refitting is a reversal of the removal procedure but refer to Chapters 7 and 8 respectively when refitting the driveshaft, and brake disc and caliper.

7 Front hub and bearing - renewal

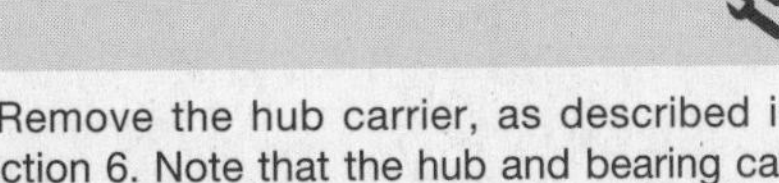

1 Remove the hub carrier, as described in Section 6. Note that the hub and bearing can be renewed with the hub carrier attached to the track rod and lower suspension arm.

2 Clean away all external dirt with a wire brush.

3 Using circlip pliers, extract the bearing retaining circlip from the inner side of the hub carrier (photo).

4 The hub must now be pressed or driven from the bearing using force from the inner side of the hub carrier. if available, use the Peugeot bearing removal tool for your model (Fig. 9.7) which locates in the circlip groove, otherwise use a suitable soft metal drift. Note that the bearing becomes unsuitable for further use after removal of the hub.

5 Using a puller, remove the bearing inner track half from the hub and refit it to the outside of the bearing.

6 Press or drive the bearing from the hub carrier. It is possible that the bearing is so tight that it cannot be removed with hand tools, in which case have your dealer remove it on a press.

7 Clean the hub and bearing recess in the carrier. Do not attempt to remove the seals or plastic ring from the new bearing.

8 Smear a little grease on the bearing recess in the carrier.

9 Press or drive the new bearing into the hub carrier using force on the outer track only, then refit the circlip in the groove.

10 Press the hub into the bearing inner tracks using the special Peugeot tool shown in Fig. 9.8 or a similar tool made from metal tubing, washers, a long bolt and nut. Note that the tube must locate on the inner track and there must be a space provided to receive the plastic ring which is pushed out by the hub.

11 Refit the hub carrier with reference to Section 6.

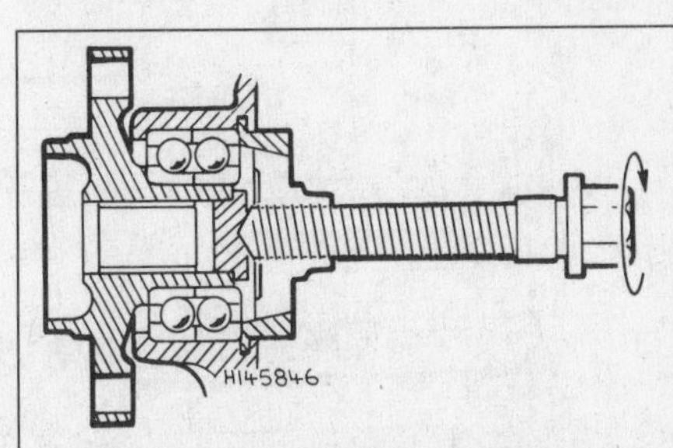

Fig. 9.7 Using Peugeot tool to remove the front hub (Sec 7)

OHV engine models – tool no 0613
OHC engine models – tool no 0606

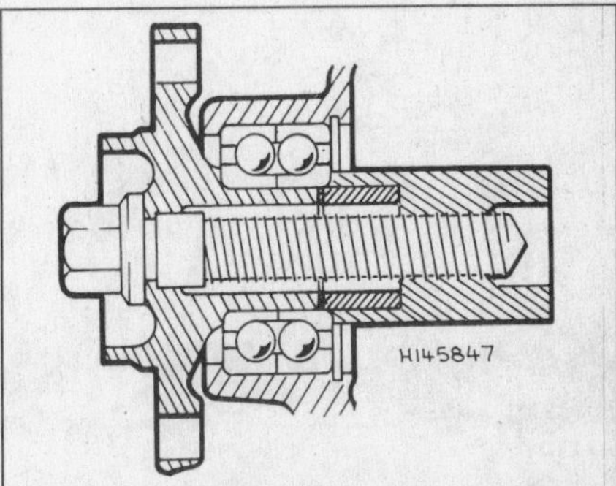

Fig. 9.8 Using Peugeot tool to refit the front hub (Sec 7)

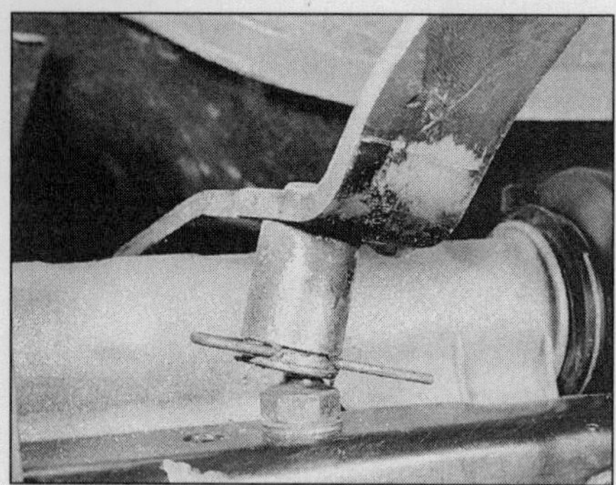

8.5 Gearchange selector rod to subframe connection – withdraw the retaining clip to detach

8.7 Subframe-to-floor mounting bolts

8.10A Lowering the front suspension assembly

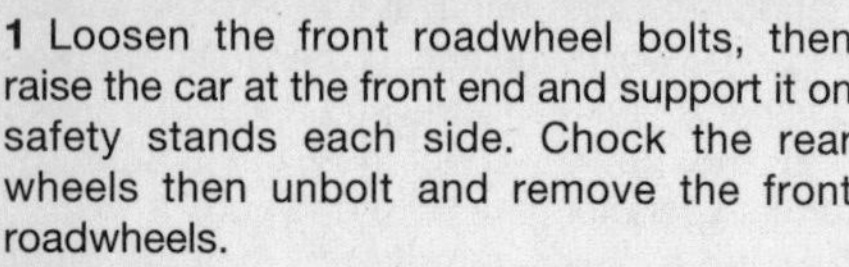

8 Front suspension assembly - removal and refitting

1 Loosen the front roadwheel bolts, then raise the car at the front end and support it on safety stands each side. Chock the rear wheels then unbolt and remove the front roadwheels.

2 Referring to Chapter 8, disconnect the brake caliper unit each side from the hub carrier. The calipers can remain attached to the hydraulic lines providing they are supported to prevent the weight of the caliper straining the hydraulic hose.

3 Disconnect the driveshaft each side from the hub carrier as described in Chapter 7. The driveshafts can be left engaged with the transmission, but suspend them to support their weight.

4 Undo and remove the steering pinion-to-column shaft coupling bolt (see Chapter 10).

5 Disconnect the gearchange selector rod unit from the subframe after extracting the retaining clip (photo).

6 Position a trolley jack centrally under the subframe to support it. Prior to undoing the subframe retaining bolts, enlist the aid of a pair of assistants and have them support the suspension assembly on each side during the detachment and lowering of the unit.

7 Undo and remove the two rear subframe-to-floor mounting bolts each side (photo).

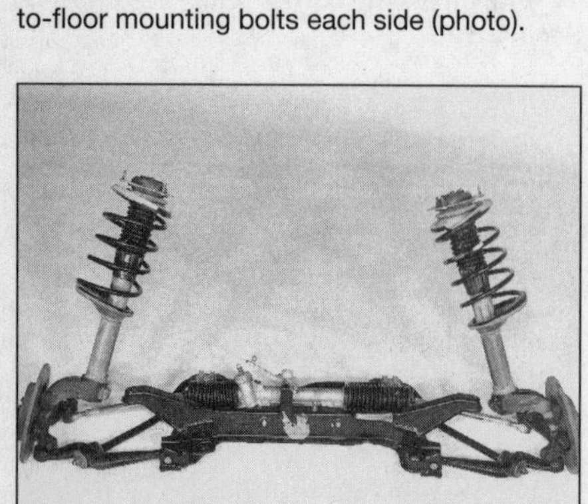

8.10B Front suspension assembly removed from the car and cleaned for inspection

8 Undo and remove the self-locking nut and special washer securing the subframe to the chassis member stud each side.

9 Unscrew and remove the three suspension strut top mounting nuts each side. Remove the flat washers and the harness location bracket on the left-hand side. Detach the earth leads from the spade connectors on the top of each strut.

10 With an assistant steadying the suspension assembly each side, slowly lower the jack under the subframe and, as the unit is lowered, check that the brake lines are clear. Withdraw the unit from under the car (photos).

11 Refitting is a reversal of the removal procedure.

12 When the assembly is initially raised into position, loosely fit the various mounting nuts and bolts, then when they are all located, tighten them to the specified torque settings.

13 Reconnect the driveshafts with reference to Chapter 7.

14 Refit the brake calipers with reference to Chapter 8.

15 Refit the steering couplings with reference to Chapter 10.

16 When the car is lowered to the ground check the brakes and steering for satisfactory action. If any of the steering and/or suspension components were removed or renewed, check the steering geometry with reference to Chapter 10.

9 Rear anti-roll bar - removal and refitting

1 Jack up the rear of the car and support on axle stands. Chock the front wheels and remove the rear wheels.

2 Working on the right-hand side, unscrew the bolt securing the anti-roll bar lever and bracket to the trailing arm. Move the bracket down, leaving it still attached to the handbrake cable.

3 Unscrew the plug from the end of the anti-roll bar then insert a well oiled bolt into the

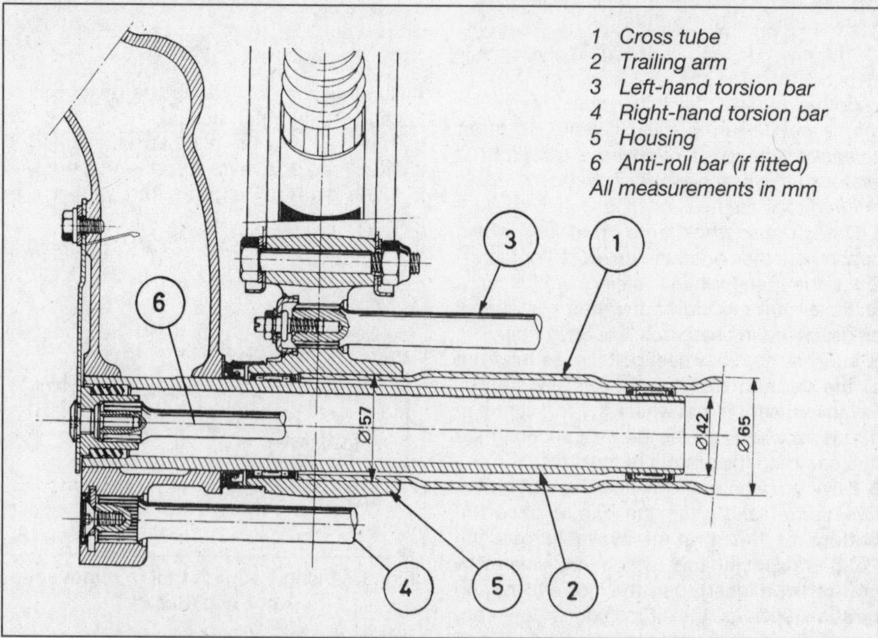

Fig. 9.9 Cross-sectional view of the rear suspension (Sec 9)

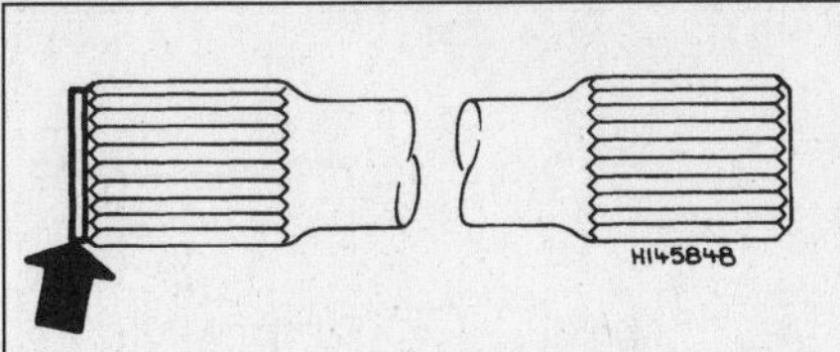

Fig. 9.10 The shoulder at the left-hand end of the rear anti-roll bar (arrowed) (Sec 9)

lever and tighten it until the lever is forced off. If available use the bolt included in the Peugeot tool kit 70908.

4 Working on the left-hand side, unscrew the bolt securing the anti-roll bar lever and bracket to the trailing arm, then move the bracket down leaving it still attached to the handbrake cable.

5 Withdraw the anti-roll bar to the left.

6 Mount the anti-roll bar in a vice with the lever uppermost then remove the lever using the procedure described in paragraph 3.

7 Before refitting the anti-roll bar, clean the splines both on the bar and levers and coat them with Esso Norva 275 grease.

8 Mount the anti-roll bar in the vice with its left-hand end uppermost. Note that the left-hand end has an additional shoulder, as shown in Fig. 9.10.

9 Fit a new sealing ring to the left-hand lever. The left-hand lever has a single identification line on its inner face. Locate the ring with the curved end facing inwards and apply some Kluber Proba grease to its outer surface.

10 Slide the lever on the bar with the identification line aligned with the line on the bar shoulder.

11 Press the lever fully onto the splines using Peugeot tool 70908 or a suitable nut, bolt and washer. If the lever is particularly tight it is permissible to drive it on with a length of metal tube.

12 Remove the tool and fit a temporary bolt in the bar to ensure the lever does not move in subsequent work.

13 Where the lever incorporates a 2 mm recess, fit a new seal; otherwise apply some sealant to the lever shoulder.

14 Insert the anti-roll bar into the left-hand side of the suspension tube then position the handbrake lever bracket, insert the bolt and tighten it to the specified torque.

15 Fit a new sealing ring to the right-hand lever. The right-hand lever has three identification lines at 120° intervals on its inner face. Locate the ring with the curved end facing inwards and apply some Kluber Proba grease to its outer surface.

16 Slide the lever on the bar so that the bolt holes in the lever and trailing arm are aligned.

17 Locate a 1.0 mm (0.039 in) spacer between the lever and trailing arm, as shown in Fig. 9.11, then press on the lever using the method described in paragraph 11. If a metal tube is used, the left-hand lever must be suitably supported.

18 Remove the tool and spacer, then

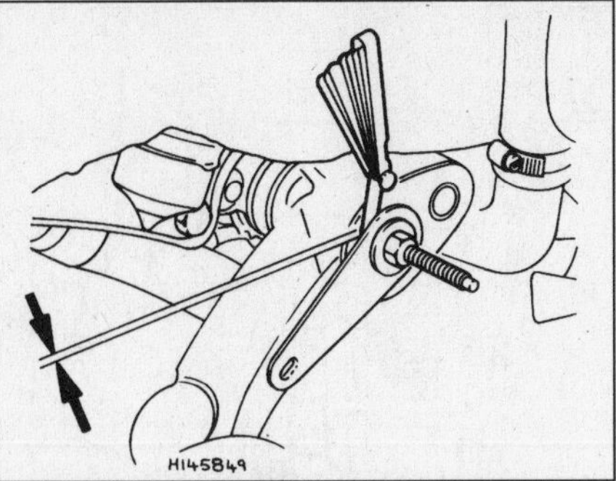

Fig. 9.11 Using feeler blades to check the rear anti-roll bar end gap (Sec 9)

position the handbrake lever bracket, insert the bolt, and tighten it.

19 Remove the temporary bolt fitted in paragraph 12.

20 Apply sealing compound to the threads and collars of the end plugs and screw them into the levers.

21 Refit the rear wheels then lower the car to the ground.

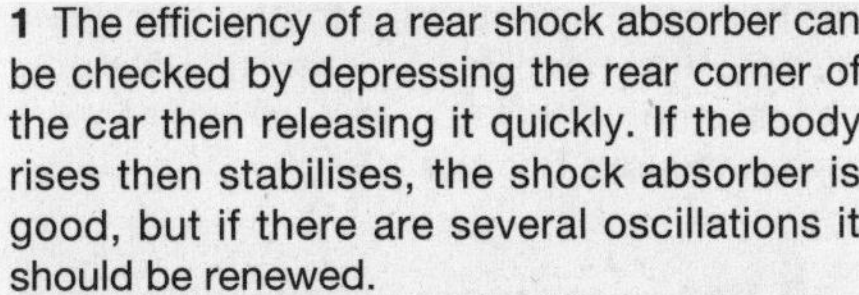

10 Rear shock absorber - testing, removal and refitting

1 The efficiency of a rear shock absorber can be checked by depressing the rear corner of the car then releasing it quickly. If the body rises then stabilises, the shock absorber is good, but if there are several oscillations it should be renewed.

2 Position the rear of the car on ramps or alternatively jack it up and support it beneath the wheels. Apply the handbrake.

3 Unscrew the shock absorber bottom mounting nut and tap the bolt outwards until it clears the shock absorber (photo). If the bolt head fouls the handbrake cable bracket, loosen the bracket bolt on the side of the trailing arm and lift the bracket as required. Do not forget to tighten the bolt after refitting the shock absorber.

4 Unscrew the upper mounting nut, remove the washer, and tap out the bolt.

5 Withdraw the shock absorber from under the car.

6 A more thorough check of the shock absorber may now be made by gripping the bottom mounting in a vice and attempting to extend and retract it. If the resistance is not firm and even in both directions, or if there are signs of leakage or damage, the shock absorber must be renewed.

7 Refitting is a reversal of removal, but renew the self-locking nuts. The nuts must be tightened when the distance between the mounting bolt centres is 288.0 mm (11.339 in). The Peugeot tool 80911 for this operation consists of a bar and adjustable bolt located beneath the lifting ramp and hooked on the suspension tube; however, loading the rear of

10.3 General view of the rear suspension assembly with the shock absorber upper and lower mounting bolts indicated (arrowed)

the car by trial and error will produce the same result.

11 Rear torsion bar - removal and refitting

The removal of the rear torsion bar will necessitate the use of a suitable slide hammer. If available use Peugeot tool 0316 and adaptor 0908.

1 Jack up the rear of the car and support on axle stands under the body. Chock the front wheels and remove the rear wheels.

2 Remove the rear anti-roll bar, as described in Section 9.

3 Remove the shock absorber on the side being worked on, with reference to Section 10.

4 In order to retain the suspension ride height it is necessary to hold the trailing arm stationary with the torsion bar relaxed. Note that the arm itself must be slightly raised to eliminate the effect of its own weight. If available use Peugeot tool 0908 fitted in place of the shock absorber, otherwise firmly support the trailing arm and record the distance between the shock absorber mounting bolt centres (Fig. 9.12).

5 Unscrew and remove the nut and washer from the torsion bar end fitted to the suspension tube.

6 Unscrew the bolt and remove the seal and thrust washer from the torsion bar end fitted to the trailing arm.

7 Using a centre punch, mark the torsion bar and trailing arm in relation to each other.

8 Support the trailing arm then extract the torsion bar using a slide hammer and adaptor screwed into the end of the bar. When

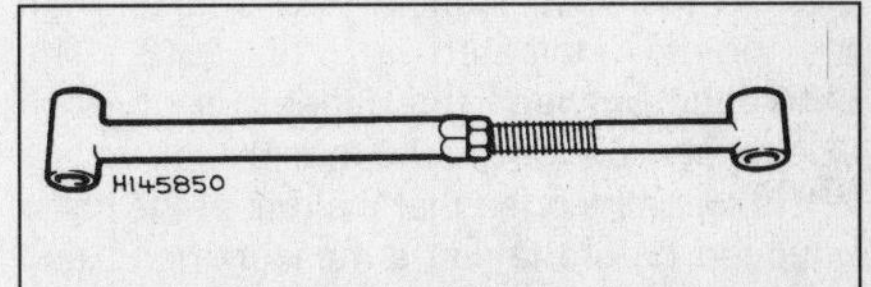

Fig. 9.12 Peugeot tool 0908 for use as a dummy rear shock absorber (Sec 11)

removing the left-hand side torsion bar take care not to damage the hydraulic brake line by supporting the suspension arm.

9 Unscrew the shouldered stud from the end of the bar.

10 Note that the right and left-hand torsion bars are different - the right one is identified by one painted ring whereas the left one has two painted rings.

11 If the original torsion bar is being refitted and the ride height is correct, check that the dimension recorded in paragraph 4 is still correct. If the ride height is being adjusted refer to Section 12 and set the dimension accordingly. If a new torsion bar is being fitted, set the dimension by raising or lowering the trailing arm to 347.5 mm (13.681 in).

12 Screw in the shouldered stud fully into the 24.2 mm diameter end of the torsion bar.

13 Coat the torsion bar splines with Esso Norva 275 grease, then insert the small end through the arm and engage it with the splines on the suspension tube bracket. It will be necessary to try the bar in several positions. If the original is not being refitted, and the bar will initially only enter by approximately 10.0 mm (0.4 in) as the splines at each end are not in the same plane. When the correct splines are engaged, drive the bar fully into position using the slide hammer and adaptor, or a suitable drift.

14 Pack the recess in the arm with grease then fit the thrust washer, a new seal and the bolt. Tighten the bolt.

15 Using a feeler gauge, check that the gap between the trailing arm and suspension tube is 0.05 mm (0.002 in). If it is greater strike the outer surface of the arm with a wooden mallet.

16 Unscrew the shouldered stud at the opposite end of the bar until it just contacts the cup. Recheck the gap, as in paragraph 15, then fit the washer and nut and tighten the nut. To prevent the stud moving hold it with a screwdriver while tightening the nut.

17 Refit the shock absorber (Section 10) and anti-roll bar (Section 9).

18 Refit the rear wheels and lower the car to the ground.

12 Rear suspension ride height - adjustment

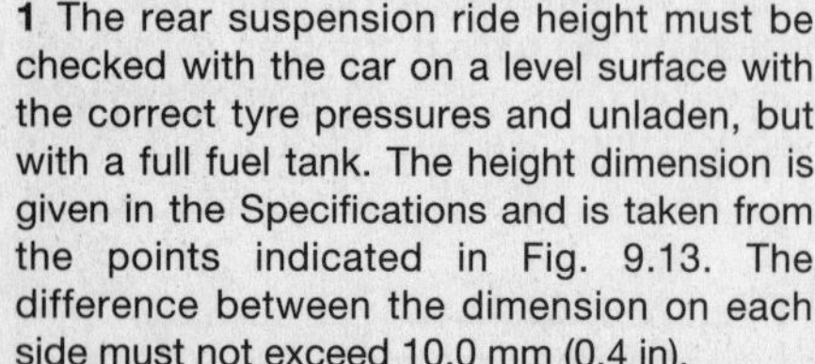

1 The rear suspension ride height must be checked with the car on a level surface with the correct tyre pressures and unladen, but with a full fuel tank. The height dimension is given in the Specifications and is taken from the points indicated in Fig. 9.13. The difference between the dimension on each side must not exceed 10.0 mm (0.4 in).

2 It is recommended that the rear of the car is bounced before taking a measurement, and that the average of three successive measurements be taken as the final reading.

3 Note that an adjustment on one side will slightly alter the ride height on the opposite side.

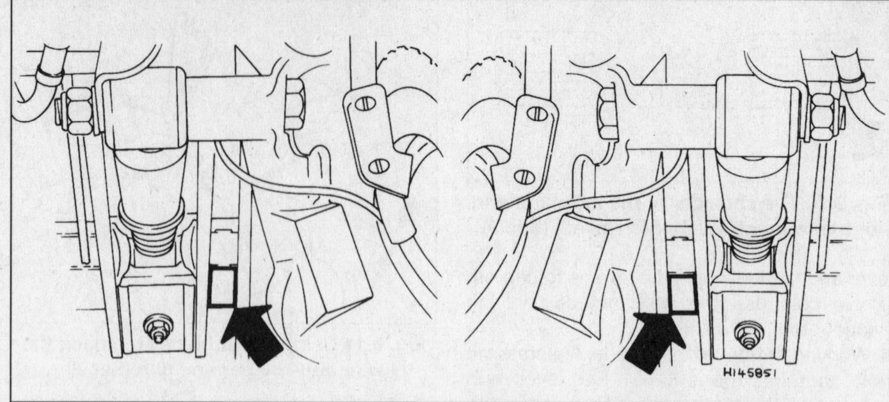

Fig. 9.13 Rear suspension ride height measurement points (arrowed) (Sec 12)

4 To adjust the ride height the torsion bar must be removed and repositioned after setting the trailing arm. A change in the dimension between the shock absorber mounting bolt centres of 2.0 mm (0.08 in) is equivalent to a change in ride height of 3.0 mm (0.12 in). Therefore it is essential to record the existing shock absorber and ride height dimensions before making an adjustment. The torsion bar removal and refitting procedure is given in Section 11.

5 After ride height adjustment has been made, the headlight beam adjustments should be checked and if necessary readjusted (see Chapter 12).

13 Rear suspension assembly - removal and refitting

1 Disconnect the handbrake cables at the lever end and withdraw them through the floor. Refer to Chapter 8 for details. Each cable can be left attached to the drums during removal/refitting.

2 Remove the exhaust system, with reference to Chapter 3.

3 Disconnect the flexible brake hoses from the rear suspension assembly, with reference to Chapter 8.

4 Unscrew the left-hand rear mounting nut, remove the exhaust bracket then temporarily refit the nut.

5 Unbolt and remove the front clamp and bracket, but do not unscrew the seat belt anchorage.

6 Support the suspension crossmember with a trolley jack (centrally located) or a safety stand each side. A trolley jack is preferable if a couple of assistants are available to help steady the suspension unit as it is detached and lowered.

7 Working in the luggage compartment, unscrew the front and rear mounting nuts (photo).

8 Lower the trolley jack supporting the suspension unit and, as it is lowered, check that the handbrake cables and the hydraulic brake lines are free. As previously mentioned, an assistant will be required on each side to help in steadying the suspension assembly as it is lowered and withdrawn (photo).

9 Refitting is a reversal of removal, but tighten all nuts and bolts to the specified torque. When tightening the front clamp make sure that the ring is centred in the seat belt anchorage bracket. Refer to Chapter 8 for information on reconnecting the brake hydraulic lines and the handbrake cables. Bleed the brake hydraulic system as described in that Chapter.

10 Refer to Chapter 3 for information on reconnecting the exhaust system.

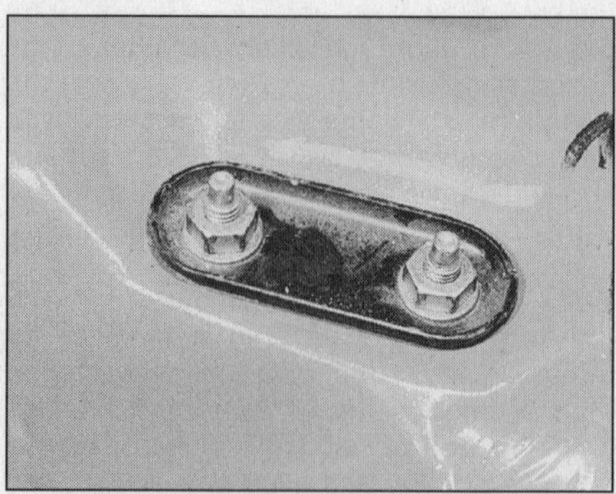

13.7 Rear suspension mounting (front) within the luggage compartment

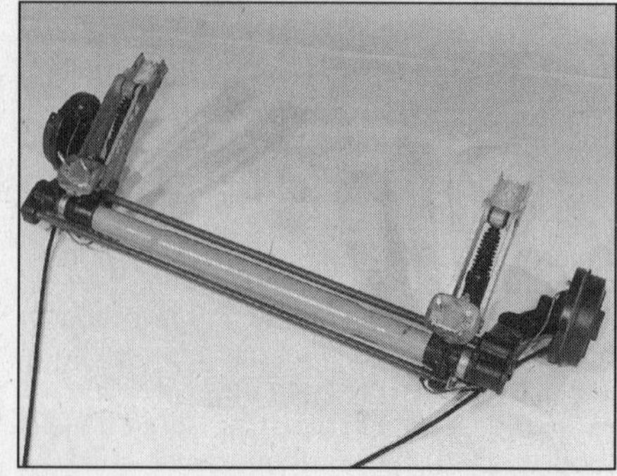

13.8 Rear suspension assembly removed from the car

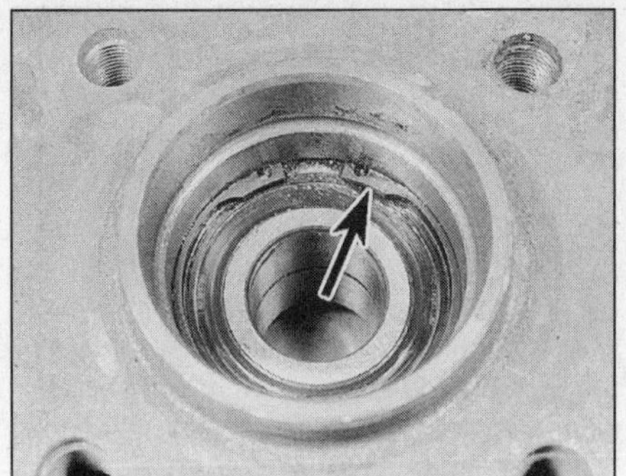

14.3 Rear hub bearing retaining circlip (arrowed)

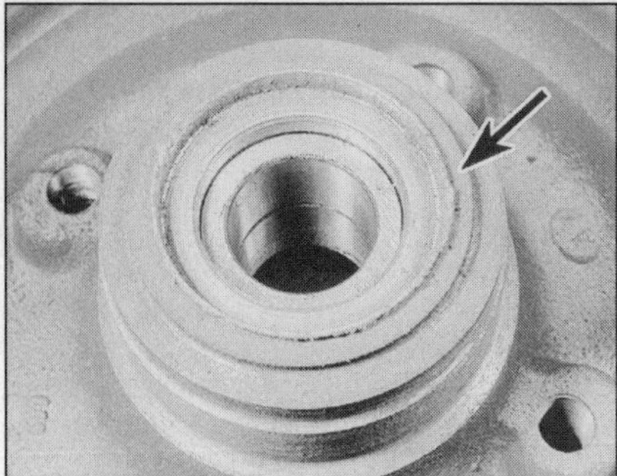

14.5 Oil seal (arrowed) in the rear hub/drum

14 Rear hub/drum - servicing

1 The removal and refitting of the rear hub/drum is described in Chapter 8, together with the inspection of the drum for wear.

2 If the bearing is to be removed from the hub/drum, a new bearing must be used on reassembly. Do not, therefore, remove the bearing unless absolutely necessary.

3 It is not possible to obtain replacement hub bearings from Peugeot although they do in fact supply a bearing retaining circlip separately (photo). If the bearings are worn excessively it will therefore be necessary to renew the complete hub/drum unless non-genuine bearings become available.

4 The bearings can be driven out using a suitable tube drift. Before fitting new bearings, the hub bearing housings must be cleaned and lubricated with Molykote 321R slip compound. The new bearing must be fitted with its lettered face towards the circlip. If pressing the bearing into position do not apply a pressure in excess of five tonnes. Fit a new circlip and carefully drive a new thrust cup into the opposing end of the hub (if removed).

5 If the hub/drum oil seal is worn or damaged it can be renewed by prising it out with a screwdriver and pressing in the new one with a metal tube (photo). Clean and grease the seal contact surface on the trailing arm before refitting the hub/drum.

15 Rear suspension trailing arm and bearings - removal and refitting

1 Jack up the rear of the car and support on axle stands. Chock the front wheels and remove the rear wheels.

2 Remove the handbrake cable and brake shoes on the side being worked on, with reference to Chapter 8.

3 Remove the anti-roll bar, as described in Section 9 (where applicable).

4 Remove the torsion bar, as described in Section 11.

5 Disconnect the hydraulic brake pipes from the wheel cylinder (with reference to Chapter 8).

6 Slide the trailing arm from the suspension tube.

7 Prise the oil seal from the end of the tube and remove the seal sleeve.

8 An extractor is required to remove both the inner and outer bearings and it is recommended that Peugeot tool 0526 is used. The tool comprises a rod and tilting washer which locates behind the bearing - the outer bearing is removed using a slide hammer attachment and the inner bearing is removed using a threaded rod, spacer and nut. If the inner bearing is very tight, a length of rod can be inserted from the opposite end of the tube to release it. Note that the inner bearing may be either plain or needle roller type.

9 If necessary the shaft may be removed from the trailing arm using a press, but first note the fitted position of the shaft, it is recessed by 2.0 mm (0.08 in) from the outer surface. Always refit the shaft in its original position. This can be achieved by inserting a 2 mm thick washer in the bore of the arm to act as a temporary distance spacer when fitting the shaft into the arm. With the shaft fitted, remove the washer.

10 To fit the bearings, first pack them with multi-purpose grease then use the special tool to pull or drive them into position. When fitting the needle bearings the side with the manufacturer's name on it must face towards the relevant open end of the tube.

11 Drive the seal sleeve into the end of the tube.

12 Locate the new seal over the trailing arm shaft, having first filled the spacers between the lips with grease.

13 Insert the trailing arm in the tube until the seal contacts the sleeve, then position a 0.05 mm (0.002 in) feeler gauge between the arm and tube and use a wooden mallet to drive the arm into position.

14 Refit the hydraulic brake pipe to the wheel cylinder and tighten the union.

15 Refit the torsion bar (Section 11) and anti-roll bar (Section 9) as applicable.

16 Refit the handbrake cable and brake shoes then bleed the brakes as described in Chapter 8 (photo).

17 Refit the wheels and lower the car to the ground.

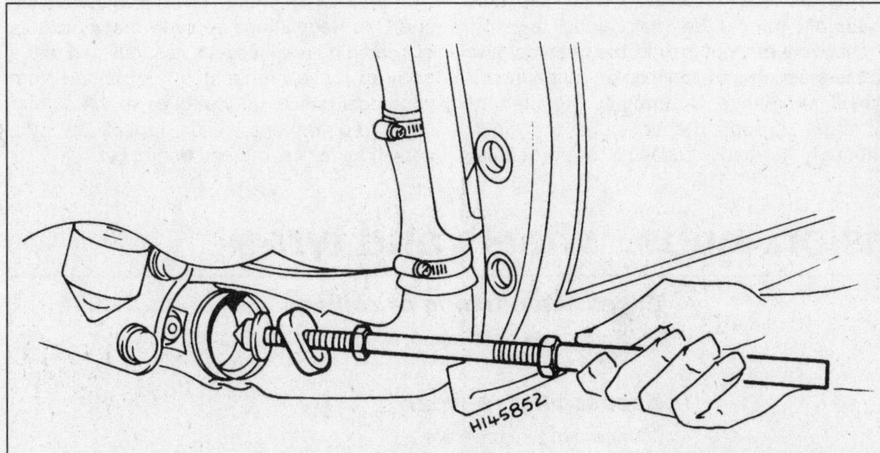

Fig. 9.14 Peugeot tool 0526 for removing the rear suspension trailing arm bearings (Sec 15)

15.16 Rear suspension arm showing handbrake cable and brake hydraulic line attachment

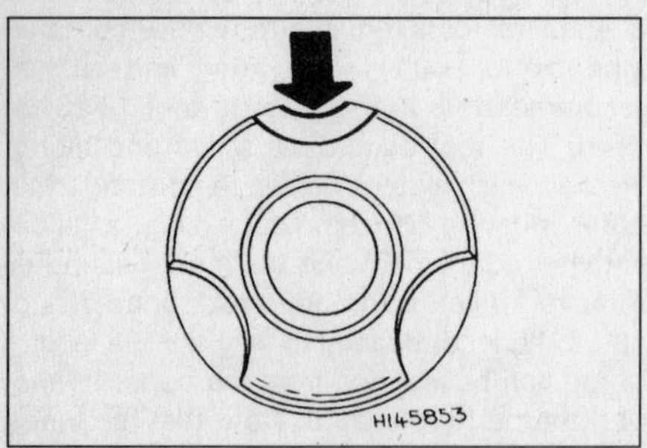

Fig. 9.15 The notch in the rear suspension mounting bushes (arrowed) must be fitted in the vertical plane (Sec 16)

16 Rear suspension mountings and bushes - renewal

1 Remove the rear suspension assembly, as described in Section 13.
2 Unbolt the rear mountings from the side-members.
3 Identify the front mounting brackets for position then unscrew the bolts and remove the brackets.
4 Saw off the ends of the front mounting bushes then drive them out with a metal bar.
5 Dip the new bushes in soapy water and press them into position using a long bolt, nut and spacers. Note that the notch in the flange must be in the vertical plane (ie facing up or down when fitted).
6 Refit the front mounting bracket, insert the bolts from the rear and tighten the nuts with the brackets horizontal.
7 Fit the new rear mountings with the studs towards the wheel side and tighten the nuts.
8 Refit the suspension assembly, with reference to Section 13.

17 Wheels and tyres - general care and maintenance

Wheels and tyres should give no real problems in use provided that a close eye is kept on them with regard to excessive wear or damage. To this end, the following points should be noted.

Ensure that tyre pressures are checked regularly and maintained correctly. Checking should be carried out with the tyres cold and not immediately after the vehicle has been in use. If the pressures are checked with the tyres hot, an apparently high reading will be obtained owing to heat expansion. Under no circumstances should an attempt be made to reduce the pressures to the quoted cold reading in this instance, or effective underinflation will result.

Underinflation will cause overheating of the tyre owing to excessive flexing of the casing, and the tread will not sit correctly on the road surface. This will cause a consequent loss of adhesion and excessive wear, not to mention the danger of sudden tyre failure due to heat build-up.

Overinflation will cause rapid wear of the centre part of the tyre tread coupled with reduced adhesion, harsher ride, and the danger of shock damage occurring in the tyre casing.

Regularly check the tyres for damage in the form of cuts or bulges, especially in the sidewalls. Remove any nails or stones embedded in the tread before they penetrate the tyre to cause deflation. If removal of a nail *does* reveal that the tyre has been punctured, refit the nail so that its point of penetration is marked. Then immediately change the wheel and have the tyre repaired by a tyre dealer. Do *not* drive on a tyre in such a condition. In many cases a puncture can be simply repaired by the use of an inner tube of the correct size and type. If in any doubt as to the possible consequences of any damage found, consult your local tyre dealer for advice.

Periodically remove the wheels and clean any dirt or mud from the inside and outside surfaces. Examine the wheel rims for signs of rusting, corrosion or other damage. Light alloy wheels are easily damaged by 'kerbing' whilst parking, and similarly steel wheels may become dented or buckled. Renewal of the wheel is very often the only course of remedial action possible.

The balance of each wheel and tyre assembly should be maintained to avoid excessive wear, not only to the tyres but also to the steering and suspension components. Wheel imbalance is normally signified by vibration through the vehicle's bodyshell, although in many cases it is particularly noticeable through the steering wheel. Conversely, it should be noted that wear or damage in suspension or steering components may cause excessive tyre wear. Out-of-round or out-of-true tyres, damaged wheels and wheel bearing wear/maladjustment also fall into this category. Balancing will not usually cure vibration caused by such wear.

Wheel balancing may be carried out with the wheel either on or off the vehicle. If balanced on the vehicle, ensure that the wheel-to-hub relationship is marked in some way prior to subsequent wheel removal so that it may be refitted in its original position.

General tyre wear is influenced to a large degree by driving style, harsh braking and acceleration or fast cornering will all produce more rapid tyre wear. Interchanging of tyres may result in more even wear, but this should only be carried out where there is no mix of tyre types on the vehicle However, it is worth bearing in mind that if this is completely effective, the added expense of replacing a complete set of tyres simultaneously is incurred, which may prove financially restrictive for many owners.

Front tyres may wear unevenly as a result of wheel misalignment. The front wheels should always be correctly aligned according to the settings specified by the vehicle manufacturer.

Legal restrictions apply to the mixing of tyre types on a vehicle. Basically this means that a vehicle must not have tyres of differing construction on the same axle. Although it is not recommended to mix tyre types between front axle and rear axle, the only legally permissible combination is crossply at the front and radial at the rear. When mixing radial ply tyres, textile braced radials must always go on the front axle, with steel braced radials at the rear. An obvious disadvantage of such mixing is the necessity to carry two spare tyres to avoid contravening the law in the event of a puncture.

In the UK, the Motor Vehicles Construction and Use Regulations apply to many aspects of tyre fitting and usage. It is suggested that a copy of these regulations is obtained from your local police if in doubt as to the current legal requirements with regard to tyre condition, minimum tread depth, etc.

Fault finding - suspension, hubs, wheels and tyres

Car pulls to one side

- ☐ Worn front suspension lower balljoint
- ☐ Incorrect tyre pressures

Wheel wobble or vibration

- ☐ Unbalanced wheels
- ☐ Damaged wheels
- ☐ Worn wheel bearings
- ☐ Worn shock absorbers

Excessive pitching or rolling

- ☐ Worn shock absorbers

Excessive tyre wear

- ☐ Incorrect tyre pressures
- ☐ Worn front suspension lower balljoint
- ☐ Unbalanced wheels

Chapter 10 Steering

For modifications, and information applicable to later models, see Supplement at end of manual

Contents

Degrees of difficulty

Easy, suitable for novice with little experience 

Fairly easy, suitable for beginner with some experience 

Fairly difficult, suitable for competent DIY mechanic 

Difficult, suitable for experienced DIY mechanic 

Very difficult, suitable for expert DIY or professional

Specifications

General

Type	Rack and pinion. Steering column with universal joint. Power-assisted steering on some models
Steering wheel turns (lock-to-lock):	
Non-assisted steering	3.80
Power-assisted steering	3.26

Front wheel alignment

Toe-in	2 ± 1 mm (0.08 ± 0.04 in)
Castor	0°30' ± 30'
Camber	0° ± 30'
Steering axis inclination	9°30' ± 30'

Power-assisted steering

Fluid type	Dexron II type ATF

Torque wrench settings

	Nm	lbf ft
Steering gear	35	26
Column-to-pinion clamp bolt	15	11
Track rod balljoint nut	35	26
Track rod inner locknut	45	33

1 General description

The steering system is of rack and pinion type with side track rods connected to the hub carriers by balljoints. Further balljoints on the inner ends of the track rods are screwed into the rack.

The steering column incorporates a single universal joint at its lower end connected to an intermediate shaft which also incorporates a universal joint at its connection to the pinions on the steering gear. The steering column is angled to prevent direct movement into the passenger compartment in the event of a front end impact.

Power steering

Fitted to certain models only, the power assistance is derived from a pump which is driven by the alternator drivebelt. At the time of writing, limited information on the power steering system is available and therefore any repairs concerning the power steering system and components should be entrusted to your Peugeot dealer.

2 Routine maintenance

Carry out the following procedures at the intervals given in Routine Maintenance at the beginning of the manual.

1 Jack up the front of the car and support on axle stands. Apply the handbrake. Thoroughly examine the bellows at each end of the steering gear for splitting and deterioration, and renew if necessary.

2 Check the track rod ends for excessive wear by attempting to move them up and down. If there is more than the very slightest movement the track rod end should be renewed. Similarly check the track rod inner joints by gripping the track rod through the bellows and attempting to move them up and down. Track rod ends should also be renewed if the rubber boots are split or damaged.

Power steering

3 Maintenance consists of checking the fluid level in the reservoir and checking the pump drivebelt tension and condition.

3.2 Prise free the steering wheel centre pad – SRI model shown

4 The power steering pump reservoir is translucent and has level markings on it, these being 'high' and low. The fluid level must not drop below the minimum level mark (fluid cold). If topping-up becomes necessary do not fill beyond the maximum mark.
5 Topping-up should only be done with clean fluid of the correct type (see Specifications). Regular need for topping-up can only be due to a leak, which should be rectified. If the pump is run dry it will be damaged: disconnect the drivebelt rather than let this happen.
6 To check, adjust and/or renew the drivebelt refer to Chapter 12, Section 5.

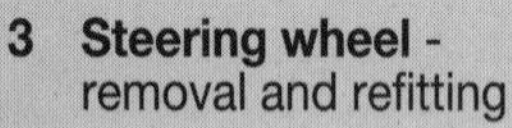

3 Steering wheel - removal and refitting

1 Set the front wheels in the straight-ahead position.
2 Prise out the centre pad (photo), then use a socket to unscrew the retaining nut. On some models the centre pad is secured by retaining screws recessed in the underside of the steering wheel.
3 Mark the hub in relation to the inner column then pull off the steering wheel. If it is tight a rocking action may release it from the splines.
4 Refitting is a reversal of removal, but check that the steering wheel is correctly centred with the front wheels straight-ahead. Tighten the nut while holding the steering wheel rim.

4 Steering column and lock - removal and refitting

Note: *To remove the steering column lock only, proceed as described in paragraphs 1, 2, 8 and 9.*
1 Remove the steering wheel, as described in Section 3.
2 Remove the lower trim panel from under the steering column.
3 Mark the column lower universal joint in relation to the intermediate shaft then unscrew and remove the clamp bolt (photo).
4 Remove the combination switches, as described in Chapter 12.

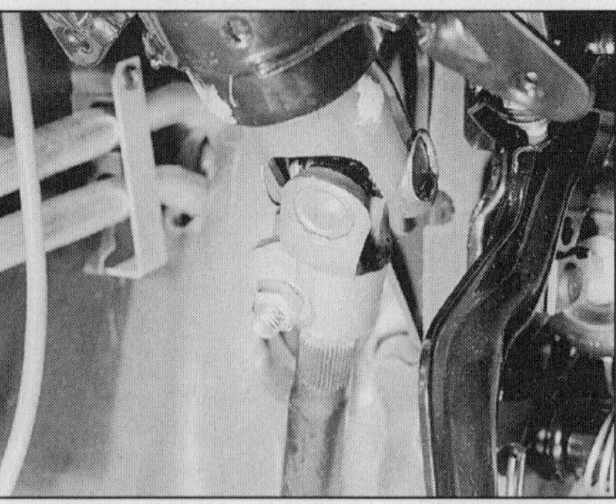

4.3 Steering column lower universal joint, clamp bolt and intermediate shaft

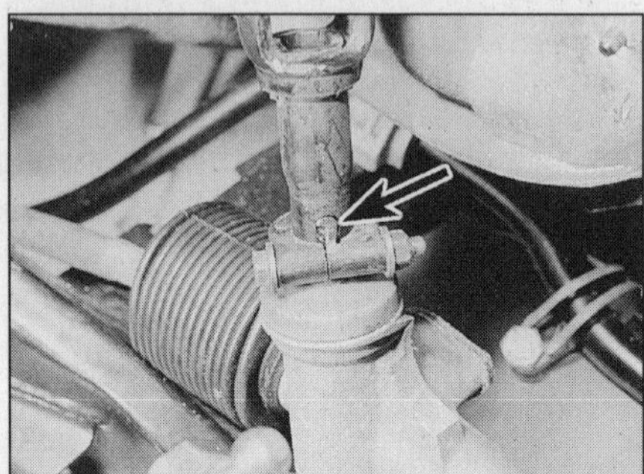

4.7 Steering column intermediate shaft, universal joint and clamp bolt. Note clamp tag location in intermediate shaft (arrowed)

4.6 Undo the steering column mounting bolt/nuts

4.8 Steering lock retaining bolt (arrowed)

5 Disconnect the ignition switch wiring multi-plugs.
6 Unscrew the mounting nuts and bolts (photo) disconnect the inner column from the intermediate shaft, and withdraw the steering column from the car. Where shear-bolts are fitted they must be drilled to remove the heads, then unscrewed after removing the column.
7 If necessary, the intermediate shaft can be removed after prising out the grommet and unscrewing the bottom clamp bolt (photo).
8 To remove the steering lock, unscrew the retaining bolt then, with the ignition key in position A, depress the plunger in the housing (photo).
9 Refitting is a reversal of removal. Renew all shear-head bolts and tighten them until the heads break off.

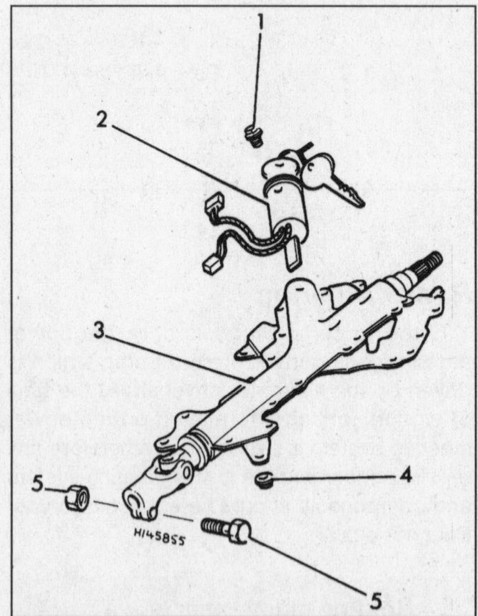

Fig. 10.1 Steering column assembly (Sec 4)

1 Bolt
2 Steering lock and ignition switch
3 Steering column
4 Mounting nut
5 Clamp bolt and nut

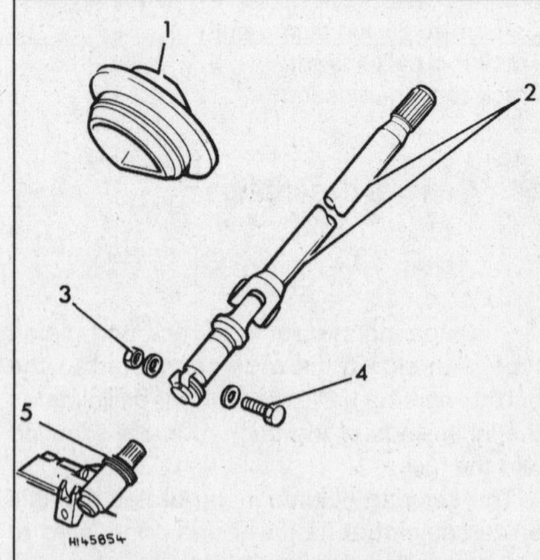

Fig. 10.2 Steering column intermediate shaft components (Sec 4)

1 Grommet
2 Intermediate shaft
3 Nut
4 Bolt
5 Steering gear

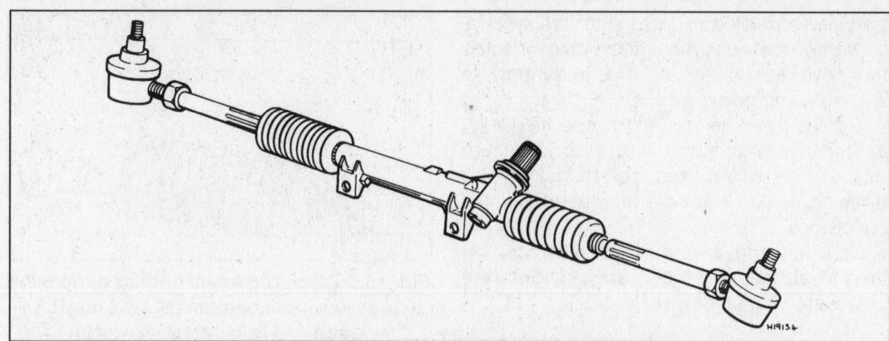

Fig. 10.3 Manual steering gear unit (Sec 5)

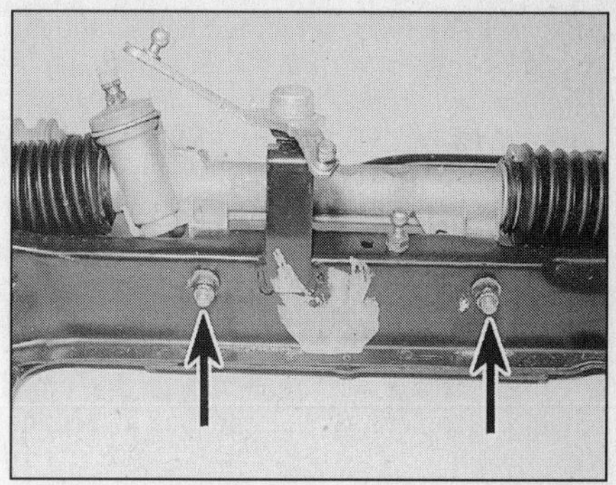

5.6 Steering gear-to-subframe mounting bolts (arrowed)

5 Steering gear - removal and refitting

1 Jack up the front of the car and support on axle stands. Apply the handbrake and remove the front wheels.

2 Unscrew the track rod end nuts then use a separator tool to detach the track rod end balljoints from the hub carriers.

3 On models fitted with power steering, disconnect the feed and return hydraulic hoses from the steering gear pinion housing by unscrewing the union connectors. As each hose is detached, allow for a certain amount of fluid spillage. Plug both the hose and pinion hydraulic ports to prevent excessive leakage of fluid and the ingress of dirt. Position the hydraulic lines out of the way.

4 Mark the lower column in relation to the pinion on the steering gear.

5 Unscrew and remove the column-to-pinion clamp bolt.

6 Unscrew and remove the two mounting bolts and withdraw the steering gear from one side of the subframe (photo).

7 Refitting is a reversal of removal, but tighten all nuts and bolts to the specified torque and check the front wheel alignment on completion. On power steering models top up and bleed the hydraulic system as described in Section 10.

6 Steering gear - overhaul

The steering gear has a very long life before any wear becomes evident, always provided that the bellows are kept in order to maintain adequate lubrication.

In view of the special tools and gauges required to overhaul the steering gear it is recommended that, when the need for this arises, the assembly should be changed for a new or factory reconditioned one rather than dismantle the worn unit.

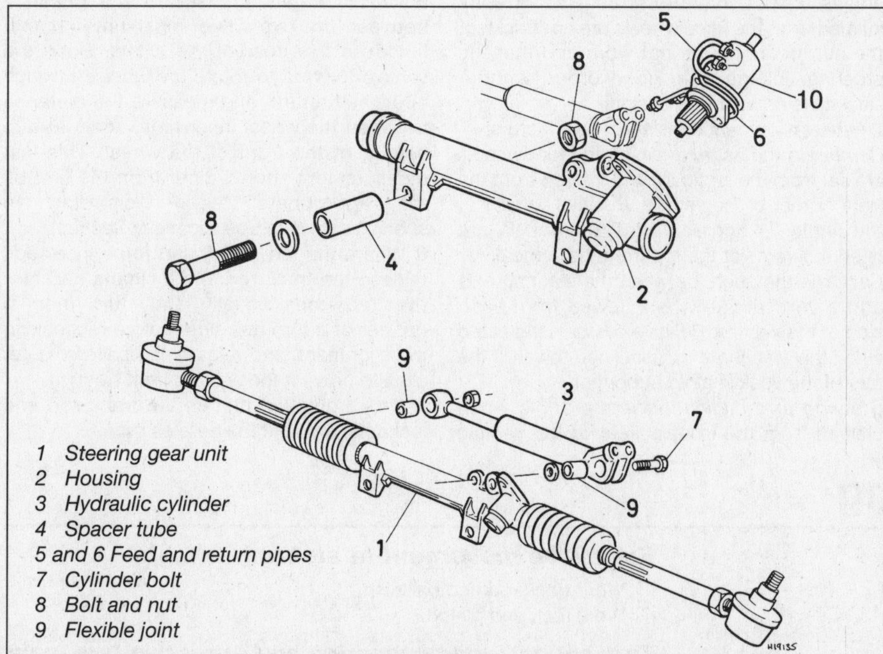

1 Steering gear unit
2 Housing
3 Hydraulic cylinder
4 Spacer tube
5 and 6 Feed and return pipes
7 Cylinder bolt
8 Bolt and nut
9 Flexible joint

Fig. 10.4 Power steering gear unit (Sec 5)

7 Track rod end - removal and refitting

1 Jack up the front of the car and support on axle stands. Apply the handbrake and remove the relevant roadwheel.

2 Loosen the locknut on the track rod.

3 Unscrew the balljoint nut and use an extractor tool to separate the taper from the hub carrier (photo).

4 Unscrew the track rod end from the track rod, noting the number of turns necessary to remove it.

5 Screw the new track rod end the same number of turns on the track rod.

6 Clean the taper surfaces then fit the

7.3 Separating the track rod end from the hub carrier

10

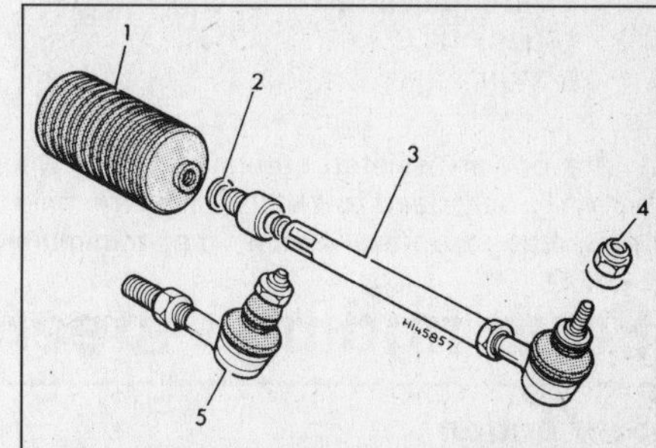

Fig. 10.5 Track rod components (Sec 7)

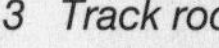

1 Bellows
2 Lock washer
3 Track rod
4 Self-locking nut
5 Track rod end

balljoint to the hub carrier and tighten the nut to the specified torque. **Note:** *If difficulty is experienced in loosening or tightening a balljoint taper pin nut due to the taper pin turning in the eye, apply pressure with a jack or long lever to the balljoint socket to force the taper pin into its conical seat.*

7 Tighten the locknut on the track rod end.

8 Refit the roadwheel and lower the car to the ground.

9 Check and if necessary adjust the front wheel toe-in setting, as described in Section 12.

8 Steering rack bellows - renewal

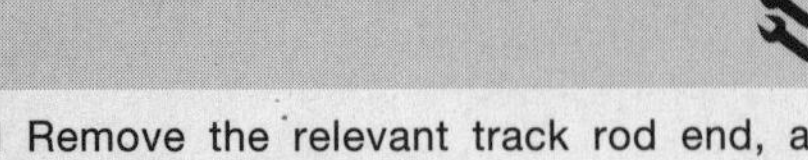

1 Remove the relevant track rod end, as described in Section 7.

2 Release the clips from each end of the bellows then ease the bellows from the steering gear and pull it from the track rod.

3 Clean the track rod and bellows location on the steering gear. If necessary, add molybdenum disulphide grease to the steering gear.

4 Slide the new bellows onto the track rod and steering gear, check that it is not twisted, then fit the clips.

5 Refit the track rod with reference to Section 7.

9 Track rod - renewal

1 Remove the steering rack bellows, as described in Section 8.

2 Using open-ended spanners, hold the rack and loosen the track rod joint socket. Unscrew the socket and withdraw the track rod.

3 Fit the new track rod using a reversal of the removal procedure, but fit a new lock washer and tighten the joint socket to the specified torque.

10 Power-assisted steering - bleeding

1 The power-assisted steering system will normally only need to be bled if (a) the fluid level has dropped below the minimum specified and allowed air to enter the system, (b) part of the system has been disconnected for any reason or (c) if the system is suspected of having air in it.

2 Top the reservoir up with the specified fluid.

3 Start the engine and allow it to idle. Turn the steering wheel from lock to lock two or three times. **Do not** hold the steering wheel on full lock.

4 Stop the engine and check the reservoir fluid level: top up if necessary. Inspect the power steering unions for leaks.

11 Power-assisted steering pump - removal and refitting

1 Remove the alternator/power steering pump drivebelt as described in Chapter 12, Section 5.

2 Syphon as much fluid as possible out of the fluid reservoir using an old poultry baster or similar item.

3 Disconnect and plug the pipe at the steering pump.

4 Unbolt and remove the pump.

5 Refit in the reverse order of removal. Tension the drivebelt (Chapter 12) and bleed the system (Section 10) to complete.

12 Steering angles and front wheel alignment

1 Accurate front wheel alignment is essential to provide good steering and roadholding characteristics and to ensure slow and even tyre wear. Before considering the steering angles, check that the tyres are correctly inflated, that the front wheels are not buckled, the hub bearings are not worn and that the steering linkage is in good order, without slackness or wear at the joints.

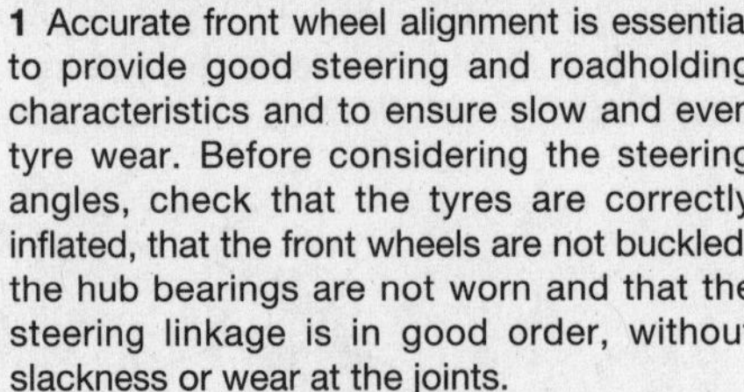

2 Wheel alignment consists of four factors:

Camber is the angle at which the roadwheels are set from the vertical when viewed from the front or rear of the vehicle. Positive camber is the angle (in degrees) that the wheels are tilted outwards at the top from the vertical.

Castor is the angle between the steering axis and a vertical line when viewed from each side of the vehicle. Positive castor is indicated when the steering axis is inclined towards the rear of the vehicle at its upper end.

Steering axis inclination is the angle when viewed from the front or rear of the vehicle between vertical and an imaginary line drawn between the upper and lower strut mountings.

Camber, castor and steering axis inclination are set during production of the car and any deviation from specified tolerance must therefore be due to gross wear in the suspension mountings or collision damage.

Toe is the amount by which the distance between the front inside edges of the roadwheel rims differs from that between the rear inside edges. If the distance between the front edges is less than that at the rear, the wheels are said to toe-in. If the distance between the front inside edges is greater than that at the rear, the wheels toe-out.

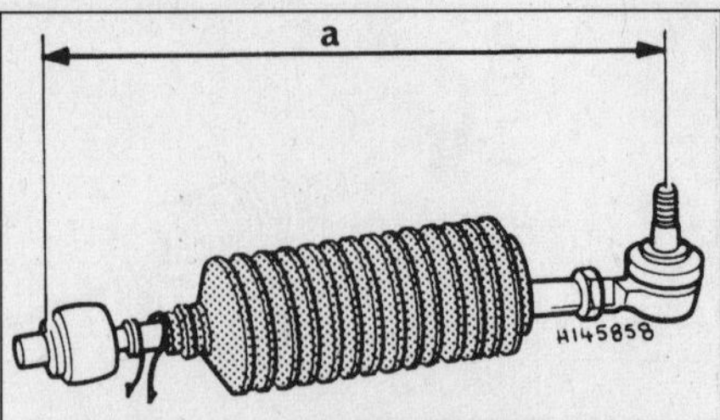

Fig. 10.6 Track rod initial setting dimension – measure between points (a). Length of each rod to be equal (Sec 12)

3 To check the front wheel alignment, first make sure that the lengths of both track rods are equal when the steering is in the straight-ahead position .

4 Obtain a tracking gauge. These are available in various forms from accessory stores or one can be fabricated from a length of steel tubing suitably cranked to clear the sump and bellhousing and having a setscrew and locknut at one end.

5 With the gauge, measure the distance between the two wheel inner rims (at hub height) at the rear of the wheel. Push the vehicle forward to rotate the wheels through 180° (half a turn) and measure the distance between the wheel inner rims, again at hub height, at the front of the wheel. This last measurement should differ from the first by the appropriate toe-in according to specification (see Specifications Section).

6 Where the toe-in is found to be incorrect, release the track rod end locknuts and turn the track-rods equally. Only turn them a quarter of a turn at a time before rechecking the alignment, and release the bellows outer clips to prevent the bellows from twisting.

7 On completion tighten the track rod end locknuts, and refit the bellows clips.

Fault finding - steering

Stiff action

- ☐ Lack of rack lubrication
- ☐ Seized track rod end balljoint
- ☐ Seized track rod inner balljoint

Excessive movement at steering wheel

- ☐ Worn track rod end balljoints
- ☐ Worn rack and pinion

Tyre squeal when cornering and excessive tyre wear

- ☐ Incorrect wheel alignment

Chapter 11 Bodywork and fittings

For modifications, and information applicable to later models, see Supplement at end of manual

Contents

Degrees of difficulty

Easy, suitable for novice with little experience 	**Fairly easy,** suitable for beginner with some experience 	**Fairly difficult,** suitable for competent DIY mechanic	**Difficult,** suitable for experienced DIY mechanic 	**Very difficult,** suitable for expert DIY or professional

1 General description

The hatchback style body has a shell which is of one-piece design and safety cell construction, whereby the outer members yield progressively and in a controlled direction in the event of impact, giving maximum protection to the passenger compartment. The body panels are of lightweight high strength steel.

The front wings are bolted to the main body for ease of removal. The complete body is given an extensive anti-corrosion treatment during manufacture; including stone chip protection and wax injection. Peugeot guarantee the body against perforation as a result of corrosion for a period of six years provided the car is given periodic inspections by a Peugeot garage.

2 Maintenance - bodywork and underframe

The general condition of a vehicle's bodywork is the one thing that significantly affects its value. Maintenance is easy, but needs to be regular. Neglect, particularly after minor damage, can lead quickly to further deterioration and costly repair bills. It is important also to keep watch on those parts of the vehicle not immediately visible, for instance the underside, inside all the wheel arches, and the lower part of the engine compartment.

The basic maintenance routine for the bodywork is washing - preferably with a lot of water, from a hose. This will remove all the loose solids which may have stuck to the vehicle. It is important to flush these off in such a way as to prevent grit from scratching the finish. The wheel arches and underframe need washing in the same way, to remove any accumulated mud, which will retain moisture and tend to encourage rust. Paradoxically enough, the best time to clean the underframe and wheel arches is in wet weather, when the mud is thoroughly wet and soft. In very wet weather, the underframe is usually cleaned of large accumulations automatically, and this is a good time for inspection.

Periodically, except on vehicles with a wax-based underbody protective coating, it is a good idea to have the whole of the

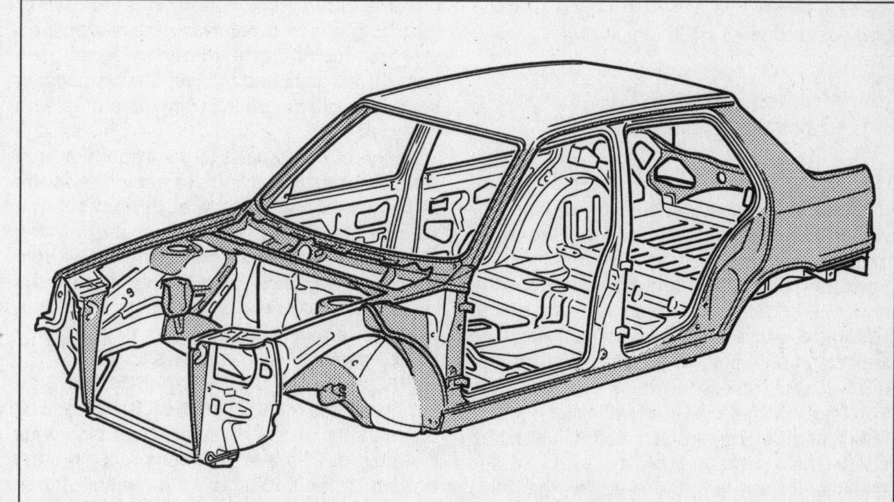

Fig. 11.1 Peugeot 309 bodyshell (5-door) (Sec 1)

11

underframe of the vehicle steam-cleaned, engine compartment included, so that a thorough inspection can be carried out to see what minor repairs and renovations are necessary. Steam-cleaning is available at many garages, and is necessary for the removal of the accumulation of oily grime, which sometimes is allowed to become thick in certain areas. If steam-cleaning facilities are not available, there are some excellent grease solvents available which can be brush-applied; the dirt can then be simply hosed off. Note that these methods should not be used on vehicles with wax-based underbody protective coating, or the coating will be removed. Such vehicles should be inspected annually, preferably just prior to Winter, when the underbody should be washed down, and any damage to the wax coating repaired. Ideally, a completely fresh coat should be applied. It would also be worth considering the use of such wax-based protection for injection into door panels, sills, box sections, etc, as an additional safeguard against rust damage, where such protection is not provided by the vehicle manufacturer.

After washing paintwork, wipe off with a chamois leather to give an unspotted clear finish. A coat of clear protective wax polish will give added protection against chemical pollutants in the air. If the paintwork sheen has dulled or oxidised, use a cleaner/polisher combination to restore the brilliance of the shine. This requires a little effort, but such dulling is usually caused because regular washing has been neglected. Care needs to be taken with metallic paintwork, as special non-abrasive cleaner/polisher is required to avoid damage to the finish. Always check that the door and ventilator opening drain holes and pipes are completely clear, so that water can be drained out (photos). Brightwork should be treated in the same way as paintwork. Windscreens and windows can be kept clear of the smeary film which often appears, by the use of proprietary glass cleaner. Never use any form of wax or other body or chromium polish on glass.

3 Maintenance - upholstery and carpets

Mats and carpets should be brushed or vacuum-cleaned regularly, to keep them free of grit. If they are badly stained, remove them from the vehicle for scrubbing or sponging, and make quite sure they are dry before refitting. Seats and interior trim panels can be kept clean by wiping with a damp cloth. If they do become stained (which can be more apparent on light-coloured upholstery), use a little liquid detergent and a soft nail brush to scour the grime out of the grain of the material. Do not forget to keep the headlining clean in the same way as the upholstery. When using liquid cleaners inside the vehicle, do not over-wet the surfaces being cleaned. Excessive damp could get into the seams and padded interior, causing stains, offensive odours or even rot.

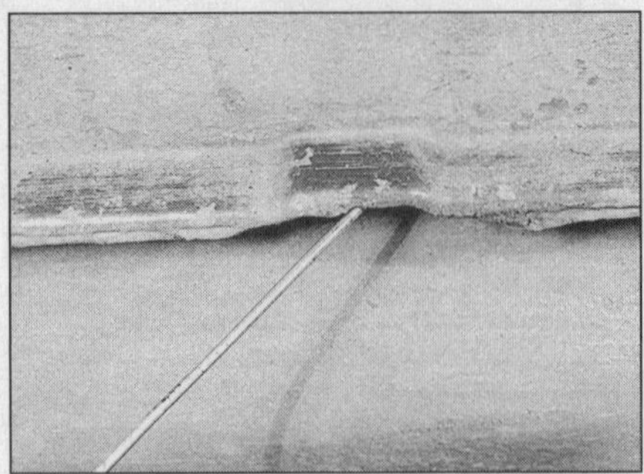

2.4A Check the sill drain points for blockage

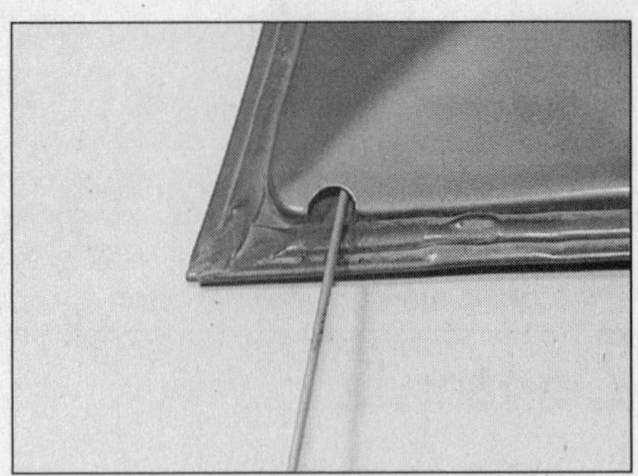

2.4B Check the door drain points for blockage

If the inside of the vehicle gets wet accidentally, it is worthwhile taking some trouble to dry it out properly, particularly where carpets are involved. Do not leave oil or electric heaters inside the vehicle for this purpose.

4 Minor body damage - repair

Note: *For more detailed information about bodywork repair, Haynes Publishing produce a book by Lindsay Porter called "The Car Bodywork Repair Manual". This incorporates information on such aspects as rust treatment, painting and glass-fibre repairs, as well as details on more ambitious repairs involving welding and panel beating.*

Repairs of minor scratches in bodywork

If the scratch is very superficial, and does not penetrate to the metal of the bodywork, repair is very simple. Lightly rub the area of the scratch with a paintwork renovator, or a very fine cutting paste, to remove loose paint from the scratch, and to clear the surrounding bodywork of wax polish. Rinse the area with clean water.

Apply touch-up paint to the scratch using a fine paint brush; continue to apply fine layers of paint until the surface of the paint in the scratch is level with the surrounding paintwork. Allow the new paint at least two weeks to harden, then blend it into the surrounding paintwork by rubbing the scratch area with a paintwork renovator or a very fine cutting paste. Finally, apply wax polish.

Where the scratch has penetrated right through to the metal of the bodywork, causing the metal to rust, a different repair technique is required. Remove any loose rust from the bottom of the scratch with a penknife, then apply rust-inhibiting paint to prevent the formation of rust in the future. Using a rubber or nylon applicator, fill the scratch with bodystopper paste. If required, this paste can be mixed with cellulose thinners to provide a very thin paste which is ideal for filling narrow scratches. Before the stopper-paste in the scratch hardens, wrap a piece of smooth cotton rag around the top of a finger. Dip the finger in cellulose thinners, and quickly sweep it across the surface of the stopper-paste in the scratch; this will ensure that the surface of the stopper-paste is slightly hollowed. The scratch can now be painted over as described earlier in this Section.

Repairs of dents in bodywork

When deep denting of the vehicle's bodywork has taken place, the first task is to pull the dent out, until the affected bodywork almost attains its original shape. There is little point in trying to restore the original shape completely, as the metal in the damaged area will have stretched on impact, and cannot be reshaped fully to its original contour. It is better to bring the level of the dent up to a point which is about 3 mm below the level of the surrounding bodywork. In cases where the dent is very shallow anyway, it is not worth trying to pull it out at all. If the underside of the dent is accessible, it can be hammered out gently from behind, using a mallet with a wooden or plastic head. Whilst doing this, hold a suitable block of wood firmly against the outside of the panel, to absorb the impact from the hammer blows and thus prevent a large area of the bodywork from being "belled-out".

Should the dent be in a section of the bodywork which has a double skin, or some other factor making it inaccessible from behind, a different technique is called for. Drill several small holes through the metal inside the area - particularly in the deeper section. Then screw long self-tapping screws into the holes, just sufficiently for them to gain a good purchase in the metal. Now the dent can be pulled out by pulling on the protruding heads of the screws with a pair of pliers.

The next stage of the repair is the removal of the paint from the damaged area, and from an inch or so of the surrounding "sound" bodywork. This is accomplished most easily by using a wire brush or abrasive pad on a power drill, although it can be done just as effectively by hand, using sheets of abrasive paper. To complete the preparation for filling, score the surface of the bare metal with a screwdriver or the tang of a file, or alternatively, drill small holes in the affected area. This will provide a really good "key" for the filler paste.

To complete the repair, see the Section on filling and respraying.

Repairs of rust holes or gashes in bodywork

Remove all paint from the affected area, and from an inch or so of the surrounding "sound" bodywork, using an abrasive pad or a wire brush on a power drill. If these are not available, a few sheets of abrasive paper will do the job most effectively. With the paint removed, you will be able to judge the severity of the corrosion, and therefore decide whether to renew the whole panel (if this is possible) or to repair the affected area. New body panels are not as expensive as most people think, and it is often quicker and more satisfactory to fit a new panel than to attempt to repair large areas of corrosion.

Remove all fittings from the affected area, except those which will act as a guide to the original shape of the damaged bodywork (eg headlight shells etc). Then, using tin snips or a hacksaw blade, remove all loose metal and any other metal badly affected by corrosion. Hammer the edges of the hole inwards, in order to create a slight depression for the filler paste.

Wire-brush the affected area to remove the powdery rust from the surface of the remaining metal. Paint the affected area with rust-inhibiting paint, if the back of the rusted area is accessible, treat this also.

Before filling can take place, it will be necessary to block the hole in some way. This can be achieved by the use of aluminium or plastic mesh, or aluminium tape.

Aluminium or plastic mesh, or glass-fibre matting, is probably the best material to use for a large hole. Cut a piece to the approximate size and shape of the hole to be filled, then position it in the hole so that its edges are below the level of the surrounding bodywork. It can be retained in position by several blobs of filler paste around its periphery.

Aluminium tape should be used for small or very narrow holes. Pull a piece off the roll, trim it to the approximate size and shape required, then pull off the backing paper (if used) and stick the tape over the hole; it can be overlapped if the thickness of one piece is insufficient. Burnish down the edges of the tape with the handle of a screwdriver or similar, to ensure that the tape is securely attached to the metal underneath.

Bodywork repairs - filling and respraying

Before using this Section, see the Sections on dent, deep scratch, rust holes and gash repairs.

Many types of bodyfiller are available, but generally speaking, those proprietary kits which contain a tin of filler paste and a tube of resin hardener are best for this type of repair. A wide, flexible plastic or nylon applicator will be found invaluable for imparting a smooth and well-contoured finish to the surface of the filler.

Mix up a little filler on a clean piece of card or board - measure the hardener carefully (follow the maker's instructions on the pack), otherwise the filler will set too rapidly or too slowly. Using the applicator, apply the filler paste to the prepared area; draw the applicator across the surface of the filler to achieve the correct contour and to level the surface. As soon as a contour that approximates to the correct one is achieved, stop working the paste - if you carry on too long, the paste will become sticky and begin to "pick-up" on the applicator. Continue to add thin layers of filler paste at 20-minute intervals, until the level of the filler is just proud of the surrounding bodywork.

Once the filler has hardened, the excess can be removed using a metal plane or file. From then on, progressively-finer grades of abrasive paper should be used, starting with a 40-grade production paper, and finishing with a 400-grade wet-and-dry paper. Always wrap the abrasive paper around a flat rubber, cork, or wooden block - otherwise the surface of the filler will not be completely flat. During the smoothing of the filler surface, the wet-and-dry paper should be periodically rinsed in water. This will ensure that a very smooth finish is imparted to the filler at the final stage.

At this stage, the "dent" should be surrounded by a ring of bare metal, which in turn should be encircled by the finely "feathered" edge of the good paintwork. Rinse the repair area with clean water, until all of the dust produced by the rubbing-down operation has gone.

Spray the whole area with a light coat of primer - this will show up any imperfections in the surface of the filler. Repair these imperfections with fresh filler paste or bodystopper, and once more smooth the surface with abrasive paper. Repeat this spray-and-repair procedure until you are satisfied that the surface of the filler, and the feathered edge of the paintwork, are perfect. Clean the repair area with clean water, and allow to dry fully.

If bodystopper is used, it can be mixed with cellulose thinners to form a really thin paste which is ideal for filling small holes.

The repair area is now ready for final spraying. Paint spraying must be carried out in a warm, dry, windless and dust-free atmosphere. This condition can be created artificially if you have access to a large indoor working area, but if you are forced to work in the open, you will have to pick your day very carefully. If you are working indoors, dousing the floor in the work area with water will help to settle the dust which would otherwise be in the atmosphere. If the repair area is confined to one body panel, mask off the surrounding panels; this will help to minimise the effects of a slight mis-match in paint colours. Bodywork fittings (eg chrome strips, door handles etc) will also need to be masked off. Use genuine masking tape, and several thicknesses of newspaper, for the masking operations.

Before commencing to spray, agitate the aerosol can thoroughly, then spray a test area (an old tin, or similar) until the technique is mastered. Cover the repair area with a thick coat of primer; the thickness should be built up using several thin layers of paint, rather than one thick one. Using 400-grade wet-and-dry paper, rub down the surface of the primer until it is really smooth. While doing this, the work area should be thoroughly doused with water, and the wet-and-dry paper periodically rinsed in water. Allow to dry before spraying on more paint.

Spray on the top coat, again building up the thickness by using several thin layers of paint. Start spraying at one edge of the repair area, and then, using a side-to-side motion, work until the whole repair area and about 2 inches of the surrounding original paintwork is covered. Remove all masking material 10 to 15 minutes after spraying on the final coat of paint.

Allow the new paint at least two weeks to harden, then, using a paintwork renovator, or a very fine cutting paste, blend the edges of the paint into the existing paintwork. Finally, apply wax polish.

Plastic components

With the use of more and more plastic body components by the vehicle manufacturers (eg bumpers. spoilers, and in some cases major body panels), rectification of more serious damage to such items has become a matter of either entrusting repair work to a specialist in this field, or renewing complete components. Repair of such damage by the DIY owner is not really feasible, owing to the cost of the equipment and materials required for effecting such repairs. The basic technique involves making a groove along the line of the crack in the plastic, using a rotary burr in a power drill. The damaged part is then welded back together, using a hot-air gun to heat up and fuse a plastic filler rod into the groove. Any excess plastic is then removed, and the area rubbed down to a smooth finish. It is important that a filler rod of the correct plastic is used, as body components can be made of a variety of different types (eg polycarbonate, ABS, polypropylene).

Damage of a less serious nature (abrasions, minor cracks etc) can be repaired by the DIY owner using a two-part epoxy filler repair material. Once mixed in equal proportions, this is used in similar fashion to the bodywork filler used on metal panels. The filler is usually cured in twenty to thirty minutes, ready for sanding and painting.

If the owner is renewing a complete component himself, or if he has repaired it with epoxy filler, he will be left with the problem of finding a suitable paint for finishing which is compatible with the type of plastic used. At one time, the use of a universal paint was not possible, owing to the complex range of plastics encountered in body component applications. Standard paints, generally speaking, will not bond to plastic or rubber satisfactorily. However, it is now possible to obtain a plastic body parts finishing kit which consists of a pre-primer treatment, a primer and coloured top coat. Full instructions are normally supplied with a kit, but basically, the method of use is to first apply the pre-primer to the component concerned, and allow it to dry for up to 30 minutes. Then the primer is applied, and left to dry for about an hour before finally applying the special-coloured top coat. The result is a correctly-coloured component, where the paint will flex with the plastic or rubber, a property that standard paint does not normally possess.

5 Major body damage - repair

The construction of the body is such that great care must be taken when making cuts, or when renewing major members, to preserve the basic safety characteristics of the structure. In addition, the heating of certain areas is not advisable.

In view of the specialised knowledge necessary for this work, and the alignment jigs and special tools frequently required, the owner is advised to consult a specialist body repairer or Peugeot dealer.

6 Bonnet - removal and refitting

1 Open the bonnet and support with the stay.
2 Using a pencil, mark the position of the hinges on the bonnet.
3 Disconnect the windscreen washer tubing.
4 Enlist the aid of an assistant to support the weight and help balance the bonnet on one side, then release the bonnet support stay.
5 Place some cloth beneath the rear corners of the bonnet, unscrew the hinge bolts and withdraw it from the car (photos).
6 Refitting is a reversal of removal, but check that the bonnet is central within its aperture and flush with the front wings. If necessary loosen the hinge bolts and move it within the elongated holes to reposition it, then adjust the bonnet lock and striker, as described in Section 7.

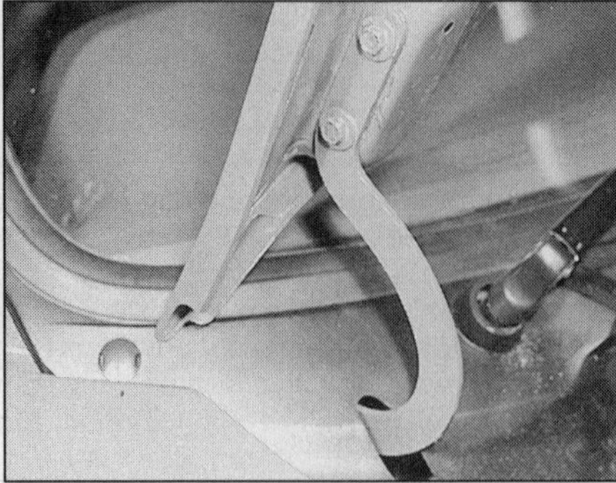

6.5 Bonnet hinge bolts

7 Bonnet lock and remote control cable - removal, refitting and adjustment

1 If the cable is broken, the bonnet lock will have to be released by deflecting the lock lever with a rod inserted through the grille slats - refer to Chapter 13.
2 Remove the front grille, as described in Section 8.
3 Unbolt the lock from the crossmember and disconnect the control cable (Fig. 11.2) .
4 Working inside the car, remove the inner trim panel forward of the nearside front door for access to the cable at the release handle end.

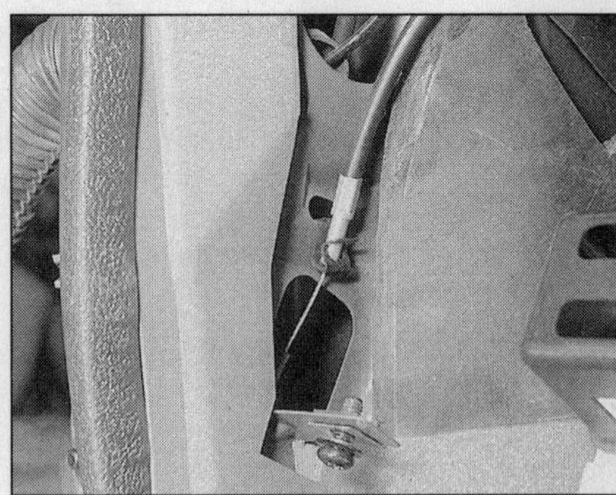

7.4 Bonnet release cable and retaining clip within the car

5 Detach the inner cable from the release handle and the outer cable from the retaining clip. Push the cable through the bulkhead and remove it from the engine compartment (photo).
6 If necessary, the bonnet striker may be unscrewed from the bonnet and the safety spring unclipped.
7 Refitting is a reversal of removal, but check that the striker enters the lock centrally and holds the front of the bonnet level with the front wings. If necessary loosen the lock bolts and move the lock within the elongated holes. Adjust the bonnet height by screwing the striker pin in or out. Adjust the rubber buffers to support the front corners of the bonnet.

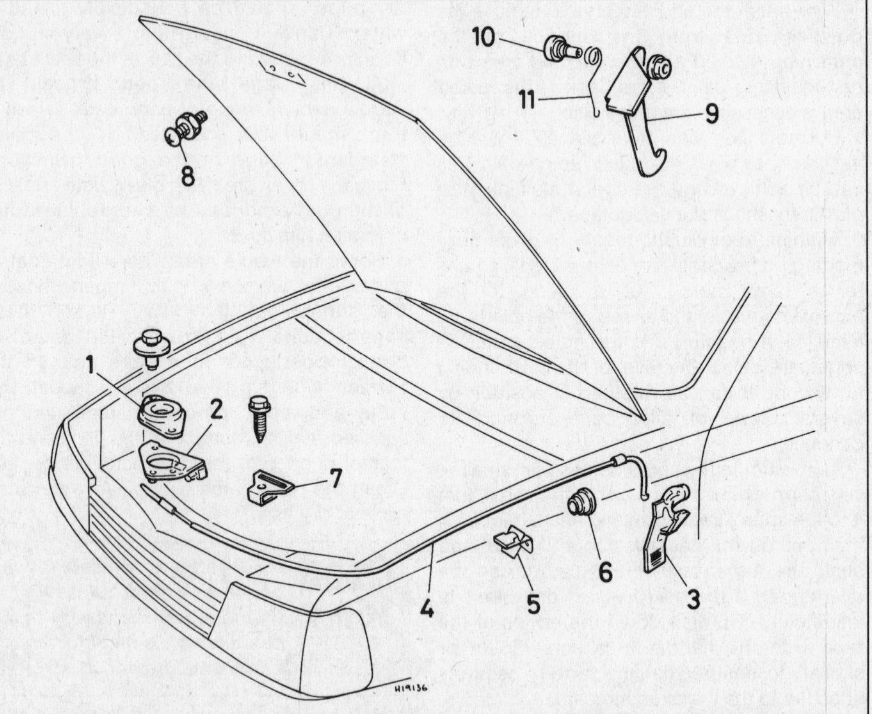

Fig. 11.2 Bonnet lock and release cable components (Sec 7)

1 Bonnet lock (upper)	*5 Clip*	*9 Safety catch*
2 Bonnet lock (lower)	*6 Grommet*	*10 Pivot*
3 Release handle	*7 Cable location clip*	*11 Spring*
4 Cable	*8 Striker*	

8 Front grille - removal and refitting

1 Open the bonnet and support it with the stay.
2 Carefully prise free the plastic retaining clips from the top edge then lift the grille clear of its location peg grommets at the bottom edge.
3 Refitting is a reversal of the removal procedure.

9 Front wing - removal and refitting

1 Remove the front indicator lamp and repeater lamp, as described in Chapters 12 and 13.
2 Remove the front bumper, as described in Section 10.
3 Unscrew the mounting bolts located on the top flange, rear flange and inner rear lower edge of the wheel arch. Access to the rear flange is gained by opening the front door (Fig. 11.3).
4 Prise the wing from the mastic bead and remove it from the car. Where applicable, detach the side indicator lamp wire as the wing is withdrawn .
5 Refitting is a reversal of removal, but apply mastic to the inner surface of the flanges. If a new wing is being fitted, paint the inside surfaces and apply an anti-corrosion sealant.

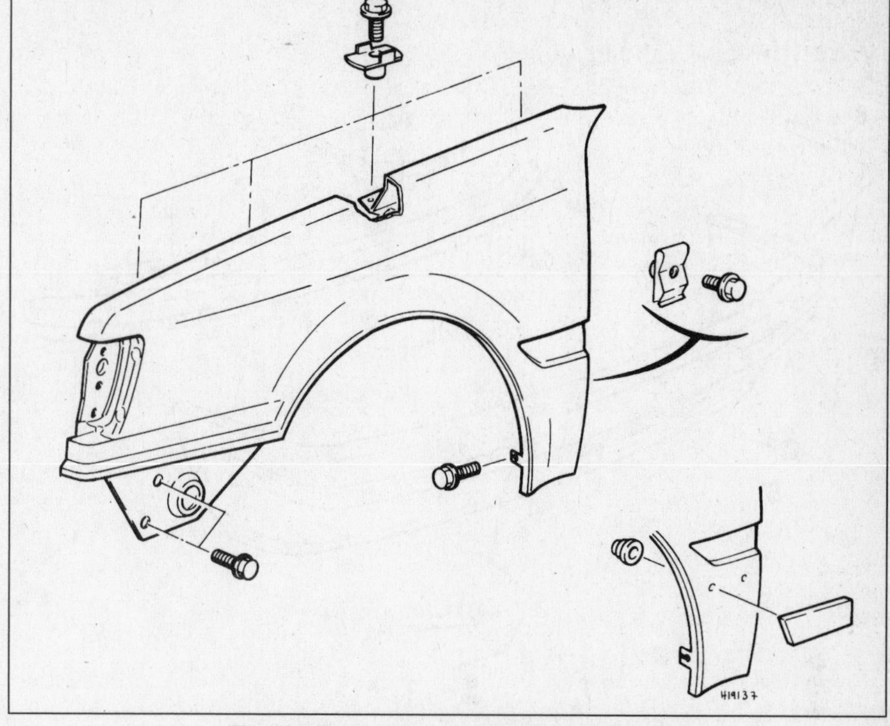

Fig. 11.3 Front wing panel and fittings (Sec 9)

10.2 Front bumper retaining bolts under the wing panel

10 Bumpers - removal and refitting

Front

1 Disconnect the battery earth lead.
2 Working under each front wheel arch in turn, unscrew and remove the bumper-to-chassis retaining bolts and the corner retaining bolt on each wing (photo).
3 Undo the bumper-to-front skirt bolts working on the front underside of the car (photo).
4 Partially withdraw the front bumper, detach the horn wire, then fully remove the bumper.
5 Refitting is a reversal of the removal procedure.

Rear

6 Disconnect the battery earth lead.
7 Undo the three retaining bolts from the underside of the bumper along the body rear edge and the single bolt from the corner section each side. Withdraw the outer bumper (photo).
8 To remove the inner rear bumper, undo the two retaining bolts within the luggage compartment (one each side), withdraw the inner bumper and detach the rear number plate wiring (photo).
9 Refit in the reverse order of removal. Check that the rear number plate lights are fully operational.

10.3 Front bumper-to-skirt retaining bolt

10.7 Rear bumper and underside support bracket

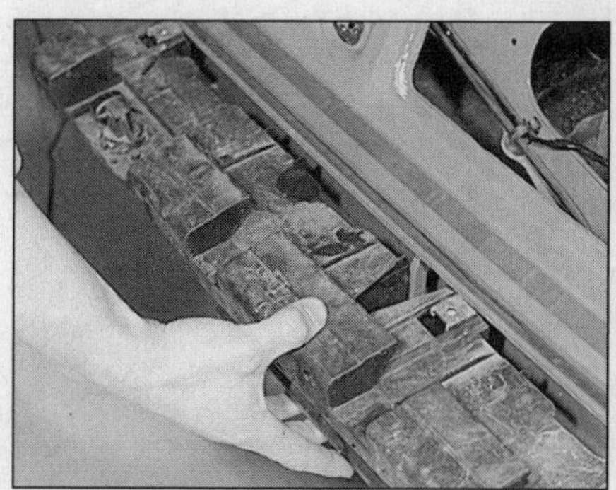
10.8 Rear inner bumper removal

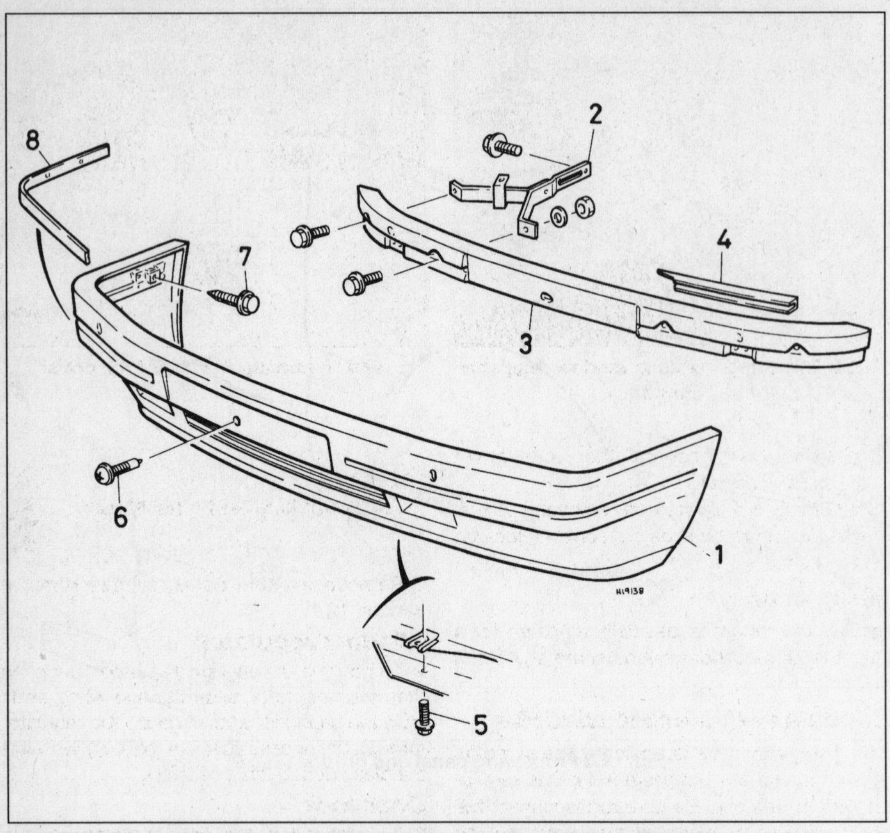

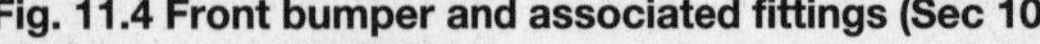
Fig. 11.4 Front bumper and associated fittings (Sec 10)

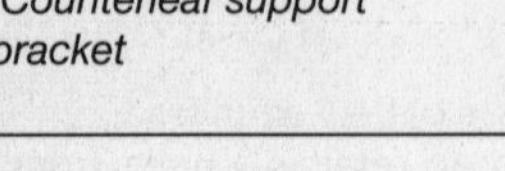
1 Bumper moulding
2 Counterleaf support bracket
3 Bumper counterleaf
4 Crossmember
5 to 7 Retaining bolts
8 Moulding inset

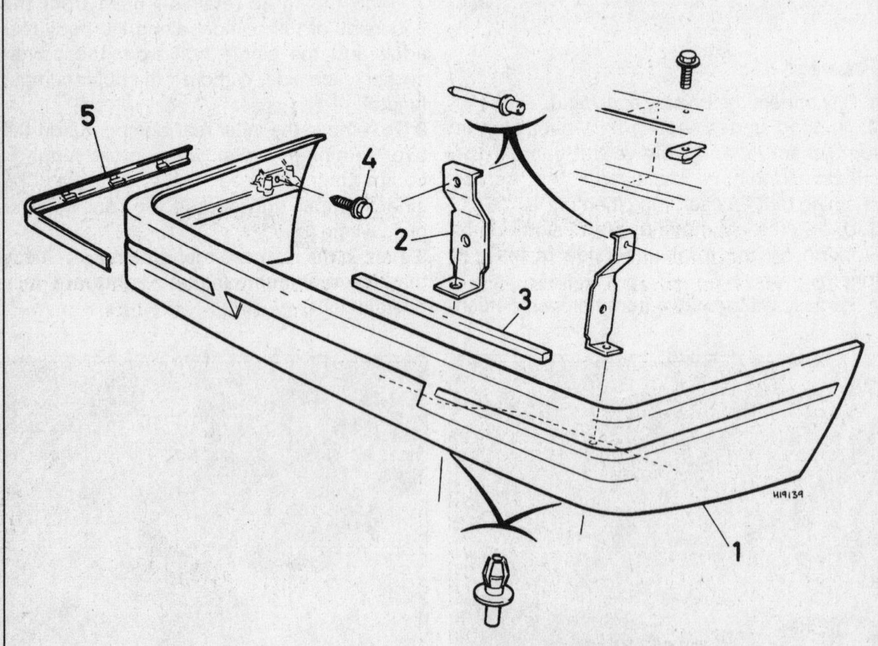

Fig. 11.5 Rear bumper and associated fittings (Sec 10)

1 Bumper 2 Support 3 Seal 4 Screw 5 Moulding (inset)

11 Door - removal and refitting

1 The door hinges are welded to the body pillar and bolted to the door (photo).
2 Remove the plastic caps from the hinge pivot pins.
3 Drive out the roll pin from the door check strap.
4 Where applicable, remove the trim panel (Section 12) and disconnect the loudspeaker wiring from the door.
5 Support the door in the fully open position by placing blocks, or a jack and a pad of rag, under its lower edge.
6 Drive out the hinge pivot pins and remove the door.
7 Refit by reversing the removal operations.
8 Where necessary, the striker on the body pillar may be adjusted to ensure correct closure of the door (photo).

12 Door trim panel - removal and refitting

Front door

Note: *Procedure given here is for 5-door models, 3-door models similar.*
1 Remove the door speaker grille, undo the retaining screws and remove the door speaker unit. Disconnect the speaker wires at the in-line connectors as it is withdrawn.

11.1 Door hinge

11.8 Front door striker

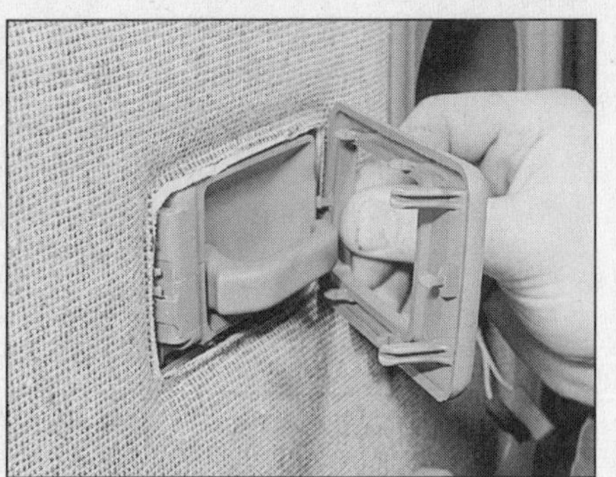
12.2 Removing the door interior handle surround

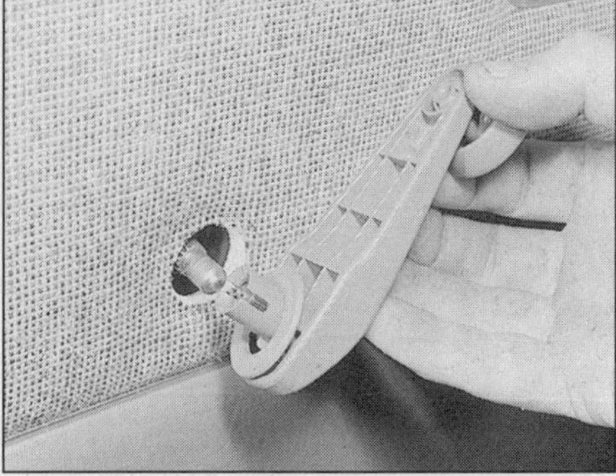
12.3 Removing the door window regulator handle

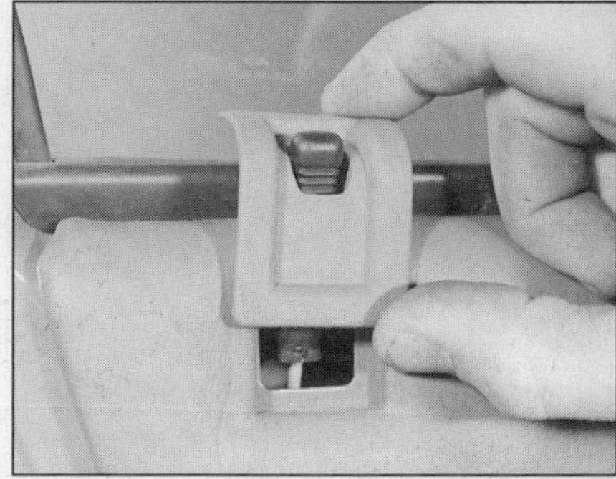
12.4 Removing the inner lock cover

2 Prise free and remove the interior door handle surround (photo).

3 Fully close the window, note the position of the winder handle with the window in the fully shut position and then pull the handle from the spindle (photo).

4 Prise free and lift clear the inner lock button surround (photo).

5 Prise free the finisher strip from the armrest, undo the two retaining screws and remove the armrest (photo).

6 Undo the door glovebox retaining screws, if applicable (photo).

7 Using a wide-bladed screwdriver, or similar tool, prise the trim panel from the door - working progressively from the bottom upwards and inserting the screwdriver adjacent to each clip.

8 Refitting is a reversal of removal, but first make sure that the clips are correctly located in the panel.

Rear door

9 The procedure is basically as given for a front door, but there will be some slight trim differences.

Models with electric windows

10 The procedure is basically the same as given previously, but there will be no regular handle to remove. Be sure to disconnect the battery before releasing the motor switch wiring.

13 Door - dismantling and reassembly

1 Remove the trim panel, as described in Section 12.

Window regulator

2 To remove the window regulator, unscrew the mounting nuts, slide the two lifting arms from the channels, and withdraw the regulator through the access aperture (photos). Support the glass during this operation.

Door lock

3 To remove the door lock and inner remote handle, disconnect the link rods as necessary

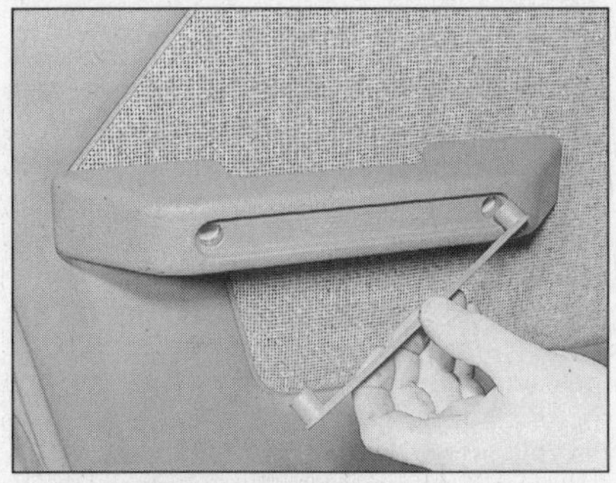
12.5 Removing the armrest finisher strip

12.6 Door panel glovebox and retaining screws

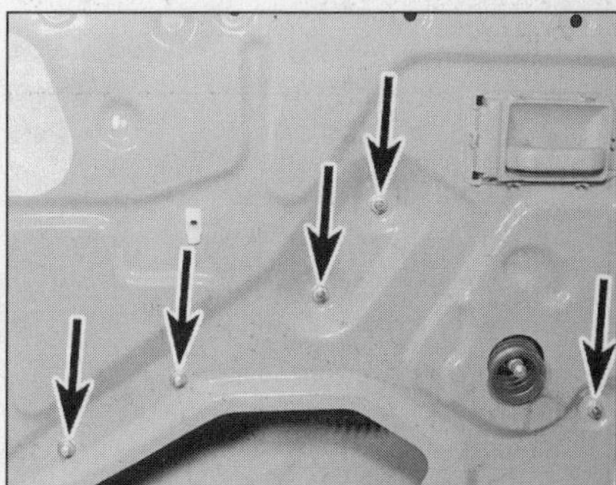
13.2A Window regulator mounting nuts (arrowed) – front door

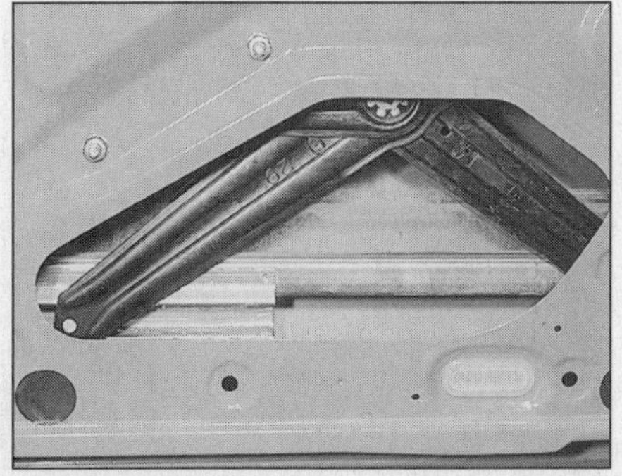
13.2B Window lift arms and glass channel

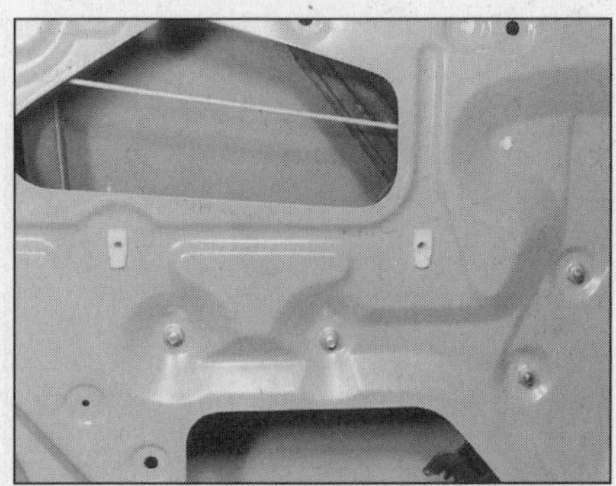
13.2C Window regulator mounting nuts – rear door

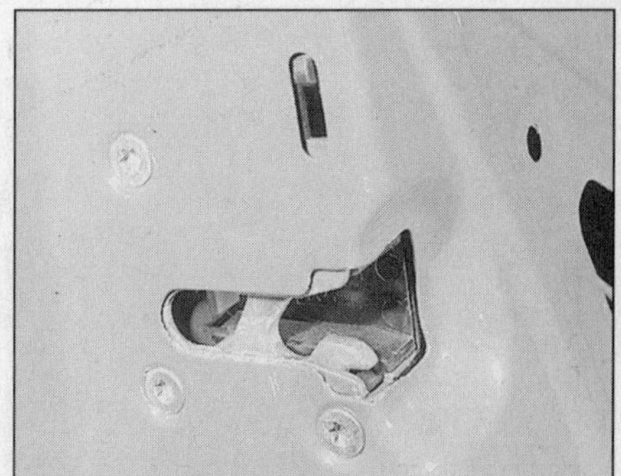
13.3A Door lock and mounting screws

13.3B Door inner remote control handle

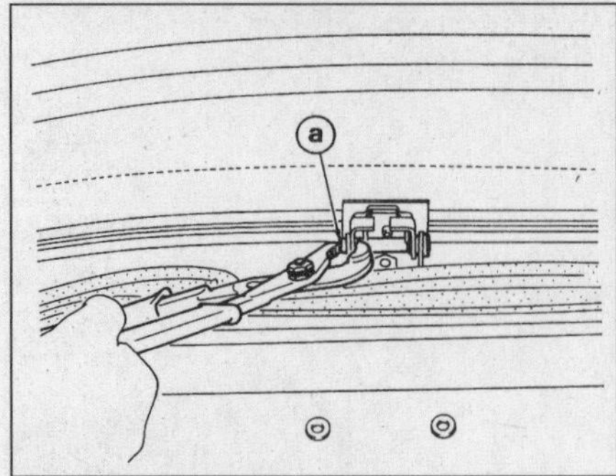

Fig. 11.6 Hinge pin removal method using slip joint pliers (a) (Sec 14)

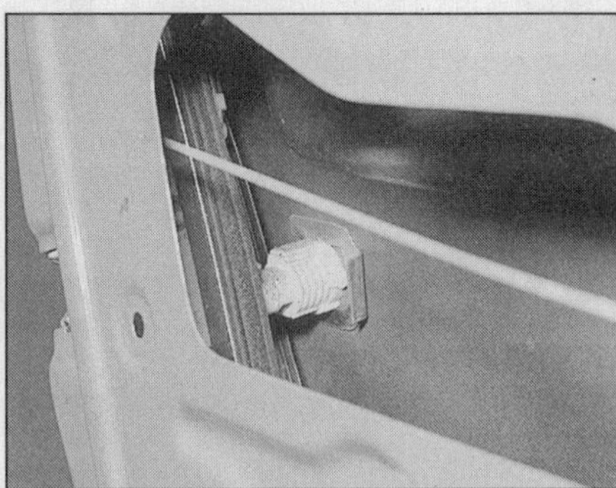

13.4 View of the private lock from inside the door

and unscrew the Torx screws retaining the lock (photos).

13.6A Prise free the mirror inner cover . . .

13.6B . . . for access to the retaining screws

Exterior handle

4 To remove the exterior handle, disconnect the link rod and unscrew the bolts. The private lock is removed by disconnecting the link rod and pulling out the retaining clip (photo).

Door glass

5 To remove the door glass, first remove the window regulator then unbolt the glass side channels, tilt the glass and withdraw it upwards.

Exterior mirror

6 To remove the exterior mirror, prise off the inner cover, prise back the rubber grommet then undo the three retaining screws and remove the mirror. If required the manual adjustment lever can be detached from the

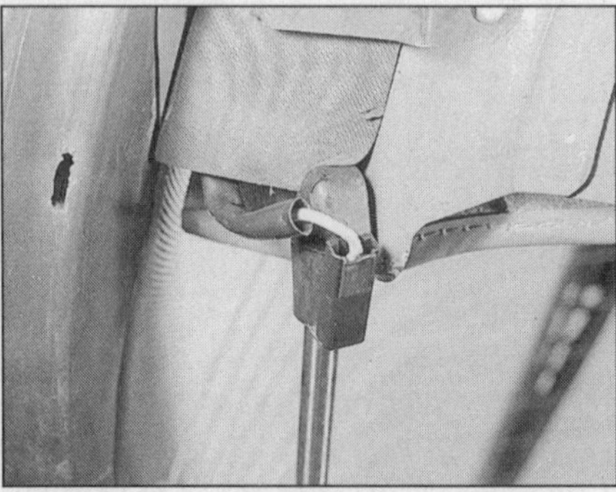

14.2A Detach the wiring connector from the strut . . .

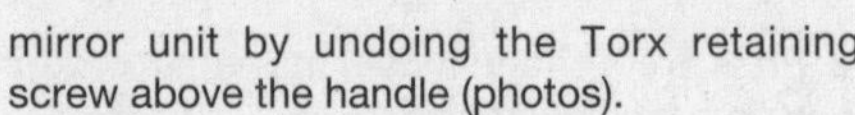

mirror unit by undoing the Torx retaining screw above the handle (photos).

General assembly

7 Reassembly of the door is a reversal of the dismantling procedure. However, when refitting the door glass, adjust the position of the side channels so that the glass moves smoothly without excessive play.

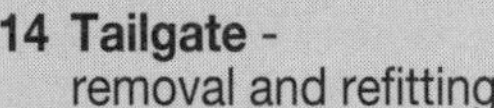

14 Tailgate - removal and refitting

1 Open the tailgate and have an assistant support it.

2 Detach the wiring connector from the strut (photo), then prise out the plastic clip and detach the strut socket (photo).

3 Disconnect the wiring for the heated rear window and tailgate wiper motor. Also disconnect the washer tube (photo).

4 Prise free the hinge pin retaining clips and then withdraw the hinge pin each side (photo). Lift the tailgate clear. New pin retaining clips must be used when refitting the tailgate (Fig. 11.6).

5 Refit in the reverse order of removal. On completion, check that the tailgate is positioned centrally in the body aperture, and make any adjustments to the lock and striker as described in Section 15. To adjust the tailgate at the hinges, loosen the retaining nuts and move the tailgate as required, then retighten the nuts.

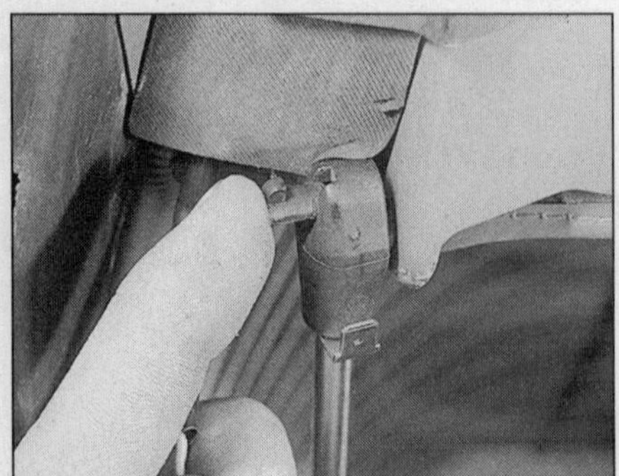

14.2B . . . and prise free the retaining clip

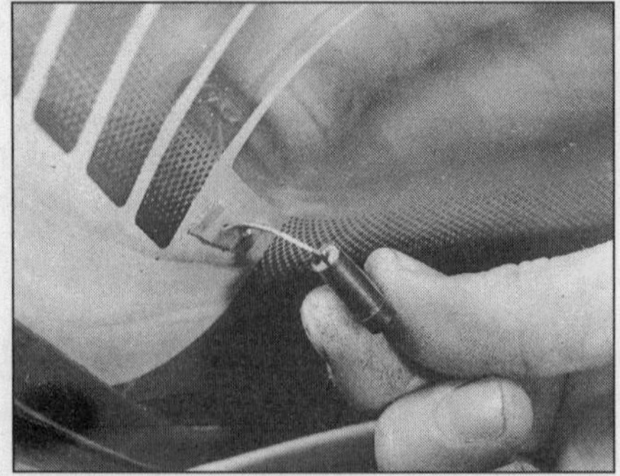

14.3 Detach the heated rear window wire connector

14.4 Tailgate hinge showing the pin retaining clip

15.1 Rear outer trim retainer nut

15.2 Tailgate lock showing three retainer rivets

15.3A Tailgate lock unit (shown with inner trim removed)

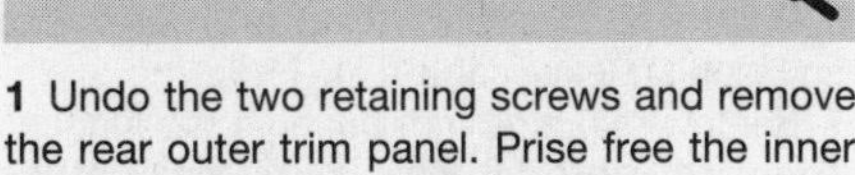

15 Tailgate lock - removal and refitting

1 Undo the two retaining screws and remove the rear outer trim panel. Prise free the inner rear trim panel for access (photo).

2 The lock unit and its retaining rivets are now accessible. Drill out the three pop rivets, withdraw the lock and detach the connecting rod through the inner rear panel aperture. Undo the rod-to-lock barrel retaining screw (photo).

3 Refit in the reverse order to removal. Use aluminium stem rivets to secure the lock unit. Check that the latch engages the striker correctly and, if necessary, adjust the striker position within the elongated bolt holes. Adjust the rubber stops so that the tailgate is supported firmly at the corners when shut (photos).

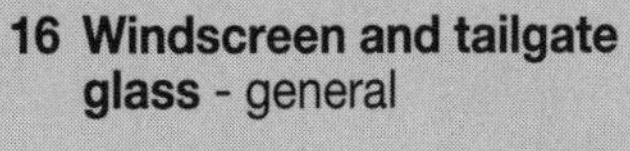

16 Windscreen and tailgate glass - general

The renewal of both the windscreen and the tailgate glass are tasks which are best entrusted to a professional fitter. In each case some specialised tools and knowledge of the safe and successful fitting of these glass panels are essential. Unless they are correctly fitted, they may well leak and at worst prove dangerous, therefore entrust renewal to a specialist.

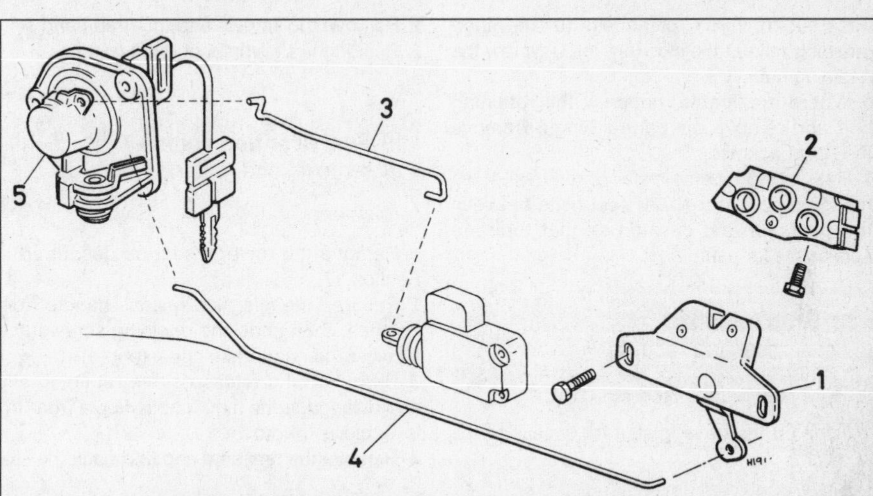

Fig. 11.7 Tailgate lock and associated components (Sec 15)

1 Lock 2 Striker 3 Actuator rod 4 Transverse rod 5 Lock barrel

17 Seats - removal and refitting

Front

1 Move the seat fully forward, then undo the retaining screws and remove the outer trim (photo).

2 Adjust the seat on the runners as required for access and remove the runner retaining bolts (Torx screws) (photos), then remove the seat.

3 Refit in the reverse order of removal. Check that the seat adjustment is satisfactory on completion.

Rear

4 To remove the cushion(s), tilt it forward and lift it clear, pulling at an angle of 45° from the retainers.

5 To remove the rear seat backrest(s), tilt the

15.3B Tailgate striker plate showing recessed retaining screws

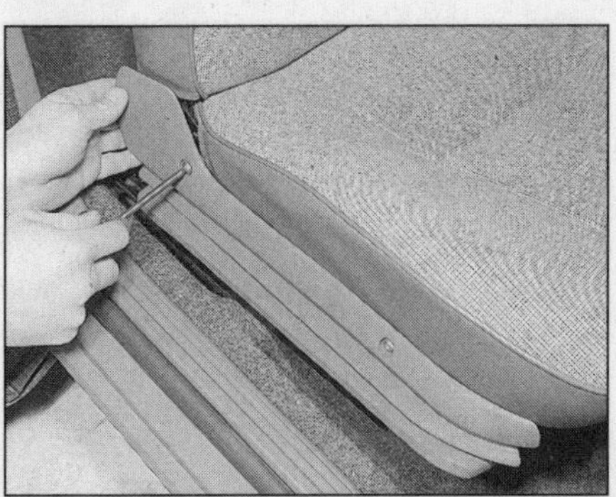

17.1 Remove the outer trim panel from the front seat . . .

17.2A . . . for access to the retaining bolts at the front . . .

17.2B . . . and rear of the seat runners

17.2C Torx screws are used, together with lock washers

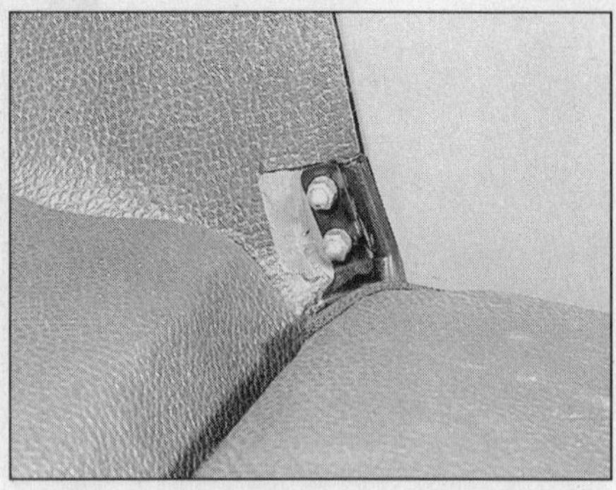
17.5 Rear seat backrest retaining nuts at the side hinge

backrest forwards for access to the hinge retaining nuts at the side (photo). Unscrew the retaining nuts.

6 Where applicable, unscrew the retaining bolt and remove the central hinge. Remove the seat backrest.

7 Refit in the reverse order of removal. Pass the fixed part of the rear seat belts between the backrest and cushion so that they are accessible for use.

18 Grab handles - removal and refitting

1 Prise up the cover plates for access to the screws.

2 Remove the screws and the grab handles.

3 Refitting is a reversal of removal.

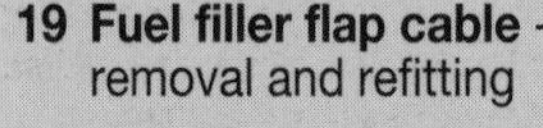

19 Fuel filler flap cable - removal and refitting

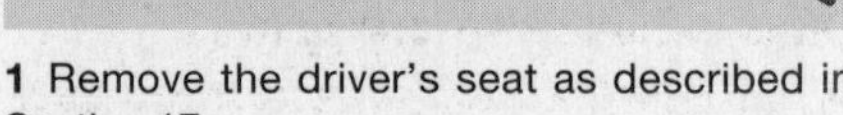

1 Remove the driver's seat as described in Section 17.

2 Pull free the filler flap release handle from its shaft, then undo the retaining screws and lift clear the handbrake cover (photo).

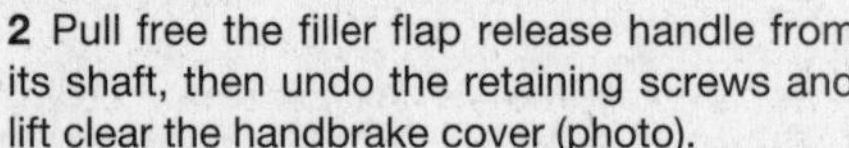

3 Prise free the release cable retaining clip and disengage the inner cable nipple from the lever clevis (photo).

4 Remove the rear seat and fold back the rear passenger compartment floor covering on the driver's side.

5 Referring to Fig. 11.8, remove the hinges, bolts and finisher panel indicated.

6 Prise free the rear wheel arch seal and unclip the release cable (Fig. 11.9).

7 Remove the side trim panel in the luggage compartment or at least fold it back at the forward upper corner to gain access to the inner body panel apertures. Reach through the inspection aperture and disengage the release cable from the flap, then withdraw the cable (photo).

8 Refit in the reverse order to removal. Check the flap for satisfactory locking and release operation before refitting the inner panels and associated items. If required, adjust the cable control at the sleeve nut (Fig. 11.10).

19.2 Withdraw the flap release handle from its shaft

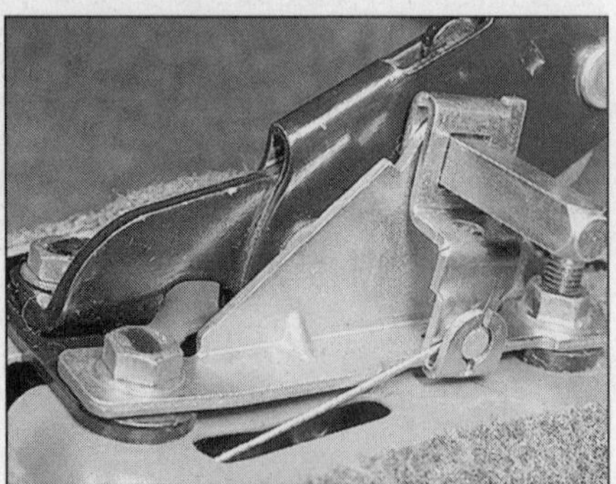
19.3 Cable connection at the release handle

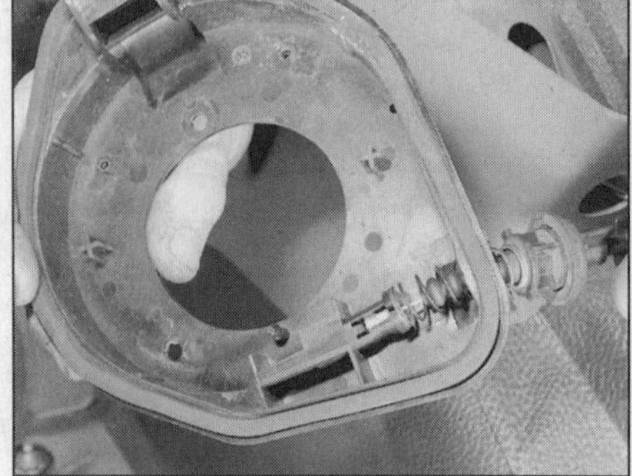
19.7 Disconnecting the cable from the petrol filler flap

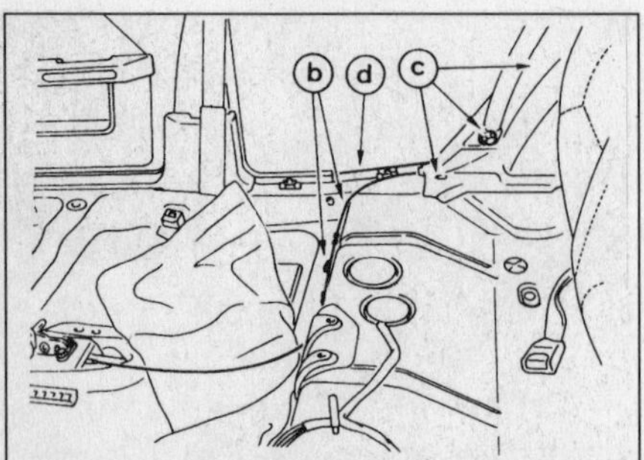

Fig. 11.8 Fuel filler flap cable removal. Detach hinges (b), bolts (c) and finisher (d) (Sec 19)

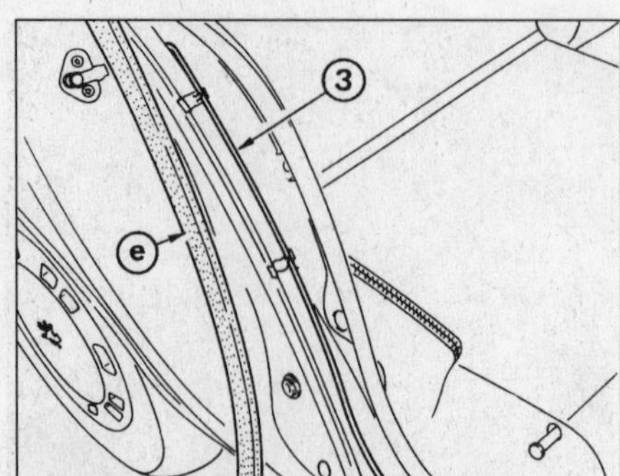

Fig. 11.9 From the rear wheel arch remove the seal (e) and cable (3) (Sec 19)

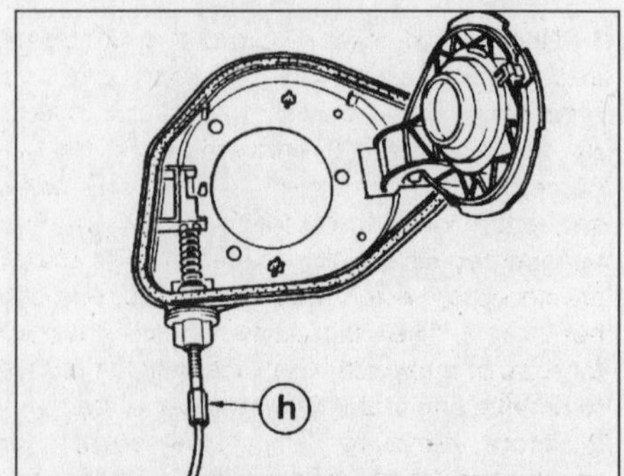

Fig. 11.10 Fuel filler flap cable control sleeve adjuster nut (h) (Sec 19)

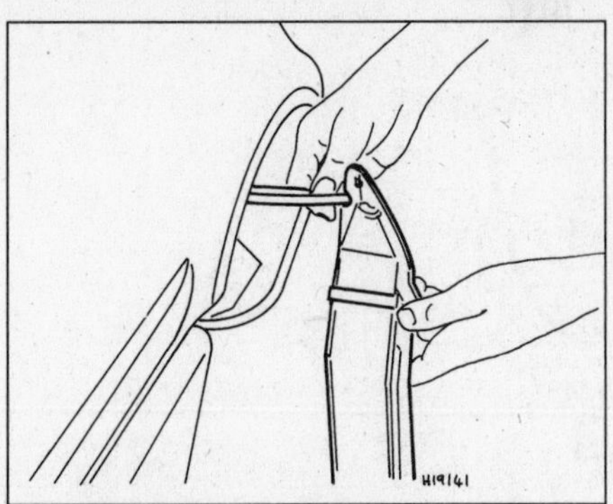

Fig. 11.11 Attach breather pipe to hose at top (Sec 20)

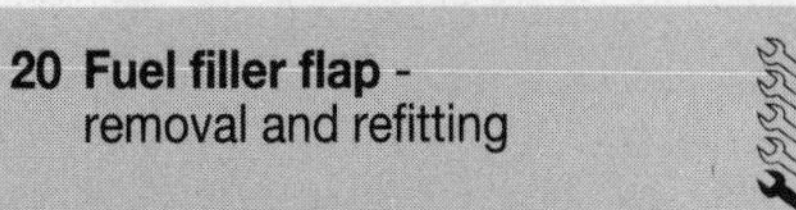

20 Fuel filler flap - removal and refitting

1 Disconnect the battery earth lead.
2 Disconnect the filler flap release cable from the filler flap as described in paragraph 7 of the previous Section.
3 Jack up and support the car at the rear on safety stands. Remove the right-hand rear roadwheel.
4 Lower but do not remove the fuel tank by undoing the tank retaining nuts down to the end of their threads - do not completely unscrew them. (Leave the bottom faces of the nuts and threads flush).
5 Unscrew and remove the three filler neck retaining screws and the two flap securing screws (photo).
6 Working under the wheel arch, release the filler pipe (photos) and then remove the filler pipe and its protective hose. Pull free the filler flap.
7 Refitting is a reversal of the removal procedure. Ensure that the breather pipe is connected to the hose at the top. If necessary adjust the control cable as described in the previous Section.

21 Facia panels - removal and refitting

1 The extent to which the various facia panels and their associated components are removed or detached is obviously dependent on the accessibility requirements of the component concerned. The following sequence describes the removal of the various panels and associated fittings which are necessary when gaining full access to the heater unit. The main items are sub-headed for ease of reference when it is only necessary to remove one or a limited number of items.
2 Before removing any facia panels or associated items, first detach the battery earth lead.
3 As the various panels are removed, note carefully the routing of the wiring harnesses. This is particularly important if removing all of the facia panels since if the harnesses are incorrectly routed when reassembling, they will not reach their various destinations for reconnection. If possible label the various wiring connections for ease of refitting.

20.5 Fuel filler flap and retaining screws
1 Filler neck screws 2 Flap retaining screws

Radio/cassette console

4 Withdraw the ashtray for access to the front retaining screws. Undo the two retaining screws from the front face and one screw each side. Withdraw the console unit and disconnect the wiring and antenna lead from the radio/cassette (photo). Refer to Fig. 11.12 for an alternative console.

Gloveboxes

5 To remove the glovebox on the passenger side, first unclip and lower the fuse/relay box unit. Unscrew and remove the upper and lower retaining screws. Disengage the glovebox lid check strap for access to the retaining screws on the right-hand side. Lift the unit at the rear edge and disengage it from the peg at the front lower edge and remove the glovebox.
6 Removal of the driver's side glovebox is similar to that described for the passenger's but prise free the surround section for access to the retaining screws.

Steering column and shrouds

7 Undo the four retaining screws and remove the lower steering column shroud. Undo the upper column mounting nuts and lower the column. Remove the upper column shroud.

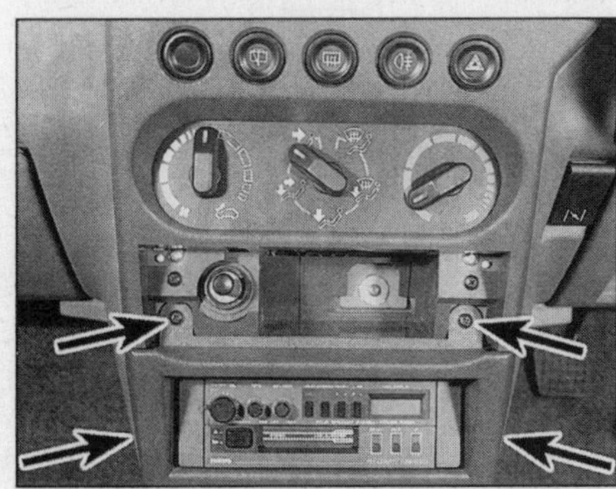

21.4 Radio/cassette console retaining screw positions (arrowed)

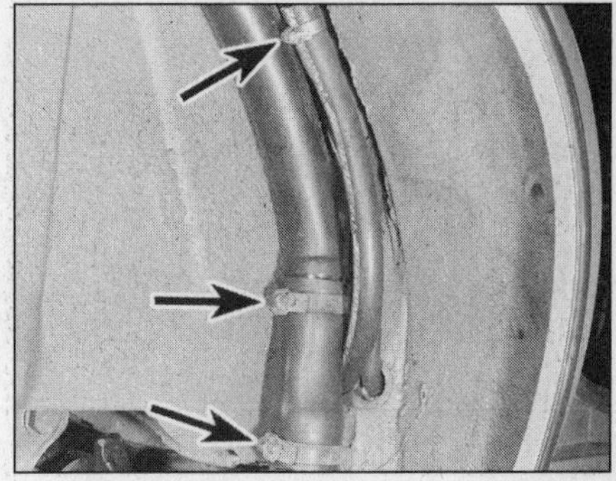

20.6A Fuel filler pipe – detach at points indicated (arrowed)

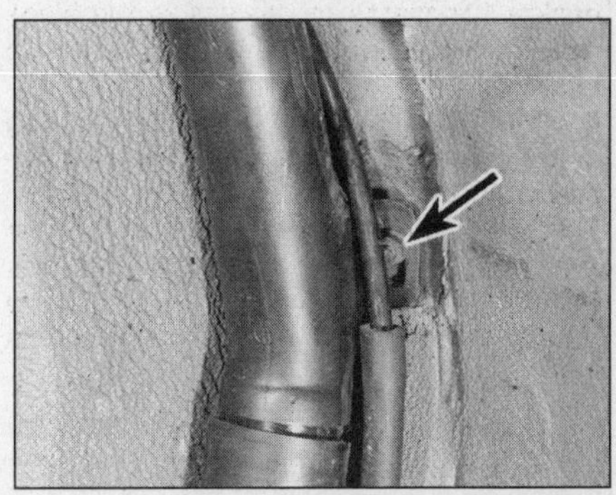

20.6B Filler pipe retaining nut (arrowed) – unscrew to remove pipe

Instrument panel and surround facia

8 Using a suitable length of 2 mm diameter rod, release the instrument facia side mouldings by inserting the rod through the holes and press on the retaining clip in each hole in turn to remove the mouldings. Each moulding is held by two clips (photo).
9 Remove the instrument panel surround facia. This facia panel is secured by six screws, two each side and two under the heater control panel. Withdraw the surround facia and disconnect the wiring to the switches (photo).
10 Unscrew the two instrument panel

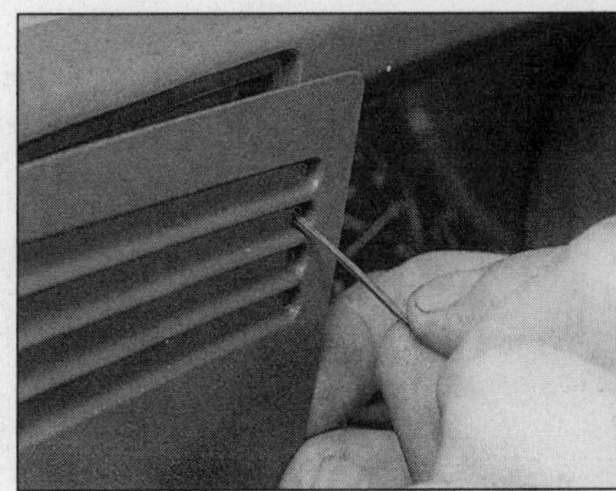

21.8 Releasing a facia panel side moulding

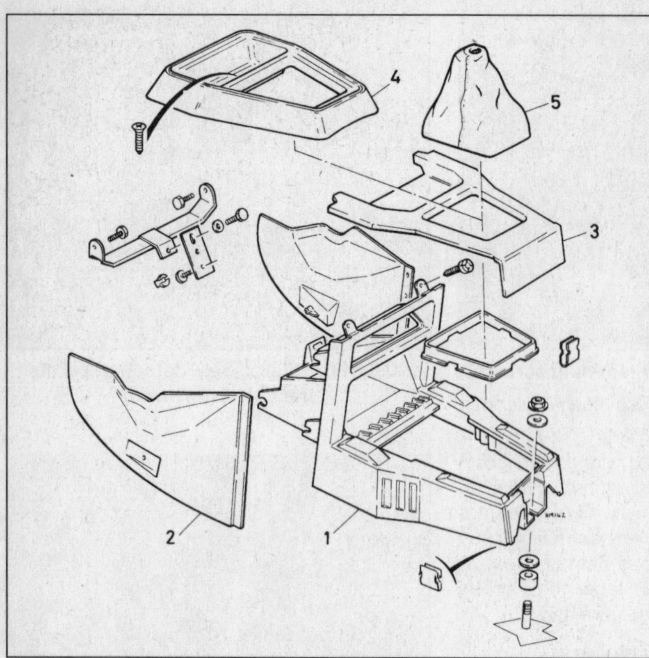

Fig. 11.12 Floor-mounted console assembly fitted to some models (Sec 21)

1 Console
2 Side face flange
3 Console trim moulding
4 Gear lever moulding
5 Gear lever gaiter

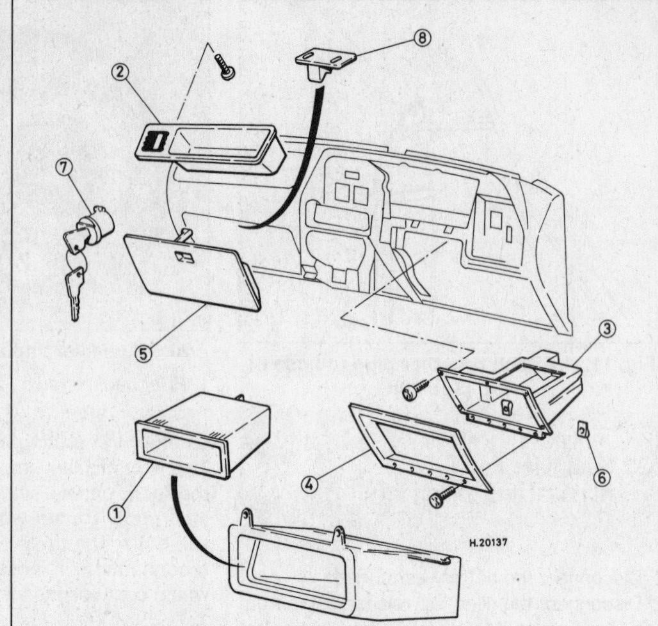

Fig. 11.13 Facia gloveboxes and trim fittings (Sec 21)

1 Central glovebox
2 Passenger glovebox
3 Driver's glovebox
4 Driver's glovebox moulding
5 Passenger glovebox lid
6 Clip
7 Lock unit
8 Striker

retaining screws (one each side) and tilt the column to partially withdraw it so that the speedometer cable and wiring connections to the instrument panel can be detached (photo).

11 Remove the panel and note how the wires are fed through the facia to it.

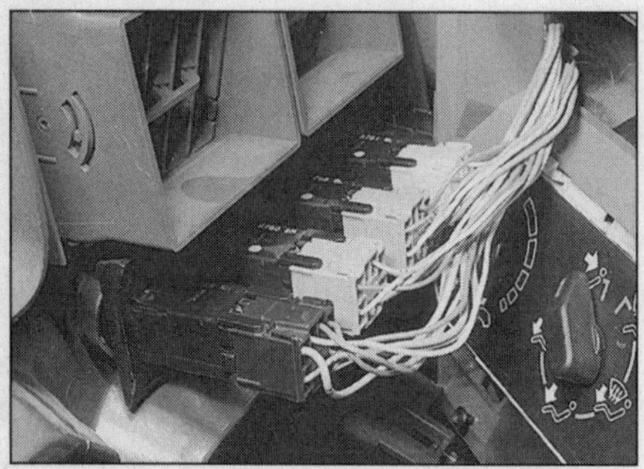

21.9 Facia panel switches and wiring connectors

Heater controls and main facia panels

12 Withdraw the choke control lever from the facia panel by pulling it sideways. The cable can be left attached if required.

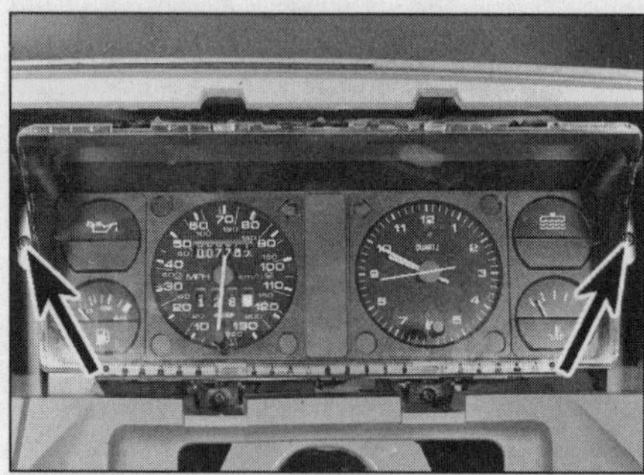

21.10 Instrument panel retaining screws (arrowed)

13 Carefully prise free the upper finisher panel from the top edge of the facia (near the windscreen). Do not damage the top of the facia when levering free the finisher panel which is secured by clips (photo).

14 Unscrew and remove the facia retaining screws, three from the top edge under the windscreen (photo), two at the bottom end on the passenger side, one on the lower end on the driver's side and six screws from the centre of the facia near the heater control panel (Fig. 11.15).

15 Withdraw the facia panel and withdraw/release the respective wiring harnesses. Note the harness routing and retaining clip locations to ensure correct reassembly.

Facia panels refitting

16 In most instances, the refitting procedures for the panels and their associated components

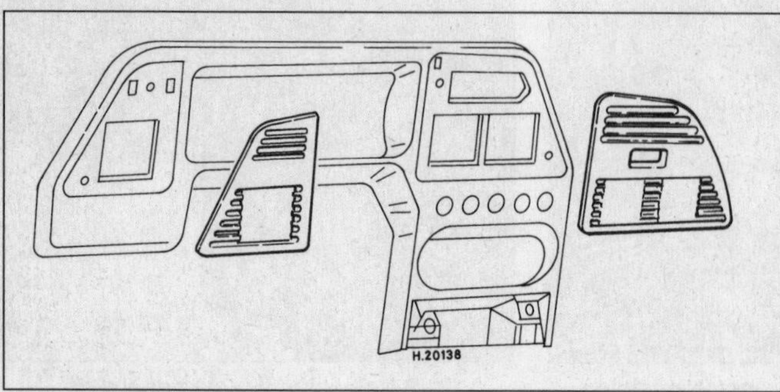

Fig. 11.14 Facia panel and side mouldings (Sec 21)

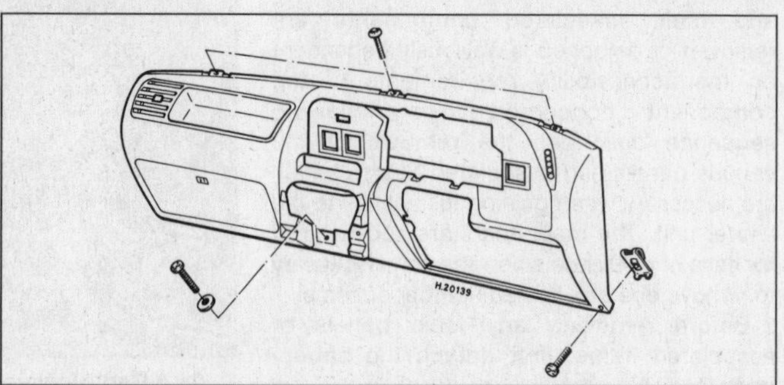

Fig. 11.15 Facia panel retaining screw locations (Sec 21)

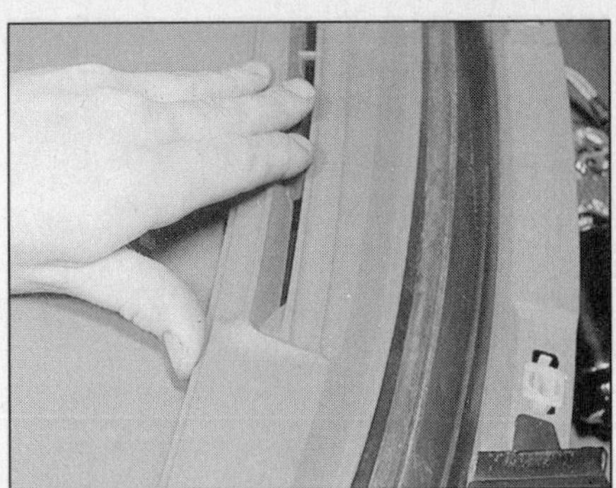
21.13 Removing the upper facia finisher panel

22.4B Heater inlet and outlet hose connections to the matrix

are a direct reversal of the removal procedure, but note the following special points:

(a) *Wiring: Ensure that the wiring harnesses and cables are correctly arranged and routed before fitting the main facia panel. The wires tend to be only just long enough and the correct routing is therefore critical. Where applicable secure the harnesses in retaining clips out of the way of adjacent components (as noted during removal). Ensure that all connections are correct and secure*

(b) *When reconnecting the steering column, ensure that the upper shroud is located before raising the column and securing the mounting bolts*

(c) *On completion, reconnect the battery earth lead and check that the various instruments and associated electrical components are fully functional*

21.14 Facia panel upper retaining screws are recessed

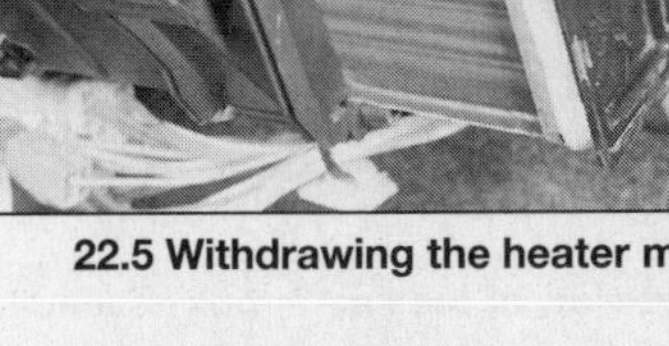
22.5 Withdrawing the heater matrix

22 Heater matrix - removal and refitting

1 Working from the engine compartment side of the bulkhead, clamp each heater hose to prevent leakage of coolant when the hoses are detached at the matrix. Alternatively, if suitable clamps are not available, drain the cooling system as described in Chapter 2.

2 Detach the hose clamp plate from the bulkhead.

3 Remove the glovebox/facia on the driver's side (see Section 21).

4 Protect the carpets and trim with suitable coverings then unclamp the heater feed and return coolant hoses from within the car. Allow for a certain amount of spillage and take care if the coolant is still hot (photos).

22.4A Heater inlet and outlet hoses showing retaining clamp (arrowed)

5 Detach the hose retaining bracket from the side of the heater, then withdraw the matrix by pulling it out of the heater unit (photo).

6 Refit in reverse. Top up the cooling system and bleed it as described in Chapter 2.

23 Heater assembly - removal and refitting

1 Remove the facia assemblies as described in Section 21, and detach the heater flow and return hoses as described in paragraphs 1 to 5 in the previous Section, but leave the matrix in position in the heater if required.

2 Disconnect the wiring harness connections to the heater control panel (photo).

3 Remove the gear lever knob, undo the retaining screws and remove the gear lever gaiter and central console panel to which it is attached.

4 Unscrew the heater retaining nuts (two each side) and the single nut at the lower rear. Withdraw the heater assembly, but note how the wiring harnesses are routed round it (photo).

5 Refitting is a reversal of the removal procedure. Ensure that the wiring connections are secure to the heater control panel and also that the harnesses are correctly routed as noted during removal. Refer to Section 21 to refit the facia (photo).

6 On completion top up and bleed the cooling system as described in Chapter 2.

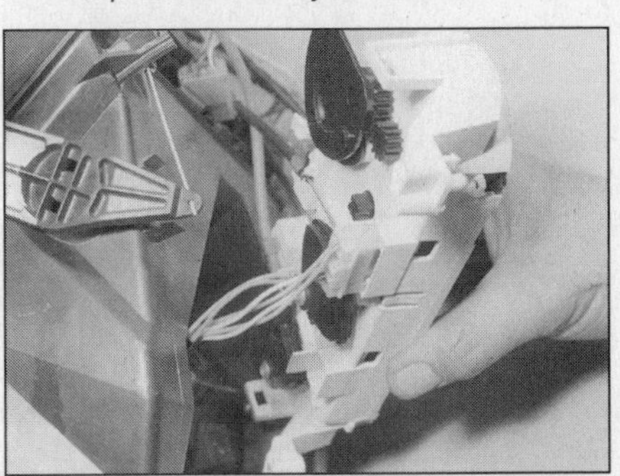
23.2 Wiring connections on rear face of heater control panel

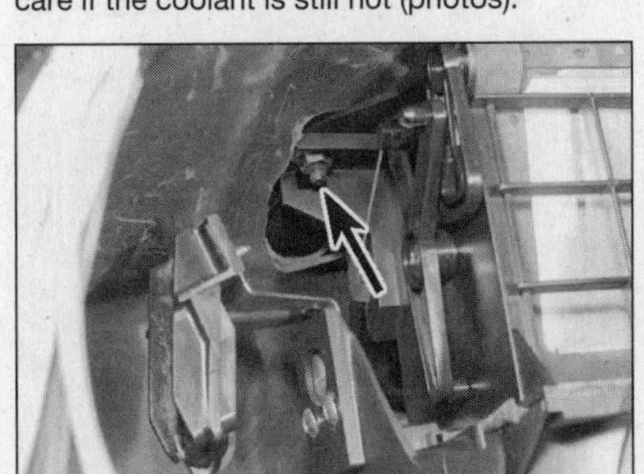
23.4 Heater unit retaining nut location – upper left side (arrowed)

23.5 Wiring loom layout is critical when refitting heater and facias

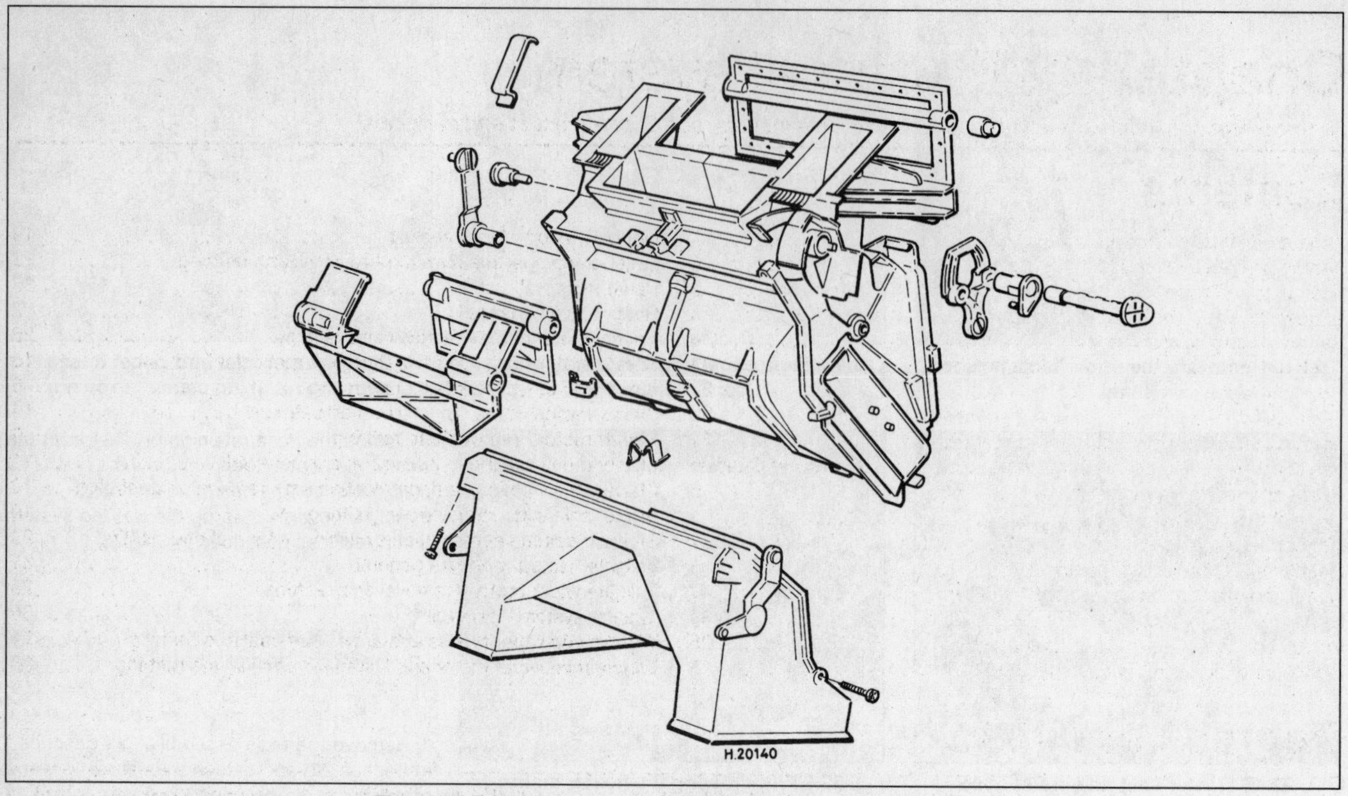

H.20140

Fig. 11.16 Exploded view of the heater box assembly (Sec 23)

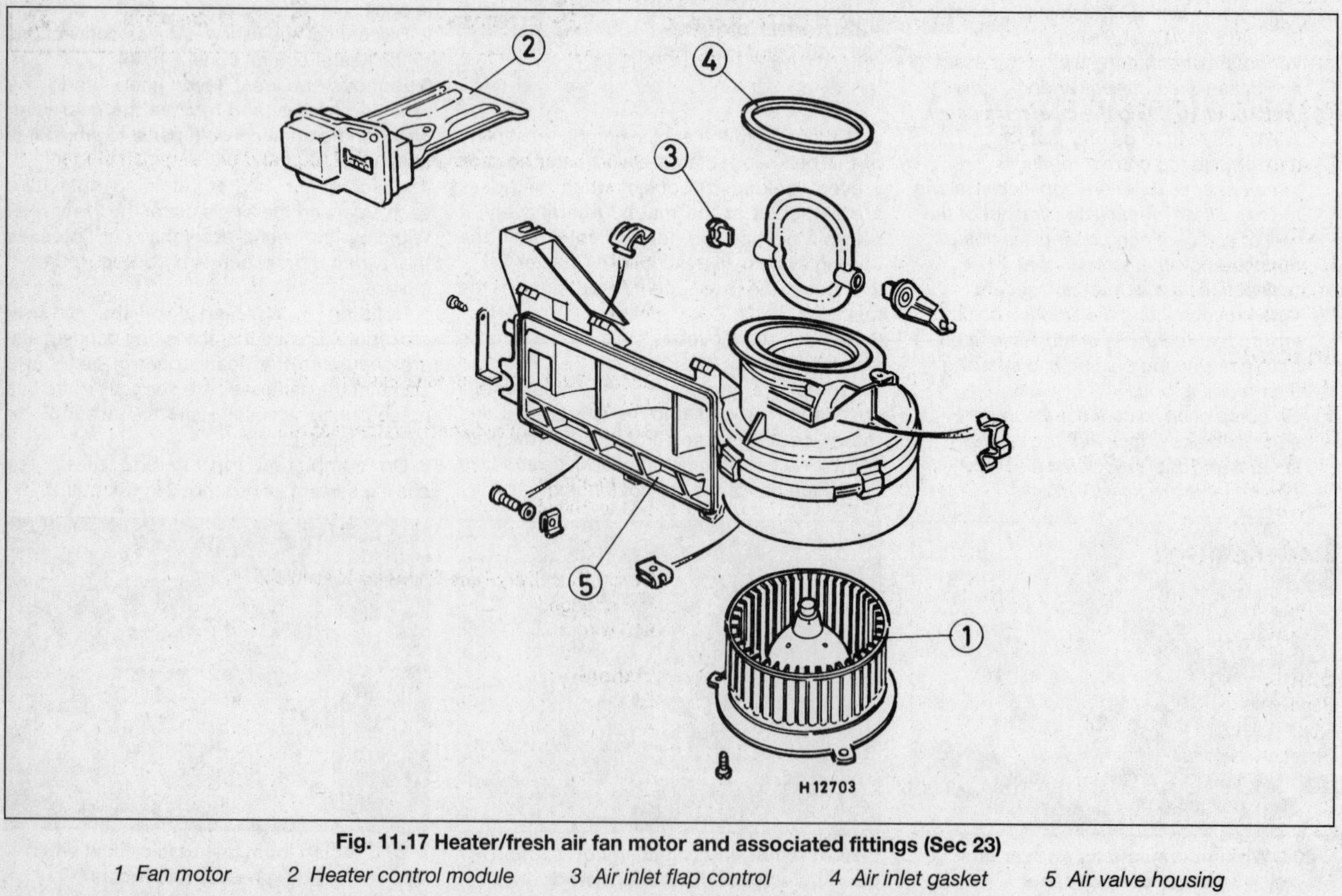

H 12703

Fig. 11.17 Heater/fresh air fan motor and associated fittings (Sec 23)

1 Fan motor *2 Heater control module* *3 Air inlet flap control* *4 Air inlet gasket* *5 Air valve housing*

Chapter 12 Electrical system

For modifications, and information applicable to later models, see Supplement at end of manual

Contents

Degrees of difficulty

Easy, suitable for novice with little experience 	**Fairly easy,** suitable for beginner with some experience 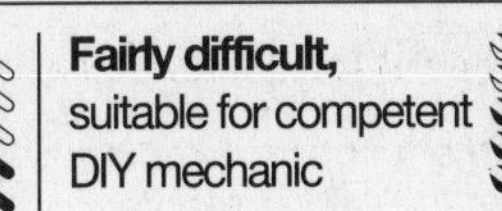	**Fairly difficult,** suitable for competent DIY mechanic	**Difficult,** suitable for experienced DIY mechanic	**Very difficult,** suitable for expert DIY or professional

Specifications

System type	12 volt, negative earth battery. Alternator and pre-engaged starter motor
Battery	
1.1 models	30 Ah
1.3 models	35 Ah
1.6 models	40 Ah
Alternator	
Make	Bosch, Paris-Rhone or Mitsubishi
Rating	750 watt
Drivebelt tension (all engines)	5.0 mm (0.20 in) deflection on longest run
Drivebelt tension using Seem C Tronic tensioner tool:	
Used belt	300 to 400 N
New belt	500 to 600 N
Starter motor	
Make	Bosch, Ducellier, Paris-Rhone or Mitsubishi
Type	Pre-engaged
Rating	850 watt
Bulbs	**Wattage**
Headlights	55
Front sidelights	4
Direction indicators (front)	21
Rear (tail) lights	5
Direction indicators (rear)	21
Rear foglight	21
Stop-lights	21
Reversing lights	21

12

Windscreen and tailgate wipers

Wiper blades	Champion X4503
Wiper arms	Champion CCA 6

Fuses

No	Circuit protected	Rating (amp)
1	Coolant level indicator, reversing lights, tachometer and clock illumination	10
2	Heater, instrument panel supply, direction indicators and cigar lighter	25
3	Windscreen wipers, front/rear washers, stop-lights and heated rear window switch	25
4	Front foglights	15
5	Hazard warning system	10
6	Spare	
7	Central door locking, battery condition indicator, radio and clock, luggage/glovebox compartment lights, interior lights	10
8	Horns and heated rear windows	25
9	Electric front windows	30
10	Rear fog light	5
11	Tail light (left-hand)	5
12	Tail light (right-hand)	5
13	Front sidelights, interior lights and instrument panel illumination, rear number plate lamps, dim-dip (where fitted)	5, 10 or 15*
14	Electric fuel pump (where fitted)	15

**Actual value depends on model, year and equipment fitted*

1 General description

The electrical system is of the 12 volt negative earth type and the major components consist of a battery, of which the negative terminal is earthed, an alternator which is belt-driven from the crankshaft pulley, and a starter motor.

The battery supplies a steady amount of current for the ignition, lighting and other electrical circuits and provides a reserve of electricity when the current consumed by the electrical equipment exceeds that being produced by the alternator.

The alternator is controlled by a regulator which ensures a high output if the battery is in a low state of charge or the demand from the electrical equipment is high, and a low output if the battery is fully charged and there is little demand for the electrical equipment.

When fitting electrical accessories it is important, if they contain silicone diodes or transistors, that they are connected correctly, otherwise serious damage may result to the components concerned. Items such as radios, tape players, electronic ignition systems, electronic tachometer, automatic dipping, etc, should all be checked for correct polarity.

It is important that both battery leads are always disconnected if the battery is to be boost charged; also if body repairs are to be carried out using electric arc welding equipment, the alternator must be disconnected, otherwise serious damage can be caused to the more delicate instruments.

2 Routine maintenance

Carry out the following procedures at the intervals given in Routine Maintenance at the beginning of the manual.

1 Check the condition of the battery and its terminals, as described in Section 3.

2 Check the general condition of the alternator drivebelt. If it shows signs of excessive wear and/or cracking, it must be renewed. Check that the drivebelt tension is as specified. If not, loosen the pivot and adjuster bolts, reposition the alternator then retighten the bolts (see Section 5 for further details).

3 Regularly top up the washer fluid reservoirs.

3 Battery - maintenance and inspection

1 The battery fitted as original equipment is of low maintenance type; however, on some models, it incorporates the standard cell covers for checking the electrolyte level. Under normal conditions it is not necessary to check the level, but if the battery is subject to severe conditions such as taxi work or extreme temperatures, the level should be checked every 10 000 miles (15 000 km).

2 When topping-up is required use only distilled water and cover the battery plates to a depth of 10.0 mm (0.40 in).

3 Acid should never be required if the battery has been correctly filled from new, unless spillage has occurred.

4 Inspect the battery terminals and mounting tray for corrosion. This is the white fluffy deposit which grows at these areas. If evident, clean it away and neutralise it with ammonia or baking soda. Apply petroleum jelly to the terminals and paint the battery tray with a suitable anti-corrosion preparation.

5 Keep the top surface of the battery casing dry.

6 An indication of the state of charge of a battery can be obtained by checking the electrolyte in each cell using a hydrometer. The specific gravity of the electrolyte for fully charged and fully discharged conditions at the electrolyte temperature indicated, is listed below.

Fully discharged	Electrolyte temperature	Fully charged
1.098	38°C (100F)	1.268
1.102	32°C (90°F)	1.272
1.106	27°C (80°F)	1.276
1.110	21°C (70°F)	1.280
1.114	16°C (60°F)	1.284
1.118	10°C (50°F)	1.288
1.122	4°C (40° F)	1.292
1.126	-1.5°C (30°F)	1.296

7 There should be very little variation in the readings between the different cells, but if a difference is found in excess of 0.025, then it will probably be due to an internal fault indicating impending battery failure. This assumes that electrolyte has not been spilled at some time and the deficiency made up with water only.

8 If electrolyte is accidentally spilled at any time, mop up and neutralise the spillage at once. Electrolyte attacks and corrodes metal rapidly; it will also burn holes in clothing and skin. Leave the addition of acid to a battery cell to your dealer or service station as the

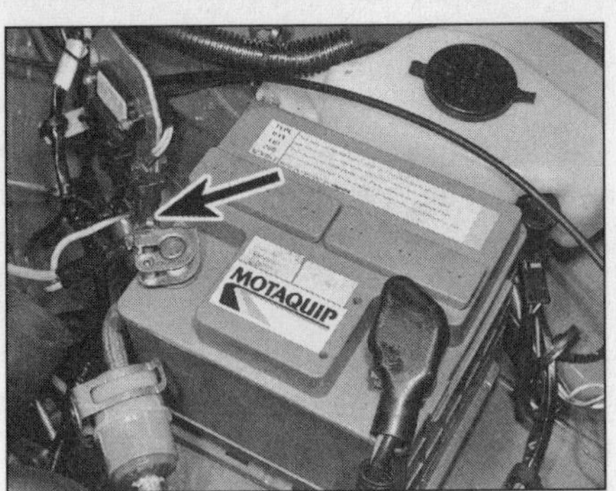

4.2 Battery and terminal lead connections with the earth lead connector securing knob indicated (arrowed)

mixing of acid with distilled water can be dangerous.

9 Never smoke or allow naked lights near the battery; the hydrogen gas which it gives off is explosive.

10 With normal motoring, the battery should be kept in a good state of charge by the alternator and never need charging from a mains charger.

11 However, if the daily mileage is low, with much use of starter and electrical accessories, it is possible for the battery to become discharged owing to the fact that the alternator is not in use long enough to replace the current consumed.

12 Also, as the battery ages, it may not be able to hold its charge and some supplementary charging may be needed. Before connecting the charger, disconnect the battery - earth lead first.

13 Specially rapid boost charges which are claimed to restore the power of the battery in 1 to 2 hours are most dangerous as they can cause serious damage to the battery plates through overheating.

14 While charging the battery note that the temperature of the electrolyte should never exceed 38°C (100° F).

15 When charging a low maintenance battery **do not** remove the cell covers; however, on other types of battery, the cell covers should be removed.

4 Battery - removal and refitting

1 The battery is located in the front left-hand corner of the engine compartment.

2 Disconnect the battery leads, negative lead first (photo). On some batteries the negative lead has a wing type terminal nut which, if unscrewed two or three turns, will isolate the battery without the need for complete removal. This is a useful facility when undertaking routine electrical jobs on the car.

3 Release the battery clamp and lift the battery carefully from the engine compartment (photo).

4 Refitting is a reversal of removal, but smear the terminals with petroleum jelly on completion. Ensure that the negative lead is reconnected last.

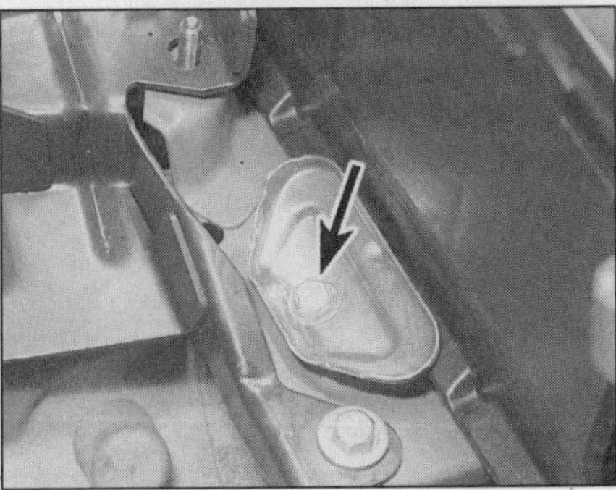

4.3 Battery retaining clamp

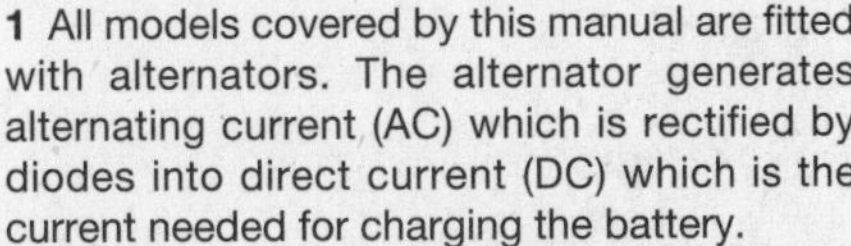

5 Alternator and drivebelt - general description and maintenance

1 All models covered by this manual are fitted with alternators. The alternator generates alternating current (AC) which is rectified by diodes into direct current (DC) which is the current needed for charging the battery.

2 The main advantage of the alternator lies in its ability to provide a high charge at low revolutions. Driving slowly in heavy traffic with a dynamo invariably means no charge is reaching the battery. In similar conditions, even with the heater, wiper, lights and perhaps radio switched on, the alternator will ensure a charge reaches the battery.

3 The alternator is of the rotating field ventilated design and comprises principally a laminated stator, on which is wound the output winding, a rotor carrying the field winding and a diode rectifier.

4 The rotor is belt-driven from the engine through a pulley keyed to the rotor shaft. A fan adjacent to the pulley draws air through the unit. Rotation is clockwise when viewed from the drive end. On models with power-assisted steering, the drivebelt also operates the power steering hydraulic pump. Drivebelt adjustment and removal are otherwise the same.

5 The voltage regulator is mounted externally on the rear cover of the alternator.

6 The equipment has been designed for the minimum amount of maintenance in service, the only items subject to wear being the brushes and bearings.

7 Brushes should be examined after about 80 000 miles (120 000 km) and renewed if necessary. The bearings are pre-packed with grease for life, and should not require further attention.

8 Regularly check the drivebelt tension.

9 Correct tensioning of the alternator drivebelt will ensure that it has a long and useful life. If the belt is loose, alternator performance will be affected and possibly the battery could be discharged. If the belt is too tight it will cause unnecessary alternator bearing wear. In either case the belt itself will suffer and its life will be shortened.

10 The drivebelt is tensioned by pivoting the alternator out and securing it when the belt is correctly tensioned.

11 To adjust the drivebelt tension, first check that it is correctly located in both pulleys then, with the mounting and adjustment strap bolts loosened, pivot the alternator outwards to tighten the drivebelt (photo). You can use a lever to help achieve this but it must be a wooden one and it must be used only at the pulley end of the alternator. Levering on the case or at the end opposite to the drive pulley can easily cause expensive damage. On some OHC engine models, adjustment can be made by turning the special adjuster screw as required (photo).

12 Tighten the belt as much as possible (but without over stretching it) to take up any play in the belt at its mid point on the longest run between the pulleys (refer to the Specifications for deflection). Whilst a taut tension is required the belt must not be overtightened. Tighten the alternator mounting and adjuster strap bolts to set the tension.

13 If a new belt has been fitted recheck its tension after a nominal mileage has been covered.

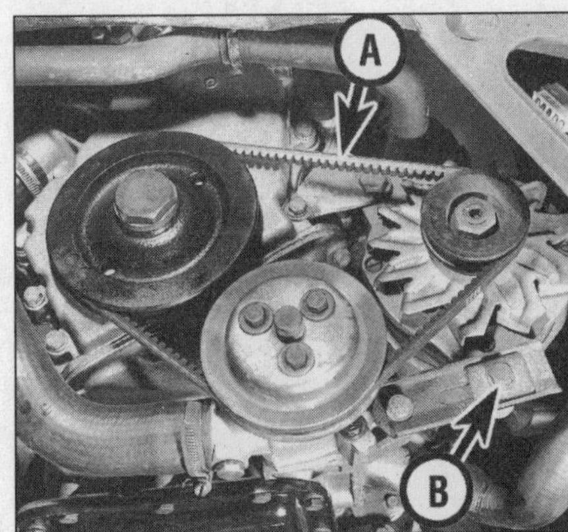

5.11A Alternator and drivebelt – OHV engine. Remove side shield for access

A Check tension at point indicated
B Adjuster

5.11B Alternator drivebelt tension adjuster – OHC engine models

6.3 Wiring connections to alternator – OHV engine

6.4A Alternator removal – OHV engine

6.4B Alternator and mounting bolts – OHC engine

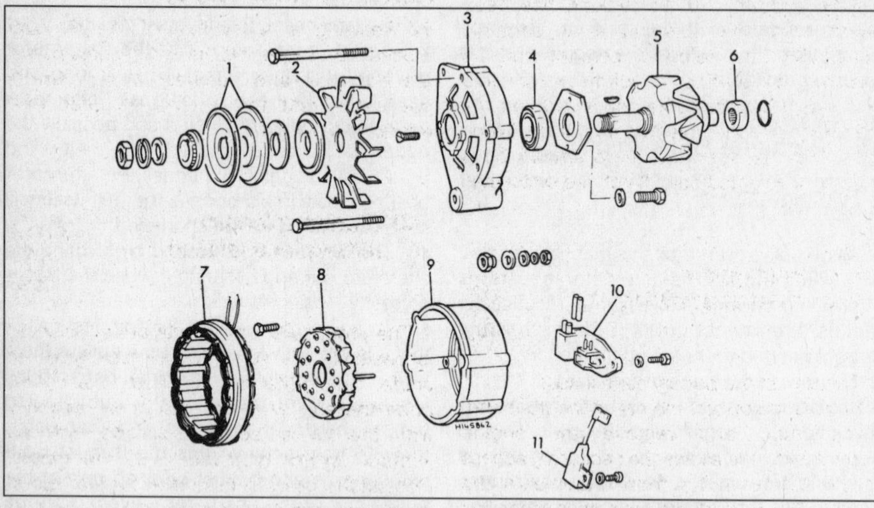

Fig. 12.1 Exploded diagram of a Bosch alternator (Sec 7)

1 Pulley
2 Fan
3 Drive end housing
4 Bearing
5 Rotor
6 Bearing
7 Stator
8 Diode plate
9 Brush end housing
10 Brush holder/regulator
11 Condenser

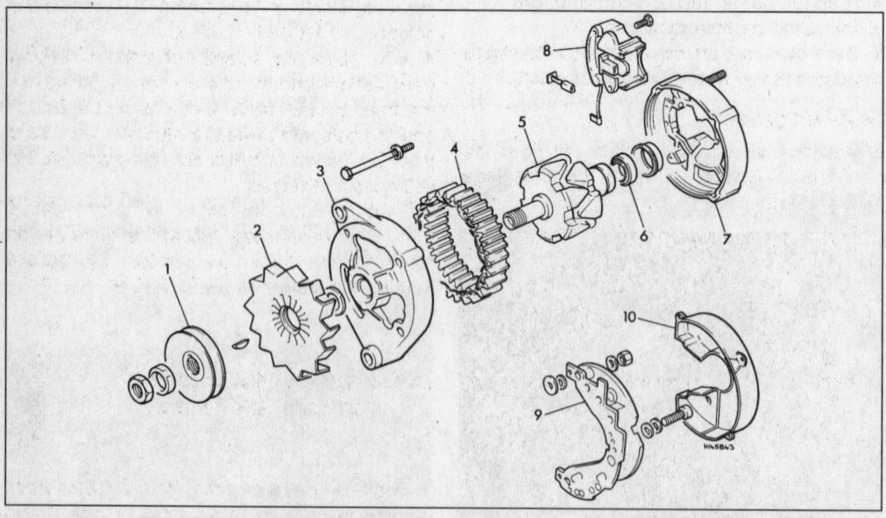

Fig. 12.2 Exploded diagram of a Paris-Rhone alternator (Sec 7)

1 Pulley
2 Fan
3 Drive end housing
4 Stator
5 Rotor
6 Bearing
7 Brush end housing
8 Brush holder/regulator
9 Diode plate
10 Cover

6 Alternator - removal and refitting

1 Disconnect the battery negative lead.

2 Loosen the pivot and adjustment bolts, swivel the alternator towards the engine then remove the drivebelt.

3 Disconnect the wiring from the alternator (photo).

4 Unscrew the pivot and adjustment bolts and lift the alternator from the engine. On OHC engine models note that the alternator front bracket is slotted to allow the pivot bolt to remain in the bracket on the engine (photos).

5 Refitting is a reversal of removal, but tension the drivebelt, as described in Section 5.

7 Alternator - brush renewal

1 Remove the alternator (Section 6) then remove the rear shield (where fitted).

2 Remove the regulator/brush holder mounting screws and withdraw the assembly. Disconnect the regulator lead, where necessary (photo).

3 With the brush holder removed, check the condition of the slip rings. If they are blackened, clean them with a fuel-moistened rag. If they are deeply scored or grooved then

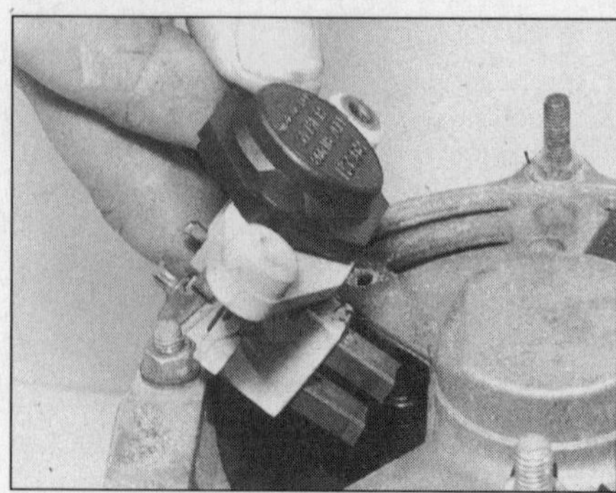

7.2 Regulator/brush holder removal

it will probably indicate that the alternator is coming to the end of its life.

4 Unsolder the old brushes and solder in the new ones. Have this done professionally if you lack skill in soldering.

5 Refit the regulator/brush holder and tighten the mounting screws. Reconnect the regulator lead, where necessary.

6 Refit the rear shield (where fitted) then refit the alternator, with reference to Section 6.

8 Starter motor - description and testing

1 The starter motor is mounted on the front of the engine and is of the preengaged type, where the drive pinion is brought into mesh with the starter ring gear on the flywheel before the main current is applied.

2 When the starter switch is operated, current flows from the battery to the solenoid which is mounted on the top of the starter motor body. The plunger in the solenoid moves inwards, so causing a centrally pivoted lever to push the drive pinion into mesh with the starter ring gear. When the solenoid plunger reaches the end of its travel, it closes an internal contact and full starting current flows to the starter field coils. The armature is then able to rotate the crankshaft, so starting the engine.

3 A special freewheel clutch is fitted to the starter drive pinion so that as soon as the engine fires and starts to operate on its own it does not drive the starter motor.

4 When the starter switch is released, the solenoid is de-energised and a spring moves the plunger back to its rest position. This operates the pivoted lever to withdraw the drive pinion from engagement with the starter ring.

5 If the starter motor fails to turn the engine when the switch is operated there are four possible reasons why:

(a) The battery is discharged or faulty

(b) The electrical connections between switch, solenoid, battery and starter motor are somewhere failing to pass the necessary current from the battery, through the starter to earth

(c) The solenoid has an internal fault

(d) The starter motor is electrically defective

To check the wiring connections at the starter motor on some models it will be necessary to raise and support the car on axle stands at the front end and remove the engine undershield.

6 To check the battery, switch on the headlights. If they go dim after a few seconds the battery is discharged. If the lamp glows brightly, next operate the ignition/starter switch and see what happens to the lights. If they go dim it is indicative that power is reaching the starter motor but failing to turn it. If the starter should turn very slowly go on to the next check.

7 If, when the ignition/starter switch is operated, the lights stay bright then the power is not reaching the starter motor. Check all connections from the battery to solenoid for cleanliness and tightness. With a good battery fitted this is the most usual cause of starter motor problems. Check that the earth cable between the engine and body is also intact and cleanly connected. This can sometimes be overlooked when the engine is taken out.

8 If no results have yet been achieved turn off the headlights, otherwise the battery will soon be discharged. It may be possible that a clicking noise was heard each time the ignition/starter switch was operated. This is the solenoid switch operating but it does not necessarily follow that the main contact is closing properly. (If no clicking has been heard from the solenoid it is certainly defective.) The solenoid contact can be checked by putting a voltmeter or bulb between the main cable connection on the starter side of the solenoid and earth. When the switch is operated there should be a reading or a lighted bulb. If not, the switch has a fault.

9 Starter motor - removal and refitting

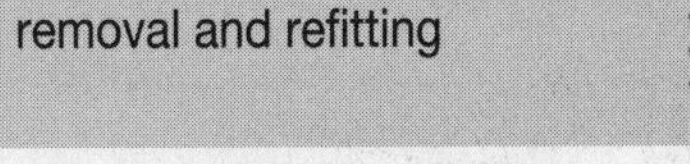

1 Disconnect the battery earth lead.

2 Raise and support the car at the front end, then unclip and remove the engine undershield. This allows the necessary access to the starter motor from underneath the vehicle. The procedures now differ according to engine type as follows:

OHV engine

3 Disconnect the wiring loom from the solenoid connections (photo).

4 Undo the starter motor support bracket bolt at the rear (from the crankcase).

5 Undo the three retaining bolts to the clutch housing, then withdraw the starter motor.

OHC engine

6 Unscrew and remove the oil filter as described in Chapter 1. Allow for oil spillage as it is withdrawn.

9.3 Starter motor wiring connections and retaining bolts (arrowed) – OHV engine

7 Detach the crankcase ventilation pipes adjacent to the starter motor.

8 On SRi models, undo the two retaining bolts and remove the inlet manifold support arm.

9 Disconnect the wiring to the starter motor solenoid.

10 Undo the starter motor support bracket bolt from the crankcase (at the rear end).

11 Undo the three retaining bolts to the clutch housing. One of these bolts will require the clutch operating lever pivot arm to be unbolted and moved out of the way so that the bolt can be withdrawn. Remove the starter motor.

Refitting (all models)

12 Refitting is a reversal of the removal procedure. Ensure that the wiring connections are correctly and securely made. Where applicable refit the engine oil filter with reference to Chapter 1.

10 Starter solenoid - removal and refitting

1 The procedure for removal of the solenoid is basically the same for all four types of starter motors that may be fitted. In all cases, once the starter motor has been removed from the car the solenoid can be removed without further dismantling of the motor. Consult the relevant illustration for the type of motor you are working on and proceed as follows.

2 First undo the terminal nut and then lift off the wire that connects the solenoid to the motor field coils.

3 Next undo and remove the nuts on the retaining studs. or the screws, that secure the solenoid to the end housing.

4 Now slide the solenoid rearward, taking care not to lose the return spring, shims or washers (where fitted). Note that on the Bosch unit the solenoid armature must be unhooked from the pinion carriage actuating arm as the solenoid is removed.

5 Refitting the solenoid is the reverse sequence to removal. Adjust the drive pinion travel as described in Section 14, before refitting the starter motor to the car.

11 Starter motor brushes - inspection and renewal

1 Begin by removing the starter motor from the car and placing it on a clean uncluttered work bench. Have some containers handy to store the small screws, washers and circlips that may otherwise be easily lost. Refer to the starter motor illustration applicable to your model.

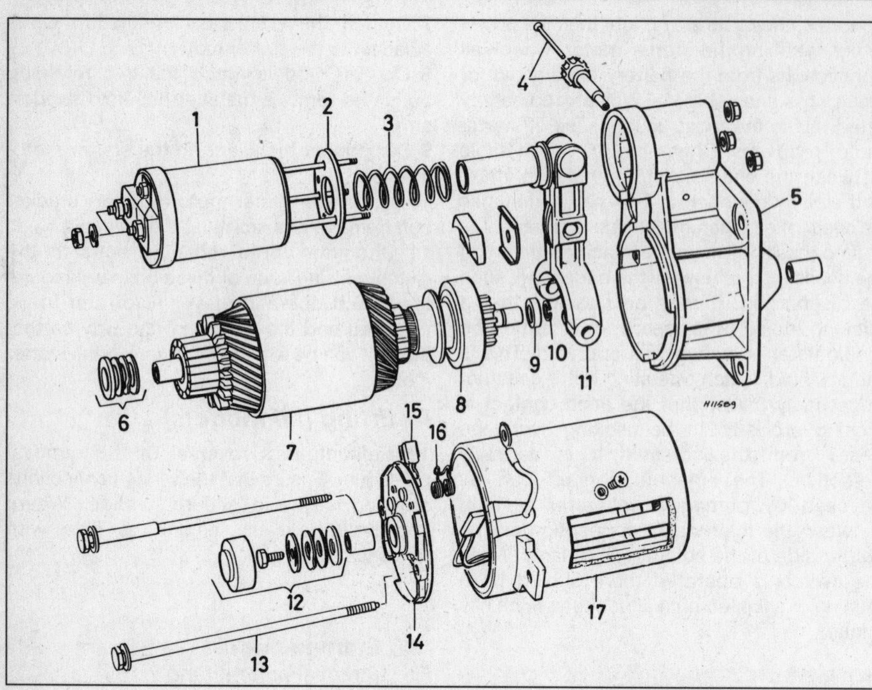

Fig. 12.3 Exploded view of the Paris-Rhone starter motor (Sec 11)

1 Solenoid
2 Spacer
3 Return spring
4 Eccentric pivot and pin
5 End housing
6 Thrust washers
7 Armature
8 Drive pinion
9 Stop collar
10 Stop ring
11 Pinion carriage operating lever
12 End cap and washers
13 Through-bolt
14 End cover
15 Brush
16 Brush spring
17 Body

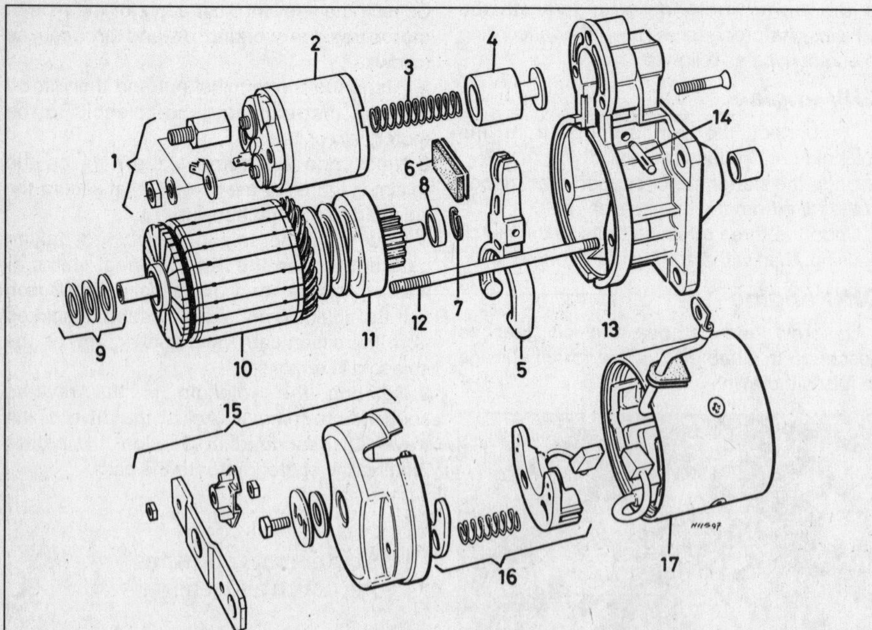

Fig. 12.4 Exploded view of the Ducellier starter motor (Sec 11)

1 Solenoid terminals
2 Solenoid
3 Return spring
4 Plunger
5 Pinion carriage operating lever
6 Dust pad
7 Stop ring
8 Stop collar
9 Thrust washer
10 Armature
11 Drive pinion
12 Retaining stud
13 End housing
14 Pivot pin
15 End cover assembly
16 Brush assembly
17 Body

Paris-Rhone

2 Remove the small cap from the centre of the commutator end cover.

3 Undo and remove the armature end bolt and recover the washer.

4 Undo and remove the two long end cover retaining bolts and carefully withdraw the end cover from the armature and starter motor body. As the end cover is withdrawn, lift up the springs and slide the two field coil brushes out of the end cover.

5 If the brushes are suspect, compare their length against new ones and renew them if worn excessively. To do this, cut off the old brush lead onto the severed end of the old one. Take care to localise the heat during the operation and do not damage the insulation of the field coils.

6 Wipe the starter motor armature and commutator clean with a non-fluffy rag, wetted with carbon tetrachloride, or other similar solvent.

7 Refit the brushes into their holders and then reassemble the starter motor using the reverse sequence to removal.

Ducellier

8 Undo and remove the two nuts and lift off the commutator end cover retaining bracket.

9 Undo and remove the armature end bolt and recover the washers.

10 Undo the second pair of retaining nuts and carefully lift off the end cover followed by the brush holders, taking care not to lose the tension springs.

11 The procedure is now the same as for the Paris-Rhone motor described in paragraphs 5 to 7 inclusive.

Bosch

12 Undo and remove the two small screws and lift off the armature end cap.

13 Extract the circlip from the end of the armature and lift off the washers and rubber sealing ring.

14 Undo and remove the two long bolts which hold the motor assembly together. The

11.17 Mitsubishi starter motor through bolts (arrowed) and support bracket

11.18 Removing the end cover

11.19 Brush removed from holder for inspection

commutator end cover can now be withdrawn to reveal the brushes and brush mounting plate.

15 Lift up the springs and slide the field coil brushes out of the mounting plate, then remove the mounting plate from the motor. Retrieve the spacer washers from the end of the armature.

16 The procedure is now the same as for the Paris-Rhone motor described in paragraphs 5 to 7 inclusive.

Mitsubishi

17 Undo and remove the two long bolts which hold the motor assembly together (photo).

18 Lift of the rear support bracket and the commutator end cover (photo) .

19 Release the springs on the two field coil brushes and slip these brushes out of their holders. Now lift off the brush holder assembly (photo) .

20 The procedure is now the same as for the Paris-Rhone motor described in paragraphs 5 to 7 inclusive.

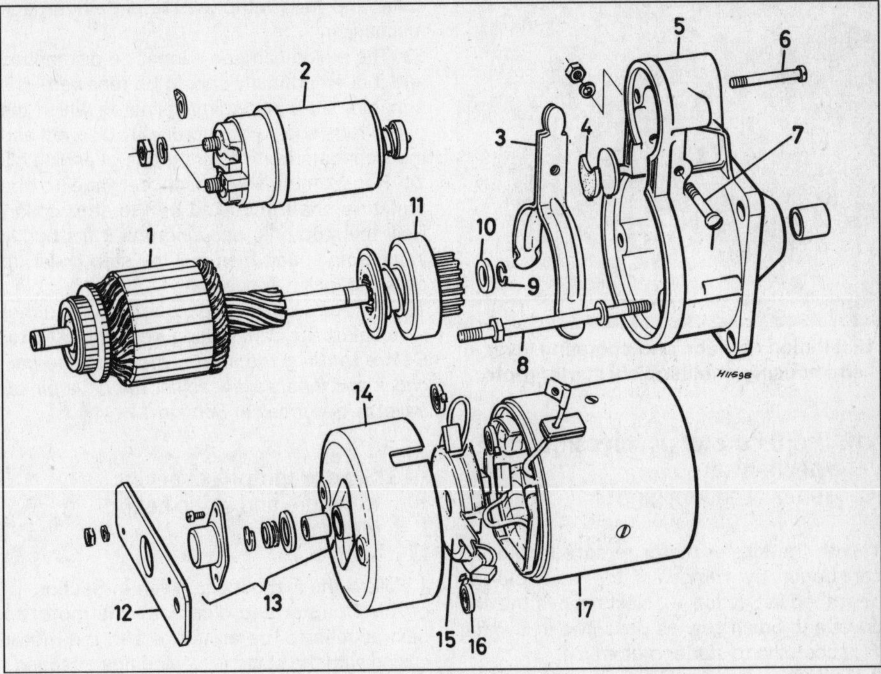

Fig. 12.5 Exploded view of the Bosch starter motor (Sec 11)

1 Armature
2 Solenoid
3 Pinion carriage operating lever
4 Dust cover
5 End housing
6 Solenoid retaining screw
7 Pivot pin
8 Retaining stud
9 Stop ring
10 Stop collar
11 Drive pinion
12 Bracket
13 End cap assembly
14 End cover
15 Brush holder
16 Brush spring
17 Field coils and body

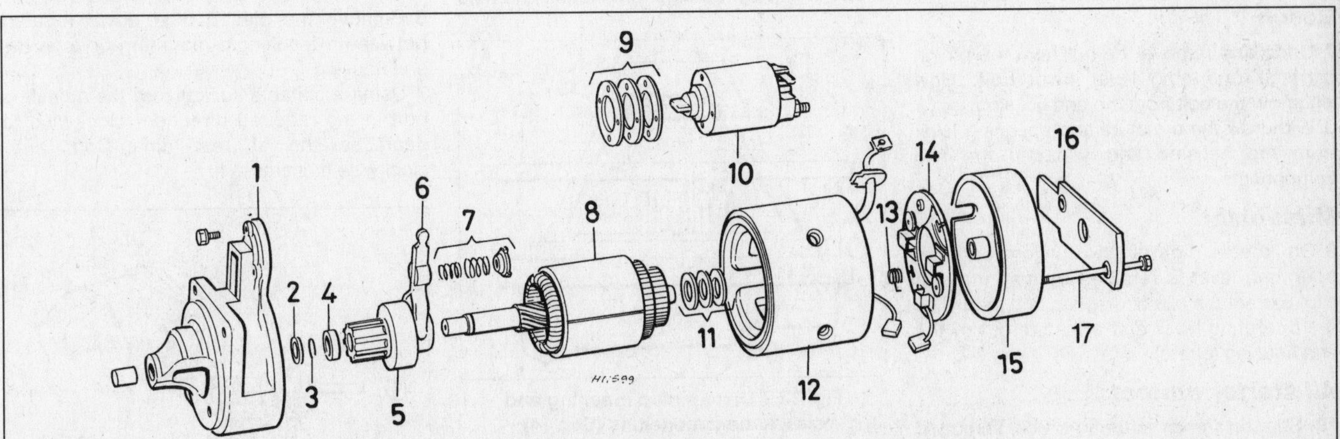

Fig. 12.6 Exploded view of the Mitsubishi starter motor (Sec 11)

1 End housing
2 Thrust washer
3 Stop ring
4 Stop collar
5 Drive pinion
6 Pinion carriage operating lever
7 Return springs
8 Armature
9 Solenoid shims
10 Solenoid
11 Thrust washers
12 Body
13 Brush spring
14 Brush and holder
15 End cover
16 End bracket
17 Retaining bolt

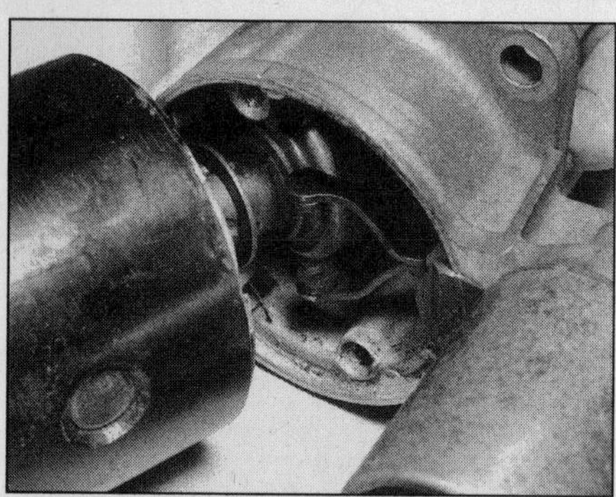

12.9 Pinion carriage and operating lever in end housing of Mitsubishi starter motor

12 Starter motor pinion carriage mechanism - removal and refitting

1 With the starter motor removed from the car begin by removing the solenoid as described in Section 10. Next remove the end cover and brush gear as described in Section 11, according to starter motor type.

2 Having carried out these operations the starter motor body can now be carefully slid rearwards off the armature.

3 The procedure now varies slightly according to motor type as described below.

Paris-Rhone

4 Drive out the expansion pin and then withdraw the pin from the end housing.

5 Slide the armature and pinion carriage operating lever out of the end housing and then lift the lever off the armature.

Ducellier

6 Drive out the pinion carriage operating lever pivot pin from the end housing and then slide the armature and operating lever out of the housing. Lift the lever off the armature.

Bosch

7 Undo and remove the nut from the pinion carriage operating lever pivot bolt. Now withdraw the bolt from the end housing.

8 Withdraw the armature and operating lever from the housing and separate the two components.

Mitsubishi

9 On these motors the pinion carriage operating lever is retained by a spring and clip. Extract the clip and spring and then slide the operating lever and armature out of the end housing (photo).

All starter motors

10 Support the armature in a vice, vertically, taking care not to damage the commutator.

11 Using a hammer and tube of suitable diameter, tap the stop collar on the end of the armature shaft down just far enough to reveal the stop ring.

12 Hook out the stop ring, slide off the stop collar and then withdraw the pinion carriage mechanism.

13 The pinion carriage cannot be dismantled and if deemed faulty should be renewed. The armature shaft and spiral spline on which the pinion runs should be thoroughly cleaned and then lubricated with a light grade of engine oil.

14 Reassemble the pinion carriage to the armature shaft, followed by the stop collar. Refit the stop ring, ensuring that it fits tightly in its groove, and then pull the stop collar up over it to lock it in position.

15 The remainder of reassembly is a direct reversal of the dismantling sequence. **Note:** *Before refitting the starter motor to the car, check and if necessary adjust the drive pinion travel as described in Section 14.*

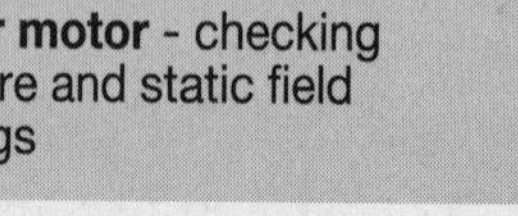

13 Starter motor - checking armature and static field windings

1 Follow the instructions given in Section 12 of this Chapter and dismantle the motor to gain access to the armature and the motor casing with the static field windings attached.

2 The armature windings may be checked for a short onto the motor shaft/armature core, and for an open-circuit in the windings.

3 Using a test circuit comprising two probes, a bulb and 12v battery, touch the commutator bars with one probe, whilst holding the other against the armature metal. The test bulb should not light up.

4 To check the armature windings for open circuit, replace the bulb with an ammeter (0 to 10 amp). Touch commutator bars (90° spaced) with the probes and note the ammeter reading. The readings should all be the same; considerable deviation (25%) indicates open-circuits or windings insulation breakdown.

5 The battery and bulb circuit is used to check the static field windings. Touch one probe onto each winding termination and hold the other against the metal motor casing. The test bulb must not light up. Remember to touch the positive brushes to check for short-circuits properly.

6 Faulty armatures or field windings should be renewed, though individual new spares may be difficult to obtain, and it will be possibly be necessary to purchase an exchange motor unit.

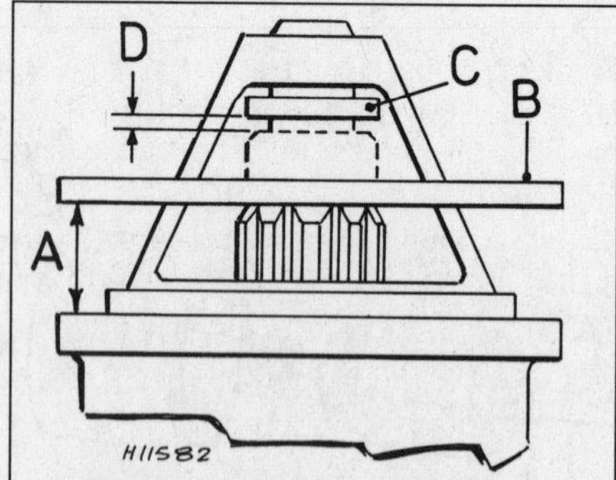

Fig. 12.7 Drive pinion meshing and clearance dimensions (Sec 14)

A Dimension with solenoid at rest = 14 mm (0.55 in)
B Straight- edge
C Pinion stop
D Clearance with solenoid energised = 0.5 to 1.5 mm (0.019 to 0.059 in)

14 Starter motor - drive pinion travel adjustment

1 Whenever the starter motor has been dismantled, or if a new or reconditioned unit is being fitted, it is necessary to adjust the drive pinion travel to obtain the correct mesh and clearance between the pinion teeth and the teeth on the flywheel ring gear.

2 With the starter solenoid at rest, the dimension from the end housing flange to the outer edge of the pinion must be 14 mm (0.55 in).

3 With the solenoid energised, the clearance between the end of the pinion and the pinion stop must be 0.5 to 1.5 mm (0.019 to 0.059 in). To energise the solenoid and enable this check to be carried out, connect one lead from a 12 volt battery to a small spade terminal on the solenoid. Using a switch in the circuit, connect the other battery terminal lead to one of the solenoid fixing studs.

4 If the pinion travel is incorrect, the adjustment procedure is as follows.

Paris-Rhone

5 Drive out the steel locking pin and rotate the plastic pivot pin until the at rest dimension is obtained. Check that the clearance with the solenoid energised is satisfactory and then refit the locking pin.

Ducellier

6 Remove the plastic dust cover located between the solenoid mounting bolts in the end housing.

7 Using a suitable socket turn the adjusting bolt in the required direction, clockwise to decrease the at rest dimension, anti-clockwise to increase it.

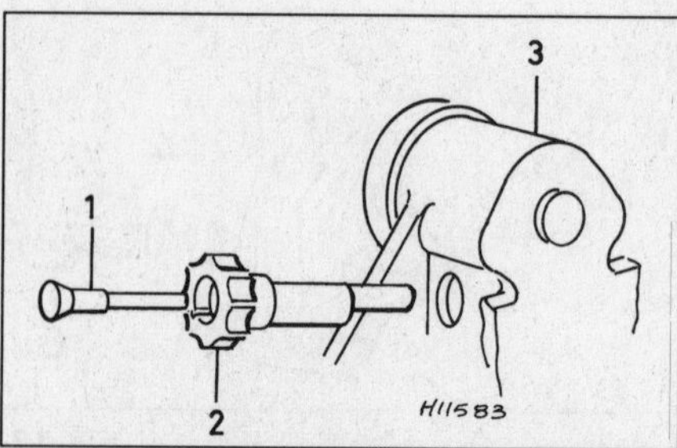

Fig. 12.8 Pinion mesh adjustment – Paris-Rhone starter motor (Sec 14)

1 Expansion pin
2 Eccentric pin
3 End housing

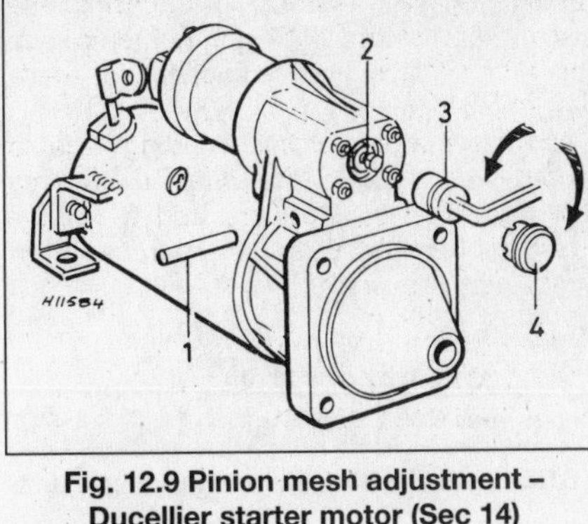

Fig. 12.9 Pinion mesh adjustment – Ducellier starter motor (Sec 14)

1 *Pivot pin*
2 *Adjusting bolt and locknut*
3 *Socket spanner*
4 *Dust cap*

8 Check the clearance with the solenoid energised and if satisfactory refit the dust cover.

Bosch and Mitsubishi

9 If the dimensions are outside the tolerance given, adjustment is by removing the solenoid (see Section 10), and adding or subtracting shims between the solenoid and end housing until the at rest and energised positions of the drive pinion are correct.

15 Fuses and relays - general

1 The main fuse/relay box is located under the lower trim panel on the passenger side. Other relays such as the fuel injection system tachymetric relay are located in the engine compartment (photo), or elsewhere.

2 The circuits protected by the fuses, together with their rating, are given in the Specifications at the start of this Chapter.

3 Access to the fuses is gained by pulling the release handle and swinging the box down (photo).

4 Always renew a fuse with one of similar rating and never renew it more than once without finding the source of trouble. If necessary, refer to the wiring diagrams at the end of this Chapter.

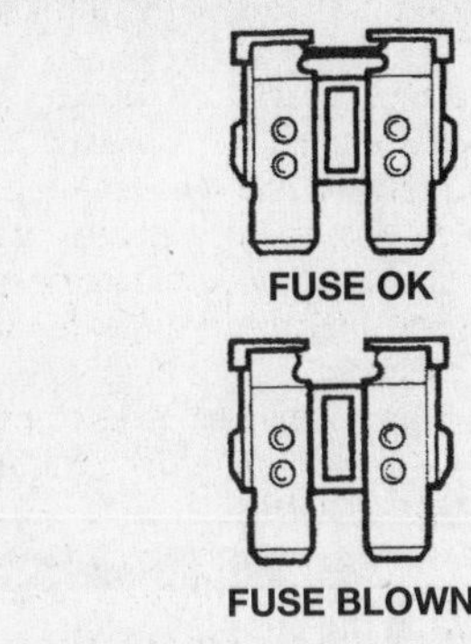

Fig. 12.10 Fuse condition check (Sec 15)

5 Relay units rarely give problems. but they can easily be renewed by pulling them from their location in the box. The relay units and their functions are also shown in the wiring diagrams at the end of this Chapter. Some relay units are connected in-line and are separate from the main fuse/relay box unit.

6 The direction indicator/hazard warning flasher unit is located on the fuse board and controls both the direction indicator and hazard warning functions.

7 In the event of either system not operating, or one lamp flashing very quickly, carry out the following checks before renewing the flasher unit itself.

8 Inspect the circuit fuse and renew it if it is blown.

9 Check the condition of all wiring and the security of the connections.

10 Check the lamp which is malfunctioning for a broken bulb.

11 Make sure that the lamp casing or bulb earth connection is making a good contact.

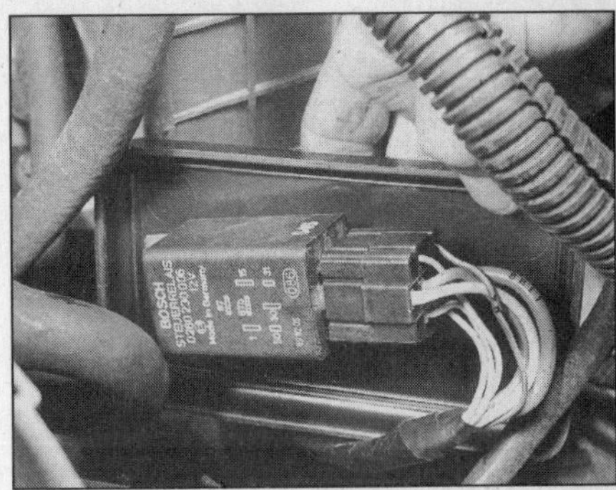

15.1 Tachymetric relay unit clipped to underside of the protector box lid in engine compartment

15.3 Fuse/relay box with spare fuse locations (arrowed)

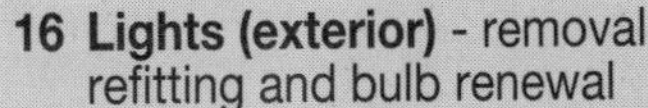

16 Lights (exterior) - removal, refitting and bulb renewal

Headlight

1 The bulbs are renewed from the rear of the headlamp unit, access being from the engine compartment.

2 Pull free the wiring connector, release the bulb retaining clip and withdraw the bulb (photos).

3 Where halogen bulbs are fitted, do not touch the glass with your fingers or with a fluffy cloth and, if necessary, allow the bulb to cool before removing it.

If the headlamp bulb glass is inadvertently touched, clean it with methylated spirit.

4 Refitting is a reversal of the removal procedure. When inserting the bulb into position it must be correctly aligned with the location notches. Check the headlights for satisfactory operation and alignment on completion.

16.2A Pull free the wiring connector and rubber cover . . .

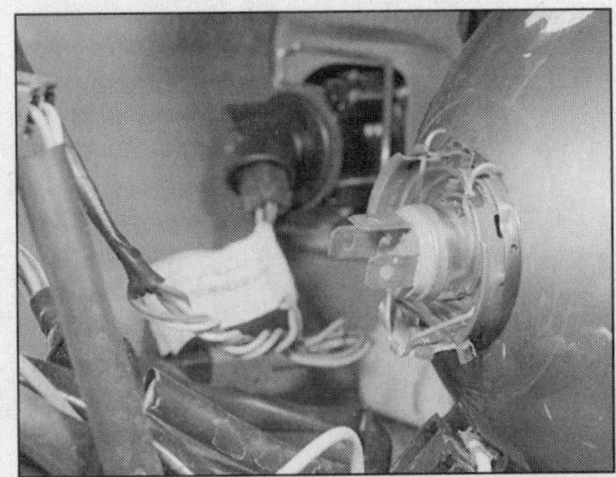

16.2B . . . release the bulb retaining clips . . .

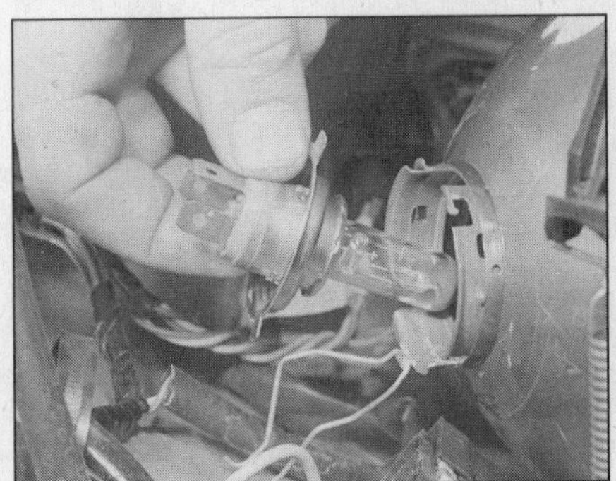

16.2C . . . and withdraw the bulb from the headlamp

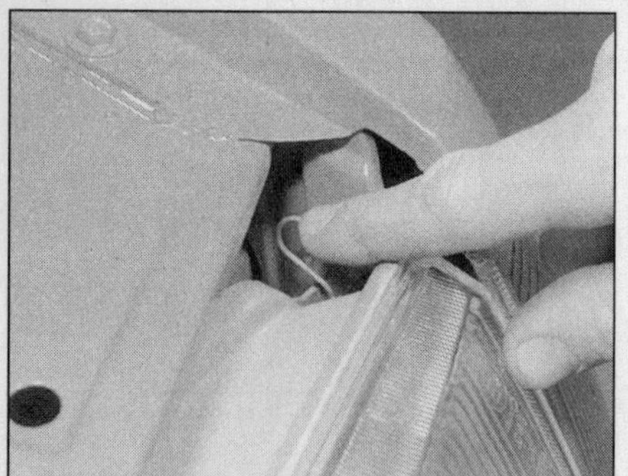
16.6A Depress the wire retaining clips . . .

16.6B . . . detach the support (where fitted) . . .

16.6C . . . and withdraw the headlamp unit

Removal and refitting

5 Raise the bonnet, and pull free the headlamp wiring connector and the sidelight bulbholder.

6 From the front side of the headlamp, depress the retaining wire clip and withdraw the headlamp unit. Access to the inner clip is made easier if the front grille is removed. Detach the support spring (where fitted) from the rear (photos).

7 Refitting is a reversal of removal. Check lamp operation and alignment on completion.

Sidelight

8 This bulb is located in the rear of the headlight unit. Pull free the bulbholder, complete with wiring connections, from the headlamp unit then withdraw the bulb from its holder (photo).

9 Refit in the reverse order to removal and check the operation of the sidelights.

Front indicator

10 Reach down within the front corner of the engine compartment on the side concerned, untwist the bulbholder and withdraw it from the light unit. Remove the bulb from the holder (photo).

11 Renew the bulb if necessary and refit in reverse order of removal.

Removal and refitting

12 Detach the wiring to the bulbholder then release and remove the wire retaining clip from within the engine compartment. Withdraw the indicator light unit (photos).

13 Refit in the reverse order of removal and check that the indicator operates in a satisfactory manner.

Front foglamps

14 Undo the retaining screws and remove the rim and lens. The bulb can now be removed from its holder within the lamp. Renew and refit the bulb as necessary and check for satisfactory operation to complete.

Removal and refitting

15 Detach the wiring connectors to the foglamp, undo the retaining bolts to the rear of the unit and withdraw the foglamp. Refit in the reverse order of removal. Check for satisfactory operation.

Rear combination lights

16 Prise free the black plastic cover from the rear panel directly in front of the rear combination light unit (in the luggage compartment).

17 Unclip and remove the combination bulbholder unit from the aperture (photo). Remove the bulb(s) as required and if necessary detach the wiring harness connector to the unit and remove it.

Removal and refitting

18 If required the lens unit can be unclipped and removed as shown (photo).

19 Refit in the reverse order of removal and

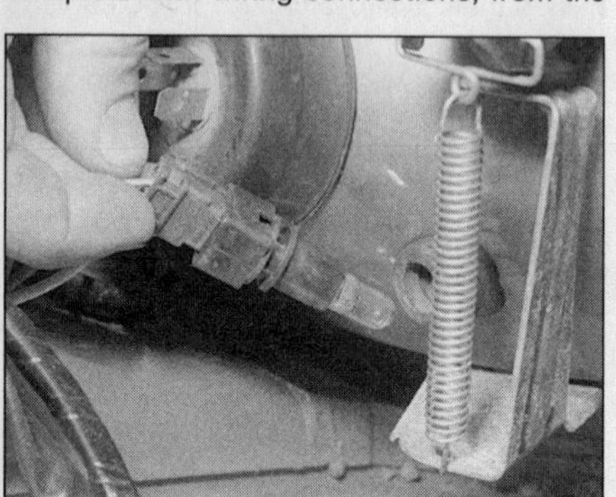
16.8 Sidelight bulb and holder removal

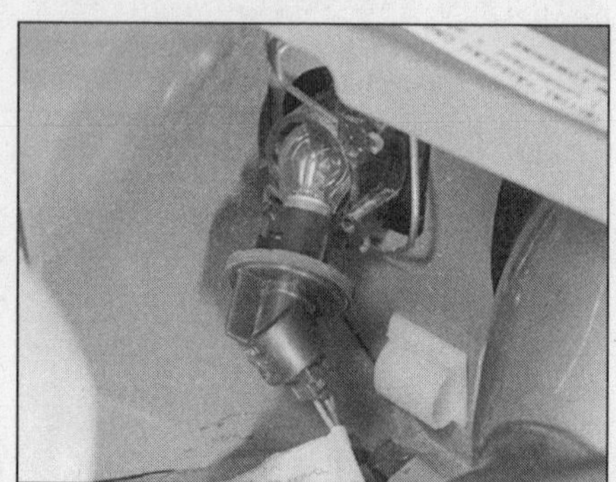
16.10 Front indicator bulb removal

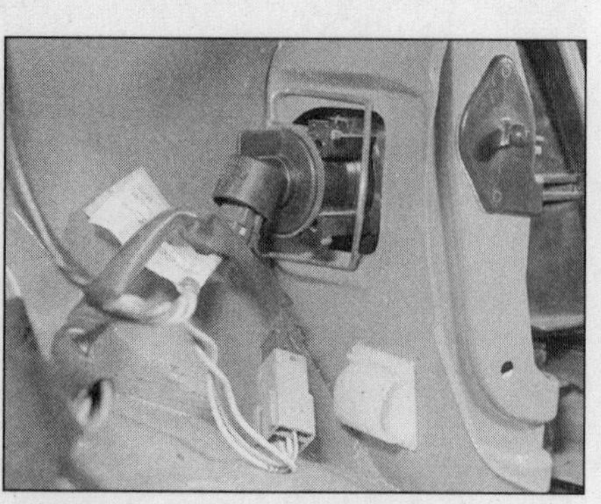
16.12A Front indicator wiring connector and unit retaining clip

16.12B Removing the front indicator light unit

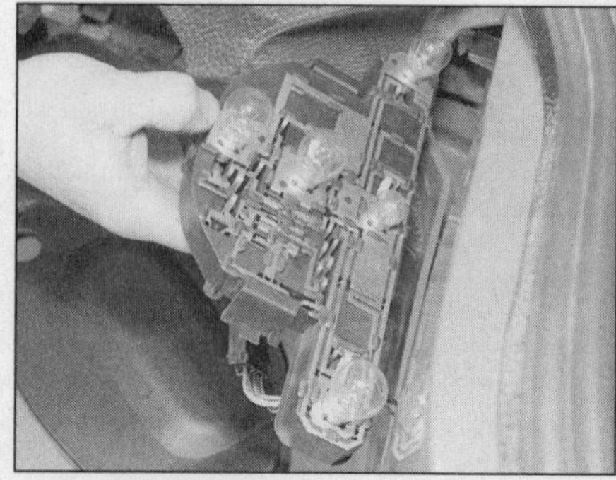
16.17 Rear combination light bulbholder unit

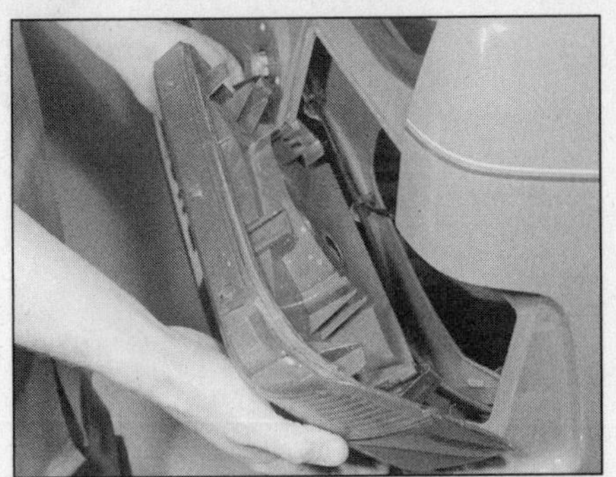

16.18 Rear combination light lens removal

16.21A Undo the retaining screws . . .

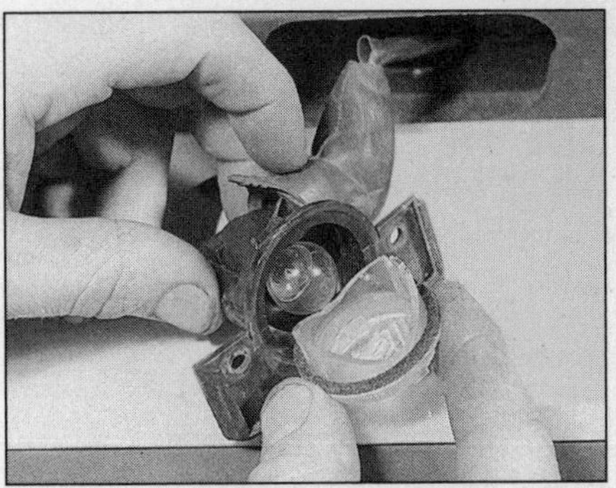

16.21B . . . and remove the number plate lens and unit for bulb renewal

check for satisfactory operation on completion.

Rear number plate

20 These units are accessible from the apertures in the underside face of the rear bumper.

21 Undo the two retaining screws, withdraw the unit and remove the lens. Renew the bulb if necessary (photos).

Removal and refitting

22 To fully remove the unit, detach the wiring connections.

23 Refit in the reverse order of removal and check for satisfactory operation.

Side indicator repeater lamp

24 Carefully pull or prise free the lamp unit from the body panel and withdraw it sufficiently to enable the bulb to be removed.

25 Refit in reverse and check operation.

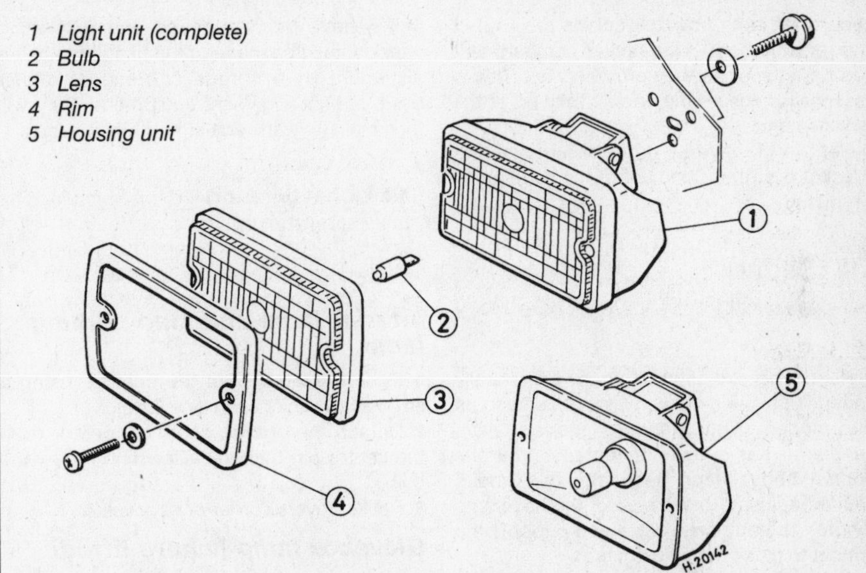

Fig. 12.11 Foglamp assembly components (Sec 16)

17 Headlamp interior adjustment cable(s) - removal and refitting

1 Access to the adjuster unit can be gained after removing the lower glovebox on the driver's side (see Chapter 11). Pull free the switch control for access to the retaining screws. Undo the screws and withdraw the switch from the instrument panel surround facia (photos).

2 To disconnect the cable from the adjuster at the headlamp, remove the black plastic domed cover, then grip and pull free the flat retainer (photo).

3 If the switch unit or cables are defective, they cannot be repaired and must be renewed as a unit. This unfortunately entails the removal of the facia panels and possibly the heater, as the adjuster cables pass through the bulkhead on the lower left-hand side, and are routed across the bulkhead on the inside to the switch control unit. If removal is

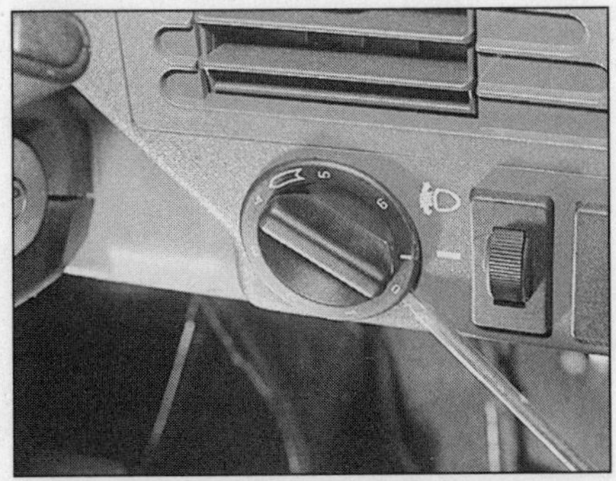

17.1A Prise and remove the headlamp adjuster control knob . . .

17.1B . . . undo the two retaining screws . . .

17.1C . . . and remove the control unit

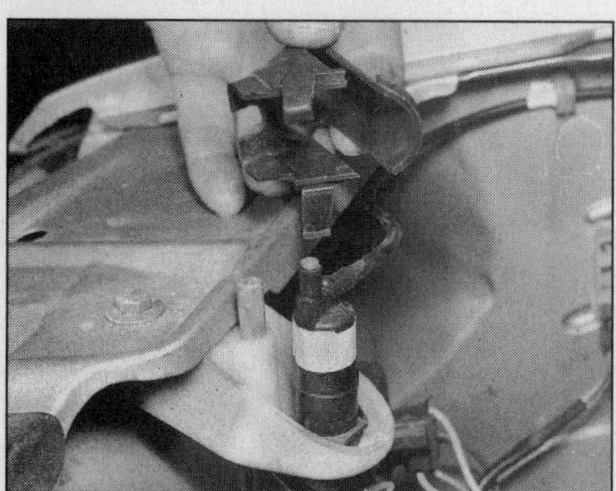

17.2 Remove headlamp adjuster cover and pull free the retainer (arrowed) to release the unit

necessary, note how the cables are routed and retained both in the engine compartment and car interior as they are removed. This is essential to ensure the correct refitting of the replacements.

4 Refit in the reverse order of removal and check/adjust the alignment of the headlamps if required.

18 Headlamp - beam adjustment

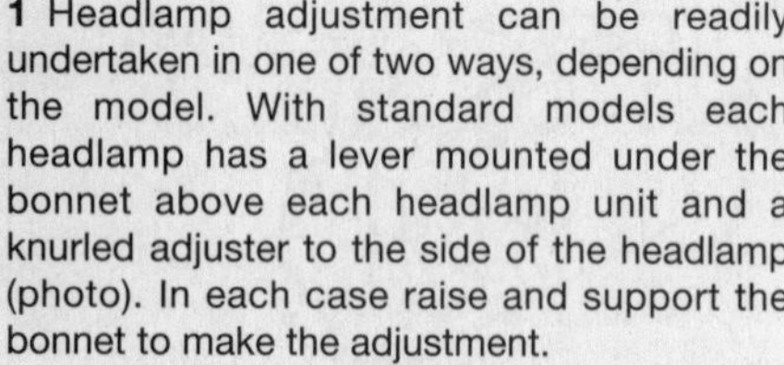

1 Headlamp adjustment can be readily undertaken in one of two ways, depending on the model. With standard models each headlamp has a lever mounted under the bonnet above each headlamp unit and a knurled adjuster to the side of the headlamp (photo). In each case raise and support the bonnet to make the adjustment.

2 An alternative method of adjustment available on some models is the remote control type, with a cable to each headlamp unit from a control unit on the instrument panel facia. This has three basic setting positions: (1) vehicle unladen - normal setting (2) vehicle with average loading and (3) vehicle with full loading at rear.

3 The above setting adjusters are convenient and should be used according to vehicle loading. When the standard beam settings are thought to be incorrect or the headlamp

19.7 Instrument panel bulbholders – round type holder removed

18.1 Headlamp adjuster knob in engine compartment

unit(s) have been removed and refitted, a check should be made of the headlamp beam alignment by a garage or Peugeot dealer using optical alignment equipment. They will then make any fine adjustments necessary.

19 Lights (interior) - bulb renewal

Interior lamp and map reading lamp

1 Prise the lamp from the console using a small screwdriver each side (photo).

2 Detach the orange cable connector from the centre pin then withdraw and renew the bulb.

3 Refit in reverse order of removal.

Glovebox lamp (where fitted)

4 This lamp is located in the centre of the top rail. Remove the bulb by pressing it inwards and unscrewing it.

5 Refit in reverse order of removal.

Instrument panel lamps

6 Remove the instrument panel, as described in Section 25.

7 Two types of bulb are fitted. Pull out the square type bulbholder and remove the wedge type holder. Twist the round type bulbholder through 90° to remove it, but on

19.9 Heater control panel rear face bulbholders (arrowed)

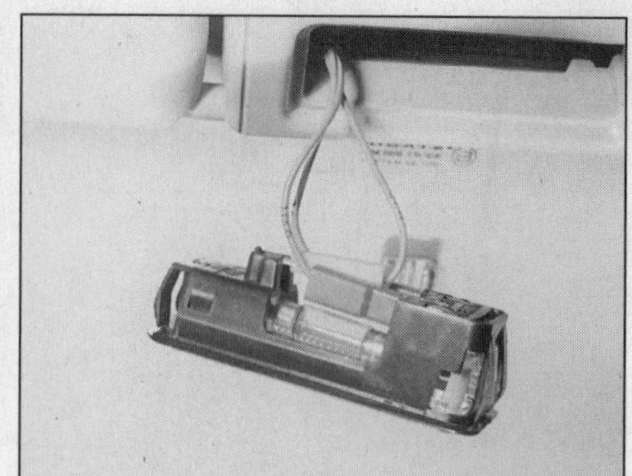

19.1 Interior light unit removed to show its wiring connections and the festoon type bulb

this type the bulb cannot be separated from the holder (photo). Refit in reverse order of removal.

Heater control panel lamps

8 Remove the facia panel as described in Chapter 11.

9 Untwist and pull the bulbholder from the rear face of the heater control panel and extract the bulb (photo).

10 Refit in reverse order of removal.

Digital clock

11 Remove the facia moulding as described in Chapter 11.

12 Untwist the bulbholder from the rear of the clock and remove the bulb.

13 Refit in the reverse order of removal.

Luggage compartment lamp

14 Prise free the lamp from the trim panel in the luggage compartment, then remove the bulb (photo).

15 Refit in the reverse order.

Facia switch illumination bulbs

16 Remove the instrument facia panel as described in Chapter 11.

17 Untwist and remove the bulbholder from the appropriate switch and renew the bulb.

18 Refit in the reverse order of removal.

Cigar lighter illumination bulb

19 Proceed as described for the facia switches above (photo).

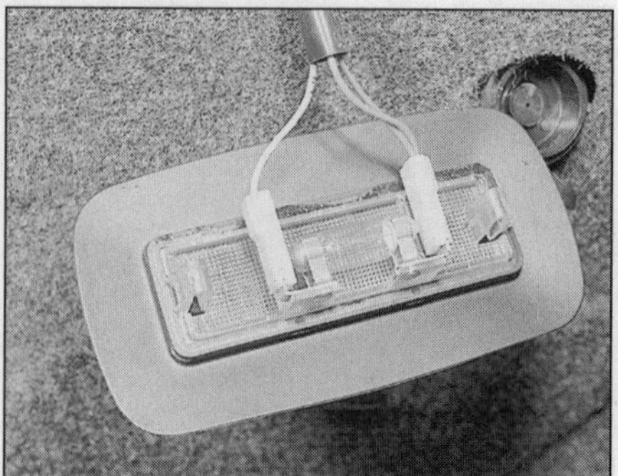

19.14 Luggage compartment lamp unit

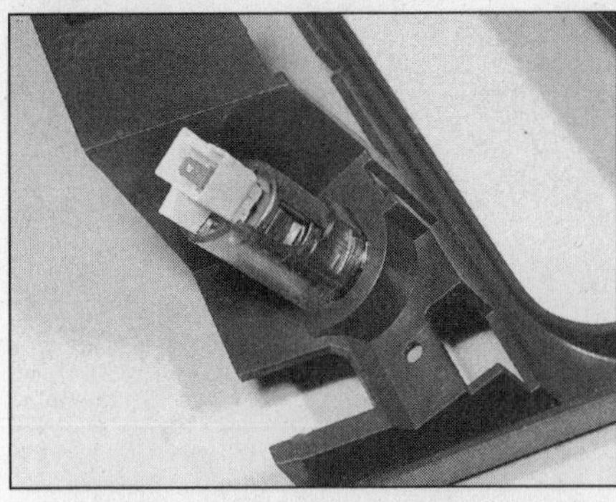

19.19 Cigar lighter unit shown with facia panel removed for access

20.3 Steering column switch retaining screws

21.3 Rear view of the facia panel switches

20 Steering column combination switches - removal and refitting

1 Disconnect the battery earth lead.
2 Remove the steering column shrouds as described in Chapter 11.
3 Detach the wiring connector, undo the retaining screws and remove the switch (photo).
4 Refit in the reverse order of removal. Check for satisfactory operation of the switch on completion.

21 Facia panel switches - removal and refitting

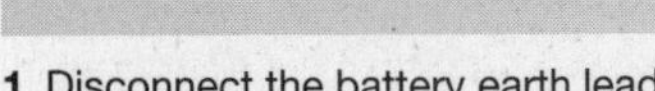

1 Disconnect the battery earth lead.
2 Remove the instrument panel surround facia as described in Chapter 11.
3 Disconnect the wiring from the switch concerned then depress the retaining lugs and withdraw the switch from the panel (photo).
4 Refitting is a reversal of the removal procedure. Check for satisfactory operation of the switch(es) on completion.
5 To remove the instrument panel lights rheostat switch, reach behind the panel and compress the retaining lugs whilst simultaneously pushing the switch through its aperture.

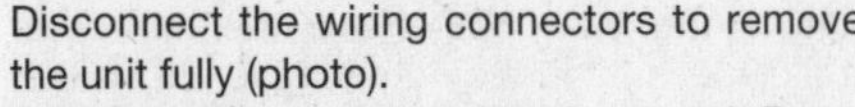

Disconnect the wiring connectors to remove the unit fully (photo).
6 Refit in the reverse order of removal. Press the unit into the panel so that the retaining lugs engage.

22 Courtesy lamp switch - removal and refitting

1 The switch is secured to the door pillar by a self-tapping screw. Extract the screw and withdraw the switch and leads.
2 If the leads are disconnected, tape them to the pillar to prevent them from slipping inside the pillar cavity.
3 It is recommended that the metal contacts of the switch are smeared with petroleum jelly as a precaution against corrosion.
4 Refit by reversing the removal operation.

23 Luggage compartment switch - removal and refitting

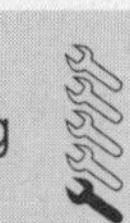

1 Carefully prise free the switch from the tailgate aperture surround panel on the left-hand side (photo).
2 If the leads are disconnected, tape them and retain them so that they are readily available for reconnection.
3 Refit in the reverse order of removal.

24 Handbrake warning switch - removal and refitting

Refer to Chapter 8, Section 17 for details.

25 Instrument panel - removal and refitting

1 Disconnect the battery earth lead.
2 Refer to Section 21 in Chapter 11 and proceed as described in paragraphs 8 to 11 inclusive to remove the instrument panel.
3 The instrument panel and its wiring connections are shown in the accompanying photos.

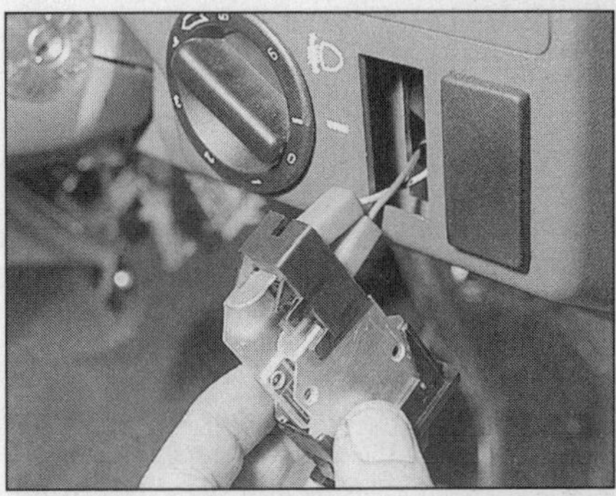

21.5 Instrument lighting rheostat removal

23.1 Luggage compartment switch removed from its aperture

25.3A Instrument panel and wiring connections

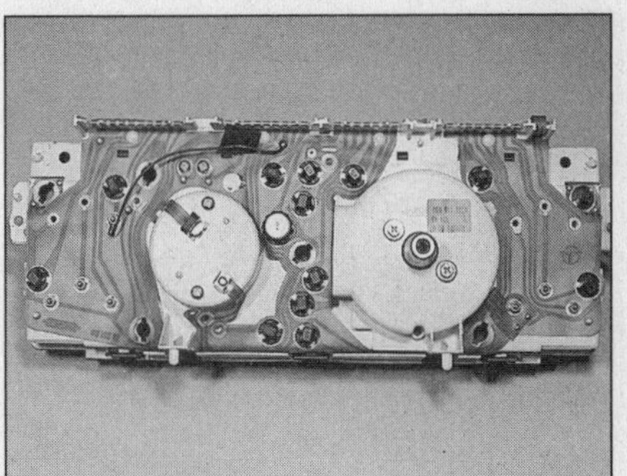

25.3B Instrument panel rear face

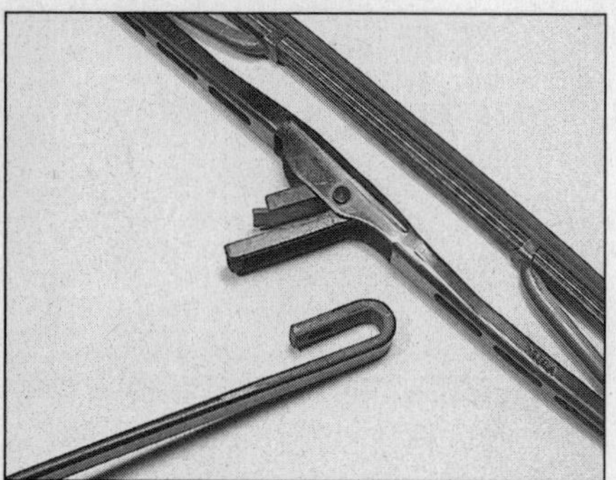

27.2 Windscreen wiper arm and blade separated

4 Refit in the reverse order of removal. Ensure that the wiring connections are securely made.

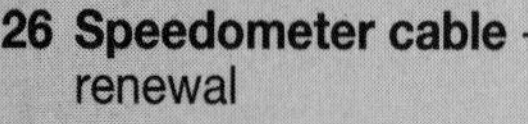

26 Speedometer cable - renewal

1 Disconnect the speedometer cable from the transmission by removing the retaining bolt or rubber plug.

2 Remove the instrument panel, as described in Section 25.

3 Prise the rubber grommet from the bulkhead beneath the facia.

4 Remove the retaining clips, where fitted, and withdraw the speedometer cable.

5 Refitting is a reversal of removal.

27 Windscreen wiper blades and arms - removal and refitting

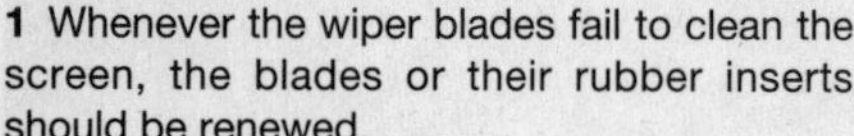

1 Whenever the wiper blades fail to clean the screen, the blades or their rubber inserts should be renewed.

2 To remove a blade, pull the arm from the glass, swivel the blade, pinch the two sides of the U-shaped block together and slide the assembly out of the hook of the arm (photo).

3 When refitting, note the pivot pin in the blade is offset to allow the blade to swivel fully against the glass. Make sure, therefore, that the blade is fitted the right way round so that the 'pip' on the plastic block locates in the cut-out in the hook of the wiper arm.

28.5 Windscreen wiper motor and wiring multi-plug connector

27.4 Windscreen wiper arm removal from the drive spindle

Before removing a wiper arm, note or mark its position on the windscreen using a felt tip pen so that its parked position on the windscreen can be restored when the arm is being refitted to the spindle splines.

4 Flip up the plastic cover, unscrew the nut and pull the arm from the spindle (photo).

5 Refitting is a reversal of removal.

28.4 Wiper spindle body

28 Windscreen wiper motor and linkage - removal and refitting

1 Remove the wiper blades and arms, as described in Section 27.

2 Disconnect the battery negative lead.

3 Open the bonnet then remove the air intake grille by removing the screws and easing the grille from the windscreen weatherstrip.

4 Unscrew the nuts from the wiper spindle bodies (photo).

5 Disconnect the wiper motor multi-plug (photo).

6 Unscrew the mounting bolt and disengage

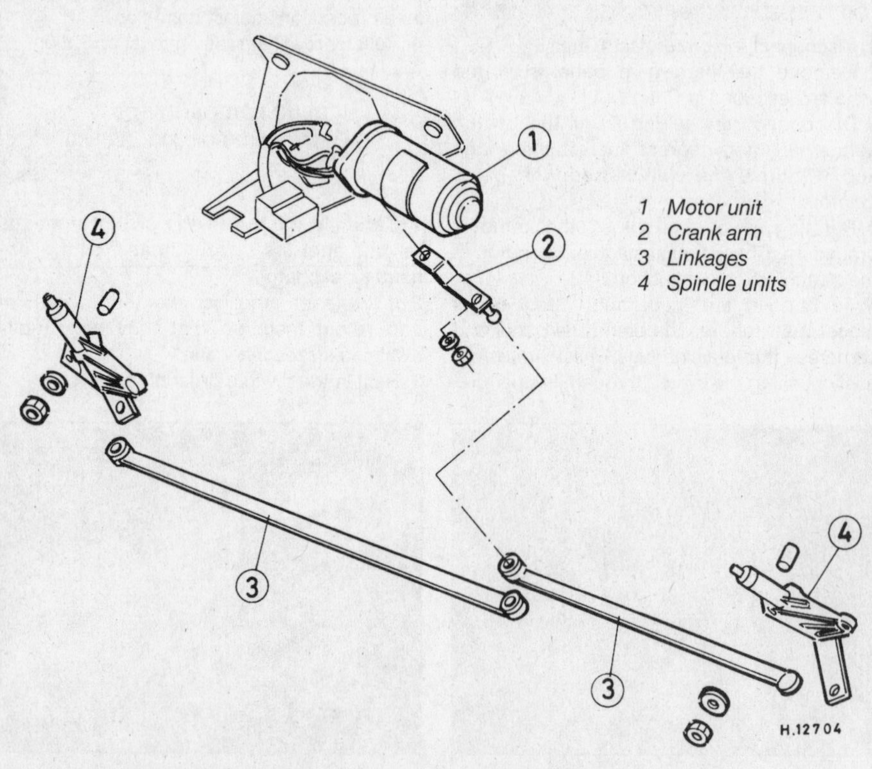

Fig. 12.12 Windscreen wiper motor and linkages (Sec 28)

28.8 Inserting the intake grille beneath the weatherstrip

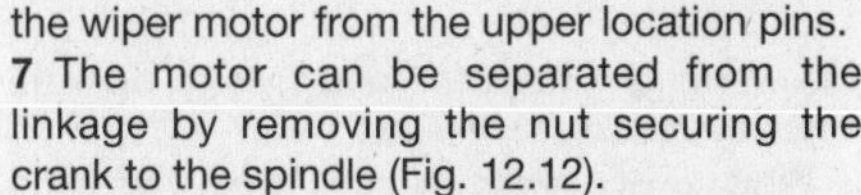

the wiper motor from the upper location pins.

7 The motor can be separated from the linkage by removing the nut securing the crank to the spindle (Fig. 12.12).

8 Refitting is a reversal of removal, but use a screwdriver to lift the weatherstrip as the grille is inserted (photo).

9 On completion wet the screen and check the wipers for satisfactory operation and parking.

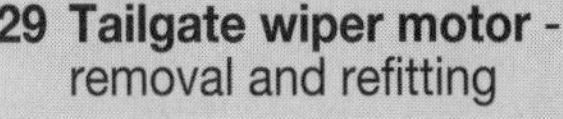

29 Tailgate wiper motor - removal and refitting

1 Remove the wiper arm and blade, as described for the windscreen in Section 27.

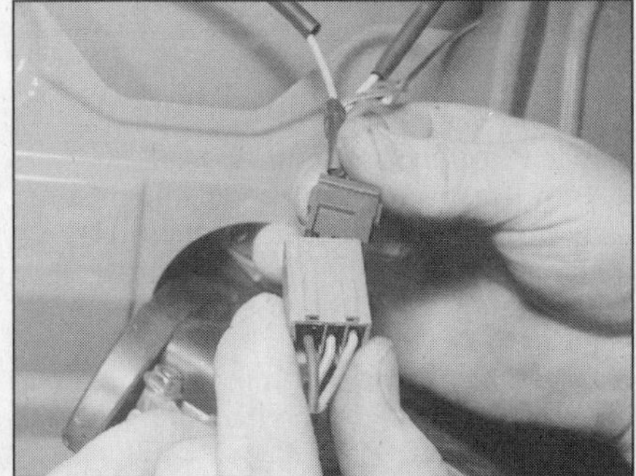

29.4C . . . and detach the wiring multi-plug

29.5 Tailgate wiper motor and mounting cover

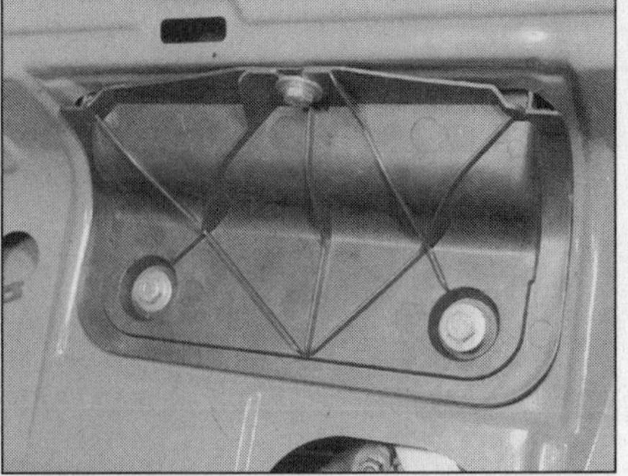

29.4A Undo the three retaining bolts . . .

2 Prise free and unclip the tailgate trim panel.

3 Disconnect the battery earth lead.

4 Undo the three motor retaining bolts, prise free the link arm and withdraw the motor. As the motor is being removed detach the wiring connectors and detach the earth lead (photos).

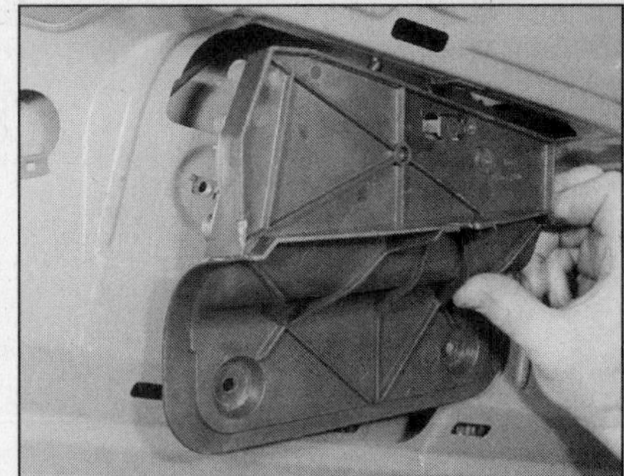

29.4B . . . withdraw the mounting plate and motor . . .

5 Undo the three bolts to remove the wiper motor unit from the mounting cover (photo) (Fig. 12.13).

6 Refit in the reverse order of removal. On completion wet the tailgate window, then check the wiper for satisfactory operation and parking.

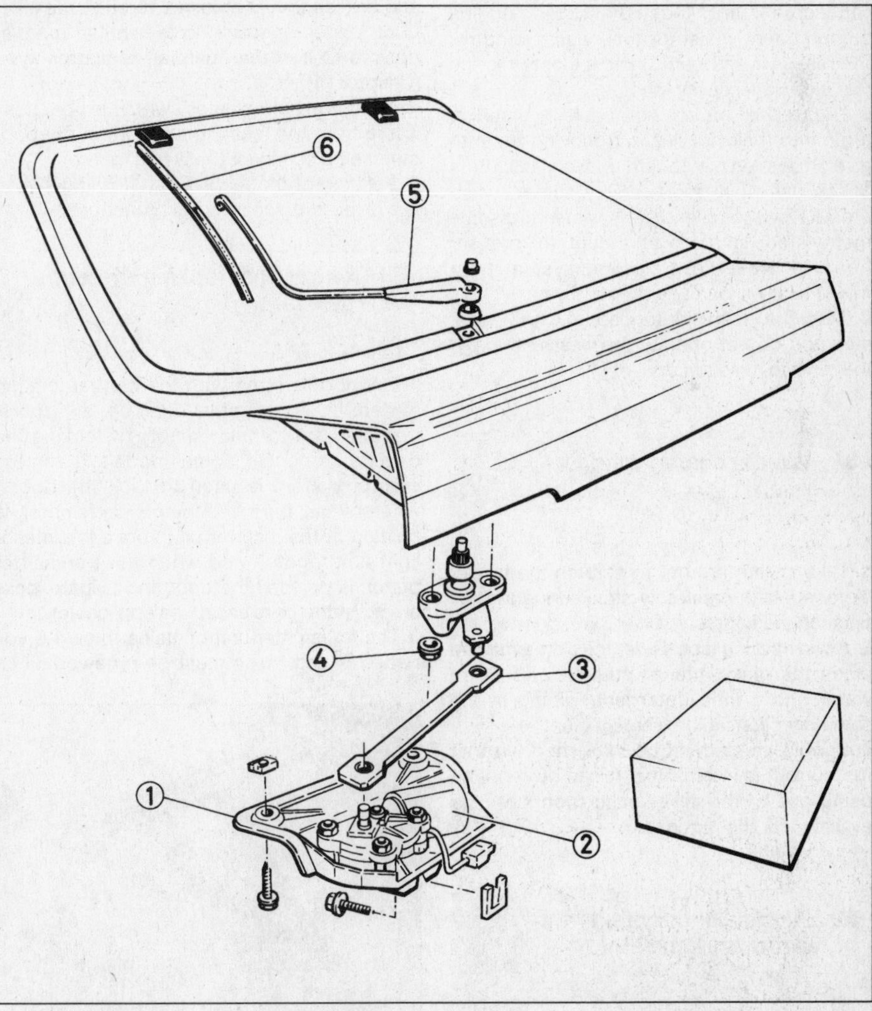

Fig. 12.13 Tailgate wiper motor and wiper arm assembly (Sec 29)

1 Motor support
2 Wiper motor
3 Connecting link and spindle unit
4 Spindle unit retaining nut
5 Wiper arm
6 Wiper blade

30.1A Windscreen washer reservoir and pump unit (arrowed) – SRi model

30.1B Tailgate washer reservoir located in the luggage compartment

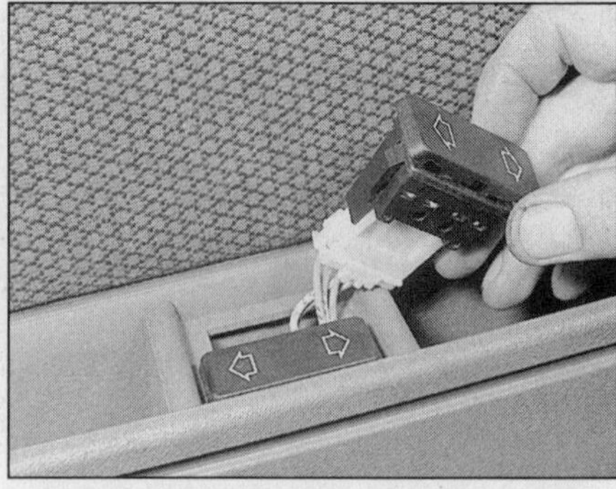

32.5 Electric window regulator switch removal

30 Washer system - general

1 The washer fluid reservoir and pump for the windscreen are located in the engine compartment whilst for the tailgate window, the reservoir and pump unit is located in the rear side panel cavity (photos).

2 The washer jets are adjustable by inserting a pin into their nozzles and moving them to give an acceptable pattern on the glass.

3 The use of a good quality screen wash product is recommended. In winter add some methylated spirit to the fluid to prevent freezing. **Never** use cooling system anti-freeze as it will damage the paintwork.

4 Keep the reservoirs topped up with washer fluid and do not operate the washer pump if the reservoir has run dry.

31 Tailgate heated window - general

1 Take great care not to scratch the heater elements with carelessly stacked luggage or rings on the fingers.

2 Avoid sticking labels over the elements, and clean the glass interior surface with warm water and a little detergent, wiping in the same direction as the elements run.

3 Should an element be scratched, so that the current is interrupted, it can be repaired using one of the silver paint products now available for the purpose.

32 Electrically-operated front windows - general

1 Operation of the front door windows on some models is by electric motors controlled by two switches on the driver's door and a single switch on the passenger door.

2 Access to the motors is gained by dismantling the doors, as described in Chapter 11.

3 Before removing the regulator motor or a switch, first disconnect the battery earth lead.

4 The regulator motor is bolted in position and access to it is obtained through the inner door panel aperture in a similar manner described for the manual regulator type (Chapter 11).

5 To remove a regulator switch, simply prise it free from the location aperture in the door trim then disconnect the wiring (photo).

6 Refitting of the regulator motor and switch is a reversal of the removal procedure.

33 Central door locking system - general

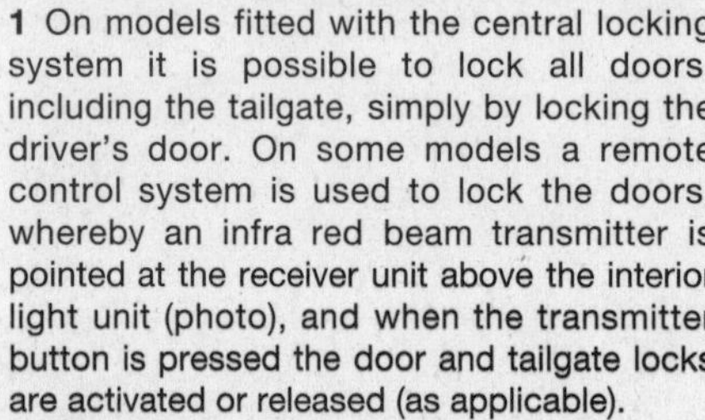

1 On models fitted with the central locking system it is possible to lock all doors, including the tailgate, simply by locking the driver's door. On some models a remote control system is used to lock the doors, whereby an infra red beam transmitter is pointed at the receiver unit above the interior light unit (photo), and when the transmitter button is pressed the door and tailgate locks are activated or released (as applicable).

2 The transmitter unit contains three 1.5 volt batteries and these must be renewed when the warning light in the unit fails to operate when the button is pressed.

3 Whichever system is fitted, electric actuators are used to operate the door/tailgate lock mechanisms. The actuators are accessible for inspection and if necessary removal after removing the door trim and/or the tailgate trim panel(s).

4 If removing an actuator unit, first disconnect the battery earth lead, then disconnect the lock connecting rod from the actuator unit, unbolt the unit and withdraw it. As it is being removed detach the wiring.

5 Refit in reverse order and check for satisfactory operation before refitting the trim panel.

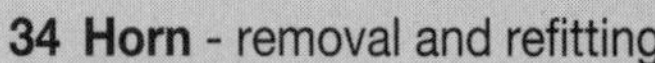

34 Horn - removal and refitting

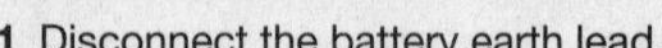

1 Disconnect the battery earth lead.

2 Remove the relevant headlamp unit for access to the horn (see Section 17). On standard models with a single horn, this is normally on the left-hand side beneath the headlamp (photo).

3 Disconnect the wiring from the horn, undo the mounting bolt, detach the earth lead and remove the horn.

4 Refitting is a reversal of the removal procedure.

33.1 Infra red receiver location (central locking system) shown with interior light removed

34.2 Horn and retaining bracket. Note earth lead

35.2A Door-mounted speaker grille

35.2B Door-mounted speaker with grille removed

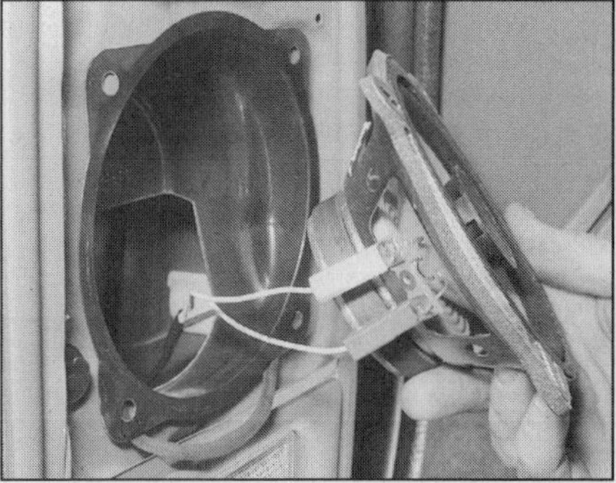

35.2C Door-mounted speaker removal showing wiring connections

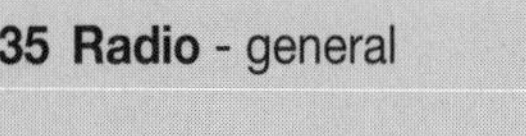

35 Radio - general

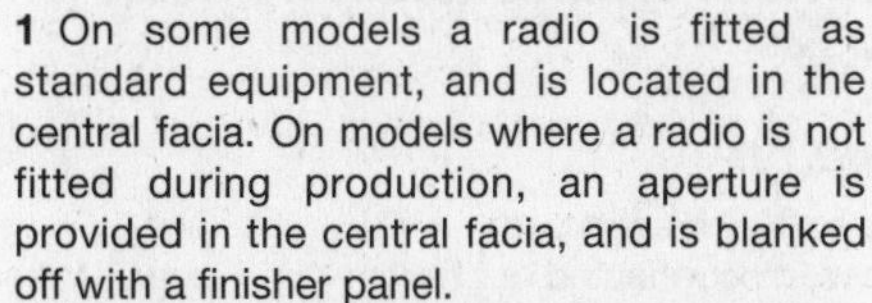

1 On some models a radio is fitted as standard equipment, and is located in the central facia. On models where a radio is not fitted during production, an aperture is provided in the central facia, and is blanked off with a finisher panel.

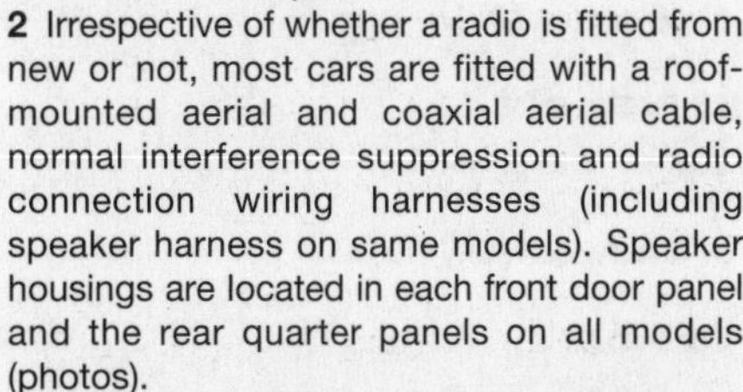

2 Irrespective of whether a radio is fitted from new or not, most cars are fitted with a roof-mounted aerial and coaxial aerial cable, normal interference suppression and radio connection wiring harnesses (including speaker harness on same models). Speaker housings are located in each front door panel and the rear quarter panels on all models (photos).

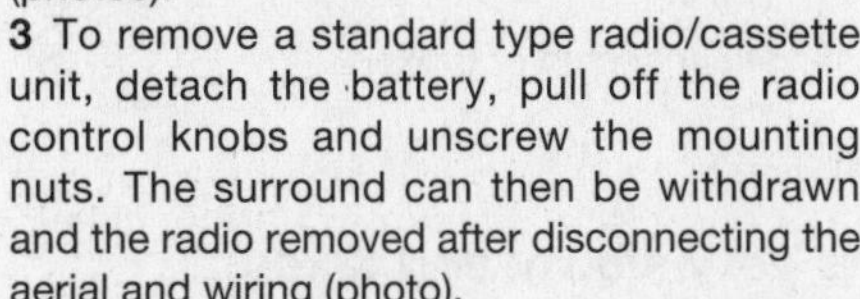

3 To remove a standard type radio/cassette unit, detach the battery, pull off the radio control knobs and unscrew the mounting nuts. The surround can then be withdrawn and the radio removed after disconnecting the aerial and wiring (photo).

4 If a radio/cassette unit is to be installed where one was not fitted before proceed as follows. First disconnect the battery earth lead.

5 Prise free the radio aperture trim finisher.

6 Withdraw the various radio wiring harness connections and the aerial. Identify and connect the wiring to the radio/cassette unit in accordance with the following and with reference to Fig. 12.14.

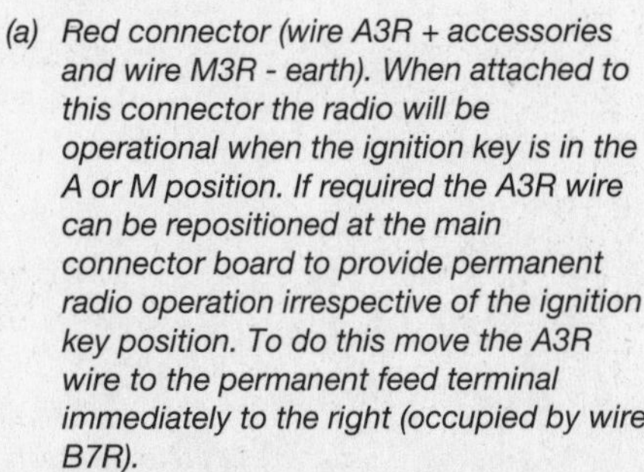

(a) *Red connector (wire A3R + accessories and wire M3R - earth). When attached to this connector the radio will be operational when the ignition key is in the A or M position. If required the A3R wire can be repositioned at the main connector board to provide permanent radio operation irrespective of the ignition key position. To do this move the A3R wire to the permanent feed terminal immediately to the right (occupied by wire B7R).*

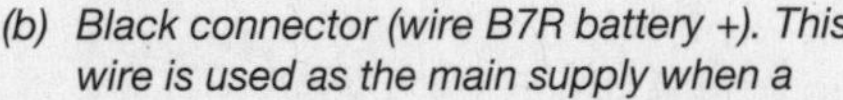

(b) *Black connector (wire B7R battery +). This wire is used as the main supply when a*

35.2D Speaker unit location in the rear quarter panel

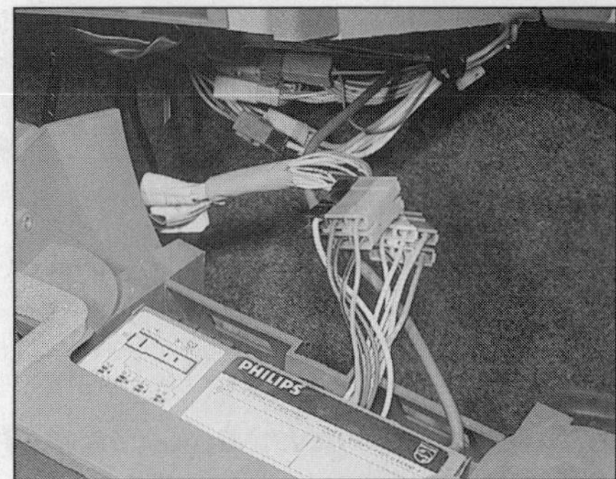

35.3 Radio and wiring connections

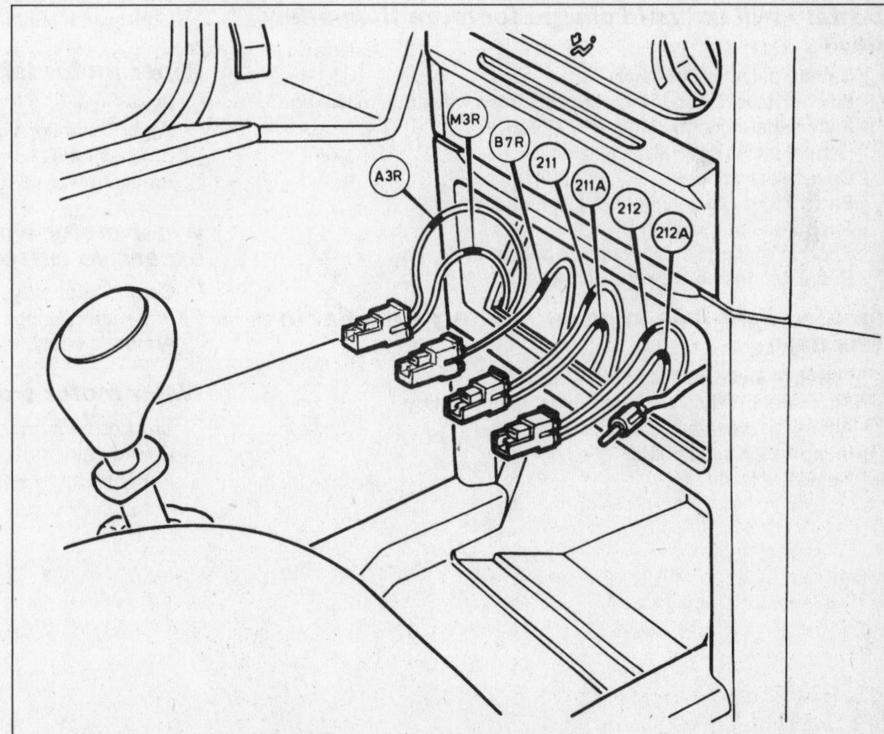

Fig. 12.14 Radio and speaker wiring connections which are accessible with the finisher panel removed (Sec 35)

A3R	+ accessories	211	LH speaker wire	212	RH speaker wire
M3R	– earth	211A	LH speaker wire	212A	RH speaker wire
B7R	Battery +				

12

permanent supply is required - such as for radios with memory functions

(c) *White connector (wire 211 and 211A). This is the left-hand speaker wire*

(d) *Yellow connector (wire 212 and 212A). This is the right-hand speaker wire*

7 When fitting speaker units to the standard partitions mentioned they should fit the 120 mm (4.7 in) apertures. Ensure that the speakers are connected with the correct polarity in accordance with the manufacturer's instructions.

8 When the radio and speakers are connected, reconnect the battery, switch the radio on and trim the reception in accordance with the manufacturer's instructions. It should be noted that the standard roof-mounted aerial gives the best reception when set rearwards at an angle of 45°.

Fault finding - electrical system

Starter fails to turn engine

- ☐ Battery discharged
- ☐ Battery defective internally
- ☐ Battery terminal leads loose or earth lead not securely attached to body
- ☐ Loose or broken connections in starter motor circuit
- ☐ Starter motor switch or solenoid faulty
- ☐ Starter brushes badly worn, sticking, or brush wires loose
- ☐ Commutator dirty, worn or burnt
- ☐ Starter motor armature faulty
- ☐ Field coils earthed

Starter turns engine very slowly

- ☐ Battery in discharged condition
- ☐ Starter brushes badly worn, sticking or brush wires loose
- ☐ Loose wires in starter motor circuit

Starter motor noisy or excessively rough engagement

- ☐ Pinion or flywheel gearteeth broken or worn
- ☐ Starter motor retaining bolts loose

Battery will not hold charge for more than a few days

- ☐ Battery defective internally
- ☐ Electrolyte level too low or electrolyte too weak due to leakage
- ☐ Plate separators no longer fully effective
- ☐ Battery plates severely sulphated
- ☐ Drivebelt slipping
- ☐ Battery terminal connections loose or corroded
- ☐ Alternator not charging
- ☐ Short in lighting circuit continual battery drain
- ☐ Regulator unit not working correctly

Ignition light fails to go out, battery runs flat in a few days

- ☐ Drivebelt loose and slipping or broken
- ☐ Alternator brushes worn, sticking, broken or dirty
- ☐ Alternator brush springs worn or broken
- ☐ Internal fault in alternator
- ☐ Regulator faulty

Horn operates all the time

- ☐ Horn push either earthed or stuck down
- ☐ Horn cable to horn push earthed

Horn fails to operate

- ☐ Cable or cable connection loose, broken or disconnected
- ☐ Horn has an internal fault
- ☐ Blown fuse

Horn emits intermittent or unsatisfactory noise

- ☐ Cable connections loose

Lights do not come on

- ☐ If engine not running, battery discharged
- ☐ Wire connections loose, disconnected or broken
- ☐ Light switch shorting or otherwise faulty

Lights come on but fade out

- ☐ If engine not running, battery discharged
- ☐ Wire connections loose
- ☐ Light switch shorting or otherwise faulty

Wiper motor fails to work

- ☐ Blown fuse
- ☐ Wire connections loose, disconnected or broken
- ☐ Brushes badly worn
- ☐ Armature worn or faulty

Wiper motor works very slowly and takes excessive current

- ☐ Commutator dirty, greasy or burnt
- ☐ Armature bearings dirty or unaligned
- ☐ Armature badly worn or faulty

Wiper motor works slowly and takes little current

- ☐ Brushes badly worn
- ☐ Commutator dirty, greasy or burnt
- ☐ Armature badly worn or faulty

Chapter 13 Supplement:
Revisions and information on later models

Contents

Degrees of difficulty

Easy, suitable for novice with little experience 	**Fairly easy,** suitable for beginner with some experience 	**Fairly difficult,** suitable for competent DIY mechanic	**Difficult,** suitable for experienced DIY mechanic 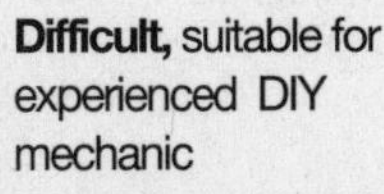 	**Very difficult,** suitable for expert DIY or professional

1 Introduction

This Supplement contains information on changes and modifications which have taken place since 1987. The major items include the TU series engine, the MA manual gearbox, the automatic transmission, and the 309 GTI models.

To use this Supplement to its best advantage, it is suggested that it is referred to before the main Chapters of the manual; this will ensure that any relevant information can be noted and incorporated within the procedures given in Chapters 1 to 12.

Some of the following information is based on the model (or production) year of a car; this is not necessarily the same as its date of registration. If the model year is not known, any Peugeot dealer will have the information required to identify exactly when a particular vehicle was built, using the details recorded on its vehicle identification plate.

Project vehicles

The vehicles used in the preparation of this Supplement, and appearing in many of the photographic sequences, were a 1989-model GTI (XU9JA/K engine) and a 1992-model Style 1.4 (TU3.2/K engine).

2 Specifications

The specifications given below are supplementary to, or revisions of, those given at the beginning of the preceding Chapters. The TU3F, or TU3FM/L, engine fitted to 1993 model year 1.4 litre models has a cast-iron cylinder block - full details were not available at the time of writing. Refer to a Peugeot dealer for specifications applicable to this engine - see text, Section 5.

Engine - TU series

General

Description	Four cylinder, in-line, overhead camshaft. All alloy with wet cylinder liners. Mounted transversely and inclined 6° to the front. Transmission mounted on left-hand end of engine.
Codes and production dates:	
TU1/K (H1A)	1991-on 1.1 litre (carburettor-engined) models
TU1M/Z (HDZ)	1991-on 1.1 litre (fuel injection-engined) models, with catalytic converter
TU3.2/K (K2D)	1991-on 1.4 litre (carburettor-engined) models
TU3M/Z (KDY)	1991-on 1.4 litre (fuel injection-engined) models, with catalytic converter
Displacement:	
TU1 engines	1124 cc
TU3 engines	1360 cc
Bore and stroke:	
TU1 engines	72.0 mm x 69.0 mm
TU3 engines	75.0 mm x 77.0 mm
Compression ratio:	
TU1 engines	9.4:1
TU3 engines	9.3:1
Firing order	1 - 3 - 4 - 2 (No 1 at flywheel end)

Cylinder block

Material	Aluminium alloy
Height:	
TU1 engines	187.43 to 187.53 mm
TU3 engines	206.93 to 207.03 mm

Crankshaft

Number of main bearings	Five
Main journal diameter	49.965 to 49.981 mm
Regrind undersize	0.30 mm
Crankpin diameter	44.975 to 44.991 mm
Regrind undersize	0.30 mm
Endfloat	0.052 to 0.452 mm
Thrustwasher thicknesses	2.40, 2.50, 2.55 and 2.60 mm

Cylinder liners

Type	Wet, removable, matched to piston, sealed by O-ring to cylinder block
Installation dimensions - without seal:	
Protrusion from block	0.03 to 0.10 mm
Maximum permissible difference in (each liner's) height	0.02 mm
Maximum permissible difference in (each liner's) protrusion	0.02 mm
Maximum permissible difference in liner protrusion, between any two adjacent liners	0.05 mm
Piston grade/liner marking:	
A	One file mark
B	Two file marks
C	Three file marks

Pistons

Type	Aluminium alloy, with two compression rings and one oil control ring
Piston diameter (standard):	
TU1 engines	71.960 to 76.990 mm, in three grades
TU3 engines	74.960 to 76.990 mm, in three grades
Piston-to-liner clearance	0.03 to 0.05 mm

Connecting rods

Length (between centres):	
TU1 engines	112.30 to 112.37 mm
TU3 engines	126.80 to 126.97 mm
Maximum weight difference on any engine	3 g

Gudgeon pin

Fit	Clearance in piston, interference in connecting rod

Cylinder head

Material	Aluminium alloy
Maximum permissible distortion	0.05 mm
Height	111.12 to 111.28 mm

Camshaft

Drive	Toothed belt
Actuation	Rocker arms
Valve lift	8.2 mm

Valves

Head diameter:		
Inlet	36.8 mm	
Exhaust	29.4 mm	
Stem diameter:		
Inlet	6.99 mm	
Exhaust	6.97 mm	
Valve length:		
Inlet	110.76 mm	
Exhaust	110.60 mm	
Seat angle (inclusive):		
Inlet	120°	
Exhaust	90°	
Valve timing (at nominal clearance of 0.7 mm):	**TU1 engines**	**TU3 engines**
Inlet opens (BTDC)	5° 19'	5° 55'
Inlet closes (ABDC)	43° 50'	44° 26'
Exhaust opens (BBDC)	32° 58'	32° 22'
Exhaust closes (ATDC)	-0° 6'	0° 42'
Valve clearances - engine cold (ie stopped for at least two hours):		
Inlet	0.20 mm	
Exhaust	0.40 mm	

Lubrication system

Oil pump type	Gear type, chain-driven from crankshaft
Oil filter type	Champion F104
Minimum oil pressure at 90°C (194°F):	
650 rpm	1.5 bars (21.8 lbf/in^2)
4000 rpm	4.0 bars (58.0 lbf/in^2)
Oil pressure warning light operates at	0.8 bars (11.6 lbf/in^2)
Lubricant type/specification	Multigrade engine oil, viscosity SAE 10W/40 or 15W/40

Torque wrench settings

Note: *Refer to a Peugeot dealer for torque wrench settings applicable to the TU3F engine - see text, Section 5.*

	Nm	**lbf ft**
Crankshaft pulley	100	74
Crankshaft sprocket	80	59
Big-end bearing cap	38	28
Flywheel	67	49
Distributor/fuel pump housing	8	6
Camshaft thrust fork	15	11
Thermostat housing	8	6
Main bearing cap casting main bearing cap bolts (models with plain No 5 bearing half-shell fitted to cylinder block - see text):		
Stage 1	20	15
Stage 2	Angle-tighten a further 45°	Angle-tighten a further 45°
Main bearing cap casting main bearing cap bolts (models with grooved No 5 bearing half-shell fitted to cylinder block - see text):		
Stage 1	20	15
Stage 2	Angle-tighten a further 55°	Angle-tighten a further 55°
Stage 3	Loosen bolt fully	Loosen bolt fully
Stage 4	20	15
Stage 5	Angle-tighten a further 45°	Angle-tighten a further 45°
Oil pump	8	6
Sump	8	6
Main bearing cap casting to block	8	6
Water pump housing:		
8 mm bolts	30	22
10 mm bolts	50	37

Torque wrench settings

	Nm	lbf ft
Cylinder head bolts:		
Stage 1	20	15
Stage 2	Angle-tighten a further 240°	Angle-tighten a further 240°
Timing belt tensioner	20	15
Timing cover	6	4
Valve cover	5	4
Dipstick tube	15	11
Oil pressure switch	28	21
Oil filter	15	11

Engine - XU series

General

The following information applies to all XU-series engines (except where otherwise noted) - note that information is given ***only*** *where different from that given for the OHC engine in the Specifications section of Chapter 1.*

Codes and production dates:	
XU52C (B2A)	1988-on 1.6 litre (carburettor-engined) models
XU52C/K (B2B)	1990-on 1.6 litre (carburettor-engined) models
XU5M2/Z (BDY)	1991-on 1.6 litre (fuel injection-engined) models, with catalytic converter
XU5M3/Z (BDY)	1991 GL 1.6 Automatic model
XU5M3/L (BDY)	1992-on GL 1.6 Automatic model
XU5JA/K (B6E)	1991 GR Injection model
XU9JA/K (D6B)	1987-on GTI models
XU9JA/Z (DKZ)	1991/92 GTI model, with catalytic converter
XU9JA/L (DKZ)	1992-on GTI model, with catalytic converter
Bore and stroke:	
XU5 engines	83.0 mm x 73.0 mm
XU9 engines	83.0 mm x 88.0 mm
Displacement:	
XU5 engines	1580 cc
XU9 engines	1905 cc
Compression ratio:	
XU52C (B2A), XU52C/K (B2B), XU5M2/Z, XU5M3/Z and XU5M3/L (BDY) engines	8.95:1
XU5JA/K (B6E) engine	9.25:1
XU9JA/K (D6B) engine	9.60:1
XU9JA/Z, XU9JA/L (DKZ) engines	9.20:1

Crankshaft - XU9JA engines

Crankpin diameter - new	49.684 to 50.000 mm

Cylinder liners - all XU engines, October 1987 on

Protrusion from block (without seal) - liners identified by notch in top edge rim	0.03 to 0.10 mm

Valves - XU9JA engines

Valve head diameter:	
Inlet	41.60 mm
Exhaust	34.05 mm

Valve timing - XU9JA engines

Inlet opens	11° 30' BTDC
Inlet closes	43° ATDC
Exhaust opens	46° BBDC
Exhaust closes	2° ATDC

Torque wrench settings

	Nm	lbf ft
Torx-type cylinder head bolts - all XU engines, October 1987 on:		
Stage 1 - All bolts, in sequence	60	44
Stage 2 - Slacken bolt 1, then	20, then angle-tighten a further 300°	15, then angle- tighten a further 300°
Repeat stage 2 on remaining bolts in sequence		
Timing belt eccentric roller-type tensioner bolt	20	15
Sump spacer plate bolt - XU9JA engines	10	7
Oil cooler union nuts - XU9JA engines	20	15

Under-bonnet view of TU engine (airbox removed)

1 *Right-hand engine mounting*
2 *Brake master cylinder*
3 *Brake fluid reservoir filler cap*
4 *Brake vacuum servo unit*
5 *Cooling system bleed screw*
6 *Air filter assembly*
7 *Carburettor*
8 *Fuel pump*
9 *Battery*
10 *Battery negative terminal*
11 *Washer fluid filler cap*
12 *Air temperature control unit*
13 *Ignition coil*
14 *Engine oil filler cap*
15 *Engine oil level dipstick*
16 *Bonnet lock*
17 *Cooling system filler cap*
18 *Alternator*

Front underside view of TU engine model (engine undershield and sideshields removed)

1 *Radiator*
2 *Front towing eye*
3 *Disc caliper*
4 *Track rod*
5 *Anti-roll bar*
6 *Exhaust intermediate pipe*
7 *Gearchange rod*
8 *Subframe*
9 *Lower suspension arm*
10 *Alternator*
11 *Engine oil filter*
12 *Exhaust front downpipe*
13 *Right-hand driveshaft*
14 *Rear lower engine mounting*
15 *Engine oil drain plug*

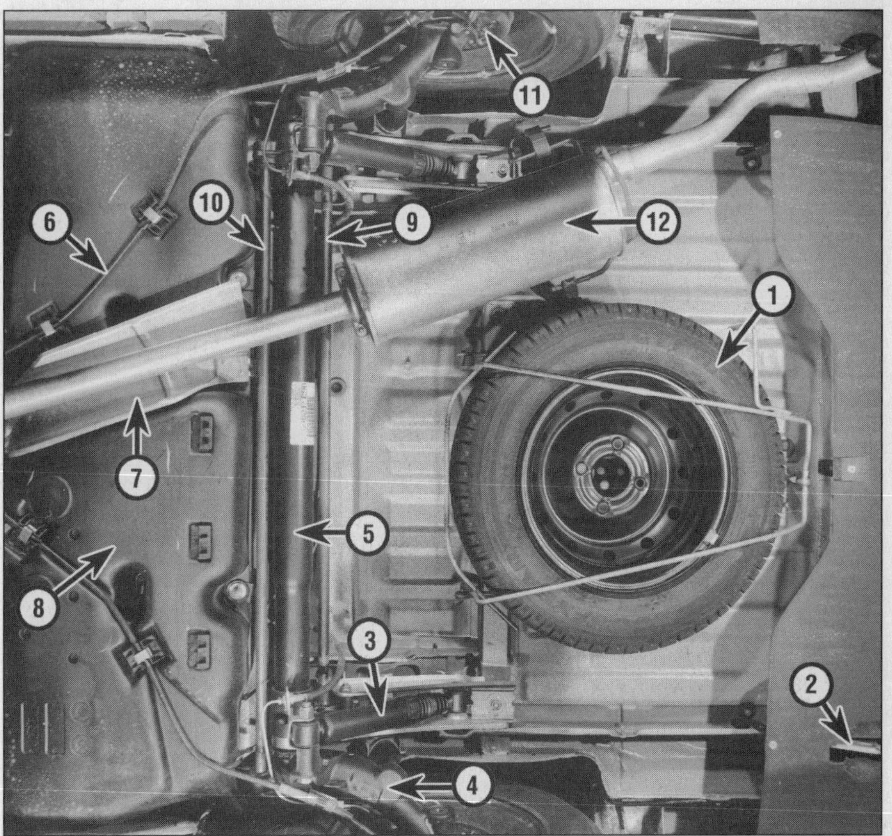

Rear underside view of TU engine model

1 Spare wheel
2 Towing eye
3 Shock absorber
4 Suspension arm
5 Suspension cross tube
6 Handbrake cable
7 Heat shield
8 Fuel tank
9 Torsion bar (right-hand)
10 Torsion bar (left-hand)
11 Brake backplate
12 Exhaust rear silencer

Cooling system

General

System capacity:	
TU1 engines	5.7 litres (10.0 pints)
TU3 engines	7.5 litres (13.2 pints)
XU5M3/Z, XU5M3/L engines	6.1 litres (10.7 pints)
All other XU engines	7.5 to 8.0 litres (13.2 to 14.1 pints)

Thermostat opening temperature

Note: *The actual temperature rating may differ, depending on model and year, from that given below - if thermostat renewal is ever necessary, always check the rating stamped on the original unit, and replace it with one of the same rating.*

TU engines	89°C
Later G1A (1G1A) engines, some later XU51C (B1A/A) engines	88°C
All other XU engines	82°C

Radiator cooling fan operating temperature	On	Off
TU1 engines	95°C	86°C
TU3 engines, early XU51C/2C/MZ/M3 engines, and XU9JA/Z or XU9JA/L engines:		
1st stage	93°C	88°C
2nd stage	97°C	92°C
XU5JA, XU9JA, and later XU51C/2C/MZ/M3 engines:		
1st stage	97°C	92°C
2nd stage	101°C	96°C

Torque wrench settings (TU engines)	Nm	lbf ft
Water pump upper stud	16	12
Water pump lower bolt	8	6
Housing inlet elbow	8	6
Housing to block:		
8 mm bolts	30	22
10 mm bolts	50	37

Fuel and exhaust systems

Carburettor

Type:		
TU1/K (H1A) and XU51C (B1A/A) - automatic transmission	Single-barrel fixed-jet, downdraught	
TU3.2/K (K2D), XU52C (B2A) and XU52C/K (B2B)	Double-barrel progressive, fixed-jet downdraught	
Application:		
TU1/K (H1A)	Solex 32 PBISA 16-1 (411-1)	
TU3.2/K (K2D)	Solex 32-34 Z2 (528-1)	
XU51C (B1A/A) - automatic transmission	Weber 36 TLC 1/100	
XU52C engines	Solex 34-34 Z1 (473/485-1)	
Calibration and settings:		
Solex 32 PB1SA and Weber 36 TLC	**Solex**	**Weber**
Venturi diameter	25	28
Main jet	127.5	140 ± 2/3
Air correction jet	175	150 ± 10
Emulsion tube	EM	F80
Enrichener drilling	55	-
Idling fuel jet	45	47 +2/-0
Idling air jet	165	150
Accelerator pump injector	40	40
Fuel inlet needle valve	1.6	-
Float setting	38 mm	28 mm
Idle speed	700 rpm	650 to 750 rpm
CO @ idle speed	1.0 to 2.0 %	1.0 to 2.0 %
Solex 32-34 Z2	**Primary**	**Secondary**
Venturi	24	25
Main jet	120	122
Air correction jet	175	180
Emulsion tube	6Z	ZC
Enrichener drilling	45	-
Needle	1.8	-
Accelerator pump injector	50	-
Idling fuel jet	40	-
Idle speed	750 rpm	
CO @ idle speed	1.5 %	
Solex 34-34 Z1	**Primary**	**Secondary**
Venturi	25	27
Main jet	112 ± 5	130 ± 5 (B2A), 112 ± 5 (B2B)
Air correction jet	145 ± 20	160 ± 20 (B2A), 140 ± 20 (B2B)
Emulsion tube	18	ZC
Accelerator pump injector	40	35
Idling fuel jet	46 ± 3 (B2A), 44 ± 3 (B2B)	50 ± 10 (B2A), 70 ± 10 (B2B)
Idling air jet	145 ± 20	145 ± 20
Enrichener drilling	50 ± 20	50 ± 20
Needle	1.8	-
Idle speed	700 to 750 rpm	
CO @ idle speed	0.8 to 1.5 %	
Air cleaner element	Champion V401	
Fuel type/octane rating	Refer to Section 7	

Fuel injection system

System type:	
TU1M/Z (HDZ), TU3M/Z and TU3FM/L (KDY)	Bosch Mono-Jetronic A2.2
XU5M2/Z (BDY)	MMBA G5
XU5M3/Z and XU5M3/L (BDY)	MMBA G6
XU5JA/K (B6E) and XU9JA/K (D6B)	Bosch LE2-Jetronic
XU9JA/Z and XU9JA/L (DKZ)	Bosch Motronic M1.3
Air cleaner element	Champion V401 or W175
Fuel filter	Champion L205
Fuel type/octane rating	Refer to Section 8
Idle speed - engine fully warmed-up:	
TU1M/Z (HDZ), TU3M/Z and TU3FM/L (KDY)	850 ± 50 rpm*
XU5M2/Z, XU5M3/Z and XU5M3/L (BDY)	800 ± 50 rpm*
XU9JA/K (D6B)	900 rpm
XU9JA/Z and XU9JA/L (DKZ)	900 ± 50 rpm

**Nominal value, given for reference only - not adjustable, and may vary constantly under ECU control.*

Fuel injection system (continued)

CO @ idle speed:

TU1M/Z (HDZ), TU3M/Z and TU3FM/L (KDY)	0.4 % maximum*
XU5M2/Z, XU5M3/Z and XU5M3/L (BDY)	-*
XU5JA/K (B6E) and XU9JA/K (D6B)	1 ± 0.5 %
XU9JA/Z and XU9JA/L (DKZ)	0.5 % maximum*

**Nominal value given, where available, for reference only - not adjustable.*

Fuel pressure:

TU1M/Z (HDZ), TU3M/Z and TU3FM/L (KDY)	1.0 to 1.2 bars (14.5 to 17.4 lbf/in²)
XU5M2/Z, XU5M3/Z and XU5M3/L (BDY)	0.7 to 0.9 bars (10.1 to 13.1 lbf/in²)
XU9JA/Z and XU9JA/L (DKZ)	2.8 to 3.2 bars (40.6 to 46.4 lbf/in²)

Ignition system

Ignition timing (vacuum hose disconnected and plugged)

TU1/K (H1A)	8° BTDC @ 850 rpm
TU1M/Z (HDZ), TU3M/Z and TU3FM/L (KDY)	8 ± 1° BTDC @ idle speed
TU3.2/K (K2D)	8° BTDC @ idle speed
XU52C (B2A), XU52C/K (B2B)	10° BTDC @ idle speed
XU5M2/Z, XU5M3/Z and XU5M3/L (BDY)	-*
XU5JA/K (B6E)	10° BTDC @ idle speed
XU9JA/K (D6B)	5° BTDC @ 700 rpm
XU9JA/Z and XU9JA/L (DKZ)	10 ± 2° BTDC @ idle speed*

**Nominal value given, where available, for reference only - ignition timing is under control of engine management system ECU, and may vary constantly at idle speed - adjustment is not possible.*

Spark plugs

TU1 engines	Champion C9YCC or C9YCX
TU3 engines	Champion RC9YCC or C9YCX
All 1.6 litre models with automatic transmission, from 1988 model year onwards	Champion C9YCC or C9YCX
All other 1.6 and 1.9 litre models, from 1988 model year onwards	Champion C7YCC or CY7CX
Electrode gap	0.80 mm (0.032 in)

Clutch - TU engines

Driven plate diameter	180 mm

Manual transmission

BE1 gearbox (January 1987 on) - general

Gear ratios (except GTI):	
1st	3.25:1
2nd	1.85:1
Gear ratios (GTI):	
1st	2.92:1
2nd	1.85:1
3rd	1.36:1
4th	1.07:1
5th	0.87:1
Reverse	3.33:1
Final drive	3.69:1

BE3 gearbox

Gear ratios (carburettor engines):	
1st	3.45:1
2nd	1.85:1
3rd	1.28:1
4th	0.97:1
5th	0.76:1
Reverse	3.33:1
Final drive	4.06:1
Gear ratios (fuel-injected engines):	
1st	2.92:1
2nd	1.85:1
3rd	1.36:1
4th	1.07:1
5th	0.87:1
Reverse	3.33:1
Final drive	3.69:1

BE-series gearboxes - lubrication

Lubricant type/specification (October 1987 on)	Gear oil, viscosity SAE 75W/80

MA gearbox - general

Type	Five speeds (all synchromesh) and reverse
Gear ratios:	
1st	3.42:1
2nd	1.81:1
3rd	1.28:1
4th	0.98:1
5th	0.78:1
Reverse	3.58:1
Final drive (TU1)	3.94:1
Final drive (TU3)	3.77:1

MA gearbox - lubrication

Oil capacity (drain and refill)	2.0 litres (3.5 pints)
Lubricant type/specification	Gear oil, viscosity SAE 75W/80

Torque wrench settings - MA gearbox	Nm	lbf ft
Gearbox housing to clutch/final drive housing	18	13
Intermediate plate to clutch/final drive housing	50	37
Pressed-steel housing	18	13
Bearing half-rings	18	13
Output shaft nut (5-speed gearbox)	140	103
Drain and filler plugs	25	18
Gearbox to engine	45	33

Automatic transmission

General

Type	ZF 4HP 14
Gear ratios:	
1st	0.398:1
2nd	0.701:1
3rd	0.960:1
4th	1.300:1
Reverse	0.339:1
Final drive	3.820:1

Lubrication

Fluid capacity:	
At overhaul	6.2 litres (10.9 pints)
At fluid change	2.4 litres (4.2 pints)
Fluid type/specification	Dexron II type ATF

Torque wrench settings	Nm	lbf ft
Inhibitor switch	41	30
Fluid cooler centre bolt	50	37
Dipstick tube union nut	45	33
Selector cable bracket	30	22
Torque converter-to-driveplate bolts	35	26
Torque converter housing to engine	45	33
Transmission mounting bracket to body	18	13
Mounting bracket to transmission	35	26

Braking system - 1.9 GTI

General

Type: Ventilated front and solid rear servo-assisted disc brakes, rear brake compensators, cable-operated handbrake on rear wheels. Anti-lock Braking System (ABS) available as an option

	Front	Rear
Disc diameter	247 mm	247 mm
Disc thickness:		
New	20.4 mm	8.0 mm
Minimum (after resurfacing)	18.5 mm	7.0 mm
Disc run-out (maximum	0.07 mm	0.07 mm
Disc pad minimum lining thickness	2.0 mm	2.0 mm
Master cylinder diameter	26.0 mm	
Servo diameter	228.6 mm	

Torque wrench settings	Nm	lbf ft
Front brake:		
Caliper mounting bolts	100	74
Caliper guide bolts	35	26
Rear brake caliper mounting bolts	120	89
ABS regulator unit mounting bolts	20	15
ABS wheel sensor bolt (with locking fluid)	10	7

Suspension, hubs, wheels and tyres

Rear wheel alignment

Toe-in per wheel - models up to 1990:	
GTI	1.90 ± 0.75 mm
All other models	1.55 ± 0.75 mm
Toe-in per wheel - models from 1990 on:	
GTI	2.50 ± 1.25 mm
All other models	1.80 ± 0.75 mm
Camber:	
1990-on GTI models	1°15' ± 30' negative
All other models	0°50' ± 30' negative

Roadwheels and tyres - 1.9 GTI

Roadwheel type	6J 15
Tyre size	185/55 VR 15

Tyre pressures - tyres cold - lbf/in² (bars)	Front	Rear
145 SR 13, 165/70 SR 13 (with manual transmission)	28 (1.9)	31 (2.1)
165/70 SR 13 (with automatic transmission)	31 (2.1)	32 (2.2)
155 R 14	29 (2.0)	32 (2.2)
175/65 HR 14	28 (1.9)	26 (1.8)
185/55 VR 15	29 (2.0)	29 (2.0)

Note: *The above is intended as a guide only; it is suggested that the car's tyre pressure label (usually stuck to the rear edge of one of the front doors) is consulted for recommendations specific to the tyres actually fitted.*

Steering

Front wheel alignment

Toe-in - per wheel:	
GTI	1.0 ± 0.5 mm
All other models	0.5 ± 0.5 mm
Castor:	
All GTI models, 1990-on SRI and GR Injection models	2°10' ± 30' positive
All other models	2°0' ± 30' positive
Camber:	
All GTI models, 1990-on SRI and GR Injection models	0°40' ± 30' negative
All other models	0°30' ± 30' negative
Steering Axis Inclination (SAI) - also known as KingPin Inclination (KPI):	
All GTI models, 1990-on SRI and GR Injection models	10°40' ± 30' positive
All other models	10°15' ± 30' positive

Torque wrench settings	Nm	lbf ft
Steering column mounting nuts	15	11
Column-to-pinion clamp bolt - all models, January 1992 on	25	18

3 Routine maintenance

Fuel filter renewal

1 On all models fitted with XU5M2/Z, XU5M3/Z or XU5M3/L engines (MMBA engine management system), the fuel filter must be renewed every 48 000 miles (80 000 km).

Manual gearbox oil - renewal

2 The interval for changing the oil in pre-October 1987 BE1 gearboxes has been extended to 36 000 miles (60 000 km).

3 On cars manufactured after October 1987, all gearboxes are filled with a special gear oil, which does not require draining at the previously-stated intervals. However, it is necessary to carry out an oil level check every 36 000 miles (60 000 km) and, if topping-up is necessary, it is important to use only the specified type of oil.

4 Engine (except TU series)

Oil consumption - general

1 The emission of blue smoke from the exhaust may be due to bore wear if the engine has covered a high mileage. On a low-mileage engine, smoke emission is more likely to be due to one of the following causes:

(a) *Blockage in crankcase ventilation components.*
(b) *Worn valve stem oil seals.*
(c) *Second piston ring fitted upside-down (refer to Figs. 1.17 or 1.32).*

2 If worn valve stem oil seals are to be renewed, fit polyacrylate ones (part number 0956.18).

3 An engine oil consumption figure of 700 miles per pint (1000 miles per 0.5 litre) is acceptable.

Engine right-hand mounting (all engines)

4 The section of the engine right-hand mounting which is attached to the bodyshell incorporates a notched tubular-shaped bush. It is essential that it is tightened to 40 Nm (30 lbf ft).

5 Although a special tool is available (Fig. 13.1) to enable a torque wrench to be used, it should be possible to fabricate something similar. Alternatively, use an oil filter strap wrench to obtain the correct tightness.

Engine right-hand mounting (XU engines)

6 To eliminate a knock which may occur in the right-hand flexible mounting, a spring plate has been fitted between the rubber snubber and the mounting bracket on later models.

7 The spring may be fitted to earlier cars, noting that the notch in the spring must be towards the right-hand side of the car.

Engine lower rear mounting (XU engines)

8 While the flexible rubber bush fitted to this mounting is now available as a separate replacement part, it is preferable to entrust its renewal to a Peugeot dealer; a press is required to remove the old bush from the mounting bracket, and a pair of Peugeot service tools are needed to ensure that the new bush is correctly located when pressing it into the bracket.

Oil filler cap (XU engines)

9 Due to the likelihood of corrosion occurring in the steel mesh within the engine oil filler cap, it is recommended that the mesh is removed and discarded.

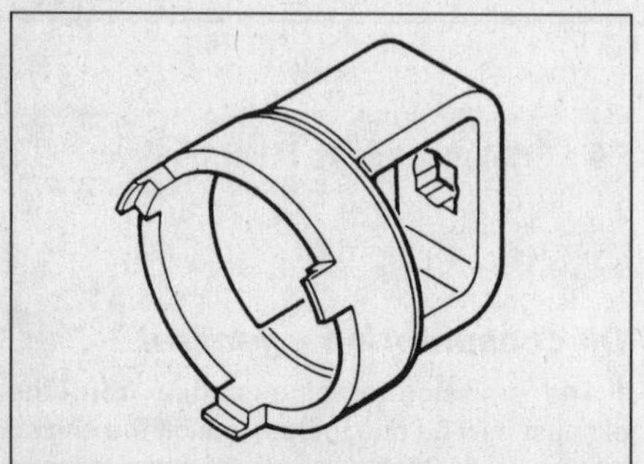

Fig. 13.1 Engine right-hand mounting tightening tool (Sec 4)

Camshaft lubrication pipe (XU engines)

10 A modified camshaft bearing lubrication pipe has been introduced, to reduce tappet noise.

11 The pipe incorporates O-ring seals, and may be fitted to earlier models.

Inlet manifold gasket (XU engines)

12 Two inlet manifold gaskets are supplied in the Peugeot decoke set; one for carburettor engines, the other for fuel-injected engines.

13 It is most important that the correct gasket is fitted, otherwise loss of power will occur in the lower engine speed range.

Cylinder head modifications (XU engines)

14 As from October 1987, the cylinder head bolts are of the Torx (T55) socket-headed type, with thicker washers.

15 The cylinder liner height has been reduced by 0.05 mm, and in consequence, the liner protrusion has also been reduced - refer to the Specifications.

16 The final tightening angle for the cylinder head bolts has been revised (refer to the Specifications); once the bolts have been tightened as specified, subsequent re-tightening is not required.

17 Lightly grease the bolt threads, and the undersides of their heads, before tightening in the sequence shown in Fig. 1.27.

Camshaft (timing) drivebelt tensioner modification (XU engines)

18 XU engines produced from late 1992 onwards are fitted with a modified timing belt, which is adjusted by an eccentric roller-type tensioner. This modification is accompanied by minor changes to several other components, including the crankshaft (pulley end) oil seal carrier plate, the coolant pump, the engine right-hand mounting bracket and the timing belt covers (the three plastic covers being replaced by two components on the modified engines).

19 The modified cylinder block has an extra threaded hole tapped in it to accept the eccentric roller-type of tensioner, but retains the fixing points for the earlier type, so that all early-type components can be fitted to replacement cylinder blocks.

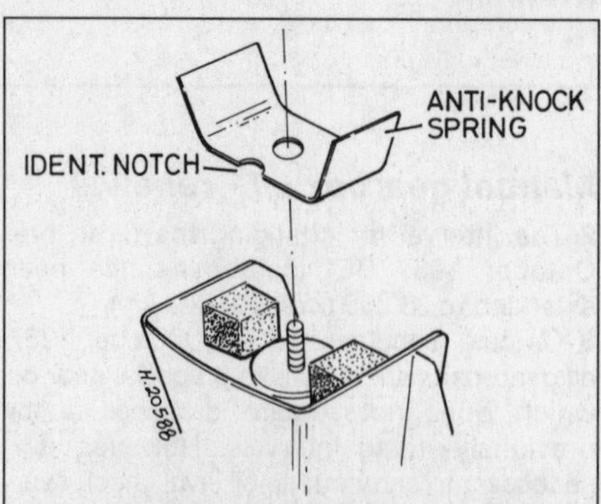

Fig. 13.2 Right-hand engine mounting anti-knock spring (Sec 4)

20 The modified timing belt (identifiable by having 114 teeth and orange markings, instead of 113 teeth and white markings) is removed and refitted as described in Section 59 of Chapter 1, noting the following differences (paragraphs 21 to 31).

21 Note: *Peugeot specify the use of their special equipment (SEEM C.TRONIC type 105 or 105.5) to set correctly the timing belt tension. If this equipment is not available, an approximate setting can be achieved using the method described below.* ***However****, it is stressed that if this is done, the vehicle must be taken to a dealer at the earliest possible opportunity to have the belt's tension set correctly using the proper equipment. Do not drive the vehicle over any long distance, and do not use high engine speeds, until the belt tension is known to be correct.*

22 The crankshaft pulley timing dowel must be of 10 mm diameter, stepped down to 8 mm (for an unspecified length) at one end, to engage with the smaller notch in the modified oil seal carrier plate.

23 With the timing belt covers removed, slacken the tensioner bolt to relax the belt tension, and remove the crankshaft pulley timing dowel before extracting the pulley itself; withdraw the belt as described, noting the direction of fitting and the markings.

24 On fitting the belt, slip it first over the camshaft sprocket, followed by the crankshaft sprocket, the coolant pump sprocket, and finally over the tensioner roller.

25 Rotate the tensioner roller anti-clockwise as far as possible by hand to take up any slack in the belt, then tighten the tensioner bolt just sufficiently to hold the roller in that position.

26 Temporarily refit the crankshaft pulley, and remove the camshaft sprocket timing dowel. Turn the crankshaft through two full turns in the normal direction of rotation, then check that the valve timing is still correct by refitting both timing dowels. If all is well, remove the dowels and turn the crankshaft through two further turns in the normal direction of rotation. **Never** turn the crankshaft backwards during this procedure.

27 Remove the crankshaft pulley, refit the camshaft sprocket timing dowel, and check that the timing belt can just be twisted through 90° (using the thumb and forefinger only to apply moderate pressure), midway between the camshaft and crankshaft sprockets on the belt's front run. If in doubt about this setting, it is better to err on the tight side until the tension can be checked by a Peugeot dealer, as if the belt is too slack, it may jump on the sprockets; this could result in serious engine damage.

28 If adjustment is required, slacken the tensioner bolt and rotate the tensioner roller clockwise to slacken the belt, or anti-clockwise to tighten it. When the setting is correct, tighten the bolt to the specified torque wrench setting, ensuring that the tensioner position is not disturbed.

29 Refit the timing belt covers.

30 Refit the crankshaft pulley; when it is finally secured, apply thread-locking compound to the bolt threads, and tighten the bolt to the specified torque wrench setting.

31 Refit all other disturbed components (Chapter 1).

XU52C engines - general

32 The XU52C (B2A) engine was introduced during the 1988 model year to replace the XU51C (B1A/A) engine, and was fitted to all 1.6 litre carburettor models with manual transmission.

33 During the 1990 model year, the XU52C/K (B2B) engine was introduced to replace the earlier units; it was fitted to 1.6 litre carburettor models with both manual and automatic transmission.

34 The XU52C engines are essentially the same as the XU51C (detailed in Chapter 1), but revisions, including the fitment of a Solex 34-34 Z1 carburettor, have resulted in an increased power output.

35 Overhaul and repair procedures are as described in Chapter 1 for the XU51C engine, noting any differences mentioned in this Section and/or in the Specifications at the beginning of this Chapter.

XU5M engines - general

36 The XU5M2/Z (BDY) engine, fitted with the MMBA G5 engine management system (which includes 'distributorless' ignition), was introduced in January 1991. This was followed by the XU5M3/Z version during the 1992 model year, and the XU5M3/L version for the 1993 model year, these having the MMBA G6 system.

37 Overhaul and repair procedures are as described in Chapter 1 for the XU5JA engine, noting any differences mentioned in this Section and/or in the Specifications at the beginning of this Chapter.

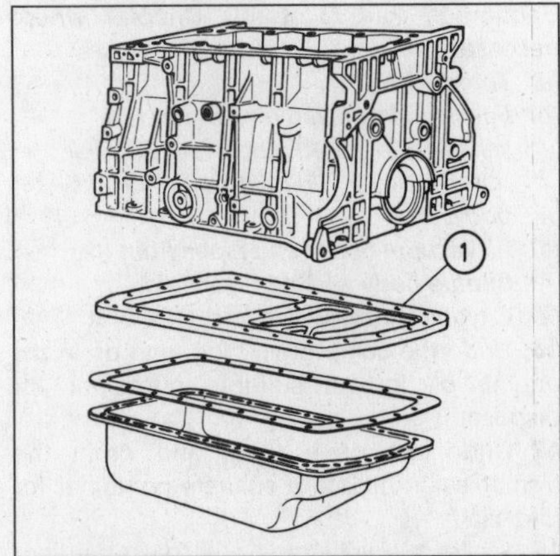

Fig. 13.3 Spacer plate (1) fitted to the sump on XU9JA engines (Sec 4)

XU5JA/K engine - general

38 During the 1991 model year, the XU5JA/K (B6E) engine was introduced to replace the XU5JA (B6D) unit. Revisions included a lower compression ratio, to allow the engine to run on 95 RON unleaded fuel without adjustment.

39 Overhaul and repair procedures are as described in Chapter 1 for the XU5JA engine, noting any differences mentioned in this Section and/or in the Specifications at the beginning of this Chapter.

XU9JA engines - general

40 The XU9JA/K (D6B) engine was introduced with the GTI model in the 1987 model year, fitted with the Bosch LE2-Jetronic fuel injection system described for the XU5JA engine in Chapter 3, and the separate electronic ignition system covered in Chapter 4.

41 During the 1991 model year, a catalytic converter was made available as an optional extra; this required the fitting of a sophisticated engine management system (Bosch Motronic M1.3) to the engine. The engine designation was accordingly changed to XU9JA/Z (DKZ) for 1991/2, the XU9JA/L version appearing for the 1993 model year.

42 Apart from the differences outlined in the Specifications and above, the main changes from the XU5JA engine concern the camshaft, sump, and pistons, and the addition of an oil cooler. Camshaft endfloat is controlled by machined shoulders on the No 1 bearing, instead of by a thrustplate. The height of the sump is reduced to accommodate a spacer plate, which acts as a stiffener and oil baffle. The pistons have special dished crowns. The oil cooler is mounted between the crankcase and the oil filter element.

43 Overhaul and repair procedures are as described in Chapter 1 for the XU5JA engine, noting any differences mentioned in this Section and/or in the Specifications at the beginning of this Chapter.

Oil cooler (XU9JA engines) - removal and refitting

44 Remove the engine oil filter.

45 Note the angle at which the coolant hoses are set, then disconnect the hoses and plug their ends to minimise coolant loss. if necessary, drain the cooling system.

46 Using a ring spanner or socket, undo and remove the threaded sleeve.

47 Remove the oil cooler and its gasket.

48 Refitting is the reverse of the removal procedure, but always use a new gasket.

Sump spacer plate (XU9JA engines) - removal and refitting

49 Remove the sump, and discard its gasket.

50 Unscrew the two bolts from the diagonally-opposite corners, and remove the spacer plate from the cylinder block. If it is stuck, use a thin knife to cut into the jointing compound.

51 Thoroughly clean the surfaces of the block, spacer plate and sump.

52 Apply silicone jointing compound to the upper mating surface of the spacer plate, position the plate on the block, then insert and tighten the two bolts to the specified torque.

53 Refit the sump with a new gasket, and tighten the bolts to the specified torque.

5 Engine (TU series)

Engine - general description

1 The TU engine is a development of the OHC unit described in Chapter 1. Apart from the fact that the TU engine is inclined forward by 6° (with the exhaust manifold mounted on the front of the cylinder head and the inlet manifold mounted on the rear), the most significant difference is that the main bearing caps are formed by a single casting that is bolted to the bottom of the cylinder block/crankcase. Note that since the two castings are machined together on manufacture, they are a matched pair, and must not be used separately; for this reason, they are only available as a single unit from Peugeot dealers.

Operations possible without removing the engine from the car

2 The following components can be removed and refitted with the engine in the car:

(a) Cylinder head.
(b) Timing belt and camshaft.
(c) Sump and oil pump.
(d) Clutch and flywheel (after removal of transmission).

3 Since the sump and cylinder head can be removed with the engine *in situ*, it is possible to remove/replace the pistons, liners and big-end bearings without removing the engine. However, this work is not recommended, since it can be performed more easily with the engine on the bench.

Engine - removal and refitting

4 The engine and transmission assembly is removed by lowering it down from the engine compartment. The transmission is separated from the engine on the bench.

5 Open the bonnet, and support in the fully-open position. It is advisable (though not absolutely necessary) to unbolt and remove the bonnet, to prevent damaging it, and to improve access.

6 Disconnect and remove the battery.

7 Remove the air cleaner unit and trunking.

8 Disconnect the following items, referring to the relevant Chapters where necessary:

(a) Coolant temperature sensor(s).
(b) Oil pressure switch.
(c) Distributor wiring.
(d) Reversing light switch.

Fig. 13.4 Cutaway view of the TU engine (Sec 5)

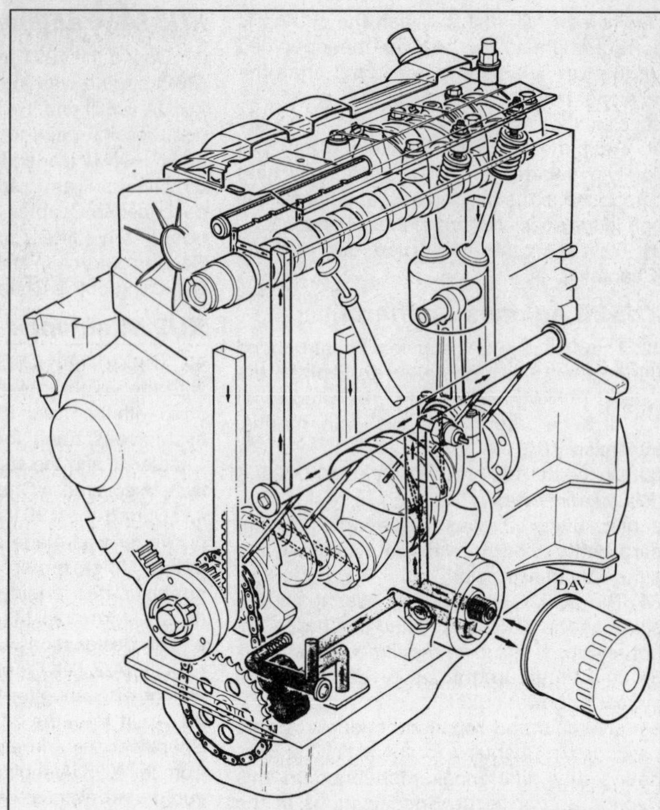

Fig. 13.5 Lubrication system on the TU engine (Sec 5)

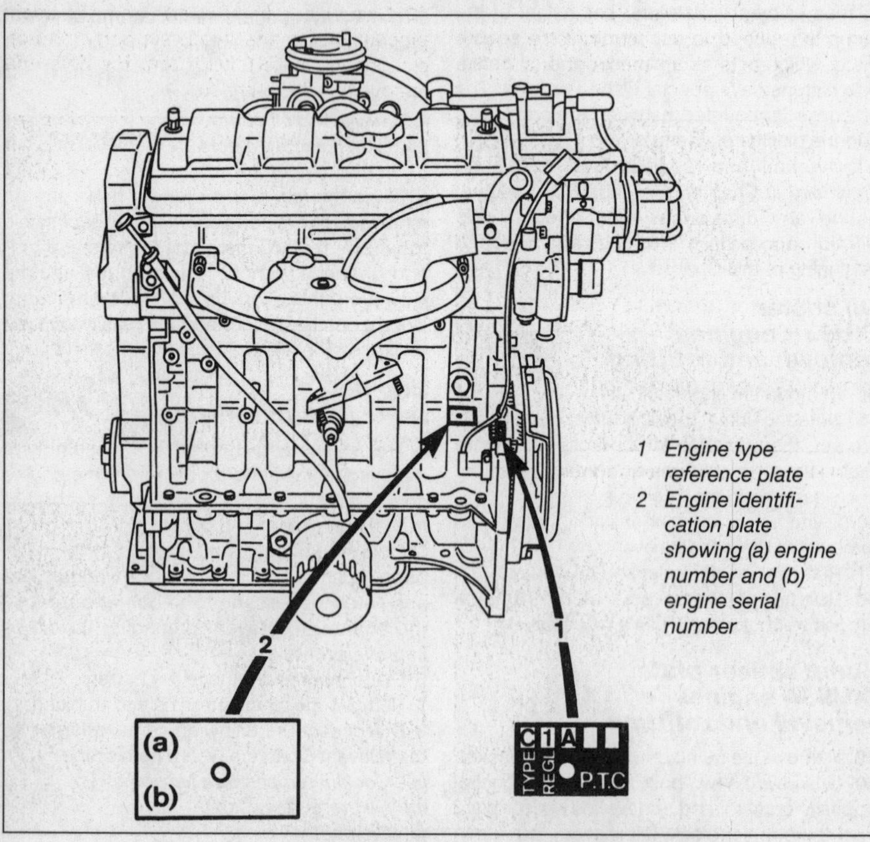

Fig. 13.6 Location of TU engine identification plates (Sec 5)

9 Disconnect the brake servo vacuum hose.

10 Disconnect and plug the fuel supply and return hoses.

11 Remove the engine undershields and sideshields, then drain the cooling system.

12 Disconnect and remove the radiator top and bottom hoses.

13 Disconnect the heater hoses from the engine.

14 On carburettor engines, disconnect the throttle and (where fitted) choke cables, and also the carburettor wiring connector.

15 On fuel-injected engines, remove or disconnect the following items, referring to Section 8, Part C of this Chapter where necessary:

(a) Throttle cable.

(b) Fuel injector/intake air temperature sensor, idle speed motor and throttle potentiometer wiring from the throttle body.

(c) All vacuum hoses and pipes from the throttle body and inlet manifold.

(d) Oxygen sensor wiring.

16 Undo the sump drain plug, and drain the engine oil into a suitable container for disposal.

17 Undo the drain plug, and drain the transmission oil into a suitable container for disposal.

18 Whilst the vehicle is still free-standing, loosen (but do not remove) the front wheel hub nuts.

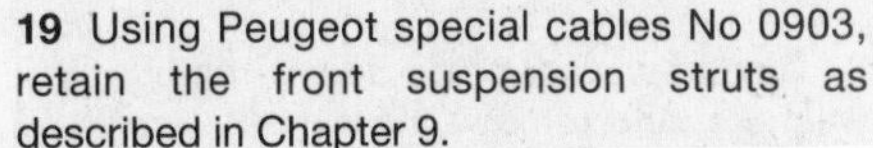

5.21 Gearchange control rods (arrowed) – engine removed for clarity

19 Using Peugeot special cables No 0903, retain the front suspension struts as described in Chapter 9.

20 Raise and securely support the vehicle at the front end and rear end on axle stands. There should be a minimum front skirt-to-ground clearance of about 27 ins (700 mm), to allow engine and transmission removal clearance.

21 Disconnect the gearchange control rods (photo).

22 Pull out the rubber cotter, and disconnect the speedometer cable from the gearbox.

23 Disconnect the clutch cable.

24 Unscrew the nut, and remove the earth cable from the gearbox (photo).

25 Detach the wiring connectors from the alternator and starter motor.

26 Undo the clamp bolt from the steering stub axle lower balljoint on each side, and withdraw the bolts. Note that the bolts are fitted from the front. With the bolts removed, prise free the joints by levering down on the suspension arm. Take care not to damage the gaiters.

27 Remove the balljoint protector shields. If strut retaining cables (suggested in paragraph 19) were not fitted, it will be necessary to unbolt and remove the suspension arm inner pivot bolt, in order to allow the full separation of the balljoint. Turn the hub onto full-lock when separating the balljoint in this manner.

28 Undo the left-hand front hub nut, then detach and remove the left-hand driveshaft (see Chapter 7).

5.38B . . .and remove the starter motor

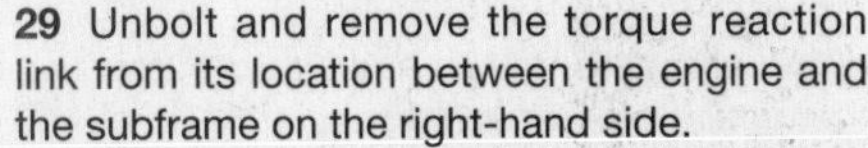

5.24 Earth cable attachment on gearbox (arrowed)

29 Unbolt and remove the torque reaction link from its location between the engine and the subframe on the right-hand side.

30 Remove the right-hand driveshaft as described in Chapter 7.

31 Unbolt and remove the exhaust downpipe.

32 Connect a hoist to the engine and transmission lifting eyes, and support the weight of the engine and gearbox.

33 Unscrew the left-hand mounting nuts, including the nut on the centre stud, and remove the mounting (photo).

34 Unscrew the right-hand mounting centre nut. If necessary, unscrew the nuts and remove the bracket completely (photo).

35 Check that all attachments are clear of the engine and transmission, then carefully lower the engine and transmission unit.

36 When fully lowered, withdraw the engine and transmission from the front end of the vehicle.

5.34 Right-hand engine mounting bracket

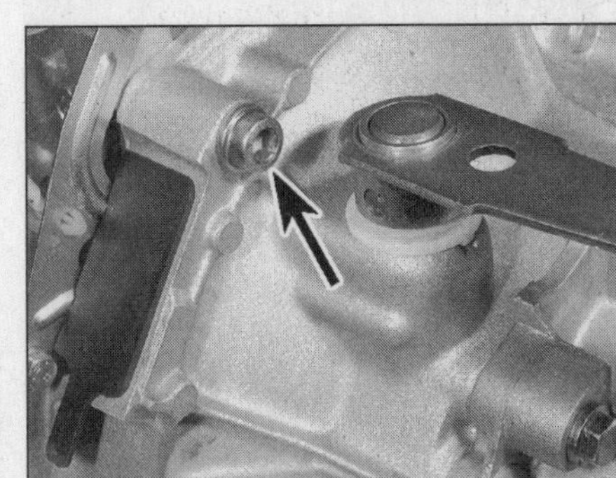

5.39 Gearbox-to-engine bolt (arrowed)

5.33 Left-hand engine mounting

37 Refitting is the reverse of the removal procedure.

Engine - separation from transmission

38 Unbolt and remove the starter motor together with the air cleaner bracket (photos).

39 Unscrew and remove the gearbox-to-engine bolts (photo).

40 Support the engine and lift the gearbox away from it. Recover any loose dowels.

Engine dismantling - general

41 Refer to Chapter 1, Section 10.

Engine - complete dismantling

42 Disconnect the HT leads from the spark plugs, unbolt the lead support (photo), disconnect the HT lead from the coil, and remove the distributor cap.

5.38A Unscrew the bolts. . .

5.42 Removing the HT lead support

5.45 Hose from water pump to thermostat housing (arrowed)

5.46 Removing the inlet manifold complete with carburettor

5.48A Alternator pivot (A), adjustment (B) and tension (C) bolts

43 Remove the spark plugs.
44 Disconnect the vacuum hose between the distributor and carburettor.
45 Disconnect the hoses between the fuel pump and carburettor, and water pump and thermostat housing (photo).

5.48B Removing the alternator pivot bolt

46 Unscrew the nuts, and remove the inlet manifold complete with carburettor from the studs on the cylinder head (photo). Note that there is no gasket.
47 Unbolt and remove the fuel pump, and remove the gasket.
48 Loosen the alternator pivot and adjustment bolts, then unscrew the tension bolt and slip the drivebelt from the pulleys. Remove the pivot and adjustment bolts, and remove the alternator (photos).
49 Unbolt the pulley from the front of the crankshaft (photo).
50 Unbolt and remove the coil, after unclipping the TDC connector (photos).
51 Unbolt the exhaust manifold hot air shroud.
52 Unscrew the brass nuts, remove the washers, and remove the exhaust manifold from the studs on the cylinder head. Remove the gaskets.
53 Remove the distributor with reference to Chapter 4.
54 Remove the thermostat with reference to Section 6.
55 Unbolt the thermostat housing from the cylinder head (photos).
56 Unbolt the distributor mounting flange from the cylinder head (photo).
57 Unbolt the TDC sensor from the flywheel end of the cylinder block, and unclip the lead from the timing plate (photos).
58 Unbolt and remove the timing plate (photo).
59 Unscrew and remove the oil filter, using a removal strap if necessary (photo).

5.49 Unbolting the crankshaft pulley

5.50A TDC connector on the coil (arrowed)

5.50B Coil location over the distributor

5.55 Removing the thermostat housing

5.56 Distributor mounting flange

5.57A TDC sensor wiring clip (arrowed). . .

5.57B . . . and mounting bolt (arrowed)

5.58 Timing plate (arrowed)

5.59 Removing the oil filter

60 Unscrew and remove the oil pressure switch (photo).

61 Unscrew the mounting bolt, and pull the engine oil dipstick holder from the main bearing cap casting. Remove the dipstick from the holder (photo).

62 Unscrew the nuts and remove the valve cover. Remove the rubber gasket from the cover.

63 Remove the two spacers and baffle plate from the studs (photos).

64 Unbolt the upper timing cover, followed by the intermediate cover and lower cover (photos).

65 Turn the engine clockwise, using a socket on the crankshaft pulley bolt, until the small hole in the camshaft sprocket is aligned with the corresponding hole in the cylinder head. Insert the shank of a closefitting twist drill (eg a 10 mm drill) into the holes (photo).

66 Align the TDC holes in the flywheel and cylinder block rear flange, and insert a further twist drill or long bolt (photo).

67 Loosen the timing belt tensioner roller nut (photo), turn the tensioner clockwise using a screwdriver or square drive in the special hole, then retighten the nut.

5.60 Oil pressure switch

5.61 Unscrewing the dipstick holder mounting bolt

5.63A Removing the spacers (arrowed). . .

5.63B. . . and baffle

5.64A Unscrew the bolts. . .

5.64B. . . remove the upper timing cover. . .

5.64C. . . intermediate cover . . .

5.64D. . . and lower cover

13

5.65 Camshaft sprocket set to TDC

5.66 Bolt (arrowed) inserted through cylinder block rear flange into the flywheel TDC hole

5.67 Loosening the timing belt tensioner roller nut

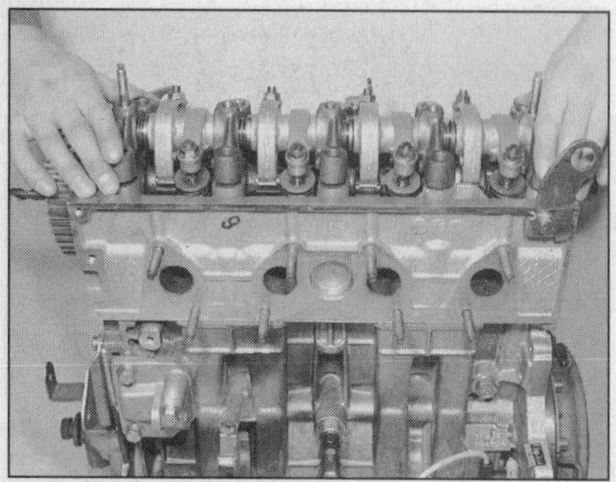

5.71 Removing the rocker arm assembly

68 Mark the normal direction of rotation on the timing belt, then remove it from the camshaft, water pump, and crankshaft sprockets.

69 Unscrew the tensioner nut and remove the tensioner roller.

70 Progressively loosen the cylinder head bolts using the reverse sequence to that shown in Fig. 13.7, then remove all the bolts.

71 Lift off the rocker arm assembly (photo).

72 Rock the cylinder head to free it from the block, then lift it from the location dowels (photo). Two angled metal rods, shown in Fig. 13.8, may be used for this purpose.

73 Remove the cylinder head gasket from the block.

74 Fit the liner clamps (see Chapter 1, Section 6) if it is not proposed to remove the pistons and liners.

75 Progressively loosen the clutch pressure plate bolts, and remove the pressure and friction disc from the flywheel (photo).

76 Unbolt the water pump housing from the side of the block, and prise out the O-ring.

77 Have an assistant hold the flywheel stationary with a wide-bladed screwdriver inserted between the starter ring gear teeth, then unscrew the crankshaft pulley bolt, and remove the hubs/sprocket and oil seal flange (photos).

78 Using a screwdriver, prise out the front oil

5.72 Lifting the cylinder head from the block

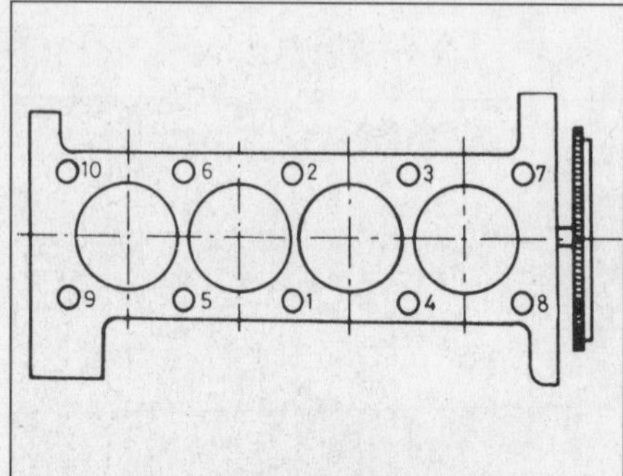

Fig. 13.7 Cylinder head bolt tightening sequence – TU engine (Sec 5)

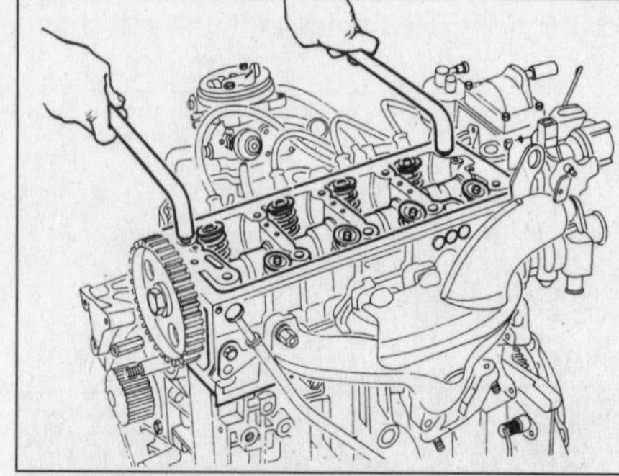

Fig. 13.8 Using two angled metal rods to free the cylinder head from the block – TU engine (Sec 5)

5.75 Removing the clutch pressure plate and friction disc

5.77A Unscrew the crankshaft pulley bolt. . .

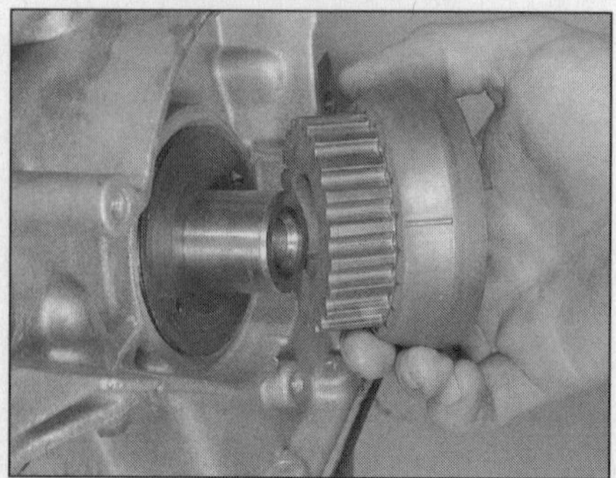

5.77B. . . and remove the hub/sprocket. . .

5.77C. . . and oil seal flange

5.78 Prising out the crankshaft front oil seal

5.82A Unscrew the nuts and bolts . . .

seal from the block and main bearing casing (photo).

79 Hold the flywheel stationary as described in paragraph 77 and unscrew the flywheel bolts. Lift the flywheel from the dowel on the crankshaft rear flange.

80 Prise out the crankshaft rear oil seal using a screwdriver.

81 Invert the engine, and support on blocks of wood.

82 Unscrew the nuts and bolts securing the sump to the main bearing casting, and remove it by carefully prising it free of the jointing compound (photos).

83 Unbolt the oil pump, and tilt it to release the drive sprocket from the chain (photos).

84 Support the block on its flywheel end.

85 Mark the liners for position, starting with No 1 (at the flywheel end). Similarly mark the big-end bearing caps.

86 Temporarily refit the crankshaft pulley bolts, and turn the crankshaft so that Nos 1 and 4 pistons (No 1 at flywheel end) are at bottom dead centre (BDC).

87 Unscrew the nuts and remove the big-end bearing caps (photo). Remove the lower big-end shells, keeping them identified for position.

88 Remove the clamps and withdraw the liners, complete with pistons, from the block (photo).

89 Remove the liner bottom O-rings (photo).

90 Repeat the procedure for Nos 2 and 3 pistons and liners.

91 Invert the engine again, and unscrew the bolts securing the main bearing cap casting to the block (photos).

5.82B. . . and remove the sump

5.83 Unscrewing an oil pump securing bolt

5.87 Removing a big-end bearing cap

5.88 Removing a liner and piston assembly

5.89 Liner bottom O-ring (arrowed)

5.91A Unscrew the main bearing cap casting front bolts. . .

5.91B. . . and side bolts (arrowed)

5.93 Removing the oil pump sprocket and chain

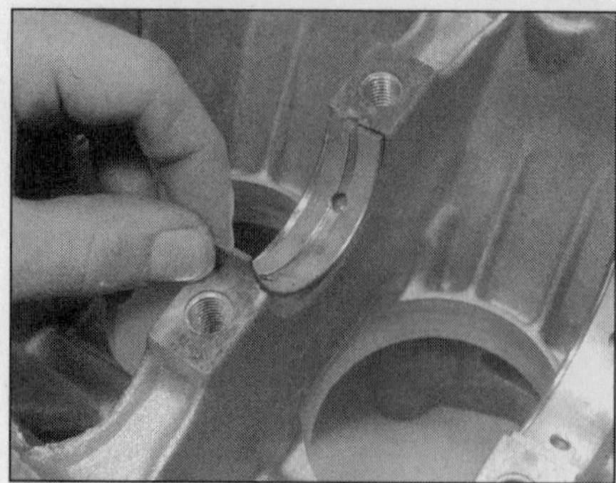
5.94A Removing a main bearing shell . . .

5.94B. . . and endfloat ring

5.95 Removing the camshaft sprocket – note location peg and cutout (arrowed)

5.96 Camshaft thrust fork (arrowed)

92 Progressively unscrew the main bearing bolts, and lift the main bearing cap casting from the block. Gently tap it with a wooden or softheaded mallet to release it. Prise out the main bearing shells, keeping them identified for location.

93 Remove the oil pump sprocket and chain from the crankshaft (photo).

94 Lift the crankshaft from the block, and remove the main bearing shells, keeping them identified for location. Also remove the endfloat rings from No 2 bearing location (photos).

Cylinder head - dismantling, decarbonising and reassembly

95 Remove the twistdrill from the camshaft sprocket, then hold the sprocket stationary using an oil filter strap wrench or tool as shown in photo 5.102. Unscrew the bolt and remove the sprocket (photo).

96 Unbolt and remove the camshaft thrust fork (photo).

97 Prise out the oil seal, and carefully withdraw the camshaft from the cylinder head (photos).

98 Remove the valves and springs, clean and check the cylinder head, and refit the valves and springs with reference to Chapter 1, Sections 74 (paragraphs 8 and 9), 77 and 88 (photos).

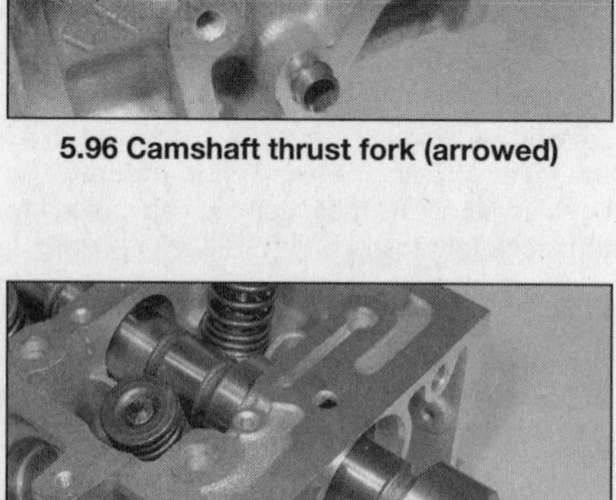
5.97A Prise out the oil seal . . .

5.97B . . .and withdraw the camshaft

5.98A Compress the valve spring and remove the collets. . .

5.98B . . .retainer. . .

5.98C . . .spring. . .

5.98D. . .spring seat. . .

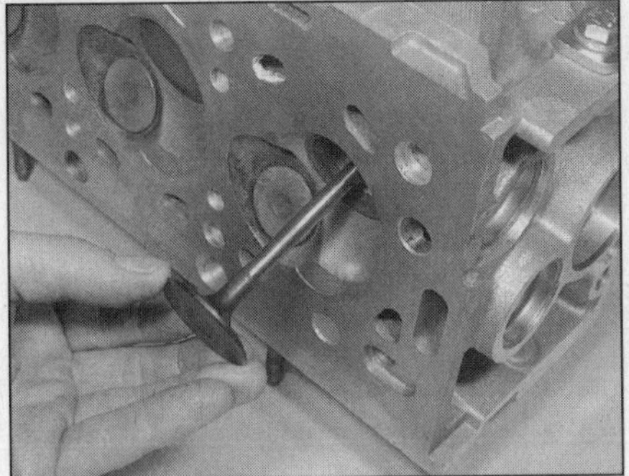
5.98E. . .and valve

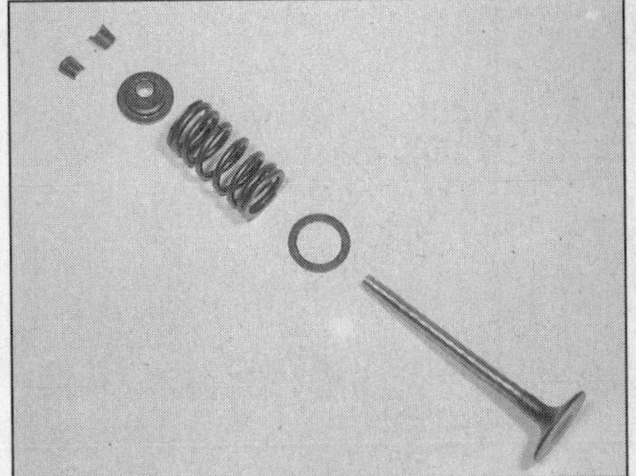
5.98F Valve components removed from the cylinder head

99 Oil the camshaft bearings, and insert the camshaft into the cylinder head.

100 Refit the camshaft thrust fork, and tighten the bolt.

101 Dip the new oil seal in oil, and press it into the cylinder head until flush, using a metal tube or large socket and hammer.

102 Refit the camshaft sprocket so that the location peg enters the cut-out. Insert and tighten the bolt while holding the sprocket stationary using either method described in paragraph 95 (photo).

Engine components - examination and renovation (general)

103 Refer to Chapter 1, Section 23.

Examination and renovation of dismantled components

104 Refer to Chapter 1, Section 75, but note that there is no camshaft lubrication manifold, as the camshaft runs in an oil bath. Also note that although the timing belt should be renewed when the engine is overhauled or if it is contaminated with oil, there is no specified replacement mileage. When handling the timing belt, do not bend it as this may damage the internal fibres.

Engine - complete reassembly

Note: *For important details of modified main bearing shells fitted to all TU engines, refer to the end of this Section.*

105 With the block upside-down on the bench, press the main bearing upper shells into position. Note that the grooved bearings are fitted to positions No 2 and 4.

106 Smear a little grease on the endfloat rings, and locate them each side of No 2 bearing with their grooves facing outwards.

107 Oil the bearings, and lower the crankshaft into position (photo).

108 Check that the crankshaft endfloat is as given in the Specifications, using a feeler blade between an endfloat ring and the crankshaft web. The rings are available in four thicknesses.

109 Fit the oil pump sprocket and chain to the front of the crankshaft, locating the sprocket on the Woodruff key.

110 Press the main bearing lower shells into position in the main bearing cap casting, noting that the grooved bearings are fitted to positions No 2 and 4.

111 Apply jointing compound to the mating face, then lower the main bearing cap casting into position over the crankshaft. At the same time, feed the oil pump chain through the aperture (photo).

112 If you have not already done so, refer to paragraph 194 onwards before proceeding. Insert the main bearing bolts dry, then tighten them evenly to the initial torque wrench setting. Angle-tighten the bolts further, by the specified angle (photos).

113 Refit the bolts securing the main bearing cap casting to the block, and tighten them to the specified torque.

114 Support the block on its flywheel end.

5.102 Using a home-made tool to hold the camshaft sprocket while tightening the bolt

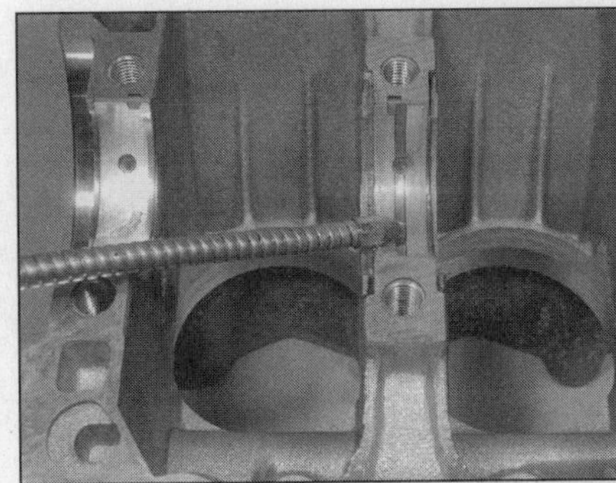
5.107 Oiling the main bearing shells

5.111A Apply jointing compound to the mating faces. . .

5.111B . . .then lower the main bearing cap casting into position

5.112A Torque tighten the main bearing bolts. . .

5.112B. . .then angle tighten a further 45°

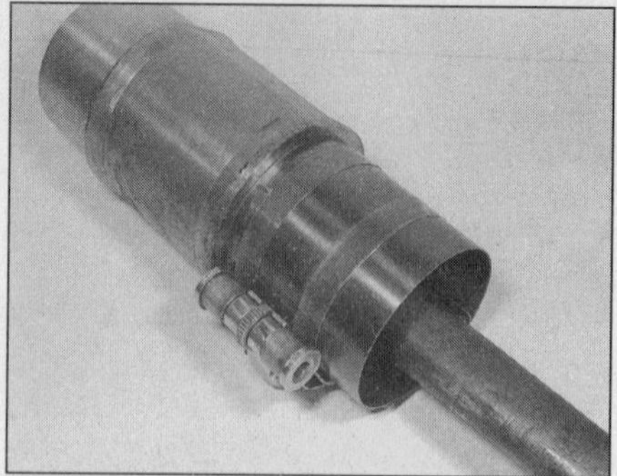
5.118 Using a hammer handle to push the piston into the liner

5.121 Tightening a big-end bearing cap nut

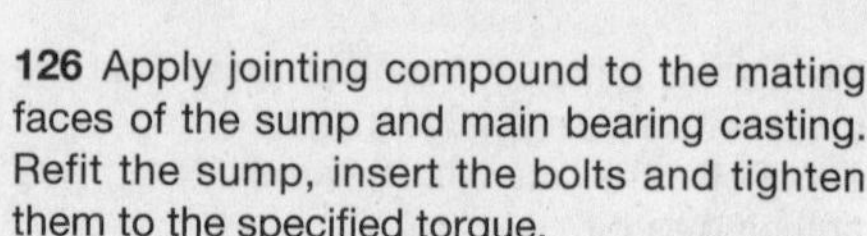

115 Check that the lower big-end bearing shells are fitted to the big-end caps and the upper shells to the connecting rods.

116 Oil the liner bores and piston rings.

117 Position the piston ring end gaps at 120° from each other, so that neither is in line with another.

118 Fit a piston ring compressor to each piston in turn, and push the pistons in their respective liners using a hammer handle (photo). Make sure that the arrows on the piston crowns face the front (timing belt end) of the liners.

119 Fit the bottom O-rings to the liners, taking care not to twist them.

120 Check that the crankshaft rotates freely, then position Nos 1 and 4 crankpins at bottom dead centre (BDC). Oil the crankpins.

121 Insert No 1 liner/piston into the block, and guide the connecting rod big-end onto the crankpin. Refit the big-end bearing cap, and tighten the nuts evenly to the specified torque (photo).

122 Check that the crankshaft rotates freely, while holding the liner in position with a clamp. Temporarily refit the crankshaft pulley bolt to turn the crankshaft.

123 Repeat the procedure to fit the remaining pistons and liners.

124 Support the block upside-down on the bench.

125 Check that the oil pump location pin is fitted to the main bearing casting, then refit the oil pump while tilting it to engage the drive sprocket with the chain. Insert and tighten the bolts.

126 Apply jointing compound to the mating faces of the sump and main bearing casting. Refit the sump, insert the bolts and tighten them to the specified torque.

127 Dip the new crankshaft rear oil seal in oil, and locate it over the rear of the crankshaft (photo).

128 Peugeot dealers use their special tool (0132 U) to fit the oil seal, however it may be fitted by using the flywheel. Temporarily locate the flywheel on the crankshaft using four bolts, then tighten the bolts evenly until the flywheel contacts the rear flange (photo). Remove the flywheel and use a metal tube or block of wood to drive the oil seal fully into position.

129 Apply locking fluid to the threads of the flywheel bolts, locate the flywheel on the crankshaft dowel, then insert the bolts and tighten them to the specified torque while holding the flywheel as described in paragraph 77 (photos).

130 Support the engine upright on the bench.

131 Dip the crankshaft front oil seal in oil, locate it over the front of the crankshaft, and drive it in flush with the front of the block using a metal tube or socket. There is no seating, so take care not to drive it in too far.

132 Fit the oil seal flange, followed by the hubs/sprocket. Insert the pulley bolt and spacer, and tighten the bolt to the specified torque while holding the flywheel stationary.

133 Refit the water pump housing together with a new O-ring, and tighten the bolts to the specified torque.

5.127 Crankshaft rear oil seal located over crankshaft

5.128 Using the flywheel and four bolts to the crankshaft rear oil seal

5.129A Apply locking fluid to the flywheel bolts. . .

5.129B . . . and tighten to the specified torque

5.135 Using a universal clutch centralising tool

5.136 Tightening the pressure plate bolts

5.140 Camshaft sprocket held at TDC

5.143 Tighten the cylinder head bolts to the specified torque. . .

134 Locate the clutch friction disc and pressure plate on the flywheel with the dowels engaged. Insert the bolts finger-tight.
135 Centralise the friction disc, using a universal tool, or by making a wooden adaptor to the dimensions shown in Fig. 5.3 - page 115 (photo).
136 Tighten the pressure plate bolts evenly to the specified torque (photo).
137 Clean the cylinder head and block joint faces thoroughly. Also clean the cylinder head bolt holes.
138 Locate the new cylinder head gasket on the block dowels with the manufacturer's name uppermost.
139 Align the TDC holes in the flywheel and block rear flange, and insert a twist drill or long bolt.
140 Align the small hole in the camshaft sprocket with the hole in the cylinder head, and insert a twist drill or bolt (photo).
141 Lower the cylinder head onto the block so that it engages the two dowels.
142 Refit the rocker arm assembly.
143 Lubricate the cylinder head bolt threads and heads with molybdenum disulphide grease. Insert them and tighten to the initial torque using the sequence given in Fig. 13.7 (photo).
144 Using the same sequence, angle-tighten the bolts through the specified angle (photo).
145 Refit the timing belt tensioner roller, turn it clockwise, and tighten the nut.
146 Engage the timing belt with the crankshaft sprocket then, keeping it taut, feed it onto the camshaft sprocket, around the tensioner pulley, and onto the water pump socket.
147 Loosen the nut, and turn the tensioner roller anti-clockwise by hand. Tighten the nut.
148 Peugeot dealers use the special tool shown in Fig. 13.9, to tension the timing belt. A similar tool may be fabricated using an 8.0 cm long arm and a 1.5 kg weight. The torque applied to the roller will approximate 12 kgf cm (10.5 lbf in). Pre-tension the timing belt with the tool and tighten the nut, then remove the timing pins and rotate the crankshaft through two complete turns. Loosen the nut and allow the roller to re-position itself. Tighten the nut.
149 If the special tool is not available, an approximate setting may be achieved by turning the roller hub anti-clockwise, until it is just possible to turn the timing belt through 90° by finger and thumb midway between the crankshaft and camshaft sprockets. The square in the roller hub should then be directly below the adjustment nut, and the deflection of the belt in the midway position should be approximately 6.0 mm (0.24 in). If using this method, the tension should be re-checked by a Peugeot dealer at the earliest opportunity.
150 Refit the lower, intermediate, and upper timing covers, and tighten the bolts (photo).
151 Adjust the valve clearances as described in paragraphs 181 to 190.
152 Refit the baffle plate with its edges pointing downwards, followed by the two spacers.
153 Fit the rubber gasket to the valve cover, locate the cover in position and tighten the nuts.
154 Apply a little sealant to the end of the engine oil dipstick holder, and insert it in the main bearing cap casting. Insert and tighten the mounting bolt.
155 Insert and tighten the oil pressure switch.
156 Smear a little oil on the sealing ring, and tighten the oil filter into position by hand only.
157 Refit the timing plate and tighten the bolts.
158 Refit the TDC sensor and tighten the bolt. Fix the lead in the plastic clip on the timing plate. Note that the main body of the TDC sensor should be 1.0 mm from the flywheel.
159 Apply jointing compound to the distributor mounting flange, then refit it to the cylinder head, and tighten the bolts.
160 Apply jointing compound to the thermostat housing, then refit it to the cylinder head, and tighten the bolts.

5.144. . .then angle tighten a further 240°

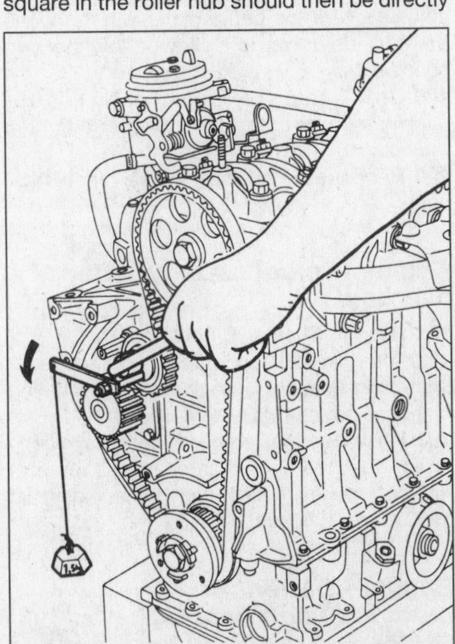
Fig. 13.9 Using Peugeot tool 0132 X to tension the timing belt (Sec 5)

5.150 Timing covers refitted

161 Refit the thermostat with reference to Section 6.
162 Refit the distributor with reference to Chapter 4.
163 Refit the exhaust manifold together with new gaskets. Refit the nuts and washers, and tighten the nuts.
164 Refit the exhaust manifold hot air shroud, and tighten the bolts.
165 Locate the coil and bracket over the distributor, and tighten the bolts.
166 Position the pulley on the front of the crankshaft. Insert and tighten the bolts.
167 Refit the alternator, and insert the pivot and adjustment bolts. Slip the drivebelt onto the pulleys, and tighten the tension bolt until the deflection of the belt midway between the pulleys is approximately 6.0 mm (0.24 in) under firm thumb pressure. Tighten the pivot and adjustment bolts.
168 Refit the fuel pump together with a new gasket, and tighten the bolts.
169 Thoroughly clean the mating faces of the inlet manifold and cylinder head, and apply jointing compound.
170 Refit the inlet manifold complete with carburettor, and tighten the nuts.
171 Reconnect the hose between the fuel pump and carburettor, and tighten the clips.
172 Reconnect the vacuum hose between the distributor and carburettor.
173 Refit and tighten the spark plugs.
174 Refit the HT leads and distributor cap.

Engine - reconnection to transmission

175 Check that the clutch release bearing is correctly fitted to the release fork. To prevent the bearing being disconnected while fitting the gearbox to the engine, tie the external release arm in the released position.
176 Lubricate the input shaft splines, clutch release bearing sleeve and fork fingers with molybdenum disulphide grease.
177 Refit any location dowels removed, then offer the gearbox to the engine so that the input shaft enters the clutch friction disc and engages the splines.
178 Push the gearbox fully onto the engine location dowels.
179 Insert and tighten the gearbox-to-engine bolts, noting that the hose bracket with the two cable ties locates on the top right-hand bolt (viewed from gearbox end).
180 Refit the starter motor, together with the air cleaner bracket, and tighten the bolts.

5.186 Adjusting a valve clearance

Valve clearances - checking and adjustment (engine cold)

181 Disconnect the crankcase ventilation hose from the valve cover.
182 Unscrew the nuts and remove the valve cover.
183 Remove the two spacers and baffle plate from the studs.
184 Prepare to rotate the crankshaft, either by jacking up one front wheel and turning the wheel with 4th or 5th gear engaged, or by using a spanner on the crankshaft pulley bolt. Rotation will be easier if the spark plugs are first removed.
185 Rotate the crankshaft until No 1 exhaust (flywheel end) is fully open. No 3 inlet valve and No 4 exhaust valve clearances may now be checked and adjusted.
186 Insert a feeler blade of the correct thickness between the rocker arm and valve stem. It should be a firm sliding fit if the clearance is correct. If adjustment is necessary, loosen the adjuster nut with a ring spanner, turn the adjuster as required with a screwdriver, then retighten the nut (photo).
187 Adjust the valve clearances in the following sequence:

Valve fully open	Adjust valve
No 1 Exhaust	*No 3 inlet and No 4 Exhaust*
No 3 Exhaust	*No 4 inlet and No 2 Exhaust*
No 4 Exhaust	*No 2 inlet and No 1 Exhaust*
No 2 Exhaust	*No 1 inlet and No 3 Exhaust*

188 When all the valve clearances have been adjusted, refit the baffle plate with its edges pointing downwards, followed by the two spacers.
189 Check that the rubber gasket is re-usable, then refit the valve cover and tighten the nuts.
190 Reconnect the crankcase ventilation hose.

Engine - initial start-up after overhaul

191 Refer to Chapter 1, Section 52.
192 The cylinder head bolts do not require re-tightening on the TU engine, and the timing belt does not require re-tensioning.
193 If new bearings and/or pistons have been fitted, treat the engine as new, and run it at reduced speeds. Also change the engine oil at 1000 miles (1500 km).

Engine - fitment of modified main bearing shells

194 It is possible that some engines may be fitted with modified main bearing shells, incorporating a grooved No 5 main bearing half-shell fitted to the cylinder block.
195 When reassembling an engine fitted with the modified bearing shells, the following procedure must be observed.
196 Fit the special grooved bearing shell to the No 5 bearing location in the cylinder block.
197 Fit the remaining bearing shells to the cylinder block, noting that the grooved bearing shells should be fitted to the No 2 and 4 bearing locations.
198 Proceed as described in paragraphs 106 to 110 inclusive.
199 Apply a thin coat of jointing compound to the mating faces, then without the centring dowels in place, lower the main bearing cap casting into position over the crankshaft. At the same time, feed the oil pump chain through the aperture.
200 Insert the main bearing bolts dry, then tighten them evenly to the Stage 1 torque wrench setting (see Specifications).
201 Angle-tighten the bolts to the Stage 2 torque wrench setting.
202 Refit the bolts securing the main bearing cap casting to the cylinder block, and tighten them to the specified torque.
203 Working on each bearing cap in turn, starting with No 3, loosen the bearing cap bolts, and then tighten them to the Stage 4 and then Stage 5 torque wrench settings.
204 Refit the centring dowels, and continue engine reassembly as described previously in this Section.

TU3F engine - general description

205 The TU3F engine was introduced for the 1993 model year, and is a development of the TU engine described previously in this Section. The most significant differences are that the TU3F engine has a cast-iron cylinder block without cylinder liners, and conventional main bearing caps are fitted instead of the one-piece main bearing cap casting.
206 The engine is fitted with Mono-Jetronic A2.2 single-point fuel injection in place of a carburettor. Details of the fuel injection system components are given in Section 8.
207 The modifications incorporated on the TU3F engine are likely to affect many of the procedures described previously in this Section for earlier TU engines, although no information was available at the time of writing. In particular, it is likely that revised torque wrench settings for various components (such as the big-end bearing caps) are specified for the TU3F engine.
208 Although the information given previously in this Section for dismantling and reassembly can be used as a guide, it is suggested that a Peugeot dealer be consulted if there is any doubt as to procedures or specifications for the TU3F engine.

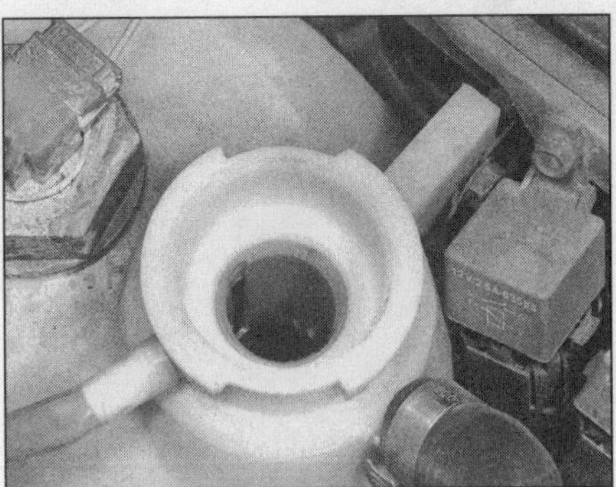

6.3 Coolant expansion tank level guide tube

6.5 Radiator filler cap

6.11 Air bleed screw on heater hose

6 Cooling system

Cooling system pressure (except TU engines)

1 From April 1987, the cooling system pressure in all engines is increased to 14 lbf/in² (1 bar). In consequence, a higher-rated expansion tank cap is used. A higher-rated temperature coolant temperature switch and radiator fan thermal switch are also fitted.

2 A guide-tube type of level indicator is fitted in the neck of the expansion tank.

3 The top of the slot in the tube is the maximum coolant level (photo).

Cooling system (TU engines) - description

4 The cooling system is similar to that described in Chapter 2.

Cooling system (TU engines) - draining, flushing and refilling

5 With the engine cold, unscrew the filler caps from the expansion tank and radiator (photo).

6 Place a suitable container beneath the left-hand side of the radiator, then unscrew the drain plug and drain the coolant.

7 Drain the cylinder block by removing the drain plug located on the front left-hand side of the block.

8 To flush the radiator, disconnect the top and bottom hoses, and insert a garden hose in the top inlet. Flush with cold water until there are no traces of sediment.

9 With the system clean, refit the hoses and tighten the drain plugs.

10 Release the rubber ring, and tie the expansion tank to the bonnet as high as possible.

11 Loosen the bleed screws on the thermostat housing and heater hose (photo).

12 Fill the radiator with coolant. Tighten the thermostat housing bleed screw when the water flows free of air bubbles.

13 Fill the radiator to overflowing, then refit and tighten the radiator cap.

14 Fill the expansion tank to the maximum level mark, then tighten the heater hose bleed screw when the water flows free of air bubbles.

15 Add more coolant to the expansion tank until the level is about 30 mm above the maximum mark. Refit and tighten the filler cap.

16 Start the engine, and run it at about 2000 rpm until the electric cooling fan cuts in.

17 Let the engine idle, then when the cooling fan stops, slowly and carefully unscrew the expansion tank filler cap (using a thick cloth over the cap as a precaution against scalding).

18 Slowly loosen the radiator filler cap until coolant flows, then retighten it. Similarly purge any air from the bleed screws on the thermostat housing and heater hose.

19 Top-up the expansion tank to 30 mm above the maximum mark, and refit the filler cap. The high level is necessary at this stage because the coolant is hot; when the system is cool, the level will fall to the maximum mark.

20 Refit the expansion tank in its normal position, and secure with the rubber ring. Check the level in the expansion tank when cold, and top-up if necessary (photo).

Radiator (TU engines) - removal and refitting

21 The procedure is as described in Chapter 2. However, additionally, the cooling fan relay must be removed from the clip on the top of the radiator (photo).

6.20 Topping-up the expansion tank

6.21A Disconnecting the low coolant level sensor wiring

6.21B Cooling fan relay (arrowed)

6.21C Radiator thermo-switch (arrowed)

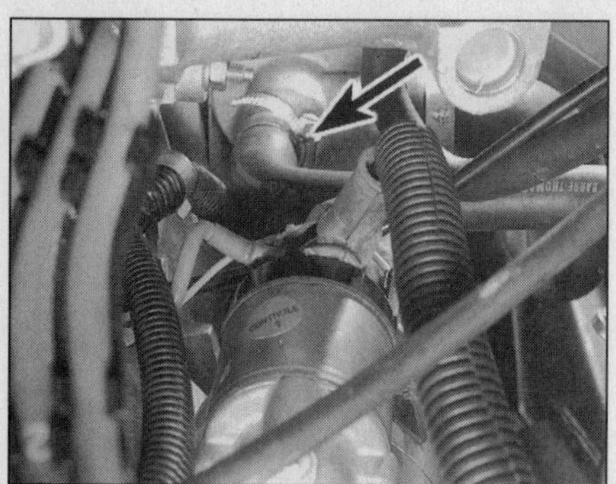
6.31A Bypass hose connection to water pump housing (arrowed)

6.31 B Water pump housing and bolts

6.32A Removing the water pump from the housing

Water pump (TU engines) - removal and refitting

22 Drain the cooling system as previously described.

23 Unbolt and remove the upper and intermediate timing covers, leaving the lower cover in position.

24 Turn the engine clockwise, using a socket on the crankshaft pulley bolt, until the small hole in the camshaft sprocket is aligned with the corresponding hole in the cylinder head. Insert a close-fitting twist drill or bolt into the holes.

25 Align the TDC holes in the flywheel and cylinder block rear flange, and insert a further twist drill or long bolt.

26 Loosen the timing belt tensioner roller nut, turn the tensioner clockwise using a screwdriver or square drive in the special hole, then retighten the nut.

27 Release the timing belt from the water pump sprocket.

28 Unscrew the nut from the right-hand engine mounting.

29 Using a trolley jack and block of wood, lift the right-hand side of the engine as far as possible.

30 Unscrew the nuts and remove the mounting bracket from the water pump housing.

31 Disconnect the hoses from the housing, then unbolt the housing from the block. Remove the O-ring seal (photos).

32 Unbolt the water pump from the housing, and remove the O-ring (photos). If necessary, similarly remove the inlet elbow.

33 Refitting is the reverse of the removal procedure, noting the following points:

(a) *Renew the O-rings.*
(b) *Make sure that the housing-to-block location dowels are in position.*
(c) *Tighten all nuts and bolts to their specified torque wrench settings.*
(d) *Refit and tension the timing belt (Section 5).*

Cooling fan thermo-switch (TU engines) - testing

34 With the thermo-switch removed, connect an ohmmeter between the terminals.

35 Suspend the thermo-switch in a container of water which is being heated. Check the temperature of the water with a thermometer. With the unit cold, there should be no continuity, but when the cut-in temperature is reached, the internal contacts should close, and the ohmmeter should register nil resistance.

36 Allow the water to cool, and check that the switch cuts out within the specified temperature range.

Thermostat (TU engines) - removal, testing and refitting

37 The procedure is as given in Chapter 2, but note the different housing on the TU engine.

7 Fuel and exhaust systems - carburettor engines

PART A: GENERAL

Unleaded fuel

1 Unleaded 95 RON fuel may be used in all Peugeot 309 carburettor-engined models. Most carburettor models can use unleaded fuel without any adjustment, but refer to the table below.

Engine	Model years	Ignition timing adjustment
E1A (1E1A)	*1986 to 1989*	*None*
TU1/K (H1A)	*1991 on*	*None*
G1A (1G1A)	*1986 to 1991*	*None*
TU3.2/K (K2D)	*1991 on*	*None*
XU51C (B1A/A)	*1986 to 1989*	*Retard by 4° when fitted with manual transmission*
XU52C (B2A)	*1988 to 1989*	*None*
XU52C/K (B2B)	*1990 on*	*None*

2 The nearest equivalent to 95 RON fuel is the 'Premium'-grade unleaded petrol most often found on sale in UK filling stations. Note that 98 RON 'Super/Superplus'-grade unleaded petrol may also be used if wished, in all carburettor-engined models. It should be possible to use the 'Super' unleaded fuel

6.32B Water pump O-ring (arrowed)

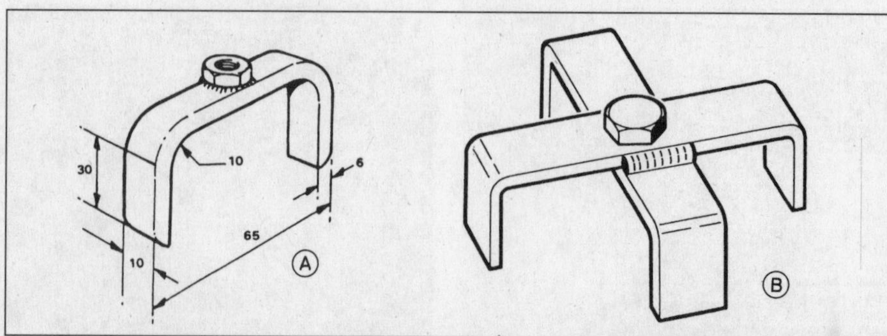

Fig. 13.10 Typical tools for removing fuel pump and sender unit ring nuts (Sec 7)
A For sender unit (dimensions in mm) *B For fuel pump*

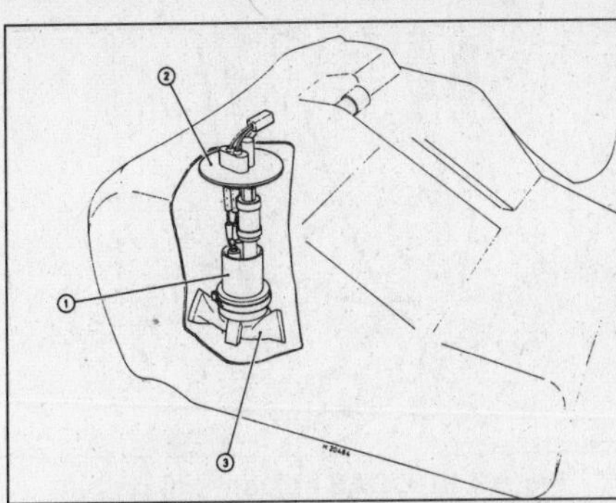

Fig. 13.11 Electrically-operated submerged type fuel pump (Sec 7)

1 Pump 2 Cover 3 Fuel filter

without any ignition timing adjustment, even in those models which would need an adjustment for 95 RON unleaded fuel - check with a Peugeot dealer for the latest information.

Fuel pump - electrically-operated type

3 This type of pump is similar to that fitted to models with fuel injection, and is covered in Section 24 of Chapter 3. The pump is submerged in the fuel tank, and incorporates a gauze filter.

4 The pump is controlled by two relays. One relay incorporates a safety feature, in that its primary windings are short-circuited to earth via the engine oil pressure switch. When the engine is stationary, this relay will not operate the fuel pump, but as soon as the engine is running, it will supply current to the pump. The other relay operates in conjunction with the starter motor.

5 If the pump is to be removed, disconnect the battery and proceed as described in Chapter 3, Section 7; where more than one fuel hose is connected, ensure that each is marked so that it can be correctly identified and reconnected before disturbing any of the connections. In theory, it should be possible to remove the pump and the sender unit after taking out the cover under the rear seats, but as the holes are usually out of alignment, the securing rings cannot be rotated. Tools similar to the ones shown in Fig. 13.10 will be required to unscrew the rings.

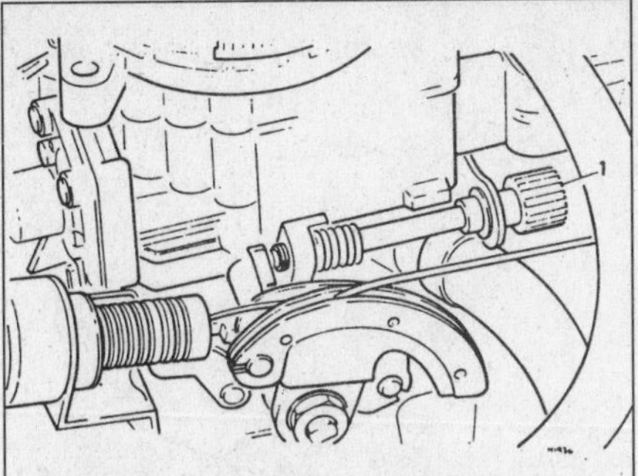

Fig. 13.12 Idle speed screw (1) on the Weber 36 TLC carburettor (Sec 7)

Fuel pump - later models

6 It would appear that some later models are fitted with a mechanical pump, with a return line and degas tank, similar to that described in Chapter 3. No further details were available at the time of writing; owners will have to seek the advice of a Peugeot dealer if such a system is encountered.

7 As far as can be ascertained at the time of writing, all TU carburettor engines are fitted with mechanical pumps; servicing procedures are as described in Chapter 3, Sections 4, 5 and 6.

Inlet and exhaust manifolds (TU engines) - removal and refitting

8 The procedure for removing and refitting manifolds is similar to that described in Chapter 3.

PART B: WEBER 36 TLC CARBURETTOR

Description

1 This carburettor is fitted to models with an XU51C engine and automatic transmission. It is of single-barrel downdraught type, incorporating an automatic choke, and a temperature-controlled air cleaner is fitted.

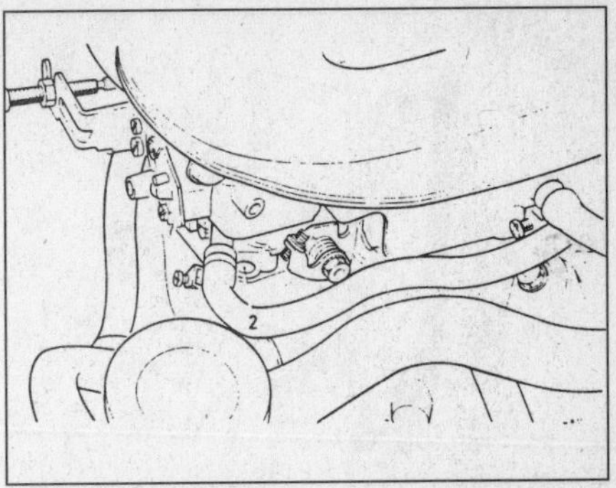

Fig. 13.13 Mixture screw location (2) on the Weber 36 TLC carburettor (Sec 7)

Idle speed and mixture - adjustment

2 Where fitted, remove the tamperproof cap from the mixture screw.

3 Select the Park (P) position with the transmission selector lever, then run the engine to its normal operating temperature. Do not remove the air cleaner.

4 Connect a tachometer to the engine.

Without an exhaust gas analyser

5 With the engine idling, adjust the idle speed screw so that the engine speed is 950 rpm.

6 Adjust the **mixture** screw to obtain the highest engine speed.

7 Repeat the procedure given in paragraphs 5 and 6 until the highest engine speed is 950 rpm.

8 Screw in the mixture screw until the engine idling speed is as specified.

With an exhaust gas analyser

9 With the engine idling, adjust the idle speed screw until the engine speed is 900 rpm.

10 Adjust the mixture screw to obtain the specified CO reading.

11 Repeat the procedure given in paragraphs 9 and 10 as necessary.

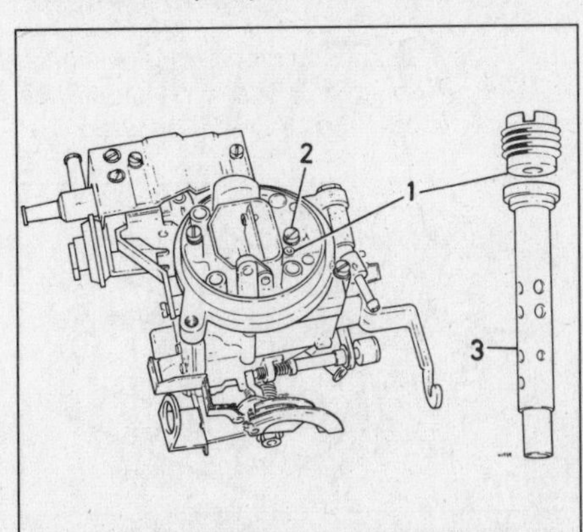

Fig. 13.14 Top view of the Weber 36 TLC carburettor (Sec 7)

1 Air correction jet 3 Emulsion tube
2 Idling jet

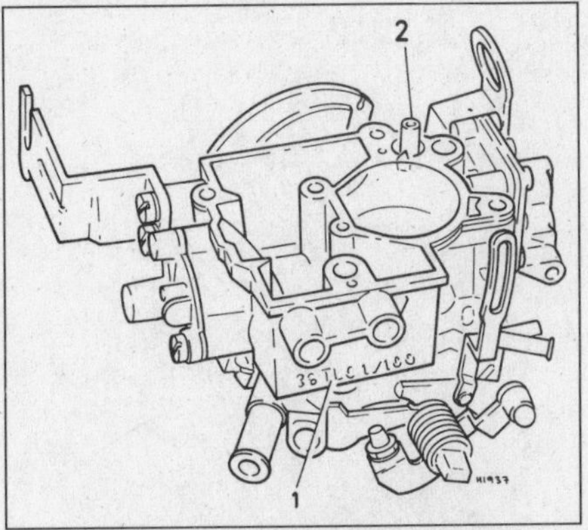

Fig. 13.15 Top cover removed from Weber 36 TLC carburettor (Sec 7)

1 Type number
2 Accelerator pump injector

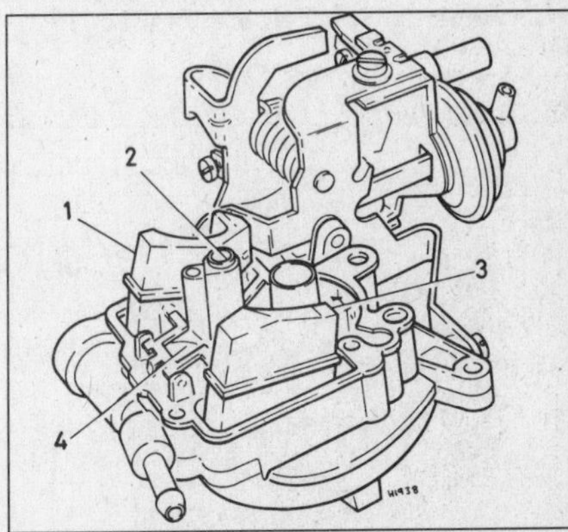

Fig. 13.16 Top cover inverted – Weber 36 TLC carburettor (Sec 7)

1 Float 3 Secondary venturi
2 Main jet 4 Fuel inlet needle valve

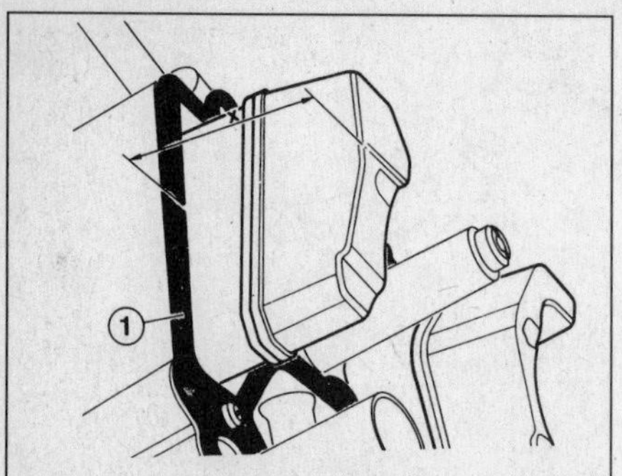

Fig. 13.17 Float level setting diagram – Weber 36 TLC carburettor (Sec 7)

1 Gasket X = 28.0 mm (1.1 in)

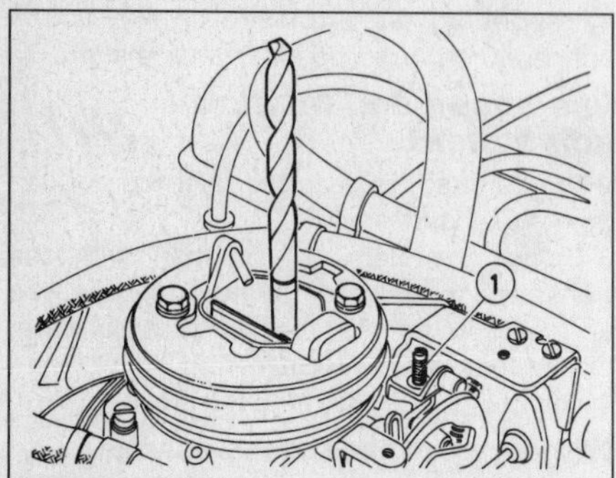

Fig. 13.20 COAS adjusting screw (1) on the Weber 36 TLC carburettor (Sec 7)

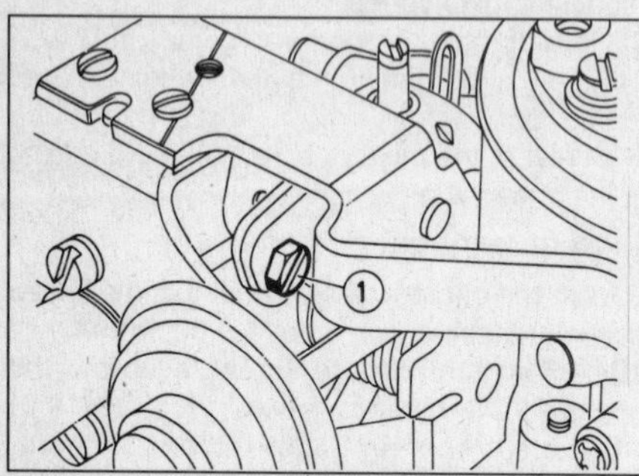

Fig. 13.22 COAS adjustment on the Weber 36 TLC carburettor (Sec 7)

1 Screw

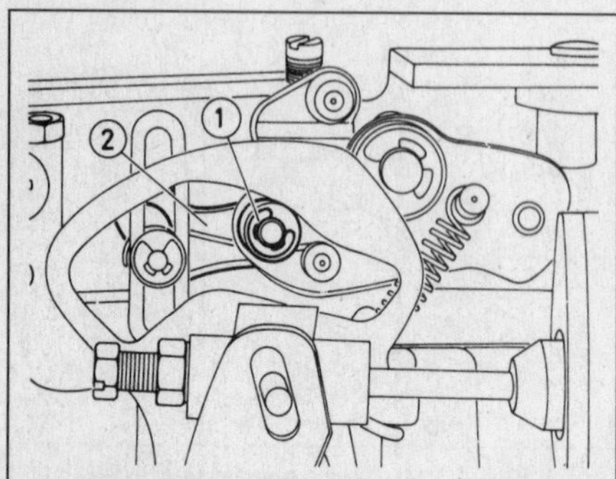

Fig. 13.23 COAS adjustment on the Weber 36 TLC carburettor (Sec 7)

1 Roller 2 Lever

Fig. 13.18 Peugeot tool 0.145 G (Sec 7)

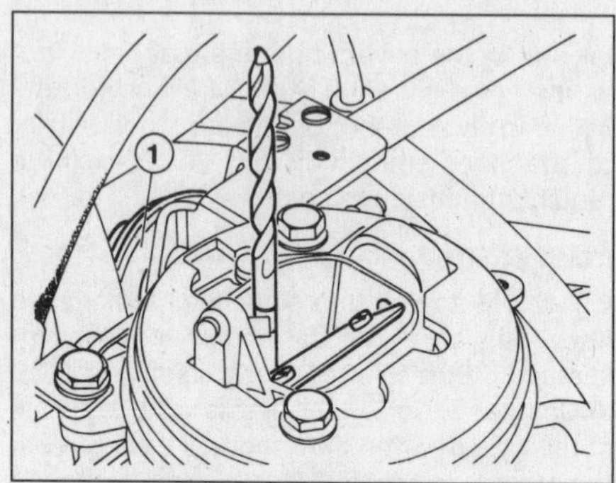

Fig. 13.21 COAS adjustment on the Weber 36 TLC carburettor (Sec 7)

1 Hose

Removal and refitting

12 The removal and refitting procedure is similar to that described for the Weber TLP carburettor in Chapter 3.

Overhaul

13 The overhaul procedure is similar to that described for the Weber TLP carburettor in Chapter 3.

14 The procedure is straightforward, but refer to the accompanying illustrations for the positions of the various jets.

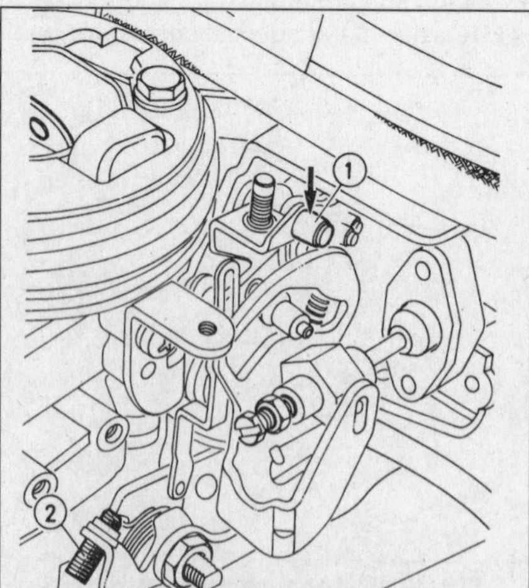

Fig. 13.24 PTO adjustment on the Weber 36 TLC carburettor (Sec 7)

1 Roller 2 Adjusting screw

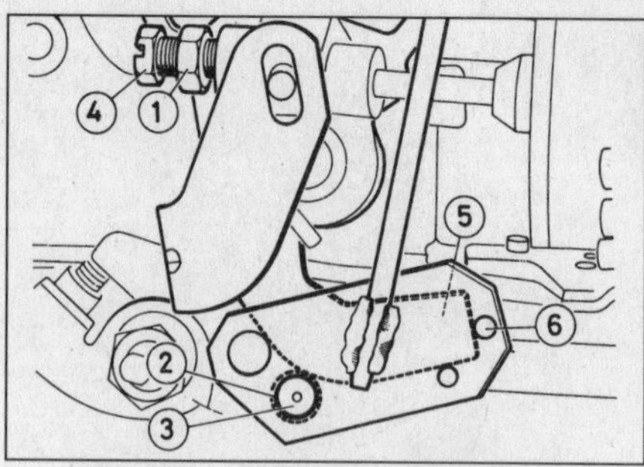

Fig. 13.19 COAS adjustment on the Weber 36 TLC carburettor (Sec 7)

1 Locknut
2 Hole
3 Roller
4 Adjusting screw
5 Cam
6 Peg on tool

15 To check the float level, hold the cover vertically with the gasket in place. Check that the dimension shown in Fig. 13.17 is as specified, and if necessary bend the tongue of the float arm to correct it.

16 To adjust the cold start device choke opening after starting (COAS), the engine must be hot and idling, the air cleaner hose removed, and the cold start device cover removed. Peugeot tool 0.145G is essential to make this adjustment.

17 Refer to Fig. 13.19 and fit the tool as shown, then turn screw (4) until the cam (5) contacts the tool peg (6). Using a 9.5 mm drill, check that the choke flap has opened by 9.5 mm - if not adjust screw (1) (Fig. 13.20).

18 Disconnect and plug the hose (1) shown in Fig. 13.21, and check now that the choke flap is open by 5.5 mm - if not, loosen screw (1) (Fig. 13.22), hold the roller (1) (Fig. 13.23) against the top of the cam, and adjust lever (2). Retighten the screw and reconnect the hose afterwards.

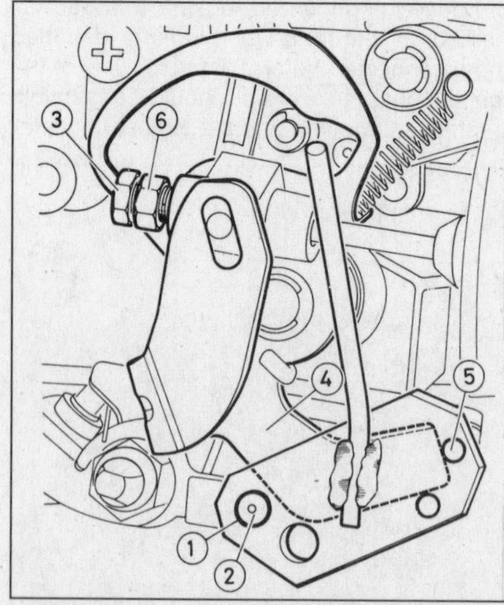

Fig. 13.25 Choke cam adjustment on the Weber 36 TLC carburettor (Sec 7)

1 Hole
2 Roller
3 Adjusting screw
4 Cam
5 Peg on tool
6 Locknut

7.8 Idle speed adjustment screw (arrowed)

7.9 Idle mixture adjustment screw (arrowed)

7.18 Disconnecting the float chamber breather pipe

19 To adjust the positive throttle opening (PTO), press the roller to open the choke flap, and check that the engine speed is 2000 rpm (make sure that the electric fan is not running). If necessary, adjust screw (2) (Fig. 13.24).

20 To adjust the choke cam, fit the tool 0.145G as shown in Fig. 13.25 and adjust screw (3) until the cam (4) contacts peg (5). Tighten the locknut (6).

21 Stop the engine, refit the cold start device cover and air cleaner hose.

PART C: SOLEX 32-34 Z2 AND 34-34 Z1 CARBURETTORS

Description

1 These carburettors are fitted to models with the TU3.2/K and XU52C engines.

2 They are of the twin-barrel downdraught type, with an automatic choke which operates on the primary barrel only.

3 A vacuum-operated choke unloader, accelerator pump and full-load enrichener device are fitted, to govern the fuel requirements of the engine over its full operating range.

Idle speed and mixture - adjustment

4 Where fitted, remove the tamperproof cap from the mixture screw.

5 If the vehicle is equipped with automatic transmission, select the Park (P) position with the transmission selector lever, then run the engine to its normal operating temperature. Do not remove the air cleaner.

6 If the vehicle is equipped with manual transmission, ensure the gear lever is in the neutral position, then run the engine to its normal operating temperature. Do not remove the air cleaner.

7 Connect a tachometer to the engine.

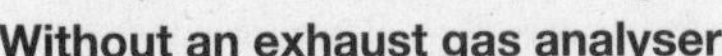

Without an exhaust gas analyser

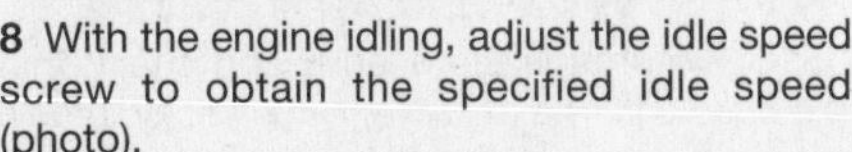

8 With the engine idling, adjust the idle speed screw to obtain the specified idle speed (photo).

9 Adjust the mixture screw to obtain the highest engine speed (photo).

10 Readjust the idle speed to that specified using the idle speed adjustment screw.

11 Repeat paragraphs 9 and 10 until no further increase in speed using the mixture screw is possible.

With an exhaust gas analyser

12 With the engine idling, adjust the idle speed screw until the engine speed is as specified.

13 Adjust the mixture screw to obtain the specified CO reading.

14 Repeat the procedure given in paragraphs 12 and 13 as necessary.

Removal and refitting

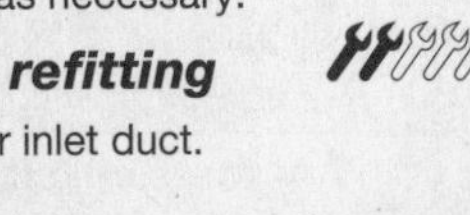

15 Remove the air inlet duct.

7.19A Automatic choke coolant pipe connection. . .

16 Disconnect the accelerator cable.

17 Disconnect the distributor vacuum pipe.

18 Disconnect the float chamber breather pipes (photo).

19 Either drain the cooling system, or clamp the automatic choke and carburettor base heating pipes, then disconnect the pipes (photos).

20 Disconnect the float chamber solenoid valve wiring.

21 Disconnect the fuel inlet pipe, either at the fuel pump or the fuel reservoir on the side of the carburettor, and plug the hose.

22 Remove the carburettor securing nut, and lift off the fuel reservoir.

23 Remove the remaining carburettor securing nuts, and lift the carburettor from the inlet manifold (photos).

7.19B . . .and carburettor base heating pipes

7.23A Remove remaining securing nuts. . .

7.23B. . .and lift off the carburettor

7.24 Removing carburettor spacer

7.28 Fuel inlet union and filter

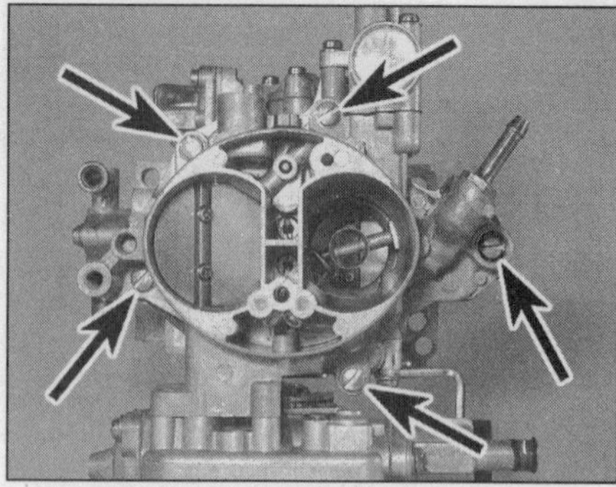
7.31 Carburettor top cover screws (arrowed)

24 Remove the carburettor spacer (photo).
25 Refitting is the reverse of the removal procedure; renew the carburettor spacer if it appears to be split or cracked.

Overhaul

Note: *Special gauges are needed to adjust the throttle valves and automatic choke. Without these gauges, do not attempt to adjust the primary or secondary barrel throttle adjuster screws. Similarly, the float height is set using a special gauge; however, the dimensions of the gauge are given, and an alternative method described.*
26 Remove the carburettor as previously described.
27 Thoroughly clean the carburettor in solvent, and dry it off before placing on a clean bench.

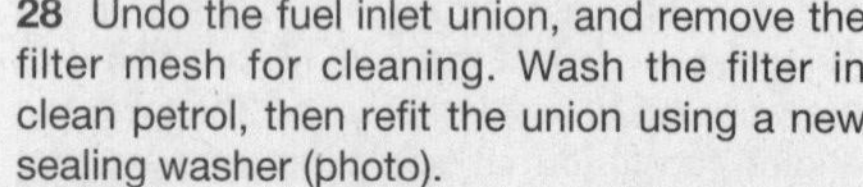

28 Undo the fuel inlet union, and remove the filter mesh for cleaning. Wash the filter in clean petrol, then refit the union using a new sealing washer (photo).
29 Remove the throttle return spring, noting how it is located on the quadrant.
30 Unscrew the link rod pin.
31 Remove the top cover screws, and lift off the cover (photo).
32 Tap out the pivot pin, and lift off the floats.
33 Unscrew the needle jet.
34 Clean out the float chamber in the main body.
35 Blow through the needle, and check that the needle is free to move; if it is sticky, renew the jet.
36 Shake the floats to ensure they are not holed and full of fuel. Renew them if this is the case.
37 Refit the needle valve using new sealing washer.
38 Ensure that no trace of old gasket remains on the top cover or main body, then fit a new gasket to the top cover.
39 Fit the floats, pushing in the pivot pin until it protrudes equally at both ends (photo).
40 To check the float height, use the gauge shown in Figs. 13.26 and 13.27; the floats should just make contact with the gauge. Note that the gasket must be fitted.
41 We measured the distance from the face of the gasket to the apex of the floats, which was 33.5 mm (photo).
42 To adjust the float height, bend the tongues of the float arm.
43 Lift out the accelerator pump injector from the main body (photo), and blow through it to ensure it is not obstructed.
44 Check that the O-ring seal is in good condition, and refit the injector, pushing it fully down into the main body.
45 Unscrew and remove the air correction jets - these can also be removed with the top cover in place (photo). The main jets are located under the air correction jets, and can be retrieved using a long thin instrument, but be careful not to score the jets during this operation.
46 Clean the jets by blowing through them. Do not attempt to clean out the jets using wire, as this may enlarge them. Refit the jets to their original bores on completion.
47 The primary and secondary venturis can be removed for cleaning if required (photo).

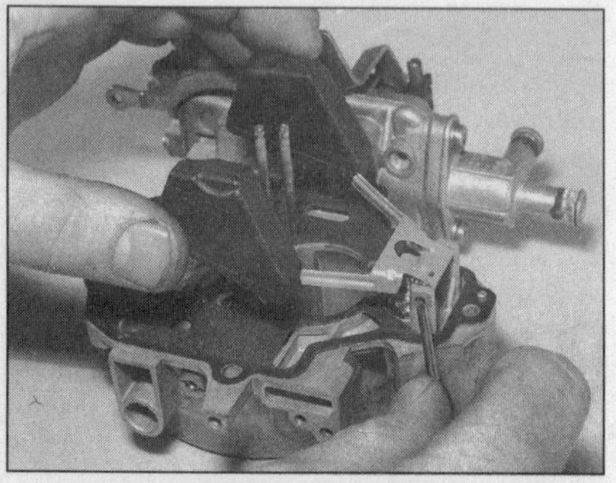
7.39 Pushing in the float pivot pin

7.41 Measuring float height

7.43 lifting out accelerator injector

7.45 Removing an air correction jet

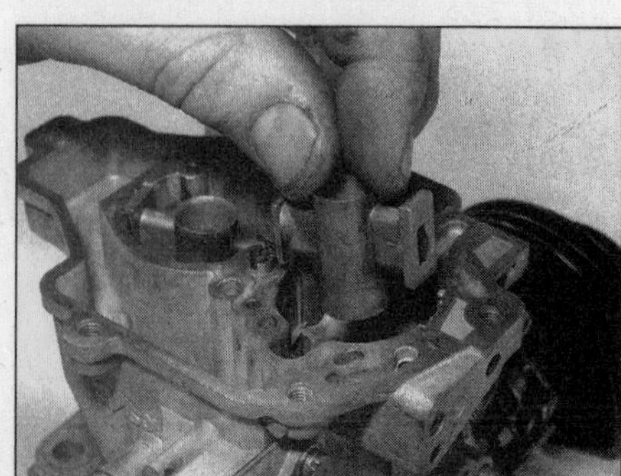
7.47 Removing a venturi

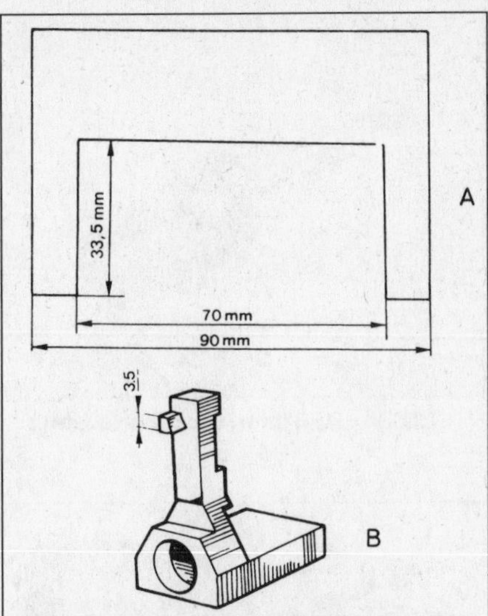

Fig. 13.26 Float setting gauge (A) and automatic choke adjustment gauge (B) (Sec 7)

All dimensions in mm

48 Unscrew the idle jet from the side of the main body, and clean it (photo).
49 Remove the retaining screw, and lift off the float chamber breather solenoid valve.
50 Dismantle the valve, and check the needle tip for deformation, renewing it as necessary.
51 Fit a new washer to the valve, and refit the needle, ensuring it locates in the washer (photos).
52 Fit the spring and screw on the solenoid, ensuring the washer is in place (photos).
53 Refit the valve to the carburettor using a new gasket (photos).
54 Remove the securing screws from the vacuum reservoir, and lift off the reservoir (photo).
55 Check the integrity of the reservoir by blowing into it, and renew the O-ring seal (photo).
56 Remove the automatic choke water housing, and lift out the thermostat (photos).
57 The operation of the thermostat can be checked in the same manner as the cooling system thermostat (Chapter 3).

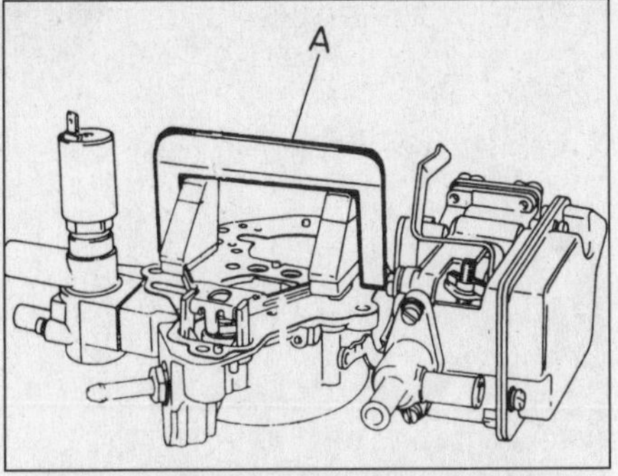

Fig. 13.27 Checking float height using the special gauge (A) (Sec 7)

7.48 Idle jet (arrowed)

7.51A Fit a new washer. . .

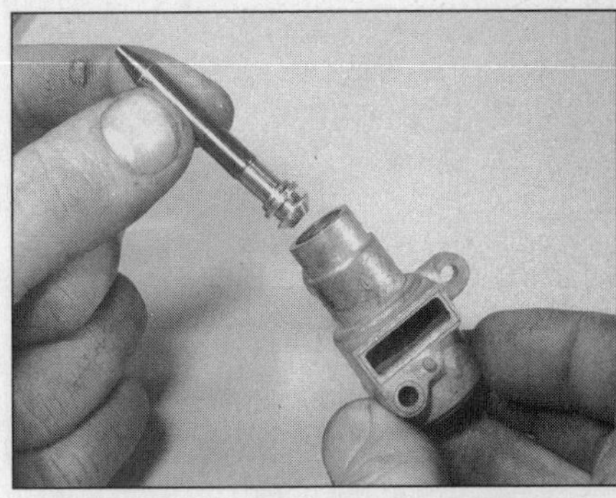

7.51B. . .then insert the needle

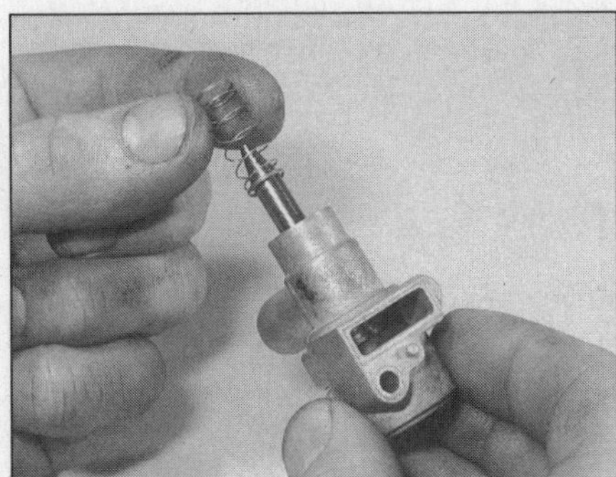

7.52A Fit the spring. . .

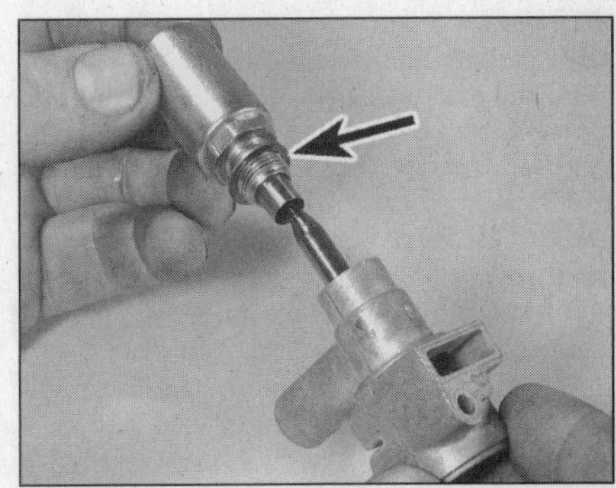

7.52B. . .and screw on the solenoid ensuring that the washer (arrowed) is in place

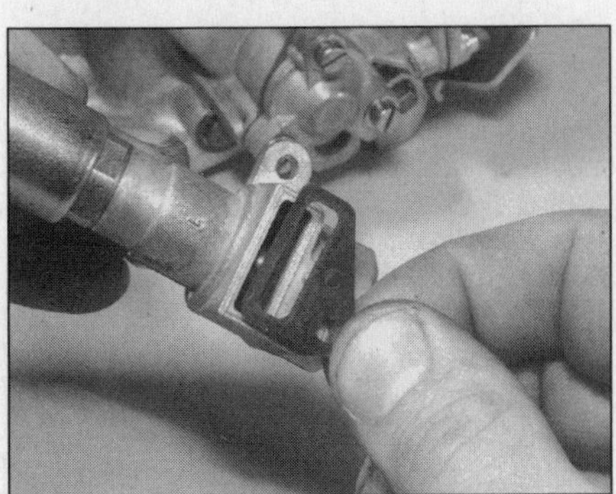

7.53A Use a new gasket. . .

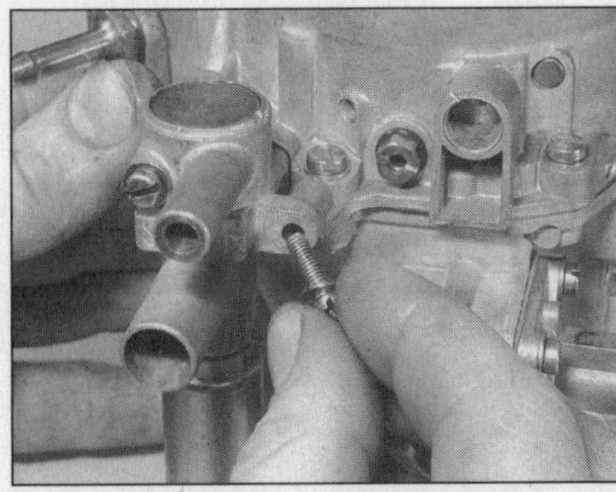

7.53B. . .when refitting the valve

7.54 Vacuum reservoir securing screws (arrowed)

7.55 Reservoir O-ring seal

7.56A Remove the automatic choke housing

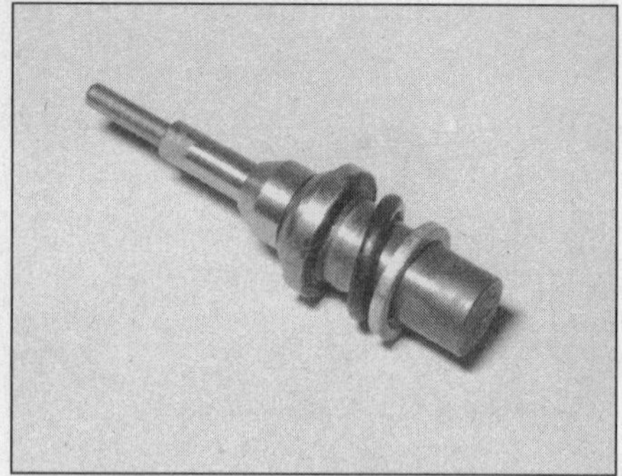
7.56B . . .and lift out the thermostat

7.63 Adjusting the choke opening after starting (COAS) screw

7.64A Enrichener device (arrowed). . .

7.64B . . .and accelerator pump (arrowed)

58 Renew the O-ring seal, and refit the thermostat to the water housing.
59 Refit the water housing to the carburettor, renewing the gasket.
60 Remove the choke unloader by undoing the four screws.
61 Check that the diaphragm is intact, renewing as necessary.
62 Refit the unloader and the vacuum reservoir.
63 The choke opening after starting (COAS) adjustment screw can be reached using a small screwdriver through the channel above the choke unloader (photo), but a special gauge is required for adjustment.
64 Similar inspections can be made on the enrichener device and the accelerator pump diaphragms (photos).
65 Refit the top cover to the main body, which is the reverse of removal.
66 Refit the carburettor to the manifold.

PART D: SOLEX 32 PBISA CARBURETTOR

General

1 The overhaul and adjustment procedures for the Solex 32 PBISA carburettor fitted to the TU1/K engine are similar to those given for the 32 BISA unit in Chapter 3.
2 Note the differences in settings, and other details listed in the Specifications Section of this Chapter.

8 Fuel and exhaust systems - fuel injection engines

PART A: GENERAL

Unleaded fuel

1 Except for the (non-catalytic converter-equipped) 1.9 GTI, all Peugeot 309 models with fuel injection engines may be operated on unleaded 95 RON fuel. Most of those models which can run on unleaded 95 RON fuel can do so without any ignition timing adjustment, but refer to the table below.

Engine	Model years	Ignition timing adjustment
*TU1M/Z (HDZ)**	*1991 on*	*None*
*TU3M/Z, TU3FM/L (KDY)**	*1991 on*	*None*
*XU5M2/Z, XU5M3/Z, XU5M3/L (BDY)**	*1991 on*	*None*
XU5JA (B6D)	*1986 to 1990*	*Retard by 2°*
XU5JA/K (B6E)	*1991 on*	*None*
XU9JA/K (D6B)	*1987 on*	*95 RON unleaded unsuitable***
*XU9JA/Z, XU9JA/L (DKZ)**	*1988 on*	*None*

***Note:** *This engine is equipped with a catalytic converter, and must be operated on unleaded fuel at all times. Leaded fuel* **must not** *be used.*
****Note:** *95 RON fuel cannot be used - use only 97 RON leaded or 98 RON ('Super' or 'Superplus') unleaded fuel - no adjustment is then required.*

2 The nearest equivalent to 95 RON fuel is the 'Premium'-grade unleaded petrol most often found on sale in UK filling stations. Note that 98 RON 'Super/Superplus'-grade unleaded petrol may also be used if wished, in all fuel injection models. It should be possible to use the 'Super' unleaded fuel without any ignition timing adjustment, even in those models which would need an adjustment for 95 RON unleaded fuel - check with a Peugeot dealer for the latest information.
3 As noted above, the (non-catalytic converter-equipped) 1.9 GTI should be run only on petrol of 97/98 RON octane rating; this means using either leaded four-star or 'Super/Superplus' unleaded petrol, as desired.
4 Note that this recommendation supersedes that given in some editions of the Owner's Handbook; while the engine is capable of running on 95 RON unleaded fuel, the amount of ignition timing retardation required to allow this resulted in too great a loss of performance, and the Handbook recommendation (to retard the ignition by 4°) was withdrawn by Peugeot.

Depressurising the fuel system

Warning: The following procedures will merely relieve the pressure in the fuel system - remember that fuel will still be present in the system components, and take precautions accordingly before disconnecting any of them.

5 As well as the metal fuel lines and flexible hoses between the various components, the fuel system referred to in this sub-Section is defined as the tank-mounted fuel pump, the fuel filter, the fuel pulsation damper (if fitted) and either the fuel rail, injectors and pressure regulator (LE2-Jetronic, Motronic M1.3 systems) or the fuel injector and the pressure regulator in the throttle body (Mono-Jetronic, MMBA systems). All these contain fuel which will be under pressure while the engine is running and/or while the ignition is switched on.

6 The pressure will remain for some time after the ignition has been switched off, and must be relieved before any of these components is disturbed for servicing work.

7 Remove either the fuel pump fuse (number 14) or the fuel pump relay (whichever is convenient) and start the engine; allow the engine to idle until it dies. Turn the engine over once or twice on the starter to ensure that all pressure is released, then switch off the ignition; do not forget to refit the fuse or relay when work is complete.

Air cleaner - description and servicing

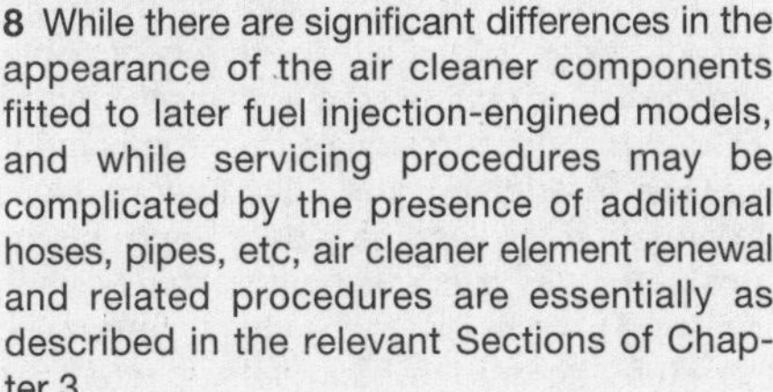

8 While there are significant differences in the appearance of the air cleaner components fitted to later fuel injection-engined models, and while servicing procedures may be complicated by the presence of additional hoses, pipes, etc, air cleaner element renewal and related procedures are essentially as described in the relevant Sections of Chapter 3.

9 In some cases, the end (or top) cover is retained by a number of spring clips; ensure that the cover is correctly seated to prevent air leaks before fastening the clips on reassembly.

10 If any hoses or pipes are disturbed during servicing work, ensure that all are correctly reconnected, and clipped or secured so that they are not kinked.

Throttle cable - removal and refitting

11 Refer to Chapter 3, Sections 31 and 14.

Fuel pump - removal and refitting

12 Refer to Chapter 3, Section 24; where more than one fuel hose is connected, ensure that each is marked so that it can be correctly identified and reconnected before disturbing any of the connections. In theory, it should be possible to remove the pump and the sender unit after taking out the cover under the rear seats, but as the holes are usually out of alignment, the securing rings cannot be rotated. Tools similar to the ones shown in Fig. 13.10 will be required to unscrew the rings.

Fuel level transmitter - removal and refitting

13 Refer to Chapter 3, Section 7.

Fuel tank - removal and refitting

14 Refer to Chapter 3, Section 30.

Electronic Control Unit (ECU) - removal and refitting

15 Disconnect the battery earth lead.

16 The ECU is located behind the facia, just above the driver's footwell. On early models, it will be necessary to remove the driver's side glovebox (Chapter 11, Section 21) to reach the unit; on models built from October 1989 onwards, it may be possible to reach the unit

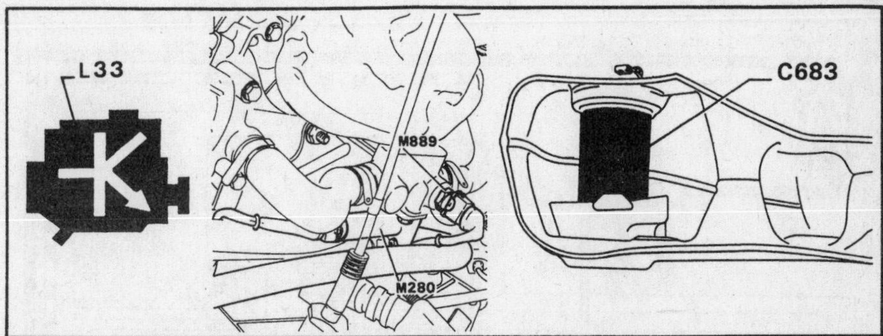

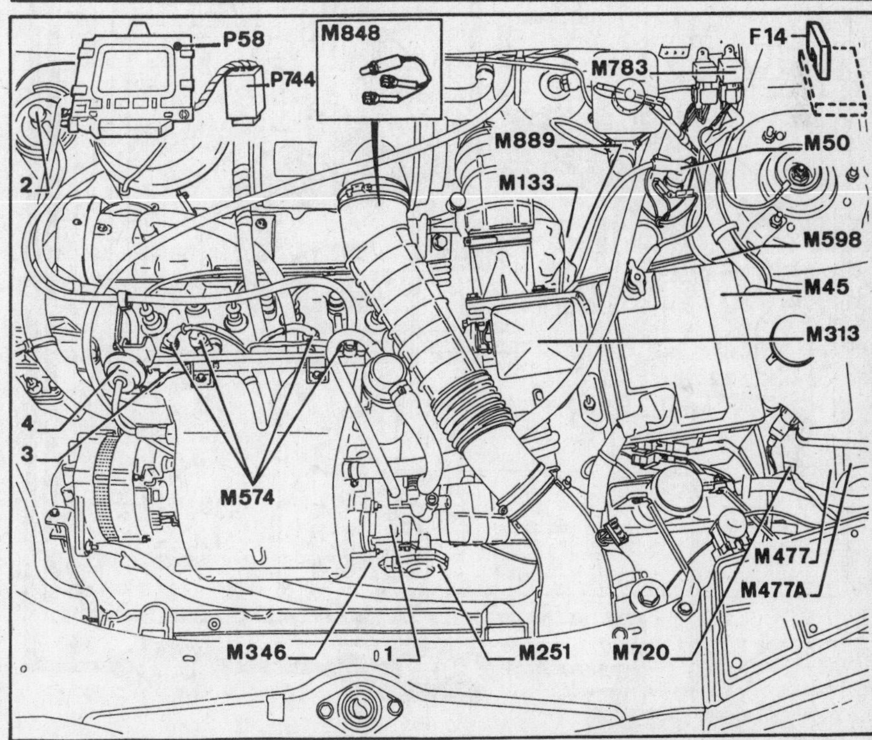

Fig. 13.28 Bosch Motronic M1.3 engine management system component location – left-hand drive model shown (Sec 8)

C683 Fuel pump – submerged in fuel tank
F14 Fuel pump fuse – in fusebox
L33 Diagnostic indicator lamp – in instrument panel
M45 Battery
M50 Ignition HT coil – early type shown
M133 Crankshaft speed/position sensor
M251 Throttle switch
M280 Supplementary air device
M313 Airflow sensor
M346 Charcoal canister-purge solenoid valve
M477 ECU supply fuse holder
M477A Lambda sensor heater supply fuse holder
M574 Fuel injectors
M598 Ignition amplifier module
M720 Diagnostic socket
M783 System main relay
M848 Lambda sensor
M889 Coolant temperature sensor
P58 Electronic Control Unit (ECU) – behind facia
P744 Fuel pump relay
1 Throttle housing
2 Fuel filter
3 Fuel rail
4 Fuel pressure regulator

13

without disturbing the parcel shelf - if not, refer to Section 20, paragraph 26 of this Chapter.

17 Unbolt the unit from its mountings, and withdraw it until the wiring plugs' locking clips or lugs can be released and the plugs can be disconnected.

18 Refitting is a reversal of the removal procedure, ensuring that the wiring plugs are correctly reconnected, and that the unit is located securely.

Fuel injection system relays and fuses - general

19 The relays are located in marked holders around the engine compartment (as noted, where details are available, in this Section) or on the fusebox panel itself, as described in Chapter 12.

20 While most fuses are mounted in the main fusebox inside the car, some are mounted in a holder located in the front left-hand corner of the engine compartment. Details of fuses actually fitted will vary depending on year and model but, for example, the fuses protecting the ECU and Lambda sensor supplies are usually included in this holder.

Manifolds and exhaust system - general

21 The procedure for removing and refitting the manifolds and the exhaust system components is similar to that described in Chapter 3. Refer to the relevant Sections of this Chapter for details of fuel injection system and catalytic converter component removal and refitting.

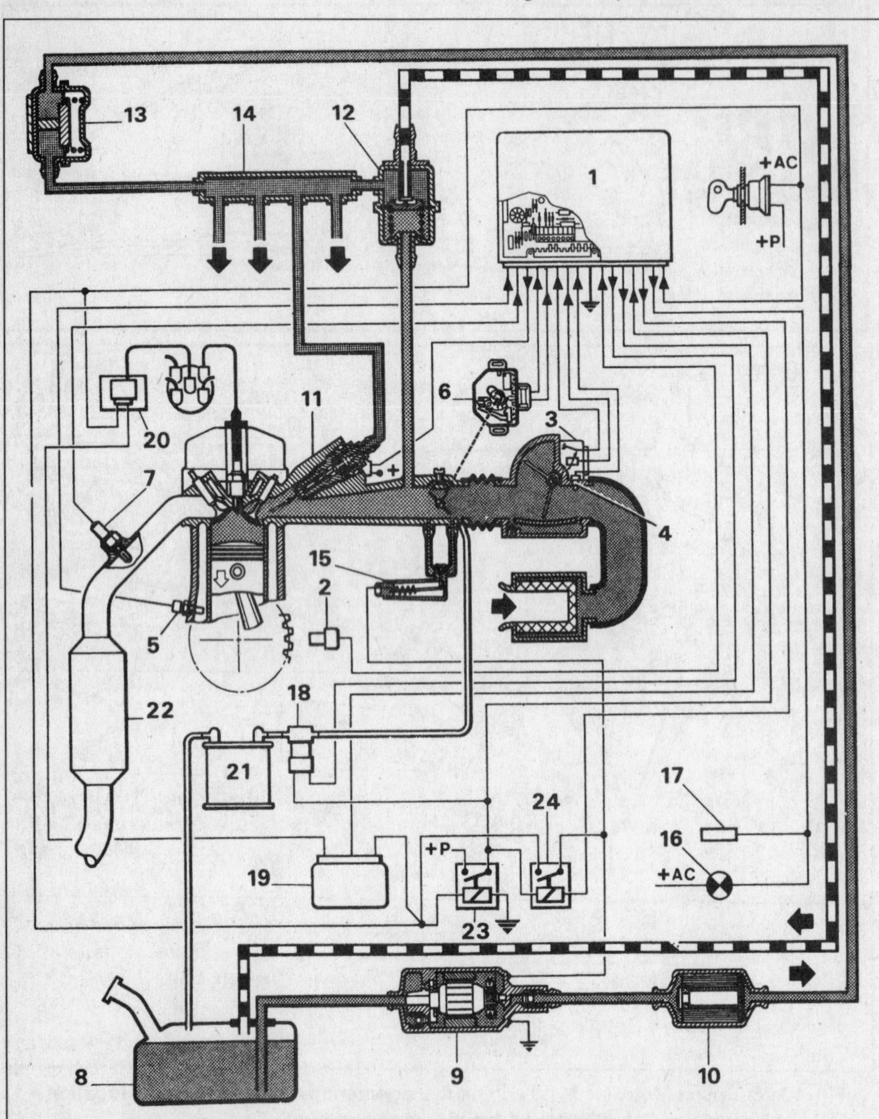

Fig. 13.29 Bosch Motronic M1.3 engine management system (Sec 8)

1 Electronic Control Unit (ECU)
2 Crankshaft speed/position sensor
3 Airflow sensor
4 Intake air temperature sensor
5 Coolant temperature sensor
6 Throttle switch
7 Lambda sensor
8 Fuel tank
9 Fuel pump – actually submerged in fuel tank
10 Fuel filter
11 Fuel injector(s)
12 Fuel pressure regulator
13 Fuel damper
14 Fuel rail
15 Supplementary air device
16 Diagnostic indicator lamp
17 Diagnostic socket
18 Charcoal canister-purge solenoid valve
19 Ignition amplifier module
20 Ignition HT coil – later type shown
21 Charcoal canister
22 Catalytic converter
23 System main relay
24 Fuel pump relay

PART B: BOSCH MOTRONIC M1.3

General description and precautions

This engine management system is fitted to the XU9JA/Z and XU9JA/L engines, and combines fuel injection and ignition systems under the control of the same ECU, to give the fine degree of engine control necessary for operation with a catalytic converter.

The fuel injection system is similar to that described for the LE2-Jetronic system in Chapter 3, Section 17, with the following differences.

The fuel supply system is essentially exactly the same, but on some models, a damper may be fitted to the feed line between the fuel filter and the fuel rail, to reduce the noise arising from pressure variations in the system as the injectors open and close.

The fuel/air metering system differs in that no adjustment of the idle mixture is possible; the mixture is controlled automatically by the ECU in response to signals from the Lambda sensor. In addition, the ECU now receives information on engine speed and piston position from a crankshaft speed/position sensor. This is bolted to the clutch housing, to register with the flywheel teeth; a reference point defined by a zone equal to two missing teeth (the flywheel has 60) allows the ECU to calculate engine speed, and to recognise the TDC position.

The Lambda sensor, screwed into the exhaust front section in front of the catalytic converter, provides the ECU with constant feedback which enables it to adjust the mixture continuously - 'closed-loop' control - to provide the best possible conditions for the catalytic converter to operate.

Until the sensor is fully warmed-up, it gives no feedback so, when the engine is started from cold, the ECU energises the sensor's heating element to speed up its response, thus reducing the amount of engine running time before closed-loop control is instigated. Meanwhile, the ECU uses pre-programmed values ('open-loop' control) to determine the correct injector pulse width. When the sensor reaches its normal operating temperature, its tip (which is sensitive to oxygen) sends the ECU a varying voltage depending on the

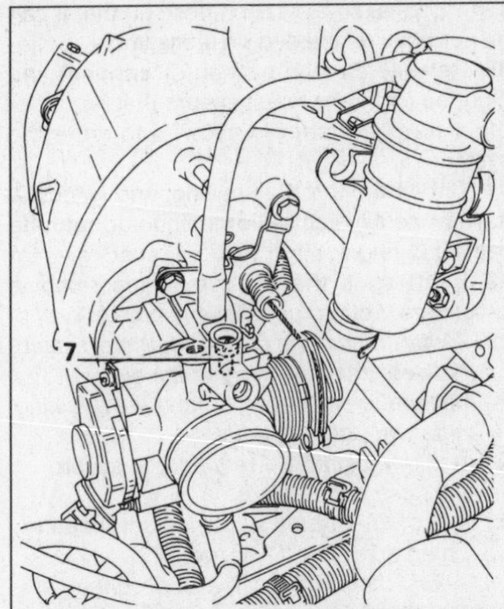

Fig. 13.30 Idle speed adjustment screw (7) – Motronic M1.3 (Sec 8)

amount of oxygen in the exhaust gases; if the intake air/fuel mixture is too rich, the exhaust gases are low in oxygen, so the sensor sends a low-voltage signal, the voltage rising as the mixture weakens and the amount of oxygen rises in the exhaust gases. Peak conversion efficiency of all major pollutants occurs if the intake air/fuel mixture is maintained at the chemically-correct ratio for the complete combustion of petrol of 14.7 parts (by weight) of air to 1 part of fuel (the 'stoichiometric' ratio). The sensor output voltage alters in a large step at this point, the ECU using the signal change as a reference point, and correcting accordingly the intake air/fuel mixture by altering the fuel injector pulse width.

In addition, the ECU energises the Evaporative Emissions Control System (see Part E of this Section), senses battery voltage, incorporates diagnostic capabilities, and can both receive and transmit information via the diagnostic connector, thus permitting engine diagnosis and tuning by Peugeot test equipment.

Refer to Chapter 3, Section 17 for precautions to be observed when working on the system components.

Throttle initial position - checking and adjustment

1 The throttle position is set in production, and will not normally require adjustment unless the throttle housing has been tampered with. Adjustment requires the use of Peugeot special tools, and should be carried out by a suitably-equipped Peugeot dealer.

Idle speed and mixture - adjustment

Note: *If the CO level reading is incorrect (or if any other symptom is encountered which causes you to suspect the presence of a fault), always check first that the air cleaner element is clean, that the spark plugs are in good condition and correctly gapped, that the engine breather and vacuum hoses are clear and undamaged, that there are no leaks in the air intake trunking, the throttle housing or the manifolds, and that the throttle cable is correctly adjusted (Chapter 3). If the engine is running very roughly, check the valve clearances and compression pressures (Chapter 1). Check also that all wiring is in good condition, with securely-fastened connectors, that the fuel filter has been renewed at the recommended intervals, and that the exhaust system is entirely free of air leaks which might upset the operation of the catalytic converter.*

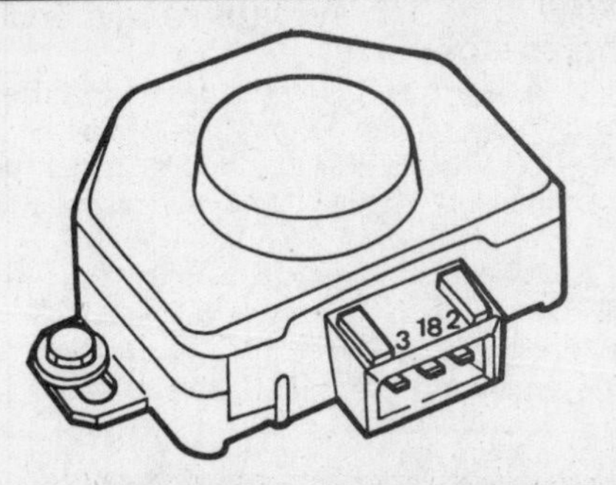

Fig. 13.31 Throttle switch and terminal numbers – Motronic M1.3 (Sec 8)

2 Before attempting to adjust the idle speed, the following conditions must be met:

(a) *The spark plugs and air cleaner must be in good condition (see note above).*
(b) *The throttle switch must be correctly adjusted.*
(c) *The engine must be at normal operating temperature, but the cooling fan must not be operating.*

3 Connect a tachometer to the engine in accordance with the equipment manufacturer's instructions, then run the engine at idle speed.

4 Turn the idle speed adjustment screw (7) in Fig. 13.30, to obtain the specified idle speed (refer to the Specifications).

5 Stop the engine and disconnect the tachometer on completion.

6 The idle mixture is not adjustable; if it is thought to be incorrect, the complete system must be checked by a Peugeot dealer using special test equipment until the fault is identified and cured.

Throttle switch - checking and adjustment

7 The throttle initial position must be correctly adjusted before attempting to adjust the throttle switch.

8 The throttle switch is located on the side of the throttle housing. To adjust it, first slacken the switch securing screws.

9 Turn the switch unit fully clockwise, then turn it back slowly until the idling contacts are heard to close.

10 Tighten the securing screws.

11 Pull the wiring plug from the switch, then connect an ohmmeter between terminals 2 and 18 in the switch - see Fig. 13.31. The ohmmeter should read zero.

12 Operate the throttle linkage, and the ohmmeter should read infinity.

13 If the readings are not correct, repeat the adjustment described in paragraphs 9 to 12 inclusive.

14 Connect the ohmmeter between switch terminals 3 and 18. The ohmmeter should read infinity.

15 Fully open the throttle; the ohmmeter should read zero.

16 If the specified reading cannot be obtained, renew the switch.

17 Reconnect the switch wiring plug on completion.

Air intake system - checking for leaks

18 Follow the procedure given in Chapter 3, Section 23, but check for leakage at the points arrowed in Fig. 13.32.

Component removal and refitting

Note: *For details of removal, refitting and servicing of components such as the air cleaner, throttle cable, fuel pump, fuel level transmitter, fuel tank, the ECU, the system relays and fuses, and the manifolds and exhaust system components, refer to Part A of this Section.*

Fuel filter

19 Refer to Chapter 3, Section 2; always depressurise the fuel system (Part A of this Section) before disturbing any of its connections.

Fuel damper

20 Depressurise the fuel system (Part A of this Section).

21 Release the clamps, then disconnect and plug the damper fuel hoses; ensure that no dirt or other foreign matter is allowed to enter the system.

22 Unbolt the damper and withdraw it.

23 Refitting is the reverse of the removal procedure; use new clamps, if required, to secure the hose connections.

Fuel pressure regulator

24 Refer to Chapter 3, Section 28; always depressurise the fuel system (Part A of this Section) before disturbing any of its connections.

Fuel rail

25 Refer to Chapter 3, Section 27; always depressurise the fuel system (Part A of this Section) before disturbing any of its connections.

Fuel injectors

Note: *If an injector is thought to be faulty, it is always worth trying the effect of a proprietary injector-cleaning treatment before renewing, perhaps unnecessarily, the injector(s). If this fails, the vehicle must be taken to a Peugeot*

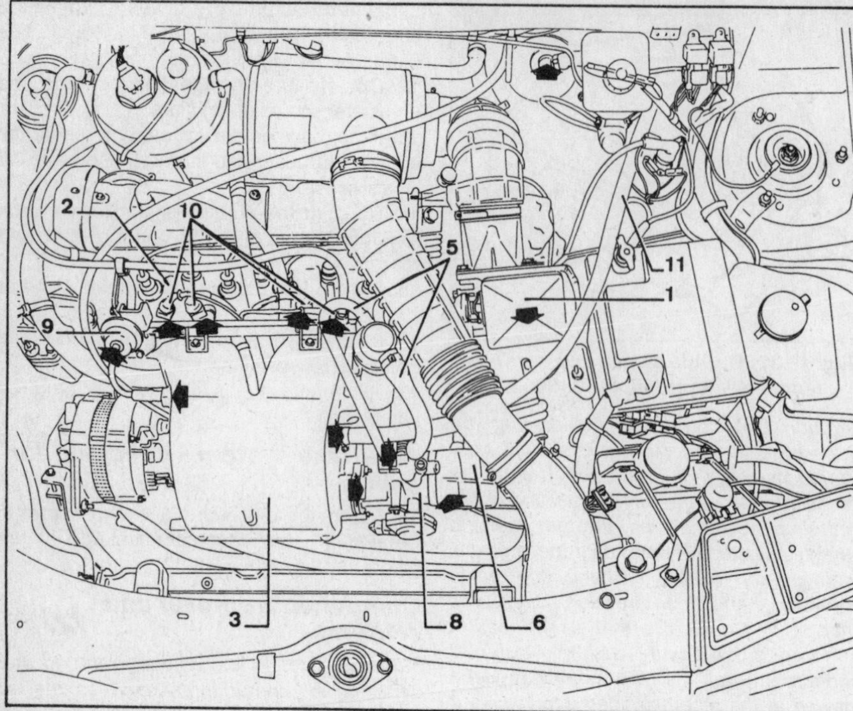

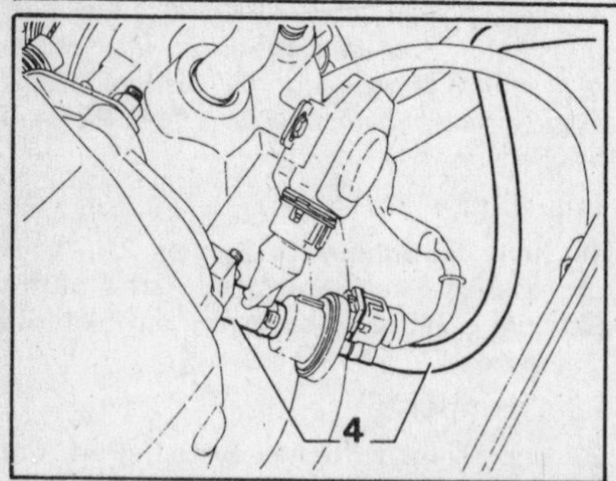

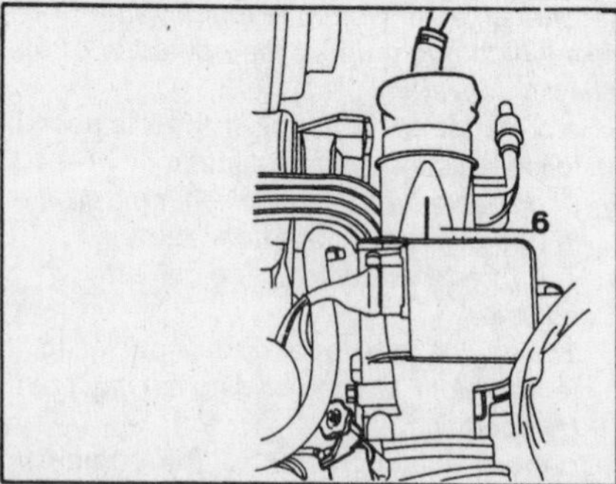

Fig. 13.32 Particular areas (arrowed) for checking air or fuel leakage – Motronic M1.3, left-hand drive model shown (Sec 8)

1 Airflow sensor
2 Cylinder head
3 Air distribution manifold
4 Charcoal canister-purge solenoid valve and hoses
5 Crankcase breather hoses
6 Air intake hose connections
8 Throttle housing
9 Fuel pressure regulator
10 Fuel injectors
11 Brake servo vacuum hose

dealer for full testing on the correct test equipment.

26 Refer to Chapter 3, Section 27; always depressurise the fuel system (Part A of this Section) before disturbing any of its connections.

Airflow sensor

27 Disconnect the battery earth lead.

28 Release the connector plug's locking clip, and disconnect the sensor wiring.

29 Release the clamps, then disconnect and plug the air intake hoses; ensure that no dirt or other foreign matter is allowed to enter the system.

30 Unbolt the sensor and withdraw it. Note that the intake air temperature sensor is not available separately from the airflow sensor; do not attempt to remove it.

31 Refitting is the reverse of the removal procedure; use new clamps, if required, to secure the hose connections.

Throttle switch

32 Disconnect the battery earth lead.

33 Release the connector plug's locking clip, and disconnect the switch wiring.

34 Unscrew the switch securing screws, and withdraw the switch.

35 Refitting is the reverse of the removal procedure; adjust the switch as described in paragraphs 7 to 17 above.

Throttle housing

36 Disconnect the battery earth lead.

37 Disconnect the throttle cable (Chapter 3).

38 Release the connector plug's locking clip, and disconnect the throttle switch wiring.

39 Disconnect all small-bore vacuum hoses and pipes connected to the housing; note the connections, or label each hose so that it can be correctly refastened on reassembly.

40 Release its clamp, then disconnect and plug the air intake hose; ensure that no dirt or other foreign matter is allowed to enter the system.

41 Unbolt the throttle housing, and withdraw it from the air distribution manifold; note the sealing O-ring.

42 Refitting is the reverse of the removal procedure, noting the following points.

(a) Always renew the O-ring sealing the joint between the housing and the air distribution manifold; tighten the retaining nuts and bolts securely.

(b) Use new clamps, if required, to secure the hose connections.

(c) Adjust the throttle switch as described in paragraphs 7 to 17 above.

(d) Adjust the throttle cable as described in Chapter 3.

Supplementary air device

43 Refer to Chapter 3, Section 25.

Coolant temperature sensor

44 This component is screwed into the coolant outlet housing on the left-hand end of the cylinder head (see Fig. 13.28); removal and refitting is as described in Chapter 2, Section 10.

Lambda sensor

45 The sensor is screwed into the exhaust front section, upstream of the catalytic converter. When handling the sensor, note that it is fragile; take care not to drop it, and do not allow it to contact fuel or silicone substances.

46 Start the engine, run it until it reaches normal operating temperature (indicated by the radiator cooling fan cutting in and out), then switch off and disconnect the battery. If access is required from below, jack up the front of the car and support it securely on axle stands, then unbolt the splash guard(s) as necessary from the underside of the engine compartment to gain access to the exhaust system from beneath.

47 Trace the wiring from the sensor itself to the connector, release it from any clips or ties, and disconnect the wiring before unscrewing the sensor.

48 Using a suitable spanner, and wearing heavy gloves to protect your hands from the hot exhaust system and sensor, unscrew the sensor and withdraw it.

49 On refitting, apply anti-seize compound to the threads of the sensor.

50 The sensor must be tightened securely; this will require the use either of a deep socket, slotted to allow for the sensor wiring, or a spanner.

Fuel injection system - complete test

51 Due to the need for specialist test equipment to carry out accurate fault diagnosis, any fault occurring with the system should be referred to a Peugeot dealer. Before doing this, however, make sure that the problem is not being caused by a disconnected or damaged hose or vacuum line, loose or disconnected wiring plug, or by some other simple fault which may become obvious under close visual inspection.

PART C: BOSCH MONO-JETRONIC A2.2

General description and precautions

This fuel injection system is fitted to models with a TU engine and catalytic converter. It is essentially a simple method of air/fuel metering, replacing the carburettor with a single injector mounted in a throttle body; this type of system is therefore also known as 'Throttle Body Injection' (TBI), 'Central Fuel Injection' (CFI) or 'single- (or mono-) point' injection. The whole system is best explained if considered as three sub-systems; the fuel delivery, air metering, and electrical control systems.

The fuel delivery system incorporates the fuel tank (with the electric fuel pump immersed inside it), the fuel filter, the fuel injector and pressure regulator (mounted in the throttle body), and the hoses and pipes connecting them. When the ignition is switched on, the pump is supplied with current, via the pump relay and fuse 14, under the control of the ECU; for safety reasons, the pump supply is maintained only for 1.5 seconds if the ignition is switched on and the engine is not running. The pump feeds through the fuel filter to the injector, fuel pressure being controlled by the pressure regulator, which lifts to allow excess fuel to return to the tank.

The air metering system includes the intake air temperature control system and the air cleaner, but its main components are in the throttle body assembly. This incorporates the injector (which sprays fuel onto the back of the throttle valve), the throttle potentiometer, the intake air temperature sensor, and the idle speed motor. The idle speed motor is controlled by the ECU to maintain the idle speed, and also incorporates an idle switch to inform the ECU when the throttle is fully released and in the idle position. **Note:** *There is no provision for adjusting the idle speed (or CO/mixture); if checking the idle speed, remember that it may vary under ECU control.*

The electrical side of the fuel injection system consists of the Electronic Control Unit (ECU) and all the sensors that provide it with information, as well as the actuators by which it controls the whole system's operation; the basic method of operation is as follows.

The ECU determines the exact volume of air entering the engine from the throttle valve potentiometer (which is linked to the throttle valve spindle, and sends the ECU information on the angle of throttle valve opening by transmitting a varying voltage) and the intake

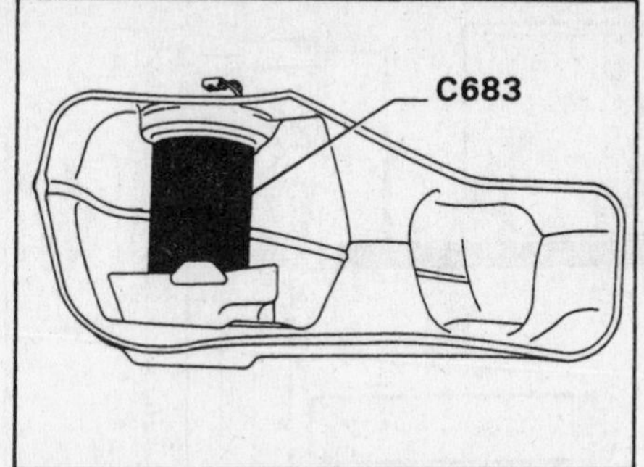

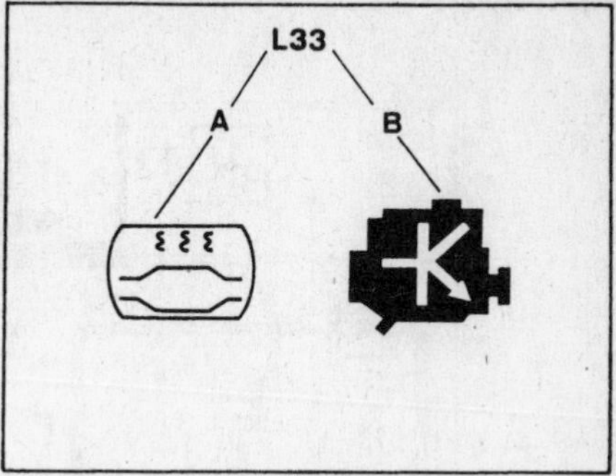

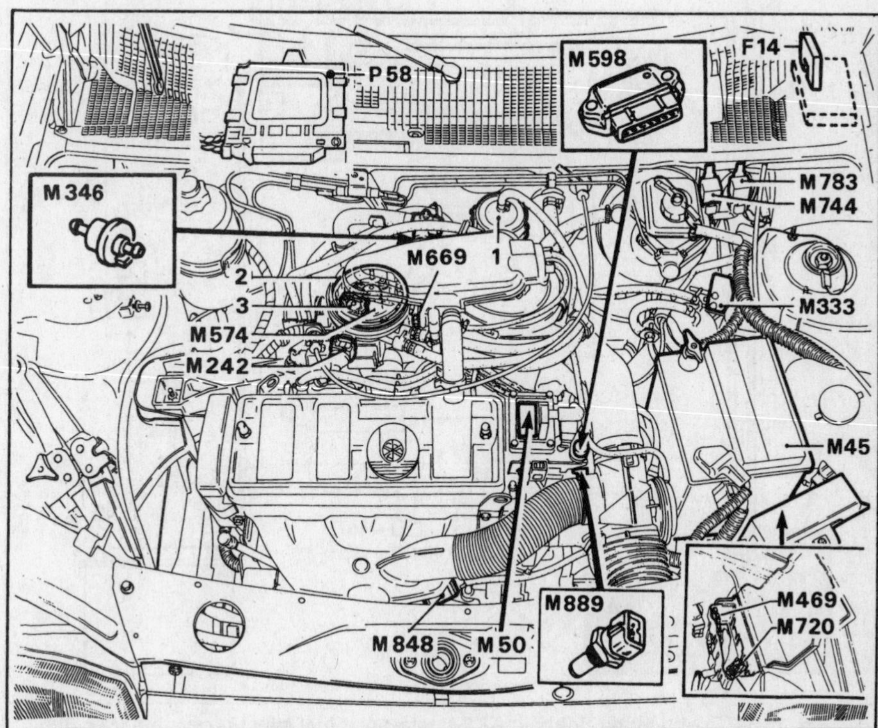

Fig. 13.33 Bosch Mono-Jetronic A2.2 single-point fuel injection system component location – left-hand drive model shown (Sec 8)

1 Fuel filter
2 Throttle body
3 Fuel pressure regulator
C683 Fuel pump – submerged in fuel tank
F14 Fuel pump fuse – in fusebox
L33 Diagnostic indicator lamps – in instrument panel:
A Catalytic converter
B Throttle body/ECU
M45 Battery
M50 Ignition HT coil
M242 Idle speed motor – incorporating idle switch
M333 Ignition timing advance cut-off solenoid valve
M346 Charcoal canister-purge solenoid valve
M469 Lambda sensor heater supply fuse holder
M574 Fuel injector (and intake air temperature sensor)
M598 Ignition amplifier module
M669 Throttle potentiometer
M720 Diagnostic socket
M744 Fuel pump relay
M783 System main relay
M848 Lambda sensor
M889 Coolant temperature sensor
P58 Electronic Control Unit (ECU) – behind facia

air temperature sensor (which informs the ECU of the temperature of the incoming air). Information on engine speed and firing position comes from the ignition HT coil, and from the idle switch (which indicates whether the throttle is in the idle position). The coolant temperature sensor supplies engine temperature information, and the Lambda sensor sends a varying voltage depending on the amount of oxygen in the exhaust gases

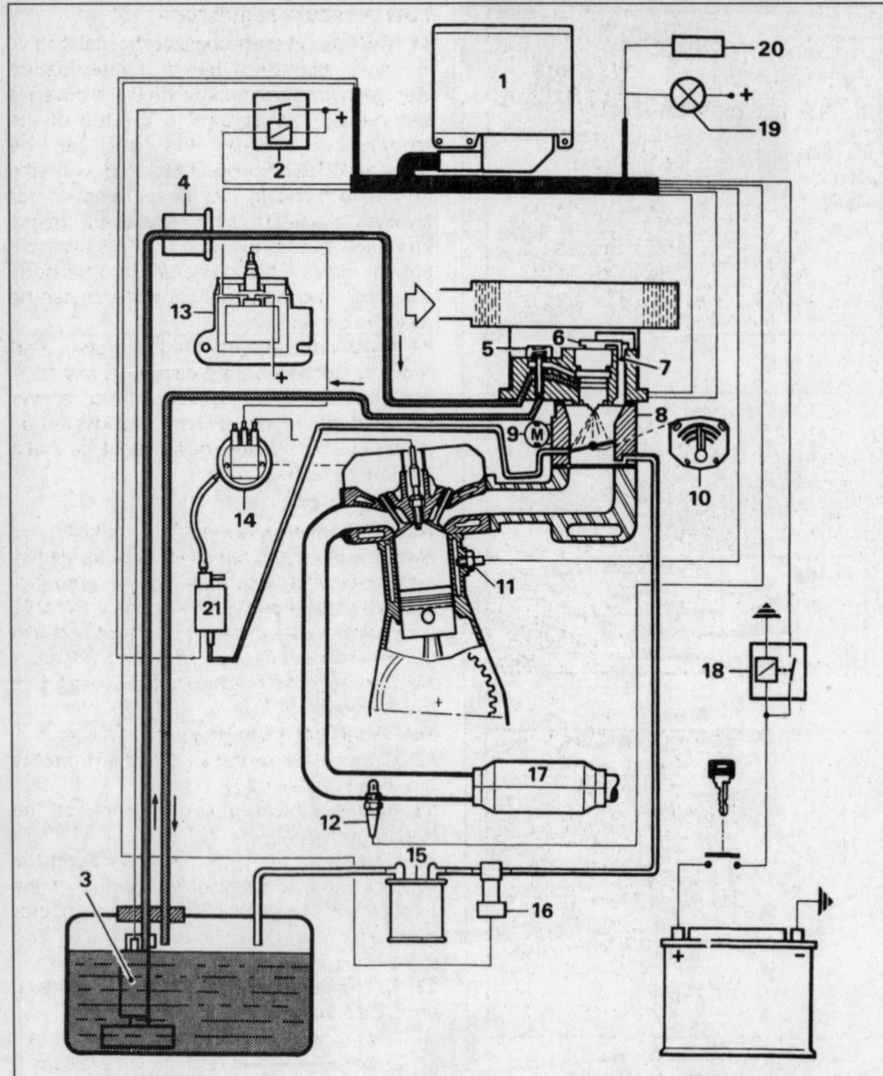

Fig. 13.34 Bosch Mono-Jetronic A2.2 single-point fuel injection system (Sec 8)

1 Electronic Control Unit (ECU)
2 Fuel pump relay
3 Fuel pump
4 Fuel filter
5 Fuel pressure regulator
6 Fuel injector
7 Intake air temperature sensor
8 Throttle body
9 Idle speed motor – incorporating idle switch
10 Throttle potentiometer
11 Coolant temperature sensor
12 Lambda sensor
13 Ignition HT coil
14 Distributor
15 Charcoal canister
16 Charcoal canister-purge solenoid valve
17 Catalytic converter
18 System main relay
19 Diagnostic indicator lamp
20 Diagnostic socket
21 Ignition timing advance cut-off solenoid valve

(for a full description of how the Lambda sensor functions, refer to Part B of this Section).

All these signals are compared by the ECU with set values pre-programmed (mapped) into its memory. Based on this information, the ECU selects the response appropriate to those values, and controls the fuel injector accordingly (opening it four times per engine cycle, and varying its pulse width - the length of time the injector is held open - to provide a richer or weaker mixture, as appropriate). The ECU also controls the idle speed motor (to control the idle speed), the fuel pump relay (controlling the fuel delivery), and the Lambda sensor. The mixture and idle speed are constantly varied by the ECU to provide the best settings for cranking, starting and engine warm-up (with either a hot or cold engine), idle, cruising and acceleration. The injector earth is switched off, both on the overrun to improve fuel economy and reduce exhaust emissions, and at maximum engine speed to prevent engine damage through over-revving. The ECU also energises the Evaporative Emissions Control System (see Part E of this Section) and, at idle speed or when decelerating, shuts off the distributor vacuum advance by earthing the ignition timing advance cut-off solenoid valve.

In addition, the ECU senses battery voltage, incorporates diagnostic capabilities, and can both receive and transmit information via the diagnostic connector, thus permitting engine diagnosis and tuning by Peugeot test equipment. If any of the sensor readings should ever be incorrect due to a fault, the ECU can also substitute fixed average values so that the engine can still run well enough for the car to be driven to a Peugeot dealer for attention.

Refer to Chapter 3, Section 17 for the precautions to be observed when working on the system components.

Idle speed and mixture - general

Note: *If the CO level reading is incorrect (or if any other symptom is encountered which causes you to suspect the presence of a fault), always check first that the air cleaner element is clean, that the spark plugs are in good condition and correctly gapped, that the engine breather and vacuum hoses are clear and undamaged, that there are no leaks in the air intake trunking, the throttle body or the manifolds, and that the throttle cable is correctly adjusted (Chapter 3). If the engine is running very roughly, check the valve clearances and compression pressures (Chapter 1). Check also that all wiring is in good condition, with securely-fastened connectors, that the fuel filter has been renewed at the recommended intervals, and that the exhaust system is entirely free of air leaks which might upset the operation of the catalytic converter.*

1 The idle speed is controlled by the idle speed motor, and is non-adjustable.

2 The idle mixture is controlled by the ECU and is non-adjustable.

3 If a fault is suspected, the vehicle should be taken to a Peugeot dealer, who will have the specialised tools and equipment to accurately test the complete system, diagnose the problem, and recommend the correct remedial action.

Throttle potentiometer - general

4 The throttle potentiometer is accurately matched to the throttle valve during manufacture, and is non-adjustable.

Warning: Do not attempt to 'adjust' the throttle potentiometer setting, or that of the stop screw on the throttle valve external linkage; if the accurately-matched relationship between these components is lost for any reason, they must be replaced. At the time of writing, this means renewing the entire throttle body assembly.

Air intake system - checking for leaks

5 Follow the procedure given in Chapter 3, Section 23, but check for leakage at the points arrowed in Fig. 13.35.

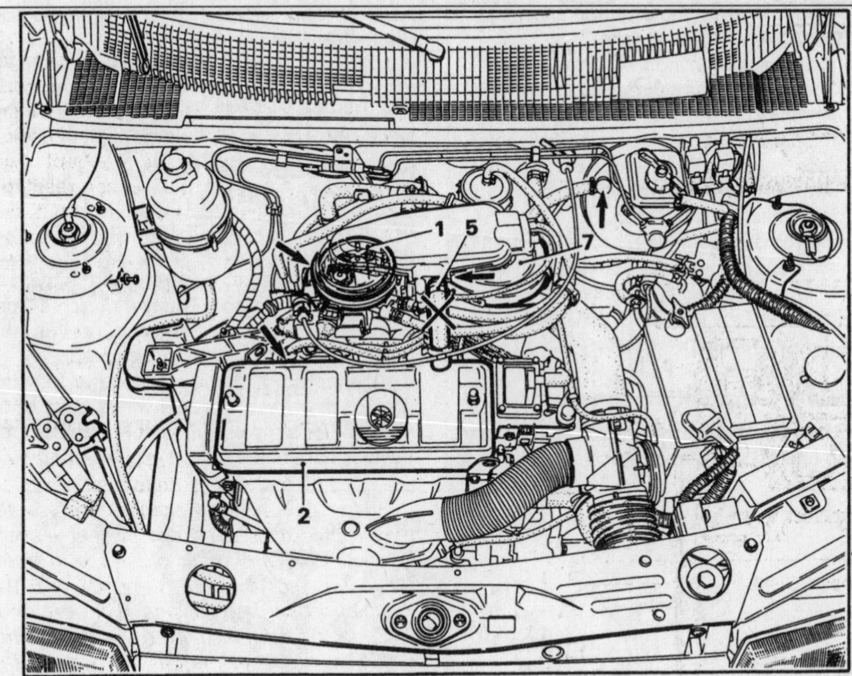

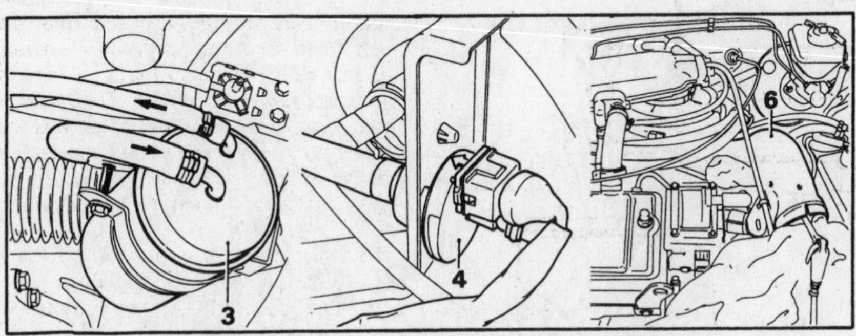

Fig. 13.35 Particular areas (arrowed) for checking air or fuel leakage – Mono-Jetronic A2.2, left-hand drive model shown (Sec 8)

1 *Throttle body*
2 *Cylinder head*
3 *Charcoal canister*
4 *Charcoal canister-purge solenoid valve*
5 *Crankcase breather pipe*
6 *Air intake hose*
7 *Air cleaner*

Component removal and refitting

Note: *For details of removal, refitting and servicing of components such as the air cleaner, throttle cable, fuel pump, fuel level transmitter, fuel tank, the ECU, the system relays and fuses, and the manifolds and exhaust system components, refer to Part A of this Section.*

Fuel filter

6 Depressurise the fuel system (Part A of this Section).

7 Place wads of rag around the filter to catch any spilled fuel.

8 Release the clamps, then disconnect and plug the filter fuel hoses; ensure that no dirt or other foreign matter is allowed to enter the system, and note the connections or label each hose so that it can be correctly reconnected on reassembly.

9 Release the filter from its clamp, and withdraw it.

10 Refitting is the reverse of the removal procedure, noting the following points:

(a) *Ensure that the filter is positioned with the arrow marking on its side (indicating direction of fuel flow) pointing upwards, and with the feed hose to the throttle body connected to the filter's upper union.*

(b) *Use new clamps, if required, to secure the hose connections.*

(c) *Start the engine, and check carefully for signs of fuel leakage from any of the disturbed components.*

(d) *Dispose safely of the old filter - it will be highly inflammable, and may explode if thrown on a fire.*

Fuel pressure regulator

11 The fuel pressure regulator (consisting of a valve operated by a spring-loaded diaphragm and secured by the unit's cover) is secured by four screws to the top of the throttle body. While the unit can be dismantled for cleaning, if required (once the air intake trunking has been removed for access), it should not be disturbed unless absolutely necessary; note that it is available only as part of the complete throttle body assembly - no individual components can be renewed separately.

12 Always depressurise the fuel system (Part A of this Section) before disturbing any of its components. If the regulator cover is ever removed, note carefully how it is located on the throttle body before disturbing it, so that it is correctly refitted.

Fuel injector

Note: *If the injector is thought to be faulty, it is always worth trying the effect of a proprietary injector-cleaning treatment before renewing, perhaps unnecessarily, the injector. If this fails, the vehicle must be taken to a Peugeot dealer for full testing on the correct test equipment.*

13 Depressurise the fuel system (Part A of this Section).

14 Disconnect the battery earth lead.

15 Remove the air intake trunking from the top of the throttle body.

16 Release the clip and disconnect the injector wiring.

17 Undo the Torx-type screw securing the injector wiring connector to the top of the throttle body, carefully lift off the connector and withdraw the injector. Remove and discard the injector sealing rings.

18 Refitting is the reverse of the removal procedure, noting the following points.

(a) *Always renew both sealing rings; apply a smear of grease to each, to ease injector refitting.*

(b) *Refit the injector so that its connector pins align with the connector's terminals when the connector is correctly located on the top of the throttle body; take care not to bend the injector's connector pins, and ensure that good contact is made.*

(c) *Apply a few drops of a suitable thread-locking compound to the screw's threads, then tighten it carefully.*

(d) *Switch on the ignition, and check carefully for signs of fuel leaks; if any signs of leakage are detected, the problem must be rectified before the engine is started.*

Intake air temperature sensor

19 This is located in the fuel injector wiring connector, and is available only as part of the connector assembly. Removal is as described in paragraphs 13 to 16 above, refitting as in paragraph 18.

Idle speed motor

20 Disconnect the battery earth lead.

21 Release the connector plug's locking clip, and disconnect the wiring plug from the motor.

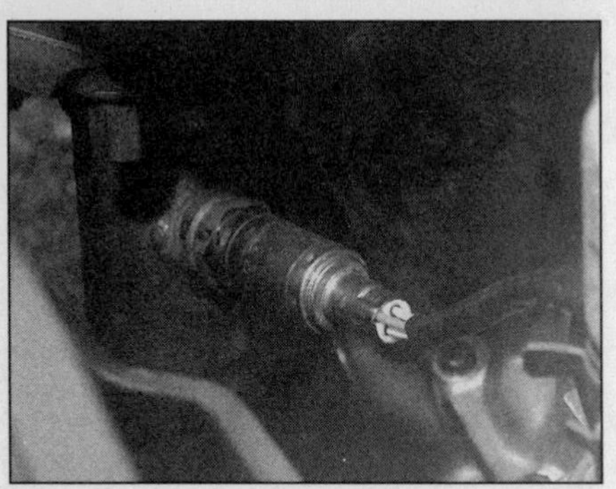

8C.36 Location of Lambda sensor – TU1 M/Z engine

22 Unscrew the securing screws and withdraw the motor.

23 Refitting is the reverse of the removal procedure; the motor will reset itself as soon as the engine is restarted.

Throttle potentiometer

24 As noted above, this component must not be disturbed, and is available only as part of the complete throttle body assembly.

Throttle body

25 Depressurise the fuel system (Part A of this Section).

26 Remove the air intake trunking from the top of the throttle body.

27 Disconnect the battery earth lead.

28 Disconnect the throttle cable (Chapter 3).

29 Release the connector plug's locking clips, then disconnect the wiring plugs from the fuel injector (removing the rubber throttle body/trunking seals to release the wiring), from the idle speed motor, and from the throttle potentiometer.

30 Disconnect the fuel hoses from their unions, and plug them to prevent loss of fuel and the entry of dirt; note the connections, and label them to ensure correct refitting. Be prepared for fuel spillage, and take suitable safety precautions.

31 Disconnect the vacuum hoses and pipes from the body unions; note the connections, or label each so that it can be correctly refastened on reassembly.

32 Undo the large screws securing the throttle body to the inlet manifold, and withdraw the body assembly; peel off and discard the gasket.

33 If required, the throttle body's upper and lower sections may be separated by removing the securing screws; note that a new gasket must be fitted on reassembly. As noted above, **do not** disturb the throttle potentiometer. The fuel inlet and return unions may be unscrewed and the vacuum hose unions may be detached, but note that new sealing rings must be fitted on reassembly, and the unions must be fastened securely.

34 Refitting is the reverse of the removal procedure, noting the following points.

(a) Renew all gaskets and seals, and use suitable thread-locking compound where applicable.

(b) Check the throttle cable operation and adjustment (Chapter 3).

(c) When reconnecting the vacuum hoses and pipes, ensure that they are correctly fastened, as noted on removal.

(d) Ensure that the fuel hoses are correctly reconnected; the direction of fuel flow is shown by arrows cast into the throttle body next to each union.

(e) Switch on the ignition, and check carefully for signs of fuel leaks from all disturbed unions; if any signs of leakage are detected, the problem must be rectified before the engine is started.

Coolant temperature sensor

35 This component is screwed into the left-hand end of the cylinder head (see Fig. 13.33); removal and refitting is as described in Chapter 2, Section 10.

Lambda sensor

36 The procedure is as described in Part B (paragraphs 45 to 50) of this Section (photo).

Fuel injection system - complete test

37 Due to the need for specialist test equipment to carry out accurate fault diagnosis, any fault occurring in the system should be referred to a Peugeot dealer. Before doing this, however, make sure that the problem is not being caused by a disconnected or damaged hose or vacuum line, loose or disconnected wiring plug, or by some other simple fault which may become obvious under close visual inspection.

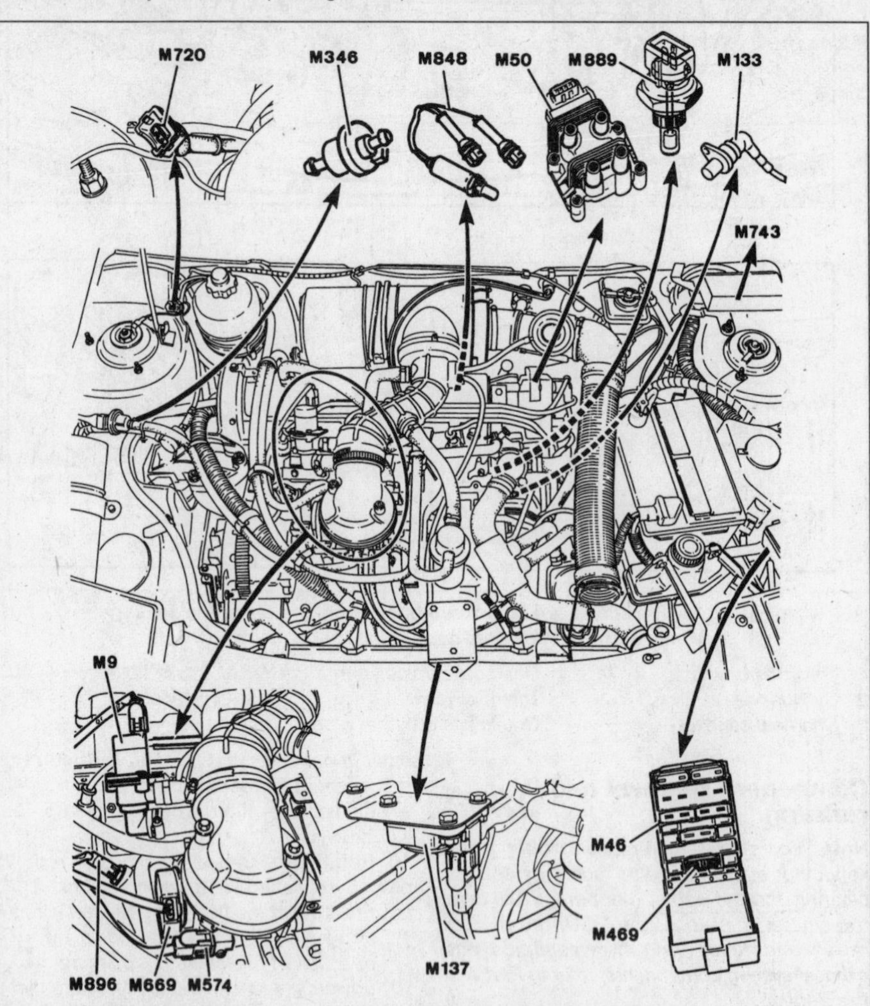

Fig. 13.36 MMBA G5 engine management system component location – left-hand drive model shown (Sec 8)

M9 Idle regulation solenoid valve
M46 Battery plus unit
M50 Ignition HT coil
M133 Crankshaft speed/position sensor
M137 Manifold absolute pressure sensor
M346 Charcoal canister-purge solenoid valve
M469 Lambda sensor heater supply fuse
M574 Fuel injector
M669 Throttle potentiometer
M720 Diagnostic socket
M743 Not fitted
M848 Lambda sensor
M889 Coolant temperature sensor
M896 Intake air temperature sensor

PART D: MMBA G5 AND G6

General description and precautions

This engine management system was developed by the MMBA company (a consortium formed by Magneti Marelli, Solex and Weber); it is fitted to the XU5M engines, and combines fuel injection and ('distributorless') ignition systems under the control of the same ECU, to give the fine degree of engine regulation necessary for operation with a catalytic converter.

There are two versions of the system, differing principally in the device used to maintain the idle speed; the first (MMBA G5) is fitted to the XU5M2/Z (BDY) engine, and uses an idle regulation solenoid valve. The second (MMBA G6), a development of the G5 version, is fitted to the XU5M3/Z and XU5M3/L (BDY) engines, and uses a stepper motor for this function.

The fuel injection side of the system is essentially a simple method of air/fuel metering, replacing the carburettor with a single injector mounted in a throttle body; this type of system is therefore also known as 'Throttle Body Injection' (TBI), 'Central Fuel Injection' (CFI) or 'single- (or mono-) point' injection. The whole system is best explained if considered as three sub-systems; the fuel delivery, air metering, and electrical control systems.

The fuel delivery system incorporates the fuel tank (with the electric fuel pump immersed inside it), the fuel filter, the fuel injector and pressure regulator (mounted in the throttle body), and the hoses and pipes connecting them. When the ignition is switched on, the pump is supplied with current, via the pump relay and fuse 14, under the control of the ECU; for safety reasons, the pump supply is maintained only for 1 to 2 seconds if the ignition is switched on and the engine is not running. The pump feeds through the fuel filter to the injector, fuel pressure being controlled by the pressure regulator, which lifts to allow excess fuel to return to the tank.

The air metering system includes the intake air temperature control system and the air cleaner, but its main components are in the throttle body assembly. This incorporates the injector, which sprays fuel on to the back of the throttle valve, and the throttle potentiometer. The idle speed is controlled by the ECU, using either an idle regulation solenoid valve (MMBA G5) or an idle regulation stepper motor (MMBA G6) to alter the amount of air that is allowed to bypass the throttle valve. **Note:** *There is no provision for the adjusting the idle speed; if checking the idle speed, remember that it may vary under ECU control.*

The electrical side of the fuel injection system consists of the Electronic Control Unit (ECU) and all the sensors that provide it with information, as well as the actuators by which it controls the whole system's operation; the basic method of operation is as follows - note that the ignition system is controlled by the same ECU, and is described in Section 9 of this Chapter.

The manifold absolute pressure (MAP) sensor is connected by a hose to the inlet manifold; variations in manifold pressure are converted into graduated electrical signals, which are used by the ECU to determine the load on the engine. The throttle valve potentiometer is linked to the throttle valve spindle, and sends the ECU information on the rate of throttle opening by transmitting a varying voltage. Information on engine speed and crankshaft position comes from the crankshaft speed/position sensor. The intake air temperature sensor informs the ECU of the temperature of the incoming air, while the coolant temperature sensor gives it the engine temperature. The Lambda sensor sends a varying voltage depending on the amount of oxygen in the exhaust gases (for a full description of how the Lambda sensor functions, refer to Part B of this Section).

All these signals are compared by the ECU with set values pre-programmed (mapped) into its memory. Based on this information, the ECU selects the response appropriate to those values, and accordingly controls the ignition HT coil (varying the ignition timing as required), the fuel injector (varying its pulse width - the length of time the injector is held open - to provide a richer or weaker mixture, as appropriate), the idle regulation device (controlling the idle speed), the fuel pump relay (controlling the fuel delivery), and the Lambda sensor. The mixture, idle speed and ignition timing are constantly varied by the ECU, to provide the best settings for cranking, starting and engine warm-up (with either a hot or cold engine), idle, cruising and acceleration. The injector earth is switched off on the overrun, to improve fuel economy and

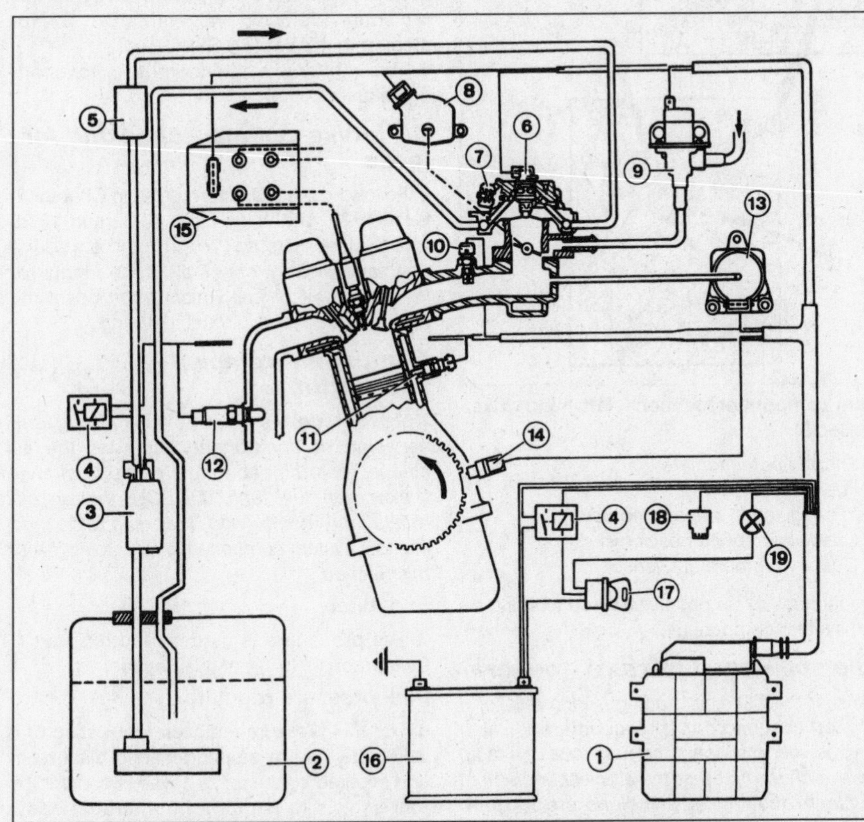

Fig. 13.37 MMBA G5 engine management system (Sec 8)

1 Electronic Control Unit (ECU) – behind facia
2 Fuel tank
3 Fuel pump – actually submerged in fuel tank (not as shown)
4 System main relay and fuel pump relay – next to ECU
5 Fuel filter
6 Fuel injector
7 Fuel pressure regulator
8 Throttle potentiometer
9 Idle regulation solenoid valve
10 Intake air temperature sensor
11 Coolant temperature sensor
12 Lambda sensor
13 Manifold absolute pressure sensor
14 Crankshaft speed/position sensor
15 Ignition HT coil
16 Battery
17 Ignition switch
18 Diagnostic socket
19 Diagnostic indicator lamp
***Note:** Refer to Fig. 13.39 for details of Evaporative Emission Control System components.*

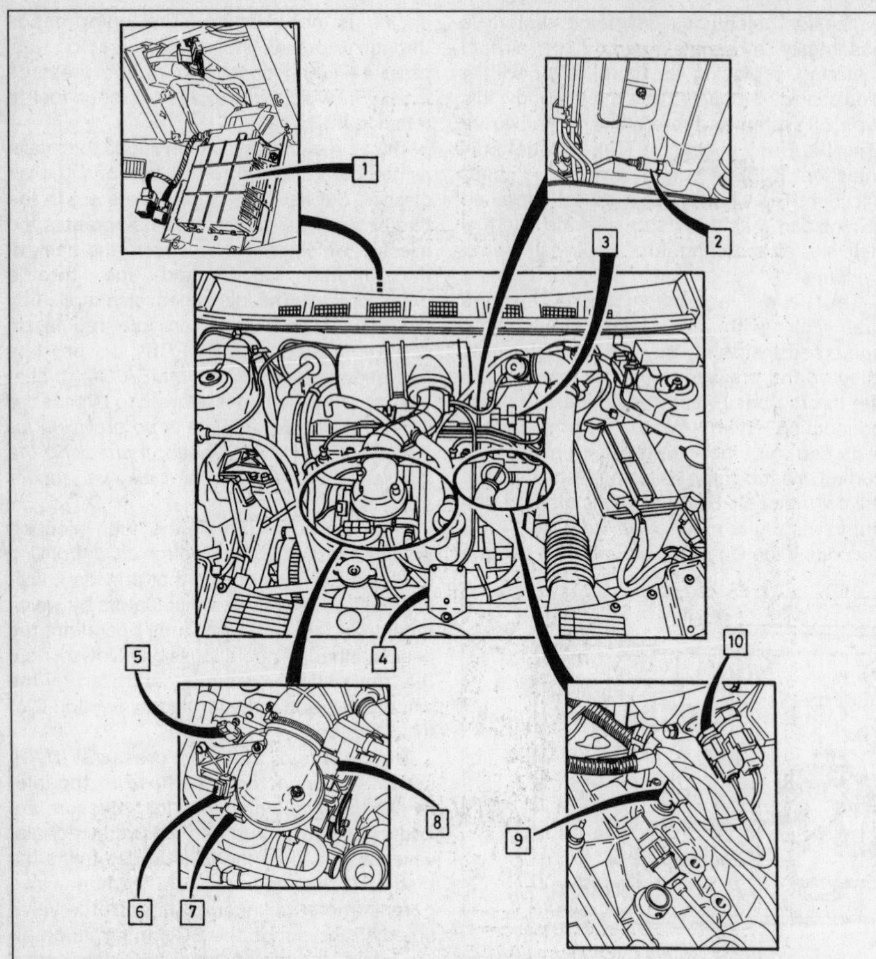

Fig. 13.38 MMBA G6 engine management system component location – left-hand drive model shown (Sec 8)

1 *Electronic Control Unit (ECU)*
2 *Lambda sensor*
3 *Ignition HT coil*
4 *Manifold absolute pressure sensor*
5 *Intake air temperature sensor*
6 *Throttle potentiometer*
7 *Fuel injector*
8 *Idle regulation stepper motor*
9 *Crankshaft speed/position sensor*
10 *Coolant temperature sensor*

reduce exhaust emissions. The ECU also energises the Evaporative Emissions Control System (see Part E of this Section) and, on models equipped with automatic transmission, receives signals from the transmission selector lever control and starter inhibitor switches, modifying its outputs according to the selector position engaged by the driver, to provide smoother transmission operation.

In addition, the ECU senses battery voltage, incorporates diagnostic capabilities, and can both receive and transmit information via the diagnostic connector, thus permitting engine diagnosis and tuning by Peugeot test equipment. If any of the sensor readings should ever be incorrect due to a fault, the ECU can also substitute fixed average values so that the engine can still run well enough for the car to be driven to a Peugeot dealer for attention.

Refer to Chapter 3, Section 17 for the precautions to be observed when working on the system components.

Idle speed and mixture - general

Note: *If the CO level reading is incorrect (or if any other symptom is encountered which causes you to suspect the presence of a fault) always check first that the air cleaner element is clean, that the spark plugs are in good condition and correctly gapped, that the engine breather and vacuum hoses are clear and undamaged, that there are no leaks in the air intake trunking, the throttle body or the manifolds, and that the throttle cable is correctly adjusted (Chapter 3). If the engine is running very roughly, check the valve clearances and compression pressures (Chapter 1). Check also that all wiring is in good condition, with securely-fastened connectors, that the fuel filter has been renewed at the recommended intervals, and that the exhaust system is entirely free of air leaks which might upset the operation of the catalytic converter.*

1 The idle speed is controlled by the idle regulation solenoid valve (MMBA G5) or stepper motor (MMBA G6), and is non-adjustable.

2 The idle mixture is controlled by the ECU, and is non-adjustable.

3 If a fault is suspected, the vehicle should be taken to a Peugeot dealer, who will have the specialised tools and equipment accurately to test the complete system, diagnose the problem, and recommend the correct remedial action.

Throttle settings - general

Note: *Do not attempt to 'adjust' the throttle potentiometer setting, or that of the stop screw on the throttle valve external linkage.*

4 The throttle valve is set in production, and must **not** be disturbed. Remember that the valve opening at idle is a basic setting only, all idle speed control being carried out by the idle regulation solenoid valve (MMBA G5) or stepper motor (MMBA G6).

5 The throttle potentiometer is non-adjustable.

Air intake system - checking for leaks

6 Following the procedure given in Chapter 3, Section 23, and using Figs. 13.32 and 13.35 for guidance as to which points require special attention, check all components for leakage of air or fuel which might upset the system's electronic air/fuel metering.

Component removal and refitting

Note: *For details of removal, refitting and servicing of components such as the air cleaner, throttle cable, fuel pump, fuel level transmitter, fuel tank, the ECU, the system relays and fuses, and the manifolds and exhaust system components, refer to Part A of this Section.*

Fuel filter

7 The procedure is as described in Part C (paragraphs 7 to 10) of this Section.

Fuel pressure regulator

8 The fuel pressure regulator (consisting of a valve operated by a spring-loaded diaphragm and secured by the unit's cover) is secured by four screws to the top of the throttle body. While the unit can be dismantled for cleaning, if required (once the air intake trunking has been removed for access), it should not be disturbed unless absolutely necessary; note that it is available only as part of the complete throttle body assembly, no individual components can be renewed separately.

9 Always depressurise the fuel system (Part A of this Section) before disturbing any of its components. If the regulator cover is ever removed, note carefully how it is located on the throttle body before disturbing it, so that it is correctly refitted.

Fuel injector

Note: *If the injector is thought to be faulty, it is always worth trying the effect of a proprietary injector-cleaning treatment before condemning the injector. If this fails, the vehicle must be taken to a Peugeot dealer for full testing on the correct test equipment. Note that (at the time of writing), the injector does not appear to be available separately from the throttle body upper section assembly.*

10 Depressurise the fuel system (Part A of this Section).

11 Disconnect the battery earth lead.

12 Remove the air intake trunking from the top of the throttle body.

13 Release the locking clip and disconnect the injector wiring.

14 Undo the Torx-type screw securing the injector retainer plate to the top of the throttle body, lift off the retainer and withdraw the injector. The injector sealing rings should be renewed as a matter of course whenever the injector is disturbed (if they are available separately).

15 Refitting is the reverse of the removal procedure, noting the following points.

(a) *Always renew both sealing rings (see note above); apply a smear of grease to each, to ease injector refitting.*

(b) *Refit the injector so that its wiring terminals point to the front of the vehicle, and locate the edge of the retainer securely in the groove at the top of the injector.*

(c) *Apply a few drops of a suitable thread-locking compound to the screw's threads, then tighten it carefully.*

(d) *Switch on the ignition, and check carefully for signs of fuel leaks; if any signs of leakage are detected, the problem must be rectified before the engine is started.*

Throttle potentiometer

16 Disconnect the battery earth lead.

17 Release the locking clip, then disconnect the wiring plug from the potentiometer.

18 Unscrew the two securing screws, and withdraw the potentiometer.

19 Refitting is the reverse of the removal procedure, noting the following points.

(a) *Install the potentiometer when the throttle valve is fully closed, and ensure that the potentiometer adaptor seats correctly on the throttle valve spindle.*

(b) *Tighten the screws carefully.*

Idle regulation solenoid valve - MMBA G5

20 If improved access is required, remove the air intake trunking.

21 Disconnect the battery earth lead.

22 Release the locking clip, then disconnect the wiring plug from the valve.

23 Slacken the clamps and disconnect the air hoses from the valve, noting carefully their connections.

24 Unbolt the valve and withdraw it.

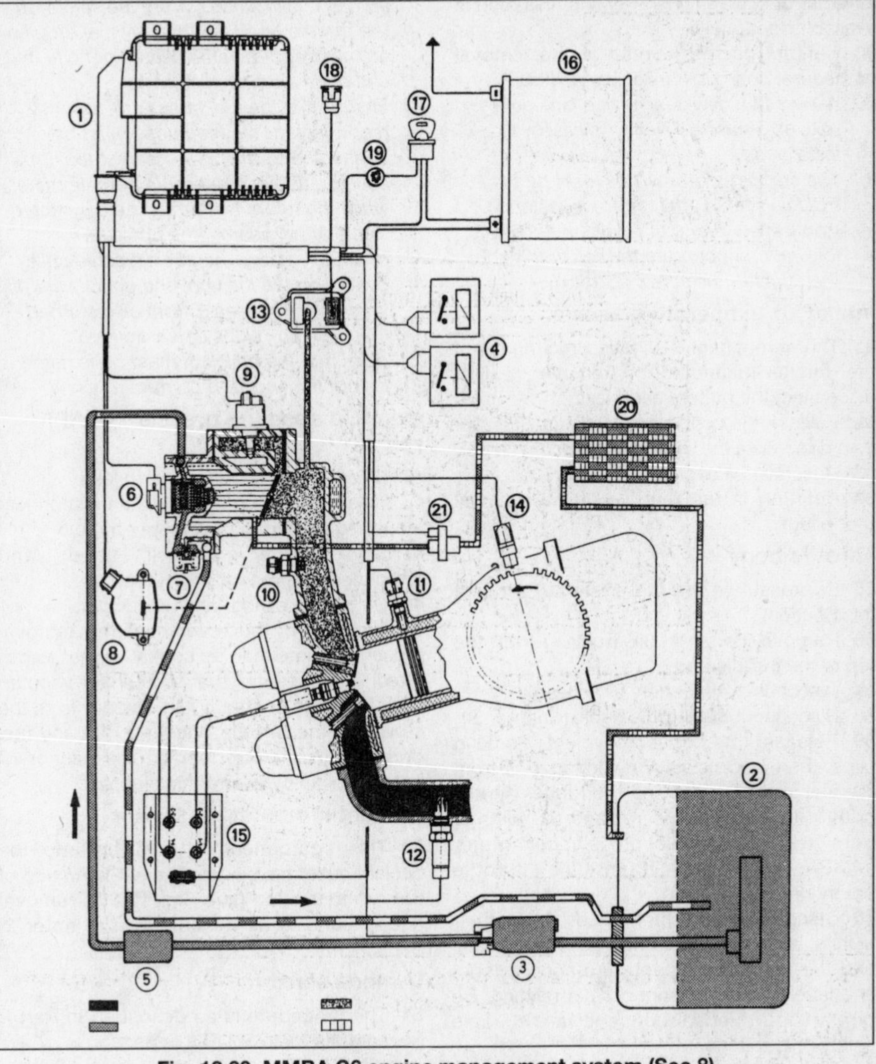

Fig. 13.39 MMBA G6 engine management system (Sec 8)

1 Electronic Control Unit (ECU) – behind facia
2 Fuel tank
3 Fuel pump – actually submerged in fuel tank (not as shown)
4 System main relay and fuel pump relay – next to ECU
5 Fuel filter
6 Fuel injector
7 Fuel pressure regulator
8 Throttle potentiometer
9 Idle regulation stepper motor
10 Intake air temperature sensor
11 Coolant temperature sensor
12 Lambda sensor
13 Manifold absolute pressure sensor
14 Crankshaft speed/position sensor
15 Ignition HT coil
16 Battery
17 Ignition switch
18 Diagnostic socket
19 Diagnostic indicator lamp
20 Charcoal canister
21 Charcoal canister-purge solenoid valve

25 Refitting is the reverse of the removal procedure, noting that the arrows cast on the valve's unions show the direction of airflow through the valve; from the air intake trunking into the valve, and out of the valve to the throttle body union. Ensure that the air hoses are securely fastened, so that there are no air leaks in the system.

Idle regulation stepper motor - MMBA G6

Note: *At the time of writing, it is not clear whether the stepper motor is available separately from the throttle body assembly or not; owners are advised to seek the advice of a Peugeot dealer before deciding on the course of action they wish to adopt if the stepper motor is thought to be faulty.*

26 If improved access is required, remove the air intake trunking.

27 Disconnect the battery earth lead.

28 Release the locking clip, then disconnect the wiring plug from the stepper motor.

29 Undo the two screws securing the stepper motor, then withdraw the stepper motor. The sealing ring should be renewed as a matter of course, whenever it is disturbed (if available separately).

30 Refitting is the reverse of the removal procedure, noting the following points.

(a) *Always fit a new sealing ring (see note above), greasing it lightly to ease installation.*
(b) *The stepper motor will be reset by the ECU as soon as the engine is restarted.*
(c) *Apply a few drops of a suitable thread-locking compound to the screw threads, then tighten the screws carefully.*

Intake air temperature sensor

31 This component is screwed into the top of the intake manifold. To remove it, first disconnect the battery earth lead.

32 Release the connector plug's locking clip, then disconnect the wiring plug from the sensor.

33 Unscrew the sensor and withdraw it.

34 Refitting is the reverse of the removal procedure.

Throttle body

35 Depressurise the fuel system (Part A of this Section).

36 Remove the air intake trunking from the top of the throttle body.

37 Disconnect the battery earth lead.

38 Disconnect the throttle cable (Chapter 3).

39 Release the connector plug's locking clips, then disconnect the wiring plugs from the fuel injector (removing the rubber throttle body/trunking seals to release the wiring), from the idle regulation stepper motor (MMBA G6), and from the throttle potentiometer.

40 Disconnect the fuel hoses from their unions, and plug them to prevent loss of fuel and the entry of dirt; note the connections, and label them to ensure correct refitting. Be prepared for fuel spillage, and take suitable safety precautions.

41 Disconnect the vacuum hoses and pipes from the body unions; note the connections, or label each so that it can be correctly refastened on reassembly.

42 Using a spanner on the hexagonal sections, unscrew the large studs securing the throttle body to the inlet manifold, and withdraw the body assembly; peel off and discard the gasket.

43 If required, the throttle body's upper and lower sections may be separated by removing the securing screws; note that a new gasket must be fitted on reassembly.

44 Refitting is the reverse of the removal procedure, noting the following points.

(a) *Renew all gaskets and seals, and use suitable thread-locking compound where applicable.*
(b) *Check the throttle cable operation and adjustment (Chapter 3).*
(c) *When reconnecting the vacuum hoses and pipes, ensure that they are correctly fastened, as noted on removal.*
(d) *As no fuel vapour trap is fitted, it is essential that the manifold absolute pressure sensor vacuum hose is routed so that it falls steadily from the sensor to the throttle body, so that any fuel droplets are not trapped in the sensor or hose, but can drain into the inlet port.*
(e) *Ensure that the fuel hoses are correctly reconnected; the feed hose must be connected to the union nearest the injector, above the throttle potentiometer, while the return hose must be connected to the union nearest the pressure regulator, above the throttle cable pulley.*
(f) *Switch on the ignition, and check carefully for signs of fuel leaks from all disturbed unions; if any signs of leakage are detected, the problem must be rectified before the engine is started.*

Manifold absolute pressure (MAP) sensor

45 Disconnect the battery earth lead.

46 Release the locking clip, then disconnect the wiring plug from the stepper motor.

47 Slacken the clamp (if fitted), and disconnect the sensor's vacuum hose.

48 Unbolt the sensor and withdraw it.

49 Refitting is the reverse of the removal procedure; note that, as no fuel vapour trap is fitted, it is essential that the sensor vacuum hose is routed so that it falls steadily from the sensor to the throttle body, so that any fuel droplets are not trapped in the sensor or hose, but can drain into the inlet port.

Coolant temperature sensor

50 This component is screwed into the coolant outlet housing on the left-hand end of the cylinder head (see Fig. 13.38); removal and refitting is as described in Chapter 2, Section 10.

Lambda sensor

51 The procedure is as described in Part B (paragraphs 45 to 50) of this Section.

Starter inhibitor switch - automatic transmission

52 The switch is screwed into the front of the transmission casing (see Fig. 13.40). It serves two functions; to prevent the starter motor from operating if any selector position other than 'P' or 'N' is selected, and to actuate the reversing lights when selector position 'R' is selected.

53 To remove the switch, disconnect the battery earth lead and the switch wires, then unscrew the switch - plug the aperture swiftly, to minimise the loss of transmission fluid.

54 Refitting is the reverse of the removal procedure; tighten the switch to the specified torque wrench setting, reconnect the wiring and check the transmission fluid level (Section 14 of this Chapter), replacing any lost fluid.

Selector lever control switch - automatic transmission

55 At the time of writing, no information was available concerning the location, removal and refitting, or adjustment of this component.

Fuel injection system - complete test

56 Due to the need for specialist test equipment to carry out accurate fault diagnosis, any fault occurring in the system should be referred to a Peugeot dealer. Before doing this, however, make sure that the problem is not being caused by a disconnected or damaged hose or vacuum line, loose or disconnected wiring plug, or by some other simple fault which may become obvious under close visual inspection.

PART E: EVAPORATIVE EMISSIONS CONTROL SYSTEM

General description

An evaporative emissions control system is fitted, to minimise the escape into the atmosphere of unburned hydrocarbons. The system consists of a charcoal canister and a canister-purge solenoid valve mounted in the engine compartment, with a pair of valves and a degas tank (a small fuel vapour separator unit) located next to the fuel tank and filler tube, as well as the hoses connecting these components.

The fuel tank filler cap is sealed; the charcoal canister collects the petrol vapours generated in the tank when the vehicle is parked, and stores them until they can be cleared from the canister into the inlet tract, to be burned by the engine during normal combustion.

To ensure that the engine runs correctly when it is cold and/or idling, and to protect the catalytic converter from the effects of an over-rich mixture, the canister-purge solenoid valve is not opened by the ECU until the engine is under partial- or full-load; the valve solenoid is then modulated on and off to allow the stored vapour to pass into the inlet tract.

The valves allow air to enter the fuel tank in the normal way to replace fuel consumed when the engine is running.

Routine maintenance

1 No special maintenance operations are required, other than a general check of the security and condition of the system's components when the other fuel system components are checked at the intervals given in '*Routine maintenance*' at the front of this manual.

2 If any of the components are found to be worn, damaged or faulty, they must be renewed.

Component removal and refitting

3 The canister-purge solenoid valve is located either beneath the throttle switch (Motronic M1.3 - see Fig. 13.28), to the rear of the throttle body (Mono-Jetronic A2.2 - see Fig. 13.33), or on the right-hand inner wing panel (MMBA systems - see Fig. 13.36).

4 To remove the valve, first disconnect the battery earth lead and the valve wiring plug, then carefully note the connections of the two vent hoses before disconnecting them. Either remove the valve from its mounting bracket, or unbolt the bracket, as required.

5 To remove the canister, trace the hose from the canister-purge solenoid valve to the canister and note the canister's hose connections, or label them, to ensure that they are reconnected to their original unions. Disconnect the hoses, and unbolt the canister mounting clamp from the vehicle body. Dismantle the clamp and withdraw the canister.

6 The location of the valves and degas tank vary according to model and year, but can be traced from the fuel tank or the canister, along the underside of the vehicle. Release any clamps or ties securing the hoses, and unfasten the clips to disconnect the hoses from each component.

7 Refitting is the reverse of the removal procedure; renew any clamps, ties or clips damaged during removal.

PART F: EXHAUST SYSTEM

Catalytic converter - general information and precautions

The exhaust gases of any internal combustion engine (however efficient or well-tuned) which burns petrol consist largely (approximately 99%) of nitrogen (N_2), carbon dioxide (CO_2), oxygen (O_2), other inert gases, and water vapour (H_2O). The remaining 1% is made up of the noxious materials which are currently seen (CO_2 apart) as the major polluters of the environment; carbon monoxide (CO), unburned hydrocarbons (HC), oxides of nitrogen (NO_x) and some solid matter, including a small lead content.

Left to themselves, most of these pollutants are thought eventually to break down naturally (CO and NO_x, for example, break down in the upper atmosphere to release CO_2) having first caused ground-level environmental problems, but the massive increase world-wide in the use of motor cars and the current popular concern for the environment has caused the introduction in most countries of legislation, in varying stages of severity, to combat the problem.

The device most commonly used to clean up car exhausts is the catalytic converter. It is fitted into the car's exhaust system, and uses precious metals (platinum and palladium or rhodium) as catalysts to speed up the reaction between the pollutants and the oxygen in the car's exhaust gases. The carbon monoxide (CO) and hydrocarbons (HC) are oxidised to form carbon dioxide and water vapour (CO_2 and H_2O), and (in the 'three-way' type of catalytic converter) the oxides of nitrogen (NO_x) are reduced to nitrogen (N_2). **Note:** *The catalytic converter is not a 'filter' in the physical sense; its function is to promote a chemical reaction, but it is not itself affected by that reaction.*

The converter consists of an element (or 'substrate') of ceramic honeycomb, coated with a combination of precious metals in such a way as to produce a vast surface area over which the exhaust gases must flow; the whole being mounted in a stainless-steel box. A simple 'oxidation' (or 'two-way') catalytic converter can deal with CO and HC only, while a 'reduction' (or 'three-way') catalytic converter can deal with CO, HC and NO_x. Three-way catalytic converters are further sub-divided into 'open-loop' (or 'uncontrolled') converters, and 'closed-loop' (also known as 'controlled' or 'regulated') converters. 'Open-loop' converters can remove 50 to 70% of pollutants, while the 'closed-loop' type (fitted to the models covered in this manual) can remove over 90% of pollutants.

The catalytic converter is a reliable and simple device, which needs no maintenance in itself, but there are some facts of which an owner should be aware, if the converter is to function properly for its full service life.

(a) *DO NOT use leaded petrol in a car equipped with a catalytic converter - the lead will coat the precious metals, reducing their converting efficiency, and will eventually destroy the converter; it will also seriously affect the operation of the Lambda sensor. Opinions vary as to how much leaded fuel is necessary to affect the converter's performance, and whether it can recover even if only unleaded petrol is used afterwards; the best course of action is, therefore, to assume the worst and to ensure that NO leaded petrol is used at any time. Note that Peugeot specify that the Lambda sensor must be renewed if the vehicle has been run for any time at all on leaded petrol.*

(b) *Always keep the ignition and fuel systems well-maintained in accordance with the manufacturer's schedule (see 'Routine maintenance') - particularly, ensure that the air cleaner filter element, the fuel filter(s) and the spark plugs are renewed at the correct interval - if the intake air/fuel mixture is allowed to become too rich due to neglect, the unburned surplus will enter and burn in the catalytic converter, overheating the element and eventually destroying the converter.*

(c) *If the engine develops a misfire, do not drive the car at all (or at least as little as possible) until the fault is cured - the misfire will allow unburned fuel to enter the converter, which will result in its overheating, as noted above. For the same reason, do not persist too long if the engine ever refuses to start (either trace the problem and cure it yourself, or have the car checked immediately by a qualified mechanic).*

(d) *Never allow the car to run out of petrol.*

(e) *The diagnostic indicator light (the outline of an engine with a symbol superimposed - where fitted) will light when the ignition is switched on and the engine is started, then will go out. While it may light briefly while the engine is running, provided it goes out again immediately and stays out, this is unimportant. If it lights and stays on while the engine is running, however, seek the advice of a Peugeot dealer as soon as possible; a fault has occurred in the fuel injection/ignition system which, apart from increasing fuel consumption and impairing the engine's performance, may damage the catalytic converter.*

(f) *DO NOT push- or tow-start the car - this will soak the catalytic converter in unburned fuel, causing it to overheat when the engine does start - see (b) above.*

(g) *DO NOT switch off the ignition at high engine speeds (ie, do not 'blip' the throttle immediately before switching off the engine). If the ignition is switched off at anything above idle speed, unburned fuel will enter the (very hot) catalytic converter, with the possible risk of its igniting on the element and damaging the converter.*

(h) *Try to avoid repeated successive cold starts with short journeys - if the converter is never allowed to reach its proper working temperature, it will gather unburned fuel, allowing some to pass into the atmosphere and the rest to soak the element, causing it to overheat when the engine does start - see (b) above.*

(i) *DO NOT use fuel or engine oil additives - these may contain substances harmful to the catalytic converter.*

(j) *DO NOT continue to use the car if the engine burns oil to the extent of leaving a visible trail of blue smoke - the unburned carbon deposits will clog the converter passages and reduce its efficiency; in severe cases, the element will overheat.*

(k) *Remember that the catalytic converter operates at very high temperatures - hence the heat shields on the car's underbody - and the casing will become hot enough to ignite combustible materials which brush against it. DO NOT, therefore, park the car in dry undergrowth, over long grass or piles of dead leaves.*

(l) *Remember that the catalytic converter is FRAGILE (it contains ceramics) - do not strike it with tools during servicing work, take great care when working on the exhaust system, ensure that the converter is well clear of any jacks or other lifting gear used to raise the car, and do not drive the car over rough ground, road humps, etc., in such a way as to 'ground' the exhaust system.*

(m) *In some cases, particularly when the car is new and/or is used for stop/start driving, a sulphurous smell (like that of* *rotten eggs) may be noticed from the exhaust. This is common to many catalytic converter-equipped cars, and seems to be due to the small amount of sulphur found in some petrols reacting with hydrogen in the exhaust to produce hydrogen sulphide (H_2S) gas; while this gas is toxic, it is not produced in sufficient amounts to be a problem. Once the car has covered a few thousand miles, the problem should disappear - in the meanwhile, a change of driving style or of the brand of petrol used may effect a solution.*

(n) *The catalytic converter, used on a well-maintained and well-driven car, should last for between 50 000 and 100 000 miles - from this point on, careful checks should be made at all specified service intervals of the CO level, to ensure that the converter is still operating efficiently - if the converter is no longer effective, it must be renewed.*

Catalytic converter - removal and refitting

1 Note that the only test of the catalytic converter's effectiveness is to check the level of CO in the exhaust gas, comparing the level in front of the converter with that at the tailpipe; if there is no significant decrease, the fault must lie in the converter, which must be renewed.

2 The exhaust system of a catalytic converter-equipped vehicle is similar in layout to that outlined in Chapter 3, except that the front section incorporates the catalytic converter and Lambda sensor.

3 To remove the catalytic converter, disconnect the Lambda sensor wiring, then undo the nuts securing the front section to the manifold and unfasten the clamp at its rear end. Prise away the rear part of the system until the converter can be withdrawn; collect any gaskets fitted.

4 On refitting, clean the mating surfaces carefully, fit new gaskets (where applicable) and tighten the nuts as described in Chapter 3, Section 16.

5 When working on any other part of the system, note that the underbody of the vehicle is protected by heat shields from the very high operating temperatures of a catalytic converter; these may have to be unbolted before the exhaust system itself can be removed from the vehicle.

9 Ignition system

Spark plugs - 1988-on XU5 engines

1 Until October 1987, taper-seat spark plugs (without sealing washers) were fitted to XU5JA and XU51C engines. After this date, conventional plugs with sealing washers were fitted.

2 Refer to the Specifications Section of this Chapter for spark plug types and electrode gaps.

Ignition coil (TU engines) - removal and refitting

3 Remove the air cleaner inlet ducting.

4 Disconnect the HT cables from the coil.

5 Disconnect the LT wiring.

6 Unhook the TDC connector from the coil bracket.

7 Unbolt the mounting bracket, and remove the coil.

8 Refitting is the reverse of the removal procedure.

Distributor (TU engines) - removal and refitting

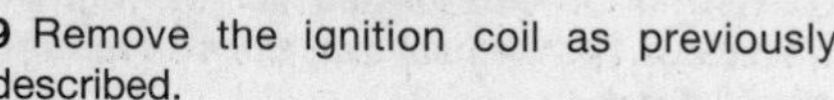

9 Remove the ignition coil as previously described.

10 Identify the HT leads for position, then disconnect them from the spark plugs.

11 Unbolt the HT lead support from the cylinder head.

12 Pull back the plastic cover, then extract the screws and remove the distributor cap.

13 Disconnect the wiring at the connector.

14 Pull the hose from the vacuum advance unit.

15 Mark the distributor mounting flange in relation to the distributor housing.

16 Unscrew the mounting nuts, unscrew the small plates, and withdraw the distributor.

17 Check the condition of the O-ring on the mounting flange, and renew it if necessary.

18 Refitting is the reverse of the removal procedure, but turn the rotor as required to align the lugs with the offset slot in the camshaft. If the old distributor is being refitted, align the previously-made marks before tightening the mounting nuts. If fitting a new distributor, initially set the distributor in the middle of the slotted holes, follow the procedure given in Chapter 4, then finally adjust the ignition timing.

Ignition amplifier module (all models) - removal and refitting

19 The module is either bolted to its own mounting bracket, next to the ignition HT coil (for example, see photo 1.2 in Chapter 4), or is attached to the side of the distributor (as on TU engines, for example). First disconnect the battery earth lead, then the module wiring at its connector.

20 Remove the two screws and withdraw the module, taking care not to bend the terminals.

21 Do not wipe away the special heat-conductive grease, as this protects the semi-conductor components within the module. If necessary, obtain new grease from a Peugeot dealer.

22 Refitting is the reverse of the removal procedure, but make sure that the special grease is spread evenly over the mating surfaces, and be careful not to overtighten the screws, or the module may be cracked.

Distributorless ignition system - description

This is an integral part of the MMBA engine management system (see Section 8, Part D, of this Chapter). The conventional distributor is replaced by the Electronic Control Unit (ECU), which incorporates the functions of the ignition amplifier module, and the crankshaft speed/position sensor.

The ignition HT coil unit combines a double-ended pair of coils; each time a coil receives an ignition signal, two sparks are produced, one at each end of the secondary windings. One spark goes to a cylinder on compression stroke, and the other goes to the corresponding cylinder on its exhaust stroke. The first will ignite the fuel/air mixture in the normal way, but the second will have no effect; this type of ignition is therefore sometimes known as 'wasted-spark' ignition.

The crankshaft speed/position sensor is bolted to the clutch housing to register with the flywheel teeth; a reference point defined by a zone equal to two missing teeth (the flywheel has 60) allows the ECU to calculate engine speed, and to recognise the TDC position.

The ECU receives information from the crankshaft speed/position sensor, the coolant temperature sensor, the throttle potentiometer and the manifold absolute pressure (MAP) sensor. It compares these inputs with the set values pre-programmed (mapped) into its memory; based on this information, it selects the optimum ignition advance to suit the prevailing engine conditions, and accordingly controls the ignition HT coil.

The ignition timing is non-adjustable, as all settings are controlled by the ECU.

Distributorless ignition system - component removal and refitting

Note: *For details of removal, refitting and servicing of all other system components, including the ECU, refer to Section 8 of this Chapter.*

Ignition HT coil

23 Remove the air intake trunking as necessary to reach the coil, which is bolted to the left-hand end of the cylinder head.

24 Disconnect the battery earth lead.

25 Release the locking clip, and disconnect the coil's wiring connector plug.

26 Unplug the HT leads, noting their connections, or labelling them so that they can be correctly reconnected.

27 Unbolt and withdraw the coil unit.

28 Refitting is the reverse of the removal procedure.

Crankshaft speed/position sensor

29 Refer to Chapter 4, Section 7.

Fault finding - distributorless ignition system

30 Specialist test equipment is required to carry out accurate fault diagnosis, therefore any fault occurring with the system should be referred to a Peugeot dealer.

Ignition system (XU9JA/Z and L engines) - description

On these engines, the ignition system is an integral part of the Bosch Motronic M1.3 engine management system (see Section 8, Part B, of this Chapter).

The Electronic Control Unit (ECU) receives information from the crankshaft speed/position sensor, the coolant temperature sensor, the throttle switch and the airflow sensor. It compares these inputs with the set values pre-programmed (mapped) into its memory; based on this information, it selects the optimum ignition advance to suit the prevailing engine conditions, and accordingly controls the ignition HT coil via the amplifier module.

The ignition timing is non-adjustable, as all settings are controlled by the ECU; note that the distributor is now just that - a distributor of the HT pulse to the appropriate spark plug; it has no effect whatever on the ignition timing.

Ignition system (XU9JA/Z and L engines) - component removal and refitting

Note: *For details of removal, refitting and servicing of all other system components, including the ECU, refer to Section 8 of this Chapter.*

Ignition HT coil

31 On models built up to December 1989, the coil is as described in Chapter 4, Section 8.

32 On later models, the coil is a square-shaped moulded plastic unit, surrounded by a thick mounting bracket. It is secured by four screws, and is located behind the battery.

Crankshaft speed/position sensor

33 Refer to Chapter 4, Section 7.

Ignition amplifier module

34 Noting that the module is located next to the ignition HT coil, refer to paragraphs 19 to 22 above.

Fault finding - ignition system (XU9JA/Z and L engines)

35 Specialist test equipment is required to carry out accurate fault diagnosis, therefore any fault occurring with the system should be referred to a Peugeot dealer.

10 Clutch

Clutch release mechanism (MA and BE 3/5 gearbox) - overhaul

1 Remove the gearbox as described in Chapter 6 or 13.

2 Pull the clutch release bearing from the guide sleeve, then release the spring clips from the fork ends.

3 Using a suitable punch, drive out the roll pin securing the release lever to the pivot shaft, then withdraw the release lever.

4 Prise the upper pivot shaft bush from the bellhousing.

5 Lift the lower end of the release lever pivot shaft from the lower bush in the bellhousing, then lower the pivot shaft into the bellhousing, and manipulate it as necessary to enable removal.

6 If desired, the lower pivot bush can be prised from the bellhousing.

7 Reassembly is the reversal of dismantling, but ensure that the pivot bushes are correctly located in the bellhousing.

8 Refit the transmission as described in the relevant Chapter.

11 Manual transmission (BE 1)

Gearchange linkage - modification

1 As from early 1987, the selector and engagement levers are secured to their shafts by roll pins, instead of the splines and nuts used previously.

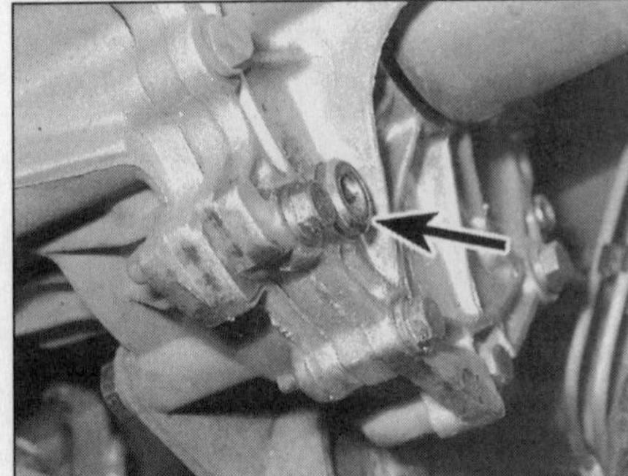

13.5A Gearbox drain plug (arrowed)

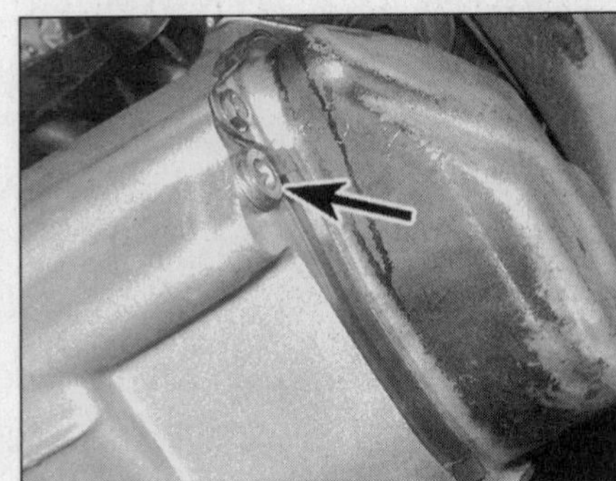

13.5B Gearbox filler plug (arrowed)

Gearbox oil - renewal

2 Refer to Section 3 of this Supplement for details of revisions to the routine maintenance requirements.

12 Manual transmission (BE 3/5)

General description

1 The BE 3/5 gearbox is a development of the BE 1/5 unit, and was introduced during the 1990 model year.

2 Most of the procedures described in Chapter 6 for the BE 1/5 gearbox are applicable to the BE 3/5 type, although many of the components have been modified, as detailed in the following paragraphs.

3 When ordering spare parts, ensure that the correct new components are obtained, as many of the BE 1/5 and BE 3/5 gearbox components are not interchangeable.

4 BE 3/5 gearboxes can be identified by the revised gearchange pattern, with reverse gear positioned behind 5th gear.

13 Manual transmission (MA)

Transmission - general description

1 The MA gearbox is fitted to the left-hand side of the TU series engine, and may be removed separately, leaving the engine in the car. It has five forward gears, all with synchromesh, and one reverse gear. All the synchromesh units are located on the output shaft, and the differential unit is located in the main gearbox casing.

Transmission - routine maintenance

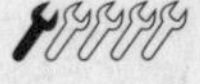

2 While there are no oil change requirements, oil level checks should be carried out every 36 000 miles (60 000 km). Make sure that all topping-up is made using only the specified grade of oil.

Transmission - removal and refitting

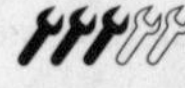

3 Remove the battery as described in Chapter 12.

4 Remove the engine undershield and sideshields.

5 Unscrew the drain and filler plugs (photos), and drain the gearbox oil into a suitable container.

6 Retain the suspension strut each side at the front using the Peugeot special tool (Chapter 9, Section 4).

7 Undo the front hub nut each side, then raise

and support the front of the vehicle on axle stands.

8 Remove the air cleaner.

9 Unscrew the nut and detach the battery negative cable from the gearbox.

10 Disconnect the wiring from the reversing light switch.

11 Pull out the rubber cotter, and remove the speedometer cable from the gearbox.

12 Prise the two gearchange control rods from the gearbox levers. A small open-ended spanner is useful for this.

13 Disconnect the clutch cable, and place it to one side.

14 Unbolt and remove the starter motor.

15 Using Peugeot special cables No 0903, retain the front suspension struts as described in Chapter 9, Section 4.

16 Disconnect the suspension arm from the steering knuckle, referring to Chapter 10 for details.

17 Remove the driveshafts with reference to Chapter 7.

18 Unscrew and remove the lower rear bolt securing the gearbox to the engine.

19 Support the left-hand side of the engine, using a hoist on the left-hand lifting eye, or a trolley jack and block of wood beneath the sump.

20 Unscrew the left-hand mounting nuts, including the nut on the centre stud, and remove the mounting.

21 Unscrew the nuts and remove the left-hand mounting bracket from the gearbox.

22 Lower the engine slightly, and unscrew the remaining bolts securing the gearbox to the engine.

23 Support the gearbox with a trolley jack or suitable sling, then withdraw it from the engine. When the two units are fully disengaged, lower the gearbox to the ground.

24 Refitting is the reverse of the removal procedure, but note the following points:

(a) It is recommended that the driveshaft oil seals and filler/drain plug washers are renewed.

(b) Tighten all nuts and bolts to their specified torque wrench settings.

(c) Lubricate the input shaft splines, clutch release bearing sleeve and fork fingers with molybdenum disulphide grease.

(d) Refill the gearbox with the correct grade and quantity of oil.

(e) Adjust the clutch cable (Chapter 5).

(f) The gearchange control rods cannot be adjusted.

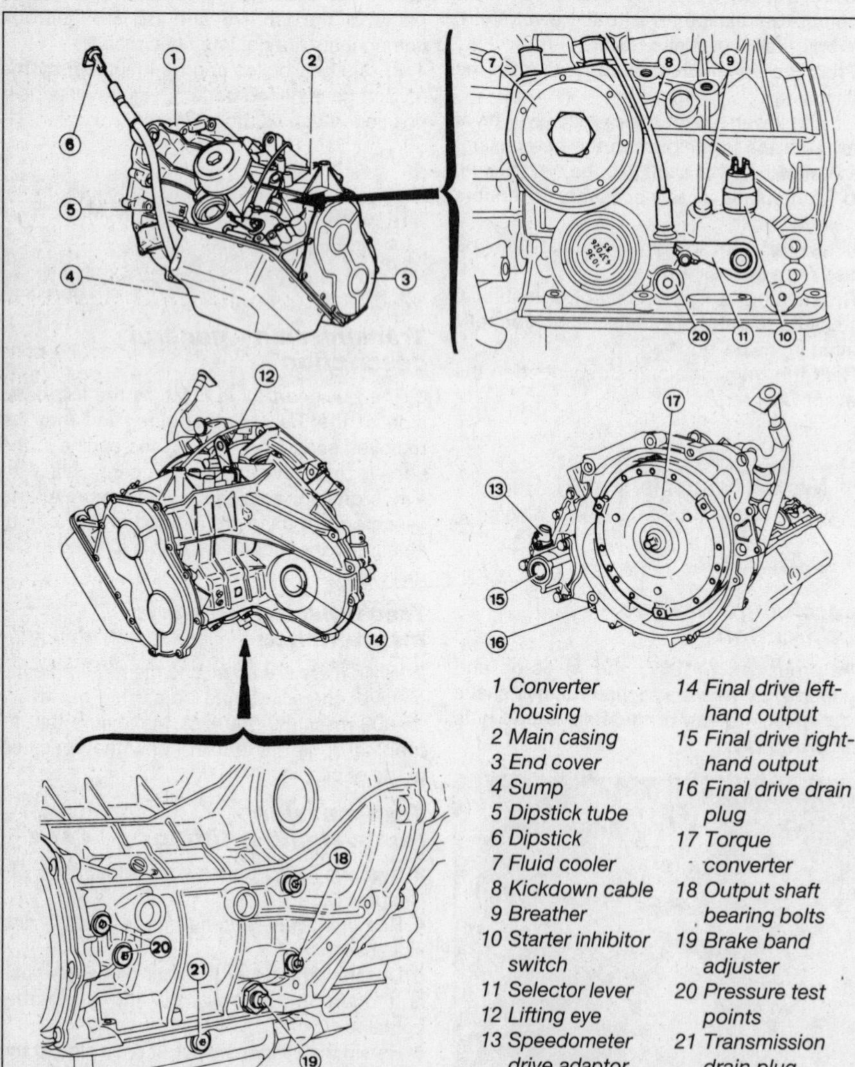

Fig. 13.40 External components of the ZF 4 HP 14 automatic transmission (Sec 14)

14 Automatic transmission

Description

1 Automatic transmission became available in June 1987, and further details are given in the Specifications in this Supplement.

2 Vehicles with this transmission are equipped with a Weber 36 TLC carburettor (XU51C engines), Solex 34-34 Z1 carburettor (XU52C engines) or the MMBA engine management system (XU5M engines).

3 Apart from modified front suspension coil springs, all other mechanical details are similar to other models with the XU5 engine.

4 In the interests of fuel economy the torque converter is completely bypassed in top (4th) gear and partially bypassed in 3rd, this reduces losses due to torque converter slip.

5 Gearchange is automatic in use, the transmission responding to changes in speed and load. The usual kickdown facility is provided for enhanced acceleration when the throttle is depressed fully.

6 Instead of the customary oil cooler mounted in the radiator, cooling is by means of a coolant/oil heat exchanger mounted on the side of the transmission.

Safety precautions

7 The following safety precautions must be adhered to where an automatic transmission is fitted. Whenever the vehicle is parked, or is being serviced or repaired, ensure that the handbrake is fully applied and the selector lever is in 'P'.

8 If it is necessary to tow a vehicle with automatic transmission, the towing speed must be restricted to 30 mph and the distance to 30 miles. If these conditions cannot be met, or if transmission damage is the reason for seeking a tow, the vehicle must be transported on a trailer, or with the front wheels off the ground.

Fluid level - checking

9 This check should be made directly after the vehicle has been used so that the transmission oil is at its normal operating temperature.

10 With the vehicle parked on level ground and the engine running, move the selector lever through all positions a number of times then finally leave it in 'P'. The handbrake must be fully applied throughout the check procedure.

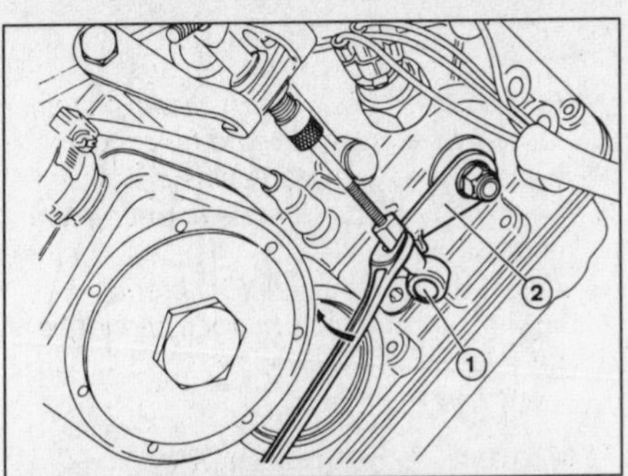

Fig. 13.41 Disconnecting the selector control rod balljoint (1) from the transmission lever (2) (Sec 14)

11 With the engine still running, remove the transmission fluid dipstick, wipe it clean, reinsert it fully then withdraw it again and check the fluid level. The fluid level must be between 'Min' and 'Max' levels.

12 If required, top-up the fluid level (but do not overfill) through the dipstick guide tube.

13 Stop the engine and refit the dipstick on completion.

Fluid - draining and refilling

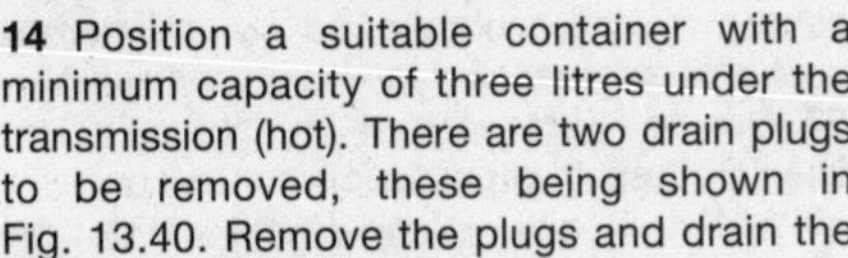

14 Position a suitable container with a minimum capacity of three litres under the transmission (hot). There are two drain plugs to be removed, these being shown in Fig. 13.40. Remove the plugs and drain the fluid, then refit the plugs.

15 Refill through the dipstick guide tube.

16 Recheck the fluid level after a nominal mileage has been covered and, if necessary, top-up the fluid, as described in paragraphs 9 to 13 inclusive.

Selector control - adjustment

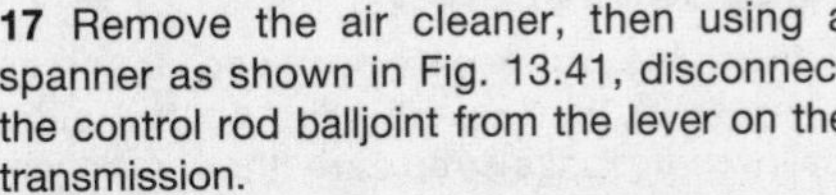

17 Remove the air cleaner, then using a spanner as shown in Fig. 13.41, disconnect the control rod balljoint from the lever on the transmission.

18 Move the lever on the transmission fully forwards to the 'P' position.

19 Inside the car, move the selector lever fully forwards to the 'P' position.

20 The control rod balljoint should align exactly with the coupling ball on the selector lever, so that when reconnected, neither the selector lever within the vehicle nor the selector lever on the gearbox move. Adjust the position of the balljoint on the connecting rod if necessary.

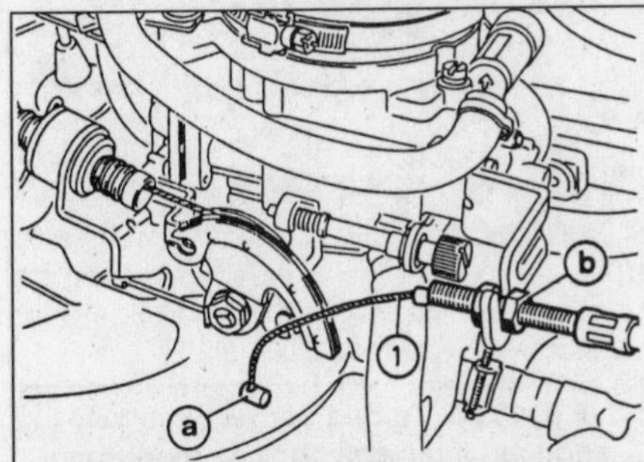

Fig. 13.44 Kickdown cable (1), nipple (a) and end fitting locknut (b) (Sec 14)

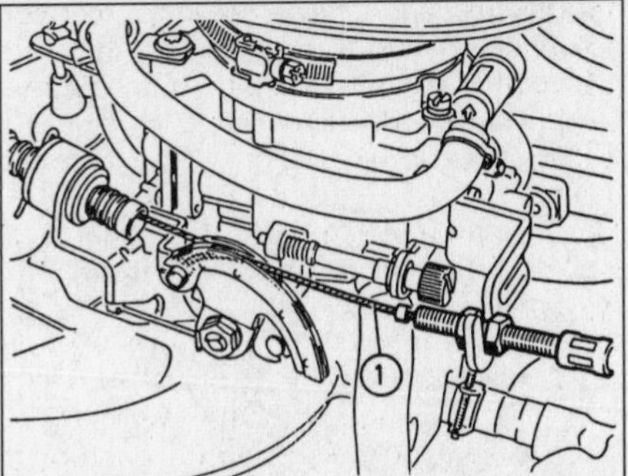

Fig. 13.42 Kickdown cable (1) showing crimped stop and clearance (Sec 14)

21 If the selector control was adjusted, check the setting by starting the engine and, when it has reached its normal operating temperature move the selector lever within the vehicle to 'P'. The vehicle should be stationary, and the gearbox parking pawl fully engaged.

22 Now move the lever to 'R' with the handbrake off. The vehicle should move rearwards, the pawl having been released.

23 If either of the checks in paragraphs 21 and 22 is unsatisfactory, unscrew the control rod balljoint one complete turn and repeat the checks until satisfactory.

24 Refit the air cleaner.

Kickdown cable - adjustment

25 Check the adjustment of the accelerator cable as described in Chapter 3, Section 14.

26 Check that there is a small clearance between the crimped stop and the end fitting of the kickdown cable. The clearance should not exceed 0.5 mm (0.020 in). Adjust if necessary, using the nuts on the threaded fitting at the support bracket.

27 Kickdown cable renewal is best left to your Peugeot dealer, as it involves removal of the valve block.

Brake band - adjustment

28 This is not a routine operation, and should only be required if the transmission appears to be malfunctioning.

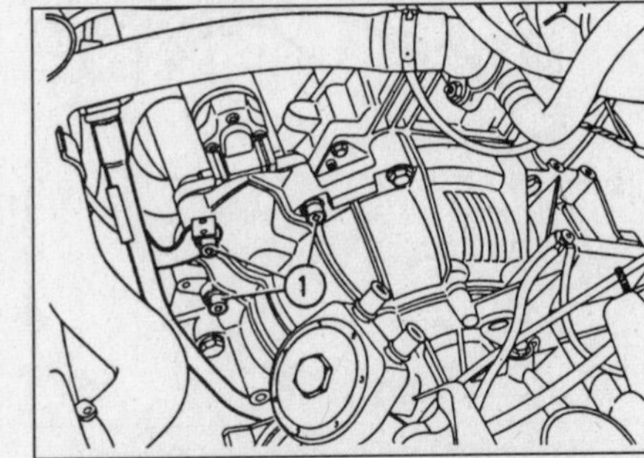

Fig. 13.45 Socket-headed starter motor fixing bolts (1) (Sec 14)

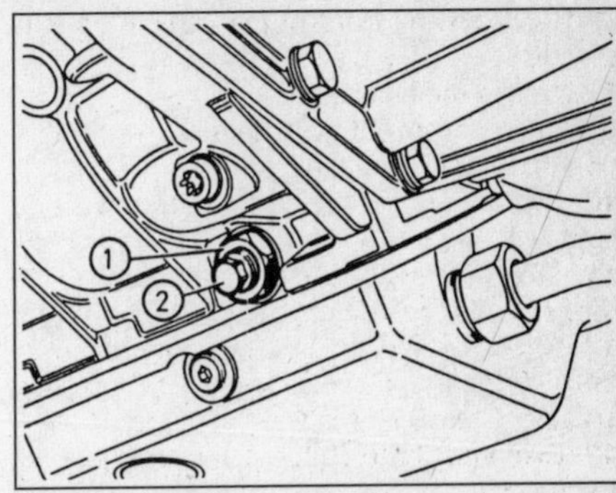

Fig. 13.43 Brake band adjuster locknut (1) and bolt (2) (Sec 14)

29 Slacken the locknut (1) (Fig. 13.43) on the side of the transmission casing, and unscrew the nut and the bolt (2) two turns.

30 Tighten the bolt to a torque of 10 Nm (7 lbf ft), and then unscrew it through two complete turns.

31 Tighten the locknut without disturbing the setting of the bolt.

Transmission unit - removal and refitting

32 The transmission is removed downwards and out from under the car.

33 Open the bonnet.

34 Drain the transmission fluid through both the drain plugs provided.

35 Disconnect the air intake hose.

36 Disconnect the battery and remove it.

37 Disconnect the earth strap (transmission-to-body).

38 Using self-locking pliers or brake hose clamps, clamp the coolant hoses down at the fluid cooler, and disconnect them from the cooler.

39 Disconnect the selector cable from the lever on the transmission by releasing the balljoint with an open-ended spanner, and then free the cable from its support bracket.

40 Disconnect the leads from the starter inhibitor switch.

41 Disconnect the kickdown cable from the throttle spindle quadrant and the support bracket.

42 Remove the socket-headed bolts (1) (Fig. 13.45).

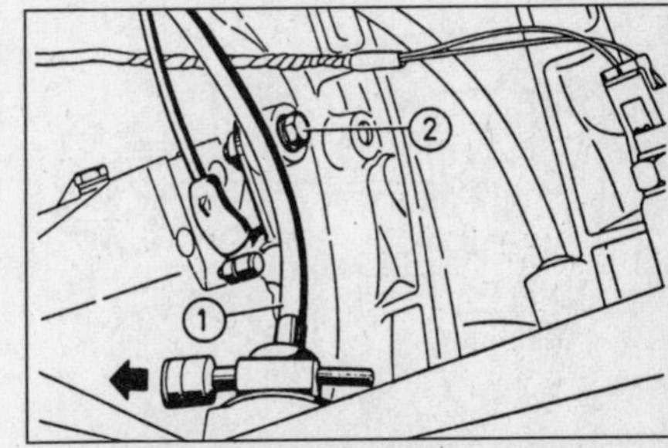

Fig. 13.46 Speedometer drive cable (1) at transmission, and crankshaft speed/position sensor bracket bolt (2) (Sec 14)

Fig. 13.47 Engine support crossbeam (Sec 14)

43 With the vehicle raised and securely supported, remove the front roadwheels and then withdraw both driveshafts as described in Chapter 7.

44 Disconnect the speedometer drive cable from the transmission by pulling out the rubber tapered cotter pin.

45 Remove the crankshaft speed/position sensor bracket (Fig. 13.46).

46 Unscrew the dipstick guide tube nut and remove the tube.

47 Remove the cover plate from the lower part of the torque converter housing.

48 Unscrew the torque converter-to-driveplate connecting bolts. The crankshaft will have to be turned to bring each bolt into view.

49 Support the weight of the engine on a crossbeam, with its hook engaged in the left-hand engine lifting eye, as shown in Fig. 13.47.

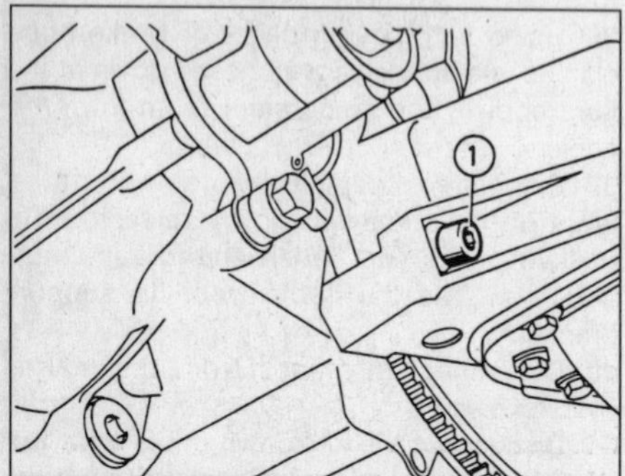

Fig. 13.50 Stiffener bolt (1) (Sec 14)

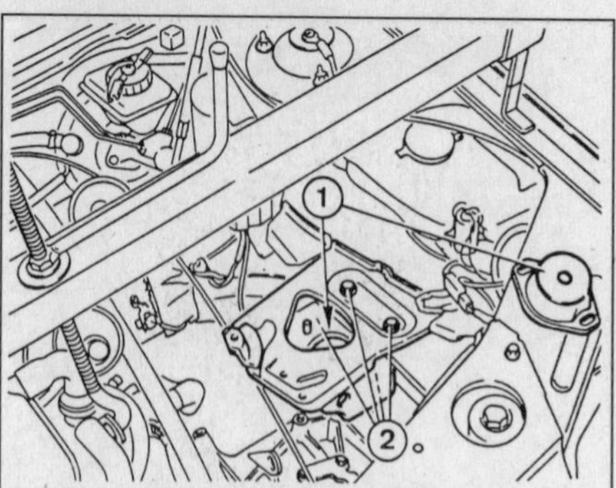

Fig. 13.48 Transmission flexible mounting (1) and battery tray bolts (2) (Sec 14)

50 Remove the flexible mounting (1) (Fig. 13.48).

51 Remove the battery tray.

52 Unscrew and remove the three engine-to-transmission connecting bolts.

53 Working under the car, unscrew and remove the socket-headed stiffener bolt (1) (Fig. 13.50).

54 Withdraw the transmission from the engine, supporting its weight on a trolley jack or on a hoist.

55 Fit a suitable retainer to prevent the torque converter being displaced.

56 Remove the transmission from under the car. The car may have to be raised to clear the transmission under the left-hand body member.

57 Lower the transmission to the floor, and remove it from under the car.

58 Before refitting the transmission, check the condition of the spigot bush in the rear of the crankshaft, and apply a little grease to aid entry of the torque converter. Also check that the two locating dowels are in place on the engine. Apply a little grease to the differential/driveshaft seals.

59 Make sure that the torque converter is fully engaged by checking the dimension shown in Fig. 13.53. If necessary, rotate the torque converter until it is correctly engaged.

Fig. 13.49 Transmission converter housing-to-engine connecting bolts (1) (Sec 14)

60 Refitting is a reversal of removal, but tighten all nuts and bolts to the specified torque, and adjust the kickdown cable and selector control as previously described. Fill the transmission as previously described, and bleed the cooling system.

Fault finding - automatic transmission

61 Faults not due to incorrect fluid level or adjustment of the selector and kickdown cables must be diagnosed by a Peugeot dealer or automatic transmission specialist.

62 Do not remove the transmission for specialist repair without allowing the specialist to test it *in situ*. Some faults cannot be diagnosed with the transmission removed.

15 Driveshafts

Driveshaft rubber bellows - renewal

1 With the driveshaft removed (refer to Chapter 7), loosen the clips on the outer bellows. If plastic straps are fitted, cut them free with snips (photo).

2 Prise the bellows large diameter end from the outer joint housing (photo), then tap the centre hub outwards using a soft metal drift in order to release it from the retaining circlip.

Fig. 13.51 Home-made retainer and bolt (1) for keeping torque converter fully engaged in housing (Sec 14)

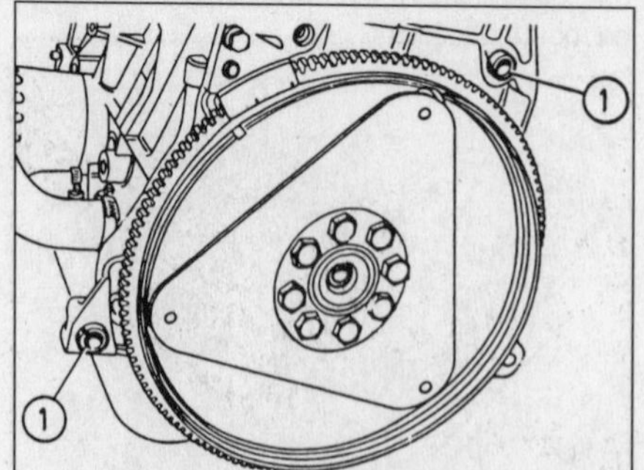

Fig. 13.52 Transmission-to-engine locating dowels (1) (Sec 14)

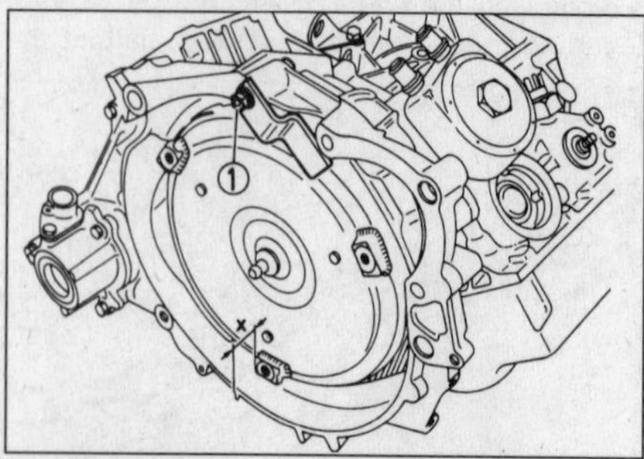

Fig. 13.53 Torque converter is fully engaged if dimension 'X' is more than 7.0 mm (0.28 in) (Sec 14)

1 Home-made retainer and bolt

15.1 Plastic straps on the driveshaft bellows

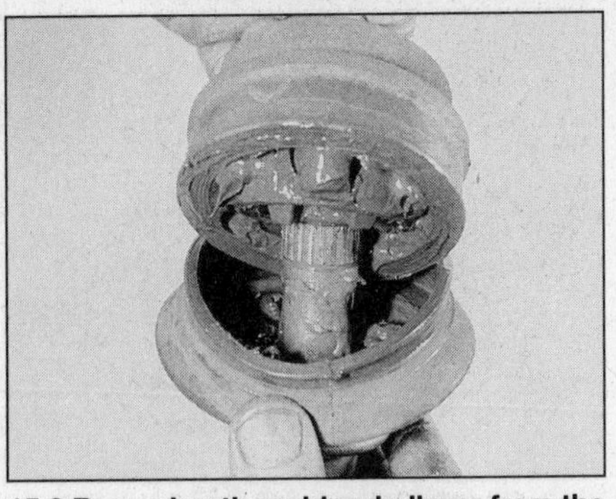
15.2 Removing the rubber bellows from the outer joint housing

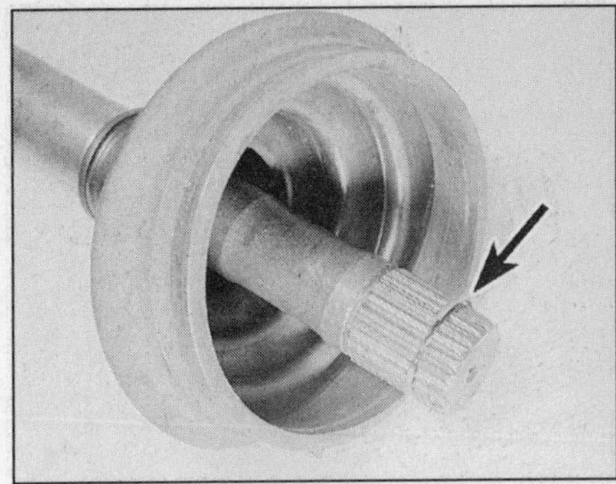
15.3 Driveshaft outer joint clip (arrowed)

Slide the outer joint from the driveshaft splines.

3 Extract the circlip from the groove in the driveshaft (photo).

4 Prise off the rubber bellows. If necessary, remove the plastic seating from the recess in the driveshaft (photos).

5 Loosen the clips on the inner rubber bellows. If plastic straps are fitted, cut them free.

6 Prise the bellows large diameter end from the inner joint housing, and slide the rubber bellows off the outer end of the driveshaft (photo).

7 Mark the driveshaft and inner joint housing in relation to each other, then separate them, keeping the rollers engaged with their respective spigots (photo).

8 Clean away the grease, then retain the rollers using adhesive tape (photo).

9 Remove the pressure pad and spring from inside the inner joint housing (photo).

10 Clean away the grease, then commence reassembly by inserting the pressure pad and spring into the inner joint housing, with the housing mounted upright in a soft-jawed vice.

11 Inject half the required amount of grease into the inner joint housing (photo).

12 Locate the new inner rubber bellows halfway along the driveshaft (photo).

13 Remove the adhesive tape and insert the driveshaft into the housing.

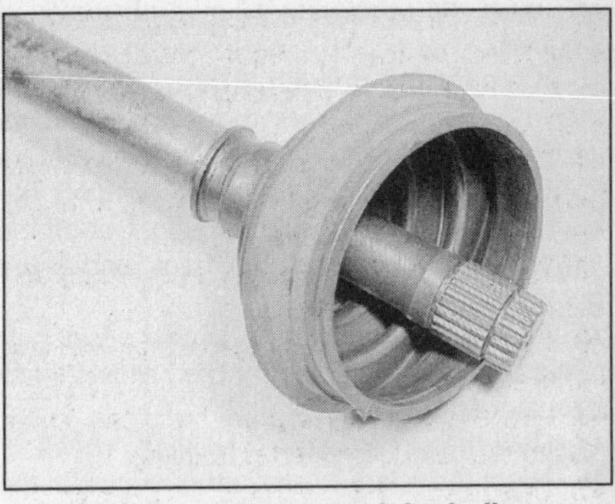
15.4A Removing outer joint bellows

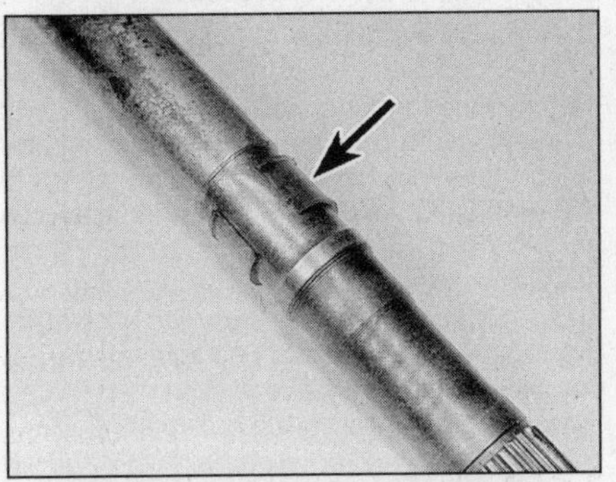
15.4B Plastic seating (arrowed) for the outer joint bellows

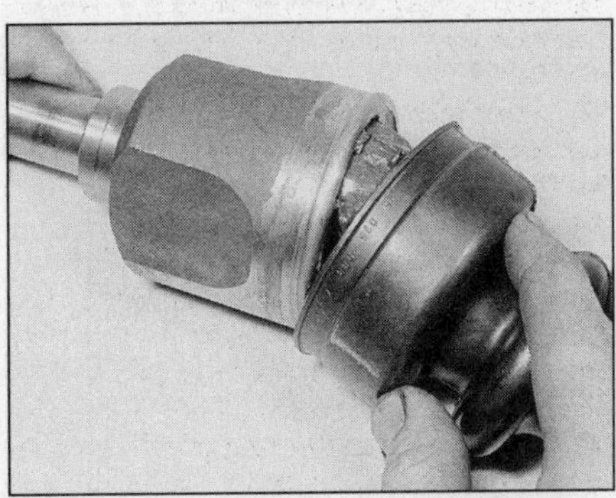
15.6 Removing the inner joint bellows

15.7 Separating driveshaft and rollers from the inner joint housing

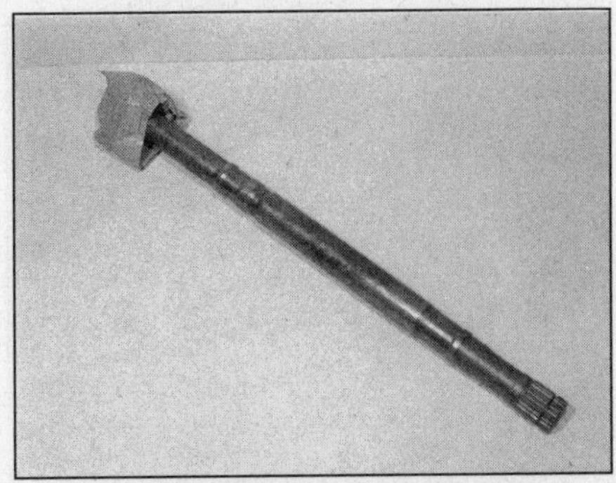
15.8 Left-hand driveshaft with rollers retained with adhesive tape

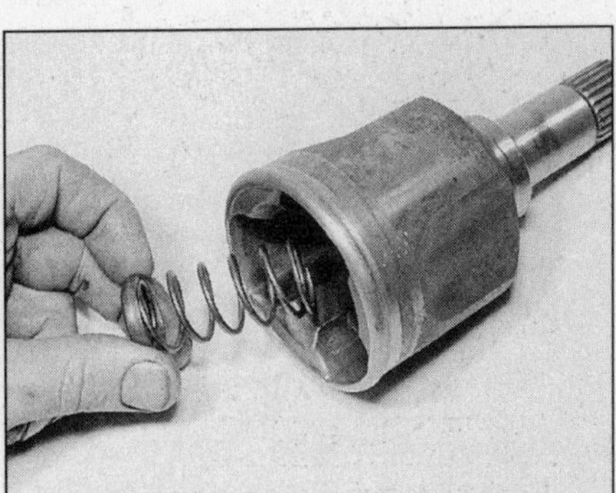
15.9 Removing the pressure pad and spring from the inner joint

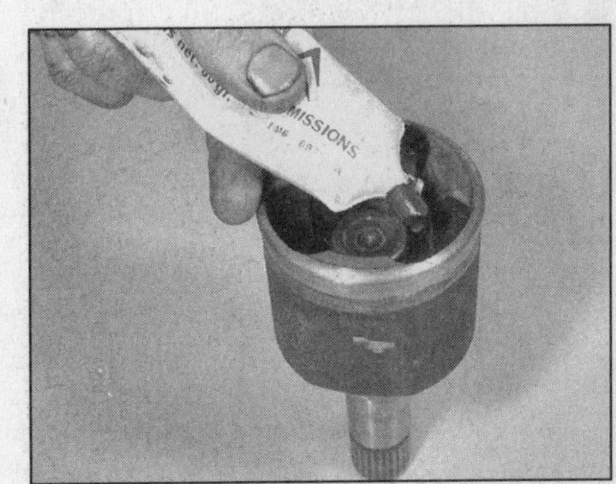
15.11 Injecting grease into the inner joint housing

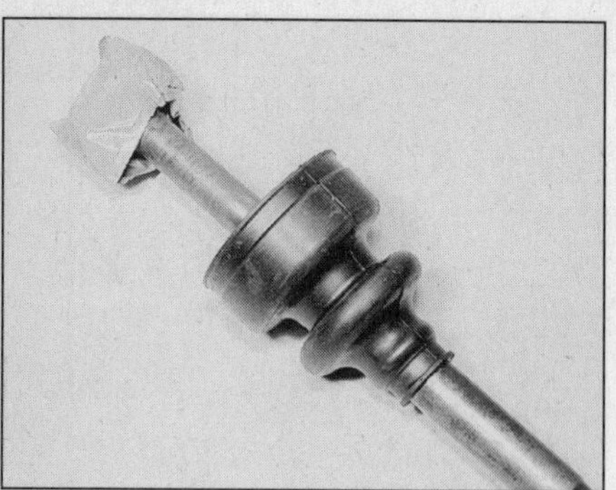
15.12 Inner joint bellows located on the driveshaft

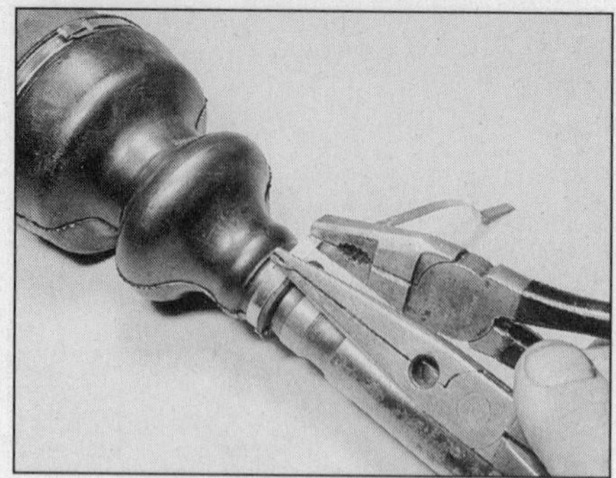
15.15A Tightening metal type bellows clip

15.15B Bellows clip correctly fitted

14 Inject the remaining amount of grease in the joint.

15 Keeping the driveshaft pressed against the internal spring, refit the rubber bellows and tighten the clips. Metal type clips can be tightened using two pliers, by holding the buckle and pulling the clip through. Cut off the excess, and bend the clip back under the buckle (photos).

16 Fit the plastic seating in the driveshaft recess, and refit the new rubber bellows small diameter end on it.

17 Refit the circlip in the driveshaft groove.

18 Inject the required amount of grease in the outer joint, then insert the driveshaft, engage the splines, and press in until the circlip snaps into the groove.

19 Ease the rubber bellows onto the outer joint, and fit the two clips, tightening them as previously described.

Differential/driveshaft oil seals (BE 1/5 gearbox) - modifications

20 During 1988, the differential/driveshaft oil seals were modified. The earlier seals are no longer available, and the revised seals will be supplied as spares for all models.

21 When fitting the later type of seal, do not drive the seal fully into the final drive housing, as the seal lip may fail to contact the driveshaft, causing oil leaks.

22 The oil seals must be fitted with the correct protrusion, as shown in Fig. 13.54. Note the different protrusions for left and right-hand seals.

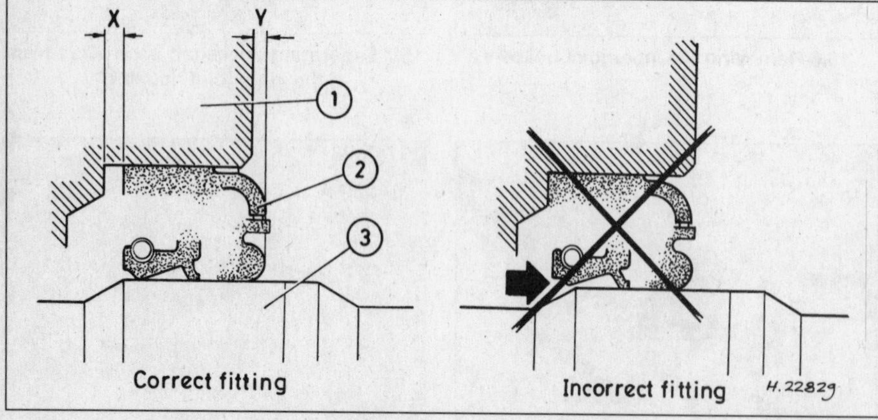

Fig. 13.54 Correct fitting of modified differential/driveshaft oil seals – BE 1 gearbox (Sec 15)

1 Casing
2 Seal
3 Shaft
X Related to Y
Y = 1.5 mm (RH), 1.0 mm (LH)

16 Conventional braking system

Girling front disc caliper - modification

1 To eliminate brake knock when parking, a welded thrust stop and a reinforced support plate have been incorporated in the caliper.

2 On earlier vehicles, the lower guide pin can be changed for one of larger diameter, which should cure the problem.

3 The guide pin kit (part number 443909) will service both calipers.

Pad wear indicator - modification

4 On all models (except GTI) from 1991, VIN 1 025 2426 approximately, the pad wear indicator is incorporated in the outer pad.

5 Peugeot dealers now supply only the revised front pad set, which is fully interchangeable with the previous type. The procedure for replacement remains as described in Chapter 8, Section 3, but refer to Fig. 13.55 for details of revised pad wear lead routing.

Braking system (1.9 GTI) - description

6 The 1.9 GTI braking system differs from the system fitted to other models, in that the circuit is split diagonally, the Girling front caliper is modified, DBA rear disc calipers are fitted, and two rear brake compensators are fitted in the two rear hydraulic circuits.

Front disc pads (1.9 GTI) - inspection and renewal

7 Apply the handbrake, then jack up the front of the car and support on axle stands. Remove the front roadwheels.

8 Viewing through the hole in the caliper, check if the friction material has worn down to 2.0 mm (0.079 in) or less. This is indicated by the central groove in the pads, which will not be visible when the wear limit is reached.

9 To remove the pads, first disconnect the wire for the pad wear warning light (photo).

10 Hold the lower guide stationary with one spanner, then unscrew the bolt (photo).

11 Swivel the caliper upwards, then withdraw the two disc pads from the bracket (photos).

12 Clean away all dust and dirt, however do not inhale the dust as it may be injurious to

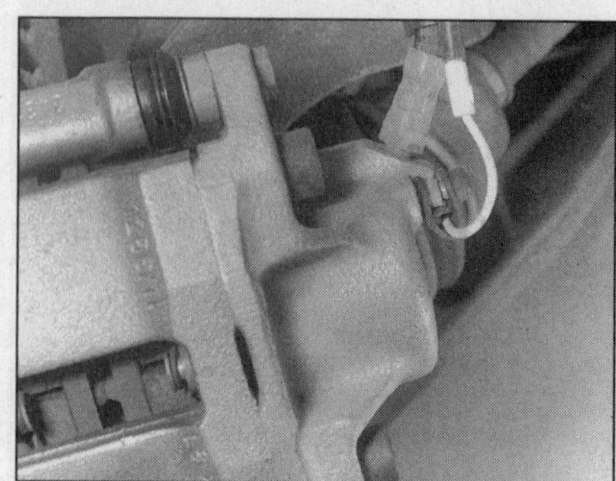
16.9 Pad wear warning light wire and connector

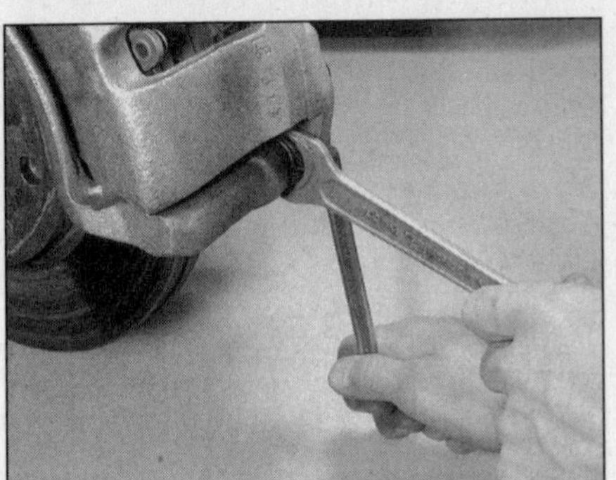

16.10 Unscrewing the lower caliper guide bolt

16.11A Swivel the caliper upwards . . .

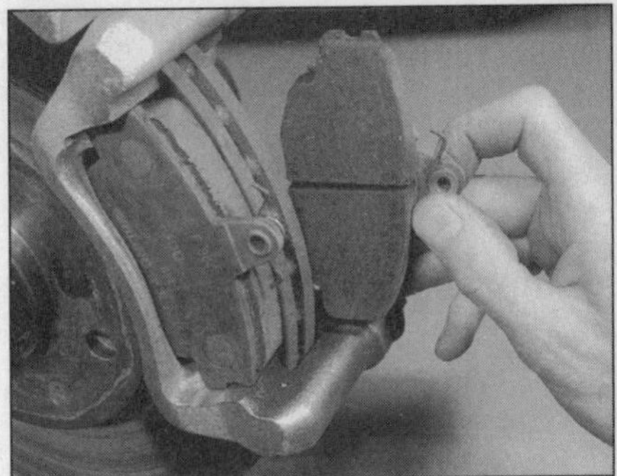

16.11B . . . and withdraw the disc pads

16.24 Spring clip (arrowed) retaining locking key

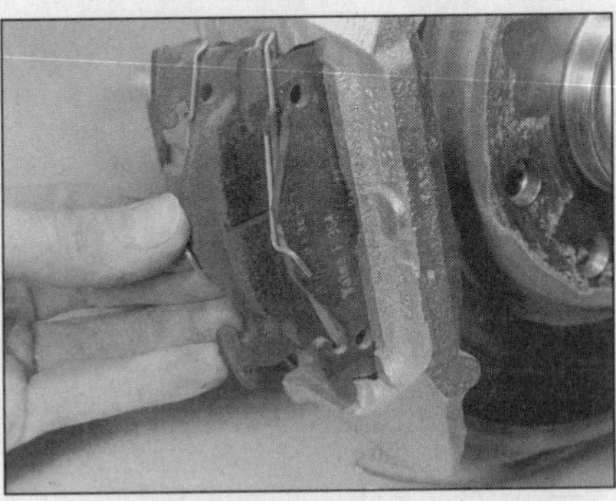

16.25 Removing the rear disc pads

16.27 Turning the rear caliper piston with a screwdriver

health. Check for brake fluid leakage around the piston dust seal and, if evident, overhaul the caliper with reference to Chapter 8. Check the brake disc for wear, and also check that the rubber bellows on the guides are in good condition.

13 Push the piston fully into the caliper.

14 Clean the backs of the disc pads and apply a little anti-squeal brake grease. Refit the inner pad (with the pad wear warning wire), then the outer pad.

15 Lower the caliper. Apply locking fluid to the lower guide bolt, insert it, and tighten to the specified torque while holding the guide stationary with another spanner.

16 Reconnect the pad wear warning light wire.

17 Fully depress the brake pedal several times to set the disc pads in their normal position.

18 Check the fluid level in the reservoir, and top-up if necessary.

19 Repeat the operations on the opposite disc caliper.

20 Refit the roadwheels and lower the car to the ground.

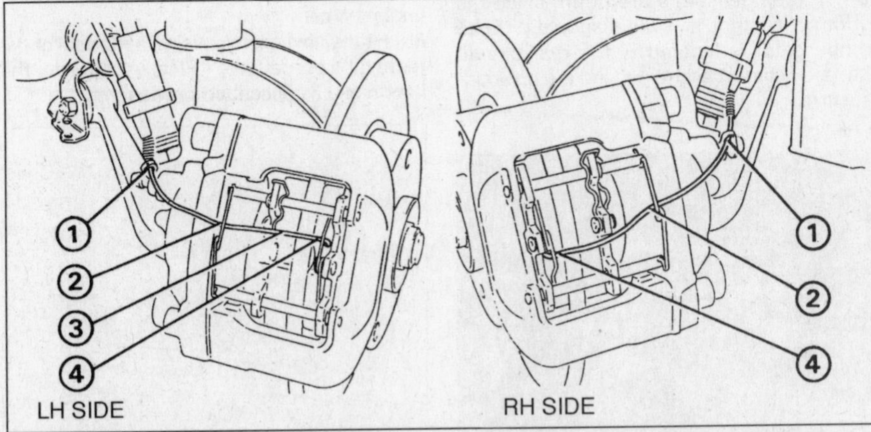

Fig. 13.55 Modified cable routing for brake pad wear warning lead (Sec 16)

1 Lead passing above the bleed screw
2 Lead passing below the pin
3 Lead passing above the spring
4 Lead passing below the spring

Rear disc pads (1.9 GTI) - inspection and renewal

21 Chock the front wheels, then jack up the rear of the car and support on axle stands. Remove the rear wheels.

22 Release the handbrake.

23 Check the disc pads for wear as described in paragraph 8.

24 To remove the pads, extract the spring clip (photo) and slide out the locking key retaining the bottom of the pads.

25 Withdraw the disc pads using pliers, while pressing down on the upper locating ears (photo).

26 Clean away all dust and dirt, taking care not to inhale it as it may be injurious to health. Check for brake fluid leakage around the piston dust seal, and if evident, overhaul the caliper using the basic procedure described in Chapter 8. Check the brake disc for wear, and also check that the rubber bellows on the guides are in good condition.

27 The automatic handbrake adjustment must now be reset, by retracting the piston, in order to accommodate the new disc pads. To do this, turn the piston using a screwdriver in the grooves (photo), at the same time using a second screwdriver to apply an outward force to the caliper. Do not damage the brake disc while carrying out this procedure.

28 Set the piston so that the mark (Fig. 13.57) is horizontal, and either above or below the piston groove.

29 Apply a little anti-squeal brake grease to the pad contact areas on the caliper.

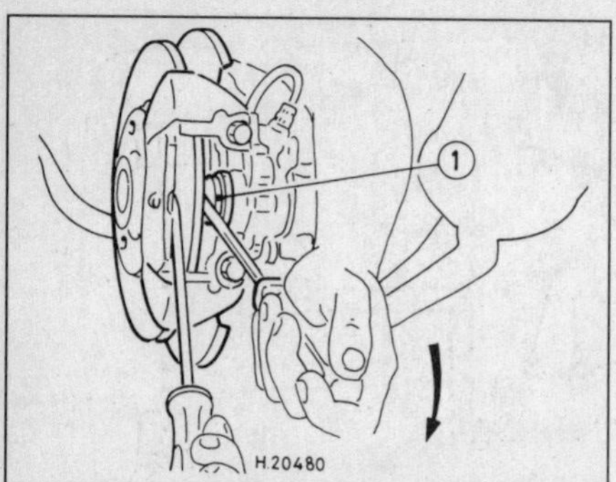

Fig. 13.56 Retracting the piston (1) to reset the automatic handbrake adjustment on a 1.9 GTI model (Sec 16)

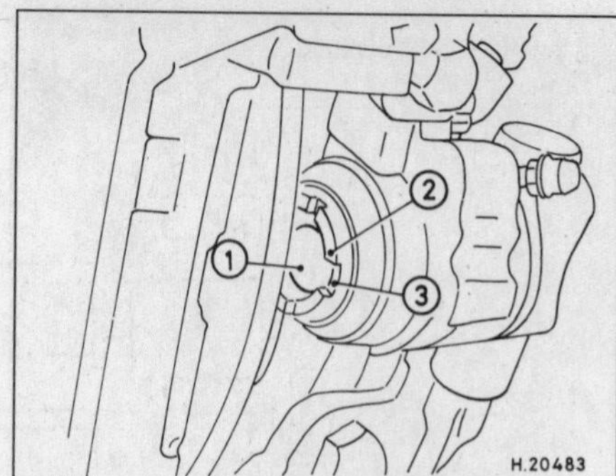

Fig. 13.57 Correct final position of piston on a 1.9 GTI rear caliper (Sec 16)

1 Piston 2 Mark 3 Groove

30 Locate the two disc pads in the caliper, pressing the upper ears fully into position.

31 Slide the locking key into the caliper, and secure with the spring clip.

32 Fully depress the brake pedal several times, to set the automatic adjuster and position the disc pads in their normal position.

33 Check the fluid level in the reservoir, and top-up if necessary.

34 Repeat the operations on the opposite disc caliper.

35 Refit the roadwheels and lower the car to the ground.

Rear disc caliper (1.9 GTI) - removal and refitting

36 Remove the disc pads as previously described.

37 Fit a brake hose clamp to the flexible hose connected to the caliper. Alternatively, where possible, remove the filler cap from the brake fluid reservoir, then tighten it down onto a piece of polythene sheeting.

38 Loosen the brake hose union at the caliper (photo).

39 Unhook the handbrake cable from the lever on the caliper, and withdraw the outer cable (photo).

40 Unscrew the two mounting bolts, withdraw the caliper from the disc, then unscrew the caliper from the brake hose. Plug the hose to prevent loss of fluid.

41 To refit the caliper, first screw it onto the brake hose and locate it over the brake disc, so that the hose is not twisted.

42 Clean the mounting bolt threads and apply a little locking fluid. Insert the bolts together with the anti-rotation plate and tighten them to the specified torque.

43 Tighten the brake hose union.

44 Insert the handbrake outer cable and re-connect the inner cable to the lever.

45 Refit the disc pads as previously described.

46 Remove the brake hose clamp or polythene sheeting, and bleed the hydraulic system with reference to paragraph 52.

47 Check and if necessary adjust the handbrake as described in paragraphs 53 to 60.

Brake discs (1.9 GTI) - removal and refitting

48 The procedure is as given in Chapter 8, Section 6. However, before removing the front disc, the caliper must be unbolted and tied to one side. There is no need to disconnect the hydraulic hose.

49 Refer to Chapter 8, Section 5 when refitting the caliper.

Rear brake compensators (1.9 GTI) - general

50 Two compensators are fitted, since the hydraulic system is split diagonally. Each compensator is located in the rear circuit. They are of fixed calibration, and are not load-sensitive.

51 Removal and refitting procedures are basically as given in Chapter 8, Section 10. It should be noted that compensators **must** be replaced in pairs.

Hydraulic system (1.9 GTI) - draining and bleeding

52 Refer to Chapter 8, Section 12.

Handbrake (1.9 GTI) - adjustment

53 Chock the wheels and fully release the handbrake.

54 Apply the brake pedal hard several times.

55 Working inside the car, remove the screw and lift the cover from the handbrake lever, as described in Chapter 8, Section 14.

56 Working beneath the rear of the car, measure the distance between the operating levers on the calipers and the end stops on the inner cables.

57 Inside the car, loosen the nut on the handbrake lever until the distance measured in paragraph 56 is 5.0 mm (0.197 in) on both sides.

58 Check that the operating levers on both calipers move freely and return positively to their stops.

59 Now tighten the nut on the handbrake lever so that the handbrake is fully applied between 7 and 9 notches. Do not over-adjust so that the handbrake is fully applied over fewer notches, otherwise the automatic adjusters will not operate correctly.

60 Refit the cover over the handbrake lever.

Handbrake cables (1.9 GTI) - renewal

61 Working inside the car, remove the screw and lift the cover from the handbrake lever, as described in Chapter 8, Section 14.

62 Unhook the cable from the compensator.

63 Chock the front wheels, then jack up the rear of the car and support on axle stands.

64 Release the cable(s) from the retaining clips, the floor, the fuel tank, the bracket(s), and the caliper lever(s), and withdraw from under the car.

65 Fit the new cable(s) using a reversal of the removal procedure. Finally adjust the handbrake as described previously.

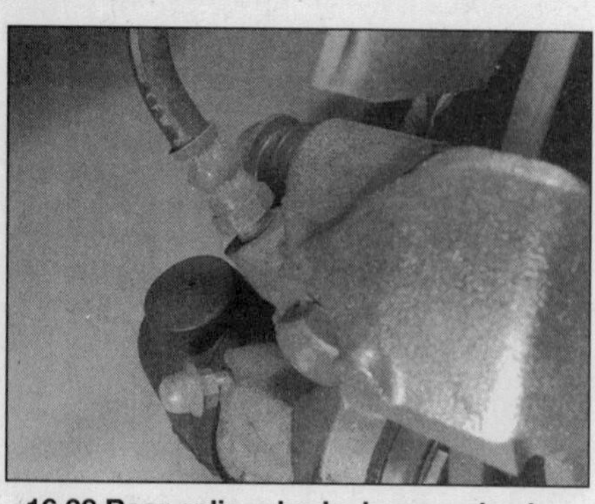

16.38 Rear caliper brake hose and union

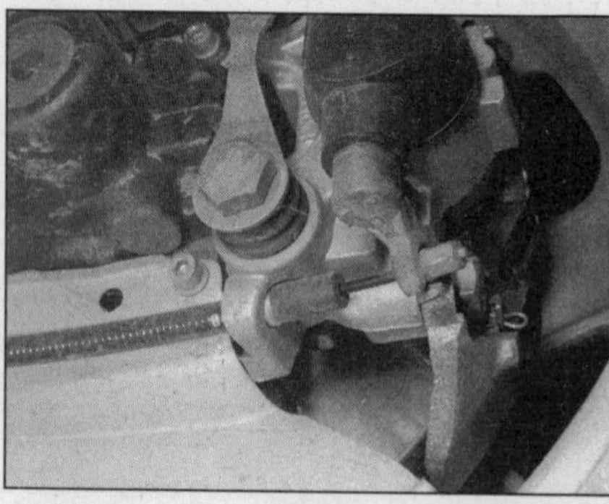

16.39 Handbrake cable attachment at rear caliper

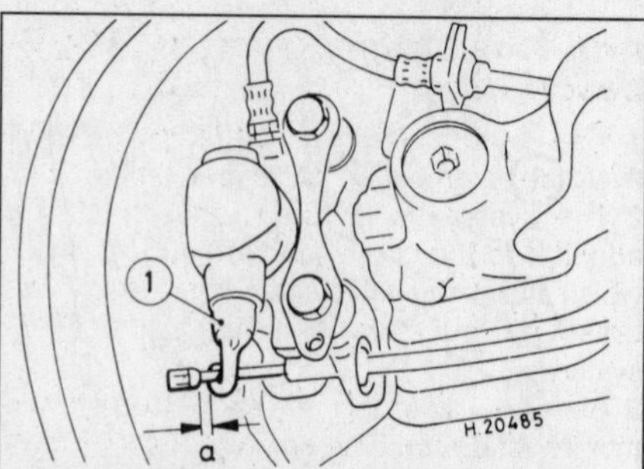

Fig. 13.58 Handbrake adjustment on a 1.9 GTI model (Sec 16)

1 Handbrake operating lever on the caliper
a = 5.0 mm

16.67 Stop-lamp switch and wiring plug (arrowed)

Stop-lamp switch - removal and refitting

66 Remove the lower facia panel from the steering column.
67 Disconnect the two wires (photo).
68 Unscrew the locknut nearest the pedal, and withdraw the switch from the bracket.
69 Refitting is a reversal of removal, but adjust the locknuts so that the distance between the end of the switch threaded body and the pedal (fully released) is 3.5 mm

17 Anti-lock braking system (ABS)

Warning: It is strongly recommended that any work involving components of the braking system on a vehicle equipped with ABS is entrusted to a Peugeot dealer, who will have the necessary specialist knowledge and equipment to carry out the work safely and effectively. Before starting any work on the ABS hydraulic system, the battery negative lead must be disconnected, and the brown three-way, brown five-way and green five-way wiring connectors must be disconnected from the regulator unit, to prevent the possibility of air entering the system. The connectors must not be reconnected until the hydraulic system has been bled.

Anti-lock braking system (ABS) - description

1 The Bendix anti-lock braking system is available as an option on later GTI models.
2 The system is fail-safe, and is fitted in addition to the conventional braking system, which allows the vehicle to retain conventional braking in the event of a failure in the ABS system.
3 Sensors mounted at each front wheel monitor the rotational speeds of the wheels, and are thus able to detect when there is a risk of the wheel locking (low rotational speed). When a wheel is about to lock up, the braking pressure to that wheel is reduced (by a solenoid valve), which allows the wheel to keep turning, and full steering control to be maintained. Solenoid valves are positioned in the brake circuits to all four wheels, and solenoid valves are incorporated in the regulator unit, which is controlled by an electronic control unit. The electronic control unit controls modulation of the braking effort applied to each wheel, according to the information supplied by the wheel sensors.

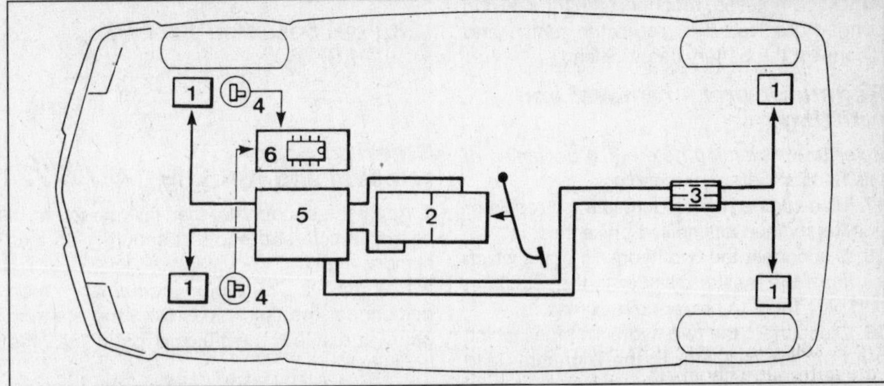

Fig. 13.59 Schematic layout of Anti-lock Braking System (ABS) (Sec 17)

1 *Brake calipers*
2 *Master cylinder*
3 *Rear brake compensators*
4 *Wheel sensors*
5 *Regulator unit*
6 *Electronic control unit*

4 Should a fault develop in the system, a self-diagnosis facility is incorporated in the electronic control unit, which can be used in conjunction with specialist diagnostic equipment available to a Peugeot dealer to determine the nature of the fault.
5 The brake components used on models fitted with ABS are similar to those used on models with a conventional braking system. Rear disc brakes are fitted to all ABS-equipped models, and all procedures for the rear brake and handbrake components are as described for 1.9 GTI models in Section 16. Refer to the following paragraphs for details of the additional ABS components, and for the special hydraulic system bleeding procedure to be observed.

Hydraulic system - draining and bleeding

Refer to the warning note at the beginning of this Section before proceeding.
6 During the bleeding procedure, the following points must be observed:
(a) *The hydraulic fluid level must be kept above the 'MIN' mark at all times.*
(b) *Use only clean, bubble-free hydraulic fluid from a freshly-opened container.*
(c) *Take extreme care to prevent dirt from entering the hydraulic system.*
7 If the hydraulic system is to be drained, follow the procedure given in Chapter 8, Section 12, but bleed the system with reference to this Section. If the master cylinder, regulator unit or connecting pipes have been removed, the complete hydraulic system must be bled, and it is recommended that the complete system is bled if a caliper is removed.
8 Bleed the four brake calipers using the method described in Chapter 8, Section 12.
9 Connect a suitable length of tubing to the bleed screw ('1' in Fig. 13.60) on the ABS regulator unit.
10 Have an assistant depress the brake pedal and hold it down.
11 Open the bleed screw, then close the screw and tighten it. Take care not to overtighten the bleed screw - as a guide, the recommended torque wrench setting is 6.5 Nm (5.0 lbf ft).
12 Have the assistant release the brake pedal.
13 Repeat the procedure given in paragraphs 10 to 12 inclusive until hydraulic fluid free from air bubbles flows from the bleed screw.
14 Now repeat the procedure for the remaining bleed screw ('2' in Fig. 13.60).
15 Proceed as described in Chapter 8, Section 12, paragraph 21 onwards.

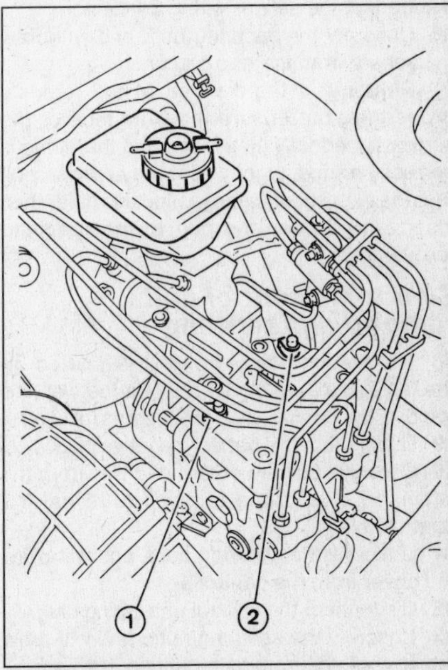

Fig. 13.60 Bleed screws (1 and 2) on ABS regulator unit (Sec 17)

16 On completion, reconnect the three wiring connectors to the regulator unit, and reconnect the battery negative lead.

Regulator unit - removal and refitting

Refer to the warning note at the beginning of this Section before proceeding.

17 Place some rags underneath the regulator unit, to soak up any spilled brake fluid.

18 Disconnect the two hydraulic pipes which run from the master cylinder to the regulator, and plug them to prevent dirt ingress.

19 Disconnect the two hydraulic pipes which run from the regulator to the T-junction, and plug them to prevent dirt ingress.

20 Similarly plug the open ports on the regulator.

21 Unbolt the regulator from its mounting bracket, and withdraw it from the engine compartment.

22 Refitting is the reversal of the removal procedure, observing the following points:

(a) *Ensure the regulator unit is correctly positioned on its flexible stops before tightening the mounting bolts to the specified torque. Tighten the hydraulic pipe unions securely.*

(b) *Bleed the brake system as described in paragraphs 6 to 16 of this Section.*

(c) *Do not reconnect the wiring connectors until the system has been fully bled.*

Wheel sensor - removal and refitting

23 The wheel sensors are mounted in the rear of the hub carriers. To remove a wheel sensor, proceed as follows.

24 Disconnect the battery negative lead.

25 Carefully pull the sensor wire from its retaining clips, then working under the wing, disconnect the sensor wiring connector.

26 Unscrew the securing bolt, and withdraw the sensor from the hub carrier.

27 Refitting is the reverse of the removal procedure, but ensure the front face of the sensor is perfectly clean, and that the wiring is correctly routed. Lightly coat the securing bolt threads with suitable thread-locking fluid, then insert and tighten the bolt to the specified torque.

Electronic control unit - removal and refitting

28 The electronic control unit is located on the left-hand side of the driver's footwell. To remove the control unit, proceed as follows.

29 Disconnect the battery negative lead.

30 Carefully pull the carpet and trim from the left-hand side of the footwell to reveal the control unit.

31 Unscrew the securing nuts, and withdraw the cover from the control unit.

32 Disconnect the control unit wiring plug.

33 Unscrew the securing nuts, and withdraw the control unit from its mounting bracket.

34 Refitting is the reverse of the removal procedure.

18 Power-assisted steering (PAS)

Steering gear - removal and refitting

1 Apply the handbrake, then jack up the front of the vehicle and support securely on axle stands.

2 Prepare a suitable container, then disconnect the fluid pipes from the steering gear, and allow the fluid to drain into the container.

3 Unscrew the track rod end balljoint nuts, then use a separator tool to detach the track rod end balljoints from the hub carriers.

4 Mark the lower column in relation to the pinion on the steering gear.

5 Unscrew and remove the column-to-pinion clamp bolt.

6 Disconnect the three gearchange control rods from the levers on the gearbox.

7 Extract the spring clip (Fig. 13.61) from the gearchange linkage, then unclip the gearbox selector and engagement rods, and support them in an upright position out of the way, using wire or string.

8 Remove the two steering gear securing bolts, recover the spacer tubes from the subframe, then disconnect the steering gear pinion from the steering column shaft.

9 Support the front subframe using a trolley jack and interposed block of wood positioned under the subframe crossmember.

10 Refer to Fig. 13.62 and remove the four bolts securing the rear of the subframe to the body, and the two nuts or bolts, as applicable, securing the front of the subframe to the body. Also remove the nut and bolt from the lower engine mounting.

11 Carefully lower the subframe sufficiently to enable removal of the steering gear, ensuring that the subframe is adequately supported.

12 Rotate the steering gear towards the rear of the vehicle, and withdraw the assembly over the rear of the subframe, taking care not to damage the rack bellows.

13 Refitting is the reverse of the removal procedure, bearing in mind the following points:

(a) *Do not forget to fit the spacer tubes to the steering gear securing bolts.*

(b) *Tighten all fixings to the specified torque.*

(c) *Ensure that the marks made on the steering gear pinion and the lower column during removal are aligned.*

(d) *When reconnecting the fluid pipes to the steering gear, the high-pressure fluid pipe (Fig. 13.63) must be vertical.*

(e) *Secure the hose (10, Fig. 13.63), to the high-pressure fluid pipe using a cable tie.*

(f) *Check the gearchange mechanism for correct operation after reconnecting the linkages.*

(g) *Bleed the system (Chapter 10).*

(h) *Check, and adjust as necessary, the front wheel alignment (Chapter 10).*

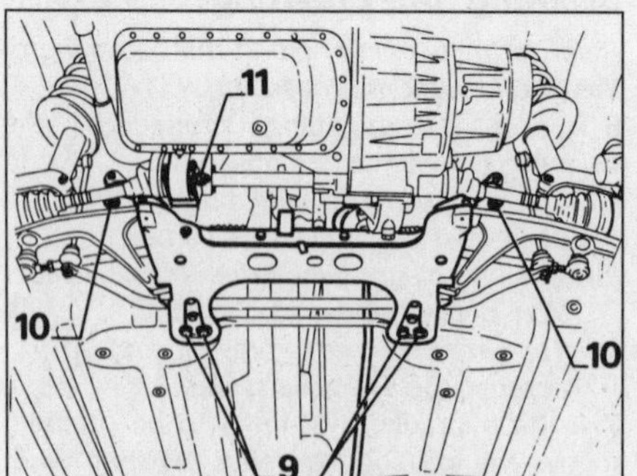

Fig. 13.62 The front subframe must be lowered to enable removal of the power steering gear (Sec 18)

9 Rear subframe securing bolts
10 Front subframe securing bolts
11 Lower engine mounting nut

Steering gear and pump - overhaul

14 Overhaul of these components is not recommended for the home mechanic, even if the parts are available. Obtain a new or reconditioned unit from a Peugeot dealer or other specialist.

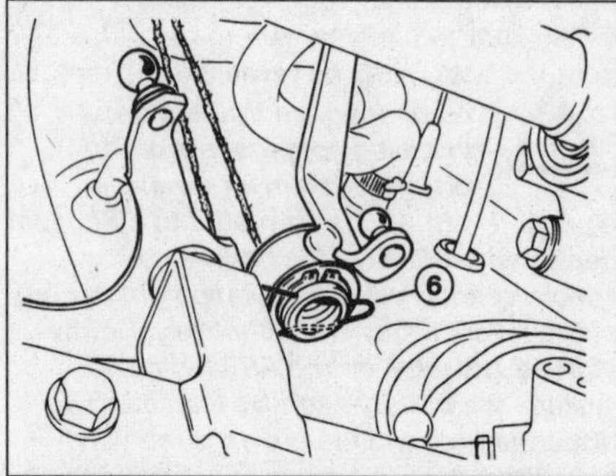

Fig. 13.61 Extract the spring clip (6) from the gearchange linkage (Sec 18)

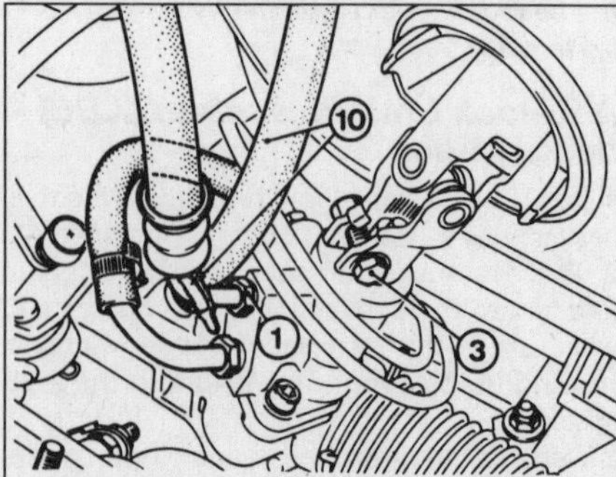

Fig. 13.63 Correct refitting of power steering gear (Sec 18)

1 High-pressure pipe
3 Column-to-pinion clamp bolt
10 Hose secured with cable tie

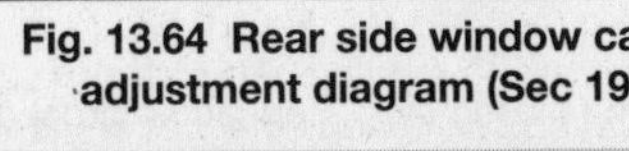

Fig. 13.64 Rear side window cable adjustment diagram (Sec 19)

19 Bodywork and fittings

Rear door quarterlight (5-door models) - removal and refitting

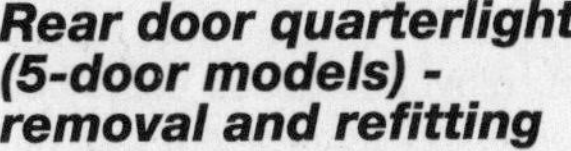

1 Remove the main glass from the door, as described in Chapter 11, Section 13.

2 Extract the fixing screw from the top of the quarterlight divider channel, and press the quarterlight glass, weatherseal and channel away from the door edge.

3 The quarterlight can then be withdrawn from the door. Refit by reversing the removal operations.

Rear side window (3-door models) - cable adjustment

4 The rear side window on the 3-door versions is controlled by a cable.

5 To ensure proper operation, the adjuster should be set to 18.0 mm (0.711 in) as shown in Fig. 13.64.

6 Access to the adjuster can be obtained in the following way.

7 Remove the rear parcel shelf, and fold the seat back down.

8 Unscrew the rear seat release knob from its rod.

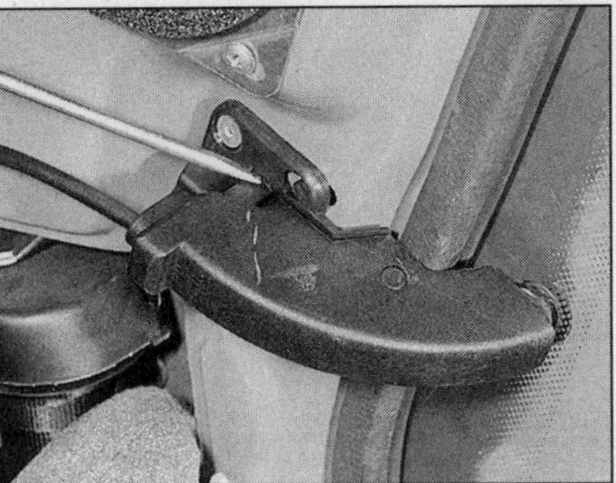

19.13 Prise off the latch plastic cover

9 Extract the six fixing screws from the rear side interior trim panel, and withdraw the panel.

10 Open the rear side window.

11 Turn the cable adjuster to provide the specified setting.

12 Close the window, and check that it seals all round. If necessary, turn the adjuster a little more until a good seal is obtained.

Rear side window (3-door models) - removal and refitting

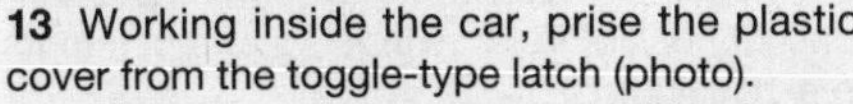

13 Working inside the car, prise the plastic cover from the toggle-type latch (photo).

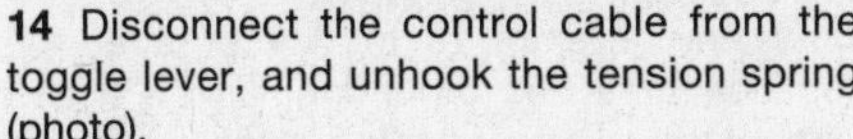

14 Disconnect the control cable from the toggle lever, and unhook the tension spring (photo).

15 Slide the latch arm off the ball-stud on the glass.

16 Using the fingers, prise off the plastic hinge cover from the forward edge of the window, to expose the hinges (photo).

17 Drill out the pop-rivets, remove the glass, and unscrew the nuts which hold the hinges to the glass.

18 Fit the hinges to the rear glass, but do not tighten the nuts excessively.

19 Pop-rivet the hinges to the body pillar.

20 Reconnect all the disconnected items, and then check the adjustment of the control cable as described earlier (photo).

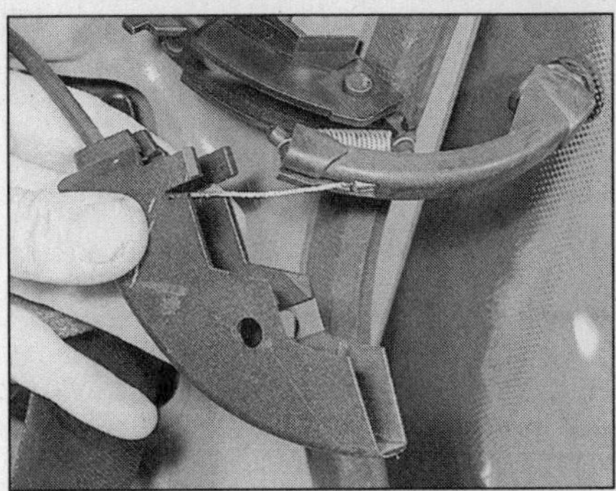

19.14 Disconnecting the window opening control cable

19.16 Plastic hinge cover

Bonnet lock cable renewal - emergency opening of bonnet

21 In the event of the bonnet lock cable breaking, the bonnet can be opened if a large hole, diameter 12.5 mm is drilled in the plate behind the radiator grille slats as shown. Take care not to damage the radiator (photo).

22 Insert a long screwdriver at the angle shown, and deflect the lever on the bonnet lock to release the lock (photo).

23 Fitting a new cable is described in Chapter 11, Section 7.

Body side rubbing strip - removal and refitting

24 The side rubbing strip can be removed by prising with a flat blade. Be prepared for some

19.20 Opening rear side window cable adjuster

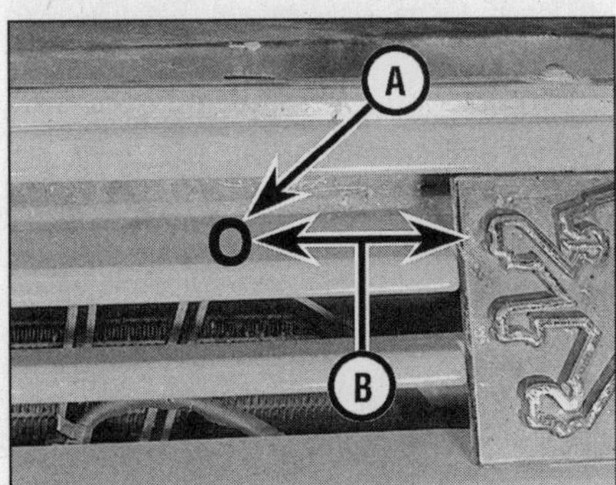

19.21 Hole drilling dimensions for emergency opening of bonnet

A = 12.5 mm (0.5 in) diameter
B = 54.0 mm (2.1 in)

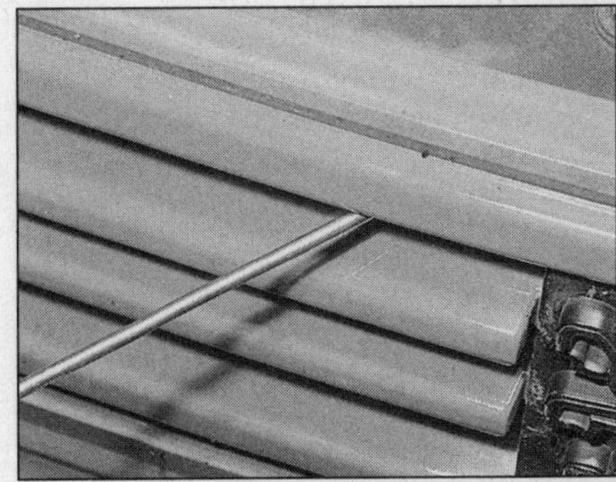

19.22 Inserting screwdriver to deflect bonnet lock lever

13

19.35A Typical seat belt anchorage components

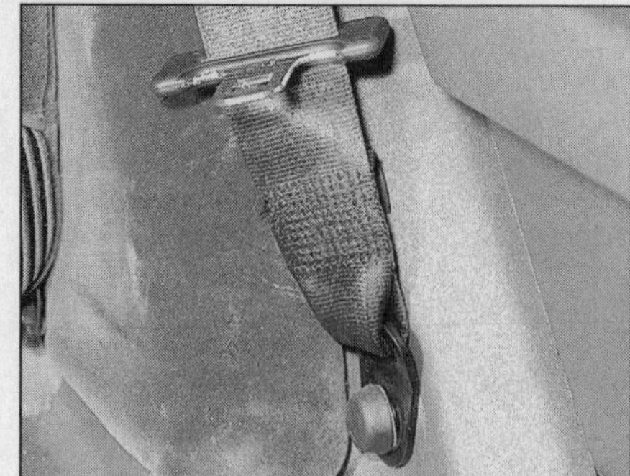
19.35B Lower seat belt anchorage

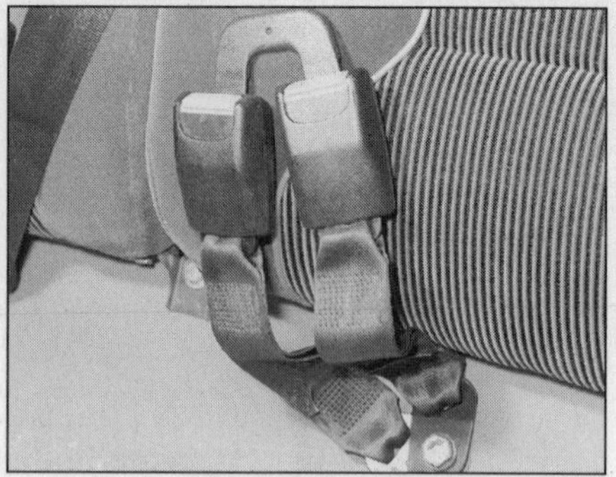
19.35C Rear seat belt anchorage

clips to break, and take care to protect the paintwork from damage when using the blade.

Exterior mirrors - removal and refitting

25 To remove the mirror, extract the grub screw and take off the control handle.
26 Prise out the triangular trim plate.
27 Extract the mirror fixing screws, and remove the mirror. Refitting is a reversal of removal.
28 Some later models have heated mirrors, and the wiring will have to be disconnected before removal. This will require removal of the door trip panel (see Chapter 11).

Interior mirror - removal and refitting

29 This is bonded directly to the windscreen.
30 The mirror can be removed by using a hot-air gun while an assistant applies a cutting action with a piece of nylon or terylene cord between the glass and the mirror base.
31 Adhesive patches and special glues are available to bond the new mirror to the glass.

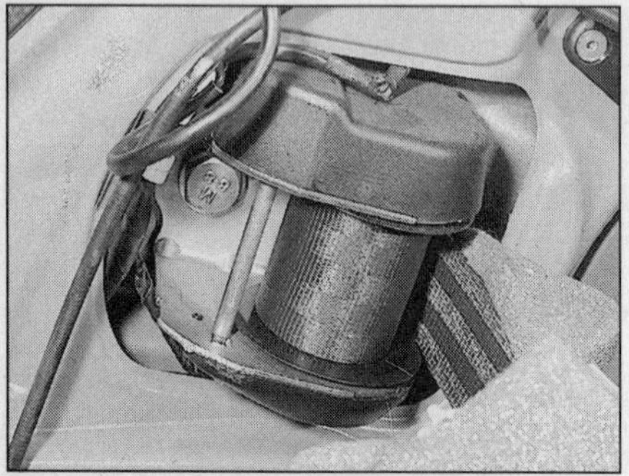
19.36 Rear seat belt inertia reel

Seat belts - maintenance, removal and refitting

32 Periodically examine the belts for signs of fraying or other damage.
33 Any cleaning required should be done using warm water and liquid detergent. Do not use solvents of any kind.
34 Retain the belt in its extended position until dry or before allowing it to retract into its reel housing.
35 Never attempt to modify or alter the location of a belt mounting, and if a belt anchorage is disconnected, always refit the mounting components in their original sequence (photos).
36 Access to the front seat belt reels is obtained after removing the interior quarter trim panel. Access to the rear belts involves removing the trim panel inside the rear corner body pillar (photo).

Glovebox (models from October 1989) - removal and refitting

Glovebox lid

37 Open the glovebox lid.
38 Insert a small flat-bladed screwdriver into the slot alongside the left-hand lid stay, and release the plastic tang. Repeat the procedure for the right-hand side.
39 With the stays released, tilt the lid downwards whilst pulling it towards you. Remove the lid.
40 Refitting is the reverse of the removal procedure.

Glovebox

41 Remove the glovebox lid as described above.
42 Undo and remove the six screws retaining the glovebox in the facia, and remove the glovebox (photo).
43 Refitting is the reverse of the removal procedure.

Facia (models from October 1989) - removal and refitting

44 Disconnect the battery negative lead.
45 Remove the centre wiper arm as described in Chapter 12.
46 Unscrew and remove the four screws securing the air inlet grille (photo).
47 Open the bonnet and remove the central clip from the air inlet grille (photo).
48 Disengage the air inlet grille from its two side fixings, and remove it.
49 Undo the three nuts securing the facia to the bulkhead, one of which is hidden by the centre wiper arm spindle.
50 On vehicles with manual chokes, detach the choke cable from the carburettor.
51 From inside the vehicle, remove the radio as described in Chapter 12.

19.42 Removing the glovebox

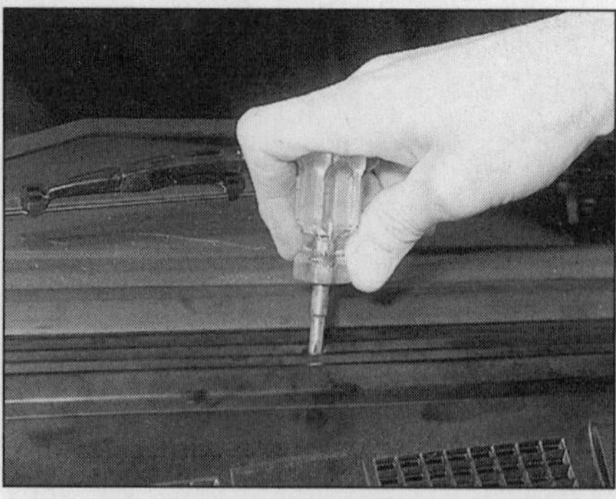
19.46 Remove the screws securing the air inlet grille

19.47 Remove the central clip from the air inlet grille

19.52 Removing a heater control knob

19.60 Removing the facia

19.63 Removing the tailgate inner trim panel

52 Remove the heater control knobs by pulling them from their spindles (photo).

53 Undo the two screws and remove the outer heater control panel.

54 Undo and remove the four screws securing the inner heater control panel to the facia. Push the inner heater control panel inwards towards the bulkhead.

55 Unscrew the four securing screws, and withdraw the lower trim panel which houses the ashtray. Two of these screws can be found either side of the panel, the other two are concealed behind the ashtray flap.

56 Remove the instrument panel as described in Section 20 of this Chapter.

57 Remove the glovebox as described earlier in this Section.

58 Remove the fusebox as described in Section 20 of this Chapter.

59 Undo and remove the two screws and the nut securing the lower part of the facia, and withdraw the facia into the vehicle.

60 Disconnect the choke cable from the choke lever, where fitted, and remove the facia from the vehicle (photo).

61 Refitting is the reverse of the removal procedure, but note the following points:

(a) *Ensure that the wiring harnesses and cables are correctly arranged and routed before fitting the facia panel. The wires tend to be only just long enough, and the routing is therefore critical. Where applicable, secure the harnesses in retaining clips out of the way of adjacent components (as noted during removal). Ensure that all connections are correct and secure.*

(b) *On completion, reconnect the battery earth lead, and check that the various instruments and associated electrical components are fully functional.*

Tailgate lock components (models from October 1989) - removal and refitting

Tailgate lock

62 Open the tailgate.

63 Remove the tailgate inner trim panel by unscrewing the nine Torx screws (photo).

64 Disconnect the lock-to-latch connecting rod.

65 Carefully unclip the tailgate outer trim panel from its five retaining clips.

66 Wearing suitable protective clothing, carefully drill out the four pop rivets securing the lock to the tailgate (photo).

67 Refitting is the reverse of the removal procedure, ensuring that the lock is positioned squarely on the tailgate before using new rivets to secure it.

Tailgate latch

68 Open the tailgate.

69 Remove the tailgate inner trim panel by unscrewing the nine Torx screws.

70 Disconnect the latch-to-lock connecting rod.

71 Unscrew the two screws securing the latch to the tailgate, and remove the latch.

72 Refitting is the reverse of the removal procedure.

Tailgate striker plate

73 Open the tailgate.

74 Unhook and remove the striker plate finisher trim. A length of bent welding rod may be used to good effect (photo).

75 Unscrew the two screws securing the striker plate, and remove the striker plate.

76 Refitting is the reverse of the removal procedure.

20 Electrical system

Alternator (Paris-Rhone) - brush renewal

1 If the brushes have been renewed (see Chapter 12), then the action of removing and refitting the regulator/brush holder may prevent the alternator 'self-exciting', to commence charging when the engine is started.

2 Should this happen, carry out the following remedial action.

3 Disconnect the charge warning light lead from the terminal 'L' on the regulator.

4 Briefly touch the end of a temporary lead from the battery positive terminal to the 'L' terminal on the regulator.

5 Reconnect the charge warning light lead to terminal 'L', and remove the temporary lead.

Alternator (Valeo) - regulator renewal

6 There are two types of regulator fitted to Valeo alternators, and although they are interchangeable, care must be taken when fitting, as they are of different dimensions.

7 The regulators carry the identifying marks 'YV' or 'YH' on their bodies.

8 The baseplate of the YV regulator is thinner than that of the YH type, and therefore requires shorter fixing screws. If the longer screws from the YH regulator are used to secure a YV regulator, they will foul the rotor and so prevent it from rotating.

9 Screws 20 mm long must be used to secure

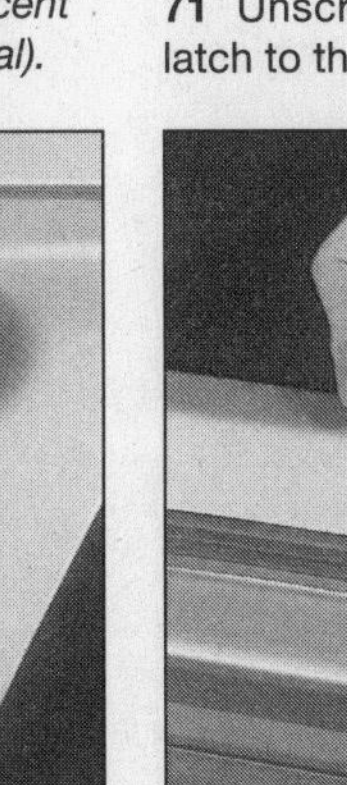

19.66 Tailgate lock and securing rivets

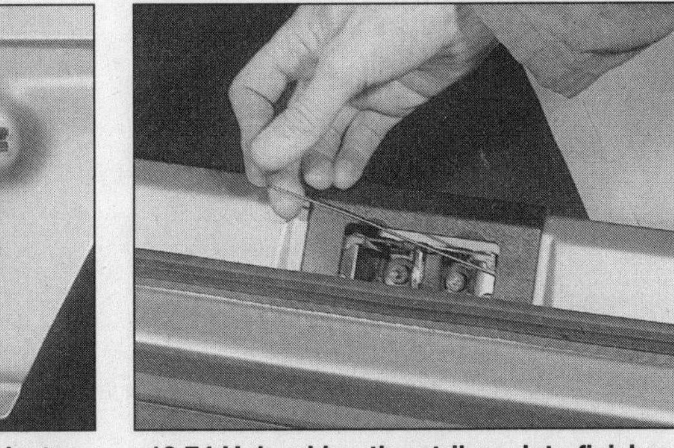

19.74 Unhooking the striker plate finisher trim

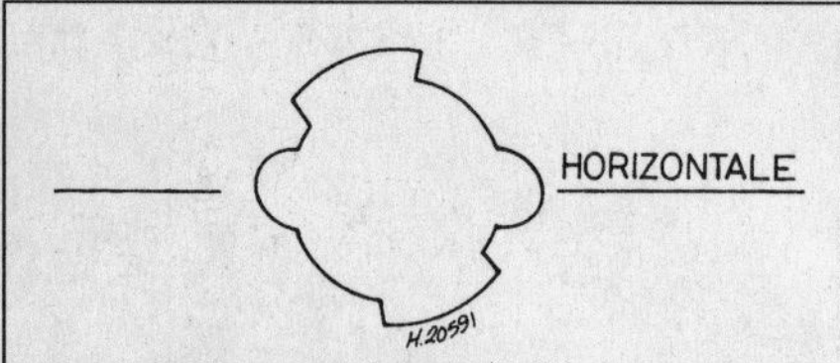

Fig. 13.65 Template for later type side repeater lamp front wing hole (Sec 20)

the YV type regulator, and 30 mm long screws must be used to secure the YH type.

Fusebox (models from October 1989) - removal and refitting

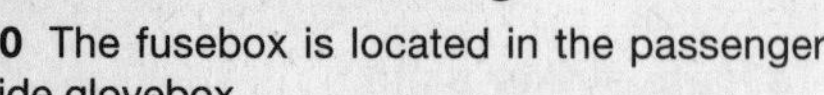

10 The fusebox is located in the passenger side glovebox.

11 Disconnect the battery negative lead.

12 Remove the glovebox as described in Section 19 of this Chapter.

13 Pull back the plastic retaining clip and lower the fusebox.

14 Gently prise apart the ball-and-socket joints securing the fusebox to the facia, and pull the fusebox into the vehicle as far as possible, taking care not to strain any wires.

15 Disconnect the wiring connectors, taking note of their relative positions, and remove the fusebox.

16 Refitting is the reverse of the removal procedure.

Side repeater lights

17 The direction indicator side repeater lights on later models have a 'bayonet' type fitting instead of the clips used previously, and are secured in the wing by twisting (photo).

18 Only the later type lights are available as replacements, and their fitting on early models will necessitate filing out the hole in the wing using the template shown in Fig. 13.65.

Headlight dim-dip system

19 This is fitted to all later models (from late 1986 onwards), and prevents the car being driven on parking (side) lights only. When the sidelights are switched on with the ignition also switched on, the headlight dipped beams will come on at approximately one-sixth intensity (hence the term 'dim-dip').

20 The headlight beam intensity is reduced by means of a relay and a power resistor unit.

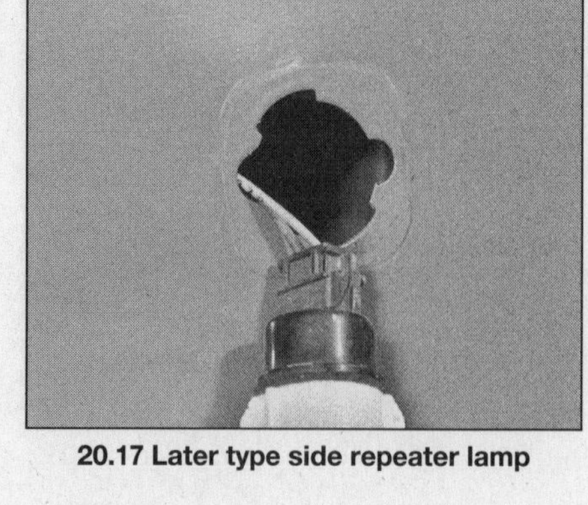

20.17 Later type side repeater lamp

Facia switches (models from October 1989) - removal and refitting

21 Disconnect the battery negative lead.

22 Remove the instrument panel cowl as described in paragraphs 25 to 31 below.

23 From the back of the switch depress the two plastic tangs, and remove the switch through the front of the cowl.

24 Refitting is the reverse of the removal procedure.

Instrument panel (models from October 1989) - removal and refitting

25 Disconnect the battery negative lead.

26 Remove the parcel shelf below the steering wheel by undoing the four screws securing it to the facia, and the nut securing it to the bulkhead.

27 Remove the steering column lower shroud by removing the four securing screws (photo).

28 Undo the four nuts securing the steering column, and lower the column to the floor.

29 Disconnect all the electrical connectors from the steering column, noting their relative positions.

30 Lever off the small trim panel which is situated between the two central heater vents (photos).

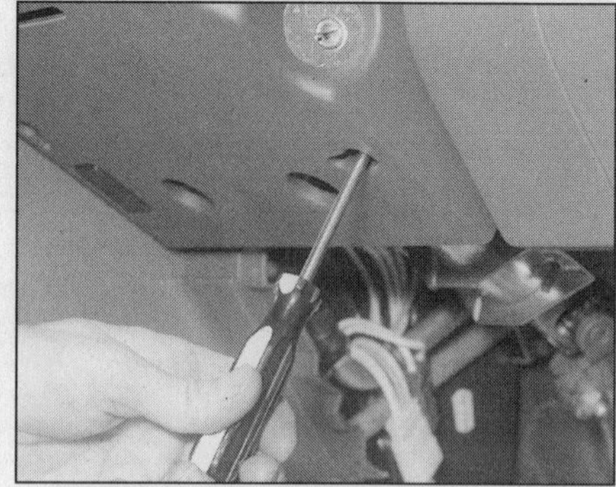

20.27 Undo the four screws to enable removal of the steering column lower shroud

31 Unscrew the five screws securing the instrument cowl to the facia, and remove the cowl. Note that one of the screws was hidden by the trim panel removed in paragraph 30.

32 Unscrew the four screws retaining the instrument panel, and pull it towards you a few inches, taking care not to strain any wiring.

33 Disconnect the speedometer drive cable and the instrument panel wiring connectors, taking note of their relative routings and connections (photo).

34 Withdraw the instrument panel.

35 The procedure for replacing panel bulbs is the same as that outlined in Chapter 12. Removal and refitting of any instruments should be self-explanatory.

36 Refitting is the reverse of the removal procedure, noting the following points:

(a) *Ensure that the wiring harnesses and cables are correctly arranged and routed before fitting the instrument panel. The wires tend to be only just long enough, and the routing is therefore critical. Where applicable, secure the harnesses in retaining clips out of the way of adjacent components (as noted during removal). Ensure that all connections are correct and secure.*

(b) *It is advisable to retighten the steering column securing nuts to the specified torque after fitting the steering column*

20.30A Lever off the trim panel. . .

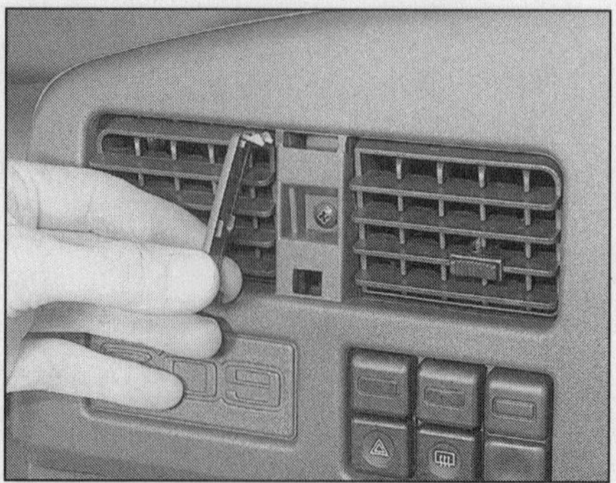

20.30B. . .to reveal one of the instrument cowl retaining screws

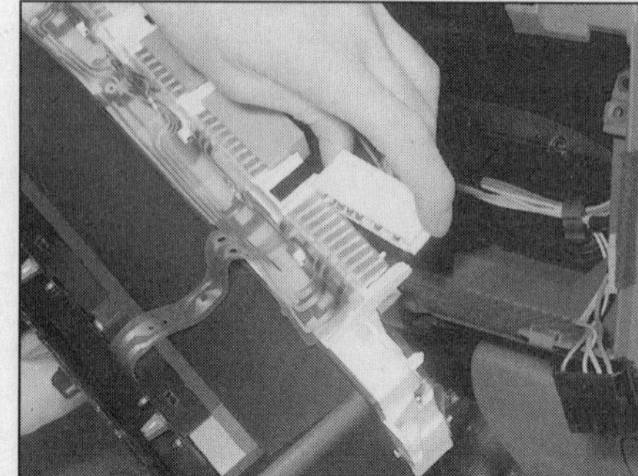

20.33 Disconnecting the instrument panel wiring connectors

lower shroud. Peugeot have provided holes in the lower shroud for this purpose (photo).

(c) *On completion, reconnect the battery earth lead, and check that the various instruments and associated electrical components are fully functional.*

Roof-mounted aerial - removal and refitting

37 Using a small screwdriver, prise out the map reading light from the roof lining above the windscreen.

38 Extract the fixing screws, and lower the light housing.

39 The aerial fixing nut is now exposed (photo). An open-ended spanner may be bent at right-angles to engage on the two flats of the nut, or a forked tool may be fabricated from a piece of sheet metal.

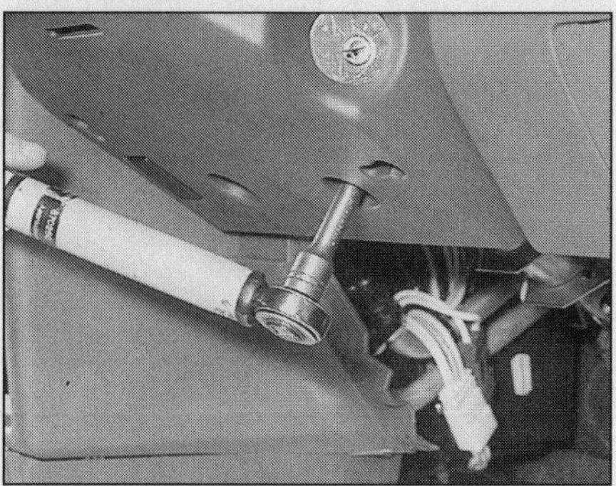

20.36 Tighten the steering column nuts to the specified torque

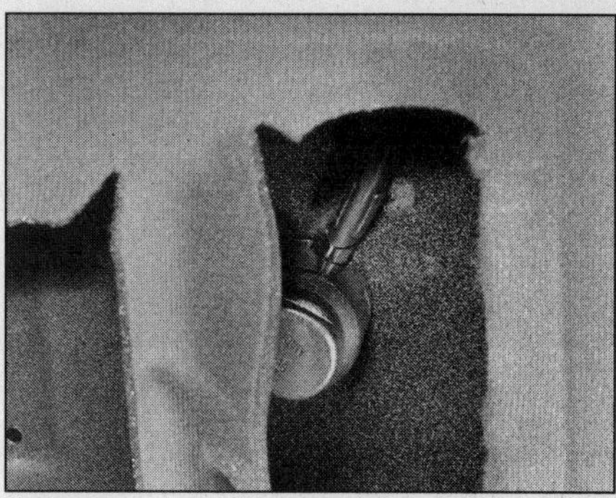

20.39 Roof-mounted aerial securing nut

40 The aerial coaxial lead is fed down the right-hand side windscreen pillar. If it is to be withdrawn, tape or tie some string to its end, then withdraw the lead, leaving the string in place to facilitate installing the new lead.

41 If a new aerial is fitted, trim the aerial in accordance with the radio or aerial manufacturer's instructions.

Notes

NOTES:

1. All diagrams are divided into numbered circuits depending on function e.g. Diagram 2: Exterior lighting.
2. Items are arranged in relation to a plan view of the vehicle.
3. Items may appear on more than one diagram so are found using a grid reference e.g. 2/A1 denotes an item on diagram 2 grid location A1.
4. Complex items appear on the diagrams as blocks and are expanded on the internal connections page.
5. Brackets show how the circuit may be connected in more than one way.
6. Not all items are fitted to all models.
7. Wire identification is not by colour, but by letters or numbers appearing on the wire at each end.

INTERNAL CONNECTION DETAILS

d c b a a7 e a6 f a5 g a4 h a3 i a2 j a1 k (88) z l y m x n w o v p u q r s t

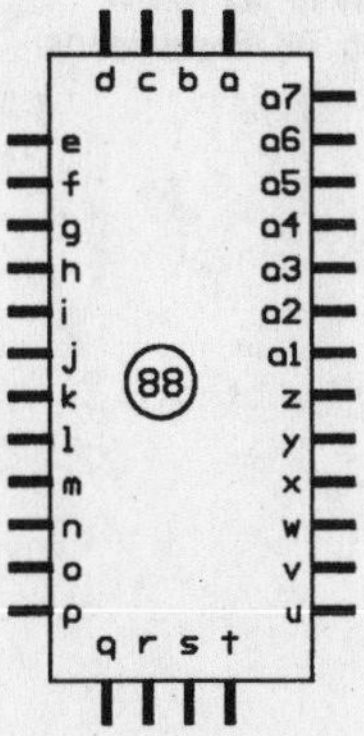

KEY TO INSTRUMENT CLUSTER (ITEM 88)

a = +VE Supply
b = Earth
c = Tachometer
d = Tachometer
e = No Charge Warning Lamp
f = Stop Warning Lamp
g = Low Brake Fluid Warning Lamp
h = Earth
i = Direction Indicator Warning Lamp
j = Sidelamp Warning Lamp
k = Dipped Beam Warning Lamp
l = Oil Pressure Gauge
m = High Temp. Warning Lamp
n = Earth
o = Coolant Temperature Gauge
p = Oil Temperature Gauge
q = Water In Fuel Warning Lamp
r = Diagnosis Warning Lamp
s = Earth
t = Clock
u = Instrument Illumination
v = Earth
w = Choke Warning Lamp
x = + VE Supply
y = Coolant Level Warning Lamp
z = Direction Indicator Warning Lamp
a1 = Pre Heater Warning Lamp
a2 = Oil Pressure Warning Lamp
a3 = Brake Pad Wear Warning Lamp
a4 = Main Beam Warning Lamp
a5 = Fuel Gauge
a6 = Low Fuel Warning Lamp
a7 = Earth

FUSE	RATING	CIRCUIT
1	10A	Coolant level indicator, reversing lamps, tachometer and clock illumination
2	25A	Heater blower, instrument panel supply, direction indicator, cigar lighter, glove box and hazard warning lamps
3	25A	Wipers, washers, stop lamps, heated rear window, clock and map reading lamp
4	15A	Front foglamps
5	10A	Hazard warning lamps
6		Spare
7	10A	Central locking, battery condition indicator, radio, clock, luggage/glove box/interior lamps and cigar lighter
8	25A	Horns and heated rear window
9	30A	Electric windows
10	5A	Rear fog lamp
11	5A	Tail lamp LH
12	5A	Tail lamp RH
13	15A	Front Side lamps, number plate lamps, interior lamps and dim/dip system
14	15A	Fuel pump

KEY TO SYMBOLS

PLUG-IN CONNECTOR
EARTH
BULB
DIODE
LINE CONNECTOR
FUSE/ FUSIBLE LINK
EARTH POINT
P121C

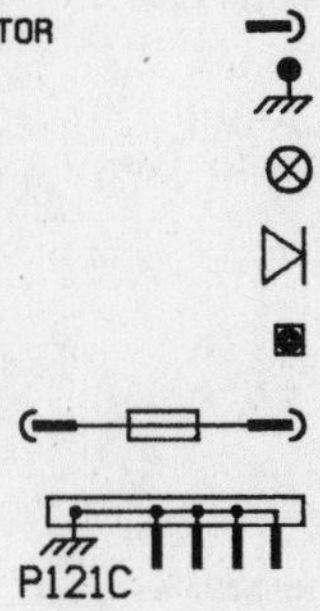

Notes, fuses, internal connection details and key to symbols

H24269
T.M.MARKE

ITEM	DESCRIPTION	DIAGRAM/ GRID REF.
1	Air Flow Sensor	1b/B6, 1d/B3
2	Air Horn Compressor	3/B5
3	Air Horn Compressor Relay	3/C5
4	Alternator	1/C3
5	Ashtray Illumination	2b/D4
6	Audible Warning Device	2b/H6
7	Auto. Trans. Inhibitor Relay	1/F5
8	Auto. Trans. Inhibitor Switch	1/E7
9	Auto. Trans. Switch Stage Illumination	2b/H4
10	Battery	1/D7, 1a/H8, 1b/C7, 1c/B7, 1d/C7, 2/C8, 2a/B7, 2b/B7, 3/B7, 3a/B7
11	Brake Pad Wear Sensor	1/D1, 1/D8
12	Cannister Purge Solenoid	1b/E3, 1c/C3, 1d/F3
13	Carburettor Breather Solenoid - XU52C Models Only	1a/D2
14	Central Locking Actuator LH Front	3a/K8
15	Central Locking Actuator LH Rear	3a/L8
16	Central Locking Actuator RH Rear	3a/L1
17	Central Locking Actuator Tailgate	3a/M5
18	Central Locking Control Switch	3a/K1
19	Central Locking Control Unit	3a/K4
20	Central Locking Infra-red - Signal Receiver	3a/K6
21	Choke Switch	1/K2
22	Cigar Lighter	2b/D4
23	Clock	2b/C5
24	Combination Switch - Lighting, Direction Indicators And Horn	2/J2, 2a/G3, 2b/F3, 3/F3, 3a/D3
25	Combination Switch - Wash/Wipe	3/J2
26	Compressor	1c/C7, 1d/A7
27	Coolant Level Indicator Unit	1/A3
28	Coolant Temp. Gauge Sender Unit	1/E5
29	Coolant Temp. Switch	1/E5
30	Cooling Fan Motor	1/A4, 1/A6
31	Cooling Fan Resistor	1/B3
32	Cooling Fan Switch	1/B4, 1/B7
33	Diagnostic Socket	1/C4
34	Dim/Dip Relay	2/D5
35	Dim/Dip Resistor	2/A8
36	Direction Indicator Flasher Relay	2a/E6
37	Direction Indicator LH Front	2a/A8
38	Direction Indicator LH Side Repeater	2a/D8
39	Direction Indicator RH Front	2a/A1
40	Direction Indicator RH Side Repeater	2a/D1

ITEM	DESCRIPTION	DIAGRAM/ GRID REF.
41	Distributor	1a/A5, 1a/A7, 1a/B1, 1a/E1, 1a/E5, 1a/F6, 1a/G1, 1a/K1
42	Driving Lamp LH	2/A6
43	Driving Lamp Relay	2/D4
44	Driving Lamp RH	2/A3
45	Electric Window Motor LH Front	3a/J8
46	Electric Window Motor RH Front	3a/K1
47	Electric Window Relay	3a/D6
48	Electric Window Switch LH	3a/H8
49	Electric Window Switch RH (Drivers)	3a/J1
50	Electric Window Switch RH (Passengers)	3a/H1
51	Engine Speed Sensor	1c/C5, 1d/C4
52	Foglamp Front	2/A3, 2/A6
53	Foglamp Relay	2/G6
54	Foglamp Switch Front	2/H3
55	Foglamp Switch Rear	2/H2
56	Fuel Gauge Sender Unit	1/M4
57	Fuel Injection ECU	1b/H6, 1b/J2, 1c/H3, 1d/J4
58	Fuel Injectors	1b/C2, 1b/E6, 1c/B4, 1d/D2
59	Fuel Pump	1b/M5, 1c/M6, 1d/M6
60	Fuse - Cooling Fan	1/C7
61	Fuse - Fuel Injection Ecu	1d/B7
62	Fuse - Lambda Sensor	1b/D4, 1c/A7, 1d/B7
63	Glove Box Lamp	2b/J8
64	Glove Box Lamp Switch	2b/J8
65	Handbrake Warning Switch	1/L5
66	Hazard Warning Lamp Switch	2a/H3
67	Headlamp Unit LH	2/A7
68	Headlamp Unit RH	2/A2
69	Heated Door Mirror LH	3/J8
70	Heated Door Mirror RH	3/J1
71	Heated Rear Window	3/L4
72	Heated Rear Window Relay	3/F6
73	Heated Rear Window Switch	3/J3
74	Heater Blower Motor	3/J5
75	Heater Blower Motor Control Unit	3/D8
76	Heater Blower Motor Switch	3/J4
77	Horn	3/A2, 3/A5, 3/A6, 3/A7
78	Idle Solenoid	1b/B1, 1c/C4

H24270

T.M.MARKE

Key to wiring diagrams

ITEM	DESCRIPTION	DIAGRAM/ GRID REF.
79	Ignition Coil	1a/A8, 1a/B3, 1a/C5, 1a/E2, 1a/G5, 1a/G7, 1a/J3, 1a/M2
80	Ignition Module	1a/B3, 1a/B5, 1a/B8, 1a/F5, 1a/F8
81	Ignition Switch	1/J1, 1a/M3, 1b/L1, 1c/K1, 1d/K1, 2/F1, 2a/G1, 2b/H1, 3/H1, 3a/F1
82	Injection Cut-off Solenoid	1b/F4
83	Injection Matching Resistor	1b/E4, 1d/E2
84	Injection Supply Relay	1b/H4, 1c/G7, 1d/F7
85	Injection Temp. Sensor	1b/D3, 1b/F7, 1c/C6, 1d/D4
86	Inlet Air Temp. Sensor	1c/B2
87	Inlet Manifold Pressure Sensor	1c/C5
88	Instrument Cluster	1/J4, 1a/K5, 1c/K3, 1d/K3, 2/E3, 2a/E3, 2b/D2
89	Instrument Illumination Control	2b/F4
90	Interior Lamp Door Switch LH Front	2b/C8
91	Interior Lamp Door Switch LH Rear	2b/K8
92	Interior Lamp Door Switch RH Front	2b/C1
93	Interior Lamp Door Switch RH Rear	2b/K1
94	Interior Lamp Front	2b/G4
95	Interior Lamp Rear	2b/J3
96	Lambda Sensor	1b/H3, 1c/D6, 1d/D5
97	Lamp Cluster LH Rear	2/M7, 2a/M7
98	Lamp Cluster RH Rear	2/M2, 2a/M2
99	Low Brake Fluid Sender Unit	1/F2
100	Low Coolant Sender Unit	1/F7
101	Luggage Comp. Lamp	2b/M6
102	Luggage Comp. Lamp Switch	2b/L5
103	Map Reading Lamp	2b/H4
104	Number Plate Lamp	2/M4, 2/M5

ITEM	DESCRIPTION	DIAGRAM/ GRID REF.
105	Oil Pressure Sender Unit	1/D5
106	Oil Pressure Switch	1/D5
107	Oil Temp. Sender Unit	1/E5
108	Radio/Cassette Unit	3a/F4
109	Reversing Lamp Switch	2/D5
110	Spark Plugs	1a/A1, 1a/B4, 1a/B7, 1a/D1, 1a/F4, 1a/G6, 1a/H1, 1a/L1
111	Speaker LH Front	3a/C8
112	Speaker LH Rear	3a/M8
113	Speaker RH Front	3a/C1
114	Speaker RH Rear	3a/M1
115	Starter Motor	1/C7, 1b/B7, 1d/A6
116	Stop-Lamp Switch	2a/C3
117	Supplementary Air Device	1b/F6, 1d/D4
118	Suppressor	1a/A2, 1a/E3, 1a/F5, 1a/F8, 1a/H3, 1a/L2
119	Tachymetric Relay	1b/A8, 1b/H4, 1c/G6, 1d/G7
120	TDC Position Sensor	1/C5
121	Throttle Potentiometer	1b/E2, 1c/C5
122	Throttle Switch	1b/A6, 1d/A3
123	Washer Pump Front	3/C8
124	Washer Pump Rear	3/L8
125	Wiper Motor Front	3/C3
126	Wiper Motor Rear	3/M5
127	Wiper Relay Front	3/F7
128	Wiper Relay Rear	3/M6

H24271
T.M.MARKE

Key to wiring diagrams (continued)

Connector colours

A Yellow
B White
BA White
C Brown
D Yellow
E Blue
F White
G White
H Brown
H706 Black
J White
K Brown
L Brown
M Yellow
MR Brown
P White
R Yellow
S Yellow
T White
V White
W Blue

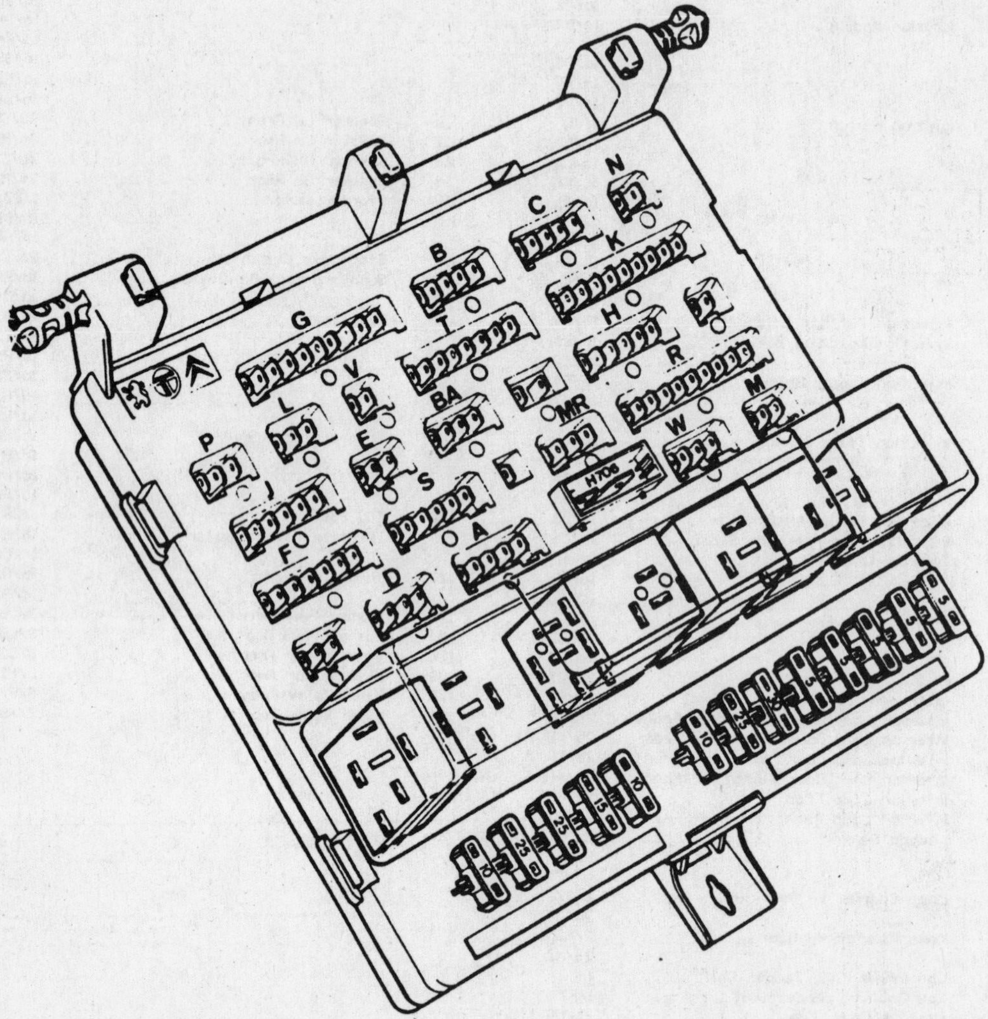

Wiring socket locations (on fuse/relay board)

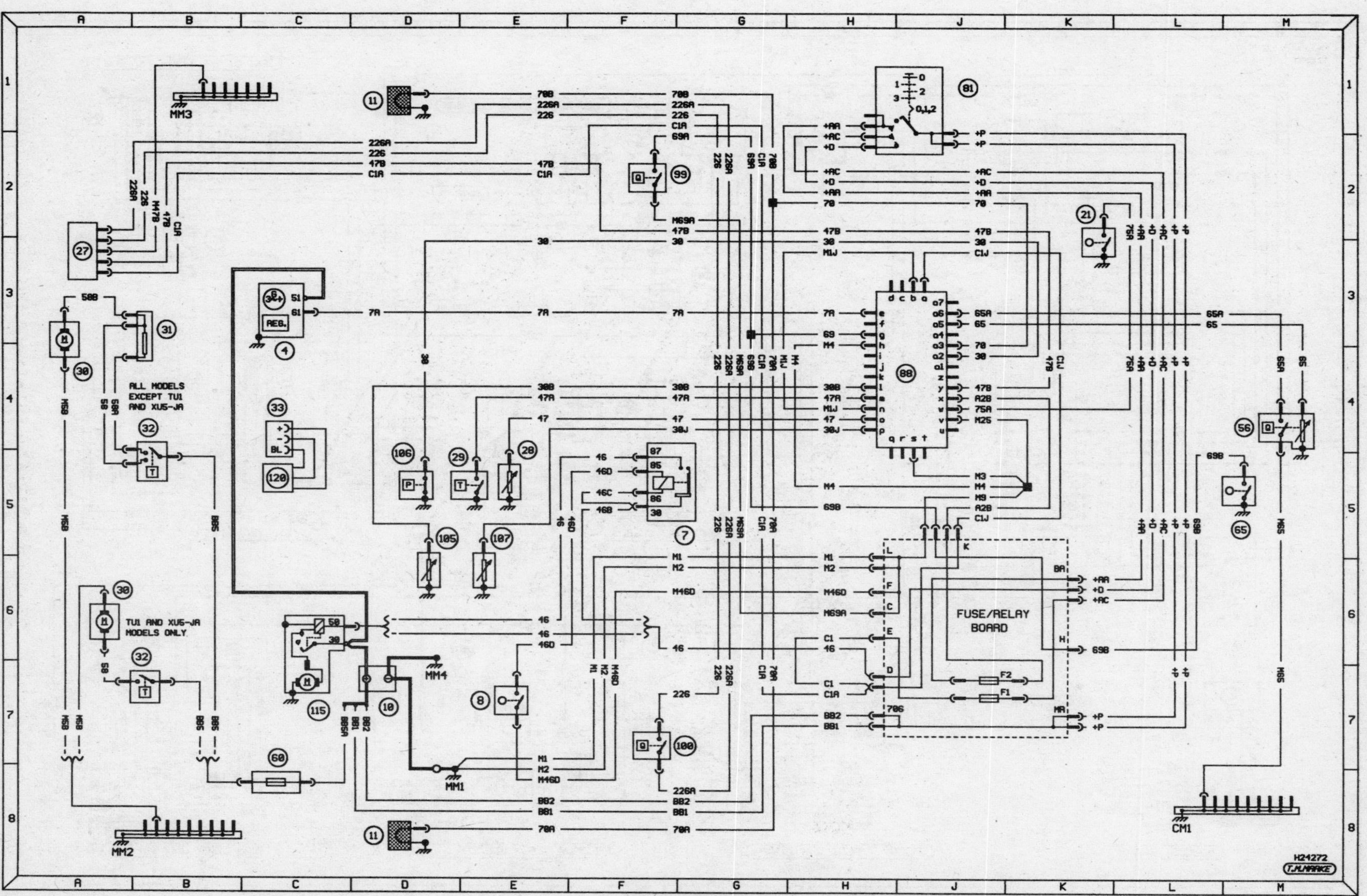

Diagram 1: Typical starting, charging, cooling fan, warning lamps and gauges (including automatic transmission)

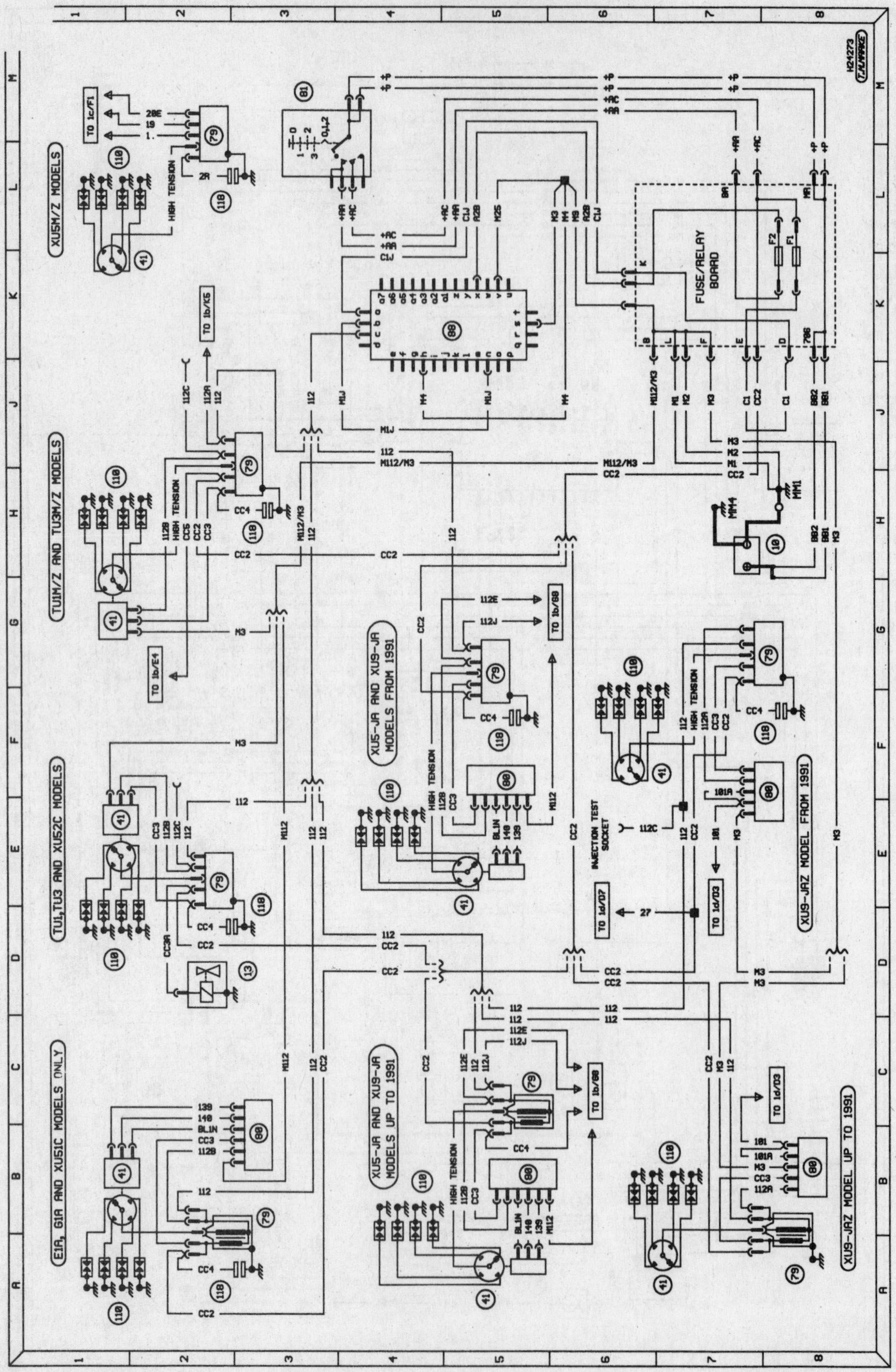

Diagram 1a: Typical ignition variation

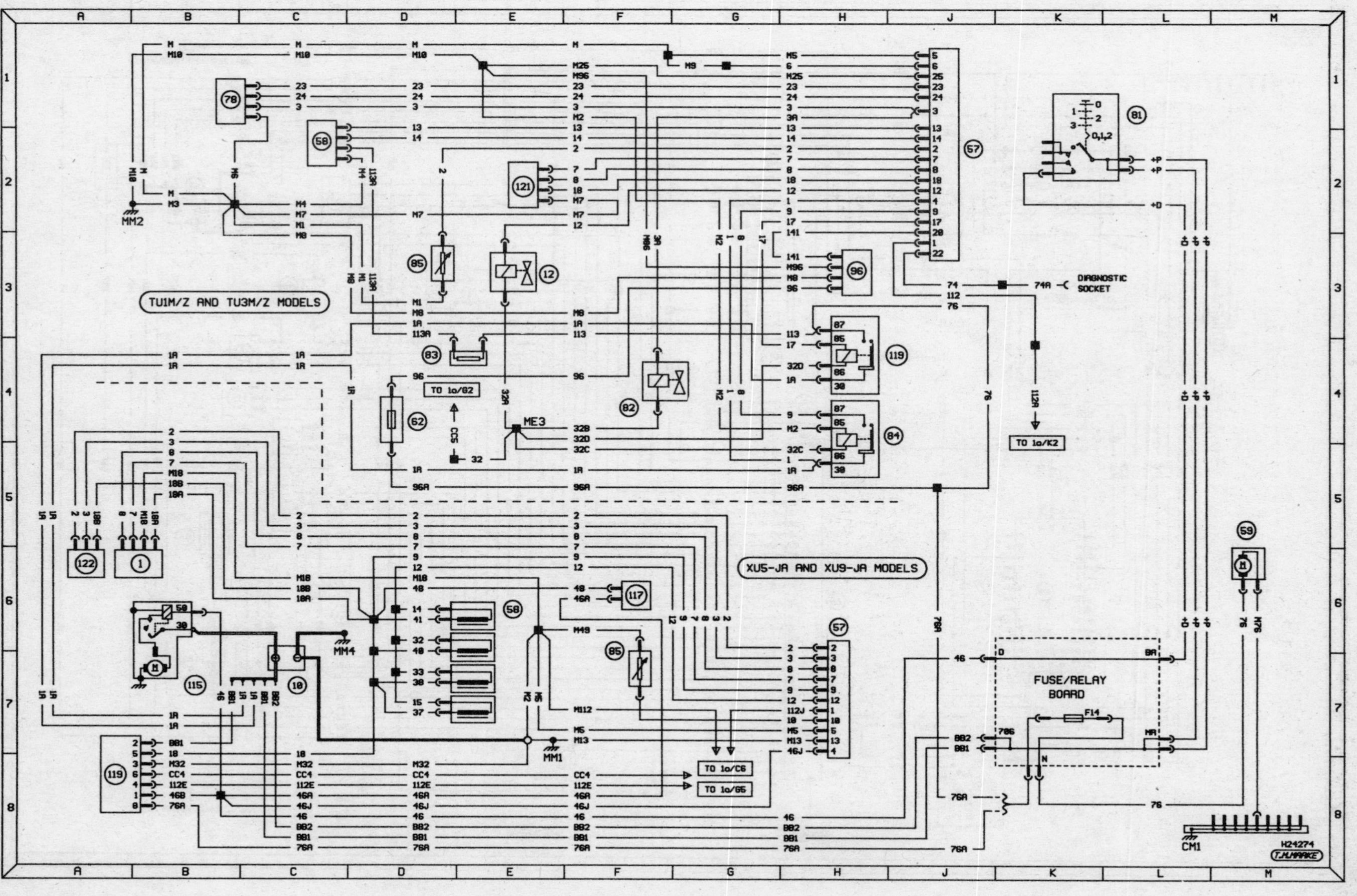

Diagram 1b: Typical engine management system (TU1M/Z, TU3M/Z, XU5-JA and XU9-JA models)

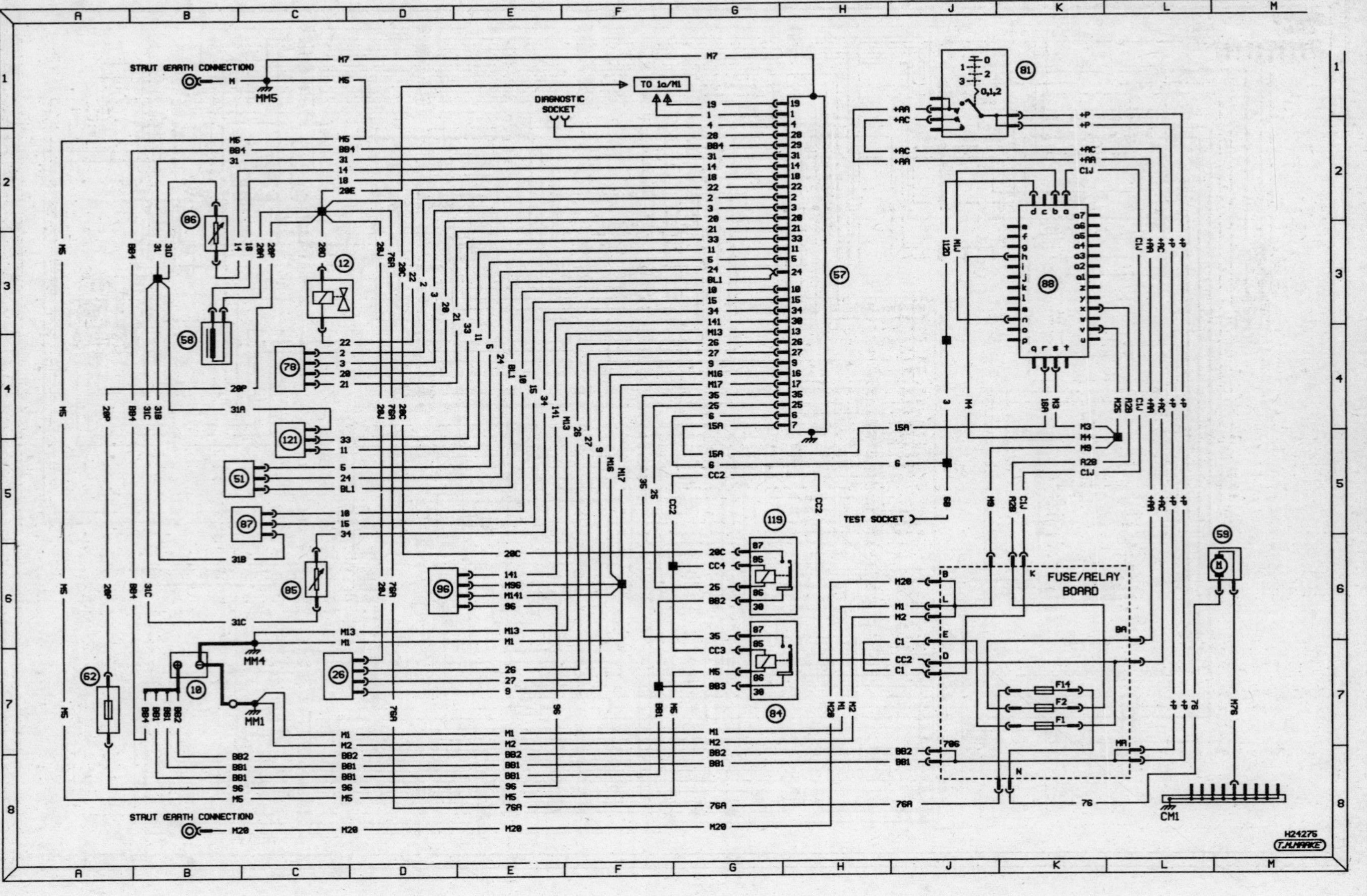

Diagram 1c: Typical engine management system (XU5M/Z catalyst models)

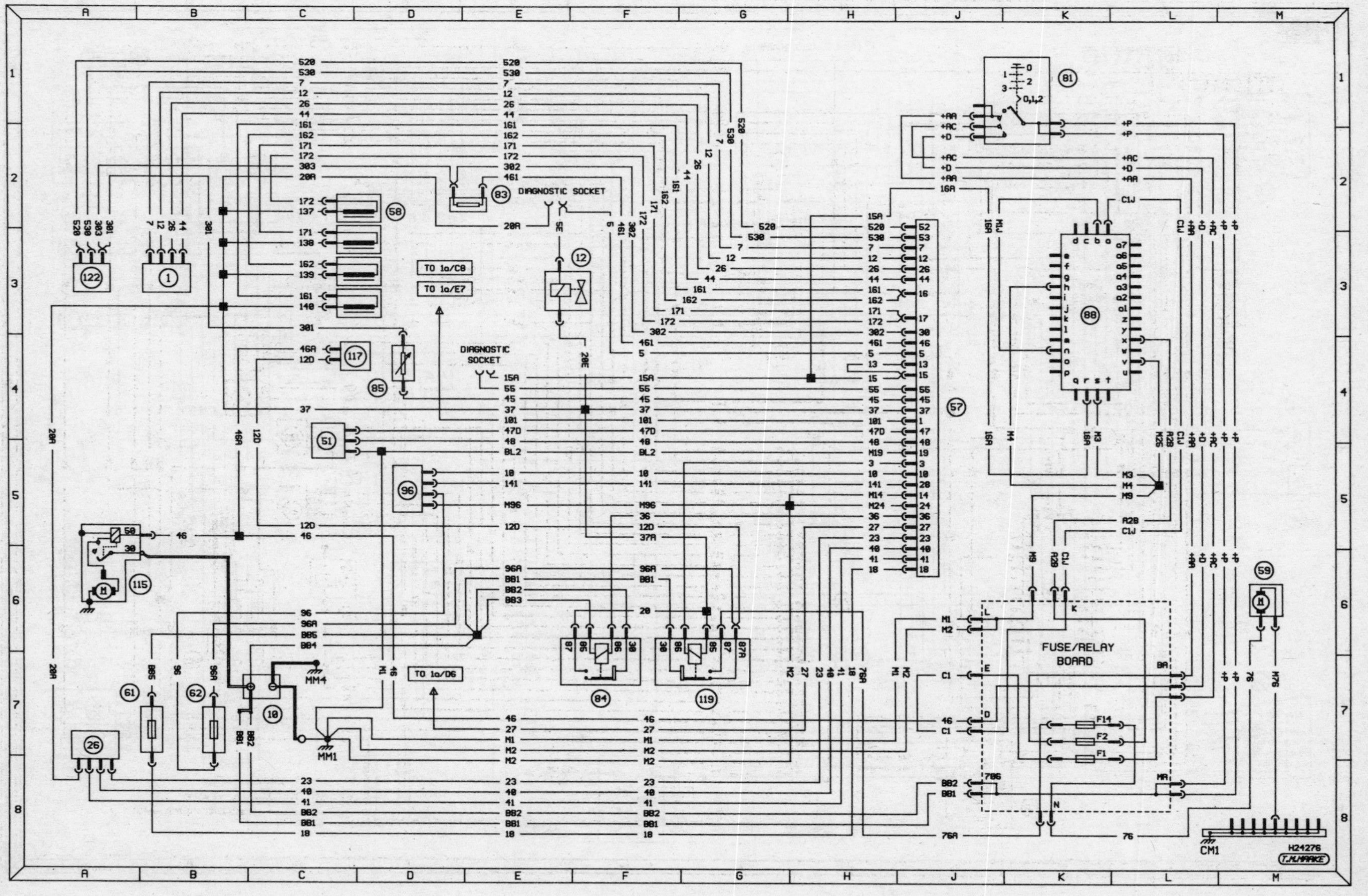

Diagram 1d: Typical engine management system (XU9-JAZ catalyst models)

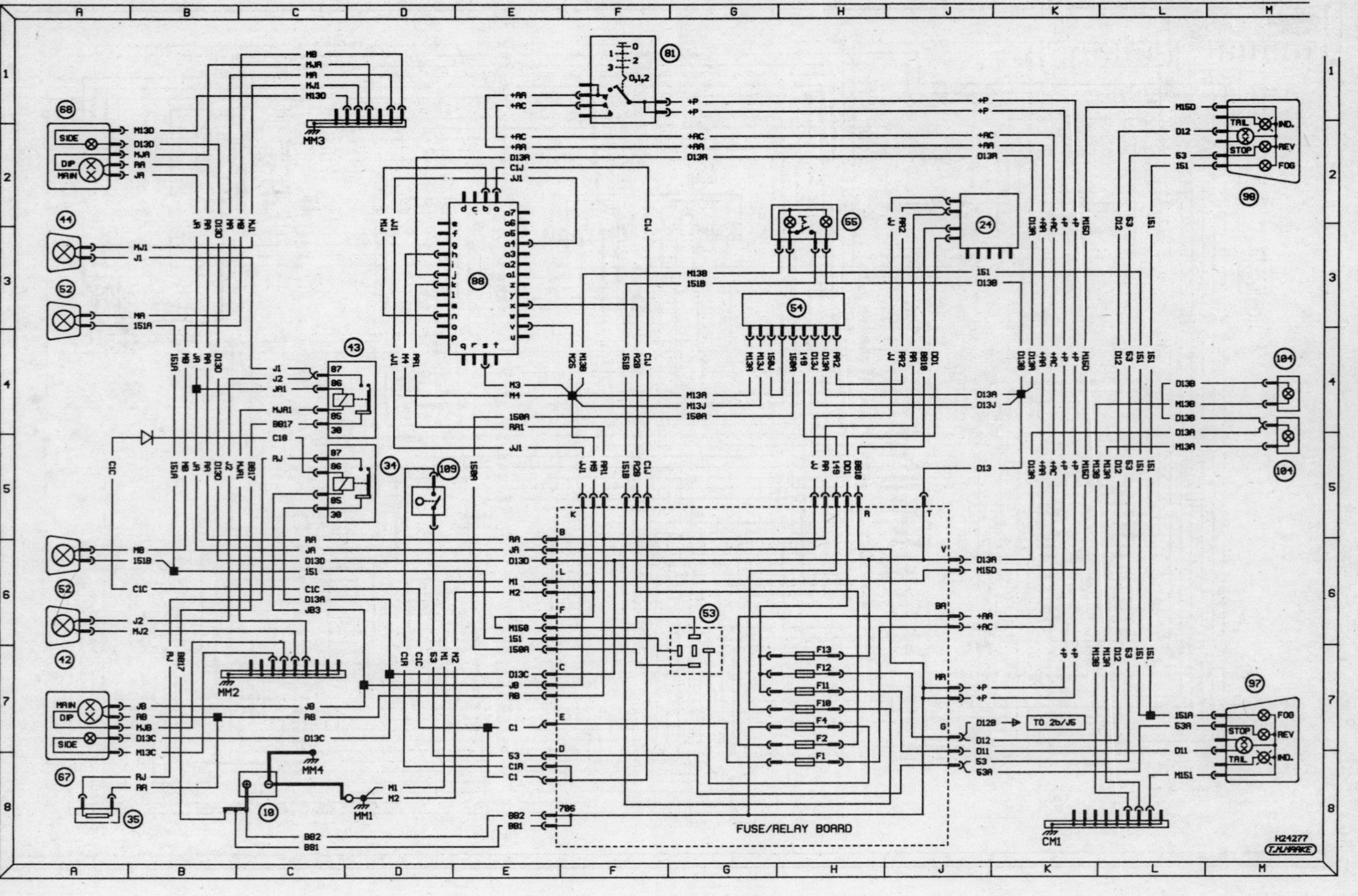

Diagram 2: Typical exterior lighting – reversing, side, fog and headlamps

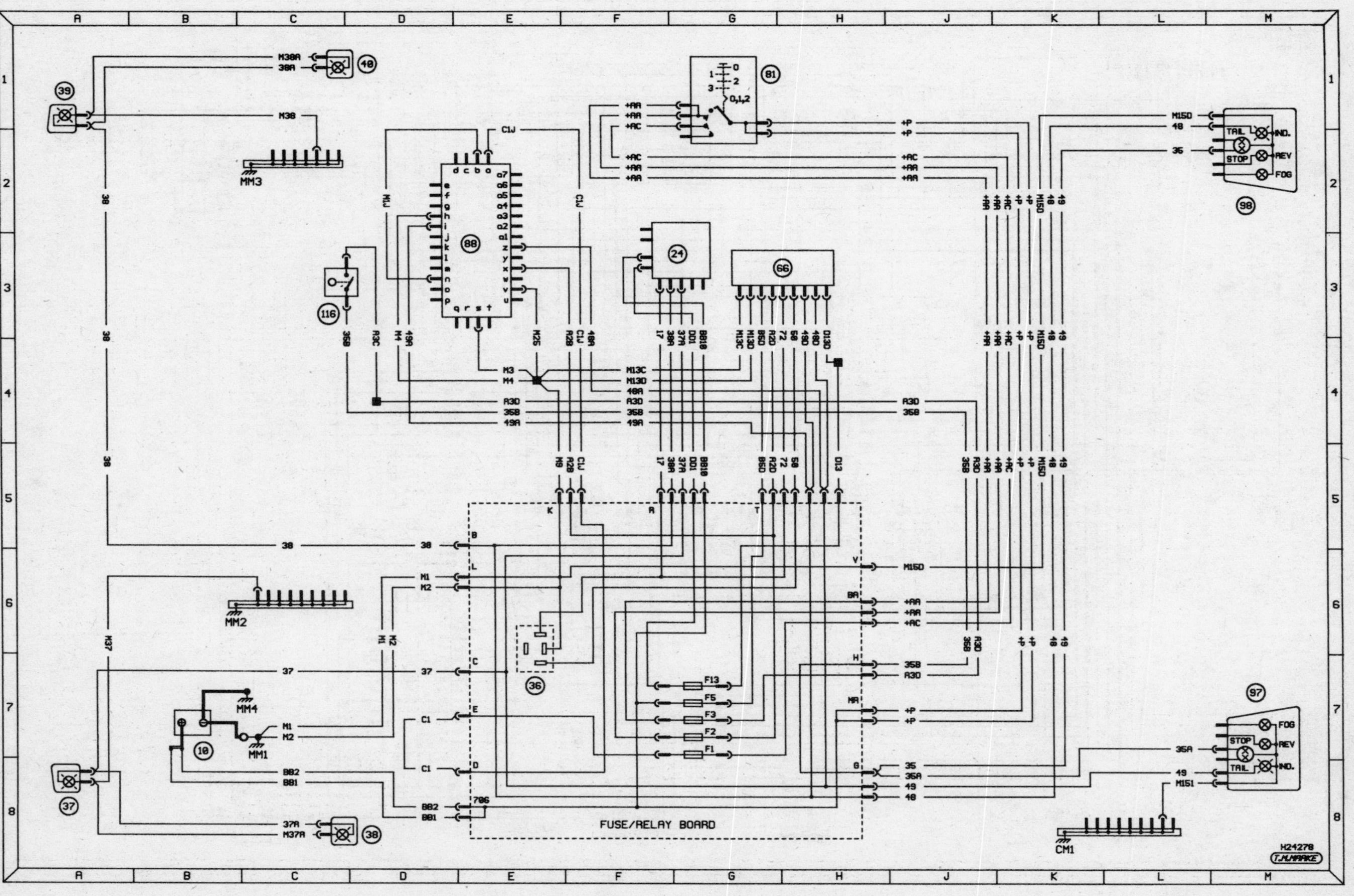

Diagram 2a: Typical exterior lighting – direction indicators and stop lights

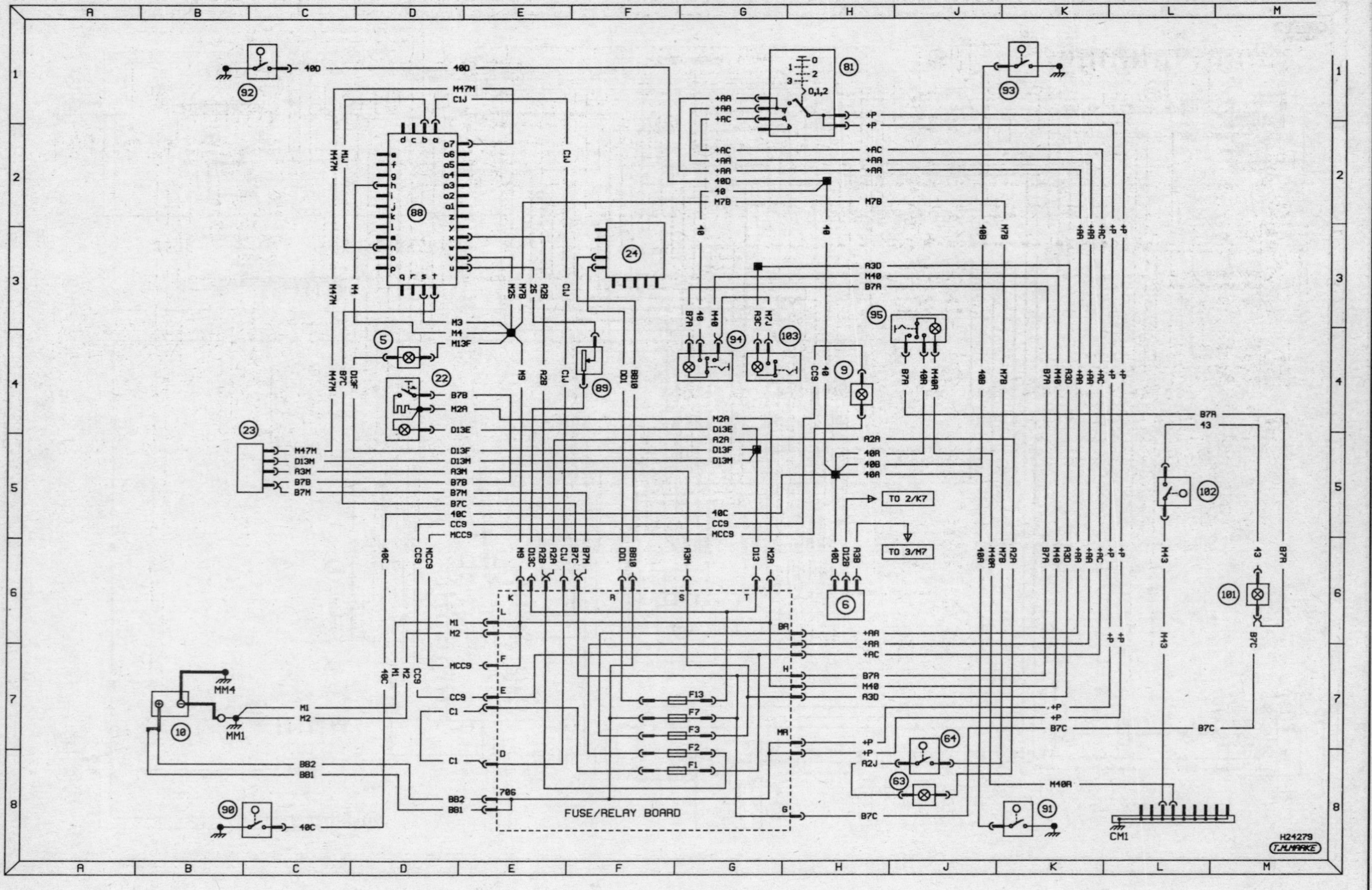

Diagram 2b: Typical interior lighting and associated circuits

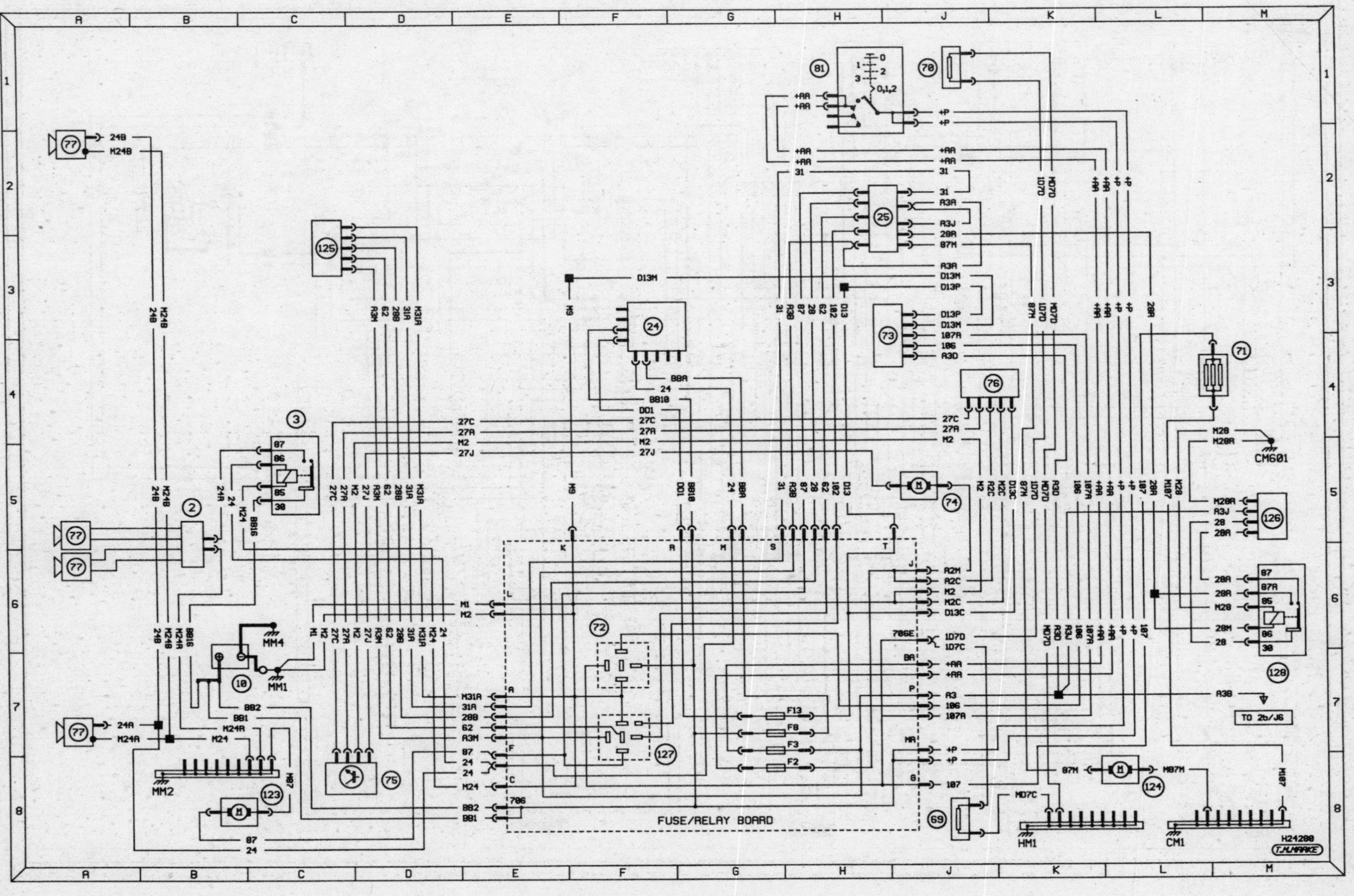

Diagram 3: Typical ancillary circuits – wash/wipe, horn, heater/blower, heated rear window and heated door mirrors

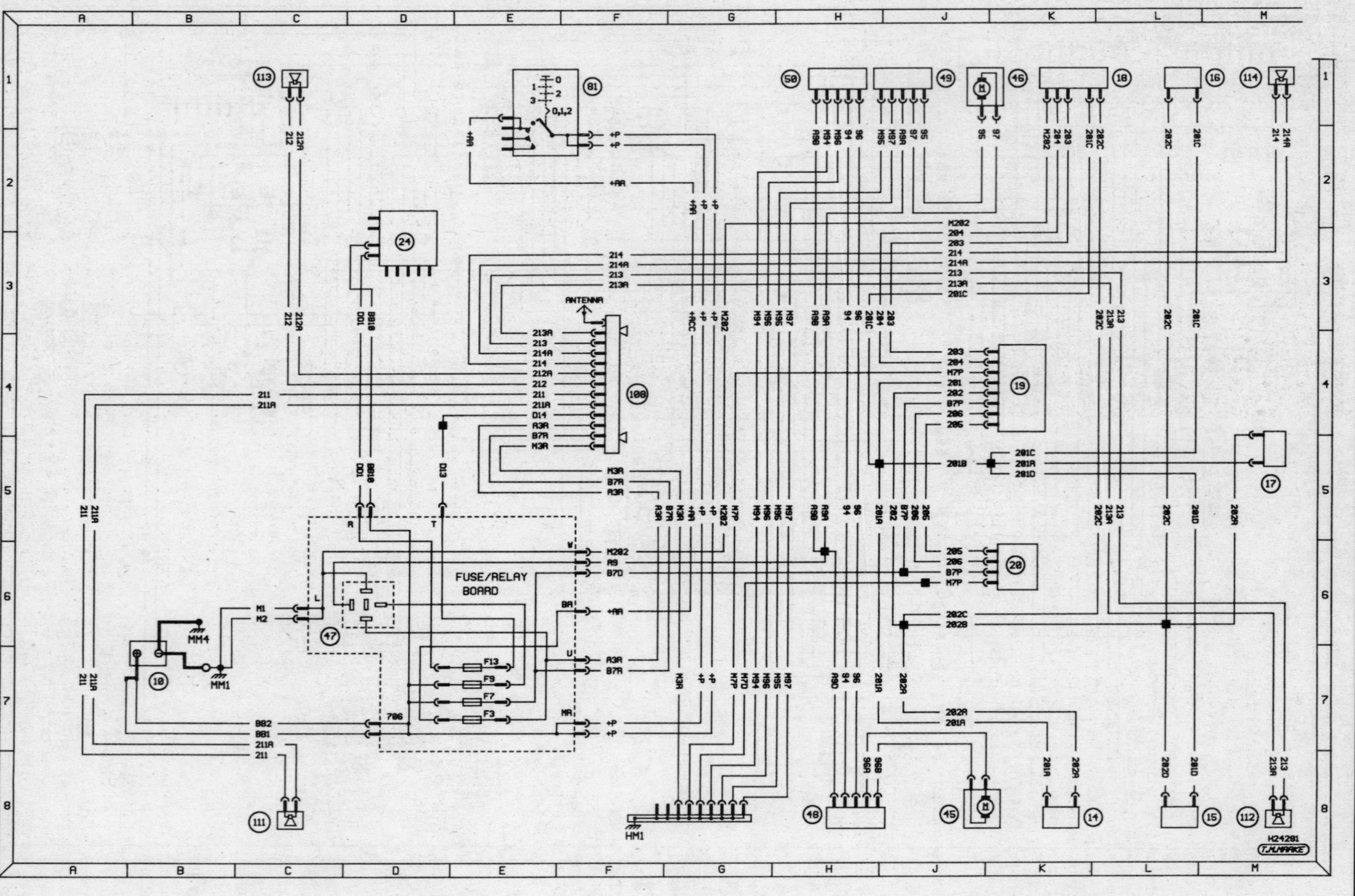

Diagram 3a: Typical ancillary circuits – electric windows, central locking and radio/cassette

This is a guide to getting your vehicle through the MOT test. Obviously it will not be possible to examine the vehicle to the same standard as the professional MOT tester. However, working through the following checks will enable you to identify any problem areas before submitting the vehicle for the test.

Where a testable component is in borderline condition, the tester has discretion in deciding whether to pass or fail it. The basis of such discretion is whether the tester would be happy for a close relative or friend to use the vehicle with the component in that condition. If the vehicle presented is clean and evidently well cared for, the tester may be more inclined to pass a borderline component than if the vehicle is scruffy and apparently neglected.

It has only been possible to summarise the test requirements here, based on the regulations in force at the time of printing. Test standards are becoming increasingly stringent, although there are some exemptions for older vehicles. For full details obtain a copy of the Haynes publication Pass the MOT! (available from stockists of Haynes manuals).

An assistant will be needed to help carry out some of these checks.

The checks have been sub-divided into four categories, as follows:

1 Checks carried out **FROM THE DRIVER'S SEAT**

2 Checks carried out **WITH THE VEHICLE ON THE GROUND**

3 Checks carried out **WITH THE VEHICLE RAISED AND THE WHEELS FREE TO TURN**

4 Checks carried out on **YOUR VEHICLE'S EXHAUST EMISSION SYSTEM**

1 Checks carried out FROM THE DRIVER'S SEAT

Handbrake

☐ Test the operation of the handbrake. Excessive travel (too many clicks) indicates incorrect brake or cable adjustment.

☐ Check that the handbrake cannot be released by tapping the lever sideways. Check the security of the lever mountings.

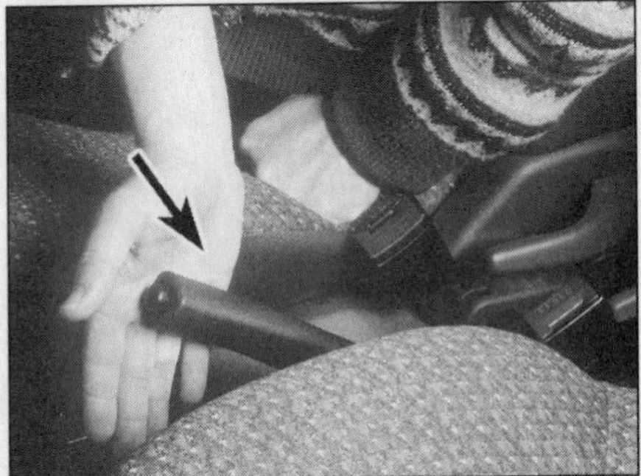

Footbrake

☐ Depress the brake pedal and check that it does not creep down to the floor, indicating a master cylinder fault. Release the pedal, wait a few seconds, then depress it again. If the pedal travels nearly to the floor before firm resistance is felt, brake adjustment or repair is necessary. If the pedal feels spongy, there is air in the hydraulic system which must be removed by bleeding.

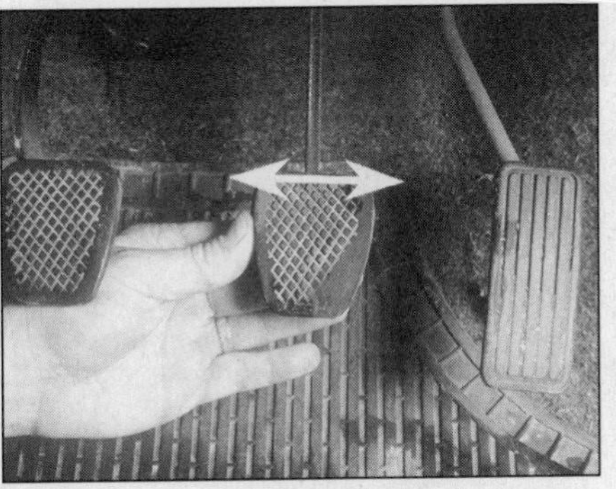

☐ Check that the brake pedal is secure and in good condition. Check also for signs of fluid leaks on the pedal, floor or carpets, which would indicate failed seals in the brake master cylinder.

☐ Check the servo unit (when applicable) by operating the brake pedal several times, then keeping the pedal depressed and starting the engine. As the engine starts, the pedal will move down slightly. If not, the vacuum hose or the servo itself may be faulty.

Steering wheel and column

☐ Examine the steering wheel for fractures or looseness of the hub, spokes or rim.

☐ Move the steering wheel from side to side and then up and down. Check that the steering wheel is not loose on the column, indicating wear or a loose retaining nut. Continue moving the steering wheel as before, but also turn it slightly from left to right.

☐ Check that the steering wheel is not loose on the column, and that there is no abnormal

movement of the steering wheel, indicating wear in the column support bearings or couplings.

Windscreen and mirrors

☐ The windscreen must be free of cracks or other significant damage within the driver's field of view. (Small stone chips are acceptable.) Rear view mirrors must be secure, intact, and capable of being adjusted.

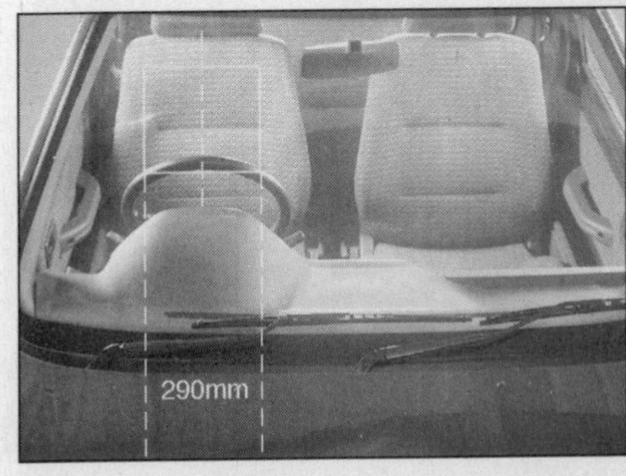

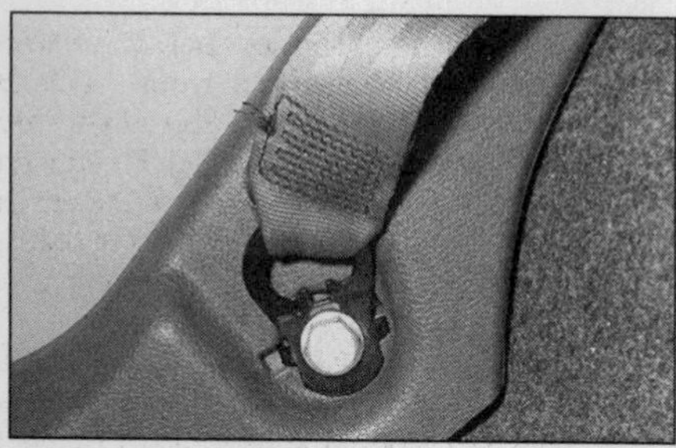

Seat belts and seats

Note: *The following checks are applicable to all seat belts, front and rear.*

☐ Examine the webbing of all the belts (including rear belts if fitted) for cuts, serious fraying or deterioration. Fasten and unfasten each belt to check the buckles. If applicable, check the retracting mechanism. Check the security of all seat belt mountings accessible from inside the vehicle.

☐ The front seats themselves must be securely attached and the backrests must lock in the upright position.

Doors

☐ Both front doors must be able to be opened and closed from outside and inside, and must latch securely when closed.

2 Checks carried out WITH THE VEHICLE ON THE GROUND

Vehicle identification

☐ Number plates must be in good condition, secure and legible, with letters and numbers correctly spaced – spacing at (A) should be twice that at (B).

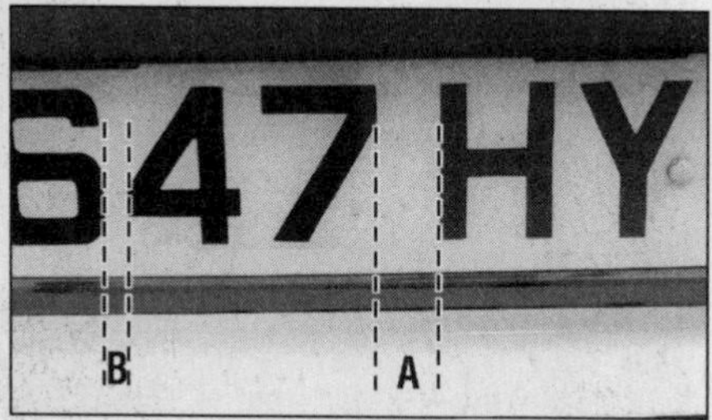

☐ The VIN plate and/or homologation plate must be legible.

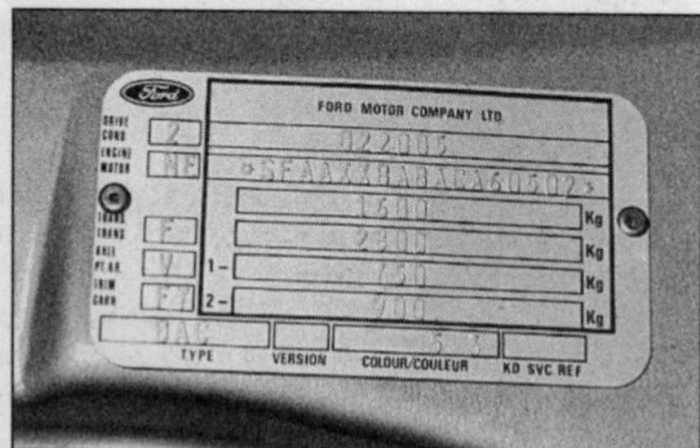

Electrical equipment

☐ Switch on the ignition and check the operation of the horn.

☐ Check the windscreen washers and wipers, examining the wiper blades; renew damaged or perished blades. Also check the operation of the stop-lights.

☐ Check the operation of the sidelights and number plate lights. The lenses and reflectors must be secure, clean and undamaged.

☐ Check the operation and alignment of the headlights. The headlight reflectors must not be tarnished and the lenses must be undamaged.

☐ Switch on the ignition and check the operation of the direction indicators (including the instrument panel tell-tale) and the hazard warning lights. Operation of the sidelights and stop-lights must not affect the indicators - if it does, the cause is usually a bad earth at the rear light cluster.

☐ Check the operation of the rear foglight(s), including the warning light on the instrument panel or in the switch.

Footbrake

☐ Examine the master cylinder, brake pipes and servo unit for leaks, loose mountings, corrosion or other damage.

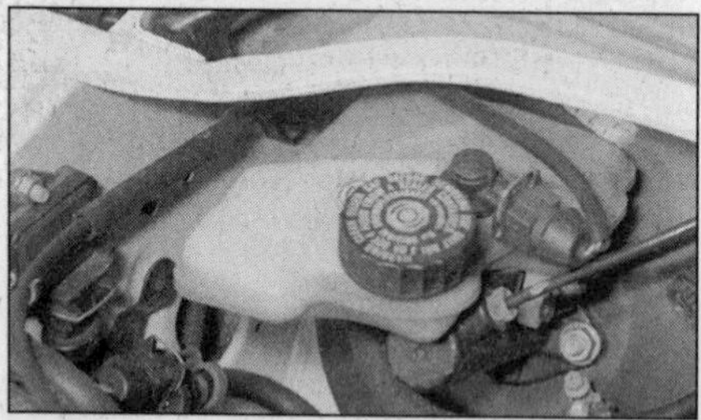

☐ The fluid reservoir must be secure and the fluid level must be between the upper (**A**) and lower (**B**) markings.

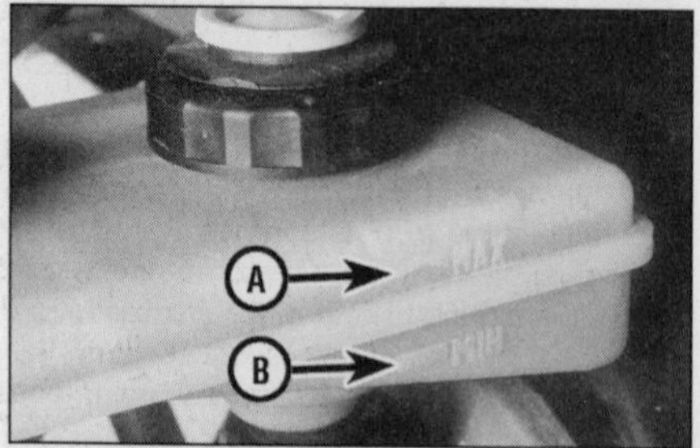

☐ Inspect both front brake flexible hoses for cracks or deterioration of the rubber. Turn the steering from lock to lock, and ensure that the hoses do not contact the wheel, tyre, or any part of the steering or suspension mechanism. With the brake pedal firmly depressed, check the hoses for bulges or leaks under pressure.

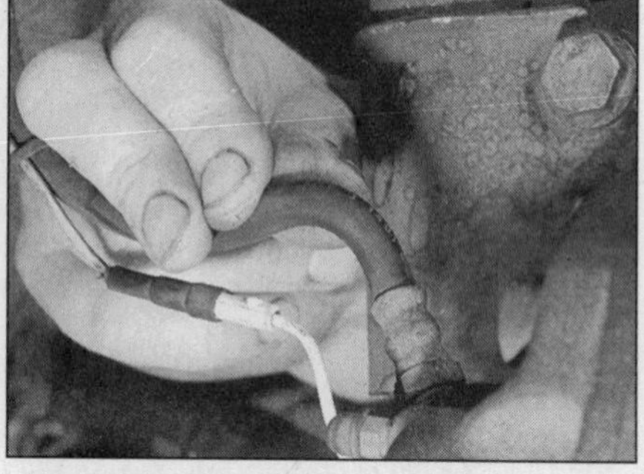

Steering and suspension

☐ Have your assistant turn the steering wheel from side to side slightly, up to the point where the steering gear just begins to transmit this movement to the roadwheels. Check for excessive free play between the steering wheel and the steering gear, indicating wear or insecurity of the steering column joints, the column-to-steering gear coupling, or the steering gear itself.

☐ Have your assistant turn the steering wheel more vigorously in each direction, so that the roadwheels just begin to turn. As this is done, examine all the steering joints, linkages, fittings and attachments. Renew any component that shows signs of wear or damage. On vehicles with power steering, check the security and condition of the steering pump, drivebelt and hoses.

☐ Check that the vehicle is standing level, and at approximately the correct ride height.

Shock absorbers

☐ Depress each corner of the vehicle in turn, then release it. The vehicle should rise and then settle in its normal position. If the vehicle continues to rise and fall, the shock absorber is defective. A shock absorber which has seized will also cause the vehicle to fail.

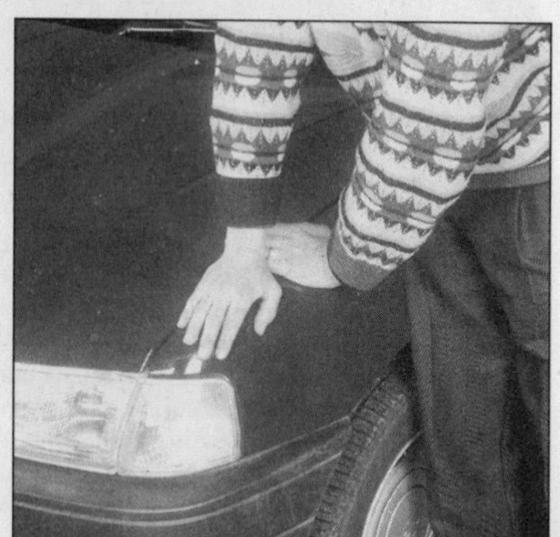

Exhaust system

☐ Start the engine. With your assistant holding a rag over the tailpipe, check the entire system for leaks. Repair or renew leaking sections.

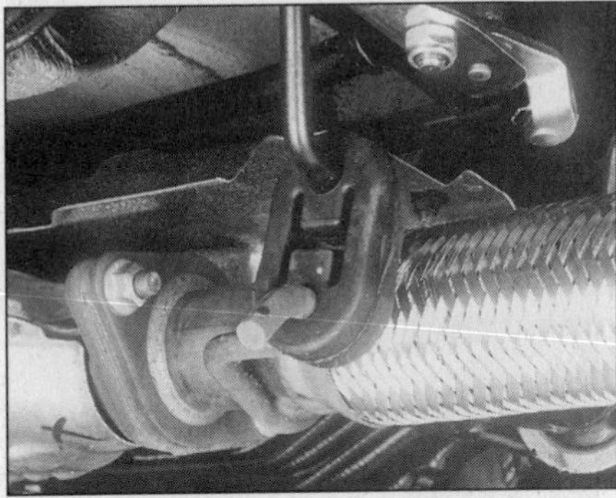

3 Checks carried out WITH THE VEHICLE RAISED AND THE WHEELS FREE TO TURN

Jack up the front and rear of the vehicle, and securely support it on axle stands. Position the stands clear of the suspension assemblies. Ensure that the wheels are clear of the ground and that the steering can be turned from lock to lock.

Steering mechanism

☐ Have your assistant turn the steering from lock to lock. Check that the steering turns smoothly, and that no part of the steering mechanism, including a wheel or tyre, fouls any brake hose or pipe or any part of the body structure.

☐ Examine the steering rack rubber gaiters for damage or insecurity of the retaining clips. If power steering is fitted, check for signs of damage or leakage of the fluid hoses, pipes or connections. Also check for excessive stiffness or binding of the steering, a missing split pin or locking device, or severe corrosion of the body structure within 30 cm of any steering component attachment point.

Front and rear suspension and wheel bearings

☐ Starting at the front right-hand side, grasp the roadwheel at the 3 o'clock and 9 o'clock positions and shake it vigorously. Check for free play or insecurity at the wheel bearings, suspension balljoints, or suspension mountings, pivots and attachments.

☐ Now grasp the wheel at the 12 o'clock and 6 o'clock positions and repeat the previous inspection. Spin the wheel, and check for roughness or tightness of the front wheel bearing.

☐ If excess free play is suspected at a component pivot point, this can be confirmed by using a large screwdriver or similar tool and levering between the mounting and the component attachment. This will confirm whether the wear is in the pivot bush, its retaining bolt, or in the mounting itself (the bolt holes can often become elongated).

☐ Carry out all the above checks at the other front wheel, and then at both rear wheels.

Springs and shock absorbers

☐ Examine the suspension struts (when applicable) for serious fluid leakage, corrosion, or damage to the casing. Also check the security of the mounting points.

☐ If coil springs are fitted, check that the spring ends locate in their seats, and that the spring is not corroded, cracked or broken.

☐ If leaf springs are fitted, check that all leaves are intact, that the axle is securely attached to each spring, and that there is no deterioration of the spring eye mountings, bushes, and shackles.

☐ The same general checks apply to vehicles fitted with other suspension types, such as torsion bars, hydraulic displacer units, etc. Ensure that all mountings and attachments are secure, that there are no signs of excessive wear, corrosion or damage, and (on hydraulic types) that there are no fluid leaks or damaged pipes.

☐ Inspect the shock absorbers for signs of serious fluid leakage. Check for wear of the mounting bushes or attachments, or damage to the body of the unit.

Driveshafts (fwd vehicles only)

☐ Rotate each front wheel in turn and inspect the constant velocity joint gaiters for splits or damage. Also check that each driveshaft is straight and undamaged.

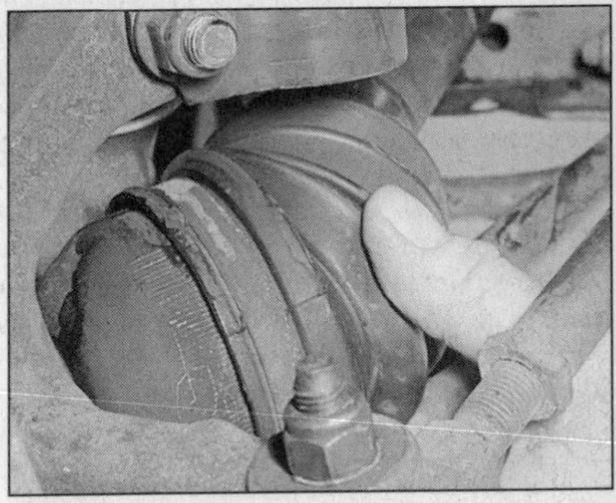

Braking system

☐ If possible without dismantling, check brake pad wear and disc condition. Ensure that the friction lining material has not worn excessively, (A) and that the discs are not fractured, pitted, scored or badly worn (B).

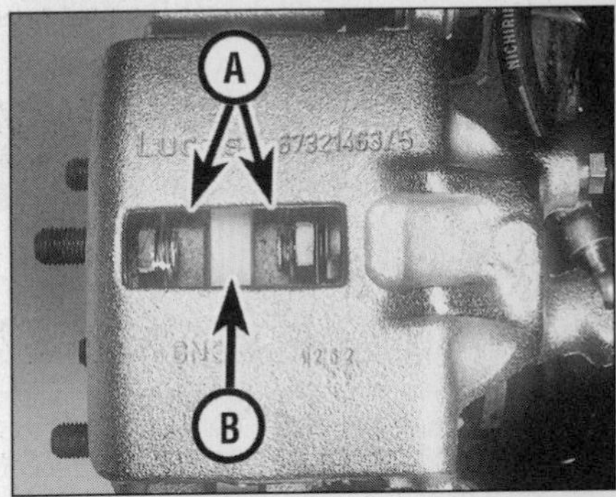

☐ Examine all the rigid brake pipes underneath the vehicle, and the flexible hose(s) at the rear. Look for corrosion, chafing or insecurity of the pipes, and for signs of bulging under pressure, chafing, splits or deterioration of the flexible hoses.

☐ Look for signs of fluid leaks at the brake calipers or on the brake backplates. Repair or renew leaking components.

☐ Slowly spin each wheel, while your assistant depresses and releases the footbrake. Ensure that each brake is operating and does not bind when the pedal is released.

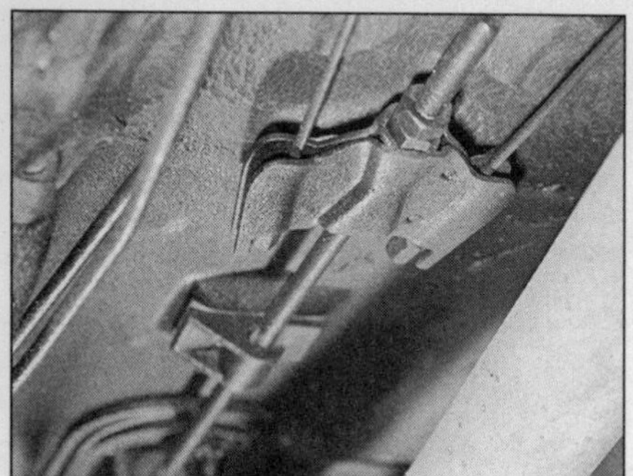

☐ Examine the handbrake mechanism, checking for frayed or broken cables, excessive corrosion, or wear or insecurity of the linkage. Check that the mechanism works on each relevant wheel, and releases fully, without binding.

☐ It is not possible to test brake efficiency without special equipment, but a road test can be carried out later to check that the vehicle pulls up in a straight line.

Fuel and exhaust systems

☐ Inspect the fuel tank (including the filler cap), fuel pipes, hoses and unions. All components must be secure and free from leaks.

☐ Examine the exhaust system over its entire length, checking for any damaged, broken or missing mountings, security of the retaining clamps and rust or corrosion.

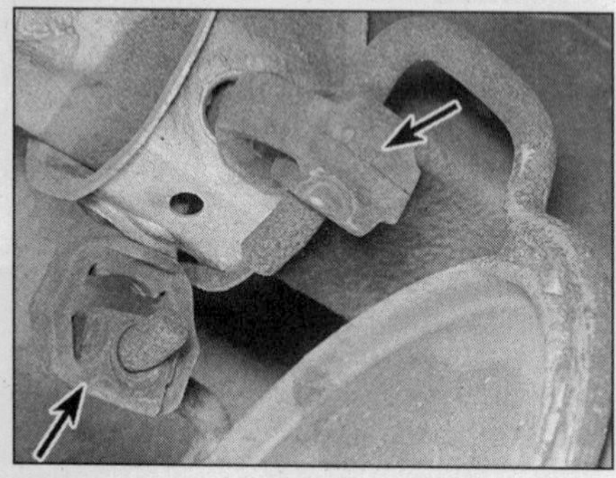

Wheels and tyres

☐ Examine the sidewalls and tread area of each tyre in turn. Check for cuts, tears, lumps, bulges, separation of the tread, and exposure of the ply or cord due to wear or damage. Check that the tyre bead is correctly seated on the wheel rim, that the valve is sound and

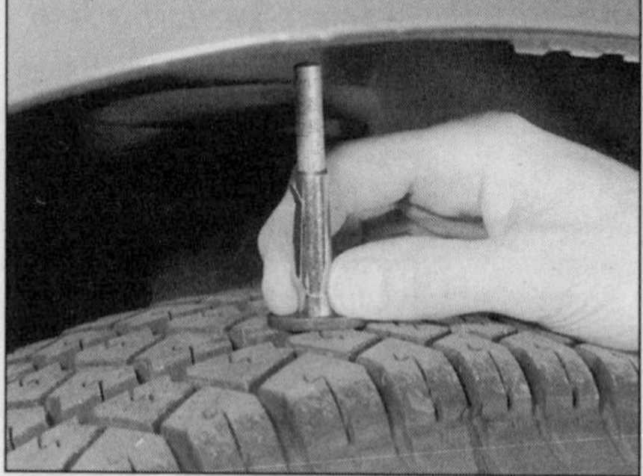

properly seated, and that the wheel is not distorted or damaged.

☐ Check that the tyres are of the correct size for the vehicle, that they are of the same size and type on each axle, and that the pressures are correct.

☐ Check the tyre tread depth. The legal minimum at the time of writing is 1.6 mm over at least three-quarters of the tread width. Abnormal tread wear may indicate incorrect front wheel alignment.

Body corrosion

☐ Check the condition of the entire vehicle structure for signs of corrosion in load-bearing areas. (These include chassis box sections, side sills, cross-members, pillars, and all suspension, steering, braking system and seat belt mountings and anchorages.) Any corrosion which has seriously reduced the thickness of a load-bearing area is likely to cause the vehicle to fail. In this case professional repairs are likely to be needed.

☐ Damage or corrosion which causes sharp or otherwise dangerous edges to be exposed will also cause the vehicle to fail.

4 Checks carried out on YOUR VEHICLE'S EXHAUST EMISSION SYSTEM

Petrol models

☐ Have the engine at normal operating temperature, and make sure that it is in good tune (ignition system in good order, air filter element clean, etc).

☐ Before any measurements are carried out, raise the engine speed to around 2500 rpm, and hold it at this speed for 20 seconds. Allow the engine speed to return to idle, and watch for smoke emissions from the exhaust tailpipe. If the idle speed is obviously much too high, or if dense blue or clearly-visible black smoke comes from the tailpipe for more than 5 seconds, the vehicle will fail. As a rule of thumb, blue smoke signifies oil being burnt (engine wear) while black smoke signifies unburnt fuel (dirty air cleaner element, or other carburettor or fuel system fault).

☐ An exhaust gas analyser capable of measuring carbon monoxide (CO) and hydrocarbons (HC) is now needed. If such an instrument cannot be hired or borrowed, a local garage may agree to perform the check for a small fee.

CO emissions (mixture)

☐ At the time of writing, the maximum CO level at idle is 3.5% for vehicles first used after August 1986 and 4.5% for older vehicles. From January 1996 a much tighter limit (around 0.5%) applies to catalyst-equipped vehicles first used from August 1992. If the CO level cannot be reduced far enough to pass the test (and the fuel and ignition systems are otherwise in good condition) then the carburettor is badly worn, or there is some problem in the fuel injection system or catalytic converter (as applicable).

HC emissions

☐ With the CO emissions within limits, HC emissions must be no more than 1200 ppm (parts per million). If the vehicle fails this test at idle, it can be re-tested at around 2000 rpm; if the HC level is then 1200 ppm or less, this counts as a pass.

☐ Excessive HC emissions can be caused by oil being burnt, but they are more likely to be due to unburnt fuel.

Diesel models

☐ The only emission test applicable to Diesel engines is the measuring of exhaust smoke density. The test involves accelerating the engine several times to its maximum unloaded speed.

Note: *It is of the utmost importance that the engine timing belt is in good condition before the test is carried out.*

☐ Excessive smoke can be caused by a dirty air cleaner element. Otherwise, professional advice may be needed to find the cause.

Introduction

A selection of good tools is a fundamental requirement for anyone contemplating the maintenance and repair of a motor vehicle. For the owner who does not possess any, their purchase will prove a considerable expense, offsetting some of the savings made by doing-it-yourself. However, provided that the tools purchased meet the relevant national safety standards and are of good quality, they will last for many years and prove an extremely worthwhile investment.

To help the average owner to decide which tools are needed to carry out the various tasks detailed in this manual, we have compiled three lists of tools under the following headings: *Maintenance and minor repair*, *Repair and overhaul*, and *Special*. Newcomers to practical mechanics should start off with the *Maintenance and minor repair* tool kit, and confine themselves to the simpler jobs around the vehicle. Then, as confidence and experience grow, more difficult tasks can be undertaken, with extra tools being purchased as, and when, they are needed. In this way, a *Maintenance and minor repair* tool kit can be built up into a *Repair and overhaul* tool kit over a considerable period of time, without any major cash outlays. The experienced do-it-yourselfer will have a tool kit good enough for most repair and overhaul procedures, and will add tools from the *Special* category when it is felt that the expense is justified by the amount of use to which these tools will be put.

Maintenance and minor repair tool kit

The tools given in this list should be considered as a minimum requirement if routine maintenance, servicing and minor repair operations are to be undertaken. We recommend the purchase of combination spanners (ring one end, open-ended the other); although more expensive than open-ended ones, they do give the advantages of both types of spanner.

- ☐ *Combination spanners: 10, 11, 12, 13, 14 & 17 mm*
- ☐ *Adjustable spanner - 35 mm jaw (approx)*
- ☐ *Engine sump drain plug key*
- ☐ *Set of feeler gauges*
- ☐ *Spark plug spanner (with rubber insert)*
- ☐ *Spark plug gap adjustment tool*
- ☐ *Brake bleed nipple spanner*
- ☐ *Screwdrivers: Flat blade and cross blade – approx 100 mm long x 6 mm dia*
- ☐ *Combination pliers*
- ☐ *Hacksaw (junior)*
- ☐ *Tyre pump*
- ☐ *Tyre pressure gauge*
- ☐ *Oil can*
- ☐ *Oil filter removal tool*
- ☐ *Fine emery cloth*
- ☐ *Wire brush (small)*
- ☐ *Funnel (medium size)*

Repair and overhaul tool kit

These tools are virtually essential for anyone undertaking any major repairs to a motor vehicle, and are additional to those given in the *Maintenance and minor repair* list. Included in this list is a comprehensive set of sockets. Although these are expensive, they will be found invaluable as they are so versatile - particularly if various drives are included in the set. We recommend the half-inch square-drive type, as this can be used with most proprietary torque wrenches. If you cannot afford a socket set, even bought piecemeal, then inexpensive tubular box spanners are a useful alternative.

The tools in this list will occasionally need to be supplemented by tools from the *Special* list:

- ☐ *Sockets (or box spanners) to cover range in previous list*
- ☐ *Reversible ratchet drive (for use with sockets)* **(see illustration)**
- ☐ *Extension piece, 250 mm (for use with sockets)*
- ☐ *Universal joint (for use with sockets)*
- ☐ *Torque wrench (for use with sockets)*
- ☐ *Self-locking grips*
- ☐ *Ball pein hammer*
- ☐ *Soft-faced mallet (plastic/aluminium or rubber)*
- ☐ *Screwdrivers:*
  Flat blade - long & sturdy, short (chubby), and narrow (electrician's) types
  Cross blade - Long & sturdy, and short (chubby) types
- ☐ *Pliers:*
  Long-nosed
  Side cutters (electrician's)
  Circlip (internal and external)
- ☐ *Cold chisel - 25 mm*
- ☐ *Scriber*
- ☐ *Scraper*
- ☐ *Centre-punch*
- ☐ *Pin punch*
- ☐ *Hacksaw*
- ☐ *Brake hose clamp*
- ☐ *Brake bleeding kit*
- ☐ *Selection of twist drills*
- ☐ *Steel rule/straight-edge*
- ☐ *Allen keys (inc. splined/Torx type if necessary)*
- ☐ *Selection of files*
- ☐ *Wire brush*
- ☐ *Axle stands*
- ☐ *Jack (strong trolley or hydraulic type)*
- ☐ *Light with extension lead*

Special tools

The tools in this list are those which are not used regularly, are expensive to buy, or which need to be used in accordance with their manufacturers' instructions. Unless relatively difficult mechanical jobs are undertaken frequently, it will not be economic to buy many of these tools. Where this is the case, you could consider clubbing together with friends (or joining a motorists' club) to make a joint purchase, or borrowing the tools against a deposit from a local garage or tool hire specialist. It is worth noting that many of the larger DIY superstores now carry a large range of special tools for hire at modest rates.

The following list contains only those tools and instruments freely available to the public, and not those special tools produced by the vehicle manufacturer specifically for its dealer network. You will find occasional references to these manufacturers' special tools in the text of this manual. Generally, an alternative method of doing the job without the vehicle manufacturers' special tool is given. However, sometimes there is no alternative to using them. Where this is the case and the relevant tool cannot be bought or borrowed, you will have to entrust the work to a franchised garage.

- ☐ *Valve spring compressor* **(see illustration)**
- ☐ *Valve grinding tool*
- ☐ *Piston ring compressor* **(see illustration)**
- ☐ *Piston ring removal/installation tool* **(see illustration)**
- ☐ *Cylinder bore hone* **(see illustration)**
- ☐ *Balljoint separator*
- ☐ *Coil spring compressors (where applicable)*
- ☐ *Two/three-legged hub and bearing puller* **(see illustration)**

REF

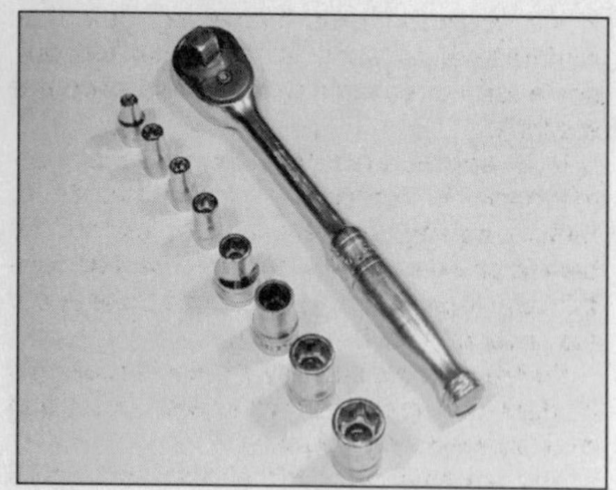
Sockets and reversible ratchet drive

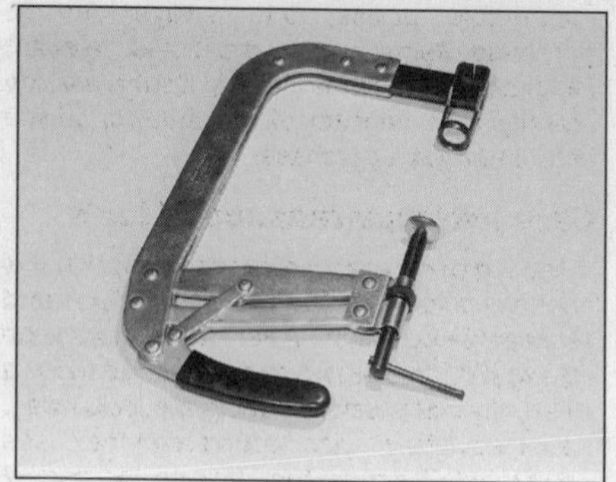
Valve spring compressor

Piston ring compressor

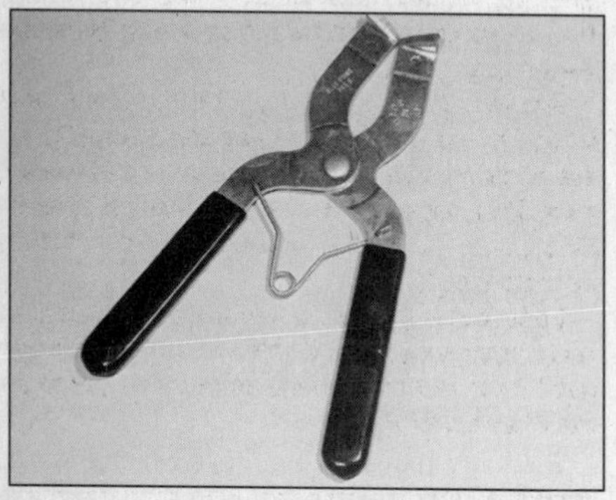
Piston ring removal/installation tool

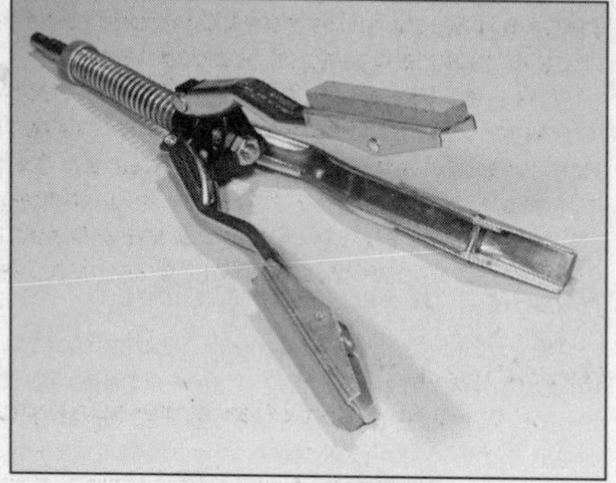
Cylinder bore hone

Three-legged hub and bearing puller

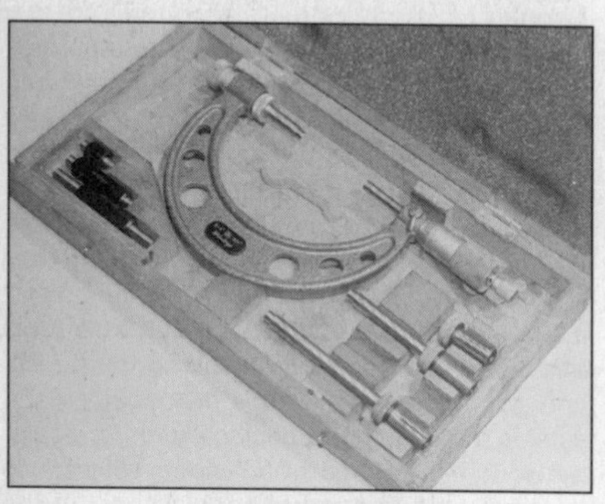
Micrometer set

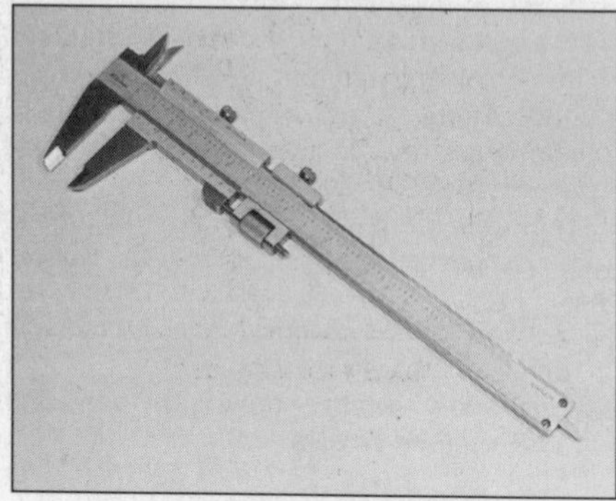
Vernier calipers

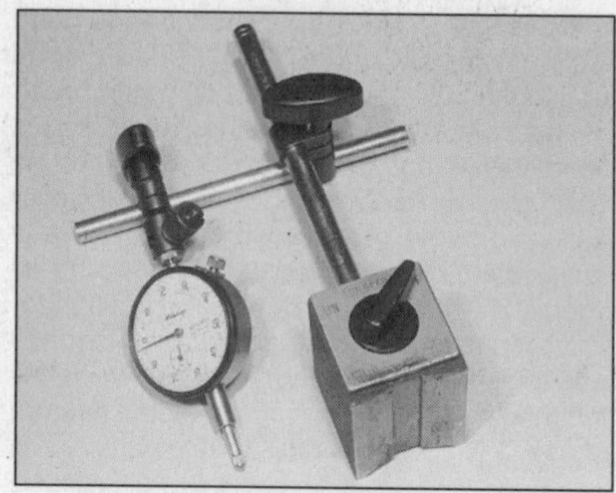
Dial test indicator and magnetic stand

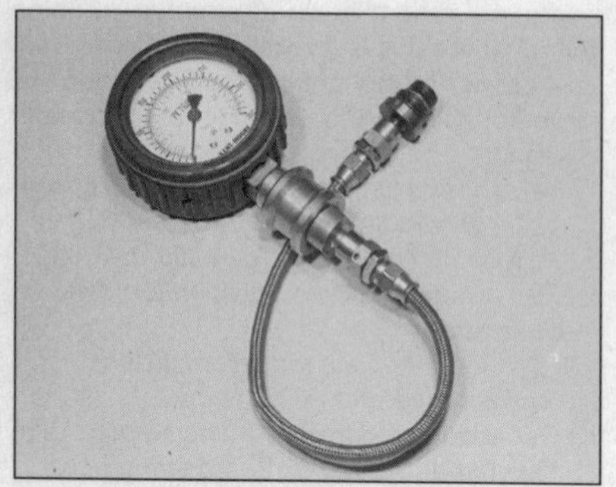
Compression testing gauge

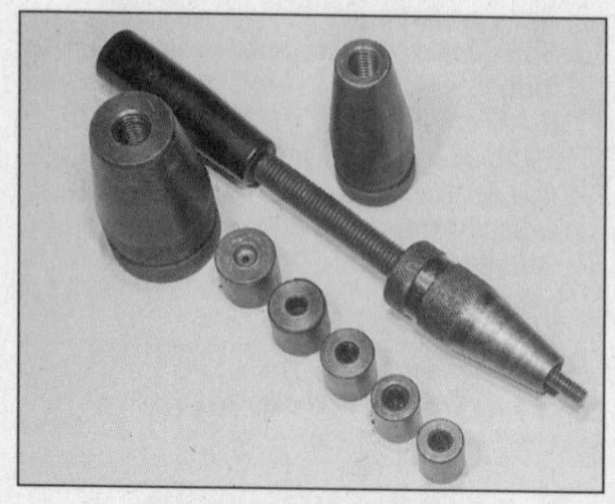
Clutch plate alignment set

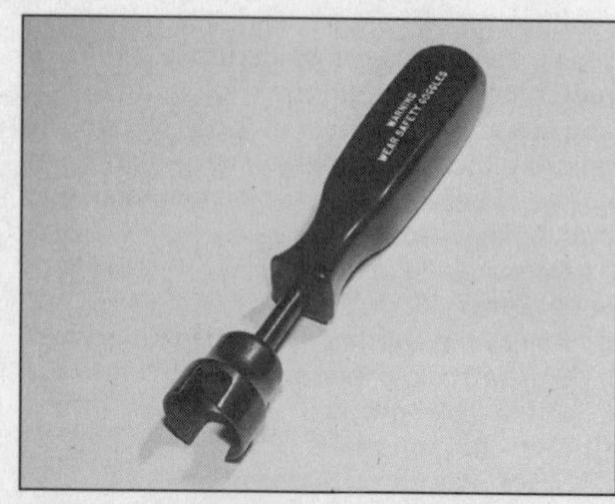

Brake shoe steady spring cup removal tool

- ☐ *Impact screwdriver*
- ☐ *Micrometer and/or vernier calipers* ***(see illustrations)***
- ☐ *Dial gauge* ***(see illustration)***
- ☐ *Universal electrical multi-meter*
- ☐ *Cylinder compression gauge* ***(see illustration)***
- ☐ *Clutch plate alignment set* ***(see illustration)***
- ☐ *Brake shoe steady spring cup removal tool* ***(see illustration)***
- ☐ *Bush and bearing removal/installation set* ***(see illustration)***
- ☐ *Stud extractors* ***(see illustration)***
- ☐ *Tap and die set* ***(see illustration)***
- ☐ *Lifting tackle*
- ☐ *Trolley jack*

Buying tools

For practically all tools, a tool factor is the best source, since he will have a very comprehensive range compared with the average garage or accessory shop. Having said that, accessory shops often offer excellent quality tools at discount prices, so it pays to shop around.

Remember, you don't have to buy the most expensive items on the shelf, but it is always advisable to steer clear of the very cheap tools. There are plenty of good tools around at reasonable prices, but always aim to purchase items which meet the relevant national safety standards. If in doubt, ask the proprietor or manager of the shop for advice before making a purchase.

Care and maintenance of tools

Having purchased a reasonable tool kit, it is necessary to keep the tools in a clean and serviceable condition. After use, always wipe off any dirt, grease and metal particles using a clean, dry cloth, before putting the tools away. Never leave them lying around after they have been used. A simple tool rack on the garage or workshop wall for items such as screwdrivers and pliers is a good idea. Store all normal spanners and sockets in a metal box. Any measuring instruments, gauges, meters, etc, must be carefully stored where they cannot be damaged or become rusty.

Take a little care when tools are used. Hammer heads inevitably become marked, and screwdrivers lose the keen edge on their blades from time to time. A little timely attention with emery cloth or a file will soon restore items like this to a good serviceable finish.

Working facilities

Not to be forgotten when discussing tools is the workshop itself. If anything more than routine maintenance is to be carried out, some form of suitable working area becomes essential.

It is appreciated that many an owner-mechanic is forced by circumstances to remove an engine or similar item without the benefit of a garage or workshop. Having done this, any repairs should always be done under the cover of a roof.

Wherever possible, any dismantling should be done on a clean, flat workbench or table at a suitable working height.

Any workbench needs a vice; one with a jaw opening of 100 mm is suitable for most jobs. As mentioned previously, some clean dry storage space is also required for tools, as well as for any lubricants, cleaning fluids, touch-up paints and so on, which become necessary.

Another item which may be required, and which has a much more general usage, is an electric drill with a chuck capacity of at least 8 mm. This, together with a good range of twist drills, is virtually essential for fitting accessories.

Last, but not least, always keep a supply of old newspapers and clean, lint-free rags available, and try to keep any working area as clean as possible.

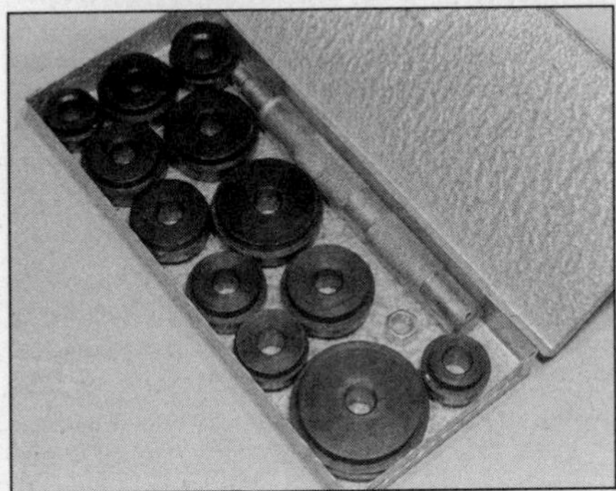

Bush and bearing removal/installation set

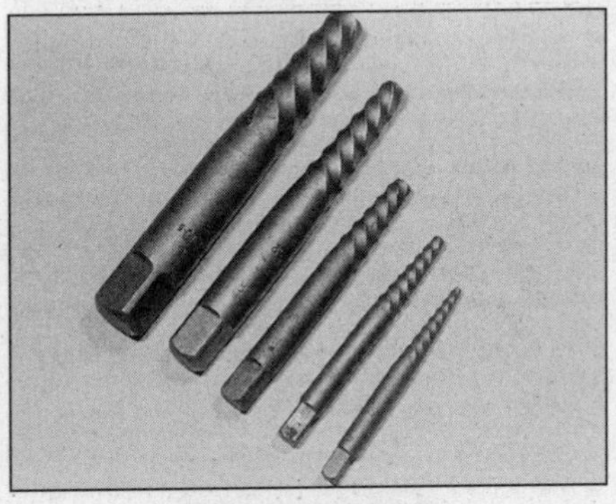

Stud extractor set

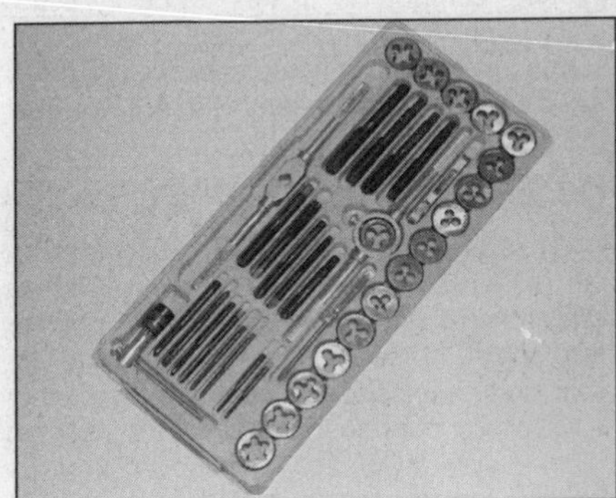

Tap and die set

Whenever servicing, repair or overhaul work is carried out on the car or its components, observe the following procedures and instructions. This will assist in carrying out the operation efficiently and to a professional standard of workmanship.

Joint mating faces and gaskets

When separating components at their mating faces, never insert screwdrivers or similar implements into the joint between the faces in order to prise them apart. This can cause severe damage which results in oil leaks, coolant leaks, etc upon reassembly. Separation is usually achieved by tapping along the joint with a soft-faced hammer in order to break the seal. However, note that this method may not be suitable where dowels are used for component location.

Where a gasket is used between the mating faces of two components, a new one must be fitted on reassembly; fit it dry unless otherwise stated in the repair procedure. Make sure that the mating faces are clean and dry, with all traces of old gasket removed. When cleaning a joint face, use a tool which is unlikely to score or damage the face, and remove any burrs or nicks with an oilstone or fine file.

Make sure that tapped holes are cleaned with a pipe cleaner, and keep them free of jointing compound, if this is being used, unless specifically instructed otherwise.

Ensure that all orifices, channels or pipes are clear, and blow through them, preferably using compressed air.

Oil seals

Oil seals can be removed by levering them out with a wide flat-bladed screwdriver or similar implement. Alternatively, a number of self-tapping screws may be screwed into the seal, and these used as a purchase for pliers or some similar device in order to pull the seal free.

Whenever an oil seal is removed from its working location, either individually or as part of an assembly, it should be renewed.

The very fine sealing lip of the seal is easily damaged, and will not seal if the surface it contacts is not completely clean and free from scratches, nicks or grooves. If the original sealing surface of the component cannot be restored, and the manufacturer has not made provision for slight relocation of the seal relative to the sealing surface, the component should be renewed.

Protect the lips of the seal from any surface which may damage them in the course of fitting. Use tape or a conical sleeve where possible. Lubricate the seal lips with oil before fitting and, on dual-lipped seals, fill the space between the lips with grease.

Unless otherwise stated, oil seals must be fitted with their sealing lips toward the lubricant to be sealed.

Use a tubular drift or block of wood of the appropriate size to install the seal and, if the seal housing is shouldered, drive the seal down to the shoulder. If the seal housing is unshouldered, the seal should be fitted with its face flush with the housing top face (unless otherwise instructed).

Screw threads and fastenings

Seized nuts, bolts and screws are quite a common occurrence where corrosion has set in, and the use of penetrating oil or releasing fluid will often overcome this problem if the offending item is soaked for a while before attempting to release it. The use of an impact driver may also provide a means of releasing such stubborn fastening devices, when used in conjunction with the appropriate screwdriver bit or socket. If none of these methods works, it may be necessary to resort to the careful application of heat, or the use of a hacksaw or nut splitter device.

Studs are usually removed by locking two nuts together on the threaded part, and then using a spanner on the lower nut to unscrew the stud. Studs or bolts which have broken off below the surface of the component in which they are mounted can sometimes be removed using a stud extractor. Always ensure that a blind tapped hole is completely free from oil, grease, water or other fluid before installing the bolt or stud. Failure to do this could cause the housing to crack due to the hydraulic action of the bolt or stud as it is screwed in.

When tightening a castellated nut to accept a split pin, tighten the nut to the specified torque, where applicable, and then tighten further to the next split pin hole. Never slacken the nut to align the split pin hole, unless stated in the repair procedure.

When checking or retightening a nut or bolt to a specified torque setting, slacken the nut or bolt by a quarter of a turn, and then retighten to the specified setting. However, this should not be attempted where angular tightening has been used.

For some screw fastenings, notably cylinder head bolts or nuts, torque wrench settings are no longer specified for the latter stages of tightening, "angle-tightening" being called up instead. Typically, a fairly low torque wrench setting will be applied to the bolts/nuts in the correct sequence, followed by one or more stages of tightening through specified angles.

Locknuts, locktabs and washers

Any fastening which will rotate against a component or housing during tightening should always have a washer between it and the relevant component or housing.

Spring or split washers should always be renewed when they are used to lock a critical component such as a big-end bearing retaining bolt or nut. Locktabs which are folded over to retain a nut or bolt should always be renewed.

Self-locking nuts can be re-used in non-critical areas, providing resistance can be felt when the locking portion passes over the bolt or stud thread. However, it should be noted that self-locking stiffnuts tend to lose their effectiveness after long periods of use, and should then be renewed as a matter of course.

Split pins must always be replaced with new ones of the correct size for the hole.

When thread-locking compound is found on the threads of a fastener which is to be re-used, it should be cleaned off with a wire brush and solvent, and fresh compound applied on reassembly.

Special tools

Some repair procedures in this manual entail the use of special tools such as a press, two or three-legged pullers, spring compressors, etc. Wherever possible, suitable readily-available alternatives to the manufacturer's special tools are described, and are shown in use. In some instances, where no alternative is possible, it has been necessary to resort to the use of a manufacturer's tool, and this has been done for reasons of safety as well as the efficient completion of the repair operation. Unless you are highly-skilled and have a thorough understanding of the procedures described, never attempt to bypass the use of any special tool when the procedure described specifies its use. Not only is there a very great risk of personal injury, but expensive damage could be caused to the components involved.

Environmental considerations

When disposing of used engine oil, brake fluid, antifreeze, etc, give due consideration to any detrimental environmental effects. Do not, for instance, pour any of the above liquids down drains into the general sewage system, or onto the ground to soak away. Many local council refuse tips provide a facility for waste oil disposal, as do some garages. If none of these facilities are available, consult your local Environmental Health Department, or the National Rivers Authority, for further advice.

With the universal tightening-up of legislation regarding the emission of environmentally-harmful substances from motor vehicles, most vehicles have tamperproof devices fitted to the main adjustment points of the fuel system. These devices are primarily designed to prevent unqualified persons from adjusting the fuel/air mixture, with the chance of a consequent increase in toxic emissions. If such devices are found during servicing or overhaul, they should, wherever possible, be renewed or refitted in accordance with the manufacturer's requirements or current legislation.

Note: It is antisocial and illegal to dump oil down the drain. To find the location of your local oil recycling bank, call this number free.

Buying spare parts

Spare parts are available from many sources. Peugeot have many dealers throughout the UK, and other dealers, accessory stores and motor factors will also stock some spare parts suitable for Peugeot cars.

Our advice regarding spare part sources is as follows:

Officially appointed vehicle main dealers - This is the best source for parts which are peculiar to your vehicle and are otherwise not generally available (eg, complete cylinder heads, internal transmission components, badges, interior trim, etc). It is also the only place you should buy parts if your vehicle is still under warranty. To be sure of obtaining the correct parts it will always be necessary to give the storeman your vehicle's engine and chassis number, and if possible, to take the 'old' part along for a positive identification. Remember that many parts are available on a factory exchange scheme - any parts returned should always be clean. It obviously makes good sense to go straight to the specialist on your vehicle for this type of part, for they are best equipped to supply you.

Other dealers and auto accessory stores - These are often very good places to buy materials and components needed for the maintenance of your vehicle (eg, oil filters, spark plugs, bulbs, drivebelts, oils and greases, touch-up paint, filler paste, etc). They also sell general accessories, usually have the convenient opening hours, charge lower prices and can often be found not far from home.

Motor factors - Good factors will stock all the more important components which wear out relatively quickly (eg, clutch components, pistons, valves, exhaust systems, brake cylinders/pipes/ hoses/seals/ shoes and pads, etc). Motor factors will often provide new or reconditioned components on a part exchange basis - this can save a considerable amount of money.

Vehicle identification numbers

Modifications are a continuing and unpublicised process in vehicle manufacture. Spare parts manuals and lists are compiled on a numerical basis, the individual vehicle numbers being essential to identify correctly the component required.

Body serial number: This is located on the right-hand side wing valance within the engine compartment.

Vehicle identification plate: This is located on the bulkhead on the right-hand side in the engine compartment.

Engine number (1.1 and 1.3 OHV, 1.1 and 1.4 OHC engines). The number is stamped on a plate attached to the cylinder block on the spark plug side, just beneath the cylinder head at the flywheel end.

Engine number (1.6 and 1.9 OHC engines): The number is located at the timing case end of the cylinder block, just beneath the cylinder head on the spark plug side.

Vehicle identification plate locations

Manufacturer's plate (EC regulations)
a Manufacturer
b Type approval number
c Vehicle identification number
Manufacturer's identification
Vehicle type code
Model year G 1986
H 1987
Serial number
d Gross vehicle weight (GVW)
e Gross train weight (GTW)
f Maximum load on front axle
g Maximum load on rear axle
h Paint and trim code
j Factory build code

Introduction

The vehicle owner who does his or her own maintenance according to the recommended schedules should not have to use this section of the manual very often. Modern component reliability is such that, provided those items subject to wear or deterioration are inspected or renewed at the specified intervals, sudden failure is comparatively rare. Faults do not usually just happen as a result of sudden failure, but develop over a period of time. Major mechanical failures in particular are usually preceded by characteristic symptoms over hundreds or even thousands of miles. Those components which do occasionally fail without warning are often small and easily carried in the vehicle.

With any fault finding, the first step is to decide where to begin investigations. Sometimes this is obvious, but on other occasions a little detective work will be necessary. The owner who makes half a dozen haphazard adjustments or replacements may be successful in curing a fault (or its symptoms), but he will be none the wiser if the fault recurs and he may well have spent more time and money than was necessary. A calm and logical approach will be found to be more satisfactory in the long run. Always take into account any warning signs or abnormalities that may have been noticed in the period preceding the fault – power loss, high or low gauge readings, unusual noises or smells, etc – and remember that failure of components such as fuses or spark plugs may only be pointers to some underlying fault.

The pages which follow here are intended to help in cases of failure to start or breakdown on the road. There is also a Fault Diagnosis Section at the end of each Chapter which should be consulted if the preliminary checks prove unfruitful. Whatever the fault, certain basic principles apply. These are as follows:

Verify the fault. This is simply a matter of being sure that you know what the symptoms are before starting work. This is particularly important if you are investigating a fault for someone else who may not have described it very accurately.

Don't overlook the obvious. For example, if the vehicle won't start, is there petrol in the tank? (Don't take anyone else's word on this particular point, and don't trust the fuel gauge either!) If an electrical fault is indicated, look for loose or broken wires before digging out the test gear.

Cure the disease, not the symptom. Substituting a flat battery with a fully charged one will get you off the hard shoulder, but if the underlying cause is not attended to,the new battery will go the same way. Similarly, changing oil-fouled spark plugs for a new set will get you moving again, but remember that the reason for the fouling (if it wasn't simply an incorrect grade of plug) will have to be established and corrected.

Don't take anything for granted. Particularly, don't forget that a 'new' component may itself be defective (especially if it's been rattling round in the boot for months), and don't leave components out of a fault diagnosis sequence just because they are new or recently fitted. When you do finally diagnose a difficult fault, you'll probably realise that all the evidence was there from the start.

Electrical faults

Electrical faults can be more puzzling than straightforward mechanical failures, but they are no less susceptible to logical analysis if the basic principles of operation are understood. Vehicle electrical wiring exists in extremely unfavourable conditions – heat, vibration and chemical attack and the first things to look for are loose or corroded connections and broken or chafed wires, especially where the wires pass through holes in the bodywork or are subject to vibration.

All metal-bodied vehicles in current production have one pole of the battery 'earthed', ie connected to the vehicle bodywork, and in nearly all modern vehicles it is the negative (–) terminal. The various electrical components – motors, bulb holders, etc – are also connected to earth, either by means of a lead or directly by their mountings. Electric current flows through the component and then back to the battery via the bodywork. If the component mounting is loose or corroded, or if a good path back to the battery is not available, the circuit will be incomplete and malfunction will result. The engine and/or gearbox are also earthed by means of flexible metal straps to the body or subframe; if these straps are loose or missing, starter motor, generator and ignition trouble may result.

Assuming the earth return to be satisfactory, electrical faults will be due either to component malfunction or to defects in the current supply. Individual components are dealt with in Chapter 12. If supply wires are broken or cracked internally this results in an open-circuit, and the easiest way to check for this is to bypass the suspect wire temporarily with a length of wire having a crocodile clip or suitable connector at each end. Alternatively, a 12V test lamp can be used to verify the presence of supply voltage at various points along the wire and the break can be thus isolated.

If a bare portion of a live wire touches the bodywork or other earthed metal part, the electricity will take the low-resistance path thus formed back to the battery: this is known as a short-circuit. Hopefully a short-circuit will blow a fuse, but otherwise it may cause burning of the insulation (and possibly further short-circuits) or even a fire. This is why it is inadvisable to bypass persistently blowing fuses with silver foil or wire.

Spares and tool kit

Most vehicles are supplied only with sufficient tools for wheel changing; the *Maintenance and minor repair* tool kit detailed in *Tools and working facilities,* with the addition of a hammer, is probably sufficient for those repairs that most motorists would consider attempting at the roadside. In addition a few items which can be fitted without too much trouble in the event of a breakdown should be carried. Experience and available space will modify the list below, but the following may save having to call on professional assistance:

- ☐ *Spark plugs, clean and correctly gapped*
- ☐ *HT lead and plug cap – long enough to reach the plug furthest from the distributor*
- ☐ *Distributor rotor*
- ☐ *Drivebelt(s) — emergency type may suffice*
- ☐ *Spare fuses*
- ☐ *Set of principal light bulbs*
- ☐ *Tin of radiator sealer and hose bandage*
- ☐ *Exhaust bandage*
- ☐ *Roll of insulating tape*
- ☐ *Length of soft iron wire*
- ☐ *Length of electrical flex*
- ☐ *Torch or inspection lamp (can double as test lamp)*
- ☐ *Battery jump leads*
- ☐ *Tow-rope*
- ☐ *Ignition waterproofing aerosol*
- ☐ *Litre of engine oil*
- ☐ *Sealed can of hydraulic fluid*
- ☐ *Emergency windscreen*
- ☐ *Wormdrive clips*
- ☐ *Tube of filler paste*

If spare fuel is carried, a can designed for the purpose should be used to minimise risks of leakage and collision damage. A first aid kit and a warning triangle, whilst not at present compulsory in the UK, are obviously sensible items to carry in addition to the above. When touring abroad it may be advisable to carry additional spares which, even if you cannot fit them yourself, could save having to wait while parts are obtained. The items below may be worth considering:

- ☐ *Clutch and throttle cables*
- ☐ *Cylinder head gasket*
- ☐ *Alternator brushes*
- ☐ *Tyre valve core*

One of the motoring organisations will be able to advise on availability of fuel, etc, in foreign countries.

Engine will not start

Engine fails to turn when starter operated

- ☐ Flat battery (recharge use jump leads or push start)
- ☐ Battery terminals loose or corroded
- ☐ Battery earth to body defective
- ☐ Engine earth strap loose or broken
- ☐ Starter motor (or solenoid) wiring loose or broken
- ☐ Ignition/starter switch faulty
- ☐ Major mechanical failure (seizure)
- ☐ Starter or solenoid internal fault (see Chapter 12)

Starter motor turns engine slowly

- ☐ Partially discharged battery (recharge, use jump leads, or push start)
- ☐ Battery terminals loose or corroded
- ☐ Battery earth to body defective
- ☐ Engine earth strap loose
- ☐ Starter motor (or solenoid) wiring loose
- ☐ Starter motor internal fault (see Chapter 12)

Starter motor spins without turning engine

- ☐ Flywheel gear teeth damaged or worn
- ☐ Starter motor mounting bolts loose

Engine turns normally but fails to start

- ☐ Damp or dirty HT leads and distributor cap (crank engine and check for spark)
- ☐ No fuel in tank (check for delivery)
- ☐ Fouled or incorrectly gapped spark plugs (remove, clean and regap)
- ☐ Other ignition system fault (see Chapter 4)
- ☐ Other fuel system fault (see Chapter 3)

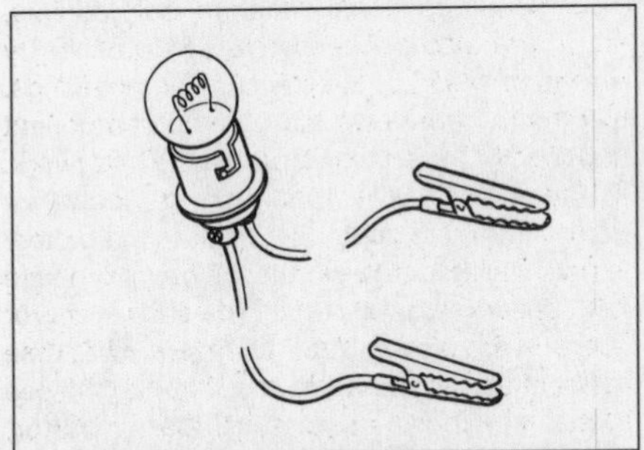

A simple test lamp is useful for checking electrical faults

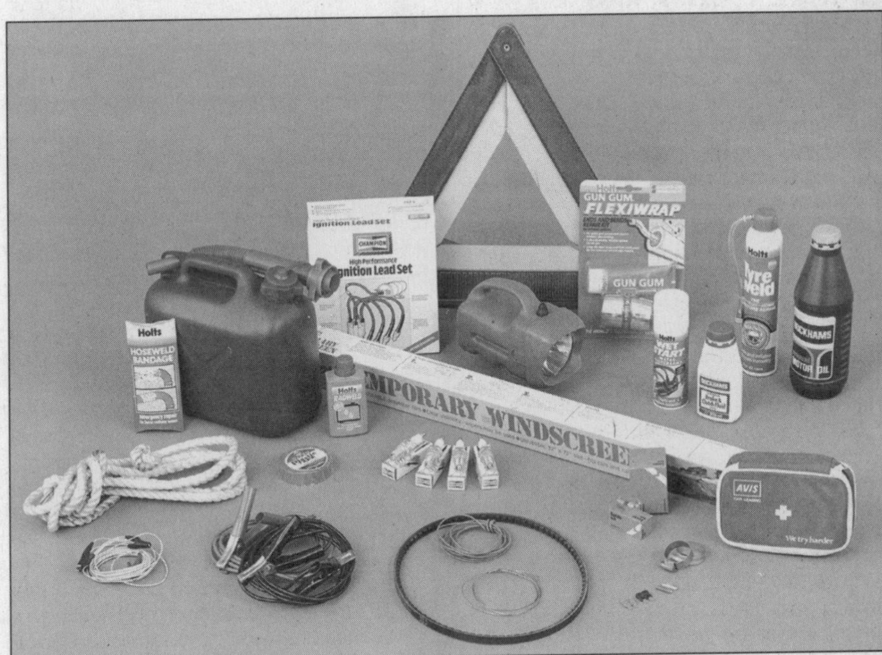

Carrying a few spares may save you a long walk!

- ☐ Poor compression (see Chapter 1)
- ☐ Major mechanical failure (eg camshaft drive)

Engine fires but will not run

- ☐ Air leaks at carburettor or inlet manifold
- ☐ Fuel starvation (see Chapter 3)
- ☐ Ignition fault (see Chapter 4)

Engine cuts out and will not restart

Engine cuts out suddenly – ignition fault

- ☐ Loose or disconnected LT wires
- ☐ Wet HT leads or distributor cap (after traversing water splash)
- ☐ Coil failure (check for spark)
- ☐ Other ignition fault (see Chapter 4)

Engine misfires before cutting out – fuel fault

- ☐ Fuel tank empty
- ☐ Fuel pump defective or filter blocked (check for delivery)
- ☐ Fuel tank filler vent blocked (suction will be evident on releasing cap)
- ☐ Carburettor needle valve sticking
- ☐ Carburettor jets blocked (fuel contaminated)
- ☐ Other fuel system fault (see Chapter 3)

H12390

Crank engine and check for spark. Note use of insulated tool

Engine cuts out – other causes

- ☐ Serious overheating
- ☐ Major mechanical failure (eg camshaft drive)

Engine overheats

Ignition (no-charge) warning light illuminated

- ☐ Slack or broken drivebelt – retension or renew (Chapter 12)

Ignition warning light not illuminated

- ☐ Coolant loss due to internal or external leakage (see Chapter 2)
- ☐ Thermostat defective
- ☐ Low oil level
- ☐ Brakes binding
- ☐ Radiator clogged externally or internally
- ☐ Engine waterways clogged
- ☐ Ignition timing incorrect or automatic advance malfunctioning
- ☐ Mixture too weak

Note: *Do not add cold water to an overheated engine or damage may result*

Low engine oil pressure

Note: *Low oil pressure in a high-mileage engine at tickover is not necessarily a cause for concern. Sudden pressure loss at speed is far more significant. In any event check the gauge or warning light sender before condemning the engine.*

Gauge reads low or warning light illuminated with engine running

- ☐ Oil level low or incorrect grade
- ☐ Defective gauge or sender unit
- ☐ Wire to sender unit earthed
- ☐ Engine overheating
- ☐ Oil filter clogged or bypass valve defective
- ☐ Oil pressure relief valve defective
- ☐ Oil pick-up strainer clogged
- ☐ Oil pump worn or mountings loose
- ☐ Worn main or big-end bearings

Engine noises

Pre-ignition (pinking) on acceleration

- ☐ Incorrect grade of fuel
- ☐ Ignition timing incorrect
- ☐ Distributor faulty or worn
- ☐ Worn or maladjusted carburettor
- ☐ Excessive carbon build-up in engine

Whistling or wheezing noises

- ☐ Leaking vacuum hose
- ☐ Leaking carburettor or manifold gasket
- ☐ Blowing head gasket

Tapping or rattling

- ☐ Incorrect valve clearances
- ☐ Worn valve gear
- ☐ Worn timing chain or belt
- ☐ Broken piston ring (ticking noise)

Knocking or thumping

- ☐ Unintentional mechanical contact (eg fan blades)
- ☐ Worn drivebelt
- ☐ Peripheral component fault (generator, water pump, etc)
- ☐ Worn big-end bearings (regular heavy knocking, perhaps less under load)
- ☐ Worn main bearings (rumbling and knocking, perhaps worsening under load)
- ☐ Piston slap (most noticeable when cold)

Length (distance)

Inches (in)	x 25.4	= Millimetres (mm)	x 0.0394	= Inches (in)
Feet (ft)	x 0.305	= Metres (m)	x 3.281	= Feet (ft)
Miles	x 1.609	= Kilometres (km)	x 0.621	= Miles

Volume (capacity)

Cubic inches (cu in; in^3)	x 16.387	= Cubic centimetres (cc; cm^3)	x 0.061	= Cubic inches (cu in; in^3)
Imperial pints (Imp pt)	x 0.568	= Litres (l)	x 1.76	= Imperial pints (Imp pt)
Imperial quarts (Imp qt)	x 1.137	= Litres (l)	x 0.88	= Imperial quarts (Imp qt)
Imperial quarts (Imp qt)	x 1.201	= US quarts (US qt)	x 0.833	= Imperial quarts (Imp qt)
US quarts (US qt)	x 0.946	= Litres (l)	x 1.057	= US quarts (US qt)
Imperial gallons (Imp gal)	x 4.546	= Litres (l)	x 0.22	= Imperial gallons (Imp gal)
Imperial gallons (Imp gal)	x 1.201	= US gallons (US gal)	x 0.833	= Imperial gallons (Imp gal)
US gallons (US gal)	x 3.785	= Litres (l)	x 0.264	= US gallons (US gal)

Mass (weight)

Ounces (oz)	x 28.35	= Grams (g)	x 0.035	= Ounces (oz)
Pounds (lb)	x 0.454	= Kilograms (kg)	x 2.205	= Pounds (lb)

Force

Ounces-force (ozf; oz)	x 0.278	= Newtons (N)	x 3.6	= Ounces-force (ozf; oz)
Pounds-force (lbf; lb)	x 4.448	= Newtons (N)	x 0.225	= Pounds-force (lbf; lb)
Newtons (N)	x 0.1	= Kilograms-force (kgf; kg)	x 9.81	= Newtons (N)

Pressure

Pounds-force per square inch (psi; lbf/in^2; lb/in^2)	x 0.070	= Kilograms-force per square centimetre (kgf/cm^2; kg/cm^2)	x 14.223	= Pounds-force per square inch (psi; lbf/in^2; lb/in^2)
Pounds-force per square inch (psi; lbf/in^2; lb/in^2)	x 0.068	= Atmospheres (atm)	x 14.696	= Pounds-force per square inch (psi; lbf/in^2; lb/in^2)
Pounds-force per square inch (psi; lbf/in^2; lb/in^2)	x 0.069	= Bars	x 14.5	= Pounds-force per square inch (psi; lbf/in^2; lb/in^2)
Pounds-force per square inch (psi; lbf/in^2; lb/in^2)	x 6.895	= Kilopascals (kPa)	x 0.145	= Pounds-force per square inch (psi; lbf/in^2; lb/in^2)
Kilopascals (kPa)	x 0.01	= Kilograms-force per square centimetre (kgf/cm^2; kg/cm^2)	x 98.1	= Kilopascals (kPa)
Millibar (mbar)	x 100	= Pascals (Pa)	x 0.01	= Millibar (mbar)
Millibar (mbar)	x 0.0145	= Pounds-force per square inch (psi; lbf/in^2; lb/in^2)	x 68.947	= Millibar (mbar)
Millibar (mbar)	x 0.75	= Millimetres of mercury (mmHg)	x 1.333	= Millibar (mbar)
Millibar (mbar)	x 0.401	= Inches of water (inH_2O)	x 2.491	= Millibar (mbar)
Millimetres of mercury (mmHg)	x 0.535	= Inches of water (inH_2O)	x 1.868	= Millimetres of mercury (mmHg)
Inches of water (inH_2O)	x 0.036	= Pounds-force per square inch (psi; lbf/in^2; lb/in^2)	x 27.68	= Inches of water (inH_2O)

Torque (moment of force)

Pounds-force inches (lbf in; lb in)	x 1.152	= Kilograms-force centimetre (kgf cm; kg cm)	x 0.868	= Pounds-force inches (lbf in; lb in)
Pounds-force inches (lbf in; lb in)	x 0.113	= Newton metres (Nm)	x 8.85	= Pounds-force inches (lbf in; lb in)
Pounds-force inches (lbf in; lb in)	x 0.083	= Pounds-force feet (lbf ft; lb ft)	x 12	= Pounds-force inches (lbf in; lb in)
Pounds-force feet (lbf ft; lb ft)	x 0.138	= Kilograms-force metres (kgf m; kg m)	x 7.233	= Pounds-force feet (lbf ft; lb ft)
Pounds-force feet (lbf ft; lb ft)	x 1.356	= Newton metres (Nm)	x 0.738	= Pounds-force feet (lbf ft; lb ft)
Newton metres (Nm)	x 0.102	= Kilograms-force metres (kgf m; kg m)	x 9.804	= Newton metres (Nm)

Power

Horsepower (hp)	x 745.7	= Watts (W)	x 0.0013	= Horsepower (hp)

Velocity (speed)

Miles per hour (miles/hr; mph)	x 1.609	= Kilometres per hour (km/hr; kph)	x 0.621	= Miles per hour (miles/hr; mph)

Fuel consumption*

Miles per gallon (mpg)	x 0.354	= Kilometres per litre (km/l)	x 2.825	= Miles per gallon (mpg)

Temperature

Degrees Fahrenheit = (°C x 1.8) + 32

Degrees Celsius (Degrees Centigrade; °C) = (°F - 32) x 0.56

** It is common practice to convert from miles per gallon (mpg) to litres/100 kilometres (l/100km), where mpg x l/100 km = 282*

A

ABS (Anti-lock brake system) A system, usually electronically controlled, that senses incipient wheel lockup during braking and relieves hydraulic pressure at wheels that are about to skid.

Air bag An inflatable bag hidden in the steering wheel (driver's side) or the dash or glovebox (passenger side). In a head-on collision, the bags inflate, preventing the driver and front passenger from being thrown forward into the steering wheel or windscreen.

Air cleaner A metal or plastic housing, containing a filter element, which removes dust and dirt from the air being drawn into the engine.

Air filter element The actual filter in an air cleaner system, usually manufactured from pleated paper and requiring renewal at regular intervals.

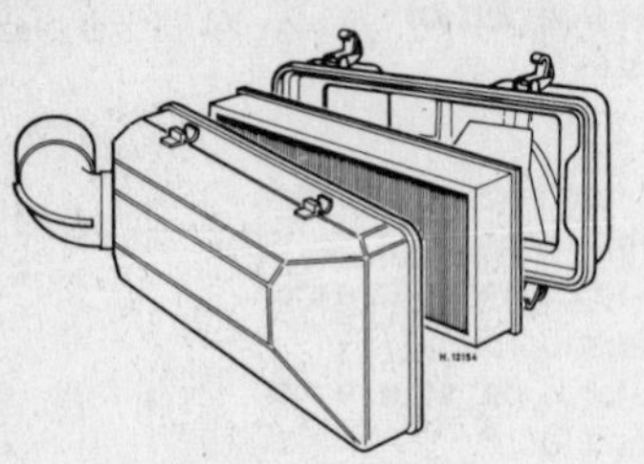

Air filter

Allen key A hexagonal wrench which fits into a recessed hexagonal hole.

Alligator clip A long-nosed spring-loaded metal clip with meshing teeth. Used to make temporary electrical connections.

Alternator A component in the electrical system which converts mechanical energy from a drivebelt into electrical energy to charge the battery and to operate the starting system, ignition system and electrical accessories.

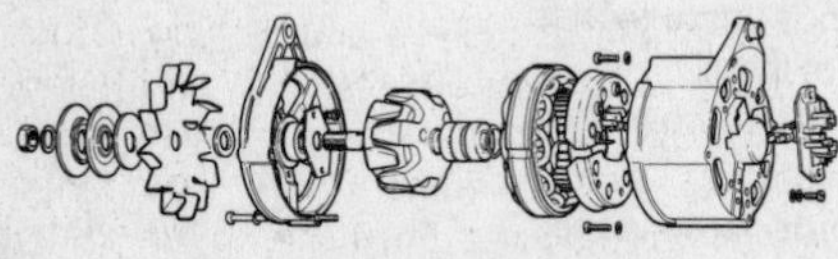

Alternator (exploded view)

Ampere (amp) A unit of measurement for the flow of electric current. One amp is the amount of current produced by one volt acting through a resistance of one ohm.

Anaerobic sealer A substance used to prevent bolts and screws from loosening. Anaerobic means that it does not require oxygen for activation. The Loctite brand is widely used.

Antifreeze A substance (usually ethylene glycol) mixed with water, and added to a vehicle's cooling system, to prevent freezing of the coolant in winter. Antifreeze also contains chemicals to inhibit corrosion and the formation of rust and other deposits that would tend to clog the radiator and coolant passages and reduce cooling efficiency.

Anti-seize compound A coating that reduces the risk of seizing on fasteners that are subjected to high temperatures, such as exhaust manifold bolts and nuts.

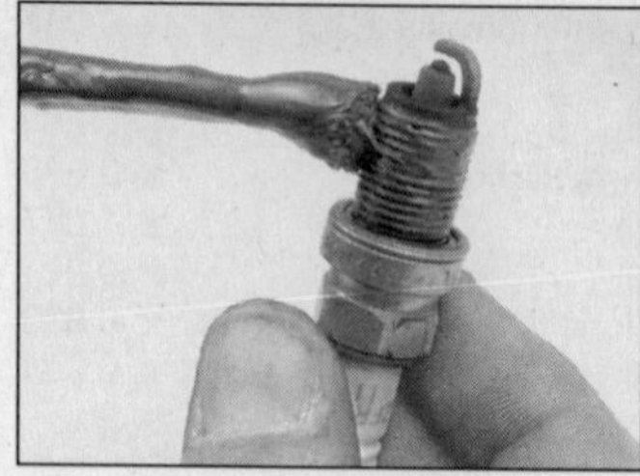

Anti-seize compound

Asbestos A natural fibrous mineral with great heat resistance, commonly used in the composition of brake friction materials. Asbestos is a health hazard and the dust created by brake systems should never be inhaled or ingested.

Axle A shaft on which a wheel revolves, or which revolves with a wheel. Also, a solid beam that connects the two wheels at one end of the vehicle. An axle which also transmits power to the wheels is known as a live axle.

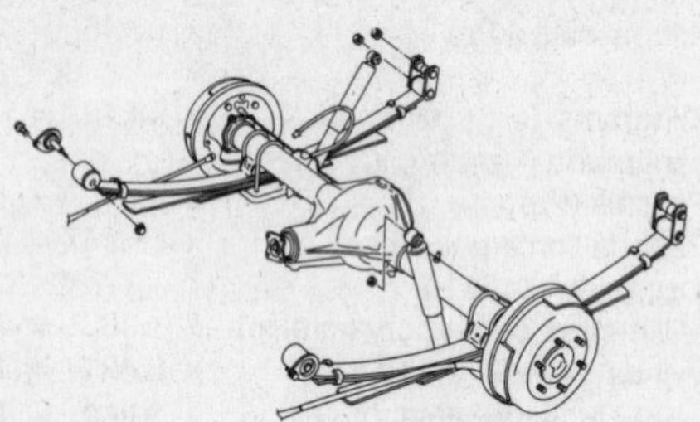

Axle assembly

Axleshaft A single rotating shaft, on either side of the differential, which delivers power from the final drive assembly to the drive wheels. Also called a driveshaft or a halfshaft.

B

Ball bearing An anti-friction bearing consisting of a hardened inner and outer race with hardened steel balls between two races.

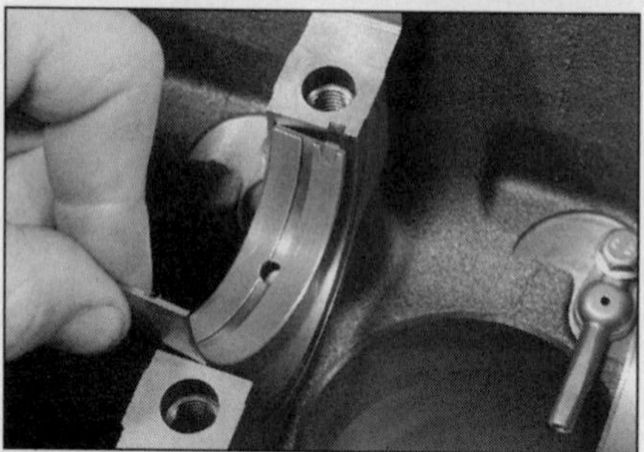

Bearing

Bearing The curved surface on a shaft or in a bore, or the part assembled into either, that permits relative motion between them with minimum wear and friction.

Big-end bearing The bearing in the end of the connecting rod that's attached to the crankshaft.

Bleed nipple A valve on a brake wheel cylinder, caliper or other hydraulic component that is opened to purge the hydraulic system of air. Also called a bleed screw.

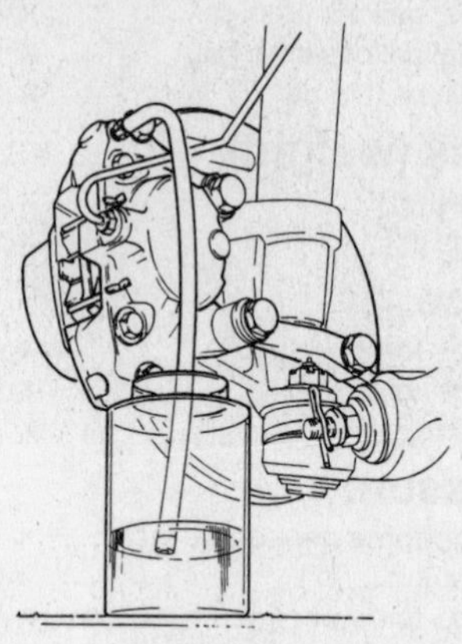

Brake bleeding

Brake bleeding Procedure for removing air from lines of a hydraulic brake system.

Brake disc The component of a disc brake that rotates with the wheels.

Brake drum The component of a drum brake that rotates with the wheels.

Brake linings The friction material which contacts the brake disc or drum to retard the vehicle's speed. The linings are bonded or riveted to the brake pads or shoes.

Brake pads The replaceable friction pads that pinch the brake disc when the brakes are applied. Brake pads consist of a friction material bonded or riveted to a rigid backing plate.

Brake shoe The crescent-shaped carrier to which the brake linings are mounted and which forces the lining against the rotating drum during braking.

Braking systems For more information on braking systems, consult the *Haynes Automotive Brake Manual*.

Breaker bar A long socket wrench handle providing greater leverage.

Bulkhead The insulated partition between the engine and the passenger compartment.

C

Caliper The non-rotating part of a disc-brake assembly that straddles the disc and carries the brake pads. The caliper also contains the hydraulic components that cause the pads to pinch the disc when the brakes are applied. A caliper is also a measuring tool that can be set to measure inside or outside dimensions of an object.

Camshaft A rotating shaft on which a series of cam lobes operate the valve mechanisms. The camshaft may be driven by gears, by sprockets and chain or by sprockets and a belt.

Canister A container in an evaporative emission control system; contains activated charcoal granules to trap vapours from the fuel system.

Canister

Carburettor A device which mixes fuel with air in the proper proportions to provide a desired power output from a spark ignition internal combustion engine.

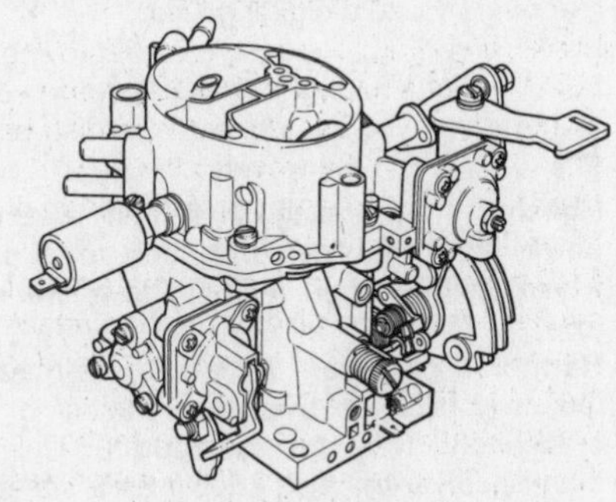

Carburettor

Castellated Resembling the parapets along the top of a castle wall. For example, a castellated balljoint stud nut.

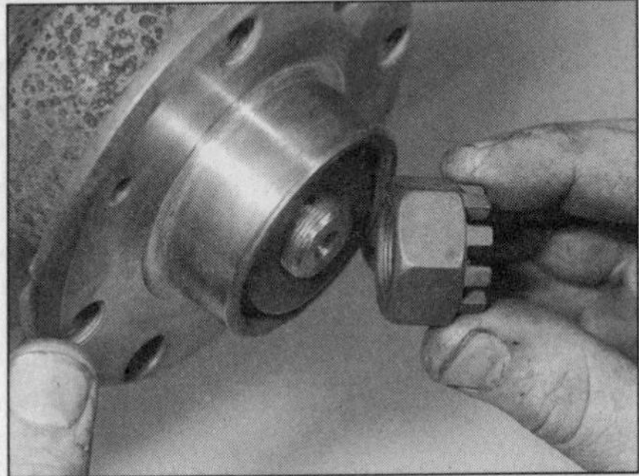

Castellated nut

Castor In wheel alignment, the backward or forward tilt of the steering axis. Castor is positive when the steering axis is inclined rearward at the top.

Catalytic converter A silencer-like device in the exhaust system which converts certain pollutants in the exhaust gases into less harmful substances.

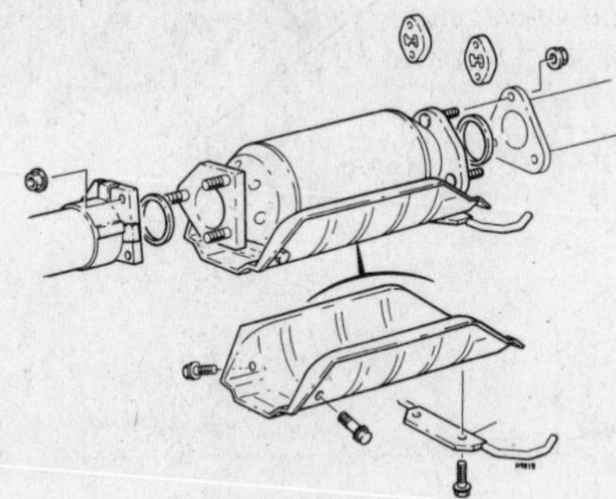

Catalytic converter

Circlip A ring-shaped clip used to prevent endwise movement of cylindrical parts and shafts. An internal circlip is installed in a groove in a housing; an external circlip fits into a groove on the outside of a cylindrical piece such as a shaft.

Clearance The amount of space between two parts. For example, between a piston and a cylinder, between a bearing and a journal, etc.

Coil spring A spiral of elastic steel found in various sizes throughout a vehicle, for example as a springing medium in the suspension and in the valve train.

Compression Reduction in volume, and increase in pressure and temperature, of a gas, caused by squeezing it into a smaller space.

Compression ratio The relationship between cylinder volume when the piston is at top dead centre and cylinder volume when the piston is at bottom dead centre.

Constant velocity (CV) joint A type of universal joint that cancels out vibrations caused by driving power being transmitted through an angle.

Core plug A disc or cup-shaped metal device inserted in a hole in a casting through which core was removed when the casting was formed. Also known as a freeze plug or expansion plug.

Crankcase The lower part of the engine block in which the crankshaft rotates.

Crankshaft The main rotating member, or shaft, running the length of the crankcase, with offset "throws" to which the connecting rods are attached.

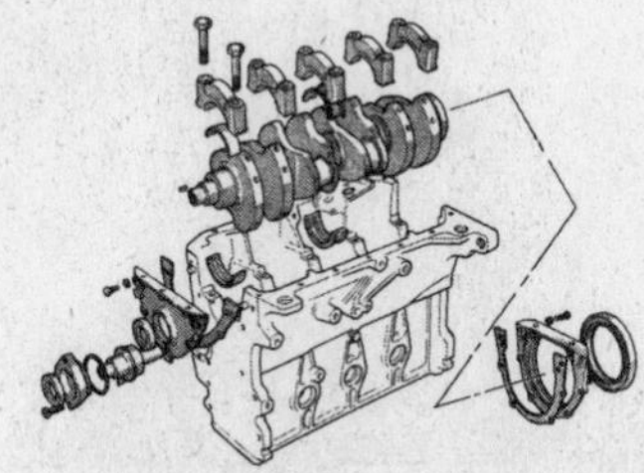

Crankshaft assembly

Crocodile clip See Alligator clip

D

Diagnostic code Code numbers obtained by accessing the diagnostic mode of an engine management computer. This code can be used to determine the area in the system where a malfunction may be located.

Disc brake A brake design incorporating a rotating disc onto which brake pads are squeezed. The resulting friction converts the energy of a moving vehicle into heat.

Double-overhead cam (DOHC) An engine that uses two overhead camshafts, usually one for the intake valves and one for the exhaust valves.

Drivebelt(s) The belt(s) used to drive accessories such as the alternator, water pump, power steering pump, air conditioning compressor, etc. off the crankshaft pulley.

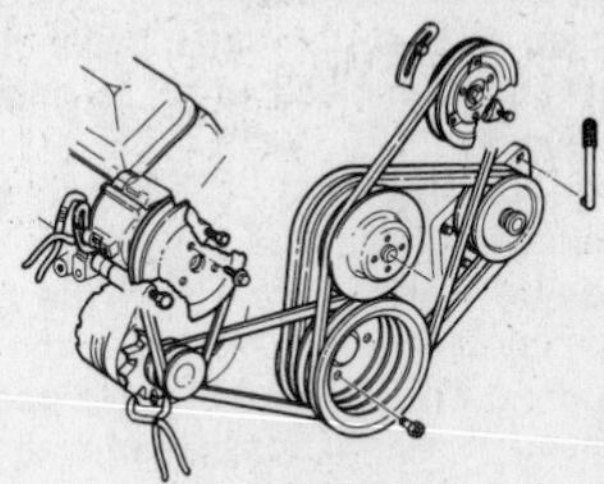

Accessory drivebelts

Driveshaft Any shaft used to transmit motion. Commonly used when referring to the axleshafts on a front wheel drive vehicle.

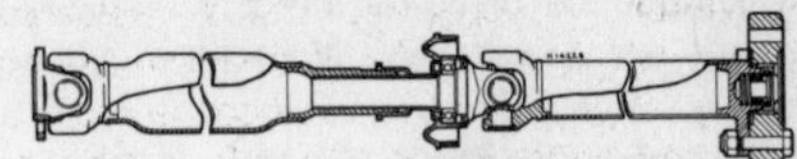

Driveshaft

Drum brake A type of brake using a drum-shaped metal cylinder attached to the inner surface of the wheel. When the brake pedal is pressed, curved brake shoes with friction linings press against the inside of the drum to slow or stop the vehicle.

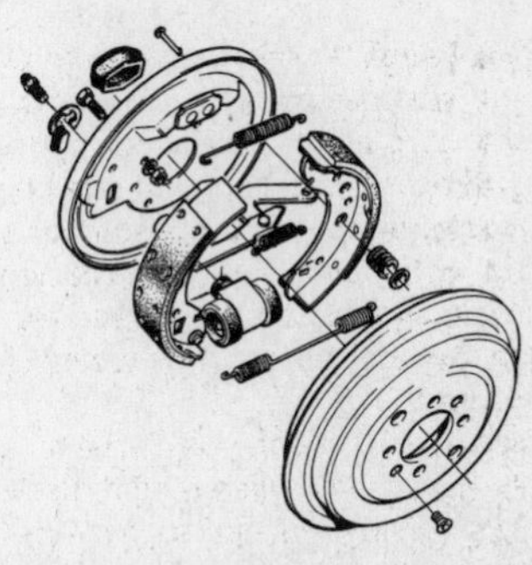

Drum brake assembly

E

EGR valve A valve used to introduce exhaust gases into the intake air stream.

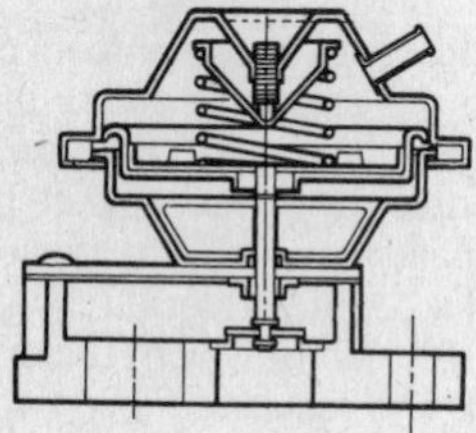

EGR valve

Electronic control unit (ECU) A computer which controls (for instance) ignition and fuel injection systems, or an anti-lock braking system. For more information refer to the *Haynes Automotive Electrical and Electronic Systems Manual.*

Electronic Fuel Injection (EFI) A computer controlled fuel system that distributes fuel through an injector located in each intake port of the engine.

Emergency brake A braking system, independent of the main hydraulic system, that can be used to slow or stop the vehicle if the primary brakes fail, or to hold the vehicle stationary even though the brake pedal isn't depressed. It usually consists of a hand lever that actuates either front or rear brakes mechanically through a series of cables and linkages. Also known as a handbrake or parking brake.

Endfloat The amount of lengthwise movement between two parts. As applied to a crankshaft, the distance that the crankshaft can move forward and back in the cylinder block.

Engine management system (EMS) A computer controlled system which manages the fuel injection and the ignition systems in an integrated fashion.

Exhaust manifold A part with several passages through which exhaust gases leave the engine combustion chambers and enter the exhaust pipe.

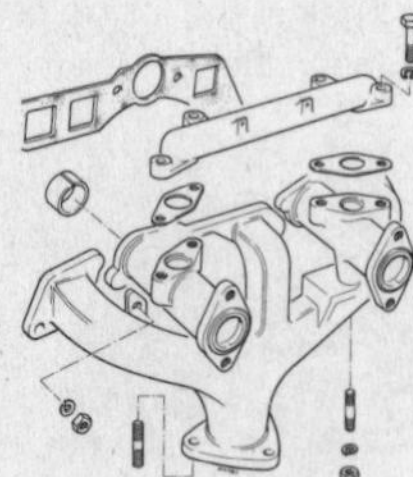

Exhaust manifold

F

Fan clutch A viscous (fluid) drive coupling device which permits variable engine fan speeds in relation to engine speeds.

Feeler blade A thin strip or blade of hardened steel, ground to an exact thickness, used to check or measure clearances between parts.

Feeler blade

Firing order The order in which the engine cylinders fire, or deliver their power strokes, beginning with the number one cylinder.

Flywheel A heavy spinning wheel in which energy is absorbed and stored by means of momentum. On cars, the flywheel is attached to the crankshaft to smooth out firing impulses.

Free play The amount of travel before any action takes place. The "looseness" in a linkage, or an assembly of parts, between the initial application of force and actual movement. For example, the distance the brake pedal moves before the pistons in the master cylinder are actuated.

Fuse An electrical device which protects a circuit against accidental overload. The typical fuse contains a soft piece of metal which is calibrated to melt at a predetermined current flow (expressed as amps) and break the circuit.

Fusible link A circuit protection device consisting of a conductor surrounded by heat-resistant insulation. The conductor is smaller than the wire it protects, so it acts as the weakest link in the circuit. Unlike a blown fuse, a failed fusible link must frequently be cut from the wire for replacement.

G

Gap The distance the spark must travel in jumping from the centre electrode to the side electrode in a spark plug. Also refers to the spacing between the points in a contact breaker assembly in a conventional points-type ignition, or to the distance between the reluctor or rotor and the pickup coil in an electronic ignition.

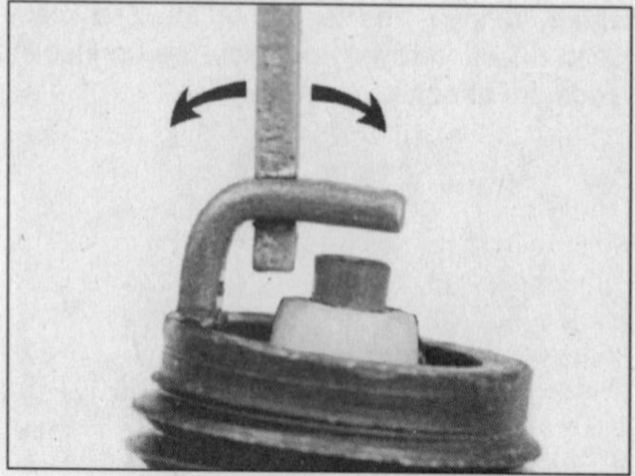

Adjusting spark plug gap

Gasket Any thin, soft material - usually cork, cardboard, asbestos or soft metal - installed between two metal surfaces to ensure a good seal. For instance, the cylinder head gasket seals the joint between the block and the cylinder head.

Gasket

Gauge An instrument panel display used to monitor engine conditions. A gauge with a movable pointer on a dial or a fixed scale is an analogue gauge. A gauge with a numerical readout is called a digital gauge.

H

Halfshaft A rotating shaft that transmits power from the final drive unit to a drive wheel, usually when referring to a live rear axle.

Harmonic balancer A device designed to reduce torsion or twisting vibration in the crankshaft. May be incorporated in the crankshaft pulley. Also known as a vibration damper.

Hone An abrasive tool for correcting small irregularities or differences in diameter in an engine cylinder, brake cylinder, etc.

Hydraulic tappet A tappet that utilises hydraulic pressure from the engine's lubrication system to maintain zero clearance (constant contact with both camshaft and valve stem). Automatically adjusts to variation in valve stem length. Hydraulic tappets also reduce valve noise.

I

Ignition timing The moment at which the spark plug fires, usually expressed in the number of crankshaft degrees before the piston reaches the top of its stroke.

Inlet manifold A tube or housing with passages through which flows the air-fuel mixture (carburettor vehicles and vehicles with throttle body injection) or air only (port fuel-injected vehicles) to the port openings in the cylinder head.

J

Jump start Starting the engine of a vehicle with a discharged or weak battery by attaching jump leads from the weak battery to a charged or helper battery.

L

Load Sensing Proportioning Valve (LSPV) A brake hydraulic system control valve that works like a proportioning valve, but also takes into consideration the amount of weight carried by the rear axle.
Locknut A nut used to lock an adjustment nut, or other threaded component, in place. For example, a locknut is employed to keep the adjusting nut on the rocker arm in position.
Lockwasher A form of washer designed to prevent an attaching nut from working loose.

M

MacPherson strut A type of front suspension system devised by Earle MacPherson at Ford of England. In its original form, a simple lateral link with the anti-roll bar creates the lower control arm. A long strut - an integral coil spring and shock absorber - is mounted between the body and the steering knuckle. Many modern so-called MacPherson strut systems use a conventional lower A-arm and don't rely on the anti-roll bar for location.
Multimeter An electrical test instrument with the capability to measure voltage, current and resistance.

N

NOx Oxides of Nitrogen. A common toxic pollutant emitted by petrol and diesel engines at higher temperatures.

O

Ohm The unit of electrical resistance. One volt applied to a resistance of one ohm will produce a current of one amp.
Ohmmeter An instrument for measuring electrical resistance.
O-ring A type of sealing ring made of a special rubber-like material; in use, the O-ring is compressed into a groove to provide the sealing action.

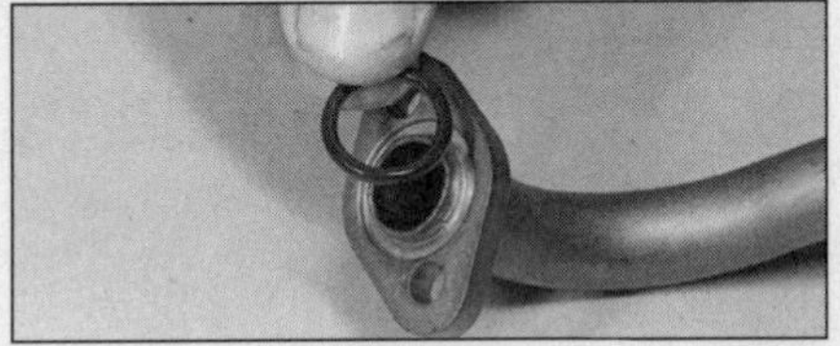

O-ring

Overhead cam (ohc) engine An engine with the camshaft(s) located on top of the cylinder head(s).
Overhead valve (ohv) engine An engine with the valves located in the cylinder head, but with the camshaft located in the engine block.
Oxygen sensor A device installed in the engine exhaust manifold, which senses the oxygen content in the exhaust and converts this information into an electric current. Also called a Lambda sensor.

P

Phillips screw A type of screw head having a cross instead of a slot for a corresponding type of screwdriver.
Plastigage A thin strip of plastic thread, available in different sizes, used for measuring clearances. For example, a strip of Plastigage is laid across a bearing journal. The parts are assembled and dismantled; the width of the crushed strip indicates the clearance between journal and bearing.

Plastigage

Propeller shaft The long hollow tube with universal joints at both ends that carries power from the transmission to the differential on front-engined rear wheel drive vehicles.
Proportioning valve A hydraulic control valve which limits the amount of pressure to the rear brakes during panic stops to prevent wheel lock-up.

R

Rack-and-pinion steering A steering system with a pinion gear on the end of the steering shaft that mates with a rack (think of a geared wheel opened up and laid flat). When the steering wheel is turned, the pinion turns, moving the rack to the left or right. This movement is transmitted through the track rods to the steering arms at the wheels.
Radiator A liquid-to-air heat transfer device designed to reduce the temperature of the coolant in an internal combustion engine cooling system.
Refrigerant Any substance used as a heat transfer agent in an air-conditioning system. R-12 has been the principle refrigerant for many years; recently, however, manufacturers have begun using R-134a, a non-CFC substance that is considered less harmful to the ozone in the upper atmosphere.
Rocker arm A lever arm that rocks on a shaft or pivots on a stud. In an overhead valve engine, the rocker arm converts the upward movement of the pushrod into a downward movement to open a valve.
Rotor In a distributor, the rotating device inside the cap that connects the centre electrode and the outer terminals as it turns, distributing the high voltage from the coil secondary winding to the proper spark plug. Also, that part of an alternator which rotates inside the stator. Also, the rotating assembly of a turbocharger, including the compressor wheel, shaft and turbine wheel.
Runout The amount of wobble (in-and-out movement) of a gear or wheel as it's rotated. The amount a shaft rotates "out-of-true." The out-of-round condition of a rotating part.

S

Sealant A liquid or paste used to prevent leakage at a joint. Sometimes used in conjunction with a gasket.
Sealed beam lamp An older headlight design which integrates the reflector, lens and filaments into a hermetically-sealed one-piece unit. When a filament burns out or the lens cracks, the entire unit is simply replaced.
Serpentine drivebelt A single, long, wide accessory drivebelt that's used on some newer vehicles to drive all the accessories, instead of a series of smaller, shorter belts. Serpentine drivebelts are usually tensioned by an automatic tensioner.

Serpentine drivebelt

Shim Thin spacer, commonly used to adjust the clearance or relative positions between two parts. For example, shims inserted into or under bucket tappets control valve clearances. Clearance is adjusted by changing the thickness of the shim.
Slide hammer A special puller that screws into or hooks onto a component such as a shaft or bearing; a heavy sliding handle on the shaft bottoms against the end of the shaft to knock the component free.
Sprocket A tooth or projection on the periphery of a wheel, shaped to engage with a chain or drivebelt. Commonly used to refer to the sprocket wheel itself.
Starter inhibitor switch On vehicles with an

automatic transmission, a switch that prevents starting if the vehicle is not in Neutral or Park.
Strut See MacPherson strut.

T

Tappet A cylindrical component which transmits motion from the cam to the valve stem, either directly or via a pushrod and rocker arm. Also called a cam follower.
Thermostat A heat-controlled valve that regulates the flow of coolant between the cylinder block and the radiator, so maintaining optimum engine operating temperature. A thermostat is also used in some air cleaners in which the temperature is regulated.
Thrust bearing The bearing in the clutch assembly that is moved in to the release levers by clutch pedal action to disengage the clutch. Also referred to as a release bearing.
Timing belt A toothed belt which drives the camshaft. Serious engine damage may result if it breaks in service.
Timing chain A chain which drives the camshaft.
Toe-in The amount the front wheels are closer together at the front than at the rear. On rear wheel drive vehicles, a slight amount of toe-in is usually specified to keep the front wheels running parallel on the road by offsetting other forces that tend to spread the wheels apart.
Toe-out The amount the front wheels are closer together at the rear than at the front. On front wheel drive vehicles, a slight amount of toe-out is usually specified.
Tools For full information on choosing and using tools, refer to the *Haynes Automotive Tools Manual.*
Tracer A stripe of a second colour applied to a wire insulator to distinguish that wire from another one with the same colour insulator.
Tune-up A process of accurate and careful adjustments and parts replacement to obtain the best possible engine performance.
Turbocharger A centrifugal device, driven by exhaust gases, that pressurises the intake air. Normally used to increase the power output from a given engine displacement, but can also be used primarily to reduce exhaust emissions (as on VW's "Umwelt" Diesel engine).

U

Universal joint or U-joint A double-pivoted connection for transmitting power from a driving to a driven shaft through an angle. A U-joint consists of two Y-shaped yokes and a cross-shaped member called the spider.

V

Valve A device through which the flow of liquid, gas, vacuum, or loose material in bulk may be started, stopped, or regulated by a movable part that opens, shuts, or partially obstructs one or more ports or passageways. A valve is also the movable part of such a device.
Valve clearance The clearance between the valve tip (the end of the valve stem) and the rocker arm or tappet. The valve clearance is measured when the valve is closed.
Vernier caliper A precision measuring instrument that measures inside and outside dimensions. Not quite as accurate as a micrometer, but more convenient.
Viscosity The thickness of a liquid or its resistance to flow.
Volt A unit for expressing electrical "pressure" in a circuit. One volt that will produce a current of one ampere through a resistance of one ohm.

W

Welding Various processes used to join metal items by heating the areas to be joined to a molten state and fusing them together. For more information refer to the *Haynes Automotive Welding Manual.*
Wiring diagram A drawing portraying the components and wires in a vehicle's electrical system, using standardised symbols. For more information refer to the *Haynes Automotive Electrical and Electronic Systems Manual.*

Note: *References throughout this index relate to Chapter•page number*

A

B

C

D

E

Haynes Manuals – The Complete List

Title	Book No.
ALFA ROMEO	
Alfa Romeo Alfasud/Sprint (74 - 88)	0292
Alfa Romeo Alfetta (73 - 87)	0531
AUDI	
Audi 80 (72 - Feb 79)	0207
Audi 80, 90 (79 - Oct 86) & Coupe (81 - Nov 88)	0605
Audi 80, 90 (Oct 86 - 90) & Coupe (Nov 88 - 90)	1491
Audi 100 (Oct 76 - Oct 82)	0428
Audi 100 (Oct 82 - 90) & 200 (Feb 84 - Oct 89)	0907
AUSTIN	
Austin Ambassador (82 - 84)	0871
Austin/MG Maestro 1.3 & 1.6 (83 - 95)	0922
Austin Maxi (69 - 81)	0052
Austin/MG Metro (80 - May 90)	0718
Austin Montego 1.3 & 1.6 (84 - 94)	1066
Austin/MG Montego 2.0 (84 - 95)	1067
Mini (59 - 69)	0527
Mini (69 - 96)	0646
Austin/Rover 2.0 litre Diesel Engine (86 - 93)	1857
BEDFORD	
Bedford CF (69 - 87)	0163
Bedford Rascal (86 - 93)	3015
BL	
BL Princess & BLMC 18-22 (75 - 82)	0286
BMW	
BMW 316, 320 & 320i (4-cyl) (75 - Feb 83)	0276
BMW 320, 320i, 323i & 325i (6-cyl) (Oct 77 - Sept 87)	0815
BMW 3-Series (Apr 91 - 96)	3210
BMW 3-Series (sohc) (83 - 91)	1948
BMW 520i & 525e (Oct 81 - June 88)	1560
BMW 525, 528 & 528i (73 - Sept 81)	0632
BMW 5-Series (sohc) (81 - 93)	1948
BMW 1500, 1502, 1600, 1602, 2000 & 2002 (59 - 77)	0240
CITROEN	
Citroen 2CV, Ami & Dyane (67 - 90)	0196
Citroen AX Petrol & Diesel (87 - 94)	3014
Citroen BX (83 - 94)	0908
Citroen CX (75 - 88)	0528
Citroen Visa (79 - 88)	0620
Citroen Xantia Petrol & Diesel (93 - Oct 95)	3082
Citroen ZX Diesel (91 - 93)	1922
Citroen ZX Petrol (91 - 94)	1881
Citroen 1.7 & 1.9 litre Diesel Engine (84 - 96)	1379
COLT	
Colt 1200, 1250 & 1400 (79 - May 84)	0600
Colt Galant (74 - 78) & Celeste (76 - 81)	0236
DAIMLER	
Daimler Sovereign (68 - Oct 86)	0242
Daimler Double Six (72 - 88)	0478
DATSUN *(see also **Nissan**)*	
Datsun 120Y (73 - Aug 78)	0228
Datsun 1300, 1400 & 1600 (69 - Aug 72)	0123
Datsun Cherry (79 - Sept 82)	0679
Datsun Pick-up (75 - 78)	0277
Datsun Sunny (Aug 78 - May 82)	0525
Datsun Violet (78 - 82)	0430

Title	Book No.
FIAT	
Fiat 126 (73 - 87)	0305
Fiat 127 (71 - 83)	0193
Fiat 500 (57 - 73)	0090
Fiat 850 (64 - 81)	0038
Fiat Panda (81 - 95)	0793
Fiat Punto (94 - 96)	3251
Fiat Regata (84 - 88)	1167
Fiat Strada (79 - 88)	0479
Fiat Tipo (88 - 91)	1625
Fiat Uno (83 - 95)	0923
Fiat X1/9 (74 - 89)	0273
FORD	
Ford Capri II (& III) 1.6 & 2.0 (74 - 87)	0283
Ford Capri II (& III) 2.8 & 3.0 (74 - 87)	1309
Ford Cortina Mk III 1600 & 2000 (70 - 76)	0295
Ford Cortina Mk IV (& V) 1.6 & 2.0 (76 - 83)	0343
Ford Cortina Mk IV (& V) 2.3 V6 (77 - 83)	0426
Ford Escort (75 - Aug 80)	0280
Ford Escort (Sept 80 - Sept 90)	0686
Ford Escort (Sept 90 - 96)	1737
Ford Escort Mk II Mexico, RS 1600 & RS 2000 (75 - 80)	0735
Ford Fiesta (inc. XR2) (76 - Aug 83)	0334
Ford Fiesta (inc. XR2) (Aug 83 - Feb 89)	1030
Ford Fiesta (Feb 89 - 93)	1595
Ford Granada (Sept 77 - Feb 85)	0481
Ford Granada (Mar 85 - 94)	1245
Ford Mondeo 4-cyl (93 - 96)	1923
Ford Orion (83 - Sept 90)	1009
Ford Orion (Sept 90 - 93)	1737
Ford Sierra 1.3, 1.6, 1.8 & 2.0 (82 - 93)	0903
Ford Sierra 2.3, 2.8 & 2.9 (82 - 91)	0904
Ford Scorpio (Mar 85 - 94)	1245
Ford Transit Petrol (Mk 1) (65 - Feb 78)	0377
Ford Transit Petrol (Mk 2) (78 - Jan 86)	0719
Ford Transit Petrol (Mk 3) (Feb 86 - 89)	1468
Ford Transit Diesel (Feb 86 - 95)	3019
Ford 1.6 & 1.8 litre Diesel Engine (84 - 96)	1172
Ford 2.1, 2.3 & 2.5 litre Diesel Engine (77 - 90)	1606
Ford Vehicle Carburettors	1783
FREIGHT ROVER	
Freight Rover Sherpa (74 - 87)	0463
HILLMAN	
Hillman Avenger (70 - 82)	0037
Hillman Minx & Husky (56 - 66)	0009
HONDA	
Honda Accord (76 - Feb 84)	0351
Honda Accord (Feb 84 - Oct 85)	1177
Honda Civic 1300 (80 - 81)	0633
Honda Civic (Feb 84 - Oct 87)	1226
Honda Civic (Nov 91 - 96)	3199
JAGUAR	
Jaguar E Type (61 - 72)	0140
Jaguar MkI & II, 240 & 340 (55 - 69)	0098
Jaguar XJ6, XJ & Sovereign (68 - Oct 86)	0242
Jaguar XJ12, XJS & Sovereign (72 - 88)	0478
JEEP	
Jeep Cherokee Petrol (93 - 96)	1943

Title	Book No.
LADA	
Lada 1200, 1300, 1500 & 1600 (74 - 91)	0413
Lada Samara (87 - 91)	1610
LAND ROVER	
Land Rover 90, 110 & Defender Diesel (83 - 95)	3017
Land Rover Discovery Diesel (89 - 95)	3016
Land Rover Series IIA & III Diesel (58 - 85)	0529
Land Rover Series II, IIA & III Petrol (58 - 85)	0314
MAZDA	
Mazda 323 fwd (Mar 81 - Oct 89)	1608
Mazda 323 rwd (77 - Apr 86)	0370
Mazda 626 fwd (May 83 - Sept 87)	0929
Mazda B-1600, B-1800 & B-2000 Pick-up (72 - 88)	0267
Mazda RX-7 (79 - 85)	0460
MERCEDES-BENZ	
Mercedes-Benz 190 & 190E (83 - 87)	0928
Mercedes-Benz 200, 240, 300 Diesel (Oct 76 - 85)	1114
Mercedes-Benz 250 & 280 (68 - 72)	0346
Mercedes-Benz 250 & 280 (123 Series) (Oct 76 - 84)	0677
Mercedes-Benz 124 Series (85 - Aug 93)	3253
MG	
MGB (62 - 80)	0111
MG Maestro 1.3 & 1.6 (83 - 95)	0922
MG Metro (80 - May 90)	0718
MG Midget & AH Sprite (58 - 80)	0265
MG Montego 2.0 (84 - 95)	1067
MITSUBISHI	
Mitsubishi 1200, 1250 & 1400 (79 - May 84)	0600
Mitsubishi Shogun & L200 Pick-Ups (83 - 94)	1944
MORRIS	
Morris Ital 1.3 (80 - 84)	0705
Morris Marina 1700 (78 - 80)	0526
Morris Marina 1.8 (71 - 78)	0074
Morris Minor 1000 (56 - 71)	0024
NISSAN *(See also Datsun)*	
Nissan Bluebird 160B & 180B rwd (May 80 - May 84)	0957
Nissan Bluebird fwd (May 84 - Mar 86)	1223
Nissan Bluebird (T12 & T72) (Mar 86 - 90)	1473
Nissan Cherry (N12) (Sept 82 - 86)	1031
Nissan Micra (K10) (83 - Jan 93)	0931
Nissan Micra (93 - 96)	3254
Nissan Primera (90 - Oct 96)	1851
Nissan Stanza (82 - 86)	0824
Nissan Sunny (B11) (May 82 - Oct 86)	0895
Nissan Sunny (Oct 86 - Mar 91)	1378
Nissan Sunny (Apr 91 - 95)	3219
OPEL	
Opel Ascona & Manta (B Series) (Sept 75 - 88)	0316
Opel Ascona (81 - 88)	3215
Opel Astra (Oct 91 - 96)	3156
Opel Corsa (83 - Mar 93)	3160
Opel Corsa (Mar 93 - 94)	3159
Opel Kadett (Nov 79 - Oct 84)	0634
Opel Kadett (Oct 84 - Oct 91)	3196
Opel Omega & Senator (86 - 94)	3157

Title	Book No.
Opel Rekord (Feb 78 - Oct 86)	0543
Opel Vectra (88 - Oct 95)	3158
PEUGEOT	
Peugeot 106 Petrol & Diesel (91 - June 96)	1882
Peugeot 205 (83 - 95)	0932
Peugeot 305 (78 - 89)	0538
Peugeot 306 Petrol & Diesel (93 - 95)	3073
Peugeot 309 (86 - 93)	1266
Peugeot 405 Petrol (88 - 96)	1559
Peugeot 405 Diesel (88 - 96)	3198
Peugeot 505 (79 - 89)	0762
Peugeot 1.7 & 1.9 litre Diesel Engines (82 - 96)	0950
Peugeot 2.0, 2.1, 2.3 & 2.5 litre Diesel Engines (74 - 90)	1607
PORSCHE	
Porsche 911 (65 - 85)	0264
Porsche 924 & 924 Turbo (76 - 85)	0397
RANGE ROVER	
Range Rover V8 (70 - Oct 92)	0606
RELIANT	
Reliant Robin & Kitten (73 - 83)	0436
RENAULT	
Renault 5 (72 - Feb 85)	0141
Renault 5 (Feb 85 - 96)	1219
Renault 6 (68 - 79)	0092
Renault 9 & 11 (82 - 89)	0822
Renault 12 (70 - 80)	0097
Renault 15 & 17 (72 - 79)	0763
Renault 16 (65 - 79)	0081
Renault 18 (79 - 86)	0598
Renault 19 Petrol (89 - 94)	1646
Renault 19 Diesel (89 - 95)	1946
Renault 21 (86 - 94)	1397
Renault 25 (84 - 86)	1228
Renault Clio Petrol (91 - 93)	1853
Renault Clio Diesel (91 - June 96)	3031
Renault Espace (85 - 96)	3197
Renault Fuego (80 - 86)	0764
Renault Laguna (94 - 96)	3252
ROVER	
Rover 111 & 114 (95 - 96)	1711
Rover 213 & 216 (84 - 89)	1116
Rover 214 & 414 (Oct 89 - 92)	1689
Rover 216 & 416 (Oct 89 - 92)	1830
Rover 820, 825 & 827 (86 - 95)	1380
Rover 2000, 2300 & 2600 (77 - 87)	0468
Rover 3500 (76 - 87)	0365
Rover Metro (May 90 - 94)	1711
Rover 2.0 litre Diesel Engine (86 - 93)	1857
SAAB	
Saab 95 & 96 (66 - 76)	0198
Saab 99 (69 - 79)	0247
Saab 90, 99 & 900 (79 - Oct 93)	0765
Saab 9000 (4-cyl) (85 - 95)	1686
SEAT	
Seat Ibiza & Malaga (85 - 92)	1609

Title	Book No.
SIMCA	
Simca 1100 & 1204 (67 - 79)	0088
Simca 1301 & 1501 (63 - 76)	0199
SKODA	
Skoda 1000 & 1100 (64 - 78)	0303
Skoda Estelle 105, 120, 130 & 136 (77 - 89)	0604
Skoda Favorit (89 - 92)	1801
SUBARU	
Subaru 1600 (77 - Oct 79)	0237
Subaru 1600 & 1800 (Nov 79 - 90)	0995
SUZUKI	
Suzuki SJ Series, Samurai & Vitara (82 - 94)	1942
Suzuki Supercarry (86 - Oct 94)	3015
TALBOT	
Talbot Alpine, Solara, Minx & Rapier (75 - 86)	0337
Talbot Horizon (78 - 86)	0473
Talbot Samba (82 - 86)	0823
TOYOTA	
Toyota 2000 (75 - 77)	0360
Toyota Celica (78 - Jan 82)	0437
Toyota Celica (Feb 82 - Sept 85)	1135
Toyota Corolla (fwd) (Sept 83 - Sept 87)	1024
Toyota Corolla (rwd) (80 - 85)	0683
Toyota Corolla (Sept 87 - 92)	1683
Toyota Hi-Ace & Hi-Lux (69 - Oct 83)	0304
Toyota Starlet (78 - Jan 85)	0462
TRIUMPH	
Triumph Acclaim (81 - 84)	0792
Triumph GT6 (62 - 74)	0112
Triumph Herald (59 - 71)	0010
Triumph Spitfire (62 - 81)	0113
Triumph Stag (70 - 78)	0441
Triumph TR2, TR3, TR3A, TR4 & TR4A (52 - 67)	0028
Triumph TR7 (75 - 82)	0322
Triumph Vitesse (62 - 74)	0112
VAUXHALL	
Vauxhall Astra (80 - Oct 84)	0635
Vauxhall Astra & Belmont (Oct 84 - Oct 91)	1136
Vauxhall Astra (Oct 91 - 96)	1832
Vauxhall Carlton (Oct 78 - Oct 86)	0480
Vauxhall Carlton (Nov 86 - 94)	1469
Vauxhall Cavalier 1300 (77 - July 81)	0461
Vauxhall Cavalier 1600, 1900 & 2000 (75 - July 81)	0315
Vauxhall Cavalier (81 - Oct 88)	0812
Vauxhall Cavalier (Oct 88 - Oct 95)	1570
Vauxhall Chevette (75 - 84)	0285
Vauxhall Corsa (Mar 93 - 94)	1985
Vauxhall Nova (83 - 93)	0909
Vauxhall Rascal (86 - 93)	3015
Vauxhall Senator (Sept 87 - 94)	1469
Vauxhall Victor & VX4/90 (FD Series) (67 - 72)	0053
Vauxhall Viva HC (70 - 79)	0047
Vauxhall/Opel 1.5, 1.6 & 1.7 litre Diesel Engines (82 - 96)	1222
VOLKSWAGEN	
VW Beetle 1200 (54 - 77)	0036
VW Beetle 1300 & 1500 (65 - 75)	0039

Title	Book No.
VW Beetle 1302 & 1302S (70 - 72)	0110
VW Beetle 1303, 1303S & GT (72 - 75)	0159
VW Golf Mk 1 1.1 & 1.3 (74 - Feb 84)	0716
VW Golf Mk 1 1.5, 1.6 & 1.8 (74 - 85)	0726
VW Golf Mk 1 Diesel (78 - Feb 84)	0451
VW Golf Mk 2 (Mar 84 - Feb 92)	1081
VW Golf Mk 3 Petrol & Diesel (Feb 92 - 96)	3097
VW Jetta Mk 1 1.1 & 1.3 (80 - June 84)	0716
VW Jetta Mk 1 1.5, 1.6 & 1.8 (80 - June 84)	0726
VW Jetta Mk 1 Diesel (81 - June 84)	0451
VW Jetta Mk 2 (July 84 - 92)	1081
VW LT vans & light trucks (76 - 87)	0637
VW Passat (Sept 81 - May 88)	0814
VW Passat (May 88 - 91)	1647
VW Polo & Derby (76 - Jan 82)	0335
VW Polo (82 - Oct 90)	0813
VW Polo (Nov 90 - Aug 94)	3245
VW Santana (Sept 82 - 85)	0814
VW Scirocco Mk 1 1.5, 1.6 & 1.8 (74 - 82)	0726
VW Scirocco (82 - 90)	1224
VW Transporter 1600 (68 - 79)	0082
VW Transporter 1700, 1800 & 2000 (72 - 79)	0226
VW Transporter with air-cooled engine (79 - 82)	0638
VW Type 3 (63 - 73)	0084
VW Vento Petrol & Diesel (Feb 92 - 96)	3097
VOLVO	
Volvo 66 & 343, Daf 55 & 66 (68 - 79)	0293
Volvo 142, 144 & 145 (66 - 74)	0129
Volvo 240 Series (74 - 93)	0270
Volvo 262, 264 & 260/265 (75 - 85)	0400
Volvo 340, 343, 345 & 360 (76 - 91)	0715
Volvo 440, 460 & 480 (87 - 92)	1691
Volvo 740 & 760 (82 - 91)	1258
Volvo 850 (92 - 96)	3260
Volvo 940 (90 - 96)	3249
YUGO/ZASTAVA	
Yugo/Zastava (81 - 90)	1453

TECH BOOKS	
Automotive Brake Manual	3050
Automotive Electrical & Electronic Systems	3049
Automotive Tools Manual	3052
Automotive Welding Manual	3053

CAR BOOKS	
Automotive Fuel Injection Systems	9755
Car Bodywork Repair Manual	9864
Caravan Manual (2nd Edition)	9894
Ford Vehicle Carburettors	1783
Haynes Technical Data Book (87 - 96)	1996
In-Car Entertainment Manual (2nd Edition)	9862
Japanese Vehicle Carburettors	1786
Pass the MOT!	9861
Small Engine Repair Manual	1755
Solex & Pierburg Carburettors	1785
SU Carburettors	0299
Weber Carburettors (to 79)	0393
Weber Carburettors (79 - 91)	1784

01/10/96

All the products featured on this page are available through most motor accessory shops, cycle shops and book stores. Our policy of continuous updating and development means that titles are being constantly added to the range. For up-to-date information on our complete list of titles, please telephone: (UK) **01963 442030** • (USA) **(805) 498-6703** • (France) **(1) 47 03 61 80** • (Sweden) **018 124016**